Gibbon and the
'Watchmen of the Holy City'

Gibbon and the 'Watchmen of the Holy City'

The Historian and his Reputation
1776–1815

DAVID WOMERSLEY

CLARENDON PRESS · OXFORD

OXFORD
UNIVERSITY PRESS

Great Clarendon Street, Oxford, OX2 6DP
Oxford University Press is a department of the University of Oxford.
It furthers the University's objective of excellence in research, scholarship,
and education by publishing worldwide in

Oxford New York

Athens Auckland Bangkok Bogotá Buenos Aires Cape Town
Chennai Dar es Salaam Delhi Florence Hong Kong Istanbul Karachi
Kolkata Kuala Lumpur Madrid Melbourne Mexico City Mumbai Nairobi
Paris São Paulo Shanghai Singapore Taipei Tokyo Toronto Warsaw

with associated companies in Berlin Ibadan

Oxford is a registered trade mark of Oxford University Press
in the UK and certain other countries

Published in the United States
by Oxford University Press Inc., New York

© David Womersley 2002

The moral rights of the author have been asserted
Database right Oxford University Press (maker)

First published 2002

British Library Cataloguing in Publication Data

Data available

Library of Congress Cataloging-in-Publication Data
Womersley, David.
Gibbon and the watchmen of the Holy City : the historian and his reputation,
1776–1815 / David Womersley
p. cm
Includes bibliographical references and index.
1. Gibbon, Edward, 1737-1794–Criticism and interpretation. 2. Gibbon, Edward, 1737-1794.
History of the decline and fall of the Roman empire. 3. Historians–England–Biography.
4. Rome–History–Empire, 284-476–Historiography. 5. Byzantine Empire–Historiography.
6. England–Intellectual life–18th century.
DG206.G5 W66 2002   937'.06'092–dc21   [aB]   2001036390

ISBN 0-19-818733-5

1 3 5 7 9 10 8 6 4 2

Typeset in Bembo
by Regent Typesetting, London
Printed in Great Britain
on acid-free paper by
Biddles Ltd, Guildford and King's Lynn

Knowledge of documents should precede final judgement upon readings.

(Westcott and Hort, 1881)

1st ed sold well, but
not because of its
religious aspect p. 40

Bentley 43-76

ACKNOWLEDGEMENTS

I first realized that this was a book which might be written, and that I might write it, when I was working on material arising out of the collation which underpinned my edition of *The Decline and Fall*. This material was first embodied in my contribution to the Royal Historical Society's 1994 conference on Gibbon, held in Magdalen College, Oxford, and organized by Roland Quinault and Rosamond McKitterick. I must therefore thank at the outset my colleague, Felicity Heal, for suggesting that I might offer something on that occasion, and for thereby imparting the first, innocent, impulse to this book.

Three of the chapters in this book have been published before in less developed forms. Chapter 1 first appeared as 'Gibbon and the "Watchmen of the Holy City": Revision and Religion in the *Decline and Fall*', in R. Quinault and R. McKitterick (eds.), *Edward Gibbon and Empire* (Cambridge: Cambridge University Press, 1997), 190–216. An early version of Chapter 5 was published as 'Gibbon's Unfinished History' in *The Historical Journal*, 35/1 (1992), 63–89. A stripped-down prototype of Chapter 6 was given an outing at the Gibbon Bicentenary Colloquium held at Jesus College, Oxford, in the summer of 1994, and I was then and am now very grateful to the select group of participants on that occasion for their valuable comments. A much enlarged version (which was nevertheless more slender than the heavyweight chapter included here) was then published in the proceedings of that colloquium as 'Gibbon's *Memoirs*: Autobiography in Time of Revolution', in D. Womersley (ed.), *Edward Gibbon: Bicentenary Essays* (Oxford: The Voltaire Foundation, 1997), 347–404.

Invitations to deliver papers at the universities of Cambridge, Birmingham, Zurich, and Boston gave me opportunities to try out the material of (respectively) Chapters 5, 2, 4, and 9 on audiences whose responses helped me to sharpen my arguments. My thanks to Howard Erskine-Hill, Marcus Walsh, Allen Reddick, and Christopher Ricks for their kindness in inviting me, and for their generous hospitality when I was in their company.

My college has been my intellectual and professional home since 1984, and in that time I and my family have benefited from its support in countless ways. It is therefore with a particular pleasure that I dedicate this book to the Principal, Fellows, and Scholars of Jesus College, Oxford.

Oxford, December 2000

CONTENTS

ABBREVIATIONS

A The Autobiographies of Edward Gibbon, ed. J. Murray (London: John Murray, 1896)

Bowersock G. W. Bowersock, John Clive, and Stephen R. Graubard (eds.), Edward Gibbon and the Decline and Fall of the Roman Empire (Cambridge, Mass., Harvard University Press, 1977)

Bury Edward Gibbon, The History of the Decline and Fall of the Roman Empire, ed. J. B. Bury, 7 vols. (London: Methuen, 1896–1900)

DF Edward Gibbon, The History of the Decline and Fall of the Roman Empire, ed. D. J. Womersley, 3 vols. (London: Allen Lane, 1994)

DF 1 Edward Gibbon, The History of the Decline and Fall of the Roman Empire, vol. i, 1st quarto edn. (1776)

DF 2 Edward Gibbon, The History of the Decline and Fall of the Roman Empire, vol. i, 2nd quarto edn. (1776)

DF 3 Edward Gibbon, The History of the Decline and Fall of the Roman Empire, vol. i, 3rd quarto edn. (1777)

EE The English Essays of Edward Gibbon, ed. P. B. Craddock (Oxford: Clarendon Press, 1972)

J1 Gibbon's Journal to January 28th. 1763, ed. D. M. Low (London: Chatto and Windus, 1929)

J2 Le Journal de Gibbon à Lausanne, ed. G. A. Bonnard (Lausanne: Librairie de l'Université, 1945)

J3 Gibbon's Journey from Geneva to Rome, ed. G. A. Bonnard (London: Thomas Nelson and Sons, 1961)

K Gibbon's Library, ed. G. Keynes (London: Jonathan Cape, 1940)

L The Letters of Edward Gibbon, ed. J. E. Norton, 3 vols. (London: Cassell and Company, 1956)

MG Miscellanea Gibboniana, ed. G. R. de Beer, L. Junod, and G. A. Bonnard (Lausanne: Librairie de l'Université, 1952)

MW 1796 Edward Gibbon, Miscellaneous Works, ed. Lord Sheffield, 2 vols. (1796)

MW 1814 Edward Gibbon, Miscellaneous Works, ed. Lord Sheffield, 5 vols. (1814)

MW 1815 Edward Gibbon, Miscellaneous Works . . . In Three Volumes, ed. Lord Sheffield, vol. iii (1815)

Norton   *A Bibliography of the Works of Edward Gibbon* (Oxford:
                Oxford University Press, 1940)
Prothero   R. E. Prothero (ed.), *The Private Letters of Edward Gibbon*, 2
                vols. (London: John Murray, 1896)
Regenstein   D 7 f. 6419
Womersley (*a*) D. J. Womersley, *The Transformation of The Decline and Fall
                of the Roman Empire* (Cambridge: Cambridge University
                Press, 1988)
Womersley (*b*) *Edward Gibbon: Bicentenary Essays*, ed. David Womersley
                (Oxford: The Voltaire Foundation, 1997)

A NOTE ON REFERENCES

Apart from those frequently cited works listed in the 'Abbreviations'
above, references in the footnotes are given in a shortened but unambiguous form, while full bibliographic details of all cited works are
supplied in the 'Bibliography'.

However, full details of books and articles are supplied in those
footnotes of which the primary purpose is bibliographical.

INTRODUCTION

On 18 February 1776 Horace Walpole wrote to William Mason with the latest literary news from London:

Lo, there is just appeared a truly classic work: . . . This book is Mr Gibbon's *History of the Decline and Fall of the Roman Empire*. He is son of a late foolish alderman, is a member of Parliament, and called a whimsical one because he votes variously as his opinion leads him . . . I know him a little, never suspected the extent of his talents, for he is perfectly modest . . . but I intend to know him a great deal more.[1]

Although this was not in fact the first occasion on which Gibbon had come before the reading public (his *Essai sur l'Étude de la Littérature* had been published in 1761), Walpole's letter reveals that at this time Gibbon had no literary character. All that even as well-placed and perceptive a student of the literary scene as Walpole can muster are a few random details about Gibbon's family background and his behaviour as a Member of Parliament. In 1776, Gibbon was without reputation.

One of Gibbon's tasks in the first volume of *The Decline and Fall* was therefore to create and display a literary character. The medium in which he chose to do so was, in part, the footnote.[2] Its literally marginal status created opportunities for allowing the reader to glimpse the personality of the author—opportunities which would have been out of place in the text of the history itself. So careful readers of the first volume of *The Decline and Fall* might have deduced from the tone, phrasing, and allusions in its footnotes that the historian was, amongst other things, a man of the world: 'The world has laughed at the credulity of Marcus [who credited the chastity of Faustina]; but Madam Dacier assures us (and we may credit a lady), that the husband will always be deceived, if the wife condescends to dissemble.'[3] They may have also noticed that his undoubted scholarship had not been

---

[1] Horace Walpole, *Correspondence*, ed. W. S. Lewis *et al.*, vol. xxviii (New Haven and Oxford: Yale University Press, 1955), 243–4.

[2] On the footnote, see Anthony Grafton, *The Footnote: A Curious History* (London: Faber and Faber, 1997). On Gibbon's footnotes, see most recently Palmeri, 'The Satiric Footnotes of Swift and Gibbon', and Cosgrove, 'Undermining the Footnote'.

[3] *DF* i. 109 n. 4.

purchased at the price of wit, and that he was capable of skewering those whose learning was less secure with an epigrammatic turn of phrase:

M. de Voltaire . . . unsupported by either fact or probability, has generously bestowed the Canary Islands on the Roman empire.

The rights, powers, and pretensions of the sovereign of Olympus, are very clearly described in the xvth book of the Iliad: in the Greek original, I mean; for Mr. Pope, without perceiving it, has improved the theology of Homer.[4]

Nor had his antiquarian labours dulled his aesthetic sensibility: 'See his [Alexander Severus's] life in the Augustan History. The undistinguishing compiler has buried these interesting anecdotes under a load of trivial and unmeaning circumstances.'[5] The literary character displayed in these footnotes unites contrasting qualities of gentility and scholarship, philosophy and erudition, and seems to exemplify Momigliano's celebrated thesis, that Gibbon's achievement in the field of historical method was to fuse the different virtues of the *érudits* and the *philosophes*.[6] It is clear, however, that the tone of these footnotes is, in comparison with that of footnotes later in the history, flat. This flatness, I would suggest, springs from the fact that they were issued into the void. That is to say, it is a consequence of Gibbon's necessary ignorance during the years of composition of the first volume of *The Decline and Fall* of how his work would be received.[7] In the later volumes of the history, the consciousness of reception and the awareness of readership seasoned Gibbon's footnotes with the vivacity of dialectic.

Therefore once we read on into the second instalment of *The Decline and Fall*, published five years later in 1781, we find new emphases at the foot of the page. There is, for instance, a tendency on Gibbon's part to defend his use of his sources, and to vindicate where possible his first-hand familiarity with them:

I may stand in need of some apology for having used, without scruple, the authority of Constantine Porphyrogenitus, in all that relates to the wars and negociations of the Chersonites. I am aware that he was a Greek of the tenth century, and that his accounts of ancient history are frequently confused and fabulous . . .

[4] *DF* i. 54 n. 87 and 57 n. 4.
[5] *DF* i. 172 n. 69.
[6] Momigliano, 'Gibbon's Contribution to Historical Method'. On gentility and scholarship in the eighteenth century, see most recently Jarvis, *Scholars and Gentlemen*.
[7] Although he was not without some shrewd hunches on that score; below, Ch. 1.

As I am *almost* a stranger to the voluminous sermons of Chrysostom, I have given my confidence to the two most judicious and moderate of the ecclesiastical critics . . .

His [Gregory of Tours's] style is equally devoid of elegance and simplicity. . . . I have tediously acquired, by a painful perusal, the right of pronouncing this unfavourable sentence.[8]

We find, too, a scrupulousness which seems born of the experience of uncharitable interpretation: 'I owe it to myself, and to historic truth, to declare, that some *circumstances* in this paragraph are founded only on conjecture and analogy. The stubbornness of our language has sometimes forced me to deviate from the *conditional* into the *indicative* mood.'[9] The metaphors in the footnotes sometimes evince an awareness of possible attack:

I shelter myself behind Maimonides, Marsham, Spencer, Le Clerc, Warburton, &c., who have fairly derided the fears, the folly, and the falsehood, of some superstitious divines.

Cambden . . . appoints him [Maximus] governor of Britain; and the father of our antiquities is followed, as usual, by his blind progeny. Pacatus and Zosimus had taken some pains to prevent this error, or fable; and I shall protect myself by their decisive testimonies.[10]

And we encounter, at moments, a testiness springing from resentment at how his habits of citation have been received by readers of the first volume: 'And here let me observe, that as the general propositions which I advance are the result of *many* particular and imperfect facts, I must either refer the reader to those modern authors who have expressly treated the subject, or swell these notes to a disagreeable and disproportioned size.'[11] In these footnotes, Gibbon's fairly frequent recourse to italicization is revealing. It suggests an affective urgency which partially eludes specifically verbal expression. It is the signature of an author on the edge of exasperation.

When we reach the third instalment, however, the tonal quality of the footnotes changes once more. Gibbon still wishes to take his reader into his confidence about the nature and extent of the scholarly labour upon which his history rests, but the mists of defensiveness have been dissipated. Geniality has taken the place of resentment: 'the numberless passages of antiquity which I have seen with my own eyes, are com-

[8] *DF* i. 658 n. 44, ii. 253–4 n. 42, and ii. 487 n. 111.
[9] *DF* ii. 232 n. 179.
[10] *DF* i. 888 n. 72 and ii. 22 n. 11.
[11] *DF* i. 759 n. 111.

4	*Introduction*

piled, digested, and illustrated, by *Petavius* and *Le Clerc*, by *Beausobre* and *Mosheim*. I shall be content to fortify my narrative by the names and characters of these respectable guides; and in the contemplation of a minute or remote object, I am not ashamed to borrow the aid of the strongest glasses . . .'.[12] The air of *détente* is palpable. Gibbon now writes out of confidence in what he revealingly calls his 'long-accustomed reader'.[13] In the footnotes to the final three volumes he is willing freely to reveal far more about his own preferences, connections, and even prejudices than had been the case in the earlier instalments:

I am happy enough to possess a splendid and interesting work, which has only been distributed in presents by the court of Madrid . . .

See Homer Iliad *B*. (I hate this pedantic mode of quotation by the letters of the Greek alphabet) . . .

To admire or despise St. Bernard [who had managed to ignore the splendours of the district of Lausanne] as he ought, the reader, like myself, should have before the windows of his library the beauties of that incomparable landskip.

On this interesting subject, the progress of society in Europe, a strong ray of philosophic light has broke from Scotland in our own times; and it is with private, as well as public regard, that I repeat the names of Hume, Robertson, and Adam Smith.[14]

And when Gibbon refers back to earlier sections of the history, we seem to catch him basking in the pleasant thought that *The Decline and Fall* is now so established in the public esteem that it has become a worthy object of its own attention:

The festival of the death of Hosein is amply described by Sir John Chardin, a traveller whom I have often praised.

Have I observed elsewhere, that this Jewish beauty [Berenice, the wife of the emperor Titus] was at this time above fifty years of age?

From these Indian stories, the reader may correct a note in my first volume . . .; or from that note he may correct these stories.[15]

The changing character of Gibbon's footnotes, as *The Decline and Fall* moves from instalment to instalment, opens a side-window onto the subject which will be more directly and fully explored in this book. For the emotional colouring of Gibbon's relationship with his reader was determined by the changing state of his reputation. Initially without a

[12] *DF* ii. 932 n. 1.
[13] *DF* iii. 471 n. 1.
[14] *DF* iii. 314 n. 195, iii. 506 n. 89, iii. 625 n. 30, and iii. 728 n. 69.
[15] *DF* iii. 227 n. 180, iii. 400 n. 60, iii. 527 n. 10.

literary character, on the publication of the first volume of *The Decline and Fall* Gibbon immediately acquired notoriety on the grounds of supposed irreligion, surreptitiously advanced (so it was alleged) by the underhand manipulation of his sources. Burdened with that reputation, Gibbon composed and published the second instalment of his history, in which he managed partially to disarm his critics, and thus regained a measure of control over his public character. Hence the greater geniality of the third instalment, a geniality born of a sense of adversity largely surmounted or resolved, and strengthened by a consciousness, not only of having now become the historian he wished to be, but of being generally so recognized. In 1788 he has become the 'luminous historian', a compliment bestowed upon him on a state occasion and 'in the presence of the British nation'.[16]

Gibbon was unabashed in acknowledging that his career as an historian was fuelled by a desire for fame: 'I have never affected, indeed I have never understood, the stoical apathy, the proud contempt of criticism, which some authors have publicly professed. Fame is the motive, it is the reward, of our labours . . .'.[17] The gods punish us by giving us what we crave. The success of *The Decline and Fall* indeed furnished Gibbon with 'a name, a rank, a character, in the World' to which he would not otherwise have been entitled.[18] Eventually this public reputation was grateful to him, and nourished that innocent vanity which even his friends acknowledged was an element in his character. Initially, however, it was a reputation he resented, and was determined to resist. In particular, the denunciation by the spokesmen for religious orthodoxy of Gibbon's treatment of Christianity, at first in respect of chapters fifteen and sixteen of *The Decline and Fall*, and subsequently in the rest of the history, was (so Gibbon contended) a vicious misrepresentation.

The subject of this book is in part the story of the conflict between Gibbon and those he mockingly dubbed the 'Watchmen of the Holy City'. It is not, however, an account merely of the attacks on *The Decline and Fall*, such as McCloy wrote over sixty years ago.[19] Rather, it

[16] *A* 336 and n. ★.

[17] From the *Vindication* (1779) (*DF* iii. 1109). Gibbon confessed to Suzanne Necker that he was indifferent to Parliament because there he would always be 'sans reputation' (*L* ii. 264). This sentiment was no affectation adopted for public effect. Similar comments occur in letters to Deyverdun and Suard: correspondents with whom Gibbon had no measures to keep, and therefore no reason for deception or dissimulation (to Deyverdun, *L* ii. 106; to Suard, *L* ii. 122).

[18] *A* 346.

[19] Shelby T. McCloy, *Gibbon's Antagonism to Christianity* (London: Williams and Norgate, 1933). The bibliography of the attacks on *The Decline and Fall* was taken further by J. E. Norton (Norton, 233–47); but even there it is still incomplete.

explores the ramifications of a more elusive aspect of authorship. By considering the sequence of interactions between the historian and his readership, we can hope to gain a more intimate understanding of what we might call Gibbon's experience of himself. At the same time, we may hope also to deepen our understanding of the conditions of English authorship during the later decades of the eighteenth and the early decades of the nineteenth centuries, from the opening of the war with the American colonies, down to the successful conclusion of the wars with revolutionary and Napoleonic France.

In the final version of his 'Memoirs' Gibbon recollected the complicated tactical situation within which the clerical attack on him was launched, and to the complexity of which that attack itself further contributed: 'Many years afterwards, when the name of Gibbon was become as notorious as that of Middleton, it was industriously whispered at Oxford that the historian had formerly "turned Papist." My character stood exposed to the reproach of inconstancy, and this invidious topic would have been handled without mercy by my opponents, could they have separated my cause from that of the University.'[20] In 1776 Gibbon's sudden notoriety, the chequered confessional past which was officiously recalled to mind, and the current politics surrounding the Church of England (to which Gibbon alludes when he notes how his case became entangled with that of Oxford), interacted in intricate and often unexpected ways. Part I of this book recovers and explains those complicated interactions, up to and including the publication of the final three volumes of *The Decline and Fall* in 1788.

At that point there occurred a development which imparted fresh vigour, and supplied new weapons, to the forces of religious orthodoxy. The French Revolution dominated the last five years of Gibbon's life. Most immediately, there was a sense of physical menace. From his drawing room in Lausanne he could see the camp fires of a revolutionary army, and hear the pounding of its cannon. However, the Revolution also posed a more intimate threat. Burke's indictment of the French *philosophes* as creators of the Revolution meant that Gibbon's adversaries could now plausibly charge the philosophic historian with being (what he certainly was not) a foe to England's *ancien régime*. Part II of this study shows how the attack on Gibbon was refreshed and to some degree reconfigured in the wake of the French Revolution. The central text here is the 'Memoirs of my Life', the six drafts of which, it

[20] *A* 88.

will be argued, can be properly understood only when positioned very exactly in the context of the literatures of revolution and counter-revolution. A study of the textual dynamics generated as Gibbon passed on from draft to draft will bring to light the extent of the measures he was prepared to take in resisting the advent of this freshly damaging interpretation of the significance and tendency of his work. At stake was nothing less than the shape and meaning of his life. It drew from him the most far-reaching reconceptualizations of both his life and work.

With Gibbon's death in 1794 the literary sequelae of his reputation for irreligion entered their third, and perhaps most interesting, phase. His friend and literary executor, Lord Sheffield, entered into possession of the historian's papers, and set about preparing what we now know as the *Miscellaneous Works*. A two-volume quarto collection published in 1796 was followed in 1814 by a five-volume octavo edition containing much new material, accompanied in 1815 by a third quarto volume which made that new material available to the purchasers of the original two volumes. It is clear, then, that this was a complicated act of publication, extending over almost two decades, embracing different formats, and embodying a number of decisions as to what should be included and what excluded. It is also an act of publication which has left behind an unusually complete archive. Gibbon's original manuscripts are in the British Library, some of the corrected proof-sheets of the first edition are in the Regenstein Library at Chicago University, and Sheffield's working papers, together with the interleaved copy of the 1796 volumes he used while preparing the enlarged 1814 edition, are in the Beinecke Library at Yale. Part III of this book elicits from these traces the series of decisions taken by Sheffield about what could be placed before the public, and when. In the brief prefatory remarks Sheffield inserted at the head of the two volumes published in 1796, he insisted on the extent to which these collected writings—and in particular the letters, journals, and 'Memoirs of my Life'—amounted to 'a complete picture of [Gibbon's] talents, his disposition, his studies, and his attainments': 'Few men, I believe, have ever so fully unveiled their own character, by a minute narrative of their sentiments and pursuits, as Mr. Gibbon will here be found to have done; not with study and labour—not with an affected frankness—but with a genuine confession of his little foibles and peculiarities, and a good-humoured and natural display of his own conduct and opinions.'[21]

---

[21] *MW 1796* i, pp. v, vii. The proofs indicate that Sheffield had originally intended to guide his

Gibbon's moral and religious character was at the heart of the controversy over the religious tendency of *The Decline and Fall*. When Sheffield advertised the central interest of the *Miscellaneous Works* as the portrait they offered of the historian, he therefore served notice that this latest publication would be a continuation of the historian's own efforts to regain control and ownership of his public reputation. Sheffield demonstrated an acute tactical sense of how that goal might best be achieved, as the political background changed from the dark days of the regicide peace to the victorious conclusion of the Napoleonic war.

So much for the subject of this book. Let me now say something brief about method. This study is methodologically promiscuous. It is so deliberately. It relies on close reading, because works of literature are formally complex. It attends to context, because authors and readers possess a social existence, and works of literature are in part acts of communication between the two. It investigates the bibliography of the works which fall within its scope, because works of literature may be physically intricate as well as formally complex, and from the details of their physical embodiment can be extracted precious, and often otherwise inaccessible, information.

However, each of these different modes of literary study requires us to conceptualize the literary work in distinct and even irreconcilable ways: as a self-sufficient verbal icon; as a message porous to, and reliant on, the conditions of its various contexts; and as the laminated product of an artisanal or industrial process. Yet to eliminate from consideration any two of these out of an itch for methodological purity (as opposed to rigour of argument) would be nothing more than intellectual priggishness. The ontological impurity of the literary work demands eclecticism in those who aspire to the fullest possible understanding. Furthermore, as I hope the arguments assembled in this book will demonstrate, these different kinds of critical and scholarly enquiry in fact reinforce one another in ways which a theoretician would be obliged to find scandalous. But the heterogeneity of the literary work silently mocks the unintelligent rigidity of the theorist. Hobbes gives us a salutary reminder that reflection on method can take us only so far: 'It happens besides, that for the finding out of equations, there is no certain method, but he is best able to do it, that has the best natural

reader yet more openly in their interpretation of Gibbon's character. The last sentence as first written had further clauses, and ended: 'opinions, such as one cannot but be delighted to see, in the intimate communication of unreserved friendship' (Regenstein, p. vii).

wit.'[22] In this respect, there is no difference between literary study and mathematics.

The three forms of literary study brought together in the making of this book might be thought to create a kind of trinity. But if so, it must be said at once that the doctrine of the literary trinity is Arian, not Athanasian. The father is bibliography, the spirit is context, but close reading is only the son. It is a later, dependent, and subordinate activity which can be practised with safety only within the boundaries marked out for it by its senior colleagues. The book's epigraph gives succinct voice to this vision of the wholesome priorities of literary study.

Oxford, December 2000

---

[22] *De Corpore*, pt. I, ch. 6.

PART I

THE HISTORIAN AND HIS REPUTATION
1776–1788

I

Revision and Religion

We may be well assured, that a writer, conversant with the world, would never have ventured to expose the gods of his country to public ridicule, had they not already been the objects of secret contempt among the polished and enlightened orders of society.

(Edward Gibbon, *The Decline and Fall*)

. . . in point of Religion she was rational that is silent.

(Edward Gibbon, on his aunt Hester)

We know, and what is better, we feel inwardly, that religion is the basis of civil society and the source of all good and all comfort. In England we are so convinced of this that there is no rust of superstition with which the accumulated absurdity of the human mind might have crusted it over in the course of all ages, that ninety nine in a hundred of the people in England would not prefer to impiety.

(Edmund Burke, *Reflections on the Revolution in France*)

Mr. Pope used to tell me, that when he had anything better than ordinary to say, and yet too bold, he always reserved it for a second or third edition, and then nobody took any notice of it.

(William Warburton to Richard Hurd)

Gibbon's struggle to determine his public reputation began with the revisions he made in chapters fifteen and sixteen for the second edition of 1776, and the third edition of 1777.[1] These chapters underwent two distinct phases of revisal: the first, completed before any attacks on the

---

[1] Gibbon made only two changes of significance for our purposes when he revised these chapters for the fourth edition of 1781. Both made more ample or more precise a reference in a footnote, and thus show a silent acknowledgement of the justice of some of Davis's strictures. Thereafter, in the editions of 1782 and 1789, he seems himself to have made no revisions, although the reader who collates the texts of these chapters in those later editions still encounters changes in accidentals. These are most probably printing house corrections, made by someone who from time to time did not understand Gibbon's prose.

supposed irreligion of the history had appeared, for the second edition published on 3 June 1776; and the second, completed in the knowledge of the first wave of attacks by Watson and Chelsum (but not Henry Davis), for the third edition published in May 1777. Moreover, the tendency of these two phases of revisal—their impact on the text of the history, and Gibbon's evident governing intention in making the revisions—is in each case coherent. That is to say, the individual corrections of the text when taken together indicate a single overall plan of revision. However, the purpose which governed the revisions made in the third edition was directly the opposite of that which had dictated the revisions made in the second edition. I shall begin by sketching how chapters fifteen and sixteen fit in to Gibbon's first volume, and how their subject connects with the broad theme of imperial decline. Then I shall discuss, in terms unavoidably minute, the character of the revisions made in the second and third editions.

II

The first volume of *The Decline and Fall* begins with three chapters surveying the political, military, and social condition of the Roman Empire in the age of the Antonines (AD 138–80). At the end of chapter fourteen, the narrative of the empire's decline has been deduced to Constantine's final defeat of his rival Licinius, and to the reunification of the empire under his sole monarchy (AD 324). Gibbon then concluded the first volume with the notorious two chapters on Christianity. Chapter fifteen described the progress of the Christian religion from its origins as a minor sect to its installation as the established religion of the empire, and explained that progress with reference to five secondary (that is to say, non-divine) causes: (i) the zeal of the early Christians, (ii) the Christian doctrine of a future life, (iii) the miraculous powers ascribed to the primitive Church, (iv) the pure morals of the first Christians, and (v) the union and discipline of the Christian republic. Chapter sixteen addressed itself to the subject of the persecutions suffered by the Christians, and suggested that the easy and tolerating temper of classical paganism could hardly have given rise to the number of martyrs which the Church subsequently claimed.

When Hume wrote to congratulate Gibbon on the publication of volume one of *The Decline and Fall*, he touched on the subject of chapters fifteen and sixteen: 'When I heard of your undertaking (which was some time ago) I own that I was a little curious to see how you would extricate yourself from the subject of your two last

chapters.'[2] The history of the decline of the empire, then, necessarily
implied some consideration of the rise of Christianity, and the relation
(if any) between the two. Historians prior to Gibbon had linked
Christianity and empire within the framework of providence. But so
roomy was that framework that it could accommodate a number of
different, even contradictory, positions. A popular explanation held
that God had delayed the birth of Christ in order that the universal
pacification brought about by the Roman Empire would make easier
the spread of the new religion. A second stated that it was necessary for
the majority of mankind to have reached a degree of intellectual
refinement before the Christian message could be properly received
and recorded. A third inverted our first explanation, and insisted that
Christianity had appeared in the world under the least propitious circumstances, and had recommended doctrines which were more likely
to repel men than to allure them; no one could doubt, therefore, that
the success of Christianity was due to divine and miraculous intervention.[3] Common to all these various interpretations, however, was
the contention that the timing and circumstances of the Christian
revelation showed evidence of design. The unmistakable upshot of
Gibbon's two last chapters—that the rise of Christianity could be fully
explained by reference to human causes, and that the fledgling faith had
not encountered opposition so extensive and determined that it could
be vanquished by only the finger of God—was an affront to all these
providential narratives.[4] Thomas Randolph put it concisely and accurately: 'The speedy and wonderful Propagation of the Gospel, under
the Circumstances in which it was first published, has been frequently
urged by Christian Writers, as an irrefragable Proof of the Truth of the
Christian Religion. But a late ingenious Historian has used his utmost
Endeavours to invalidate the Force of this Proof, and attempted to
account for the Success of the Gospel by natural Causes.'[5]

[2] *A* 312.
[3] In *The Decline and Fall* Gibbon himself alluded with mock reverence to the first of these (*DF*
i. 499). It had been most clearly advanced some years before by William Robertson, *The Situation
of the World at the Time of Christ's Appearance* (Edinburgh, 1755). For the need for refinement, see
Apthorp, *Letters*, p. vi. For the difficult doctrines of Christianity, see Salisbury, *Establishment of
Christianity*, 109 and Milner, *Gibbon's Account*, 179. For the worldly disadvantages over which it
triumphed, see Leland, *Reflections*, 96 and White, *Sermons*, 135–6.
[4] For an invocation of the finger of God, see White, *Sermons*, 105.
[5] Randolph, *Truth of the Christian Religion*, 1. Compare Milner, *Gibbon's Account*, 172: 'the
whole energy of his [Gibbon's] fifteenth chapter is directed to establish positions, tending to
account for its [Christianity's] progress by methods merely human. What consequences sub-
versive of its divine authority would thence be deduced, its enemies will tell with pleasure.'
Dalrymple countered Gibbon's analysis by maintaining that 'the things which Mr Gibbon considered as secondary or human causes, efficaciously promoting the Christian religion, either

The first volume of *The Decline and Fall* was published on 17
February 1776.[6] Writing to his stepmother on 26 March, Gibbon conveyed two important pieces of information: 'my book has been very
well received . . . by every set of people except perhaps by the Clergy
who seem (I know not why) to shew their teeth on the occasion. A
thousand Copies are sold, and we are preparing a second Edition,
which in so short a time is, for a book of that price a very uncommon
event.'[7] This is the first indication that Gibbon knew he had provoked
'the Clergy', although for the time being he knew neither who would
enter the lists against him, nor what they would write.[8] In the same
breath, he reports that the second edition is in preparation. It is of the
first importance to appreciate that the revisions Gibbon made for the
second edition were planned and executed in this period of uncertainty.
On 24 May, once again to his stepmother, he returned to the subject of
the second edition: 'My mornings have been very much taken up with
preparing and correcting (though in a minute and almost imperceptible
way) my new Edition which will be out the first of June.'[9] April and
May 1776 were thus the months given over to revision. The second
edition appeared on 3 June. The revisions it embodied, though minute,
were however far from imperceptible.[10] Moreover, they demonstrate
that, despite his protestation to the contrary, Gibbon had a very good
idea of where and how he had offended the orthodox.

Gibbon composed two accounts of this controversy: the first, in the
Vindication of 1779, the second in draft 'E' of the 'Memoirs', completed
on 2 March 1791. The image he created of himself was in each case
slightly different. In the *Vindication*, Gibbon is a Lear of the world of
historiography, more sinned against than sinning:

---

tended to retard its progress, or were the manifest operations of the wisdom and power of God'
(Dalrymple, *Secondary Causes*, 210).

[6] Norton, 37.

[7] *L* ii. 100.

[8] Even as late as June 1776 Gibbon was unsure about the identities of those who were to
oppose him. On 6 June he wrote to Holroyd that 'I now understand from pretty good authority
that Dr Porteous the friend and chaplain of St Secker is actually sharpening his goosequill against
the two last Chapters' (*L* ii. 111). Porteous never published an attack on Gibbon, although
Travis's *Letters* were dedicated to Porteous, and it may be that the hand of the bishop of Chester
guided the pen of his archdeacon.

[9] *L* ii. 110.

[10] Gibbon's revisions to the second, third, and fourth editions of *The Decline and Fall* produced
several thousand variants. Many of these are very small, and in general Gibbon restricted his revisions so that in virtually all cases the pagination, and very often even the lineation, of the text
could be preserved. This was clearly convenient for the compositor setting up the new edition;
it may be that Strahan and Cadell requested Gibbon so to restrict his revisions.

When I delivered to the world the First Volume of an important History, in which I had been obliged to connect the progress of Christianity with the civil state and revolutions of the Roman Empire, I could not be ignorant that the result of my inquiries might offend the interest of some and the opinions of others. If the whole work was favourably received by the Public, I had the more reason to expect that this obnoxious part would provoke the zeal of those who consider themselves as the Watchmen of the Holy City. These expectations were not disappointed . . .[11]

'I could not be ignorant': Gibbon admitted here what he would later deny, namely that he was aware that he ran the risk of offending those he mockingly called 'the Watchmen of the Holy City'. In the *Vindication* he professed to be unperturbed by the 'ordinary, and indeed obsolete charges of impious principles'.[12] He had been stung to reply only because Davis had attempted 'the ruin of my moral and literary character'.[13] In draft 'E' of the *Memoirs*, however, composed twelve years later, Gibbon would retouch this self-portrait. The outcry of the orthodox was now entirely unforeseen by the innocent historian: 'I had likewise flattered myself that an age of light and liberty would receive, without scandal, an enquiry into the *human* causes of the progress and establishment of Christianity.' The pose of necessity struck in the *Vindication* ('I had been obliged to connect . . .') was also moderated into an admission that the author had of course enjoyed scope for a certain discretion. The subject might indeed have received a different and more emollient handling: 'Had I believed that the majority of English readers were so fondly attached even to the name and shadow of Christianity, had I foreseen that the pious, the timid, and the prudent would feel, or affect to feel, with such exquisite sensibility, I might perhaps have softened the two invidious Chapters, which would create many enemies and conciliate few friends.'[14] Gone, too, was the proud and unshaken defiance of the *Vindication*. In the 'Memoirs', Gibbon explained the sequence of his emotions differently: 'Let me frankly own that I was startled at the first vollies of this Ecclesiastical ordnance; but as soon as I found that this empty noise was mischievous only in the intention, my fear was converted to indignation, and every feeling of indignation or curiosity has long since subsided in pure and placid

---

[11] *DF* iii. 1109. Cf. Apthorp, *Letters*, p. vi: 'the Jewish and Christian revelations were *providentially* connected with the great revolutions in civil history' in order that their proofs should be written into the historical record without 'doubt, mistake, or ambiguity' (my emphasis).

[12] *DF* iii. 1110.

[13] *DF* iii. 1110.

[14] *A* 316.

indifference.'[15] The findings of collation corroborate some of these assertions (although, as we shall see below, there are good reasons to doubt that Gibbon composed his 'Memoirs' in a mood of 'pure and placid indifference' to his religious reputation). However, it is difficult to see how the heroic figure of the *Vindication* and the inadvertent figure of the 'Memoirs' can both be true; indeed, Gibbon's revisions show them both to be in some measure false. The *Vindication* is misleading in its suggestion that Gibbon stoically endured the assaults of his detractors until his character as a gentleman was challenged: but the revisions to the second and third editions show him anticipating, eluding, and rejecting his adversaries on points of religious history. The 'Memoirs' are less than candid in their suggestion that the unaware historian was overtaken by a controversy the possibility of which had not occurred to him: but the revisions to the second edition, made before any attack had been published, show that Gibbon possessed a very accurate sense of which areas of his history would be offensive, and why.[16]

III

As we have seen, Gibbon probably spent the months of April and May 1776 in revising the text of his first volume for its second edition.[17] The character of the changes he made in chapters fifteen and sixteen are evinced by an amendment he made in the text of chapter eight, the chapter devoted to the Persians.[18] In the course of that chapter, Gibbon paid close attention to the refashioning of the religion of Zoroaster into a civil religion at the hands of Artaxerxes, the great founder of the dynasty of the Sassanides. The theology of the Magian religion was clarified on the basis of the intoxicated vision of 'Erdaviraph, a young

---

[15] *A* 319. Cf. also: 'The freedom of my writings has, indeed, provoked an implacable tribe; but as I was safe from the stings, I was soon accustomed to the buzzing of the hornets . . .' (*A* 346).

[16] Sheffield records that 'before the publication of the Work & while it was in hand He [Gibbon] had often said there would be much Difficulty and Delicacy in respect to that part which gives the History of the Christian Religion' (Beinecke Library, MS Vault, Sect. 10, Drawer 3, Sect. B 11 ii; transcribed in Appendix 1, below). It was for reassurance on this very point that Gibbon had allowed some of his friends to read the manuscript of volume one before publication (see *MW 1796* i. 496 and *L* ii. 81). The potential for religious controversy in the subject of *The Decline and Fall* was immediately obvious to a contemporary such as Hume, as is shown by the congratulatory letter to Gibbon which 'overpaid the labour of ten years' and in which Hume comments knowingly on 'the subject of your two last chapters' (*A* 311–12).

[17] Norton suggested that the third edition of 1777 appeared to be more heavily revised than the second of 1776 (Norton, 43). Collation reveals that in fact the text of *The Decline and Fall* was more substantially revised in 1776.

[18] This variant is not noted by Bury (Bury, i, pp. xxxii–xxxiv).

but holy prelate'; its church government was remodelled into a regular hierarchy; and rival sects or religions were methodically suppressed.[19] This persecution of heterodoxy was described as follows in the first edition: 'The majesty of Ormusd [the embodiment of the principle of good in the Magian religion], who was jealous of a rival, was seconded by the despotism of Artaxerxes, who could not suffer a rebel; and with the assistance of what his prelates no doubt called wholesome severities, the schismatics within his vast empire were soon reduced to the inconsiderable number of eighty thousand.'[20] In the second edition, Gibbon made a small but significant deletion: 'The majesty of Ormusd, who was jealous of a rival, was seconded by the despotism of Artaxerxes, who could not suffer a rebel; and the schismatics within his vast empire were soon reduced to the inconsiderable number of eighty thousand.'[21] By removing the incidental blow aimed at the prelates of Zoroastrianism ('with the assistance of what his prelates no doubt called wholesome severities'), Gibbon muted the deistical character of the passage, reducing it almost to a mere statement of fact. It had of course been one of the principal tenets of the late seventeenth- and early eighteenth-century freethinkers that priestcraft might arise in any religion, and that, wherever it arose, it would display its essential characteristic of oppression by employing 'wholesome severities'.[22] Such a sentiment lay behind the passage Gibbon deleted when preparing his second edition. Moreover, when the deleted phrase was taken together with the echo of the jealous God of the Old Testament in the statement that Ormusd was 'jealous of a rival', the Magian clergy appeared for a moment to be close to the Christian priesthood. The intention which motivated the deletion of the phrase which detonated that injurious potential—an intention of removing language which suggested an affinity with writers such as Collins, Toland, and Tindal— was dominant also in Gibbon's revisions to chapters fifteen and sixteen.

The substantive changes Gibbon introduced into these chapters in the second edition were of three kinds: (i) the adducing of fresh evidence in support of positions or contentions which, in the know-

[19] *DF* i. 216.

[20] *DF 1* 208.

[21] *DF 2* 208.

[22] 'Wholesome severities' was an expression with some history in eighteenth-century English religious controversy, as it 'had been the cant phrase of the Tory party in the controversy on toleration in 1688' (Pattison, *Essays*, ii. 143): Gibbon's father's library was, it will be remembered, 'stuffed with much trash of the last age, with much High Church divinity and politics' (*A* 248). In Nicholas Amhurst's Whiggish *Terræ-Filius* the phrase is used mockingly to describe the actions of an arbitrary and oppressive proctor (p. 286). It recurs later in *The Decline and Fall* (*DF* ii. 95 n. 84), as an ironic periphrasis for bigoted persecution.

ledge of imminent attack, appeared unguarded; (ii) the elimination of sceptical turns of phrase which were inessential to the central lines of argument; (iii) the excision of deistical language. Common to all three kinds of revision, however, was the aim of confusing or obscuring the affiliations which existed between the topics, language, and arguments of *The Decline and Fall*, and those perceived to be typical of deism and freethought.

The first kind of revision can be most promptly dealt with. The branding of the Christian Jews with the 'contemptuous epithet of Ebionites' is supported in the footnotes of the first edition with nothing more than a scoff at a mistaken etymology: 'Some writers have been pleased to create an Ebion, the imaginary author of their sect and name. But we can more safely rely on the learned Eusebius than on the vehement Tertullian, or the credulous Epiphanius.'[23] In the second edition, the note was amplified by the addition of the following: 'According to Le Clerc, the Hebrew word *Ebjonim* may be translated into Latin by that of *Pauperes*. See Hist. Ecclesiast. p. 477.'[24] When Gibbon came to look again at this footnote in the spring of 1776, his allegation that 'Ebionite' was a term of contempt seemed to require some justification: without such justification, that passage and its note ran the risk of seeming an instance of that scorn for the Jews for which freethinkers and deists such as Shaftesbury and Bolingbroke had been frequently reproached.

A very similar revision occurred when Gibbon looked again at his relation of the Gnostics' reservations about the character of the God of the Old Testament, in whom 'they could discover none of the features of the wise and omnipotent father of the universe'.[25] In the first edition, the footnote simply spelled out the Gnostics' misgivings with greater specificity: 'The milder Gnostics considered Jehovah, the Creator, as a Being of a mixed nature between God and the Dæmon. Others confounded him with the evil principle.'[26] The difficulty arose here because, in the late and mid-eighteenth century, religious sceptics were sometimes seen as the heirs of ancient Gnosticism, and were occasionally referred to as 'modern Gnostics'.[27] The danger Gibbon ran here was

---

[23] *DF 1*, p. xcvii n. 22.

[24] *DF 2*, pp. lxvi–lxvii n. 22.

[25] *DF* i. 457.

[26] *DF 1*, p. lxvii n. 28.

[27] See Howes, *A Discourse*; these philosophic Christians operate 'a revised plan of the ancient Gnostics' (p. 8), to the point where they may be said to comprise 'a modern sect of Gnostics' (p. 11). That modern sceptics were simply warming over the long-exploded objections of ancient enemies of Christianity was a common topic of the orthodox opponents of freethinking.

that of seeming to place his own doubts about Jehovah in the mouth of the ancient Gnostics. In the second edition, therefore, he ensured that this passage could be read as nothing more than a reporting of the sentiments of an historical sect by producing an authority. The following sentence was added to the existing text of the note: 'Consult the second century of the general history of Mosheim, which give a very distinct, though concise, account of their strange opinions on this subject.'[28] By calling their opinions 'strange' Gibbon explicitly distanced himself from the Gnostics. At the same time, he contrived to shelter himself behind the irreproachably orthodox figure of Mosheim, the Lutheran and church historian, whose *Vindiciae antiquae christianorum disciplinae* (1720) had, conveniently enough, been a riposte to Toland, the freethinker.[29] A moment which a hostile reader might have seized on as evidence of infidelity has been made safe.

There were moments, then, when Gibbon brought forward corroborating authorities to prevent a point being read as simply his surrendering to a freethinking and irreverent disposition. There were also moments, however, when Gibbon apparently realized that the wording he had used was pointlessly offensive. In these instances, he was prepared to rephrase. In the first edition, when relating the views of the early Christians on chastity, he wrote that: 'It was their favourite opinion, that if Adam had preserved his obedience to the Creator, he would have lived and died in a state of virgin purity . . .'.[30] In the second edition, 'lived and died' became 'lived for ever'.[31] The revision accommodated *The Decline and Fall* to the orthodox Christian belief that it had been man's disobedience which had brought death into the world. The implication in the text of the first edition that Adam would have died even had he remained in a state of innocence could have been construed as a step towards the mortalist materialism with which freethinkers were routinely charged.[32]

There was a similar trimming away of loose language in the passage towards the end of chapter fifteen in which Gibbon had explained the mutually reinforcing effect of the five secondary causes of the progress

[28] *DF 2*, p. lxvii n. 28.

[29] Johann Lorenz von Mosheim (*c.*1694–1755); ecclesiastical historian; Gibbon owned his *De Rebus Christianorum ante Constantinum Magnum Commentarii* (Helmstadt, 1753), *Dissertationum ad Historiam Ecclesiasticam Pertinentium Volumen Primum et Alterum*, 2 vols. (Altona and Lubeck, 1767), *An Ecclesiastical History*, 2 vols. (London, 1765) and 6 vols. (London, 1782), and *Institutionum Historiæ Ecclesiasticæ Libri Quatuor* (Helmstadt, 1764).

[30] *DF 1* 484.

[31] *DF 2* 484.

[32] See e.g. Bentley, *Remarks* (1713), 14.

of Christianity. Of the fifth cause ('the union and discipline of the Christian republic'), he had said in the first edition: '[It] united their courage, directed their arms, and gave their efforts that irresistible weight, which even a small band of well-trained and desperate volunteers has so often possessed over an undisciplined multitude . . .'.[33] In the second edition, however, the 'well-trained and desperate volunteers' of the first edition were changed into 'well-trained and intrepid volunteers'.[34] It was clearly more complimentary to attribute the success of the early Christians to intrepidity, rather than to despair. Moreover, the revision moved *The Decline and Fall* slightly closer to compatibility with a providentialist account of the progress of Christianity, and to that (small) extent attenuated its infidel character.

One last example of this class of revision. In the final sentence of chapter sixteen, Gibbon questioned the credibility of Eusebius's account of the persecutions suffered by the early Church. In the first edition, the question was posed in these words: 'what degree of credit can be assigned to a courtly bishop [Eusebius], and a passionate declaimer, who, under the protection of Constantine, enjoyed the exclusive privilege of recording the persecutions which Christianity had experienced from the vanquished rivals or disregarded predecessors of their gracious sovereign.'[35] In the second edition, the 'persecutions which Christianity had experienced' became the 'persecutions inflicted on the Christians'.[36] The change was, to use Gibbon's word, 'minute'; but it was nevertheless rich in implication. The neutrality of 'experienced' was replaced by 'inflicted', with its suggestions of injustice and harm. The general term 'Christianity' gave way to the more specific 'Christians': those who had allegedly suffered the persecutions are now not refined away into an abstraction. The tendency of the conclusion was, however, unchanged. In the second edition and thereafter, Gibbon still encouraged his reader to view sceptically the number of martyrs claimed by the Church. But he also adjusted his wording so as to concede what could not be denied except at the cost of impartiality: namely, that martyrdoms had occurred, that the persecutions in which those martyrs died were endured by men and women, and that they were attended with circumstances of cruelty. Those stubborn realities had perhaps been too lightly left out of the account in the first edition. By allowing them to emerge in his second edition and thereafter, Gibbon sacrificed nothing of importance to his central objectives. But he had made it harder to argue that (in an inversion of the charge he

---

[33] *DF 1* 502.   [34] *DF 2* 502.   [35] *DF 1* 586.   [36] *DF 2* 586.

himself had levelled at Eusebius) he had indulged a mere prejudice against Christianity by relating whatever might redound to its disgrace, and suppressing all that could tend to its glory.[37]

The third kind of revision Gibbon made for the second edition involved the deletion of language drawn from the vocabulary of deism. Discussing the doctrine of the immortality of the soul in chapter fifteen, and remarking that it was more prevalent among barbarians than amongst the pagans of Greece and Rome, Gibbon noted that 'since we cannot attribute such a difference to the superior knowledge of the barbarians, we must ascribe it to the influence of an established priesthood, which employed the motives of virtue as the instrument of ambition'.[38] To this, in the first edition, he appended a note: 'The Druids borrowed sums of money on bonds made payable to the creditor in the other world. The success of such a trade is one of the strongest instances of sacerdotal art and popular credulity.'[39] The text, with its allusion to an established priesthood using virtue as the instrument of ambition, was already tinctured with deism. The footnote, however, strengthened that colouring into a virtual statement of allegiance: 'sacerdotal art' and 'popular credulity' were phrases redolent of writers such as Blount, Toland, and Tindal, which announced a hostility towards the power exerted by priests in society. In the second edition, the footnote was completely rewritten:

If we confine ourselves to the Gauls, we may observe, that they intrusted, not only their lives, but even their money, to the security of another world. Vetus ille mos Gallorum occurrit (says Valerius Maximus, l. ii. c. 6. p. 10.), quos memoria proditur est, pecunias mutuas, quæ his apud inferos redderentur, dare solitos. The same custom is more darkly insinuated by Mela, l. iii. c. 2. It is almost needless to add, that the profits of trade hold a just proportion to the credit of the merchant, and that the Druids derived from their holy profession a character of responsibility, which could scarcely be claimed by any other order of men.[40]

The inclusion of references and quotation immediately tilted the balance of the note away from polemic and towards historical scholarship, while the greater elaborateness of the syntax, and the politeness of

[37] For this charge against Eusebius, see *DF* i. 577. For the accusation of prejudice against Christianity in Gibbon, see Loftus, *Reply*, 150 and 199. This was a standard charge against deists and freethinkers: 'no writers whatsoever discover stronger signs of prejudice' (Leland, *Principal Deistical Writers*, i. 393).
[38] *DF* i. 465.
[39] *DF 1*, pp. lxviii–lxix n. 55. This detail was noted, and dismissed as 'but a silly story', by Henry Taylor (*Grand Apostacy*, 43).
[40] *DF 2*, pp. lxviii–lxix n. 56.

the language, in which Gibbon first related the institution of these loans, and then commented on them, occluded his allegiances. Whereas in the first edition a hint of deism in the text was corroborated and amplified in the note, in the second edition the note moved away from the language and polemical style of the deists, thereby neutralizing the deistical flavour of the text. The note in the second edition is, of course, 'ironic', and it would be no difficult task to unpick, for instance, the hostile implications of the comparison between the priest and the merchant. But here, as it also did at times elsewhere, Gibbon's irony seems to have strengthened as the defensive complication of a deistical impulse which had been at first more nakedly expressed.

The subject of the government of the Church was a natural source of deistical language and sentiment, and for the second edition Gibbon made a number of small changes in his treatment of this topic which all served to obscure or complicate what in the first edition might have been more easily recognizable as compatible with deism. In the first edition, Gibbon had written as follows about the 'spiritual guides of Christianity': 'while they concealed from others, and perhaps from themselves, the secret motive of their conduct, they too frequently relapsed into all the turbulent passions of active life . . .'.[41] In the second edition, the 'spiritual guides of Christianity' became the 'ecclesiastical governors of the Christians', and the 'secret motive of their conduct' was enlarged into the 'secret motives of their conduct'.[42] To move from a single 'motive' to a plural 'motives' weakened the suggestion of an organized conspiracy, common to all prelates, which had as its aim the transformation of religious into secular authority; while the revision of 'spiritual guides' to 'ecclesiastical governors' removed the implication that theological refinement might be an instrument of temporal absolutism, and that such an improper conversion of the divine into the worldly had occurred amongst the early Christians. We find a similar dilution of deistical affinity when Gibbon revised an aphoristic sentence concerning the role of church government in church conflicts. In the first edition he wrote: 'The government of the church has often been the subject as well as the instrument of religious contention.'[43] 'Instrument' suggests forethought, organization, and purpose: in a word, priestcraft. In the second edition, it was replaced by 'prize', a word which brought with it fewer injurious connotations.[44]

Gibbon's orthodox opponents were irritated by what they saw as the implication of chapters fifteen and sixteen, that there was a natural and

---

[41] *DF 1* 487–8.   [42] *DF 2* 487–8.   [43] *DF 1* 488.   [44] *DF 2* 488.

inevitable antipathy between philosophy and Christianity. Noting that Gibbon appeared to suggest that Marcus Aurelius had despised the Christians 'as a philosopher', Francis Eyre commented that 'there is no word that has been more prostituted of late than that of philosophy'.[45] One of the revisions Gibbon made in the second edition reveals that he himself realized that this opposition of philosophy and Christianity would cause offence, and that he tried in one instance at least to remove that implication. To illustrate the geographical spread of Christianity around the Mediterranean basin, Gibbon referred to the writings of Lucian. In the first edition, he did so in these words: 'From a philosophic writer who had studied mankind, and who describes their manner in the most lively colours, we may learn, that, under the reign of Commodus, his native country of Pontus was filled with Epicureans and *Christians*.'[46] In the second edition, Gibbon altered the opening phrases so that they read 'From the writings of Lucian, a philosopher who had studied mankind'.[47] The revision made it a less natural reading of the passage to see in it the unspoken suggestion that Lucian was 'philosophic' because unsympathetic to Christianity.

One of the aspects of chapter fifteen which elicited the most indignant response from Gibbon's critics was the discussion of the darkness of the passion with which it concluded. Gibbon's observation that pagan writers, although they noted the preternatural darkness which followed the death of Caesar, had said nothing about the darkness which followed the crucifixion, was read by his adversaries as an implicit denial of one of the miracles of Christ's life.[48] Joseph Milner, for example, condemned it as 'an attack upon the Gospel, the most direct of any to be met with in the book'.[49] Once again, a revision Gibbon made in the second edition indicates that he knew that this section of the chapter would be controversial, and that, while not removing or emasculating it, he deleted a word which disclosed his scepticism too broadly. In the first edition, the final paragraph of chapter fifteen began: 'But how shall we explain or excuse the supine inattention of the Pagan and philosophic world, to those evidences which were presented by the hand of Omnipotence, not to their reason, but to their senses?'[50] In the second edition, Gibbon amended

[45] [Eyre], *Remarks*, 109.
[46] *DF 1* 507.
[47] *DF 2* 507.
[48] John Brown had discussed the darkness of the passion as a miracle gracing the life of Jesus in his anti-deistical *Essays on the Characteristics of the Earl of Shaftesbury*, 280.
[49] Milner, *Gibbon's Account*, 235.
[50] *DF 1* 517.

'explain or excuse' to 'excuse'.[51] By removing the question of how the inattention of the pagans to Christian miracles could be explained, Gibbon masked the suggestion which had been more overtly displayed in his first edition, that a very natural explanation of their silence on this score was that the accounts of the Christian miracles were fictitious. The passage as it stands in the second edition still bore within it this implication, but it had been buried more deeply beneath the surface of the prose. The reader of Gibbon's second edition is not explicitly urged to consider the matter of explanation, and therefore Gibbon seems less openly to hurry his reader into areas of reflection which were bound to stimulate sceptical thoughts.

One final example of Gibbon's replacement of a more provocative comment in the first edition with a more enigmatic turn of phrase in the second edition. A common topic amongst deists and freethinkers was the absurd (as they saw it) otherworldliness of a Christian conception of virtue based on denial, abstinence, and mortification—what they commonly derided as 'monkish virtue'. Martyrdom is clearly an extreme form of this, in their eyes, perverted virtue. While the main thrust of Gibbon's sixteenth chapter was given over to arguing that there had been far fewer martyrs than the Church had claimed, in his first edition Gibbon was also prepared to reflect openly on the gloomy inversion of natural ideas of good prevalent among the early Christians. Contrasting Dionysius's escape from martyrdom with the patience of Cyprian, Gibbon wrote: 'But as he [Dionysius] escaped and survived the persecution, we must account him either more, or as he considered it himself, less fortunate than Cyprian.'[52] In the second edition, the end of this passage became 'either more or less fortunate than Cyprian'.[53] By making the preference for martyrdom over life a choice which anyone might make, rather than identifying it explicitly as the preference of Dionysius, as it was in the first edition, Gibbon made less overt the suggestion that such a preference was idiosyncratic and perverse. A measure of outspokenness was once again replaced by a greater reserve expressed through deliberate inscrutability.

IV

Taken together, then, there is a striking degree of congruence between the detailed changes Gibbon made to chapters fifteen and sixteen for the second edition. In the first edition Gibbon had in places employed

---

51 *DF 2* 517.   52 *DF 1*, p. lxxxi n. 80.   53 *DF 2*, p. lxxxi n. 80.

vocabulary and forms of expression which could be read as signs of
affiliation to the band of deists, freethinkers, and *esprits forts* who had
been attacked by the orthodox since the early years of the century as
enemies to established and revealed religion. In the second edition,
some of those signs were made ambiguous, or effaced. But let us be
clear about the extent of these revisions. There was no profound
remodelling of these two chapters. By no means all the deistical or
sceptical language was removed, and the argument was not in the least
affected. Moreover, if Gibbon's purpose in revising was that of conciliation, then he failed abjectly. Henry Davis, for example, Gibbon's
most bitter antagonist, was prompted to enter the lists after reading this
second, revised, edition.[54] But if Gibbon did not intend to remove the
occasion of offence, why did he (who was by temperament so averse to
the minutiae of correction and revisal) take trouble over these details of
expression? We know that while this very second edition was 'at the
press' Gibbon entertained the radical notion of suppressing the two
chapters altogether, and was prevented from doing so only by
Holroyd's firm advice neither to remove nor to alter.[55] If Gibbon
nerved himself to let the chapters remain, collation shows that he was
unable to follow Holroyd's advice in full and resist the temptation to
draw back where on reflection he felt he had presented his enemies
with too broad a target. In a letter to his stepmother of October 1776,
when the attacks had just begun to be published, Gibbon wrote that he
initially feared he would be 'hurt' by them. The revisions embodied in
the second edition confirm and substantiate that fear of damage.[56]

However, the tone of Gibbon's comments on his opponents underwent a marked change once the attacks began to appear in print, and

[54] In his *A Reply to Mr. Gibbon's Vindication* (1779), Davis informed his reader that 'my references answer to the second edition of Mr. Gibbon's History' (p. 14). The variants Davis printed
in *An Examination of the Fifteenth and Sixteenth Chapters of Mr. Gibbon's History . . .* (1778) suggest
that he was using the second edition then, too, and that he had collated it with the third edition
(see pp. 142–3); it is also worth noting that in the *Examination* he refers accurately to the '*three*
several editions of Mr. G's history' (p. 142). Davis seems also to have carried out *selective* colla-
tions of all three editions, for instance when he notes that what he takes to be a slip on Gibbon's
part has nevertheless 'uniformly preserved its place through the three editions of his history'
(p. 26).

[55] MS note in interleaved copy of *Miscellaneous Works*, Beinecke Library, Yale University (MS
vault, section 10, drawer 3, section B, B 11 i and ii), transcribed in Appendix 1, below. The
timing of this episode confirms the mood of anxious accommodation to prevailing opinion in
which the revisions for the second edition were made. The French translation of volume one of
The Decline and Fall appeared without chapters fifteen and sixteen, and in his letters to Suard
Gibbon made plain his willingness to make any cuts in this area of the work which Suard felt
necessary in order to avoid offending the authorities (*L* ii. 122–3 and 132: Norton, 123–6).

[56] *L* ii. 118.

Gibbon could assess the gravity of the threat they posed. During the period of suspense, in which he revised for the second edition, he wrote of the coming replies with playfulness and apparent unconcern:

I now understand from pretty good authority that Dr Porteous the friend and chaplain of St Secker is actually sharpening his goosequill against the two last Chapters.

At present *nought* but expectation. The attack on me is begun, an anonymous eighteen penny pamphlet, which will get the author more Glory in *the next World than in* this. The Heavy troops, Watson and another are on their march.

With regard to another great object of hostilities [that is to say, in addition to the war with the American colonies], *myself*, the attack has been already begun by an anonymous Pamphleteer but the heavy artillery of Dr Watson and another adversary are not yet brought into the field.[57]

However, once Gibbon had read the attacks and judged their quality, his tone was inflected into hard, unplayful accents. When he alluded to his opponents in a series of letters written in November 1776, after he had read the replies of Chelsum and Watson, he did so with a contempt unadorned by imagination or metaphor:

An anonymous pamphlet and Dr Watson out against me: both (in my opinion) feeble; the former very illiberal, the latter uncommonly genteel.

By this time Mylady may see that I have not much reason to fear my antagonists.

Two answers (which you have perhaps seen) one from Mr Chelsham [sic] of Oxford the other from Dr Watson of Cambridge, are already born and I believe the former is choleric the latter civil, and both too dull to deserve your notice; three or four more are expected; but I believe none of them will divert me from the prosecution of the second Volume . . .[58]

When the play of fancy is succeeded by simple and unemotional disregard, it is tempting to read the earlier embellishment as a sign of agitation, and the posture of *insouciance* as the guise of anxiety.

The different character of the revisions Gibbon made to chapters fifteen and sixteen for the third edition confirms this reading of his letters. The third edition was in press in March 1777, and was published in May, although Cadell had envisaged the need for a third edition as far back as May 1776.[59] The second edition was still being advertised for

---

[57] *L* ii. 111, 117, 118.
[58] *L* ii. 120, 121, 129.
[59] Third edition in press: letter to Dorothea Gibbon of 29 March 1777 (*L* ii. 141). Date of publication: Norton, 43. First envisaged: letter to Deyverdun of 7 May 1776 (*L* ii. 105).

sale in November 1776, and so was not by then exhausted.[60] Strahan and Cadell required a little over two months to reset, print, and assemble a volume of this size.[61] If we assume that Gibbon did not settle down to the work of revision until he knew that the third edition was definitely required, we can therefore suppose that he was working on the emendations for the third edition between late November 1776 and February 1777 (he was of course at the same time working on the second volume of the history).[62] The revisions for the third edition were begun, then, at just the time when Gibbon's apprehension of his adversaries had petrified into scorn. And when Gibbon wrote to Richard Watson on 2 November 1776 to say that, while he had no present intention of replying to his critics, he nevertheless reserved to himself the 'privilege of inserting in a future edition, some occasional remarks and explanations', it is reasonable to suppose that it is the revisions for the third edition which he had in mind.[63]

The different moods in which Gibbon emended for the second and third editions, and the different purposes those two phases of revisal served, are caught in the variants for a single footnote to chapter sixteen. Gibbon was in no doubt that the notorious passage in Josephus which referred to Jesus was a later interpolation.[64] In the first edition, he had expressed his disbelief as follows: 'The passage concerning Jesus Christ, which was inserted into the text of Josephus, between the time of Origen and that of Eusebius, may furnish an example of no vulgar forgery. The accomplishment of the prophecies, the virtues, miracles, and resurrection of Jesus, are fairly related. Josephus acknowledges that he was the Messiah, and hesitates whether he should call him a man.'[65] In the second edition, 'distinctly' was substituted for 'fairly'.[66] A personal judgement was deleted, and its place was taken by a more objective, and to that extent more impersonal, term. It is a revision entirely of a piece with that withdrawal from positions of exposure, which we have identified as the dominant characteristic of the second edition. Once again, Gibbon proved to have a shrewd eye for what his enemies would be unable to digest. Francis Eyre (reading Gibbon in the

---

[60] Norton, 43.

[61] This was the time required for the second edition (Norton, 42). The third edition may conceivably have taken slightly longer because of the transferral of the notes from the end of the volume to the foot of the page.

[62] Norton, 43 n. 7.

[63] *L* ii. 119.

[64] Josephus, *Jewish Antiquities*, xviii. 63–4.

[65] *DF 1*, p. lxxviii n. 35.

[66] *DF 2*, p. lxxviii n. 35.

second edition) devoted fourteen pages of his *A Few Remarks on the History of the Decline and Fall* to an elaborate defence of the authenticity of this passage of Josephus, designed to show 'how weak is the sophistry of the incredulous'.[67] William Salisbury and James Chelsum also championed the integrity of Josephus's text at length, in works published in 1776 and to which Gibbon may therefore be responding in revision made in this passage for the third edition.[68] In that third edition Gibbon allowed the correction of 'fairly' to 'distinctly' to stand, but expanded the note to almost twice its size by adding more authorities in support of his position: 'If any doubt can still remain concerning this celebrated passage, the reader may examine the pointed objections of Le Fevre (Havercamp. Joseph. tom. ii. p. 267–273.), the laboured answers of Daubuz (p. 187–232.), and the masterly reply (Bibliotheque Ancienne et Moderne, tom. vii. p. 237–288.) of an anonymous critic, whom I believe to have been the learned Abbé de Longuerue.'[69] The tone of this addition is one of impatient contempt ('if any doubt can *still* remain'); and the parade of authorities is a rhetorically crushing blow which seems to admit of no reply (the reservation of the identity of the clerical author of the decisive and dismissive contribution to the debate is a particularly effective piece of timing, which confirms the conjecture of a recent scholar that the footnote in Enlightenment historiography was as much an instrument of polemic as of scholarship).[70] The defiance of criticism Gibbon showed in this revision was the ruling passion of the corrections he made for the third edition.[71]

In two instances, Gibbon silently acknowledged that his opponents

---

[67] [Eyre], *Remarks*, 48–61; quotation from p. 61.

[68] Salisbury, *Establishment of Christianity*, 217–29. Chelsum, *Remarks*, 55–9; 2nd edn. of 1778 cited as Chelsum, *Remarks 2*.

[69] *DF* 3 639 n. 36.

[70] Champion, *Pillars of Priestcraft Shaken*, 30.

[71] The third edition allowed Gibbon in one respect greater scope for revisal. The surprisingly acceptable appearance made by putting the notes at the foot of the page, as had been done in the pirated Dublin edition, reconciled Gibbon to the same reorganization of the official editions (*L* ii. 116). In his 'Memoirs', he said that he had often regretted his compliance (*A* 339 n. 64). But the complete repagination of the volume clearly meant that the work of the compositor would now, and now only, be not greatly increased by the introduction of new material. Gibbon nevertheless restricted his revisals of the text so as to permit the retention of most of the lineation of the first two editions, thereby relieving the compositor of one consideration. However, he did take advantage of the opportunity to introduce some new footnotes. Inserted at the moment of conversion from endnotes to footnotes, they were invisible to the merely scanning eye. In his letters Gibbon seems always to have under-represented the extent of his revisions. In the 'Memoirs', as part of the fascinating myth of composition he there constructed, he contrived to suggest that, in careless facility, he eschewed revision altogether (*A* 333 and 334), while at other moments laying claim to laborious rewriting (*A* 308 (chapters fifteen and sixteen) and pp. 315–16 (the age of Constantine)).

had scored palpable, if not mortal, hits. In the first two editions, Gibbon had elaborated on the pagan disregard for the miracles of Christianity: 'The lame walked, the blind saw, the sick were healed, the dead were raised, dæmons were expelled, and the laws of Nature were perpetually suspended for the benefit of the church.'[72] Richard Watson, whose *An Apology for Christianity* Gibbon censured as polite but feeble, had queried the adverb 'perpetually'.[73] Nothing of substance to Gibbon's argument depended on the point (although it does confirm what was also indicated by the revisions to the second edition, namely that Gibbon had been betrayed into exaggerated expression in this section of the history). In the third edition, therefore, Gibbon revised 'perpetually suspended' to 'frequently suspended'.[74] A more substantial concession was made in connection with the gift of tongues, one of the miraculous powers claimed by the apostles and their first disciples. In the first two editions, Gibbon had implicitly questioned the reality of this miracle, by noting that this power had not always been granted to those whose need of it was greatest: 'The knowledge of foreign languages was frequently communicated to the contemporaries of Irenæus, though Irenæus himself was left to struggle with the difficulties of a barbarous dialect whilst he preached the gospel to the natives of Gaul.'[75] This was a passage which Chelsum had attacked, on the grounds that Gibbon had lifted a point from Middleton's *Free Enquiry*, and that the observation in any event was based on a misreading of Irenæus: 'Our author's too fond attachment to Dr. Middleton, appears to have betrayed him into one very remarkable misrepresentation.'[76] In the third edition, Gibbon left the text untouched, but introduced a new footnote which materially complicated his own implicit position towards this alleged miracle, and which demands to be understood in relation to the accusation of being merely Middleton's pupil in religious scepticism: 'Irenæus adv. Hæres. Proem. p. 3. Dr. Middleton (Free Enquiry, p. 96, &c.) observes, that as this pretension of all others was the most difficult to support by art, it was the soonest given up. The observation suits his hypothesis.'[77] Here Gibbon was unmistakably

---

[72] *DF 1* 518; *DF 2* 518.

[73] Watson, *Apology*, 147–8.

[74] *DF 3* 618.

[75] *DF 1* 475; *DF 2* 475.

[76] Chelsum, *Remarks*, 91 n. 1. Chelsum was followed by Loftus, *Reply*, 116 (ref. to the 2nd edn. of 1778); [Eyre], *Remarks*, 19; and Davis, *Examination*, 46–7. Middleton himself seems to have been following Shaftesbury; see Brown, *Essays on the Characteristics*, 297. The gift of tongues was plainly perceived by the 1770s to be one of the familiar topics of religious scepticism. The charge of being but an echo of Middleton is frequently made by Gibbon's enemies, and was in their eyes one of the clearest indications of his deistical sympathies.   [77] *DF 3* 567 n. 74.

putting distance between himself and Middleton. By reflecting criti-
cally on Middleton's hostile 'observation' about the gift of tongues, he
implied that his own (unspoken) views were different. It is difficult to
read this as anything but Gibbon responding to Chelsum's stricture by
assuming a position which might be understood (and thus attacked) less
easily. It represented a tactical retreat to safer ground.

Elsewhere, however, the revisions to the third edition show Gibbon
going on to the offensive. If he had prudently and subtly given way
before Chelsum over the gift of tongues, he felt on firmer ground over
his contention that the Christian religion devoted all pagans, no matter
how blameless their lives, to eternal punishment. In the first two
editions, Gibbon had drawn attention to the harshness of this doctrine:
'The condemnation of the wisest and most virtuous of the Pagans, on
account of their ignorance or disbelief of the divine truth, seems to
offend the reason and the humanity of the present age.' And he had
reinforced the point in an uncompromising footnote: 'And yet whatever may be the language of individuals, it is still the public doctrine of
all the Christian churches.'[78] Chelsum had objected to this, and had in
particular excepted the Church of England from so inhumane a teaching.[79] Gibbon responded by deploying the heavy troops of his scholarship, and quadrupling the size of the note:

And yet whatever may be the language of individuals, it is still the public
doctrine of all the Christian churches; nor can even our own refuse to admit the
conclusions which must be drawn from the viiith and the xviiith of her Articles.
The Jansenists, who have so diligently studied the works of the fathers, maintain this sentiment with distinguished zeal, and the learned M. de Tillemont
never dismisses a virtuous emperor without pronouncing his damnation.
Zuinglius is perhaps the only leader of a party who has ever adopted the milder
sentiment, and he gave no less offence to the Lutherans than to the Catholics.
See Bossuet, Histoire des Variations des Eglises Protestantes, l. ii. c. 19–22.[80]

The additional references revealed the previously hidden strength of
Gibbon's position, while the specific mention of the Church of
England, and of the eighth and eighteenth of the Thirty-Nine Articles,
was a silent but pointed riposte to Chelsum's special pleading.

A further instance of Gibbon's unleashing only in the third edition
the full force of his scholarly armament can be seen in the textual
history of another passage in which he touched upon one of the topics
of deism, that of the character of the Jewish nation. The propensity of

[78] *DF 1* 473 and p. lxx n. 68; *DF 2* 473 and p. lxx n. 68.
[79] Chelsum, *Remarks*, 23.
[80] *DF 3* 565 n. 70.

the Jews to idolatry during the age of miracles had been a favourite subject for the freethinkers, because the disparity between the behaviour of
the Jews and their preternatural environment was a contradiction
which called into question the historical accuracy of the Old Testament. In the first two editions, Gibbon had polished this familiar
subject into an elegant form:

The contemporaries of Moses and Joshua had beheld with careless indifference
the most amazing miracles. Under the pressure of every calamity, the belief
of those miracles has preserved the Jews of a later period from the universal
contagion of idolatry; and in contradiction to every known principle of the
human mind, that singular people seems to have yielded a stronger and more
ready assent to the traditions of their remote ancestors, than to the evidence of
their own senses.[81]

The text of this passage remained unchanged for the third edition, and
thereafter. It was sufficiently reminiscent of the deistical writing of the
earlier part of the century for Joseph Milner (who read Gibbon's first
volume in the second edition) to condemn it with mock uncertainty:
'whether it was copied from Lord Bolingbroke I must not presume to
say.'[82] But for the third edition Gibbon added a note which honed the
rusty weapon of the deists, blunted and ineffective from overuse, to a
new edge: '"How long will this people provoke me? and how long will
it be ere they *believe* me, for all the *signs* which I have shewn among
them?" (Numbers xiv. 11.). It would be easy, but it would be unbecoming, to justify the complaint of the Deity from the whole tenor
of the Mosaic history.'[83] This is one of comparatively few references
to the text of the Bible in chapter fifteen,[84] and it is one which, in this
context, jeopardizes the reliability of the Scriptures. Far from being
copied out of 'that haughty infidel' Lord Bolingbroke, Gibbon could
have retorted to Milner, the observation is nothing more than a deferential expansion of the words of God Himself.[85] It is this surprisingly
respectable genealogy for the reflection of the freethinkers and deists
which Gibbon plants, like a mine, at the foot of his page, and which
makes the assumption of decorum and dignity in the refusal to engage
in the 'unbecoming' business of dragging into the light all the support
for this view of Jewish history contained in the 'Mosaic history' so
much more deep than the play-acting it may at first seem to be.

[81] *DF 1* 452; *DF 2* 452.
[82] Milner, *Gibbon's Account*, 5.
[83] *DF 3* 539 n. 10.
[84] Cf. *DF* i. 450 n. 12, 467 n. 60, 468 n. 63.
[85] Milner, *Gibbon's Account*, 19.

One final example of Gibbon's aggressive expansion of a footnote.[86] Chelsum and Davis both resented the use that Gibbon made of a passage of Tertullian's *De Spectaculis*, in which (according to Gibbon) the 'zealous African' dilated upon the eternal punishments to be suffered by the pagans in 'a long variety of affected and unfeeling witticisms'.[87] Their objections were in essence two; that Gibbon had misunderstood this passage, and that Tertullian was in any event on this point unrepresentative of the Christian tradition.[88] The first of these Gibbon ignored, but to the second he replied using his favourite tactic of making the Church a witness against herself. In the first two editions, the footnote to this passage gave only the bare reference to the chapter of *De Spectaculis* from which Gibbon had translated Tertullian's gleeful meditations on the sufferings in store for the pagans. In the third edition, it became far more substantial:

Tertullian, De Spectaculis, c. 30. In order to ascertain the degree of authority which the zealous African had acquired, it may be sufficient to allege the testimony of Cyprian, the doctor and guide of all the western churches. (See Prudent. Hymn. xiii. 100.) As often as he applied himself to his daily study of the writings of Tertullian, he was accustomed to say, '*Da mihi magistrum*; Give me my master.' (Hieronym. de Viris Illustribus, c. 53.)[89]

This was a silent and surely decisive riposte to Chelsum, the satisfaction of which for Gibbon must in some measure have arisen from the opportunity to deploy against this modern cleric the judgement of a Church Father as important as Cyprian, as recorded by another Church Father of unassailable authority, Jerome.

Gibbon's footnotes in the third edition, then, reveal a new combativeness. However, he also revised the wording of his main text at a number of points, in a way which complemented without duplicating the more pugnacious pose he now struck at the foot of the page. As we have seen, for the second edition, Gibbon had muted or removed language which, on reflection, seemed too plainly characteristic of deism or freethinking. Those emendations were not undone for the third edition.[90] But we find him elsewhere refining and enhancing the

---

[86] Other examples can be found in the revisions made in the following notes: *DF* 3 563 nn. 64 and 65, 638 n. 32, and 642 n. 43.   [87] *DF* 3 566.

[88] Davis, *Examination*, 29–33. Chelsum, *Remarks*, 21–4: Chelsum urges the atypicality of Tertullian's writings, which sometimes 'breathe a spirit, altogether contrary to the plain dictates of Christian charity' (p. 22).   [89] *DF* 3 566 n. 72.

[90] It is a striking feature of Gibbon's successive revisals of volume one that individual revisions, once made, are almost never subsequently altered. This suggests that Gibbon prepared the next edition from a copy of the previous edition, and perhaps also that he kept no separate record of revisions made for any particular edition.

style of passages pregnant with harm for Christianity. The hallmark of Gibbonian irony—a sustained pressure of insinuation poised on the threshold of perceptibility—seems in part to have been perfected through the process of revision.[91]

An example occurs in the passage where Gibbon describes the variety, looseness, and uncertainty of the religious sentiments of the polytheists. Having suggested that 'as long as their adoration was successively prostituted to a thousand deities, it was scarcely possible that their hearts could be susceptible of a very sincere or lively passion for any of them', Gibbon then turned to the implications of this for the advent of Christianity and the appeal of the new religion to men.[92] In the first two editions, he implied that Christianity had filled the vacancy caused by the failure of polytheism: 'When Christianity appeared in the world, even these faint and imperfect impressions [the religious feelings inspired by polytheism] had been insensibly obliterated.'[93] In the third edition, Gibbon rewrote the end of that sentence in such a way that a different relation between Christianity and paganism was implied: 'When Christianity appeared in the world, even these faint and imperfect impressions had lost much of their original power.'[94] In 1777, not only was paganism more durable (in that, instead of being 'obliterated' it still maintained a presence, albeit reduced, in the minds of men); Christianity too was set in a new light, in that the reinvigoration of men's religious life which the new faith brought about now seems, not so much a replacement for the exhausted and erased religious sentiments of paganism, but a refreshment of them. The revised wording of the third edition thus touched on the topic, made notorious earlier in the century by Middleton's *Letter from Rome* (1729), of the evident and scandalous continuities between paganism and Christianity. Gibbon would return to this subject openly in chapter twenty-eight, in which he recounted the simultaneous ruin of paganism, and introduction of the worship of saints and relics among the Christians. It is unlikely that he had reached this stage of the composition of the second instalment of 1781 when revising for the third edition of volume one: he had begun work on volumes two and three only five months or so earlier, in June 1776.[95] But it may be that he had planned that far ahead, and that the subject was for that reason in his mind.

---

[91] A happy confirmation of Gibbon's maxim on style, that 'the choice and command of language is the fruit of exercise' (*A* 308).

[92] *DF* 3 601.

[93] *DF* 1 503; *DF* 2 503.

[94] *DF* 3 601.

[95] Letter to Holroyd of 29 June 1776 (*L* ii. 112).

A change as slight as the introduction of a single word could be sufficient to tilt the tone of the prose towards the disingenuousness and sly malice Gibbon, reassured as to the weakness of his opponents, seems to have been more prepared to indulge in his third edition. Commenting on the morality of self-denial forged by the 'zealous fathers' of the Church, in the first and second editions he explained its limited attractiveness amongst the polite as follows: 'A doctrine so extraordinary and so sublime must inevitably command the veneration of the people; but it was ill calculated to obtain the suffrage of those worldly philosophers, who, in the conduct of this transitory life, consult the feelings of nature and the interest of society.'[96] The sting in the tail of this paragraph was already sharp: the 'feelings of nature' and the 'interest of society', although the horizon of their concern is of course bounded to this world, are not lightly to be set aside or affronted. For the third edition, however, Gibbon inserted a word which contrived to make the phrasing less abrupt, and, by giving a more courtly turn to the expression, hit the tone of deferential regret which is so characteristic of his irony. In 1777, the worldly philosophers 'consult *only* the feelings of nature and the interest of society.'[97]

This greater willingness to allow his hostility towards Christianity (considered as a *congeries* and sequence of historical institutions, if not as a creed) to make itself felt can be seen also in the way Gibbon rewrote a sentence towards the end of chapter sixteen in which he looked forward to one of the important topics of his second volume, the conversion of Constantine and the establishment of Christianity as the religion of the empire. In the first and second editions, we read: 'The motives of his [Constantine's] conversion, as they may variously be deduced from faith, from virtue, from policy, or from remorse . . . will form a very interesting and important chapter in the second volume of this history.'[98] The various possible motives for Constantine's conversion which Gibbon listed here form a descending scale of integrity, stretching from the pure and best motive of religious faith; passing through its diminished (because secular) successor, virtue; moving on to the baser shadow of virtue, policy (which yet might be partially redeemed if its concern is for the welfare of the empire's inhabitants as a whole, rather than merely the security or comfort of the emperor); and concluding in the moral basement of remorse, the craven and unworthy corruption of repentance. Gibbon clearly entertained a number of different explanations of Constantine's conduct, some of

---

[96] *DF 1* 482; *DF 2* 482.   [97] *DF 3* 575: emphasis added.   [98] *DF 1* 576; *DF 2* 576.

them compatible with the traditions of the Church, others at variance with those traditions. But to list the motives in the form of a moral spectrum put no pressure on the reader to choose one or other, or any combination of them, as the approved explanation, for the reason that this arrangement seemed not to be the result of authorial choice, but to be determined by an internal principle of descending integrity. In the third edition, however, the motives were revised and reordered: 'The motives of his conversion, as they may variously be deduced from benevolence, from policy, from conviction, or from remorse; . . . will form a very interesting and important chapter in the second volume of this history.'[99] 'Faith' and 'virtue' have disappeared, to be replaced by an amiable but lesser moral strength, 'benevolence' (lesser, because an involuntary disposition rather than the result of conscious decision) and a neutral psychological motive, 'conviction' (which might be conviction to the good or to the bad). The top end of the range of possibility has thus been markedly diminished. But it is the revised arrangement of these four possibilities in the third edition which suggests to the reader that the less complimentary possibilities are the more likely. They now form not a continuous spectrum, but two doublets—benevolence/policy, conviction/remorse—in which the second is a base alternative to the first, and in which, furthermore, first and second seem to be related as reputation and reality. Gibbon was almost certainly composing and revising the chapters on Constantine when preparing the third edition of volume one for the press.[100] This revision is entirely in keeping with the account of Constantine's conversion which Gibbon would eventually publish in 1781.[101] The direction of influence, however, may have been from the revision to the first volume, to the work in progress. It may be that the renewed confidence Gibbon felt in tackling subjects of religious controversy in late 1776 and early 1777, the first expressions of which were the intransigent revisions to the third edition of volume one, emboldened him to treat Constantine with the severity so evident in the first four chapters of the second volume.

[99] *DF* 3 601–2.
[100] These chapters cost him a great deal of trouble, if the 'Memoirs' are to be believed on this point (*A* 315–16). Their composition and revision might therefore very probably have occupied Gibbon for the better part of a year after they were begun in June 1776 (*L* ii. 112).
[101] See chapter twenty (*DF* i. 725–65).

V

The narrative of the process of revisal Gibbon undertook when preparing the second and third editions of the first volume of *The Decline and Fall* is now clear. In the period of anticipation before any of the attacks on his supposed irreligion were published, Gibbon made in his second edition a number of small adjustments to his wording, all of which served to obscure or reduce the deistical character of his writing. Once the attacks had begun to appear, and Gibbon had found them unintimidating, the printing of the third edition became an opportunity for him to return to the conflict and press home his attack on the Christian Church by reinforcing a number of his footnotes, and honing his style. The separate stages of revisal thus distinguished, and their opposed tendencies thus established, the further question arises of what our enhanced understanding of this process of revisal allows us now to deduce more broadly about Gibbon's handling of religion in the first volume of *The Decline and Fall*.

J. G. A. Pocock, viewing *The Decline and Fall* within a series of rich and overlapping contexts formed by the political, sociological, and religious thought of the European Enlightenments, has formed the view that chapters fifteen and sixteen are unrepresentative of Gibbon's deepest concerns on the subject of religion: 'they are preliminary to Gibbon's main historical argument and . . . the controversy about them was in a sense premature.'[102] What we have discovered about the sequence of Gibbon's revisions to these chapters corroborates this speculation.

We know that Gibbon felt these two chapters to be expendable. That is the clear indication of Holroyd's unpublished note to the 'Memoirs', stating that Gibbon retained them in the second and later editions of volume one only at his insistence. It is also implied by Gibbon's frequent assurances to his French translator, Suard, that he will make any cuts in these chapters which Suard considers necessary to avoid giving offence; and also by the eventual appearance of the French translation of volume one minus the two last chapters.[103] In a letter to Suzanne Necker Gibbon even suggested that he had blundered with chapters fifteen and sixteen: 'I myself have been misguided enough to arouse the hatred of a powerful and numerous order of men, who have ever considered the forgiveness of injuries to be a point of doctrine

---

[102] J. G. A. Pocock, 'Gibbon in History', 339.
[103] Letters to Suard: *L* ii. 122–3 and 132. Publication of the French translation: Norton, 123–6.

rather than a principle of conduct.'[104] The suspicions of Henry Davis
and East Apthorp, that the first fourteen chapters were nothing but the
pretext for Gibbon's attack upon Christianity, and served but to introduce chapters fifteen and sixteen 'with a better grace, and more decent
appearance', can therefore safely be dismissed.[105]

But, at the same time, Gibbon also knew that the scandal these
chapters had stimulated had, in some quarters, done him no harm.
Calming his stepmother's fears that his reputation as an enemy to
Christianity would cause him to be arrested when he visited France in
1777, Gibbon reassured her that 'the recent fame of my book is perhaps
the circumstance which will introduce me [in Paris] with the most
favour and eclat'.[106] Gibbon wrote for fame, as he frankly confessed. His
subject he knew to be important, but he equally knew that success or
failure depended more on the adroitness of the treatment than the
intrinsic merits of the subject: 'the subject is curious and never yet
treated as it deserves . . . Should the attempt fail, it must be by the fault
of the execution.'[107] 'Execution' covers many aspects of the preparation
and composition of a work; scholarly foundations, of course, and lucid-
ity of organization and style. It might equally comprise other attractions
calculated to procure for the work favourable and plentiful notice. John
Brown, that well-known analyst of mid-eighteenth-century mores,
believed that 'no Allurements could engage the *fashionable* infidel
World to travel through a large Quarto'—and the first volume of *The
Decline and Fall* is certainly that.[108]

On the basis of the information revealed by collation, we may conjecture as follows. When preparing volume one for first publication
Gibbon's desire for literary celebrity led him to lace chapters fifteen and
sixteen with some sophisticated, but inessential, irreligious and deistical
language; by means of this allurement the fashionable infidel world
might be persuaded to traverse his large Quarto.[109] As Loftus had
speculated, reflections of 'this kind would be pleasing to many people,

---

[104] 'Moi-même j'ai été assez mal avisé pour encourir la haine d'un order puissant et nombreux
qui a toujours considéré le pardon des injures comme un dogme plutôt qu'un précepte' (*L* ii.
263).

[105] Davis, *Examination*, pp. i, 141; Apthorp, *Letters*, 16.

[106] *L* ii. 144.

[107] *L* ii. 75.

[108] John Brown, *Estimate*, 57.

[109] Gibbon's exposure to deistical thought perhaps originated in his enforced residence with
Mallet, the literary executor of Bolingbroke, after his conversion to Catholicism (*A* 130). Having
failed to make him an infidel, his father then decided to try to make him a Protestant, and sent
him to Lausanne. Gibbon's personal antipathy to religion has always been exaggerated; see
Turnbull, 'Supposed Infidelity', and more recently Womersley, 'Gibbon's Religious Characters'.

and beget a smile against the Apostles; which was an advantage not to be lost'.[110] But in the event, Gibbon underestimated the appeal of his subject in even those quarters apparently the most resistant to historical scholarship; his book sold like a sixpenny pamphlet on the news of the day.[111] Nor was that his only error. Far from being the attraction he intended, the deistical trimmings of the last two chapters had caused the only discordant notes in the chorus of admiration *The Decline and Fall* aroused in the spring of 1776. In 1775 Gibbon had gone to the trouble of consulting George Scott,[112] sending him part of the manuscript of *The Decline and Fall*, including presumably at least some of the text of chapters fifteen and sixteen, because on 29 December of that year Scott had replied, thanking Gibbon for 'the liberty of perusing part of your work', and reassuring him that 'I dare say you will be thought to have written with all due moderation and decency with respect to received (at least once received) opinions'.[113] Like many subsequent historians of the eighteenth century, Gibbon, misleadingly consoled by Scott, had undervalued the strength, depth, and prevalence of the religious sentiments of the time, and had formed too light an opinion of the willingness of the late eighteenth-century Church of England to defend its ground.[114] The whole episode was a strange reprise of what John Brown had asserted had also been the case with Hume's *History of England*:

A large Impression was published, and a small Part sold. The Author being asked, why he had so larded his Work with Irreligion, modestly replied, 'He had done it, that his Book might sell'.—It was whispered him, that he had totally mistaken the Spirit of the Times: . . . he had offended his best Customers, and ruined the Sale of his Book. This Information had a notable Effect; for a second Volume . . . hath appeared; not a Smack of Irreligion is to be found in it; and an Apology for the *first* concludes the whole.[115]

For the second edition of volume one of *The Decline and Fall* therefore, some of the most egregiously misjudged instances of tone and language were removed or moderated. The controversy thereupon broke, with

---

[110] Loftus, *Reply*, 144.

[111] See the triumphant letter to Deyverdun of 7 May 1776 (*L* ii. 104–8), in which Gibbon says that *The Decline and Fall* 's'est vendu, selon l'expression du libraire comme une brochure de six sous sur les affaires du tems' (*L* ii. 106).

[112] George Lewis Scott (1708–80), FSA, FRS; mathematician; appointed sub-preceptor to the young George III in 1750, despite being suspected of Jacobite inclinations; commissioner of excise from 1758; contributed in 1767 a paper on 'the present state of the physical and mathematical sciences' to Gibbon and Deyverdun's *Mémoires Littéraires de la Grande-Bretagne*.

[113] *MW 1796* i. 496.

[114] See Walsh, Haydon, and Taylor, *Church of England* and Clark, *English Society 1688–1832*.

[115] Brown, *Estimate*, i. 57–8.

the publication of pamphlets by Chelsum and Watson. Gibbon, having discovered that the controversy did him little harm amongst those whose opinions he valued, and that his adversaries were not in themselves formidable, moved in precisely the opposite direction for the third edition. The broad, and at times crude, deistical language which had been cut for the second edition was not restored, but the style of other passages, latent with implication embarrassing for the Church, was given a new astringency. One is suddenly put in mind of the extraordinary self-analysis in the journal entry for 8 May 1762 (Gibbon's twenty-fifth birthday): 'It appeared to me, upon this enquiry, that my Character was virtuous, incapable of a base action, and formed for generous ones; but that it was proud, violent, and disagreable in society.'[116] There was to be little violence in Gibbon's life (and perhaps still less chivalry). But pride there may have been in the revisions for the third edition. Aspects of chapters fifteen and sixteen had been gravely miscalculated. But once the dispute about those errors had become a public matter, and the indifferent prowess of his enemies had been demonstrated, then there could be no turning back.

This was the explanation for the irreligion of the two last chapters held by some of Gibbon's contemporaries. *The Gentleman's Magazine* linked Gibbon's attacks on Christianity with a desire to appeal to the world of fashion: 'Detesting its principles as much as we admire its style, we shall wave entering into farther particulars, or extracting the poison here diluted, satisfied with having warned our readers of the main design, and too fashionable principles of this too fashionable work, whose danger is enhanced by its ingenuity . . .'.[117] George Travis made the connection yet more explicitly: 'The impartial public demand it [a clear statement of religious belief] from you; or the persuasion, already entertained by many, will soon become universal, that you conceived a decent *modicum* of infidelity (no matter how prepared) to be necessary to give *fashion* to a work, pompous, yet not substantial,—specious, yet not satisfactory,—labored, yet not accurate.'[118] Travis's literary judgement was manifestly weak; yet he may have been a better reader of the human heart. His suspicions about why Gibbon wrote as he did about Christianity are, at the least, not incompatible with the textual evidence.[119] It would be one last instance of the surprisingly accurate

---

[116] *J1* 69. Gibbon is perhaps recalling *Hamlet*, III. i. 125.
[117] *The Gentleman's Magazine*, 46 (1776), 367.
[118] Travis, *Letters*, 123.
[119] One popular explanation of these chapters—that Gibbon was taking revenge on Christianity for the sufferings he had endured after his conversion to Catholicism—I find quite discountenanced by the evidence of the revisions to the first three editions of volume one. This

mutual understanding which seems, beneath the surface animosity, to have existed between Gibbon and his critics.

Gibbon himself scripted the encounter between the historian and his adversaries in two acts: dignified silence, followed by devastating rebuttal.[120] It is already clear that, in reality, this was a drama with more twists and reversals than Gibbon, reviewing his life in the 1790s, was prepared to admit. Just as Gibbon manipulated the narrative of his brush with the 'Watchmen of the Holy City' when writing his 'Memoirs', so perhaps he was tempted subtly to misconceive it. Most modern commentators have taken their line from Gibbon, and have depicted the controversy as a reprise of *The Dunciad*: the hero of literature annoyed by critic insects.[121] Here, too, there is room for another treatment, in which the vocabulary and tactics of Gibbon's adversaries would be more sympathetically assessed by relocation in the polemical tradition of which they were a part. Once the attack on Gibbon has been re-situated in that context, we can propose a new explanation for the effectiveness of the *Vindication* as a reply to them. And that is the subject of the following chapter.

interpretation seems to have arisen with Porson (*Letters*, pp. xxviii–xxxi); to have attracted Sainte-Beuve (*Causeries*, 347–78); and most recently to have ensnared Patricia Craddock (*Luminous Historian*, 62–3).

[120] *A* 316–19.

[121] For instance, see Patricia Craddock's headnote to *A Vindication* in *EE* 570, and also her *Luminous Historian*, 120–31.

2

Forging a Polemical Style: Gibbon's Vindication *and Literary Warfare, 1694–1779*

For the interest, therefore, of truth and justice . . . if it were necessary to choose, there would be much more need to discourage offensive attacks on infidelity, than on religion.

(J. S. Mill, *On Liberty*)

The style of declamation must never be confounded with the genuine sense which respectable enemies entertain of each other's merit.

(Edward Gibbon, *The Decline and Fall*)

When one looks at the pamphlets against Gibbon and at this answer in the *Vindication*, what perhaps is most striking is how narrow was the gap which, in the matter of interpretation of texts and criteria of factual accuracy, separated him from his opponents.

(Arnaldo Momigliano, 'Eighteenth-Century Prelude to Mr. Gibbon')

At some time after 1779, Robert Tyrwhitt sat down with pencil in hand to read the hybridized copy of Richard Bentley's *A Dissertation Upon the Epistles of Phalaris* which he had made by having bound together pages from the three editions of 1697, 1699, and 1777.[1] He annotated sparingly, but alongside two passages he made laconic jottings of great interest. In the margin of this passage towards the end of the 'Preface' he pencilled 'Gibbon, Vind.': 'But when I saw such a multitude of Errors concenter'd together, the sight was so deform'd and disagreeable, *Miseranda vel hosti*, that no Resentment could prevail with me to

---

[1] Robert Tyrwhitt (1735–1817); unitarian, grandson of Edmund Gibson, bishop of London; Fellow of Jesus College, Cambridge. His copy of Bentley's *Dissertation* is held at the Bodleian Library, press mark 29981 e.1; hereafter cited as Tyrwhitt, *Dissertation*.

return him his own Complement.'[2] And by this celebrated later passage, he wrote 'Gibbon, V. 422': 'When you return to these again, you feel by the emptiness and deadness of them, that you converse with some dreaming Pedant with his elbow on his desk . . .'.[3] This chapter explores what lies behind these two enigmatic annotations. As we shall see, it is no accident that an educated reader at the end of the eighteenth century should have been reminded of Gibbon's *Vindication* when reading Bentley's *Dissertation Upon the Epistles of Phalaris*. By following the implications of Tyrwhitt's laconic jottings, we will arrive at a deeper understanding both of what Gibbon was trying to do, and of the means whereby he thought he could achieve it, when in 1779 he wrote his celebrated pamphlet of retaliation against his critics.

Today it is the very completeness of the success which Gibbon's *Vindication* has enjoyed with posterity which is the chief obstacle to the literary historian. On 9 October 1850, having just read Whitaker's *Gibbon's History* [. . .] *Reviewed* (1791), Macaulay wrote in his diary: 'How utterly all the attacks on his *History* are forgotten! This of Whitaker's; Randolph's; Chelsum's; Davis's; that stupid beast Joseph Milner's; even Watson's.'[4] It was not, at the time, an unusual or an innovative judgement. Sixteen years earlier, in the course of an influential review of Guizot's edition of *The Decline and Fall*, Dean Milman had appraised the controversy surrounding Gibbon's alleged irreligion, and had concluded that it had been a grotesque mismatch: 'It is remarkable that . . . the more distinguished theological writers of the country stood aloof, while the first ranks were filled by rash and feeble volunteers. Gibbon, with a single discharge from his ponderous artillery of learning and sarcasm, laid prostrate the whole disorderly squadron.'[5] Yet the common opinion in the late eighteenth century had been that Gibbon's critics, although denied a complete victory, had nevertheless prevailed in a struggle which was, finally, yet one more setback for the forces of infidelity. Whitaker maintained that the 'tone of opinion concerning Mr. Gibbon' had been 'decisively settled among the discerning few, ever since Mr. Davis wrote'; the *Monthly Review*, the *Critical Review* and the *Annual Register* separately and on several occasions noted that Gibbon's credit as an historian had been damaged in the controversy; while in 1788 the *European Magazine* reported that Gibbon's handling of religion had been 'opposed with an ability and a success which

---

[2] Tyrwhitt, *Dissertation*, p. cxii.
[3] Ibid. 487.
[4] Quoted in Trevelyan, *Life and Letters of Lord Macaulay*, ii. 284–5.
[5] *Quarterly Review*, 50 (1834), 293.

renders our condemnation unnecessary'.[6] When from the pulpit in 1799 Christopher Hunter had stated that Chelsum, Davis *et al.* had provided 'ample and unquestionable proof' of Gibbon's culpable inaccuracies, he was therefore hardly courting controversy.[7]

The question of why the encounter between Gibbon and his critics should have looked so very different to early Victorian, rather than late Georgian, eyes is an issue which is full of interest.[8] It is, however, not an issue to be pursued in this chapter, which is concerned less to explain why Victorian commentators represented that encounter as they did than to recover the eighteenth-century actuality which they seem either to have coarsened or to have suppressed. At the level of narrative, I shall display the ebbs and flows of success and setback for both Gibbon and his detractors, prior to the handing down of the downright verdicts of the succeeding century which proclaimed their combat to have been no contest. Thereafter on the foundation of that narrative I shall propose a fresh reading of the style of the *Vindication*, in which the nature and magnitude of Gibbon's achievement in that pamphlet will be thrown into new light.

Until very recently, Milman's and Macaulay's was the version of Gibbon's clash with the forces of religious orthodoxy which modern scholarship had been content to repeat:

Gibbon, of course, demolished the foolish Mr. Davis [. . .]

. . . most of these [Gibbon's critics] were nonentities who merely let off blanks.[9]

D. M. Low admired the 'deadly polemic' of the *Vindication*, deploring Gibbon's 'furious and feeble' opponents; Hugh Trevor-Roper quoted Milman's judgement approvingly, cast a mocking eye on Gibbon's 'maimed and spluttering victims', and disdainfully pronounced that 'a controversy so finally settled does not deserve to be commemorated'; Jane Norton dismissed the charges of the orthodox as 'mere pettifogging . . . mere futilities'; while Patricia Craddock sternly reproved Davis as 'presumptuous'.[10]

In writing of the controversy in this way, these scholars echoed a

---

[6] Norton, 88–9. Patricia Craddock's view, that 'Davis's charges were unjustifiable by the standards of any age', is hard to reconcile with these late eighteenth-century readings of the dispute (*Luminous Historian*, 123).

[7] Hunter, SCEPTICISM *not separable from* IMMORALITY, 16.

[8] For an important study of the reception of Gibbon by at least one eminent Victorian, see Young, '"Religious Accuracy"'.

[9] Jordan, *Gibbon and His Roman Empire*, 144; Porter, *Edward Gibbon*, 3.

[10] Low, *Edward Gibbon*, 263; Gibbon, *A Vindication* [. . .] ed. Hugh Trevor-Roper (Oxford, 1961), p. vii; Norton, 79; Craddock, *Luminous Historian*, 120.

version of the conflict written by one of the participants. First in the *Vindication*, thereafter in his 'Memoirs', Gibbon bequeathed to us narratives of the controversy which differ from each other revealingly in emphasis, but which are agreed as to the outcome. As we have seen in the previous chapter, in both the 'Memoirs' and the *Vindication*, victory crowned the historian, while confusion descended upon his ill-bred and unscholarly enemies. When Jane Norton sought forgiveness for not having read Spedalieri's *Confutazione dell'esame del cristianismo fatto dal sig. Eduardo Gibbon* (Rome, 1784) in the very words of Gibbon himself ('Shall I be excused for not having read them?'), this was just an unusually vivid instance of the ventriloquizing of later scholars by the historian.[11]

But when the story of Gibbon's victory over his enemies is conceived as 'simple and obvious'[12] certain questions of interest and importance are lost to sight. Foremost among these are the related issues of how Gibbon's victory was achieved, and of exactly what kind of victory it was. In so far as later writers have thought about why the *Vindication* was so effective, they have concentrated on its rhetoric: 'if he [Gibbon] seriously hoped for such oblivion, he should have written differently: with less irony, less appearance of relish, fewer of those majestic, devastating phrases.'[13] However, the rhetoric of the *Vindication* has been more praised than analysed. I shall argue, first that the triumph which Gibbon secured with the *Vindication* was in fact purely rhetorical, because Gibbon's choice of language and style in that work embodied a response to the assumptions, rather than to the specific allegations, of his enemies. Secondly, I shall suggest that his response outflanked those enemies, stealing from them the rhetorical clothes in which they had dressed their attacks on *The Decline and Fall*, rather than defeating them on the substantive scholarly ground they had chosen for the contest. And finally, I will indicate how the ripostes which the *Vindication* provoked confirm this reading of the origins and tendency of Gibbon's polemical style.

Horace Walpole admired Gibbon as 'the best writer of controversial pamphlets'.[14] In order to understand why this is so, the *Vindication* must

---

[11] Norton, 83; cf. *A*, 322 n. 44. For an important assessment of Gibbon's adversaries written from a standpoint not chosen by Gibbon, see Aston, 'A "Disorderly Squadron"?'.

[12] The quoted phrase is taken from Gibbon's 'General Observations on the Fall of the Roman Empire in the West', where it is applied to the story of the ruin of Rome; *DF* ii. 509.

[13] *Vindication*, ed. Trevor-Roper, p. viii, referring to the closing words of the *Vindication*: 'I have only to request, that, as soon as my Readers are convinced of my innocence, they would forget my Vindication' (*DF* iii. 1184).

[14] Walpole, *Correspondence*, xli. 393.

be placed in two contexts. First, we must examine the situation formed
by the attacks on Gibbon before the publication of the *Vindication* in
1779. Here we must pay particular attention to the way in which
Gibbon's critics located their attack on *The Decline and Fall* in the series
of altercations between deists and the defenders of Christianity which
had occurred since the late seventeenth century. The need for such
contextualizing is suggested by a comment of William Burgh's when
defending the apparent shapelessness of his *An Inquiry into the Belief of the
Christians of the First Three Centuries*: 'A book, such as mine is, like the
architecture of a fortification which the enemy necessitates, not the
builder conceives, must derive its form and extent from the caprice of
its opponent, rather than the preconcerted plan of its writer; the mode
of attack prescribes and ascertains the mode of defence.'[15] Although
Burgh could not have used the word (and perhaps would not have
wished to even if he could), it is the intertextuality of polemical writing
which preoccupies him here. His observation that 'the mode of attack
prescribes and ascertains the mode of defence' offers important
guidance for the reader of polemic, which always has its origins, and
frequently its destination, in other books.

Once this preliminary phase is complete and we have reconstructed
the position in which Gibbon found himself on the threshold of composing the *Vindication*, we can turn to the question of precisely how
Gibbon decided to answer the charges which had been laid against him.
Here, we will review the plentiful points of contact between Gibbon's
writings before *The Decline and Fall* and the great literary controversies
of the eighteenth century. From the battle between the Ancients and
the Moderns, to the various literary duels fought by Warburton,
Gibbon's tangential involvement in, and his reading of, the often bitter
campaigns waged by men of letters earlier in the century have two
important implications. In the first place, when he sat down to write the
Vindication he already had a detailed knowledge of the controversial
terrain upon which he was obliged to fight. Secondly, he was already
thoroughly familiar with the various polemical styles and strategies
which he might now employ in his defence, since he had so employed
them in the past. The first context (that of the history of the conflict
between religious orthodoxy and deism since the late seventeenth
century) is necessary if we are to feel the polemical pressures to which
Gibbon was subjected in 1779. The second (that of the history of
scholarly polemic since Bentley's reply to Boyle) is necessary if we are

[15] Burgh, *Inquiry*, p. viii.

to be aware of the possibilities available to Gibbon—what we might
think of as the weapons in the polemical armoury which lay closest to
his hand—when he set about replying to his critics.

With these two contexts established, we shall turn to the *Vindication*
itself, and consider, first, how the rhetoric of that work was cunningly
forged from the stylistic weapons used in earlier literary warfare, and
secondly why this stylistic alloy proved so effective when wielded
against 'the Watchmen of the Holy City'. We shall indeed find that the
mode of attack prescribed and ascertained the mode of defence, and
that Gibbon proceeded in accordance with another of Burgh's principles of literary warfare: 'In the fields of controversy, it is lawful to array
against an adversary the arguments which he has himself involuntarily
contributed, or the concessions which preclude his reply . . .'.[16] Finally
we shall glance forwards to the later attacks on *The Decline and Fall*, and
see how, although the *Vindication* did not dam the flood of criticism, it
nevertheless diverted the offensive stream into different and, for a
while, more manageable channels.

II

At the very beginning of his *Remarks on the Two Last Chapters of Mr.
Gibbon's History*, James Chelsum sounded what was to be one of the
keynotes of the whole controversy:

The enemy himself [Gibbon] in the mean time, often lies hid behind the shield
of some bolder warrior; and shoots his envenomed darts, under the protection
of some avowed heretic, of the age.—It may be added, that the singular address
of the historian, has served even to make the laboured arguments of modern
writers, coincide with the description of a remote period of antiquity; and has
introduced many well-known objections to christianity, which the refined
scepticism of the present age, claims for its own.

And in the footnote to this passage, Chelsum made his charge yet more
explicit:

We are obliged to attribute to the present age, the invention of many metaphysical subtleties, and perhaps of some arguments of another kind; but for the
most part, even the licentiousness of modern infidelity, has been only able to
revive old arguments, disguised under some new form. This is a truth, which
must strike every one, versed in the history of infidelity, with the strongest
conviction.[17]

[16] Burgh, *Inquiry*, 386.
[17] Chelsum, *Remarks*, 2–3. 'Bolder warriors' and 'avowed heretics' with whom Gibbon was
compared (apart from those such as Middleton from whom he was accused of stealing) included

The same point—that modern religious scepticism was but a warmed-through version of the scepticism of antiquity, and that Gibbon was merely the latest charlatan so to pass off the old as the new—was repeated by Richard Watson, by Henry Davis, and by East Apthorp.[18] It formed a central element of the essential charge of inauthenticity which Gibbon's critics levelled against him, and which was most fully elaborated in the unholy trinity of Davis's *Examination*, where Gibbon stood triply accused of repeating the arguments of the ancient sceptics, of plagiarism, and of inaccuracy of reference caused by a failure to consult the original authorities. Those from whom Gibbon allegedly stole included Middleton, Hume, Tindal, Barbeyrac, and Bayle; and the upshot, as Davis expressed it, was that 'were I to restore to each of them the passages which Mr. G. has purloined, he would appear as naked as the proud and gaudy daw in the fable, when each bird had pinched away his own plume'.[19] The whole episode was a sad confirmation of Watson's melancholy insight into the perennial nature of infidelity, that 'there have been men, it seems, in all ages, who in affecting singularity, have overlooked truth'.[20]

To attack Gibbon on this point involved his clerical critics in some difficulties. In the first place, their accusation that Gibbon was only repeating arguments long since confuted entailed the consequence that their own refutations could hardly rise above the level of mere *rifacimenti*. Watson pointed out that 'Leland and others, in their replies

Collins (Davis, *Reply*, 97), Toland (Davis, *Examination*, 81–2, and Dalrymple, *Secondary Causes*, 14 and 19), Bolingbroke (Dalrymple, *Secondary Causes*, 14), and Tindal (*Gentleman's Magazine*, 46 (1776), 441).

[18] 'the Gnostics of modern times . . . are all miserable copiers of antiquity; and neither Morgan, nor Tindal, nor Bolingbroke, nor Voltaire, have been able to produce scarce a single new objection' (Watson, *Apology*, 35); 'Our author often proposes second, or even third handed notions as new; and has gained a name among some, by retailing objections which have been long ago started, and as long since refuted and exploded. In fact, sceptics and free-thinkers are of a date so old, and their objections were urged so early, and in such numbers, that our modern pretenders to this wisdom and philosophy can with difficulty invent any thing new, or discover, with all their malevolent penetration, a fresh flaw. The same set of men have been alone distinguished by different names and appellations, from Porphyry, Celsus, or Julian, in the first ages of Christianity; down to Voltaire, Hume, or Gibbon in the present' (Davis, *Examination*, p. iii); 'Christianity underwent a fiery trial from the wits of antiquity, not dissimilar to that which it hath sustained in Britain for a century past' and 'the late and present advocates of the modern irreligion, have not perhaps made any real improvement on the old system of infidelity' (Apthorp, *Letters*, 3 and 186). For Gibbon and the 'Deistical Writers of the Present Age', see also CUL Add. MS 8530, fo. 46^r, and Howes, who in *A Discourse on the Abuse of the Talent of Disputation in Religion* characterized modern infidelity as the 'revived plan of the ancient Gnostics' (p. 8).

[19] Davis, *Examination*, 275.
[20] Watson, *Apology*, 229.

to the modern Deists, have given very full, and, as many learned men apprehend, very satisfactory answers to every one of the objections, which you have derived from the Gnostic heresy'.[21] The more that these clergymen harped on the 'arguments and reflexions long ago exploded', upon the deists' reliance on 'such weapons as have been already blunted and shattered', and on the 'second-hand reflexions . . . stale objections [and] antiquated censures' of the infidel historian, the more they entangled themselves in a rhetorical problem.[22] It was an awkwardness to which Chelsum explicitly drew attention in the peroration to the first edition of his *Remarks*:

I cannot however conclude, without lamenting, the hard fate of those, who from sincere conviction, think it incumbent on them to oppose the attacks of infidelity. The enemies of religion assume at pleasure, a variety of shapes; and they scruple not to repeat the most partial objections, nay to collect them studiously, under the delusive appearance of novelty.

The apologist of religion, can adopt but one mode of defence; conclusive indeed, and satisfactory to those who search patiently after truth, but simple and unadorned, and destitute of the charms, either of variety or novelty, for those who seek only to be amused. He is obliged sometimes to repeat the observations of others; and he may to some perhaps, seem altogether to insist on obvious and well-known truths. It is too often forgotten, that repeated attacks require repeated answers; and that the cause of religion is too sacred and important, not to lay claim to continual defence. Not to be ready to oppose the enemy, as often as he returns to the charge, would be in some sort to abandon the field, and to acknowledge tacitly, the superiority of his forces.[23]

The corollary of the accusation of artfulness levelled against the infidel, then, was that the champions of orthodoxy were driven into high-minded repetition. While there were moral advantages accruing to

[21] Watson, *Apology*, 36.

[22] Davis, *Examination*, 168, 185, and 207. The exhaustedness of the arguments of infidelity had been remarked even in the early years of the century by Bentley in his attack on Collins, whose arguments he had mocked as 'so old and stale' and as 'threadbare obsolete Stuff' (*Remarks*, 32 and 51). (As we shall see, much of the later eighteenth-century attack on irreligion takes its rise from Bentley's reply to Collins.) It had been repeated in the 1750s by John Brown, who had noted that 'such a Writer can have little else to do, but to new model the Paradoxes of ancient *Scepticism*, in order to *figure it* in the World, and be regarded by the Smatterers in Literature and Adepts in Folly, as a prodigy of Parts and Learning' (*Estimate*, 168). And it would be taken up again in the 1780s by Joseph White: 'the absurdity of atheism has been exposed; and the atheist driven from the field he had the presumption to call his own, even by the very weapons which he chose for his defence. Deism in all its forms has been examined and detected: all its illiberal cavils have been replied to; all its haughty pretensions confounded; and even the pertinent and momentous objections, to which the best informed, and best disposed of its advocates sometimes had recourse, have been weighed with impartiality, and refuted by argument' (White, *Sermons*, 27–8).

[23] Chelsum, *Remarks*, 93–4.

Gibbon's critic when he censured 'those arts which he disdains to imitate', it was, as its practitioners ruefully acknowledged, a strategy which paid no literary dividends.[24]

Alongside that tactical quandary for Gibbon's opponents, however, there existed a more profound difficulty. For if the substantive content of both the religious sceptics' objections to Christianity and the rejoinders of the faith's defenders had been essentially unchanged since the days of the early Church, the same could not be said for the social profile of religious unbelief, at least as it had developed in England since the seventeenth century.

Gibbon's critics to a large extent shared a common understanding of the history of deism in England. It had arisen, they maintained, in the seventeenth century. Over its origins and early history, there were variations of emphasis. Some discovered its source in the writings of Lord Herbert of Cherbury, some in the philosophy of Spinoza; and for others it had strengthened only after 1688.[25] However, it was a point of common agreement that the early battles in this war between religion and unbelief had all been won by the Church, to the extent that in 1778 East Apthorp could write that, for those in the eighteenth-century Church of England, 'our chief glory is in the elaborate defence and confirmation of the gospel against the inroads of deism'.[26] Nevertheless, as Richard Watson had morosely opined, 'infidelity is a rank weed; it is nurtured by our vices, and cannot be plucked up as easily as it may be planted.'[27] And so it had proved. The early deists had been, in the main, men of low station and indifferent scholarship. It had been on these grounds that Smyth Loftus had chided Gibbon for the company he

[24] Ibid. 94. The rhetorical constraints under which the defenders of Christianity were obliged to operate was a theme taken up later by Joseph White, in his notorious Bampton Lectures, when he proclaimed that the orthodox will disdain to use 'the pointed shafts of ridicule, or . . . the poisonous arts of insinuation' (White, *Sermons*, 40).

[25] For the tracing of deism to Lord Herbert of Cherbury, see Philip Parsons, *Dialogues of the Dead with the Living* (1779), in which Dialogue I is between Hume and Herbert, to whom the former says 'You, my lord, was the founder of a noble plan of Deism, on which I have endeavoured to build a firm and durable fabric' (p. 2). This is an ascription which Herbert denies, but which was nevertheless current. Dialogue VIII is between Gibbon and Archbishop Langton, and is an item in Gibbon's early bibliography missing from Patricia Craddock's *Edward Gibbon: A Reference Guide*. For the discovery of deism's source in Spinoza, see Watson, *Apology*, 237; a judgement endorsed by Leslie Stephen, who stated that 'the whole essence of the deist position may be found in Spinoza's "Tractatus Theologico-Politicus"': *English Thought*, i. 33. For deism's invigoration after 1688, see Apthorp, *Letters*, 4.

[26] Apthorp, *Letters*, 176; cf. Stephen, *English Thought*, i. 90. Mark Pattison believed that, in the eighteenth-century controversies over free-thinking, 'public opinion was throughout on the side of the defenders of Christianity' (*Essays*, ii. 102).

[27] Watson, *Apology*, 265–6.

appeared to wish to keep: 'he must know that the most learned and worthy men of our nation, men who have done the highest honour to it by their genius, knowledge, virtue, have been staunch believers; and of how different a character from them the heads of our unbelievers have been, the world need not be told from me.'[28] But the deists, despite being defeated in argument and numerically outnumbered, had not gone away. Rather, they had taken shelter in the higher reaches of society.[29] Chelsum, in the second, enlarged and revised, edition of his *Remarks*, deplored the fact that 'in our times . . . the higher ranks of men' had embraced 'a total desertion of religion'.[30] Richard Watson concluded his *Apology* with a long address 'to a set of men, who disturb all serious company with their profane declamation against Christianity; and who having picked up in their travels, or the writings of the deists, a few flimsy objections, infect with their ignorant and irreverent ridicule, the ingenuous minds of the rising generation'.[31] The reference to 'their travels' serves to locate this 'set of men' amongst those wealthy enough to have gone on the Grand Tour, from which they had returned at once polished and corrupted, and inclined to 'infect' the next generation of the political and monied *élite*.[32] In this way a gulf had opened up between Christianity and those who possessed the social *ton* which was both indicated and censured in the words 'fashion' and 'fashionable'.[33]

[28] Loftus, *Reply* 204–5. Leslie Stephen found this attitude typical: 'the ordinary feeling for the deist was a combination of the *odium theologicum* with the contempt of the finished scholar for the mere dabbler in letters' (Stephen, *English Thought*, i. 87).

[29] 'Our infidels, as to number, are nothing, I thank God, in comparison of our Christians . . .' (Loftus, *Reply*, 136). For corroboration of the emigration of religious infidelity to the higher fractions of society by the end of the eighteenth century, consider Vicesimus Knox's assertion that 'you seldom meet with infidelity in a cottage' (*Spirit of Despotism*, 85).

[30] Chelsum, *Remarks 2* 142.

[31] Watson, *Apology*, 202. Watson was explicit that his purpose in answering Gibbon was not to indulge the hope of converting the historian, but rather 'to lessen, in the minds of others, some of that dislike to the Christian religion, which the perusal of your book had unhappily excited' (Watson, *Apology*, 199). In his Bampton Lectures of 1784 Joseph White also evinced an awareness that *The Decline and Fall* seemed to be calculated to appeal to the tastes of the young and well-bred when, in the course of his attack on Gibbon in Sermon III, he cautioned 'the younger part of my audience, against being unwarily seduced into an approbation of his [i.e. Gibbon's] sentiments, by the insinuating arts of his sophistry, and the captivating graces of his language' (White, *Sermons*, 153).

[32] For the moral paradoxes surrounding the Grand Tour, see Bruce Redford's subtle, graceful, and scholarly study, *Venice and the Grand Tour*, especially pp. 5–25. Foreign travel had been indicted as one conduit for the introduction of religious relativism, and thereby irreligion, into England since the late seventeenth century; see, for instance, Stephens, *Growth of Deism in England*, 6.

[33] Watson had noted the apparent incompatibility of Christianity and the 'standard of fashion' (Watson, *Apology*, 220); East Apthorp had linked the 'decline of religious zeal in these lukewarm

Gibbon assumed an additional significance in the eyes of the clerics who attacked him because he seemed to embody the alarming upward social mobility of 'modern infidelity'.[34] As Whitaker had put it in a letter to Gibbon of 11 May 1776, the historian displayed 'Deism in a new shape'.[35] In the eyes of the faithful this new form of unbelief was intellectually no more respectable than its predecessors. But socially it was incomparably more refined, and therefore much more threatening. Richard Bentley, in a work which came to assume a foundational status for opponents of freethinking and religious heterodoxy, had in the early years of the century mocked Anthony Collins's writing as '*Sand without Lime*', and had wondered aloud as to '*who would meddle with such dry mouldring Stuff, that with the best Handling can never take a Polish?*'[36] Gibbon's prose, however, suggested that the raw material of religious scepticism could, in the right hands, be given high gloss: even Chelsum had been obliged to acknowledge the historian's 'polished stile'.[37] Bentley had gone to particular pains to rebut Collins's conscription of Cicero into the regiments of freethinking, arguing that whenever Cicero wrote *in propria persona* 'he declares for the Being and Providence of God, for the Immortality of the Soul, for every Point that approaches to Christianity', and that he expounded these beliefs 'in a finer Dress with new Beauties of Style'.[38] Bentley had chosen to end his attack on Collins with this defence of Cicero in order to emphasize, not only the illiteracy he saw as natural to freethinking, but the mutual implication and reinforcement of religious orthodoxy and high literary culture. *The Decline and Fall* vigorously challenged the assumption that there was a natural consonance between the ability to write well and a disposition to theism. It was for this reason that East Apthorp was perturbed by the likely effect of the literary qualities which so powerfully (and, on all subjects apart from Christianity, so properly) recommended *The Decline and Fall* to the politer fractions of late eighteenth-century society: 'The decorum of this author, and the splendid elegance of his style, place him in a light so superior to that of others, who have gone before him in this unavailing hostility against

days' to 'fashionable prejudice' (Apthorp, *Letters*, pp. xi–xii). The social migration of deism upwards is repeatedly adverted to by Leslie Stephen (*English Thought*, i. 177, 375, and 445).

[34] For this phrase, see Loftus, *Reply*, 31, where it is said to be typified in Gibbon.

[35] *MW* ii. 151.

[36] Bentley, *Remarks*, sig. *2ᵛ.

[37] Chelsum, *Remarks*, 88.

[38] Bentley, *Remarks*, 81–2. It was a point about which Gibbon expressed his doubts in *The Decline and Fall*: 'From this passage alone, Bentley (*Remarks on Free-thinking*, p.250.) might have learned how firmly Cicero believed in the specious doctrines which he has adorned' (*DF* ii. 793–4 n. 56).

Heaven's best gift to man . . .'.[39] From this consideration sprang yet
further discomfort. Apthorp might wish to trace the proliferation of
modern infidelity to 'the neglect of solid literature'.[40] But Gibbon's
literature looked very solid.

It was for this reason that Gibbon's attackers were so anxious to
impugn the quality of his learning, since hitherto scholarship had been
a loyal auxiliary of the Church in its struggles with the deists.[41] It would
be intolerable if scholarship, as well as good birth, were to defect from
the cause of true religion. Yet that was very much what the example of
Gibbon suggested had come to pass. One response to this was simply to
drag in triumph, again and again, those few notable converts 'of high
rank and character' who had made the journey 'back again to religion
and the gospel': for instance, Charles Gildon, converted by Charles
Leslie's *A Short and Easie Method with the Deists* (1697), and Soame
Jenyns, whose *View of the Internal Evidence of the Christian Religion* (1776)
some nevertheless suspected to be camouflaged deism, so insipid and
half-hearted were its arguments for religious faith.[42] An alternative was
to parade polite yet orthodox authors such as George Lyttelton, author
of the *Observations on the Conversion and Apostleship of St. Paul* (1747), or
Gilbert West, whose *Observations on the Resurrection* had been published
in the same year.[43] But, either way, these elements in the attack on *The
Decline and Fall* reveal an awareness amongst those mounting it that the

[39] Apthorp, *Letters*, 2–3. Joseph White would later style Gibbon a 'living writer, the elegance
of whose style seems to have conferred a very alarming popularity on the licentiousness of his
opinions', and warned 'the younger part of my audience, against being seduced into an approbation of his sentiments, by the insinuating arts of his sophistry, and the captivating graces of his
language' (White, *Sermons*, 137–8 and 144). The same point, that the finesse of Gibbon's style
was an aggravating feature of his performance in *The Decline and Fall*, was made in 1799 by
Christopher Hunter, who associated him with Hume in this yoking of literary refinement to
irreligion: 'In works, abounding with amusing reflections, and recommended by an elegant and
engaging style, several assertions occasionally occur, tending to the disparagement of revealed
religion' (Hunter, SCEPTICISM *not separable from* IMMORALITY, 15).

[40] Apthorp, *Letters*, 178. 'Literature' here, of course, is used in the eighteenth-century sense of
'literary learning' (*OED*, 1).

[41] It is remarkable that some of Gibbon's opponents in the mid- and late-1770s go back to read
his *Essai sur l'Étude de la Littérature* (1761), presumably because the adequacy or otherwise of
Gibbon's 'literature' (in the Johnsonian sense of learning acquired through reading) is of moment
in the controversy over his religion; e.g. Chelsum, *Remarks*, 14 n. 1. In his 'Memoirs' Gibbon
remarked on this renewal of interest in his first publication, without being quite precise as to what
had caused it: 'in England my Essay was slowly circulated, little read, and soon forgotten; till the
fame of the historian enhanced the price of the remaining copies' (*A* 300–1).

[42] Apthorp, *Letters*, 191. For allusions to Jenyns and Gildon, see Maclaine, *Series of Letters*,
passim; Loftus, *Reply*, 49; and Davis, *Examination*, 167 (where Jenyns is praised as an 'eminent
writer, whose conversion does as much honour to Christianity, as his candid avowal of it does to
his heart'). For suspicion of Jenyns's motives, see Parsons, *Dialogues*, 101–49 (Dialogue V,
between Bishop Sherlock and Jenyns).   [43] Ibid., 215.

history of deism had, in their day, been deflected from its previous course, and that religious unbelief was now to be most apprehended amongst the polite. As we shall see, these two factors—the history of the resistance to deism by the Church, and questions of birth and gentility—run steadily throughout this controversy, and shape Gibbon's *Vindication* in surprising yet unmistakable ways.

III

As I have pointed out, Gibbon composed two accounts of his response to his critics. One is to be found in the opening pages of the *Vindication*, the other in draft 'E' of his 'Memoirs'. We have already seen in the previous chapter that these two witnesses are not always in perfect agreement over the events of the mid- and late-1770s. However, in this case they are in fundamental accord on what they assert to be the facts of how Gibbon came to answer his critics, although they diverge in emotional colouring and strategy. In the *Vindication* Gibbon depicted himself as a candid author, free of any affected indifference to the opinions of 'the Public', and who indeed had hoped to learn from 'the well-grounded censures of a learned adversary', until Davis's *Examination* had undertaken the 'ruin of my moral and literary character' by impugning 'my credit as an historian, my reputation as a scholar, and even my honour and veracity as a gentleman'. Such allegations it was impossible to digest, and so, with a due sense of the invidiousness of what he was about to undertake, Gibbon reluctantly buckled down to 'the odious task of controversy'.[44] In the 'Memoirs' we are given an elaborately wrought tableau in which the attack on *The Decline and Fall*, and its eventual rebuttal, form but one thread in a life rich in activities which it is hard to reconcile with the image of the socially destructive deist painted by his enemies: activities such as mixing on terms of social equality with French ministers of state, defending the cause of constitutional monarchy against irascible republican radicals in Paris, quietly studying the useful subjects of anatomy and theology in London, writing state papers against the French at the behest of the Chancellor and Secretary of State, and providing loyal support to the government through a 'stormy and perilous' session of parliament.[45]

[44] I quote from the *Vindication* as reprinted in Appendix 3 to volume three of the Penguin edition of *The Decline and Fall* (*DF* iii. 1108–84); a more correct text than that given in *EE* 229–313. The quotations in my text are taken from the introductory paragraphs (*DF* iii. 1108–12).

[45] *A* 310–22. The French minister of state is Necker (p. 313); the irascible republican is Mably (pp. 314–15 and nn. 31 and 32); and the state paper is the *Mémoire Justificatif* of 1779.

Notwithstanding this diversity of treatment, however, a crucial point on which both the *Vindication* and the 'Memoirs' are agreed is that it was the publication of Davis's *Examination* which prompted Gibbon to reply to his critics. In the words of draft 'E' of the 'Memoirs': 'I adhered to the wise resolution of trusting myself and my writings to the candour of the Public, till Mr. Davies of Oxford presumed to attack, not the faith, but the good faith, of the historian.'[46] Now, it is certainly the case that the *Vindication* takes Davis as its prime target. But it does not follow from this that the idea of writing the *Vindication* was first suggested to Gibbon by Davis's *Examination*. Indeed, close attention to the documents surrounding the publication of the *Vindication* suggests a different, and much more intriguing, story.

On 14 January 1779—the day the *Vindication* was published—Gibbon wrote to his friend the Scottish historian William Robertson:

Dear Sir
Before this you will have received by the post, a Copy of a pamphlet which has appeared to-day in London. I have not forgot the friendly advice which you gave me on this subject and you will easily credit the reluctance which I expressed to engage with such an Adversary. It was indeed one of those unpleasant circumstances in life, where it is extremely difficult or rather impossible to follow a line of conduct with which either the public or ourselves can be perfectly satisfied. However I have now made a resolution and indeed a public declaration, that nothing shall extort from me any farther prosecution of this odious Controversy.[47]

The pamphlet in question is of course the *Vindication* itself, so strong in Gibbon's mind as he writes this letter that he echoes its language.[48] But when did Robertson dispense the 'friendly advice' on the subject of replying to his critics to which Gibbon here alludes? Almost certainly when the two men met for dinner on Sunday, 15 March 1778.[49] There is no mention of Gibbon's critics in the letter Robertson wrote to Gibbon in the summer of 1777; we know from the letter Gibbon wrote to Robertson on 3 November 1779 that the Scotsman had not visited

---

[46] *A* 316. Compare the *Vindication*: 'I should have consulted my own ease, and perhaps I should have acted in stricter conformity to the rules of prudence, if I had still persevered in patient silence. But Mr. Davis may, if he pleases, assume the merit of extorting from me the notice which I had refused to more honourable foes. I had declined the consideration of their *literary Objections*; but he has compelled me to give an answer to his *criminal Accusations*' (*DF* iii. 1110).

[47] *L* ii. 203.

[48] Compare e.g. 'this odious Controversy' with the *Vindication*'s 'the odious task of controversy' (*DF* iii. 1109).

[49] 'Dr Robertson is [in] town, I shall dine with him to-morrow' (Gibbon to Holroyd, 14 March 1778: *L* ii. 177). Robertson was in London to oversee the publication of his *History of America*.

London since March 1778; and there is no indication of any correspondence between the two men during the period from Robertson's visit to London in March 1778 and the letter from Gibbon to Robertson of January 1779.[50]

Which of Gibbon's critics might the two historians have discussed over dinner that Sunday? We can say at once and as a matter of simple fact that Davis was not one of them, because his *Examination* would not be published until at the earliest 27 April, and more probably not until 2 May 1778.[51] Moreover, Robertson seems never to have read Davis's attack on Gibbon at all.[52] Three weeks before that dinner conversation, however, Gibbon had received, and had proudly rejected, a copy of the second enlarged edition of Chelsum's *Remarks*. In that letter, after acknowledging the 'candid and ingenious apology' of Richard Watson, Gibbon had gone on to contrast the literary manners of 'the Divinity Professor of Cambridge' with those of the Student of Christ Church:

A different mode of controversy calls for a different behaviour; and I should deem myself wanting in a just sense of my own honour, if I did not immediately return into the hands of Mr Batt your most extraordinary present of a book, of which almost every page is stained with the epithets, I shall take leave to say the undeserved epithets, of *ungenerous, unmanly, indecent, illiberal, partial,* and in which your adversary is repeatedly charged with *being deficient in common candour,* with *studiously concealing the truth, violating the faith of history,* &c. This consideration will not however prevent me from procuring a copy of your Remarks, with the intention of correcting any involuntary mistakes, (and I cannot be conscious of any other,) which in so large a subject your industry, or that of your colleagues, may very possibly have observed. But I must not suffer myself to be diverted from the prosecution of an important work, by the invidious task of controversy, and recrimination. Whatever faults in your performance I might fairly impute to want of attention, or excess of zeal, be

---

[50] *MW 1796* i. 521–3. 'May we not hope for the pleasure of seeing you in London? I remember a kind of engagement you had contracted to repeat your visit every second year, and I look forwards with pleasure to next spring [i.e. the spring of 1780] when your bond will naturally become due' (*L* ii. 232). The falling due of the biennial bond in the spring of 1780 indicates that Robertson's last visit to London had taken place in the spring of 1778, and that no visit had intervened.

[51] See the advertisements in the *Morning Post* for 27 April 1778 and in the *Public Advertiser* and the *Gazetteer and New Daily Advertiser* for 2 May 1778. Some have not felt the need to narrow down the dating of the *Examination* beyond the spring of 1778, a period which they have adopted from the *DNB* (Norton, 86; Craddock, *Luminous Historian*, 122). Nevertheless, the precise date is full of valuable implication.

[52] For Robertson's ignorance of Davis, see his reply to Gibbon of 10 March 1779: 'Davis's book never reached us here. Our distance from the Capital operates somewhat like time. Nothing but what has intrinsic value comes down to us. We hear sometimes of the worthless and vile things that float for a day on the stream, but we seldom see them' (*MW 1796* i. 539).

assured, Sir, that they shall sleep in peace; and you may safely inform your readers, that Suidas was a heathen four centuries after the heathenism of the Greeks had ceased to exist in the world.[53]

The strength of feeling in this letter is remarkable, particularly since less than a month before Gibbon had received a presentation copy of Smyth Loftus's *Reply* with amusement and equanimity.[54] The cleric most vigorously present in Gibbon's thoughts on 15 March 1778 was therefore undoubtedly James Chelsum.

Returning now to the language of Gibbon's letter to Robertson of 14 January 1779, it would seem that the 'friendly advice' which Robertson had given had counselled against becoming involved in controversy: 'I have not forgot the friendly advice which you gave me on this subject and you will easily credit the reluctance which I expressed to engage with such an Adversary.'[55] Despite appearances to the contrary (namely, the publication of the *Vindication*), Gibbon is anxious to reassure Robertson that he had not blithely disregarded his brother historian's opinion. And Robertson's reply meets this implication in Gibbon's language, because he there reassures Gibbon that, notwithstanding the advice he had previously dispensed, he now believes the publication of Davis's *Examination* had left Gibbon no alternative but to enter the fray:

I read your little performance with much eagerness, and some solicitude. The latter soon ceased. The tone you take with your adversary in this *impar congressus* appears to me perfectly proper; and, though I watched you with some attention, I have not observed any expression which I should, on your own account, wish to be altered. . . . I am satisfied, however, that it was necessary for you to animadvert on a man who had brought accusations against you, which no gentleman can allow to be made without notice.[56]

The implication of this exchange of letters, therefore, is of some consequence. It now appears that Gibbon first thought seriously about answering his critics once he had read, not Davis's *Examination*, but the

---

[53] *L* ii. 173–4.

[54] 'I received to-day a huge pacquet, a Theological answer written by a *mere* Irish parson' (*L* ii. 172). Before the arrival of the second edition of Chelsum's *Remarks*, Gibbon's constant attitude towards his critics had been expressed in his reassurance to Deyverdun, that 'je n'opposerai qu'un silence respectueux aux clameurs de mes Ennemis' (*L* ii. 108). To express a distaste for controversy was of course commonplace, as Watson had shown: 'It is not, in good truth, a difficult task, to chastise the froward petulance of those, who mistake personal invective for reasoning, and clumsy banter for ingenuity; but it is a dirty business at best, and should never be undertaken by a man of any temper, except when the interests of truth may suffer by his neglect' (*Apology*, 201).

[55] *L* ii. 203.

[56] *MW 1796* i. 539.

second edition of Chelsum's *Remarks*. Notwithstanding his haughty proclamation to Chelsum, that 'I must not suffer myself to be diverted from the prosecution of an important work, by the invidious task of controversy, and recrimination', it seems to have been Chelsum who had first aroused in Gibbon the strength of feeling which eventually brought forth the *Vindication*, which was so evident in his letter rejecting the present of the second edition of the *Remarks*, and which it seems was still so vivid in his conversation three weeks later that William Robertson had been obliged to pacify his brother historian, and dissuade him from writing the retort which, we may infer, he was even then meditating.[57]

Why should the second edition of Chelsum's *Remarks* have provoked, not only such a vigorous emotional response in Gibbon, but the first thoughts of a reply? As we have seen in the first chapter, Gibbon responded to the first edition of Chelsum's *Remarks* silently and subtly in the revisions he made to the second and third editions of volume one of *The Decline and Fall*. But the story told by those two sets of revisions is the reverse of the sequence of events we now see in 1778. In 1776 Gibbon had been apprehensive of his attackers, and, by means of revisions made for the second edition which muted some of the anti-clerical aspects of his language, he had trimmed his sails in anticipation of their criticisms. However, when he read their pamphlets, his fears were dispelled, and that reassurance found expression in the revisions for the third edition of 1777, which tended to sharpen the very qualities of his writing which he had softened in the previous year. That mood of complacent disregard seems to have lasted until at least January 1778, when as we have seen the unheralded arrival of Smyth Loftus's *Reply* prompted nothing more than a sardonic aside in a letter of desultory gossip to Holroyd. It was thoroughly dispelled in February by the unwelcome gift of the second, enlarged, edition of Chelsum's *Remarks*.

We know from the *Vindication* that Gibbon read with care the majority of the attacks on him. We also know that he had in his library a copy of the second edition of Chelsum's *Remarks* (he had therefore been as good as his word in buying a copy of the second edition to replace the complimentary copy he had returned), to which he keyed his references when writing the *Vindication*. And we know further that he had read the first edition of the *Remarks* with enough attention for him to be able to prophesy that it would 'get the author more Glory *in*

---

[57] *L* ii. 173. This echoes the impassive language in which Gibbon had noted the publication in 1776 of the first wave of attacks: 'I believe none of them will divert me from the prosecution of the second Volume . . .' (*L* ii. 129).

the next World than in this'.[58] It would seem, therefore, that Gibbon's strength of response to the second edition of the *Remarks* may have been caused by the revisions and enlargements which Chelsum had incorporated into the pamphlet of 1778, and which Gibbon was in a position to have noticed for himself.[59] When we look at how that second edition differs from its predecessor, we can begin to understand why it elicited such a response. Moreover, the reasons for Gibbon's resentment suggested by collation of the two editions of the *Remarks* turn out to be very different from those brandished by the indignant historian in his letter to Chelsum of 20 February 1778.[60] There, Gibbon had implied that the second edition of Chelsum's attack had marked a descent from argument into mere abuse. It was 'a book, of which almost every page is stained with the epithets, I shall take leave to say the undeserved epithets, of *ungenerous, unmanly, indecent, illiberal, partial*, and in which your adversary is repeatedly charged with *being deficient in common candour*, with *studiously concealing the truth, violating the faith of history*, &c.'[61] Inspection reveals that this is the reverse of the truth. The second edition of the *Remarks* is far more disciplined in its tone and focused in its allegations than was its predecessor. We must therefore try to explain Gibbon's vehemence of response without invoking outraged good-breeding.

[58] 'As soon as I saw the advertisement, I generally sent for them; . . . I read with attention several criticisms which were published against the Two last Chapters of my History . . .' (*DF* iii. 1109). *K* 93. *L* ii. 117; the absence of the first edition from Gibbon's library suggests that he disposed of it when the second edition was published. Gibbon had read what he owned, as he would famously state in draft 'B' of the 'Memoirs': 'The review of my library must be reserved for the period of its maturity; but in this place I may allow myself to observe that I am not conscious of having ever bought a book from a motive of ostentation; that every volume, before it was deposited on the shelf, was either read or sufficiently examined, and that I soon adopted the tolerating maxim of the elder Pliny, "Nullum esse librum tam malum ut non ex aliquâ parte prodesset"' (*A* 165; cf. p. 248 (draft 'C')).

[59] In the *Vindication* Gibbon comments dismissively on the revisions it embodied ('some alteration of form, and a large increase of bulk'): *DF* iii. 1158–81, especially pp. 1158–60; quotation on p. 1159. Although this is unfair to Chelsum, it is useful confirmation that Gibbon had compared the two editions of the *Remarks*, and had formed some opinion, no matter how slanted, about the effect of the revisions made in the second edition.

[60] The table of contents Chelsum supplied for the second edition of the *Remarks* indicates new material with an asterisk (*Remarks* 2, sigs. cʳ–c2ᵛ). However, this table misrepresents the nature and scale of the process of revision Chelsum carried out for the second edition in two respects. Firstly, it draws attention, not to all new inserted passages, but only to wholly new sections inserted into the text for the first time in 1778 (thereby ignoring the amplification of sections included in a less well-supported form in the first edition). Secondly, it takes no notice of deletions, which are of course just as important as additions for the scholar who wishes to assess the development between 1776 and 1778 in Chelsum's thought about how and where Gibbon might be vulnerable to attack. For Chelsum's own account of how the text of the first edition was remodelled to produce that of the second, see *Remarks* 2, pp. xiii–xiv, n. 7.   [61] *L* ii. 173.

The changes Chelsum made for the second edition of the *Remarks* can be grouped under two headings: the chastening of style, and the sharpening of argument. In respect of style, it would have been immediately apparent to Gibbon that Chelsum had stripped out the blatant sarcasms to which he had been unable to refuse himself in 1776. For example, in the first edition, apropos of the 'distinct chapter of Pliny' reserved for 'eclipses of an extraordinary nature and unusual duration' in which the puzzled Gibbon had been curiously unable to find mention of the darkness of the Passion, we read:

As the best solution of the difficulty, I will repeat to you, this important chapter, 'devoted' as it is, to eclipses of that kind, among which, it is contended, the preternatural darkness, in question, ought to have found a place. It will not detain you long.

'There are, says our philosopher, eclipses of an extraordinary nature, and unusual duration, such as that which followed the murder of Cesar, and in the war with Antony; when a perpetual paleness covered the sun, almost through-out the whole year.' You have the whole chapter laid before you.

You will now perhaps be surprized at the serious manner, in which this objection is proposed. It must appear surely from the whole of the chapter, that it was not the philosopher's design, to record all the most remarkable eclipses . . .[62]

In 1778 Chelsum deleted three sentences: 'It will not detain you long', 'You have the whole chapter laid before you', and 'You will now perhaps be surprized at the serious manner, in which this objection is proposed'.[63] The trimming away of such persiflage suggests, in the first place, a greater confidence on Chelsum's part that the details he is bringing forward can be allowed to make their own point; secondly, a realization that the tonal excesses of the first edition had betrayed a man too eager in the pursuit of his enemy.

The same greater self-possession in argument is evident in the fol-lowing revision, taken from that section of the *Remarks* in which Chelsum attacks Gibbon for extenuating the persecutions of the early Christians by the Roman government. In 1776 had Chelsum allowed his indignation to distract him from the consideration most useful to his line of attack, and on which he therefore ought to have squarely laid the emphasis:

Yet many of those emperors, who distinguished themselves in the persecution of Christianity, were tyrants of so odious a character, were themselves so lost to all ideas of religion, that even the pretence of their having persecuted the

---

[62] *DF* i. 512. *Remarks*, 44–5.   [63] *Remarks* 2, 164–5.

Christians in defence of the religion of their country, can scarcely be urged in
their favour. The inoffensive principles of the Christians, considered as subjects, soon became sufficiently known and experienced; . . .[64]

In revising his pamphlet, Chelsum realized that the moral failings of
the emperors were less central to his argument than was the moral
innocence of the first Christians. It was that moral innocence which
made the persecutions so criminal, while the matter of the odiousness
of the emperors was relevant only to the secondary and subordinate
purpose of fending off a possible line of justification for the persecutions. Accordingly in 1778 the language of moral outrage was deleted,
and in the second edition the paragraph begins: 'Yet the inoffensive
principles . . .'.[65]

It should already be apparent that the separation of Chelsum's stylistic revisions from the remodelling of his argument is a distinction which
cannot be taken very far. The greater vigilance over his prose which
Chelsum showed in 1778 (a vigilance which dictated the purifications
of tone we have just examined, and which is evident elsewhere in the
detailed rewriting of paragraphs substantially retained for the second
edition, as well as in the removal of paragraphs of a parenthetical nature
which served only to clog the exposition in 1776) was part of a general
raising of his game which made him a far more formidable polemicist in
1778 than he had been two years earlier.[66] Chelsum's greater discipline
and firmness of purpose are caught in the stylistic recension of an early
paragraph:

I shall now beg leave to turn your attention, to some of our author's disquisitions, as they present themselves in order. It is by no means my design to
follow him through all his researches. My remarks will be confined rather
to particular passages; and it will be more especially my object, to examine
diligently into the force of the several testimonies collected, in support of his
assertions; since should these be found to fail, the superstructure built upon
them, must fall in consequence. I shall attend particularly also, to such short but
significant reflections, not immediately relating to the subject of his history, as
our author has occasionally indulged himself in, in the course of his general
notes. From these, perhaps the true temper and design of our historian may best
be collected, since in attending to them, we follow him as it were, into his most
secret recesses, and hear him speaking in his own person. For all such reflexions

---

[64] *Remarks*, 48.

[65] *Remarks 2*, 171.

[66] For an example of such stylistic polishing, compare the paragraph at the foot of *Remarks*, 5
with its rewritten equivalent at the top of *Remarks 2*, 5. For an example of a deleted, parenthetic,
paragraph, consider the paragraph straddling *Remarks*, 81–2, which was dropped from *Remarks 2*.

too, he is more immediately accountable, should it be found, that the history itself can by no means be said to have required them.[67]

In the second edition, this became:

Thus much premised, I shall now follow our Author regularly through the course of his Inquiry: and I shall attend not only to his quotations, but to such short significant reflections also, not immediately relating to the subject of his history, as our Author has occasionally introduced in the course of his general notes. From these perhaps the true temper and design of our Historian may best be collected, since in these we hear him speaking in his own person. For all such reflections too he is more immediately accountable, should it be found that the History itself can by no means be said to have required them.[68]

What is striking here is the removal of a whole level of style, namely those decorative, at times dandyish, and often parenthetical phrases which suggested an ironic courtliness: 'I shall now beg leave', 'It is by no means my design', 'it will be more especially my object', 'in attending to them, we follow him as it were, into his most secret recesses'. This revision is richly suggestive. In the first place, it is possible to read the artificial style of the first edition of the *Remarks* as an attempt to match Gibbon on the ground he had made his own, that of elaborate irony. In the second edition, Chelsum wisely desists from a competition from which he could never emerge with laurels, and accordingly sets his language in contrast to Gibbon's enamelled prose. As a consequence of this purification of style, Chelsum appears more manly and direct. The greater terseness of his writing suggests a more confident sense of readership, a readership who do not need to be courted with 'fine' writing, and who are well disposed to hear a solid charge plainly and forcibly delivered. This intimation at the level of style of rising morale amongst Gibbon's opponents seems to have some justification, as Chelsum's own account of the different circumstances in which he revised his pamphlet indicates:

When the Author of the following Remarks therefore had observed farther what distinguished attention had actually been paid to Mr. Gibbon's work, his desire to furnish in some sort at least an antidote to the many erroneous positions contained in it, prevailed over other considerations. He was induced from the motive to submit to the public inspection remarks which were originally intended for his own private satisfaction only. He was induced to submit them even hastily, and in an imperfect state, without waiting to make farther additions, or to digest his materials in a better manner. In one respect at least his work is now rendered far more worthy attention. He has been honoured

---

[67] *Remarks*, 7–8.   [68] *Remarks* 2, 6–7.

with the communications of a distinguished writer in the most liberal and obliging manner.[69]

Haste and isolation have been happily replaced by reflection and collaboration. The revisions Chelsum made for the second edition of the *Remarks* are second thoughts, then, but not second thoughts which carry any message of retreat or compromise. Rather, they announce a determination to renew the attack by means of a different and better rhetorical strategy. That refreshed determination and more precise sense of how and where the attack should be directed are as evident in Chelsum's refinement of his argument as in his disciplining of his tone.

The most important of the changes Chelsum made to the substance of his attack on Gibbon was his muting of the charge of deism. The following passages from the first edition which press that charge were excised from its successor:

The enemy himself in the mean time, often lies hid behind the shield of some bolder warrior; and shoots his envenomed darts, under the protection of some avowed heretic, of the age.—It may be added, that the singular address of the historian, has served even to make the laboured arguments of modern writers, coincide with the description of a remote period of antiquity; and has introduced many well-known objections to christianity, which the refined scepticism of the present age, claims for its own.

I should be but ill inclined to take any notice of our author's disquisitions concerning the miraculous powers of the primitive church, had not some reflections fallen from him (not necessarily suggested by his immediate subject) which affect materially, the faith of modern Christians. 'That very free and ingenious inquiry,' which, in his own words, 'appears to have excited a general scandal among the divines of our own, as well as of the other churches of Europe,' met with many learned antagonists. To enter again into so recent a controversy, to repeat answers, so easy to be consulted, would be altogether superfluous.[70]

A related elision occurs in the footnote in which Chelsum, shrewdly comparing Gibbon's account of paganism as a 'systeme riant, mais *absurde*' in the *Essai sur l'Étude de la Littérature* with his apparent admira-

---

[69] *Remarks 2*, pp. xiii–xiv. The 'distinguished writer' was Dr Thomas Randolph, President of Corpus Christi College, Oxford and Lady Margaret's Professor of Divinity.

[70] *Remarks*, 2–3 and 24; compare *Remarks 2*, 1–2 and 67–96 respectively. The latter comparison is particularly interesting, since those thirty pages of the second edition consist of a full statement of Gibbon's debts to Middleton. If Gibbon is to be charged with being a puppet of Middleton (who is of course the author of the 'free and ingenious inquiry'), then the charge must be made at length and fully substantiated, so as to admit of no reply. It is therefore suggestive of Chelsum's removal of debating points from the *Remarks*, in favour of more solid material. I return at the end of this chapter to the question of the alleged indebtedness of Gibbon to Middleton.

tion of it in *The Decline and Fall*, drew attention to an earlier element in that youthful work:

> I am happy to seize an opportunity of acknowledging, that, that attention to the Belles Lettres, which is displayed in the course of this work, forms its least merit. It is preceded by an English dedication, which does the utmost honour to the author's heart. A dedication from A SON, distinguishing himself in literature, at an early period of life, addressed in the warmest terms of affection, to A RESPECTED FATHER. I had *almost* said, LET THIS EXPIATE![71]

In the second edition, this became: 'This work is preceded by an English dedication which does the utmost honour to the Author.—A dedication from A SON distinguishing himself in literature at an early period of life, addressed in the warmest terms of affection to A RESPECTED FATHER!'[72] The deletion of the wordy first sentence is of a piece with that general stylistic tautening we have observed already in the second edition. More interesting altogether, however, is the removal of the enigmatic final sentence of the first edition's note, 'I had almost said, LET THIS EXPIATE!' That sentence had directed the reader to Richardson's *Clarissa*, and to the last words of the morally unprincipled rake, Lovelace. Fatally wounded in his duel with Colonel Morden, at the point of death Lovelace exclaims 'LET THIS EXPIATE!'[73] In alluding to Richardson at this point, and in thereby suggesting some link between Gibbon and Lovelace, Chelsum was implicitly invoking the common prejudice of the time, that irregularity in matters of religion led inexorably to other kinds of moral depravity, in particular to sexual libertinism.[74] The deletion of the allusion in the second edition is a corollary of Chelsum's suppression of the charge of deism.

The thinking behind these deletions is illuminated by a passage from the 'Preface' to the second edition (which corresponds to nothing in the first edition). There Chelsum paid Gibbon a measured compliment:

> The work [*The Decline and Fall*] derives additional credit from the situation of it's Author, on whom . . . it reflects real honour to have spent those many hours

---

[71] *Remarks*, 14 n. 1.

[72] *Remarks 2*, 50 n. 6. For some interesting sidelights on Gibbon's actual relations with his father during the composition and publication of the *Essai*, see Ghosh, 'Gibbon's First Thoughts'.

[73] Letter 537, F. J. de la Tour to J. Belford, 18 Dec., in Samuel Richardson, *Clarissa*, ed. A. Ross (Harmondsworth: Penguin Books, 1985), 1488.

[74] On this theme, see e.g. John Ogilvie, who in his *An Inquiry into the Causes of the Infidelity and Scepticism of the Times* (1783) had asserted that 'the love of pleasure, and the gratification of sensual appetite, are causes of infidelity and of scepticism that are too conspicuous to be omitted' (pp. 441–2); or Richard Hurd, who in attacking Helvétius yoked together 'libertinism and infidelity' (*Correspondence*, 63); or Christopher Hunter, SCEPTICISM *not separable from* IMMORALITY.

in literary employments, which others of his rank and condition too often dedicate only either to frivolous or to destructive pursuits. But the very agreeable entertainment which our Author has set before us, is unhappily intermixed with a subtle poison of the most dangerous tendency.[75]

On reflection, it must have seemed idle to attempt to deny Gibbon the credit for the classical and historical scholarship so manifest in the footnotes to the first volume of *The Decline and Fall*. Equally, it must have come to seem ridiculous, once haste and indignation had yielded to calm and leisure, to compare the self-effacing and celibate MP with Richardson's Lovelace. Gibbon was manifestly not an unlearned and loose-living deist, such as former champions of orthodoxy had effectively mocked. Such exaggerations, which wore their improbability on their face, merely lent comfort to the man Chelsum wished to damage.

In the second edition of the *Remarks*, therefore, Chelsum redirected his energies. He replaced the implausible charge of reviving the deism of the earlier part of the century with a much more well-documented attack on the historical vision of *The Decline and Fall*, and the historiographic technique whereby that vision was recommended to the unwary reader. By means of greatly enlarged documentation, in the second edition of the *Remarks* Chelsum pressed home his linked contentions that the first volume of *The Decline and Fall* unjustly depreciated the first Christians, and in particular the early Fathers, while at the same time averting its attention from the moral shortcomings of paganism and the Roman administration.[76] These two issues, of the substance of Gibbon's historical vision and the technical sleights of hand on which it relied, come together in the peroration to the second edition, a sober recapitulation of the crux of the controversy which took the place of some seven rambling and miscellaneous pages in the first edition of 1776:

The spirit indeed of his [Gibbon's] remarks will perhaps appear principally to have deserved notice; but however the cause of Christianity in general had in

---

[75] *Remarks 2*, pp. xii–xiii.

[76] This augmented documentation figures prominently in Chelsum's own account of the differences between his first and second editions: 'The present tract was originally published in the month of October 1776. [*sic*] without the Author's name, under the title of A Letter to a Friend. It contained the first public strictures on Mr. Gibbon's work. It having been now thrown a into [*sic*] new form, many passages of the former tract are omitted, and others are transposed. The additions are distinguished in the table of Contents. The Reader's convenience has been consulted also, by subjoining for the most part, in every instance where it has seemed important, the entire passages out of Mr. Gibbon's work, which before, for brevity's sake, were only referred to by marking the pages' (*Remarks 2*, pp. xiii–xiv, n. 7).

reality still remained unaffected by our Author's disquisitions, it's cause was yet too sacred to subject it even in appearance to any diminution of it's proper strength and support. It became therefore necessary to endeavour to offer an antidote even to exploded objections since the interests of Religion are too important not to lay claim to continual defence; since not to advance to meet the enemy as often as he returns to the charge, would be in some sort to abandon the field, and to acknowledge tacitly the superiority of his forces.

The defects of evidence which our Author's History labours under required still farther animadversion. One of the most eminent Historians of this age has pronounced of History in general, in allusion to our Author's own opinion, that 'he who delineates the transactions of a remote period has no title to claim assent, unless he produces evidence in proof of his assertions.—Without this he may write an amusing tale, but cannot be said to have composed an authentic history.'

We shall not apply this maxim improperly, when we assert still farther, that he who abounds in partial and erroneous quotations, however he may have preserved the appearance, has yet so far in reality produced no evidence in proof of his assertions.[77]

The eminent historian whom Chelsum quoted against Gibbon was, as it happened, William Robertson; and we may suppose that this citing of one friend against another figured in their conversation over dinner on 15 March.

Such lucky hits aside, there was surely still much to occupy the two historians as they dined together that evening. The second edition of Chelsum's *Remarks* provided clear evidence that the attack on *The Decline and Fall*, far from dying down, was now better organized, and equipped with a more accurate sense of the strengths of its own position and the vulnerable points in Gibbon's. The reduction of heat in Chelsum's style menaced Gibbon with an increase in light, trained on those dark places in *The Decline and Fall* where his closeness to the deists of earlier generations was most marked. In the *Vindication* Gibbon would imply that a retort had been wrung from him only because Davis had moved the accusations from the historian's religious to his moral character. But Gibbon's moral character had always been at the very heart of the dispute, ever since Chelsum himself had published passages such as the following in October 1776: 'When important passages are misrepresented, when the characters of venerable writers are sacrificed to false criticism, neither the diligence of an impartial inquirer, the discernment of a scholar, nor the fidelity of an historian, are discoverable.'[78] Davis perhaps delivers his accusations with more puppyish

[77] *Remarks 2*, 242–3.   [78] *Remarks*, 92.

exuberance, but they are ethically no different from these of Chelsum. Gibbon was prompted to reply to his critics, not because they had suddenly impugned his honour as a gentleman, but because they suddenly looked more formidable than they had done when he had made the revisions for the third edition of his first volume in 1777. The controversy had moved on since then, and not in directions which favoured the historian. Moreover, Chelsum's ostentatiously mild reply to the stinging epistle in which Gibbon had refused the present of the second edition of the *Remarks* may only have deepened the historian's alarm:

Sir,
Permit me to assure you, with the utmost sincerity, that no insult, such as, I collect from your letter, you attribute to me, was ever intended by me.

I had reason to think, from several circumstances, that my not having sent my Remarks to you in their first form, had been considered by you as a want of attention, and I was very ready to pay what others gave me reason to expect, would be received as a mark of civility. I do not mean here to refer to Mr. Batt.

My determination was the result of a deference to the opinions of others; and it arose in no degree from an '*officious readiness*,' to which you attribute it. I may be accused of an error in judgment, but I cannot justly be accused of any greater offence.

Concerned as I am at my mistake, I am most of all concerned that so esteemed a friend as Mr. Batt should have been employed in a very unpleasant mediation between us.

As it is the sole object of this letter to give you every possible assurance of my having intended a compliment in what has unfortunately been received as an insult, I should have concluded here, but that I am anxious to do myself the justive of pointing out to you, that you have unwarily imputed to me one expression (as I apprehend) wholly without foundation.

On the most diligent recollection I cannot remember that I have any where said (and I am sure I never intended to say) that you have '*studiously*' concealed the truth.[79]

We should be wary of reading such studied moderation of tone and language as the honest signature of a genuinely moderate disposition in the author, for, as Anne Goldgar has recently shown, the style in which disputes within the Republic of Letters were managed received careful and interpretative attention from bystanders.[80] To show humility in the face of aggression might be very prudent, as the response to the quarrel between Anne Dacier and Antoine Houdar de la Motte had shown: 'the quarrel about Homer has started up again, with a great deal of

[79] *MW 1815* iii. 620.   [80] Goldgar, *Impolite Learning*.

vivacity. . . . Her [Mme Dacier's] Best Friends have blamed this trans-
port of anger against Mr. *de la Motte*, & the injurious things she says
to him. Mr. *de la Motte* has responded with much moderation, & this
moderation adds a new weight to his response.'[81] That Chelsum's composure of tone may be of this strategic kind is suggested by the fact that,
behind its indeflectible neutrality of language, this letter in fact pursues
and repeats in a different form the charge which Chelsum had levelled
at Gibbon in the *Remarks*, namely that *The Decline and Fall* had misrepresented the early Christians by means of a careless or deliberate
inattention to the evidence. Chelsum now stands in the place of those
first martyrs for the faith whom he had defended in the *Remarks*. His
pure intentions have also been misjudged, and, as were those of the
early Christians, on the basis of a *parti pris* reading of the textual evidence; for indeed Chelsum had not accused Gibbon of 'studiously'
concealing the truth.

When Davis's *Examination* did appear, probably in early May as we
have seen, it was not to Robertson that Gibbon turned for advice, but
to Horace Walpole. Walpole's letter assessing the gravity of the threat
represented by Davis is of interest, both for what Gibbon took from it
and for what he ignored.[82] Enclosing his own annotated copy of the
Examination ('to prove I did not grudge the trouble of going through
such a book, *when you desired it*'—my emphasis) Walpole began by
insisting on the insignificance, as he saw it, of Davis's indictments: 'I
have gone through your inquisitor's attack, and am far from being clear
that it deserves your giving yourself the trouble of an answer, as neither
the detail nor the result affects your argument.' Davis's charges of
plagiarism are absurd, 'for if they are so [i.e. true plagiarisms], no argument that has ever been employed, must be used again, even where the
passage necessary is applied to a different purpose.' If, however, Davis is
after all to be answered, the rhetoric of the riposte must receive special
attention: 'Upon the whole, I think ridicule is the only answer such a
work is entitled to. The ablest answer you can make (which would be
the ablest answer that could be made) would never have any authority
with the cabal, yet would allow a sort of dignity to the author. His
patrons will always maintain that he vanquished you, unless you make

[81] *Histoire Critique de la République des Lettres*, 9 (1715), 327; quoted in Goldgar, *Impolite Learning*, 215. Cf. 'The form of disputes—ideally moderate and measured—was frequently the focus of attention, and arguments were often judged on the politeness with which they were presented, rather than on their intrinsic merit' (Goldgar, *Impolite Learning*, 240).
[82] The letter itself is kept among the Gibbon papers at the British Library (Add. MS 34,886, fo. 106). It was first reprinted in the second edition of the *Miscellaneous Works* (*MW 1814* ii. 156–8). It is quoted here from *Horace Walpole's Correspondence*, ed. W. S. Lewis, xl (1980), 385–7.

him too ridiculous for them to dare to revive his name.' Here we can see encouragement to adopt that tone of mordant sarcasm so prevalent in the *Vindication* (to which Gibbon was perhaps in any event inclined); and as Walpole's fancy warms to the possibilities for mischief in such a reply ('You might divert yourself too with Alma Mater the Church employing a goujat [i.e. an army valet] to defend the citadel, while the generals repose in their tents') we also find, it may be, the metaphorical seed of that sneering phrase for Gibbon's enemies which so goaded them, and which I have incorporated in the title of this book: the 'Watchmen of the Holy City'.[83]

With Walpole's parting piece of advice, however, Gibbon evidently did not wholly agree: 'In short, dear Sir, I wish you not to lose your time; that is, either not reply, or set *your mark* on your answer, that it may always be read with the rest of your works.' Gibbon would surely set his mark upon the *Vindication*, as Walpole demanded; but he would conclude the pamphlet with the wish that it be forgotten: 'I am impatient to dismiss, and to dismiss FOR EVER, this odious controversy, with the success of which I cannot surely be elated; and I have only to request, that, as soon as my Readers are convinced of my innocence, they would forget my Vindication.'[84] That wish for oblivion found expression in a form which precludes all doubt as to its sincerity. The *Vindication* was printed in octavo, so that it could not be bound with the quarto volumes of *The Decline and Fall*.[85]

IV

It is impossible, then, to view Gibbon's resolve to set about composing the *Vindication* during the busy summer and autumn of 1778 as simply a response to the publication of Davis's *Examination*.[86] As the exchange of letters with Robertson and a close attention to dates of publication show, it can only have been the appearance of the second edition of Chelsum's *Remarks* which jolted Gibbon out of the mood of disdainful

[83] *DF* iii. 1109. For evidence that the jibe hit home, see Chelsum, *Reply*, 2, and Davis, *Reply*, 5.   [84] *DF* iii. 1184.

[85] *A* 316 n. 34. Gibbon's fastidiousness drew from Davis a rejoinder of sorts: 'I have taken care that the *Reply* should be printed in the same size as the *Examination*, that while they exist . . . they may be bound and read together, and that the latter publication may correct and confirm the former' (Davis, *Reply*, 175).

[86] Gibbon's letters during the second half of 1778 show him to have been much preoccupied with both public and private business (the war with the colonies and the liquidation of assets such as the New River share respectively), as well as with the composition of the second instalment of *The Decline and Fall*: *L* ii. 182–200.

indifference with which he had hitherto greeted all the published attacks upon him. The propelling motive behind the composition of the *Vindication*, it follows, was not moral outrage but alarm at the advent of technically more formidable attacks. The publication in May of Davis's *Examination*—more unguarded in its language than the revised version of Chelsum's pamphlet, and more extravagant in its allegations—was therefore a great stroke of luck for Gibbon. The meditated reply from which he had been temporarily dissuaded by Robertson could now be written, and directed at a much weaker figure, whose vulnerable book, in which were repeated and exaggerated precisely the charges of deism and literary theft which Chelsum's second and wiser thoughts had muted in favour of more substantive historiographical allegations, might be made to encapsulate the whole attack upon *The Decline and Fall*.

Yet even with a sophomore adversary, such as Davis, to engage in controversy might be to run risks. So Walpole's letter had counselled (in the midst, however, of at the same time indicating how the job might be done). If a reply were in the least misjudged, it might serve to strengthen rather than weaken its target. How might Gibbon have responded to the dangerous opportunity which had unexpectedly opened before him with the publication of Davis's *Examination*? It would surely have been natural both to consider how other writers had handled themselves in literary controversy, and to review the strengths and aptitudes revealed in one's own earlier work. In Gibbon's case these two fields of enquiry—that of eighteenth-century literary polemic as a whole, and his own earlier writings—merged into one another.

Although Gibbon's manner in the *Vindication* suggests that he was unaccustomed to descend to literary altercation, in fact both his earlier publications—the *Essai sur l'Étude de la Littérature* (1761) and the *Critical Observations on the Design of the Sixth Book of the Æneid* (1770)—had been contributions to literary controversies, while the third piece we shall examine in this context (his long letter in the character of 'Daniel Freeman' written to Richard Hurd in August 1772 on the subject of the prophecies of the Book of Daniel) had pursued the anti-Warburtonian line of the *Critical Observations*.

The *Essai*, as a plea for the value of studying ancient literature, steps forward as a belated bulletin in 'la fameuse dispute des anciens et des modernes', which had administered 'le coup mortel' to the study of 'Belles-Lettres'.[87] According to Gibbon, the early rounds had not been fair fights:

[87] *MW 1796* ii. 451.

Il n'y a jamais eu un combat aussi inégal. La logique exacte de Terrason, la philosophie déliée de Fontenelle, le style élégant et heureux de la Motte, le badinage léger de St. Hyacinte, travailloient de concert à réduire Homère au niveau de Chapelain. Leurs adversaires ne leur opposoient qu'un attachement au minuties, je ne sais quelles prétensions à une supériorité naturelle des anciens, des préjugés, des injures et des citations. Tout le ridicule leur demeura. Il en rejaillit une partie sur ces anciens, dont ils soutenoient la querelle: et chez cette nation aimable, qui a adopté, sans y penser, le principe de Milord Shaftsbury, on ne distingue point les torts et les ridicules.

Depuis ce tems, nos philosophes se sont étonnés que des hommes pussent passer une vie entière à rassembler des faits et des mots; et à se charger la mémoire au lieu de s'éclaircir l'esprit. Nos beaux esprits ont senti, quels avantages leur reviendroient de l'ignorance de leurs lecteurs. Ils ont comblé de mépris les anciens, et ceux qui les étudient encore.[88]

In the *Essai* he undertakes to plead again the case for the value of classical literature, and to that extent he is on the side of the 'Ancients'. However, his awareness of the weakness of his predecessors precludes him from simply restating their arguments. His own strategy is to concede to the Moderns the justness of their principles, but then to argue, through a series of case studies, that those sound principles are in fact fulfilled by the study of ancient literature.[89] It would indeed be a waste of life to 'se charger la mémoire au lieu de s'éclaircir l'esprit', but this is not what the study of ancient literature necessarily entails. The *Essai* is therefore a subtle exercise in compromise.[90] Determined to fix 'la juste valeur des Belles-Lettres', Gibbon hopes nevertheless to placate the Moderns by acknowledging the soundness of their values and the technical accomplishment of their arguments.[91] The concluding sentiment,

[88]   *MW 1796* ii. 451–2. The 'principe' of Shaftesbury alluded to is presumably the maxim, advanced in 'The Freedom of Wit and Humour', that ridicule is the test of truth.

[89]   That such is Gibbon's attitude to the Moderns is suggested by his comment on Terrasson, the anti-Homerian: 'just tho' not warm!' (*J1* 190). The *Essai* sets out to reconcile judiciousness and warmth.

[90]   D. M. Low's judgement, that in the *Essai* 'Gibbon's thesis only floats on the surface of the controversy between the ancients and moderns which stirred the liveliest and profoundest thought of France for over a hundred years' (*J1*, p. xl n. 1) correctly measures the depth of Gibbon's involvement in the substantive issues of the *querelle*, but seems to imply what was surely not the case, namely that it was Gibbon's intention to fight over the old terrain once more.

[91]   *MW 1796* ii. 452. For other accounts of the *Essai* as an attempt to resolve some of the issues in the quarrel, see in particular two works by J. M. Levine: *Humanism and History: Origins of Modern English Historiography* (Ithaca, NY: Cornell University Press, 1987) and *The Battle of the Books: History and Literature in the Augustan Age* (Ithaca, NY: Cornell University Press, 1991). Levine's opinion that 'the quarrel was not the only and probably not the most important influence upon Gibbon's thought, but it was a crucial ingredient in the formation of his mind and an essential part of that elaborate setting in which we can hope to measure his achievement' (*Humanism and History*, 178) is one to which my present argument would lend support, but on

in its elevation of general utility over personal glory, is entirely in keeping with the placatory tendency of the work as a whole: 'L'avantage de l'art m'est plus cher que la gloire de l'artiste.'[92] A sharer in the enthusiasms of the Ancients, but persuaded of the intellectual cogency of the position of the Moderns, in the *Essai* Gibbon combined within himself antagonistic characters. This was to develop into a constant feature of his polemical writing, and one which he exploited to great effect in the *Vindication.*

The *Essai* demonstrates Gibbon's familiarity with the personnel and arguments of the first great literary battle of the eighteenth century, and it shows him joining the conversation in the role of deferential peacemaker. His *Critical Observations on the Design of the Sixth Book of the Æneid*, published anonymously nine years later in 1770, shows him joining a later controversy in a quite different role. In draft 'E' of his 'Memoirs' Gibbon described the pamphlet as follows, and passed judgement:

> In the year 1770 I sent to the press some *Critical Observations on the Sixth Book of the Æneid*. This anonymous pamphlet was pointed against Bishop Warburton, who demonstrates that the descent of Æneas to the shades is an Allegory of his initiation to the Eleusinian mysteries. The love of Virgil, the hatred of a Dictator, and the example of Lowth, awakened me to arms. The coldness of the public has been amply compensated by the esteem of Heyne, of Hayley, and of Parr; but the acrimony of my style has been justly blamed by the Professor of Gottingen. Warburton was *not* an object of contempt.[93]

rhetorical and stylistic grounds, rather than on matters of substantive scholarship. There Gibbon seems to have sided generally with the Moderns, although a passage such as the following from his journal shows traces of the attitudes of the Ancients in its contempt for dictionary learning and in its embracing of the humanistic principle of the classical texts being their own best commentary: 'Indeed, more I read the Antients, more I am persuaded that the originals are our best commentators. In this article of ancient Gymnastics (for instance), when I have read with care Homer, Pausanias, and some few more ancients, M. Burette has little to teach me, excepting perhaps what he may have picked up from some obscure passages of some obscure Lexicographer' (*J1* 113; for earlier instances of the principle that the ancients are their own best commentary, see Roscommon, *An Essay on Translated Verse*, l. 186 and Pope, *An Essay on Criticism*, ll. 129–30, in Womersley (ed.), *Augustan Critical Writing*, 113 and 212). Such moments are however rare (cf. also *J1* 139 and 147–8); and the passage continues in a spirit of placatory compromise: 'What I say is not, however, to proscribe the use, but to restrain the abuse, of modern Critics.' Peter Ghosh's comments about Gibbon's 'distance from the *querelle*' are misleading. The issues of the dispute are clearly central to Gibbon's own intellectual life, even if they do not arise for him in the way they did for Bentley and Temple, and the literary embodiment of the *querelle* was of enduring significance for him, as my argument in this chapter shows ('Gibbon's Timeless Verity', 163 n. 256). In this instance I find François Furet closer to the mark, when he calls the *querelle* 'a literary controversy that . . . went to the heart of his intellectual life' ('Civilization and Barbarism', 205).

[92] *MW 1796* ii. 495.
[93] *A* 304–5.

In a later chapter we shall see that the gesture of qualified revocation in the last sentence is characteristic of this particular draft of the 'Memoirs', written as it was under the tutelary influence of Burke's *Reflections on the Revolution in France*, and entailing as it did an effort on Gibbon's part to bring his earlier life into line with counter-revolutionary scripture. Warburton's stock might well have risen in Gibbon's estimation during the 1790s, when the bishop of Gloucester's views on Church and State must have seemed consolingly robust.[94] Twenty years earlier, however, when the pressure to find and build alliances against the contagion of revolution had not existed, Gibbon had despised Warburton's *Divine Legation of Moses Demonstrated*. The strategy Gibbon chose to launch his attack against this 'object of contempt' draws on his reading in the quarrel of the Ancients and Moderns, and points forward to the strategy of the *Vindication*.

Gibbon was not by any means the first in the field against Warburton's *Divine Legation*. In 1755 John Jortin (whom in *The Decline and Fall* Gibbon would praise for 'freedom', 'learning, candour, and ingenuity', and 'becoming asperity') had attacked the very theory against which Gibbon would write some fifteen years later, and Gibbon was obliged to notice his anticipator in a slightly embarrassed post-script.[95] In addition, Gibbon indicated in a footnote an attack which Warburton had courted, but which had not actually occurred. In accepting the laws of Zaleucus as genuine the 'bishop has entered the lists with the tremendous Bentley, who treated the laws of Zaleucus and Charondas as the forgeries of a sophist . . . But Bentley is no more, and W—n may sleep in peace. I shall however disturb his repose . . .'[96] As the author of the *Dissertation Upon the Epistles of Phalaris* (1697; reprinted 1699 and 1777) Bentley had been one of the leading combatants on the English front of the Ancients and Moderns. The *Dissertation* was

[94] 'Warburton . . . based his defence of a religious establishment not on its truth but on its use-fulness to the State', albeit on the premise that 'TRUTH and PUBLIC UTILITY coincide', so that 'to provide for utility is, at the same time, to provide for truth, its inseparable associate' (Evans, *Warburton and the Warburtonians*, 44).

[95] For the postscript, see *EE* 159–62. *DF* i. 779 n. 45, i. 783 n. 58, and ii. 86 n. 54. Not every one thought Warburton's theory risible. Arthur Murphy reports that Henry Fielding, in *A Journey from This World to the Next* (1743), incorporated 'a well turned compliment to the learned author who has, with so much elegance and ability, traced out the analogy between Virgil's system and those memorable rites' in 'the surprise with which he has made Mr. Addison hear of the *Eleusinian Mysteries*, in the sixth Æneid' ('An Essay on the Life and Genius of Henry Fielding, Esq.' [1762], in Paulson (ed.), *Henry Fielding: The Critical Heritage*, 419).

[96] *EE* 135, n.(5). Bentley had died in 1742. Gibbon would touch on the laws of Zaleucus once more, in a footnote to *The Decline and Fall*: 'the laws of Zaleucus and Charondas, which imposed on Diodorus and Stobæus, are the spurious composition of a Pythagorean sophist, whose fraud has been detected by the critical sagacity of Bentley' (*DF* ii. 782, n. 16).

generally regarded as the heaviest blow landed on the Ancients, and in the *Essai* Gibbon had praised Bentley's 'pénétration hardie'.[97] It is therefore striking that, with the phrase 'I shall however disturb his repose', Gibbon enters the lists on Bentley's behalf. The *Critical Observations* is a vindication of the great critic, and Gibbon is his champion. At the same time, he might hope to acquire reputation himself. As Johnson had written in 1765, 'Dr. Warburton had a name sufficient to confer celebrity on those who could exalt themselves into antagonists.'[98]

In what sense can we see Gibbon's performance in the *Critical Observations* as Bentleian? Gibbon's prose style (whatever he may have regretted in 1790 about its 'acrimony') was always much more urbane than Bentley's pugnacious stridency: in respect of their habitual tone, Warburton was Bentley's natural heir. However, in criticizing Warburton for shoddy scholarship and for being unable to relinquish a self-serving hypothesis, Gibbon was linking the charges of technical inadequacy and vanity as Bentley had linked them against Boyle in the *Dissertation*. And when Gibbon uncovers Warburton mistaking modern forgeries for genuine ancient writings, just as Boyle and Temple had done with the *Epistles of Phalaris*, the influence of Bentley seems particularly strong.[99]

To play the part of Bentley against Warburton must have been particularly tempting, because in many quarters Warburton himself was seen as Bentley's true successor. Here we must recollect that there were two major elements in Bentley's reputation. The first was that of the great classical philologist, the editor of Horace, and the man whose precision and depth of learning had exposed beyond repair the slackness and confusion at the heart of the position of the Ancients. The second was that of the implacable foe of deism and natural religion, the Boyle lecturer, the merciless chastiser of Anthony Collins in the *Remarks Upon a Late Discourse of Freethinking* (1713; reprinted, 1743).[100] It was in this

---

[97] *MW 1796* ii. 453. Gibbon's admiration of Bentley as a natural and consummate critic endured to the very end of his life: *EE* 542 and 547.

[98] Johnson, 'Preface', 47.

[99] *EE* 137.

[100] Some saw a tension between Bentley the champion of orthodox Christianity and Bentley the classical philologist. In the burlesque section of his reply to Bentley in which he wittily cites known circumstances of Bentley's life to 'prove', in a parody of Bentley's own arguments, that Bentley could not have written the *Dissertation Upon the Epistles of Phalaris*, Boyle had drawn attention to Bentley's Boyle lectures as one such circumstance: 'that learned Doctor was chosen out by the then Fathers of the Church, as a fit Person to vindicate the Truth of Religion against Atheists, Deists, and all other Opposers of Divine Revelation' (Boyle, *Bentley's Dissertations . . . Examin'd*, 201). But also cf. below, n. 176.

second respect that Warburton was at mid-century widely recognized as having donned Bentley's mantle. Such had been the success of Bentley's attack on Collins that it had become a template for those who wished to defend religious orthodoxy against freethinking.[101] In a letter to John Devey of 23 January 1740 Richard Hurd wrote of a piece by Samuel Squire that "tis wrote a good deal in the taste and spirit of Bentley's Phileleutherus Lipsiensis [i.e. Bentley's adopted *persona* in his reply to Collins], and is expected to be a good thing'.[102] Five years later, however, and writing to the same correspondent, Hurd exulted in the advent of Bentley's true heir: 'The attention of the learned world at present turns entirely almost on the author of the Divine Legation of Moses, who is mowing down his adversaries with as great zeal and success as ever old Bentley did before him.'[103] In playing Bentley against Warburton, Gibbon was thus rebutting the cherished belief of the Warburtonians, and arguably of Warburton himself, that Bentley's mantle had fallen on their man.[104] The *Critical Observations* implied that, although Warburton might share Bentley's enemies and even his rugged literary manners, it was Gibbon who could wield the scholarly

[101] It would, for instance, serve as the model for Samuel Horsley's attacks on Joseph Priestley in the 1780s: see the account of this altercation in the article on Priestley in the *DNB*.

[102] Kilvert, *Memoirs*, 6. I owe this reference to the kindness of Isabel Rivers.

[103] Ibid. 23; Monk thought that the attack on Collins in the *Divine Legation* 'plainly emulates' that of Bentley (Monk, *Life of Bentley*, ii. 410). Compare also Hurd's praise of Warburton's effectiveness against the deists in the preface to his edition of Warburton's works. Warburton 'was the terror of the infidel world, while he lived, and will be their disgrace to future ages. His sublime reason, aided by his irresistible wit, drove them from their old fastnesses of logick and philosophy, and has forced them to take shelter in the thin cover of history and romance; whence we now see them shoot their arrows, tipt in irony and badinage'—apparently an allusion to Gibbon and Hume (Hurd, *A Discourse*, 118; I owe this reference to the kindness of Isabel Rivers).

[104] Warburton's relationship with Bentley was complex, although in retrospect not difficult to explain. In Warburton's eyes Bentley's weakness was due to the imbalance of his virtues: 'He was a great master both of the languages and the learning of polite Antiquity; whose writings he studied with no other design than to correct the errors of the text. For this he had a strong natural understanding, a great share of penetration, and a sagacity and acumen very uncommon. All which qualities he had greatly improved by long exercise and application. Yet, at the same time, he had so little of that elegance of judgment, we call *Taste*, that he knew nothing of *Style*, as it accommodates itself, and is appropriated to the various kinds of composition. And the faculties of his Understanding being infinitely better than those of his Imagination, the *style of poetry* was what he had the least idea of' (from Warburton's note to l. 104 of Pope's *Epistle to Augustus*, in *The Works of Alexander Pope Esq. . . . together with the Commentaries and Notes of Mr. Warburton*, 9 vols. (1751), iv. 157–9; quotation on p. 158). Warburton saw himself as the complete critic uniting both understanding and imagination, a self-image which required that Bentley's limitations be ever before the public: hence the anti-Bentleian strokes which Warburton both inserted himself, and encouraged Pope to insert, in the later editions of Pope's poetry (Monk, *Life of Bentley*, i. 122–3 and ii. 404–11; Jebb, *Bentley*, 202–3). In private, however, Warburton acknowledged that Bentley was 'a truly great and much injured man' (*Letters from a Late Eminent Prelate to one of his Friends*, 9).

weapons on which Bentley's claim to greatness most securely rested. Perhaps no man might again hope to be all that Bentley had been; but in that case the legacy had been divided very unequally. Warburton had perversely chosen Bentley's human failings, but Gibbon had seized his scholarly strengths.

The third work we must consider was first published only in 1811, but it is in certain respects a continuation of the *Critical Observations*, and is moreover an important document illustrating Gibbon's career as a literary polemicist before the *Vindication*. Towards the end of his life Warburton founded a series of lectures of which the purpose was to expound and defend the biblical prophecies concerning the Christian Church. The first series of these lectures had been delivered in 1768 by Warburton's ally, lieutenant, and factotum, the archdeacon of Gloucester (later bishop of Worcester) Richard Hurd. When in 1772 these lectures were published as *An Introduction to the Study of the Prophecies concerning the Christian Church*, Gibbon wrote pseudonymously to Hurd (asking for any answer to be addressed to '*Daniel Freeman, Esq. at the Cocoa Tree, Pall Mall*') posing the question '*Whether, there is sufficient evidence that the Book of Daniel is really as ancient as it pretends to be.*'[105] The point was crucial to Hurd's overall argument, for as Gibbon reminded him, 'from this point the Golden Chain of Prophecy, which you have let down from Heaven to earth, is partly suspended'.[106]

Gibbon had written once before against Hurd in 1762, albeit for his own satisfaction. Having read Hurd's edition of Horace, he composed an essay of thirty pages disputing Hurd's interpretation of these two epistles, and deplored, in passing, Hurd's 'excessive praises (not to give

---

[105] *L* i. 338 and 328. Gibbon had a good deal of accumulated thinking on this subject to hand when he decided to engage with Hurd. In August and September 1752 he had begun and then abandoned an essay entitled 'The Age of Sesostris' (*A* 79–81); in 1758 he had composed a critical account of Newton's chronology (*MW 1815* 61–73); and perhaps at the same time he was also writing his 'Mémoire sur la Monarchie des Mèdes' (*MW 1815* 1–60). All these early works would have obliged him to reflect on the historical significance of the Book of Daniel.

[106] *L* i. 328. Hurd first became aware of the identity of the author of this letter when he saw his reply published without his permission in Gibbon's *Miscellaneous Works* (*MW 1796* i. 455–63). He had evidently therefore not accepted Gibbon's offer to disclose his identity: 'if you have any scruple of engaging with a mask, I am ready, by the same channel, to disclose my real name and place of abode' (*L* i. 338–9). He then published Gibbon's original letter, together with his reply (in a version which differs slightly from that published in the *Miscellaneous Works*) in the *Works of Richard Hurd, DD, Lord Bishop of Worcester*, 8 vols. (1811), v. 363 ff. This is the only text we possess of this work of Gibbon's. He seems either not to have made, or to have destroyed, any copy for his later personal use, and Sheffield did not choose to print a text in either the five-volume octavo second edition of the *Miscellanous Works* (1814), or the supplementary third quarto volume of the *Miscellaneous Works* (1815).

them a harsher name)' of Warburton.[107] Although the letter of 1772 shares the earlier essay's distaste for 'Warburton and his bloodhounds', it is at once more succinct and more rhetorically elaborate than its predecessor, reading at certain points like a first attempt at phrases and textual manoeuvres which would later be executed with more precision in *The Decline and Fall*.[108] However, like the *Critical Observations* of two years before, the letter to Hurd on the Book of Daniel was written from within the milieu of Tory deism which perhaps came into the Gibbon family originally from its most famous exponent, Bolingbroke, by means of David Mallet, Bolingbroke's literary executor and near neighbour of the Gibbon family in Putney.[109] It was a persona well calculated to affront Hurd, who at that stage in his life had strongly Whiggish leanings.[110] In 1770 Gibbon had mocked Warburton's ideas

[107] Q. *Horatii Flacci Epistolæ, ad Pisones et Augustum*, 2nd edn. (Cambridge, 1757). *MW 1796* ii. 27–50; ii. 27. In his journal Gibbon marked the importance to his own intellectual life of this engagement with Hurd, when in the entry for 18 March 1762 he commented that it had 'started a new train of ideas upon many curious points of Criticism' (*J1* 49).

[108] *A* 304 n. 21. For phrases which read like first attempts at topics which would preoccupy Gibbon in *The Decline and Fall*, consider the following: 'This age indeed, to whom the gift of miracles has been refused, is apt to wonder at the indifference with which they were received by the ancient world' (*L* i. 333) anticipates 'When the law was given in thunder from Mount Sinai; when the tides of the ocean, and the course of the planets were suspended for the convenience of the Israelites; and when temporal rewards and punishments were the immediate consequences of their piety or disobedience, they perpetually relapsed into rebellion against the visible majesty of their Divine King' and 'But how shall we excuse the supine inattention of the Pagan and philosophic world, to those evidences which were presented by the hand of Omnipotence, not to their reason, but to their senses?' (*DF* i. 449 and 512); 'An irreligious prince may be indiscreet enough to treat with ridicule whatever is held sacred by his subjects; but he will entertain too great a contempt both for the people, and for popular superstition, ever to think of forcibly separating them from each other' (*L* i. 335) looks forward to 'We may be well assured, that a writer, conversant with the world, would never have ventured to expose the gods of his country to public ridicule, had they not already been the objects of secret contempt among the polished and enlightened orders of society (*DF* i. 58).

[109] The opposite of such Tory deism is the Whiggish piety of a writer such as Leland, who insists that the cause of the Church of England and of the Hanoverian regime are one and the same, and that Bolingbroke is the enemy of both: 'it should be the earnest desire of every true Christian, and lover of his country, that all should be united in a steady and well-regulated zeal for our holy religion, and for that establishment on which, under God, the security of our most valuable civil and religious liberties doth in a great measure depend' (Leland, *Reflections*, p. xix). Gibbon's father exposed his son to Tory and even Jacobite influences, such as that of Crop, the mayor of Southampton and simulacrum of Fielding's Squire Western, who 'drinks hard, rails against all ministers and keeps alive the small remains of Jacobitism at Southampton' (*J1* 144). It was of course to Mallet that Gibbon's father had first sent him following his conversion to Catholicism, in an attempt to drive out superstition with irreligion, but Gibbon had been 'rather scandalized than reclaimed' by his 'philosophy' (*A* 130). For a more lengthy consideration of interactions between the Mallets and the Gibbons, see Womersley, 'Gibbon's Religious Characters'.

[110] Hurd was later attacked by Samuel Parr for drifting in later life away from his initial Whig allegiances.

on Church and State, and had in deist vein ironically celebrated 'the Antient Alliance between the Avarice of the Priest and the Credulity of the People'.[111] In 1772 the name of his persona 'Daniel Freeman' is redolent of the Tory appropriation of what had been originally an Old Whig language, while the address at which 'Daniel Freeman' might be found—'*the Cocoa Tree*'—reeked of old Toryism.[112] Furthermore, the analysis 'Daniel Freeman' places before Hurd is couched in deist language, and draws upon the general account of the psychology of religion and of the wiles of priestcraft promulgated by freethinkers earlier in the century:

The eager trembling curiosity of mankind has ever wished to penetrate into futurity; nor is there perhaps any country, where enthusiasm and knavery have not pretended to satisfy this anxious craving of the human heart.

Such an extraordinary interdict [Darius's forbidding of religious worship for thirty days], by depriving the people of the comforts, and the priests of the profits of religion, must have diffused a general discontent throughout his empire; . . .[113]

In addition, the recurrent idiom of the letter is that of elaborate irony, which after 1776 would have been easily recognizable as Gibbonian, but which in 1772 must have seemed to be the signature of an unusually urbane deist:

Since you have undertaken the care and defence of this extensive province [of biblical prophecy], I may be allowed, less as an opponent than as a disciple, to propose to you a few difficulties; about which I have sought more conviction than I have hitherto obtained.

---

[111] *EE* 136.

[112] For the best available survey of the mutations of the languages of Whiggery, see Pocock, 'The Varieties of Whiggism from Exclusion to Reform'. For the political connotations of the Cocoa Tree, the coffee-house in Pall Mall at which the Tory society, Edward Harley's Board, had met every Thursday during the parliamentary session since 1727, see Colley, *Defiance of Oligarchy*, 71–5, 137, 140, 165, 206, 211, and 280. Gibbon's retrospective account of his listless town life between 1758 and 1760 confirms the political associations of the club; he was 'reduced to some dull family parties, to some old Tories of the Cocoa-tree, and to some casual connections, such as my taste and esteem would never have selected' (from draft 'C', *A* 245; cf. also *L* i. 204 and n. 2). At the time, however, he had been more enthusiastic: 'We . . . returned to the Cocoa-tree. That respectable body, of which I have the honor to be a member, affords every evening a sight truly English. Twenty or thirty, perhaps, of the first men in the kingdom, in point of fashion and fortune, supping at little tables covered with a napkin, in the middle of a Coffee-room, upon a bit of cold meat, or a Sandwich, & drinking a glass of punch. At present, we are full of Privy Counsellors and Lords of the Bedchamber; . . .' (*J*1 185: cf. also pp. 186 and 200).

[113] *L* i. 329 and 335. The prophecies of the Book of Daniel had earlier been a focus of deist controversy, and awareness of that lineage permeates this encounter between Gibbon and Hurd on both sides (cf. Stephen, *English Thought*, i. 228).

To the first of these incidents I am so far from forming any objection, that it seems to me, in the true style of the oriental customs in war and government. But the two last are embarrassed with difficulties, from which I have not been able to extricate myself.

the hopes I still entertain, that you may be able and willing to dispell the mist, that hangs, either over my eyes, or over the subject itself.[114]

Finally, 'Daniel Freeman's' credentials are put beyond doubt when we note that the criterion for belief in matters of religion which he proposes for Hurd's endorsement is substantially that of Hume in 'Of Miracles':

May I not assume as a principle equally consonant to experience, to reason, and even to true religion; 'That we ought not to admit any thing as the immediate work of God, which can possibly be the work of man; and that whatever is said to deviate from the ordinary course of nature, should be ascribed to accident, to fraud, or to fiction; till we are fully satisfied, that it lies beyond the reach of those causes?' If we cast away this buckler, the blind fury of superstition, from every age of the world, and from every corner of the globe, will invade us naked and unarmed.[115]

---

[114] *L* i. 327, 332, and 338. The pose of being a convinced Christian concerned only for the welfare of the faith had become a commonplace of deist rhetoric since Toland's *Christianity Not Mysterious* (1696), and John Leland had identified such elaborate courtesy as a sign of deism in his pamphlet on Bolingbroke: 'Any one that is conversant with those that are called the deistical writers, must have observed, that it is very usual for them to put on an appearance of respect for Christianity, at the same time that they do all in their power to subvert it' (Leland, *Reflections*, p. vi). Hurd would (perhaps not without a knowing irony himself) praise the letter as 'very elegant' and would admire its 'civility' (*MW 1796* i. 455). The coda to his reply suggests that he has accurately construed Gibbon's style, and is aware that he is dealing with an erudite dissimulator: 'if you should indulge this quality [candour] still further, so as to conceive the possibility of that being *true and reasonable*, in matters of religion, which may seem strange, or, to so lively a fancy as yours, even ridiculous, you would not hurt the credit of your excellent understanding, and would thus remove one, perhaps a principal, occasion of those mists which, as you complain, *hang over these nice and difficult subjects*' (*MW 1796* i. 463). The accusation of disingenuous courtesy Davis would later make against *The Decline and Fall*: 'I could prove, that Mr. G., like *Rousseau*, one of his famous predecessors in infidelity, while he *hypocritically* launches out in the praises of revelation, and *affects* to treat it with reverence and esteem; really endeavours to expose and place it in a ridiculous light' (*Examination*, 165). Henry Taylor's extraordinarily naive reading of this aspect of Gibbon's style is worth recording: 'I must confess, I did not see the turn of Mr. *Gibbon*, till I had read him more than once: and at length I found, or seemed to find, sufficient reason to acquit him of any evil design against the truth, and rather to consider him as being in a state of doubt and uncertainty, upon meeting with difficulties which he could not explain, and wavering in his opinions' (*Grand Apostacy*, p. xi). However, we should not overlook how genuinely confusing a style such as Gibbon's might be when its author came before the public without any reputation to guide interpretation.

[115] *L* i. 328–9. Note the proximity of this principle to that of an orthodox Christian such as Joseph White, who cautioned that 'what can be accounted for by human means, must not be hastily and indiscriminately ascribed to divine' (White, *Sermons*, 57). Chelsum would claim to

With deism, of course, Bentley himself would notoriously have no truck, while his flirtation with Toryism was brief and tactical.[116] It may therefore seem that 'Daniel Freeman's' apparent religious and political allegiances would preclude Gibbon's employing Bentleian weapons against Hurd. However, literary polemic is an art which relies more upon unlikely but effective alliances than upon intellectual hygiene. Although the stylistic surface of the letter to Hurd is so sharply at variance with Bentley's values, the essence of its argument that the Book of Daniel is of more recent date than it pretends is a scaled-down version of Bentley's argument in the *Dissertation Upon the Epistles of Phalaris*.[117] And when 'Daniel Freeman' caps his chain of scholarly argumentation with an appeal to literary sensibility—'Compare the Anabasis with the Cyropaedia; and *feel* the difference between truth and fiction; between the lively and copious variety of the one, and the elegant poverty of the other'[118]—there is an echo of Bentley's similar contrasting of the vivacity of the authentic and the lifelessness of the spurious apropos the *Epistles of Phalaris*: 'a fardle of common-places, without life or spirit from action and circumstance.... When you return to these [the *Epistles of Phalaris*] again, you feel by the emptiness and deadness of them, that you converse with some dreaming Pedant with his elbow on his desk; . . .'[119] As he had done two years earlier in the *Critical Observations*, when writing to Hurd as 'Daniel Freeman' Gibbon once more modelled the essence of his polemical strategy on the example of Bentley.

It is clear, then, that Gibbon was already a blooded polemicist before he had even thought of writing the *Vindication*. As the author of the *Essai sur l'Étude de la Littérature*, of the *Critical Observations*, and of the

have discovered 'the well known argument of Mr. Hume' on miracles in *The Decline and Fall* (Chelsum, *Remarks*, 26).

[116] Bentley's address to Anne of June 1712 congratulating her on the treaty of Utrecht was received as a manifesto in support of the Tory ministry, whose then leader, Robert Harley, Earl of Oxford, was Bentley's main protector in his battles with the fellowship of Trinity, and in the dedication to Harley of his edition of Horace Bentley announces himself as a converted Whig (Monk, *Life of Bentley*, i. 305; Jebb, *Bentley*, 111 and 127). But by 1716 Bentley seems to have been once more a Whig when he congratulated George I on the defeat of the recent Jacobite invasion; and by the mid-1720s Bentley was widely regarded as the leader of the Whig party in the Cambridge Senate (Monk, *Life of Bentley*, i. 417; Jebb, *Bentley*, 116).

[117] The anecdote that Bentley nearly alienated the affections of his fiancée by expressing doubts about the authenticity of the Book of Daniel is worth recollecting here (Monk, *Life of Bentley*, i. 151; Jebb, *Bentley*, 97–8). It was an anecdote probably unknown to Gibbon, although capable of being known, since the source was Whiston. [118] L i. 337.

[119] Bentley, *Epistles of Phalaris*, 487. This was a passage which we know caught Gibbon's attention, since he quotes it in a footnote to chapter twenty-four of *The Decline and Fall* (*DF* i. 917 n. 26).

pseudonymous letter to Richard Hurd, Gibbon was in the first place steeped in the major scholarly controversies of the eighteenth century, which organize themselves conveniently into an earlier group focusing on Bentley and a later group focusing on Warburton. Secondly, he was not only a student of these controversies, he was also a participant (albeit one with a preference for concealing his identity). In the *Essai* he had played an eirenic role, seeking to reconcile the two sides to the dispute. Thereafter with the *Critical Observations* and the letter to Hurd Gibbon's writing had became more—perhaps even culpably—aggressive.[120] But the literary vehicle which delivered that aggression bore traces of kinship with the cultural diplomacy of the *Essai*. Common to all three works is the yoking together of dissimilar characters. In the *Essai*, it is the hitherto repugnant positions of Ancients and Moderns which are ingeniously drawn together, while in the *Critical Observations* and the pseudonymous letter to Hurd we find the weapons of Bentleian scholarship in the hands of a Tory deist.

Did the situation which obtained in May 1778 after the publication of Davis's *Examination* offer Gibbon the possibility of continuing his established polemical habits? Aside from the intemperance of his language, the most notable feature of the *Examination* from Gibbon's point of view would surely have been that it revived the charge which Chelsum had wisely allowed to subside in his second edition, namely that *The Decline and Fall* was nothing more than warmed-through deism.[121] In levelling this charge against Gibbon his critics were wrapping themselves, as Warburton had done before them, in the mantle of Bentley, the dauntless foe of deism. The charge-sheet they raised against Gibbon was substantially the same as that Bentley had raised against Anthony Collins, when he had accused him of dishonesty in citation ('O Dulness, if this was done by chance! O Knavery, if it was done by design!'), of deliberately mischievous mistranslation ('the Infamy of that faulty Translation . . . Warp'd . . . to a vile and impious abuse'), and of reviving the exploded cavils of ancient scepticism ('this threadbare obsolete Stuff, the most obvious surmise that any wavering Fool catches at, when he first warps towards Atheism, is dress'd up here as if it was some new and formidable business').[122] Moreover, their

---

[120] 'the acrimony of my style [in the *Critical Observations*] has been justly blamed' (*A* 305).

[121] See above n. 18.

[122] Bentley, *Remarks*, 71; Bentley, *Remarks . . . Supplemented*, 257; Bentley, *Remarks*, 51. Note also Bentley's comment that Collins's literary carelessness 'carries in it an Air of Libertinism'; a judgement which draws together freethinking, moral slackness, and literary corruption—an unholy trinity which would also later be discovered in Gibbon (Bentley, *Remarks . . . Supplemented*, 262).

characteristic mode of preceding against *The Decline and Fall* was a deliberate imitation of the method of minute confutation practised by Bentley in his *Dissertation Upon the Epistles of Phalaris* and his reply to Collins; it was a bid to make the 'terse, manly Bentleian style' their own.[123] So it must have seemed both natural and tempting for Gibbon when writing the *Vindication* to do what he had already done with some success against Warburton: namely, to exploit the ambivalence of Bentley's reputation as both consummate scholar and resolute foe of deism, and thus turn Bentley back upon his latter-day, and unworthy, *epigones*. In so doing, he would be following Burgh's first rule of literary warfare, that 'the mode of attack prescribes and ascertains the mode of defence'.

However, what about that other recurrent characteristic of Gibbon as a polemicist, his joining together of disparate or incongruous personae. Could that too form part of his strategy in the *Vindication*? In pursuing this line of thought we shall be led to what is perhaps Gibbon's most effective stroke of polemical art in the *Vindication*. We know that the attacks on *The Decline and Fall* put Gibbon in mind of the English phase of the quarrel between the Ancients and Moderns. Writing to Priestley in 1783, following his attack on *The Decline and Fall* the previous year in his *Corruptions of Christianity*, Gibbon had concluded his letter by citing the monitory example of another Unitarian scientist who had indulged a weakness for writing on theological subjects: 'Remember the end of your predecessor Servetus, not of his life (the Calvins of our days are restrained from the use of the same fiery arguments) but I mean the end of his reputation. His theological writings are lost in oblivion; and if his book on the trinity be still preserved, it is only because it contains the first rudiments of the discovery of the circulation of the blood.'[124] Servetus's discovery of the circulation of the blood had been one of the achievements of the modern period on which the English champion of the moderns, William Wotton, had laid particular emphasis:

---

[123] Stephen, *English Thought*, i. 205. Cf. Champion, *Pillars of Priestcraft Shaken*, 30: 'A common characteristic of historical work of the period . . . was the fashion for extensive line-by-line analysis of opponents' works.'

[124] *L* ii. 321. Michael Servetus (or Miguel Servet), 1509–53; doctor and theologian; burned by Calvin for heresy. Gibbon also touches on the fate of Servetus at the end of chapter fifty-four in *The Decline and Fall* (*DF* iii. 438 nn. 35 and 36), although this chapter is likely to have been substantially written after 1783 (*DF* i, p. lxxxv). Nevertheless, Servetus is still in close proximity to Priestley, to whom Gibbon adverts on the facing page: *DF* iii. 439 n. 42. For another, and roughly contemporary, comment on the fate of Servetus, see Godwin, *Political Justice*, 2nd edn., bk. II, ch. 3 'Of Duty' (i. 100–1); this passage was dropped from the third and subsequent editions.

The first that I could ever find, who had a distinct *Idea* of this Matter [the circulation of the blood], was *Michael Servetus*, a *Spanish* Physician, who was burnt for *Arianism*, at *Geneva*, near CXL Years ago. Well had it been for the *Church of Christ*, if he had wholly confined himself to his own Profession! His Sagacity in this Particular, before so much in the dark, gives us great Reason to believe, that the World might then have had just Cause to have blessed his Memory. In a Book of his, entitled, *Christianismi Restitutio*, printed in the year MDLIII. he clearly asserts, that the Blood passes through the Lungs, from the Left to the Right Ventricle of the Heart; and not thorough the *Partition* which divides the two Ventricles, as was at that Time commonly believed.[125]

Gibbon's reproof to Priestley looks rather like a more suave version of Wotton's pious ejaculation, 'Well had it been for the *Church of Christ*, if he had wholly confined himself to his own Profession!' Moreover, there are also reasons to believe that Gibbon was rereading Bentley's contribution to the quarrel, his *Dissertation Upon the Epistles of Phalaris*, at exactly the time when he was composing the *Vindication*.[126] Now, in the literature of the Ancients and Moderns there is no character more antipathetic to Bentley than Charles Boyle, and Gibbon could hardly be unaware of the extent to which Boyle's case (a well-bred man assailed in print by those he deemed to be his social inferiors) answered to some of the circumstances of his own. In writing the *Vindication*, therefore, Gibbon determined to be both Bentley and Boyle. He would steal his opponents' clothes, show them who was the true successor of the great Bentley, and at the same time occupy in advance the ground from which a counterattack might be launched. To do so would be a brilliant extension of his established practice as a polemicist, namely to bring together and combine apparently irreconcilable characters. At the same time, it would exemplify Burgh's second law of literary warfare, namely that 'in the fields of controversy, it is lawful to array against an adversary the arguments which he has himself involuntarily con- tributed, or the concessions which preclude his reply'.

---

[125] Wotton, *Reflections*, 229–30.

[126] Patricia Craddock has pointed out that when Gibbon compares his task in the *Vindication* to a 'hostile march over a dreary and barren desert, where thirst, hunger, and intolerable weari- ness, are much more to be dreaded, than the arrows of the enemy', he seems to draw his metaphors from his own narrative of the Persian campaign of Julian the Apostate in chapter twenty-four of *The Decline and Fall* (*DF* i. 908–58); Craddock, *Luminous Historian*, 121. It is there- fore striking that in this very chapter Gibbon should apply Bentley's famous condemnation of the epistles of Phalaris, that 'you feel by the emptiness and deadness of them, that you converse with some dreaming pedant, with his elbow on his desk', to the epistles of the sophist Libanius (*DF* i. 917 n. 26). The chapter furnished metaphors to the *Vindication*; the reading Gibbon was doing for the *Vindication* supplied an illustrative quotation to the chapter. Bentley's *Dissertation* had been republished in 1777, although Keynes records no copy of this edition in Gibbon's library.

V

We can best begin our reading of the *Vindication* by citing one of Gibbon's own citations from Davis's *Examination*. At the end of his rebuttal of the accusations Davis had made of his handling of Sulpicius Severus and Paolo Sarpi, Gibbon aloofly quoted, without further comment, Davis's indictment: '"We have here an evident proof that Mr. Gibbon is equally expert in misrepresenting a modern as an ancient writer, or that he wilfully conceals the most material reason, with a design, no doubt, to instil into his Reader a notion, that the authenticity of the Apocalypse is built on the slightest foundation."'[127] In chiding Gibbon for taking a modern for an ancient writer, Davis was playing Bentley to Gibbon's Boyle. In repeating the now exploded charge, Gibbon showed that he had accepted the 'ground which he [Davis] has chosen for the scene of our combat'.[128] A number of allusions and touches of phrasing locate the *Vindication* within the topics and language associated with the quarrel between the Ancients and Moderns. For instance, when Gibbon states the nature of the charge against him as that of 'perverting the ancients, and transcribing the moderns';[129] when he calls to mind the fate of Miguel Servet—'When I recollect that the imputation of a similar error was employed by the implacable Calvin, to precipitate and to justify the execution of Servetus, I must applaud the felicity of this country, and of this age, which has disarmed, if it could not mollify, the fierceness of ecclesiastical criticism'[130]— when he employs the contrast between 'the smoothness of the Ionic, and the roughness of the Doric dialect', which had been of such importance in the dispute over the authenticity of the epistles of Phalaris, to discriminate between his detractors;[131] finally, when he cites Bentley with approval on the period of Suidas;[132] in all these details we can see a determination on Gibbon's part to keep the quarrel of the Ancients and Moderns present before his reader as a kind of filter through which to view and understand the current dispute.[133] When we follow

---

[127] *DF* iii. 1129 (slightly misquoting the original, which is to be found in Davis, *Examination*, 44).

[128] *DF* iii. 1110.

[129] *DF* iii. 1108.

[130] *DF* iii. 1122.

[131] *DF* iii. 1159.

[132] *DF* iii. 1162.

[133] This viewing of the controversy over his irreligion through the lens of the Ancients and Moderns endures into the *Memoirs*, where in draft 'E' Gibbon praises 'Mr. Porson's answer to Archdeacon Travis as the most acute and accurate piece of criticism which has appeared since the days of Bentley' (*A* 323, n. 46). Bliss Carnochan has also discovered the language of the *querelle*

Gibbon's cue and read his quarrel with his critics through the *querelle* of the Ancients and Moderns, what comes into focus?

In the first place, we notice a number of details through which Gibbon stakes his claim to being Bentley *redivivus*. His explanation that 'it is my intention to pursue in my defence the order, or rather the course, which Mr. Davis has marked out in his Examination' recalls Bentley's defence of his orderliness against Boyle's reproaches (as well, of course, as restating Burgh's maxim that in polemic 'a book . . . must derive its form and extent from the caprice of its opponent, rather than the preconcerted plan of its writer; the mode of attack prescribes and ascertains the mode of defence').[134] More substantially, Gibbon's exposure of Davis's scholarly shallowness, his patient reconstruction of the train of ignorance and error which produced Davis's blunders, and his frank admission that he had used dictionaries and other scholarly compilations for which he as well as Bentley had been reproached, all cast Gibbon in the role of Bentley, at least as the encounter with Davis is scripted in the *Vindication*.[135]

However, the alignment between Gibbon and Bentley is not made just at the level of style through echo and allusion. It is also established at the level of politics and churchmanship. Bentley had been appointed Master of Trinity as a result of the influence of Latitudinarian Whigs such as Tenison. Always an object of suspicion to High Churchmen such as Atterbury (who had suggested that Bentley's critical methods would lead to biblical scepticism), in 1702 Bentley had showed his opposition to High Church moves in convocation by obtaining Cambridge doctorates for Nicolson, Kennett, and Gibson, who had all been denied Oxford doctorates because of their opposition to Atterbury.[136] Gibbon, whose Tory allegiances seem to have evaporated

colouring that of the *Vindication*: *Gibbon's Solitude*, 299 n. 19. It may be found also in Davis, who when he speaks of Gibbon being 'stript of his glittering armour' brings to mind Swift's *Battel of the Books* (*Examination*, 185).

[134] *DF* iii. 1112.

[135] *DF* iii. 1126 (shallowness), 1149 (ignorance and error), 1152 (scholarly compilations).

[136] Gascoigne, *Cambridge in the Age of the Enlightenment*, 82–95; Bennett, *Tory Crisis*, 42. For the most recent extensive discussion of latitudinarianism, see Rivers, *Reason, Grace and Sentiment*, i. 25–88. However, one should not over-simplify Bentley's churchmanship, as Monk's persuasive explanation of Bentley's silence on the Bangorian controversy admonishes us: 'His opinions on the subject in dispute would probably have led him to take part with Sherlock, Snape, and the High-church combatants; while his acquaintance, connections, and interests, lay entirely with the opposite party' (Monk, *Life of Bentley*, ii. 23). He was a defiant advocate of the importance of sacerdotalism: 'For it ever was and ever will be true, in all Nations, under all Manners and Customs, *No Priesthood, no Letters, no Humanity*; and reciprocally again, *Society, Laws, Government, Learning, a Priesthood*' (Bentley, *Remarks*, 15). Bentley's famous comment, that 'those he wrote *for*, [were] as bad as those he wrote *against*', expresses the personal angularity which

soon after the death of his father, admired the 'latitudinarians of Cambridge' as the most recent practitioners of 'rational theology', so Bentley's Whiggish Latitudinarianism may have been genuinely congenial to him by 1779.[137] Be that as it may, in the *Vindication* Gibbon went out of his way to display his closeness to Bentley's politics and churchmanship. He was 'a firm friend to civil and ecclesiastical freedom', a celebrant of 'English freedom', a champion of the 'free inquiries of the present age'.[138] Davis had suspected Gibbon of being 'secretly inclined to the interest of the Pope', in what he called 'this strange and unnatural alliance of infidelity and superstition'.[139] To show how wide this was of the mark, Gibbon heaped praise on radical Whigs such as Walter Moyle ('a bold and ingenious critic'), and on Latitudinarians such as his old comrade-in-arms against Warburton, John Jortin ('learned and ingenuous').[140] He scorned Francis Eyre's religious opinions by noting that as they were 'principally founded on the infallibility of the Church, they are not calculated to make a very deep impression on the mind of an English reader'.[141] Even Richard Watson (whose attack on *The Decline and Fall* Gibbon was happy to dismiss in private as 'too dull to deserve . . . notice') is in the *Vindication* com-

---

makes him difficult to place within parties or groupings (Monk, *Life of Bentley*, ii. 43; Bentley, *Dissertation* (1777), 448).

[137] *DF* iii. 438 n. 38. But even in the early 1760s Gibbon's preferences in churchmanship were of this stripe, as his praise of Limborch as 'moderate and judicious, the general character of the Arminian Divines', and his approving statement of Erasmus's stance on theology, that 'he was always persuaded, that any speculative truths were dearly purchased at the expence of practical virtue and publick peace' indicate (*J1* 87 and 148–9).

[138] *DF* iii. 1158, 1124, and 1182.

[139] *DF* iii. 1142. Davis, *Examination*, 87, 122, and 158. Although perhaps 'strange and unnatural', the fear of a secret alliance between Catholics and atheists or freethinkers is nevertheless commonly found in late seventeenth-century and eighteenth-century members of the Church of England: cf. Francis Fullwood, *A Parallel: Wherein it Appears that the Socinian agrees with the Papist* (1693). The proximity between Catholic and religious sceptic was frequently exemplified by reference to the biographies of Tindal and, once the events of the 1750s became more widely known, of Gibbon himself: *Gentleman's Magazine*, 46 (1776), 441; Smyth Loftus, *Reply*, 100 and 115. The customary psychological explanation of the ease of the transition from believing anything to believing nothing was concisely expressed by Dalrymple: 'he who is once made sensible of his having believed too much, is apt to disbelieve every thing, and so exchange credulity for scepticism' (Dalrymple, *Secondary Causes*, 24: cf. Taylor, *Grand Apostacy*, p. xiii; Milner, *Gibbon's Account*, 238–9; and Smyth Loftus, *Reply*, 188–90). Leland had noted that Herbert of Cherbury had used 'precisely . . . the same way of talking, to shew that the *Laics* can have no certainty about any revelation at all, which the writers of the *Romish* Church have frequently urged to shew the necessity the people are under to rely intirely upon the authority of the Church or Pope' (*Principal Deistical Writers*, i. 10).

[140] *DF* iii. 1167 and 1169. In his *Reply* Davis noted the strenuous 'talk against popery' in the *Vindication* (p. 49).

[141] *DF* iii. 1182.

plimented on the 'liberal and philosophic cast' of his thinking.[142] As the most eminent representative in the late 1770s of the Whiggish Cambridge Latitudinarianism with which Gibbon wished to associate himself, a graceful nod towards Watson was an easy way for Gibbon to imply that less separated him from Watson, than separated Watson from Chelsum, Davis and Randolph.[143]

The corollary to Gibbon's claim that Bentley's values were his, is the demonstration that Davis, Chelsum, and Randolph have little in common with the man whose successor they implicitly claimed to be. The *Vindication* thus managed to reconfigure the conflict between Gibbon and his adversaries. They had presented it as another battle in the longstanding war between Christianity and irreligion. Gibbon re-presents it as a mirror of factional tension within the Anglican Church. Bentley himself had noted when replying to Collins that religious scepticism and Protestantism were easily confusable: '*Free-thinking* here for many Pages together is put for Common use of Reason and Judgment, a lawful Liberty of Examining, and in a word, good *Protestantism*. Then whip about, and it stands for Scepticism, for Infidelity, for bare *Atheism*.'[144] In paying homage to Jortin and gracious compliments to Watson, Gibbon availed himself of this proximity to present himself in the *Vindication* as a 'good protestant'.[145] The language he used of Davis, Randolph, and Chelsum, however, carried very different connotations. After 1776 the revival of revealed theology within the Church of England had threatened to dislodge Latitudinarianism from the position it had occupied since the early years of the century, that of the natural outcome and extension of

---

[142] *L* ii. 129. *DF* iii. 1156. D. M. Low was right to sense that Gibbon 'strengthened his position by saluting Dr. Watson as an adversary whose minds and manners commanded respect', even though his account of the controversy was unable to yield an explanation of how and why Gibbon's position was strengthened by such a gesture (Low, *Edward Gibbon*, 263).

[143] The implication is further reinforced by passages such as the following, in which there exists at least an equality of rank between Gibbon and Watson, but no sort of community with Chelsum and Randolph: 'it would be inconsistent enough, if I should have refused to draw my sword in honourable combat against the keen and well-tempered weapon of Dr. Watson, for the sole purpose of encountering the rustic cudgel of two staunch and sturdy Polemics [i.e. Chelsum and Randolph]' (*DF* iii. 1160).

[144] Bentley, *Remarks*, 13. He had earlier insisted that freethinking was a bastard child of reformation: "Twas by the price and purchase of Their [the Reformers] Blood, that this Author and his Sect have at this day, not only the Liberty, but the Power, Means, and Method of Thinking' (p. 23). The same point would be made in a less lively fashion by Leslie Stephen: 'The Protestant writers against Rome were forging the weapons which were soon to be used against themselves' (*English Thought*, i. 79).

[145] It was with this phrase that Gibbon announced to Catherine Porten his reconversion from Catholicism in 1755: *L* i. 3.

reformation.[146] Gibbon's praise of the Latitude men in 1788 at the end of the fifty-fourth chapter of *The Decline and Fall* must thus have struck a rather anachronistic note as an almost nostalgic gesture for an endangered and unfashionable, if not entirely departed, style of church-manship.[147] Davis, Chelsum, and Randolph, however, were squarely within the resurgent High Churchmanship of the later eighteenth-century Church of England. Randolph had assisted Chelsum in writing his remarks, and Gibbon turned the circumstance of 'the confederate Doctors' (a faint echo of Bentley's insistent and insulting use of the plural 'our editors' in the Phalaris controversy?) to polemical advantage:

The two friends are indeed so happily united by art and nature, that if the author of the Remarks had not pointed out the valuable communications of the Margaret Professor, it would have been impossible to separate their respective property. Writers who possess any freedom of mind, may be known from each other by the peculiar character of their style and sentiments; but the champions who are inlisted in the service of Authority, commonly wear the uniform of the regiment. Oppressed with the same yoke, covered with the same trappings, they heavily move along, perhaps not with an equal pace, in the same beaten track of prejudice and preferment.[148]

Towards the end of the *Vindication* a very similar blow is aimed at Eyre, the Catholic cast of whose thought is brought forward to emphasize once more how badly Davis had misread the confessional dimension to the quarrel:

it is not my wish or my intention to prosecute with this Gentleman a literary altercation. There lies between us a broad and unfathomable gulph; and the heavy mist of prejudice and superstition, which has in a great measure been dispelled by the free inquiries of the present age, still continues to involve the mind of my Adversary. He fondly embraces those phantoms . . . which can scarcely find a shelter in the gloom of an Italian convent; and the resentment which he points against me, might frequently be extended to the most en-lightened of the PROTESTANT, or, in his opinion, of the HERETICAL critics.[149]

It is easy to see how the terms of these oppositions ('freedom of mind', 'the most enlightened of the PROTESTANT . . . critics' and literary authenticity on one side; 'Authority', 'prejudice and preferment', 'prejudice and superstition' and oppressed uniformity on the other) hint

[146] Gascoigne, *Cambridge in the Age of Enlightenment*, 238; Nockles, *Oxford Movement in Context*, 44–103; Aston, 'Horne and Heterodoxy', 895–919.
[147] *DF* iii. 438 n. 38. For an account which depicts latidudinarianism as more resilient towards the end of the century, see Young, *Religion and Enlightenment*.
[148] *DF* iii. 1160 and 1159.
[149] *DF* iii. 1182.

at an opposition in churchmanship, between Latitudinarian and High. It was a hint amplified when Gibbon referred to the '*dogmatical* part of their [i.e. Chelsum and Randolph's] work, which in every sense of the word deserves that appellation', and commented tartly on 'the force of his [i.e. Chelsum's] dogmatic style'.[150]

However, it was not enough for Gibbon to be Bentley. He must also be Boyle, because his persona in the *Vindication* was a complex one created to meet the exigencies of a quarrel which involved not only 'my credit as an historian, my reputation as a scholar', but also 'my honour and veracity as a *gentleman*'.[151] The best way to show how Gibbon's character in the *Vindication* exceeds that of Bentley alone is to consider two passages in which it is clear that Bentleian qualities by themselves produce an insufficient matrix. Both passages come from the *Vindication*'s introductory pages:

The defence of my own honour is undoubtedly the first and prevailing motive which urges me to repel with vigour an unjust and unprovoked attack; and to undertake a tedious vindication, which, after the perpetual repetition of the vainest and most disgusting of the pronouns, will only prove that *I* am innocent; and that Mr. Davis, in his charge, has very frequently subscribed his own condemnation. And yet I may presume to affirm, that the Public have some interest in this controversy. They have some interest to know, whether the writer whom they have honoured with their favour is deserving of their confidence, whether they must content themselves with reading the History of the Decline and Fall of the Roman Empire as a *tale amusing enough*, or whether they may venture to receive it as a fair and authentic history.

Perhaps, before we separate, a moment to which I most fervently aspire, Mr. Davis may find that a mature judgment is indispensably requisite for the successful execution of *any* work of literature, and more especially of criticism. Perhaps he will discover, that a young student, who hastily consults an unknown author, on a subject with which he is unacquainted, cannot always be guided by the most accurate reference to the knowledge of the sense, as well as to the sight of the passage which has been quoted by his adversary.[152]

In the first of these passages the proud claim to scholarly integrity is Bentleian, but the stance of the reluctant polemicist drawn into the field by only a sense of his own affronted honour recalls the very similar sentiments of Charles Boyle:

The first of these Reflections, had it come single, I could easily have neglected: Had he stop'd there, I would have left the Book to shift for itself, and him to

---

[150] *DF* iii. 1160 and 1173.
[151] *DF* iii. 1110; emphasis added.
[152] *DF* iii. 1111 and 1112.

the good Opinion he has of his own Performances, without endeavouring to lessen it. But when he carried his Criticisms so far as to assert, not only of *Phalaris*, but his *Editor* too, that they neither of them wrote what was ascrib'd to them; he gave me so plain, and so publick an Affront, that I could not, with any tolerable Regard to my Reputation, quietly put it up. Thus was I, much against my Inclinations, brought into the Lists.[153]

In the second passage, Gibbon's stance as the elder and more experienced man dispensing advice to a rash and youthful opponent is reminiscent of Bentley, who had mused over 'the hardiness of this forward Writer [Boyle]; who, when he was utterly unfurnished of this part of learning, could venture so beyond his depth, without any necessity'.[154] But the tone of urbane condescension mingled with high-born bemusement is taken direct from Charles Boyle, who had begun his reply to Bentley on a note of well-bred surprise: 'I little imagin'd ever to have been engag'd in a Dispute of this Nature.'[155]

If we turn now to trace the Boylean element in Gibbon's persona in the *Vindication*, we shall find it particularly in that thread of polemic which turns on the disparity in birth and condition between Gibbon and his opponents.[156] Phrases such as the following, far from uncommon in the *Vindication*, conceive literary refinement as the product of elevated social station, and construe stylistic polish as the signature of good breeding:

I should have considered the difference of our language and manners as an unsurmountable bar of separation between us.

I shall not condescend to animadvert on the rude and illiberal strain of this passage, and I will frankly own that my indignation is lost in astonishment.

a false and ungenerous accusation, which must reflect dishonour either on the object or on the author of it.

my style, which on this occasion was more modest and moderate, has acquired, perhaps undesignedly, an illiberal cast from the rough hand of Mr. Davis.[157]

---

[153] Boyle, *Dr. Bentley's Dissertations . . . Examin'd*, sigs. A^v-A2^r. This, the fourth edition, was the edition Gibbon owned.

[154] Richard Bentley, *Epistles of Phalaris* (1777), 98.

[155] Boyle, *Dr. Bentley's Dissertations . . . Examin'd*, sig. A^r.

[156] That the Boylean persona should still have had any authority may surprise a modern reader, who sees the Phalaris controversy as a complete victory for Bentley. It is remarkable, however, that 'popular opinion' was slow to see this, and regarded the point at issue as still 'undecided' (Monk, *Life of Bentley*, i. 138; Jebb, *Bentley*, 76–83).

[157] *DF* iii. 1110, 1113, 1113–14, 1145. On his first visit to Paris after the publication of the *Essai* Gibbon had resented the fact that he had been treated 'more as a man of letters, than a man of fashion' (*J*1 202). For a most interesting and subtle exploration of the tension between learning and breeding in the eighteenth century, see Jarvis, *Scholars and Gentlemen*.

It was a polemical stroke in which Gibbon had been memorably anticipated by Boyle, who had directed similar blows at Bentley:

Surely no Man of liberal Education could put together so many unmannerly and slovenly Expressions without studying for them.

These are the Flowers, which Dr. Bentley has, with no very sparing Hand, strew'd throughout every Page almost of his learned Epistle. It can hardly be imagin'd, how one, that lives within the Air of a Court, should prevail with himself to deal in such dirty Language: . . .

The first and surest Mark of a Pedant is, to write without observing the receiv'd Rules of Civility, and common Decency: And without distinguishing the Characters of those he writes to, or against: For *Pedantry* in the Pen, is what Clownishness is in Conversation; it is *written, Ill-breeding.*[158]

From that assumption of social superiority flowed a whole range of further touches, each one calculated to put the antagonist of the moment in his place. Gibbon employs people to discharge the more menial and ancillary tasks associated with literary production, but Davis, as an impecunious and low-born hack, is obliged to take such functions upon himself:

Few objects are below the notice of Mr. Davis, and his criticism is never so formidable as when it is directed against the guilty corrector of the press, who on some occasions has shewn himself negligent of my fame and of his own. . . . I can only lament my own defects, whilst I deprecate the wrath of Mr. Davis, who seems ready to infer that I cannot either read or write. I sincerely admire his patient industry, which I despair of being able to imitate; but if a future edition should ever be required, I could wish to obtain, on any reasonable terms, the services of so useful a corrector.[159]

Such well-turned insults may of course be relished in themselves. But in so far as we surrender to that temptation, we will miss the depth and intricacy of Gibbon's polemical strategy. If we anthologize such moments and see them simply as dictated by Gibbon's own strength of feeling, we will overlook the complicated dynamics of personae to which they contribute, and we will misunderstand both what Gibbon was trying to do in the *Vindication*, and how he set about achieving it.[160]

---

[158] Boyle, *Dr. Bentley's Dissertations . . . Examin'd*, 11 (twice) and 93.

[159] *DF* iii. 1115. It is perhaps relevant that Bentley had himself been charged with considering *Paradise Lost* 'like a Corrector to the Press, [who] never looks on his Author but to spy his Faults' (Anon., *Milton Restor'd and Bentley Depos'd* (1732), in Womersley, *Augustan Critical Writing*, 328).

[160] We know that Gibbon was sensitive on the matter of birth, as his insistence on being received as a man of condition, rather than a mere author, when visiting Paris in 1763 shows (*MG* 105–6; *L* i. 132–44; *A* 200 and 261). It was a foible once more in evidence when he returned to

Is there any way in which we might corroborate this reading of Gibbon's rhetoric and strategy in the *Vindication*? Gibbon's pamphlet provoked three replies, from Chelsum, Davis, and Eyre, and I shall conclude this chapter by indicating how the first two, by Chelsum and Davis, confirm the reading of the *Vindication* set out above by trying to take back the ground which Gibbon has claimed as his own.[161] We shall see that they have a common understanding of Gibbon's strategy in the *Vindication*, and that they both set about trying to counter it in a similar fashion in their replies.

Both Chelsum and Davis show in their replies that the *Vindication* had landed some telling blows. In Chelsum we see wounded peevishness as he deplores Gibbon's accuracy in spotting the 'one unguarded place in his adversary, at which he might aim a blow', and ruefulness as he regrets his own 'accidental inadvertence, such as may be found often in the greatest writers . . . for which I have expressed a real concern'.[162] For his part, Davis was obliged to acknowledge 'some mistakes' in the *Examination*, although his attempt to turn this back against Gibbon was truly desperate: 'But is he aware of the conclusion which must be drawn from hence? Had he properly supported his claim to "the merits of *diligence* and *accuracy*," his references and quotations could not have led me into error.'[163] However unconvincing we may find that particular would-be thrust of Davis's, it is nevertheless typical of the incorrigibility of all three of those who replied to the *Vindication*. And the chief means whereby both Chelsum and Davis tried to regain the initiative, despite the setback they had suffered with the publication of the *Vindication*, was by tackling head-on the appropriation of Bentley to his cause which Gibbon had managed to bring off in that work.

Chelsum does this with some dexterity when acknowledging a slip:

Paris in 1777, as the vain postscript to his letter of 16 June to Holroyd shows (*L* ii. 151). But the desire to be considered as a man of birth, and not a man of letters, was a recurrent feature of eighteenth-century authorship. It begins with the celebrated encounter between Voltaire and Congreve (Voltaire, *Letters on England*, 99–100; cf. D. F. McKenzie: '*Mea Culpa*: Voltaire's Retraction of his Comments Critical of Congreve', and 'Richard van Bleeck's Painting of William Congreve as Contemplative (1715)'), and carries on through Thomas Gray's reluctance to be thought 'an author professed' (*Poems and Memoirs*, 335; cf. Boswell, *Correspondence between Boswell and Temple*, i. 297). Such a preference for birth over authorship was thus already invested with symbolic significance before Gibbon composed the *Vindication*.

[161] The three replies are: James Chelsum, *A Reply to Mr. Gibbon's Vindication* (Winchester, 1785); Henry Davis, *A Reply to Mr. Gibbon's Vindication . . . wherein the charges brought against him in the Examination are confirmed* (1779); [Francis Eyre], *A Short Appeal to the Public. By the Gentleman who is particularly addressed in the Postscript of the Vindication* (1779).

[162] Chelsum, *Reply*, 108 and 127.

[163] Davis, *Reply*, 2 and 3.

The acute Bentley himself was not always accurate; and argues, that 'if a mistake through mere forgetfulness, and but once or very seldom committed, were enough to disgrace a writer, nobody could escape the infamy, except those that were inspired.' I will borrow the words which he has used to his own adversary. 'I shall not go about the make the glory less' which Mr. Gibbon has acquired, 'but give him and his admirers leave to magnify it as much as they can.' It were cruel indeed to attempt in any sort to deprive Mr. Gibbon of the accidental triumph he has obtained in respect of this *single* instance of mistake in 'literary history'.

To which he appends a note: 'Had Mr. Gibbon been his Antagonist, Dr. Bentley himself might have been accused, in the same spirit of remark, of not having even "a very moderate acquaintance with that useful branch of knowledge," modern Geography.—Dr. Bentley (Dis. p.420) acknowledges himself, "by a small slip of the memory to have put Buda for Belgrade." '[164] Contrary to Gibbon's insinuations, then, it is Chelsum who is the new Bentley (here characterized surprisingly in terms of insouciance over precise detail).

In Davis's *Reply* the reappropriation of the role of Bentley involves a double act of redescription. In the first place, Gibbon is presented as the freethinking target of Bentley's invective, Anthony Collins. For Davis, it is impossible to 'consider Mr. Gibbon to be more friendly to Christianity than Collins', and all that Gibbon says on the mild temper of classical polytheism 'may be comprised in the words of Mr. Collins; whose sentiments are the same'.[165] Secondly, Davis's case against Gibbon is so close to Bentley's against Collins as to be virtually identical. At its simplest, this involves Bentley's being repeatedly laid under contribution to support Davis's argument.[166] The two champions of religious orthodoxy are so close in spirit that they are even liable to the same trifling oversights. In the ardour of his desire to convict Gibbon of plagiarism, Davis had unluckily made Gibbon take the same passage from two different authors. But an extenuating precedent was at hand: 'And here, if it were necessary, I shall be screened by the example of a writer eminent for his critical abilities. My learned reader may recollect, that *Dr. Bentley*, in his Dissertation on the Epistles of Phalaris, had represented more than one particular passage as transcribed by his opponent from two different authors.'[167] More ambitiously, the claim of identity means that Bentley's very words can, without incongruity,

---

[164] Chelsum, *Reply*, 28–9.
[165] Davis, *Reply*, 86 and 97.
[166] For example, Davis, *Reply*, 53 n. ‡ and 54 n. §.
[167] Davis, *Reply*, 161.

drop from the lips of Davis: 'I shall close this *Reply* in the very apposite words which the learned Dr. Bentley addresses to his opponent: . . .'[168] By the end of his *Reply*, Davis would have us believe that he and Bentley are one and the same. Whatever we may feel about the truth of that, it is difficult not to read Davis's insistence on the point as a countermove to the exactly parallel claim made by Gibbon in the *Vindication*. For the areas in which their replies overlap suggest that Chelsum and Davis had read Gibbon's *Vindication* with the same understanding of the origins of its style, and of the intentions that style was designed to secure, as had Robert Tyrwhitt before he sat down to read and annotate his interleaved copy of Bentley's *A Dissertation Upon the Epistles of Phalaris*.

VI

Francis Eyre was adamant that the *Vindication* was nothing more than rhetorical sleight of hand. He scorned it as 'a loose and angry declamation upon the vague and trite topic of religious prejudices sharpened with, what he [Gibbon] thought, the keenest poignancy of personal reflection'; and Eyre went on to pose the question 'does not a vindication require something beyond this slight task of assurance?'[169] Our analysis of the way in which the rhetoric of the *Vindication* sets in motion a complex intermingling of literary personae has suggested why Gibbon's opponents would have found it an awkward work to answer. Gibbon understood very well the polemical tradition within which the attacks on *The Decline and Fall* had arisen, and, drawing on both his extensive reading in eighteenth-century literary polemic and his own experience as a participant in scholarly warfare, he had artfully framed the *Vindication* so as to preclude any obvious line of retort. As a result Chelsum and Davis, as we have seen, were reduced to merely repeating Gibbon's own polemical strategy. Like the contest between Ajax and Odysseus to claim the armour of Achilles, the struggle between Gibbon and his opponents was in the end a contest over identity: who *was* the latter-day Bentley? There is little doubt that in this contest over the armour of Bentley, Gibbon shows much more literary finesse than Chelsum and Davis. His Odyssean subtlety contrasts pleasingly with the Ajax-like bluntness of their bald claims to possession. But beyond this triumphant display of superior technique, what of substance did Gibbon achieve with the *Vindication*?

---

[168] Davis, *Reply*, 177.   [169] Eyre, *Short Appeal*, 7 and 19.

The material achievement of that pamphlet has nothing to do with Gibbon's rhetorical besting of Davis and Chelsum. As Gibbon said in his 'Memoirs', 'a victory over such antagonists was a sufficient humiliation', just as Bentley had proudly declared that he would 'never be very proud of the Victory' over Boyle.[170] Gibbon's triumph was to separate for ever the question of his supposed irreligion from the integrity of his scholarship. In the attack on deism these had been regularly linked, the assumption being that only when deliberately mishandled could the literary record be made to support freethinking. Like so much in that polemical tradition, it was a line of attack which had its origin in Bentley's reply to Collins. Freethinkers were in general 'the greatest *Manglers of Authors*', and Collins was no exception: 'an Author must be mangled, Sense and Grammar distorted, all rules of Syntax perverted, to bring out a little Blasphemy.'[171] On the other hand, Bentley himself, as the greatest classical scholar and the most effective flail against the deists of his age, exemplified the congruity of sound literature and religious orthodoxy. Later in the century John Leland, whose works were arsenals of arguments against the deists, had insisted on the way literary and religious bad faith accompanied one another:

no writers whatsoever discover stronger signs of prejudice; and there is great reason to complain that they have not carried on the debate with that fairness and candour which becomes the importance of the subject.

I cannot but observe on this occasion, what must have occurred to every one that has been much conversant in the Deistical writers, that it would be hard to produce any persons whatsoever who are chargeable with more unfair and fraudulent management in their quotations, in curtailing, adding to, or altering the passages they cite, or taking them out of the connection, and making them speak directly contrary to the sentiments of the authors. It is well known that they affect frequently to quote Christian divines; but they seldom do it fairly, and often wilfully misrepresent, and pervert their meaning. Many glaring instances of this sort might be produced out of the writings of the most eminent Deistical authors, if any man should think it worth his while to make a collection to this purpose.

the unfair conduct of the Deistical Writers, and the strange liberties they take in misrepresenting the sense of the Christian Writers whom they quote.[172]

It was exactly this characteristic of deistical writing which Davis claimed to have discovered in *The Decline and Fall*, notwithstanding the apparent security of its scholarship:

---

[170] *A* 317 n. 34. Bentley, *Dissertation*, p. lxxxviii.
[171] Bentley, *Remarks*, sig. *2ᵛ and p. 23.
[172] John Leland, *Principal Deistical Writers*, i. 393; Leland, *Supplement*, 37 and 67.

Every one who had ever looked into Mr. Gibbon's history must have instantly perceived, that his principal design was to paint Christianity in odious colours. But it was not perhaps so generally known, nor could it well be conceived, that, in order to finish his picture, he could have had recourse to such an extensive system of gross misrepresentation as I have exposed to the Public in the foregoing sheets.[173]

After the *Vindication*, such a line of attack on *The Decline and Fall* was impossible.[174] Davis's attack had mingled some telling points with others which were either mistaken (as he was forced to admit) or easily deflected. By choosing to concentrate the *Vindication*'s fire on Davis's *Examination* Gibbon laid to rest the whole question of his scholarship. He might still be suspected of irreligion, but the familiar anti-deistical charge of irreligion surreptitiously promoted through literary unscrupulousness could no longer gain a hearing.[175]

In so separating Gibbon's scholarship from his irreligion, the *Vindication* blunted criticism of *The Decline and Fall*, until the advent of the French Revolution in 1789 offered Gibbon's adversaries, as we shall see, new angles of attack. However, it also throws light on a broader shift in intellect and sentiment which occurs as we move from the eighteenth to the nineteenth centuries, and which can be most easily appreciated if we review the changes which occurred in Bentley's reputation between his death and the composition of Monk's *Life of Bentley*. As we have seen, in all but the most accomplished philological circles, Bentley's victory in the Phalaris controversy was for long in doubt. At the same time, Bentley was chiefly celebrated as the assailant of the deists. So for the half century after his death the two halves of Bentley's reputation, that of the philologist and that of the religious polemicist, were in the public mind of equal preponderance. Indeed, if anything in the wake of the extravagance of his late edition of *Paradise Lost* Bentley was arguably more considerable as a writer on religious topics than as a philologist and literary scholar.[176] Moreover, Bentley himself seems not

---

[173] Davis, *Examination*, 141.

[174] Milner, writing in 1781, deplores the fact that knowledge of the classics was not 'more deep and general among real Ministers of the Gospel than it is' (*Gibbon's Account*, 259–61). At the end of the century the necessary link between scholarship and religious faith which Bentley had exemplified in the first half of the century has been broken.

[175] For example, note Milner's insistence that he is not going to impugn Gibbon's scholarship, and his defensive explanation that none of the 'mistakes' he is going to point out in *The Decline and Fall* 'are ascribed to want of capacity' (Milner, *Gibbon's Account*, 'Preface' and p. 240).

[176] These two aspects of Bentley's career were seen as complementary by many of his contemporaries. William Wotton, Bentley's ally against Boyle and Temple, remarks how it was Bentley's writings against freethinking, rather than his classical scholarship, which had encouraged him in his efforts to show 'how the World has gone on from Age to Age, Improving': 'I had

to have kept his religious and his scholarly activities in rigidly separate compartments. The first hint of his most remarkable contribution to philology, the rediscovery of the digamma, occurs in a manuscript annotation to his copy of Collins's pamphlet on freethinking—a book which thus symbolizes within itself the integrity of Bentley's interests, at least as Bentley himself pursued them.[177] However, by the time Monk published his *Life of Bentley* in 1833, the wholeness of Bentley's work had disappeared from sight. Although the attack on Collins is acknowledged to be of enduring amusement, and could even then be read 'with the same delight' as on its first appearance, it is unmistakable that in Monk's evaluation of the significance of the whole life, the emphasis has shifted dramatically towards Bentley's philological work.[178] His victory in the Phalaris controversy is now established beyond question. The grounds on which any claim for the magnitude of his achievement now most securely rest are the publications on classical philology, and even there the foundations are judged to be more robust in the Greek than the Latin work. Meanwhile, the attacks on the deists, like the vendetta with the fellows of Trinity, earn their place in the story chiefly for the human colour they supply, rather than because of their intellectual power or consequence. We have moved from a world in which sound literature and religious orthodoxy were constant and even necessary companions, to that very different nineteenth-century world in which, notwithstanding many fond and backward glances, they had separated and were encountered together only occasionally and by chance. Gibbon's *Vindication* is a crucial document in that transition.

One further aspect of the *Vindication*'s claim to being a Bentleian work deserves to be brought out here, since it points forward to Gibbon's attempts to control his public reputation during the last five years of his life in the wake of the French Revolution. A recurrent accusation in the attack on *The Decline and Fall* is that 'Mr. Gibbon . . . is but the Echo of D^r. Middleton'.[179] Smyth Loftus had insisted on this

also a fresh Inducement to this Search, when I found to how excellent purpose my most Learned and Worth Friend Dr. *Bentley*, had, in his late incomparable Discourse *against Atheism* [i.e. Bentley's Boyle Lectures], shewn what admirable Use may be made of an accurate Search into Nature, thereby to lead us directly up to its Author, so as to leave the unbelieving World without Excuse' (Wotton, *Reflections*, pp. vi and xviii–xix).

[177] Jebb, *Bentley*, 150–1.

[178] Monk, *Life of Bentley*, i. 345.

[179] CUL Add. MS 8530, fo. 15^v. This MS is probably a holograph of Francis Eyre's *A Few Remarks on the History of the Decline and Fall* (1778). Middleton was Gibbon's most obvious predecessor in polemical vindication, as Gibbon himself seems to have been aware (*DF* i. 473 n. 79).

propinquity: 'His [Gibbon's] account of the Christian inspiration is so certainly false, that the only thing to be said in his vindication is, that he never examined the matter, but trusted to Dr. Middleton, without reading the answers given to his book; which, to speak the truth of it, is written with a prejudice and disingenuity the most disgraceful to any cause, or to any author.'[180] The accusation had been repeated more than once by Davis and Chelsum.[181] But Bentley and Middleton had existed in a state of continual hostility, and their vigorous antagonism had been largely responsible for turning Bentley's mastership at Trinity into a running battle between the head of house and the fellowship. So for Gibbon the imitation of Bentley had this further attraction. Not only had Gibbon stolen the clothes of the orthodox; he had also denied one of the central contentions of his attackers by assuming the persona of the most implacable enemy of the man he was supposed to have aped. When we come to consider Gibbon's complex motives in writing his 'Memoirs', we shall see how he further widens the distance between himself and Middleton.

However, the conception of the 'Memoirs' was some way off in the future.[182] In between lay the composition of five further volumes of *The Decline and Fall*. The next two chapters examine in detail two sections from those later volumes, one from the second instalment of 1781, the other from the third instalment of 1788. These chapters reveal how, even in the midst of historical narrative, Gibbon was not unmindful of the criticisms which had been made of *The Decline and Fall*, and suggest how those very criticisms exerted a stimulating rather than a stultifying influence on the historian's imagination.

[180] Loftus, *Reply*, 117: cf. also pp. 129, 197, and 232.

[181] Davis, *Examination*, pp. iv n. ‡, 28–9, 64, and 169–85; Chelsum, *Remarks 2*, 67 and 91.

[182] The earliest suggestion—and it is no more than that—of an autobiographical project in Gibbon's letters comes with a reference to the writer on heraldry, John Gibbon, in a letter to Sheffield of 21 Nov. 1787 (*L* iii. 82). The earliest explicit reference to composition is to be found in a letter to Sheffield of 28 Dec. 1791, where Gibbon writes of 'the plan of the Memoirs I once mentioned, and as you do not think it ridiculous I believe I shall make the attempt' (*L* iii. 240). By this time, however, he had already completed no less than five drafts of the 'Memoirs'; see below, Appendix 2.

3

'Too deeply into the mud of the Arian controversy': Gibbon and the Early Church Fathers

> how calm is the voice of history compared with that of polemics.
>
> (Edward Gibbon, *The Decline and Fall*)

> In all Controversies about Religion the chief provocation to men
> of sense is to see a set of rash, dogmatical Divines, whose minds,
> prepossessed with systems and darkened with prejudices, could
> never see thro' the mists their Nurses and Mothers had spread
> about their eyes, setting themselves up for the only guides and
> teachers of truth to the Nation; requiring the learning and reason
> of mankind to submit to their arbitrary decisions, and branding
> with the name of *Sceptick and Infidel*, all who cannot admit their
> manner of explaining and defining the terms of Christian Faith.
>
> (Middleton, *A Defence of the Letter to Dr. Waterland*)

In draft 'E' of his 'Memoirs', Gibbon revealed that he had allowed two
years to elapse between the publication of volume one of *The Decline
and Fall* in 1776, and the composition of his second and third volumes,
which were eventually published in 1781. He gave four reasons in
extenuation of 'this long delay':

1. After a short holyday I indulged my curiosity in some studies of a very
different nature; a course of Anatomy which was demonstrated by Dr. Hunter,
and some lessons of Chemistry which were delivered by Mr. Higgins: the
principles of these sciences, and a taste for books of Natural history, contributed
to multiply my ideas and images, and the Anatomist or Chemist may sometimes track me in their own snow. 2. I dived perhaps too deeply into the mud
of the Arian controversy; and many days of reading, thinking, and writing were
consumed in the pursuit of a phantom. 3. It is difficult to arrange with order
and perspicuity the various transactions of the age of Constantine; and so much

was I displeased with the first Essay, that I committed to the flames above fifty sheets. 4. The six months of Paris and pleasure must be deducted from the account.[1]

It is a curious miscellany. Love of pleasure, an inclination for distraction and an encounter with technical difficulty account for the first, third, and fourth reasons. However, it is harder to fathom the motives underlying the second reason, namely Gibbon's absorption in a theological debate of late antiquity, albeit one of great intrinsic and historical significance. Why should Gibbon have become so involved in this subject? And why should he have expended such energy in an attempt (as he tells us, an ultimately unavailing attempt) to reach the bottom of it?

II

We might begin by considering the implications of the allusion embedded in Gibbon's choice of words when recollecting his frustrated attempt to understand the Arian controversy. He was alluding, of course, to the mud-diving episode in book two of *The Dunciad*.[2] It might seem that all that Gibbon wished to suggest by using the metaphor of mud-diving is that he had been overwhelmed by a distasteful subject for which he had little appetite. But Gibbon's way with allusion was rarely casual. His reading re-echoes in his writing and is fraught with significance.[3] Moreover, we know that Gibbon had an intense, if unorthodox, interest in questions of theology.[4] It is unlikely, therefore, that the full pejorative force of the allusion was directed exclusively against the subject matter of the Arian controversy. To certain kinds of enlightened mind theology may be, in a manner of speaking, mud—opaque, contaminating, and not infrequently noisome. But also blameworthy are those who, with a depraved appetite, choose mud for their element.

---

[1] *A* 315–16. One may note in passing that the third reason suggests that Gibbon's custom was to plan out in some detail the architecture of either a whole volume, or an important section of it, before beginning to compose.   [2] *The Dunciad*, ii. 269–358.

[3] On this subject, see my 'A Complex Allusion in Gibbon's Letters', and 'A Complex Allusion in Gibbon's *Memoirs*'. For an account of the uses of allusion to Pope in the works of one of Gibbon's contemporaries and friends, see Frans de Bruyn, *The Literary Genres of Edmund Burke*, especially chs. 1 and 5, pp. 19–58 and 209–82.

[4] The reading and reflection which preceded his conversion to Catholicism in 1754; his intellectual grappling with Grotius's *De Veritate Religionis Christianæ* in 1759; his fencing with Hurd over the significance of the Book of Daniel in 1772; and his 'ample dissertation on the miraculous darkness of the passion' of 1771 or 1772 (*A* 84–6, 249, and 285): all these episodes sufficiently show how Gibbon's primary historical interests repeatedly led him (albeit from a standpoint with great potential for heterodoxy) to consider theological matters of the first importance.

The mud-diving competition is, as Dulness implies in her invitation, reserved for a certain class of dunce:

> 'Here strip, my children! Here at once leap in,
> Here prove who best can dash thro' thick and thin,
> And who the most in love of dirt excel,
> Or dark dexterity of groping well.
> Who flings most filth, and wide pollutes around
> The stream, be his the Weekly Journals bound,
> A pig of lead to him who dives the best;
> A peck of coals a-piece shall glad the rest.'[5]

It is the reference to the 'Weekly Journals' which supplies the hint, and Pope's own note amplifies it: 'Papers of news and scandal intermixed, on different sides and parties, and frequently shifting from one side to the other, called the London Journal, British Journal, Daily Journal, etc. the concealed writers of which for some time were Oldmixon, Roome, Arnall, Concanen, and others; persons never seen by our author.'[6] The original mud-divers, then, were unprincipled party-writers. Oldmixon, Roome, Arnall and Concanen had all been in the pay of Walpole, and—with varying degrees of commitment: it is said that Concanen determined his political allegiances on the toss of a coin— had written on behalf of the ministry against opposition figures, such as Pope's friends Bolingbroke and the High Church Jacobite, Francis Atterbury.[7] In recollecting this episode of *The Dunciad* at this point in his 'Memoirs', Gibbon implied that his character as an historian had been contaminated by the contrasting qualities of the hack. The allusion thus conveys a measure of self-reproach.

Gibbon's account of the Arian controversy (or Trinitarian controversy, as he sometimes styled it), which had distracted and divided the Church during the fourth century, forms the core of chapter twenty-one of *The Decline and Fall*.[8] In this chapter Gibbon laid out the 'subtle and profound' opinions which men of those times (and, as we shall see, not of those times alone) entertained 'concerning the nature, the

---

[5] *The Dunciad*, ii. 275–82.

[6] Ibid. ii. 280 n.

[7] John Oldmixon (1673–1742): man of letters and Whig historian of England, who assailed the reliability of Clarendon's *History of the Great Rebellion* and supplied Whiggish narratives of the English past designed to vindicate the existence of an ancient constitution enshrining English liberty; Edward Roome (d. 1729): songwriter; collaborator with Concanen and Sir William Yonge (d. 1755), Walpole's lieutenant; William Arnall (?1715–?1741): Whig journalist paid to answer Bolingbroke's *The Craftsman*, and successor to Concanen in *The British Journal*; Matthew Concanen (1701–49): dramatist, poet, and contributor to *The Daily Courant*, in which he attacked *The Craftsman*, also an associate of Sir William Yonge.

[8] *DF* i. 766–829.

generation, the distinction, and the equality of the three divine persons of the mysterious *Triad*, or Trinity'.[9] The placing of this chapter is an example of Gibbon's ability to insinuate judgement by means of the disposal of his material. By virtue of following his narrative of the conversion of Constantine to Christianity, and the consequent establishment of Christianity as the religion of the empire (which Gibbon had deduced in chapter twenty), chapter twenty-one immediately suggests that bitter theological controversy is the child of this union between Church and State. This is indeed the chapter's keynote, and it is sounded in its first paragraph:

The edict of Milan, the great charter of toleration, had confirmed to each individual of the Roman world, the privilege of chusing and professing his own religion. But this inestimable privilege was soon violated: with the knowledge of truth, the emperor imbibed the maxims of persecution; and the sects which dissented from the Catholic church, were afflicted and oppressed by the triumph of Christianity. Constantine easily believed that the Heretics, who presumed to dispute *his* opinions, or to oppose *his* commands, were guilty of the most absurd and criminal obstinacy; and that a seasonable application of moderate severities might save those unhappy men from the danger of an everlasting condemnation.[10]

The phrase 'moderate severities'[11] echoes the cant phrases beloved of the High Church Tories in the Church and State crises which had followed 1688: crises in which unorthodox attitudes towards the doctrine of the Trinity had played a part. Gibbon knew that the subject of the Arian controversy had, in the hands of writers he admired, sustained a 'concealed parallel' with more recent events.[12] Such parallelisms were not to Gibbon's own historiographic taste, no matter how 'dextrously managed'.[13] Nevertheless, the occurrence of the phrase may suggest the memory of more recent English experience of relationships between Church and State in the back of his mind as he deduced the tribulations of the faithful under Constantine and Constantius.[14] Moreover, the

[9] *DF* i. 775.

[10] *DF* i. 766.

[11] Compare its close relation, 'wholesome severities', over which, as we saw, Gibbon hesitated when revising chapter fifteen in 1776; see above, p. 19.

[12] The writer is the Abbé de la Blétérie, who in his *Histoire de l'empereur Jovien* (1748) suggested a measure of equivalence between Athanasius and the Jansenist Arnauld (*DF* i. 812 n. 137). For Gibbon's admiration of this writer, and his possible influence on, in particular, this part of *The Decline and Fall*, see *A* 143.

[13] *DF* i. 812 n. 137.

[14] That Gibbon approached the Arian controversy of the fourth century at least partly by way of the Trinitarian disputes of the late seventeenth and early eighteenth centuries in the Church of England is revealed by some of the footnotes to chapter twenty-one, in which the protagonists

concluding words of chapter twenty-one also, albeit at one remove, send us forwards into the eighteenth century. The morale of the pagans under the new state religion was sustained, so Gibbon says, by rumours of apostasy in the ruling dynasty itself: 'their [the pagans'] hopes were revived by the well-grounded confidence, that the presumptive heir of the empire, a young and valiant hero, who had delivered Gaul from the arms of the Barbarians, had secretly embraced the religion of his ancestors.'[15] This hero is, of course, Julian the Apostate, whose story Gibbon will begin to recount in chapter twenty-two. The *Vindication*, which was published in 1779 and which Gibbon was composing during the summer and autumn of 1778,[16] is linked to the chapters on Julian by the striking metaphor which Gibbon chose to illustrate his engagement with his critics: 'And now let me proceed on this hostile march over a dreary and barren desert, where thirst, hunger, and intolerable weariness, are much more to be dreaded, than the arrows of the enemy.'[17] On the strength of this metaphor it has been suggested that the composition of chapter twenty-four, in which Gibbon describes Julian's Persian expedition in terms similar to these, was coeval with the composition of the *Vindication*.[18] If so, then we can reasonably allocate the composition of chapter twenty-one on the Arian controversy to the spring or summer of 1778. In other words, there are circumstantial grounds for believing that Gibbon was writing on the Arian controversy at just the

of the later dispute are used to illustrate points of contention in the earlier: e.g. *DF* i. 780 n. 49, where the allusion is to Samuel Clarke's *Scripture-Doctrine of the Trinity* (1712). Other such moments of proximity between the fourth century and later religious disputes occur at *DF* i. 784 (where the word 'variations' cues a glance at Bossuet's *Histoire des Variations* (1688), a book which Gibbon says played a part in his conversion to Catholicism (*A* 86); *DF* i. 793–4 (where the quotation from Ammianus Marcellinus had been earlier cited in polemical pamphlets such as Marvell's *Mr. Smirke*, in *A Short Historical Essay Touching General Councils, Creeds, and Impositions in Religion* (1676), 53, and *The Second Part of the Rehearsal Transpros'd*, ed. D. I. B. Smith (Oxford: Clarendon Press, 1971), 322: I owe these references to the kindness of Nicholas von Maltzahn); and *DF* i. 822, where Gibbon explicitly compares the Circumcellions to the Camisards. The discursive similarities between late antiquity and the eighteenth century had been noted by some of the participants in the Trinitarian controversy, such as Styan Thirlby, who had commented that 'there is a very surprizing Resemblance betwixt the Arts and Methods formerly made use of in order to the Establishment of that *Heresy* [Arianism], and those by which its *Revival* is now attempted' (*An Answer to Mr. Whiston's Seventeen Suspicions Concerning Athanasius*, p. i.).

[15] *DF* i. 829.
[16] See above, Ch. 2.
[17] *DF* iii. 1112.
[18] For example, after Julian's death, his soldiers were 'obliged to traverse a sandy desert, which, in the extent of seventy miles, did not afford a single blade of sweet grass, nor a single spring of fresh water; and the rest of the inhospitable waste was untrod by the footsteps either of friends or enemies' (*DF* i. 952). The likelihood that the metaphor which Gibbon chose to illustrate his encounter with his critics was recollected from his narrative of Julian's last campaign was first noted by Patricia Craddock (*Luminous Historian*, 121–2).

moment when, as we have seen in Chapter 2, the clerical attacks on *The Decline and Fall* had begun to assume a more effectively menacing aspect, and when his own equanimity in the face of critical disapproval was wearing thin.[19] It follows that, when composing these chapters, Gibbon had been forcibly put in mind of both those earlier eighteenth-century theological controversies which had involved the doctrine of the Trinity, and that later controversy of which his own alleged irreligion was the focus.

Gibbon was not the only writer for whom, in the late 1770s, the theological controversies of the fourth century, of the earlier eighteenth century, and of the present had come to be linked. Many of the attacks on the first volume of *The Decline and Fall* had taken the opportunity to fire some shots across Gibbon's bows in respect of the church history he would be obliged to narrate in his next volume. For instance, Smyth Loftus, in the process of disputing Gibbon's claim (embodied in the fifth cause adduced in chapter fifteen) that the coherence of the early Christian Church had contributed to its growth, cited the Trinitarian disputes of the fourth century:

when Paganism was brought to its expiring gasp, the controversy between the Trinitarians and the followers of Arius, raised such a flame in the church, and bred such animosities between the contending parties, as made them the derision and sport even of the Heathens themselves. These are incontestible facts, and will hereafter be fully proved even by Mr. Gibbon himself; and therefore this most learned writer was strangely mistaken when he made the union of the church one cause of its prodigious encrease.[20]

Earlier in his essay he had admonished Gibbon against modelling his account of later church history on the authorities he had apparently followed in his first volume:

And here I will advise Mr. Gibbon not to follow Mr. Voltaire, as he here has the Doctor [i.e. Conyers Middleton], in his future history, when he comes to the worship of images in the Christian church; because this great genius's account of this matter is totally copied from Baronius, and where the interest of the Roman church is concerned, there cannot be a more partial and unjust historian than this very great and learned cardinal.[21]

And he concluded his essay by warning the devout reader as to what he would very probably encounter in later chapters of Gibbon's history:

I think it first necessary to warn the Christian reader against being frightened from his religion, by the horrid picture which he will hereafter find to be drawn

---

[19] See above, p. 68.   [20] Loftus, *Reply*, 170–1.   [21] Ibid. 123–4.

by Mr. Gibbon, and justly too, in his history of the next and the two following centuries, when the furious dissentions, animosities, persecutions, and cruelty of the Christians against each other, and when the luxury, pride, ambition, turbulence, of their great an powerful clergy, will present a horrid scene to his view; . . .[22]

It was an emphasis taken up by others. Henry Davis's *Examination* also drew to a close on a note of menace, thinly veiled as advice concerning the handling of future ecclesiastical material:

I could wish to advise him (would he accept of such humble counsel), when he favours us with his next volume, to keep close to his department as an historian, and to drop the character of a champion of infidelity, which, he may now find, has not added to his literary fame. In the prosecution of his plan, it will fall naturally in his way to treat of the *corruptions* of Christianity; and as his *diligence* and *accuracy* will find ample materials for accounting for the rise and progress of *popery* from *natural causes*, we trust that he will not continue to attack genuine Christianity; at least, that he will, for the future, beware of such arts as have been sufficiently exposed in the foregoing sheets.[23]

Francis Eyre, in the manuscript draft of his attack on *The Decline and Fall*, echoed this note of indignant foreboding. Annotating Gibbon's *obiter dictum* towards the end of chapter sixteen, that the 'motives of his [Constantine's] conversion, as they may variously be deduced from benevolence, from policy, from conviction, or from remorse; and the progress of the revolution, which, under his powerful influence, and that of his sons, rendered Christianity the reigning religion of the Roman empire, will form a very interesting and important chapter in the second volume of this history',[24] Eyre fumed at what he took to be an impudent advertisement of yet more historiographical chicanery to come:

Answer. Especially if it be wrote with the Impartiality, Candour, & Strict Adherence to truth, with the one we have before us. It is easy to forestall his Market, & shew ev'ry misrepresentation which no doubt will appear in his 2^d. Volume. These before our Eyes are borrowed & purloin'd from the Deistical Writers of the present Age. The Sequel of the History will be no doubt grounded on the same plan.[25]

'Forestall his Market': Eyre's helpful choice of metaphor reveals very clearly what was happening when he, Davis, and Loftus allowed their

[22] Loftus, *Reply*, 234–5.
[23] Davis, *Examination*, 284.
[24] *DF* i. 571.
[25] CUL, Add. MS. 8530, fo. 45^{r-v}.

attention to move forwards to the subject matter of Gibbon's later chapters. By displaying their awareness of the kind of narrative which would result were Gibbon to continue in the same vein as he had in volume one of *The Decline and Fall*, and with the same impious authorities (as they saw it) guiding his pen, they hoped to anticipate— and therefore make unwritable—that predicted, irreligious account of the early Christian Church.

Advice about the next instalment of *The Decline and Fall* came from friends, as well as foes. Hume had concluded his letter of congratulation on the publication of volume one by revealing some prospective concern on Gibbon's account:

> I must inform you that we are all very anxious to hear that you have fully collected the materials for your second volume, and that you are even considerably advanced in the composition of it. I speak this more in the name of my friends than in my own, as I cannot expect to live so long as to see the publication of it. Your ensuing Volume will be still more delicate than the preceding, but I trust in your prudence for extricating you from the difficulties; and in all events you have courage to despise the clamour of bigots.[26]

In March 1776, when this letter was written, Gibbon had not yet begun work on the second volume, although of course—as a handful of comments in the first volume, such as that on the conversion of Constantine to which Eyre took exception, suggest—he must have already given preliminary consideration to the major subjects he would be obliged to narrate, and to his likely manner of treating them. Indeed, as his critics were quick to grasp, Gibbon's organization of his material in volume one of *The Decline and Fall* had in part dictated how some of the most sensitive material of the second volume would have to be dealt with. For instance, the decision to break the high-political narrative of volume one at the end of chapter fourteen, with the reunification of the empire under the Illyrian monarchy of Constantine in AD 324, and to insert at that point the two chapters dealing with the growth of Christianity and the exaggerated accounts of the scale and severity of persecution suffered by the first Christians, seemed (at least to Francis Eyre) virtually to announce that Gibbon's picture of the conversion of Constantine, held over as it had been to the second volume, would be drawn from the unsympathetic standpoint of a religious sceptic, and would depict the emperor's conversion as a piece of self-interested, secular, and political calculation, rather than as one of the landmarks in a providentialist view of human history.[27] Hence, perhaps, Gibbon's

---

[26] *A* 313. [27] CUL, Add. MS. 8530.

difficulties over the arrangement of the 'various transactions of the reign of Constantine' which required the redrafting of 'above fifty sheets' and which, as well as the mud of the Arian controversy, contributed to the delay in beginning the composition of his second volume.[28] In the period of 'phoney war', before any of the attacks on *The Decline and Fall* had appeared in print, but when Gibbon knew that attacks were imminent, he had affected a degree of bravado.[29] But both the difficulty he encountered with the architecture of his account of the reign of Constantine, and the trouble he took in his attempt to fathom the Arian controversy, suggest a process of renewed imaginative and critical engagement. If it was part of the purpose of critics such as Loftus and Davis to make Gibbon pause and think again, it would seem that they succeeded.

But why were at least the more dogmatic and High Church of Gibbon's clerical antagonists so concerned over what the historian might say about the early Church Fathers? It was not a prospect which had disturbed, for instance, Richard Watson, who as the foremost spokesman for Latitudinarian churchmanship in the later eighteenth century had 'determined to study nothing but my Bible, being much unconcerned about the opinions of councils, father, churches, bishops, and other men, as little inspired as myself'.[30] However, in the later eighteenth century Latitudinarianism was subjected to hostile pressure from more dogmatic members of the Church of England. They scoffingly dismissed it as 'Hoadlyism', and sought instead to reinvigorate the traditions of revealed theology within the Church of England, and to recover the engagement with patristic writings entailed by such a turn away from natural theology. Although the tide of patristic learning in England was ebbing between the seventeenth century and the advent of the Tractarians in 1833, it had nevertheless far from disappeared in the years when Gibbon composed *The Decline and Fall*.[31] Indeed, throughout the eighteenth century it remained for many central to

---

[28] *A* 315–16.

[29] See above, Ch. 1. It had been very much in that spirit of flaunted insouciance that Gibbon had written to Holroyd on 29 June 1776 and announced defiantly that 'the second Volume will not be less interesting than the first'—'interesting' here sounding very much like a deist term of art meaning 'offensive to the orthodox' (*L* ii. 112).

[30] Quoted in Gascoigne, *Cambridge in the Age of Enlightenment*, 240. Watson's conviction that belief in the orthodox doctrine of the Trinity was inessential to the condition of being a Christian is encapsulated in his remark that 'if any one thinks that an Unitarian is not a Christian, I plainly say, without myself being a Unitarian, that I think otherwise' (Young, *Religion and Enlightenment*, 75–6).

[31] 'the Church of England, with its well-established interest in the writings of the Fathers . . .' (Wiles, *Archetypal Heresy*, 137).

the Church of England, which 'so far from undervaluing the ancient Fathers, requires her clergy to consult their interpretation of the Scriptures in preaching to the people under pain of excommunication'.[32] It was for this reason that when in the 1780s the High Church champion Samuel Horsley entered the lists against Joseph Priestley over the doctrine of the Trinity (a dispute to which we shall return in Chapter 4), he took his stand on the ground that the 'reasonableness of our faith will be best understood from the writings of the Fathers of the first three centuries'.[33] This esteem of the early Fathers of the Church had taken root in England in the early seventeenth century, when English bishops, according to a surprised but delighted Isaac Casaubon, were 'deeply enamoured of the ancient church'.[34] After 1660 it had been tended by Archbishops Sheldon and Sancroft, and had developed into:

a uniquely English version of the union of a national Church and a regime of absolute monarchy . . . In it the Church of England, with its ordered worship and a conservative theology rooted in patristic learning, received from the civil power continual support and comfort in its role as guardian of the morals and religious duties of the nation. And in return the Church fostered loyalty and obedience with the ideological resources at its command: in the education of the young, in the elaboration of social and political theory, and by its influence as a major landowner.[35]

The early Church Fathers thus acquired a double importance for orthodox Anglicans during the long eighteenth century. On the one hand, the writings of the early Fathers were an indispensable guide to the interpretation of Scripture and the essential doctrines of the Christian religion. Daniel Waterland had expressed their subordinate status, yet also their importance, in a metaphor: '*Antiquity* . . . super-added to Scripture, is what we sincerely value, and pay a great Regard to; . . . *Antiquity* ought to attend as an handmaid to Scripture, to wait upon her as her Mistress, and to observe her; to keep off *Intruders* from making too bold with her, and to discourage *Strangers* from misrepresenting Her. *Antiquity*, in this ministerial View, is of very great

---

[32] John Milner, *Letters to a Prebendary . . . With Remarks on the Opposition of Hoadlyism to the Doctrines of the Church of England* (1802), 385; quoted in Nockles, *Oxford Movement*, 105.

[33] Samuel Horsley, *Tracts in Controversy with Dr. Priestley* (1789), 68; quoted in Nockles, *Oxford Movement*, 106.

[34] 'Episcopis . . . priscae Ecclesiae amantissimis'; letter of 1611 to Daniel Heinsius, quoted in Quantin, 'The Fathers in Seventeenth Century Anglican Theology', 987.

[35] Bennett, *Tory Crisis*, 295.

Use . . .'.[36] It may be that Chillingworth had famously pointed to the contradictions within the corpus of patristic writings, and had thereupon concluded that no guidance could be expected from the Fathers: 'I see plainly, and with my own eyes, that there are Popes against Popes; Councils against Councils; some Fathers against others; the same Fathers against themselves; a consent of Fathers of one age, against a consent of Fathers of another age . . .'.[37] Alluding to this passage from Chillingworth's *Religion of Protestants*, Waterland acknowledged that 'there have been *Fathers* against *Fathers*, Councils against Councils'. But he drew from this fact an alternative conclusion: nothing less than that in the light of this tendency to disagreement, 'the more Regard is to be paid to them [the Fathers] in the greater Matters wherein they all agreed'.[38]

As well as exercising a benignly constraining influence on the interpretation of Scripture, in their own persons the early Fathers embodied just the kind of 'Christian political establishment' which it had been the business of the Church of England to foster.[39] It was for this reason that even a Whiggish churchman such as Archbishop Herring would profess 'great respect for the patristic writers', since they assisted him in his efforts to steer clear of what he saw as the contending superstitions of Papists and Dissenters.[40] The *via media* of the Anglican Church thus made some acknowledgement of the authority of the Fathers hard to

---

[36] Waterland, *Importance of the Doctrine of the Holy Trinity Asserted*, 356 and 361. Later in the century John Jortin, a writer on religion much admired by Gibbon, would write more circumspectly: 'we ought to acknowledge, what truth and plain matter of fact extort from us, that . . . the Fathers, are often poor and insufficient guides in things of judgment and criticism, and in the interpretation of the Scriptures, and sometimes in points of morality also and of doctrine, as Daillé, Whitby, Barbeyrac, and others have fully shewed. The men themselves usually deserve much respect, and their writings are highly useful on several accounts; but it is better to defer too little than too much, to their decisions, and to the authority of *Antiquity*, that *Handmaid to Scripture*, as she is called. She is like *Briareus*, and has *a hundred hands*, and these hands often clash, and beat one another' (*Remarks on Ecclesiastical History*, ii. 163–4).

[37] Quoted by Middleton, *Free Inquiry*, p. xcviii.

[38] Waterland, *Importance of the Doctrine of the Holy Trinity Asserted*, 441. Later in the century Thomas Randolph was to agree, maintaining that the Fathers are 'the best Guides we can follow, where any Doubts may arise about the Sense of *Scripture*' (*Vindication of the Doctrine of the Trinity*, pt. 3, p. 1).   [39] Clark, *English Society 1688–1832*, 226.

[40] Browning, *Political and Constitutional Ideas of the Court Whigs*, 90–3. The general tension between Whiggism and patristic learning is illustrated by e.g. Nicholas Amherst's ironic advice to young Oxonians to read the Church Fathers, the implication being that a taste for such study marked you out as a High Church Tory: 'Never puzzle your brains about *philosophy, mathematicks, ethicks, history*, and such like *lay-studies*; but read the *fathers*, the *orthodox* FATHERS, I mean, (for even some of the FATHERS have been *hereticks*,) and learn from those primitive old gentlemen what a pack of *asses* and *blockheads* TILLOTSON, and BURNET, and HOADLY, and FLEETWOOD, and the rest of our *modern upstarts* are, when compared with the great LUMINARIES of those antient times' (*Terræ-Filius*, 179).

avoid, if not obligatory. To be sure, after 1660 natural theology had
arisen to challenge the primacy which had been accorded tradition in
theological argument, and under its influence men's minds had become
more receptive to forms of explanation either derived from, or bearing
an affinity to, mathematics and the natural sciences.[41] But the appeal to
tradition was never entirely driven from the field. Although George
Horne, the High Churchman and Hutchinsonian, would describe the
reign of George II as a 'time when the smoke of Arianism, Deism, and
Laodiceanism [that is, Latitudinarianism] have darkened the air', the
patristic character of the Church of England survived the lean years of
Latitudinarian ascendency to strengthen markedly in the final quarter of
the eighteenth century, at just the moment when *The Decline and Fall*
was published.[42]

If the vigilance amongst Gibbon's orthodox critics on the subject
of the historian's handling of the early Church Fathers now seems
explicable, was it the case that anything more specific than simply the
general impression of irreligion conveyed by volume one of *The Decline
and Fall* had sounded the alarm over what Gibbon might write when he
turned his attention to the church history of the fourth century?

As a younger man, Gibbon's comments on the Fathers suggest
distaste for prelatical pride, and sympathy for the secular authorities
against whom the Fathers often ranged themselves. When he had
visited Milan in May 1764, Gibbon had committed to his journal some
dry comments on details of church architecture: 'Dans le choeur de
l'Eglise on voit avec plaisir les places des Chanoines qui sont d'un beau
noyer, travaillèès en bas relief, où l'on a representè toute la suite des
actions de St Ambroise. La matiere n'est pas riche, mais l'ouvrage est
d'une grande beautè, et je m'imagine que tout ecclesiastique doit con-
siderer avec plaisir celui où le grand Theodose est humiliè au pied d'un
prelat orgeilleux.'[43] Those youthful sympathies and antipathies seem to
have carried through into the first volume of *The Decline and Fall*, and
in particular into the footnotes to chapter fifteen, where the orthodox
must have been troubled to read that 'it is much to be feared, that the
primitive fathers are very frequently calumniators'.[44] And the presence

[41] Bennett, *Tory Crisis*, 16–17.
[42] Cited by Gascoigne, *Cambridge in the Age of Enlightenment*, 248. Nockles, *Oxford Movement*, 105–6. Wiles, *Archetypal Heresy*, 130 ff.
[43] *J3* 47. For Gibbon's much more nuanced account of this transaction in chapter twenty-seven of *The Decline and Fall*, see *DF* ii. 56–60. Note in particular the Delphic conclusion, that 'the cause of humanity, and that of persecution, have been asserted, by the same Ambrose, with equal energy, and with equal success' (*DF* ii. 60).
[44] *DF* i. 458 n. 32; cf. also *DF* i. 512 n. 194.

in those footnotes of references to Jean Daillé and the 'very judicious' Jean Barbeyrac must also have been disquieting.[45] These writers had been singled out by Waterland as particularly dangerous enemies of the Fathers:

The famous *Daillé*, whom no Man can suspect of *Partiality* towards the *Antients* . . .

I do not know a warmer or keener Adversary that the *Fathers* have had, than Mons. *Barbeyrac* . . .[46]

However, a more specific and substantial irritant seems to have been the account Gibbon had given in chapter sixteen of the martyrdom of St Cyprian.[47] In a footnote in the preceding chapter Gibbon had acknowledged that Cyprian was 'the doctor and guide of all the western churches'.[48] But if Cyprian was important in the tradition of Western Christendom as a whole, he had assumed a particular importance after 1660 in the Church of England. Because of the way in which he had stood out against the pretensions of the bishop of Rome, Cyprian was the early Father upon whose teaching, above that of all others, the distinctive church government of the Church of England had been grounded.[49] For instance, in *Origines Britannicae, or the Antiquities of the British Church* (1685), Edward Stillingfleet had based his argument that the Anglican episcopate enjoyed full competence, independent of Rome, on the example of Cyprian, whose pronouncements while bishop of Carthage were developed into a full-blown doctrine, the 'Cyprian privilege'. In doing so he was following Peter Heylyn, whose *History of Episcopacy* (1657) had argued in substantially

---

[45] *DF* i. 478 n. 87. Jean Daillé (1594–1670); protestant clergyman of great influence; tutor to the grandson of Duplessis-Mornay; author of *Traicté de l'Employ des Saincts Peres* (Geneva, 1632). Jean Barbeyrac (1674–1744); legal theorist and moral philosopher in the natural law tradition; translator of the works of Pufendorf, Grotius, and Richard Cumberland; involved in controversy over the morality of the clergy and Church Fathers with Remi Ceillier (1688–1761); author of *Traité de la Morale des Pères de l'Eglise* (Amsterdam, 1728). Cf. Stephen, *English Thought*, i. 268. For an example of censure of Gibbon's reliance on Barbeyrac, see Dalrymple, *Secondary Causes*, 168–9.

[46] Waterland, *Importance of the Doctrine of the Holy Trinity Asserted*, 386 and 412–13.

[47] *DF* i. 541–5.

[48] *DF* i. 471 n. 72.

[49] 'St Cyprian, Bishop of Carthage, stood out among the early Fathers of the Church . . . The shadow of Cyprian stood behind the teachings of Hammond, Bramhall, Ferne and the others' (Spurr, *Restoration Church of England*, 129). On Cyprian see also Bettenson, *Early Christian Fathers*, and Wiles, 'The Theological Legacy of St Cyprian'. John Jortin, in a work which greatly influenced Gibbon and elicited his admiration, noted Cyprian's 'high notions of Episcopal authority and Ecclesiastical jurisdiction' and his strenuous opposition to the 'domination of one Pope' (Jortin, *Remarks on Ecclesiastical History*, ii. 298).

the same fashion, and whose biography of Archbishop Laud had borne the title *Cyprianus Anglicus* (1668).[50] The summation of this Anglican cherishing of Cyprian was John Fell's edition of the early Father's writings.[51] Fell had both used Cyprian to enforce the case of monarchical episcopacy,[52] and claimed Cyprian as a forerunner of the Anglican *via media* between schismatics and Romanists.[53]

Gibbon's account of Cyprian's government of the Church of Carthage had begun with suave praise of the bishop's ability to 'reconcile the arts of the most ambitious statesman with the Christian virtues which seem adapted to the character of a saint and martyr'. But he had then opened up a damaging perspective into the deeper past, while at the same time suggesting awkward parallels with more recent history:

The patriotic Cyprian, who ruled with the most absolute sway the church of Carthage and the provincial synods, opposed with resolution and success the ambition of the Roman pontiff, artfully connected his own cause with that of the eastern bishops, and, like Hannibal, sought out new allies in the heart of Asia. If this Punic war was carried on without any effusion of blood, it was owing much less to the moderation than to the weakness of the contending prelates. Invectives and excommunications were *their* only weapons; and these, during the progress of the whole controversy, they hurled against each other with equal fury and devotion. The hard necessity of censuring either a pope, or a saint and martyr, distresses the modern catholics, whenever they are obliged to relate the particulars of a dispute, in which the champions of religion indulged such passions as seem much more adapted to the senate or to the camp.[54]

The comparison with Hannibal, which turns this altercation in the fledgling Church into a mock-heroic version of the Punic wars ('Invectives and excommunications were *their* only weapons') imbues the prose with a tone of amused detachment. The struggles with the bishop of Rome, which had made Cyprian such a useful figure for Bishop Fell and other leaders of the Restoration Church of England, are here presented as the self-aggrandisement of an ambitious prelate in

[50] 'Bishops knew that they "stood in St Paul's place"; they identified with Early Christian figures like Cyprian or Ambrose; and these patristic fantasies were further promoted by biographies with titles like *Cyprianus Anglicus*' (Spurr, *Restoration Church of England*, 161).

[51] *Sancti Cæcilii Cypriani Opera, recogn. & illustr. per Ioannem Oxoniensem episcopum* (Oxford, 1682).

[52] For this understanding of the significance to church government of Fell's edition of Cyprian, see Rupp, *Religion in England*, 72.

[53] Fell had claimed that if only Dissenters and Romanists would read Cyprian 'it would be impossible for them to continue in their opinions, and be either Papists or Separatists' (*Of the Unity of the Church*, 40).

[54] *DF* i. 489–90.

whom the character of the statesman had taken precedence over that of the saint and martyr. The discomfiture of the modern Catholics, reduced to the 'hard necessity of censuring either a pope, or a saint and martyr', is clearly relished; but such enjoyment is far from driving Gibbon into the arms of Bishop Fell and his colleagues amongst the Anglican apologists. The sense in the writing, not so much of open irony as of irony smothered and held in reserve, is the signature of a fastidious independence of mind, scornful of partisanship in others and careful not to fall into herd-like behaviour itself.

When, in chapter sixteen, Gibbon proceeded to relate the circumstances of Cyprian's martyrdom, the note of dispassionate re-evaluation was once more struck at the outset:

During the same period of persecution [that of the reign of Decius], the zealous, the eloquent, the ambitious Cyprian governed the church, not only of Carthage, but even of Africa. He possessed every quality which could engage the reverence of the faithful, or provoke the suspicions and resentment of the Pagan magistrates. His character as well as his station seemed to mark out that holy prelate as the most distinguished object of envy and of danger. The experience, however, of the life of Cyprian, is sufficient to prove, that our fancy has exaggerated the perilous situation of a Christian bishop; and that the dangers to which he was exposed were less imminent than those which temporal ambition is always prepared to encounter in the pursuit of honours. Four Roman emperors, with their families, their favourites, and their adherents, perished by the sword in the space of ten years, during which, the bishop of Carthage guided by his authority and eloquence the counsels of the African church.[55]

Cyprian the saint and martyr, it would seem, was just another politician motivated by 'temporal ambition', albeit a politician of unusual accomplishment in self-preservation. Unsurprisingly, therefore, Cyprian had at first shunned the opportunity to seal with his blood the truth of his beliefs:

Prudence suggested the necessity of a temporary retreat, and the voice of prudence was obeyed. He withdrew himself into an obscure solitude, from whence he could maintain a constant correspondence with the clergy and people of Carthage; and concealing himself till the tempest was past, he preserved his life, without relinquishing either his power or his reputation. His extreme caution did not however escape the censure of the more rigid Christians who lamented, or the reproaches of his personal enemies who insulted, a conduct which they considered as a pusillanimous and criminal desertion of the most sacred duty. The propriety of reserving himself for the

[55] *DF* i. 541.

future exigencies of the church, the example of several holy bishops, and the divine admonitions which, as he declares himself, he frequently received in visions and extasies, were the reasons alleged in his justification.[56]

In the final phase of what Gibbon represents as, not so much a furious and violent persecution of the early Christian Church, as a sober legal challenge to the new religion conducted with a meticulous attention to due process, the same reflex of self-preservation initially asserted itself:

At length, exactly one year after Cyprian was first apprehended, Galerius Maximus, proconsul of Africa, received the Imperial warrant for the execution of the Christian teachers. The bishop of Carthage was sensible that he should be singled out for one of the first victims; and the frailty of nature tempted him to withdraw himself by a secret flight, from the danger and the honour of martyrdom: but soon recovering that fortitude which his character required, he returned to his gardens, and patiently expected the ministers of death.[57]

The hinge here is the phrase 'that fortitude which his character required'. It leaves the passage as a whole suspended between, on the one hand, the possibility that Cyprian was a genuine martyr who eventually conquered his 'frailty of nature', and on the other the rival interpretation that he was a hypocrite who had sated his worldly ambitions through the Church, and who was then trapped in the 'character' he had assumed. After relating how Cyprian had suffered 'the mildest and least painful' form of execution 'that could be inflicted on a person convicted of any capital offence', Gibbon placed exactly this hermeneutical dilemma before his reader:

It was in the choice of Cyprian either to die a martyr or to live an apostate: but on that choice depended the alternative of honour or infamy. Could we suppose that the bishop of Carthage had employed the profession of the Christian faith only as the instrument of his avarice or ambition, it was still incumbent on him to support the character which he had assumed; and, if he possessed the smallest degree of manly fortitude, rather to expose himself to the most cruel tortures, than by a single act to exchange the reputation of a whole life, for the abhorrence of his Christian brethren and the contempt of the Gentile world. But if the zeal of Cyprian was supported by the sincere con- viction of the truth of those doctrines which he preached, the crown of martyrdom must have appeared to him as an object of desire rather than of terror.[58]

Gibbon's whole account of Cyprian's martyrdom is calculated to keep in play—although not irrevocably to close with—the interpretation which here he seems to raise only to dismiss for its orthodox alternative:

[56] *DF* i. 541–2.   [57] *DF* i. 543.   [58] *DF* i. 545.

namely, that 'the bishop of Carthage had employed the profession of
the Christian faith only as the instrument of his avarice or ambition',
and that therefore his martyrdom was an instance of a paradoxical aspect
of human nature—heroic hypocrisy.[59] No wonder that, having read
this, Joseph Milner might conclude that 'Cyprian must be seriously
defended'; that Francis Eyre, in his published attack on Gibbon, should
seek to redress the balance by including a life of Cyprian calculated to
restore the saint and martyr's lustre in the wake of the 'rather dark
shades' of Gibbon's palette; and that Sir David Dalrymple should
include an account of the martyrdom of Cyprian in the second volume
of his *Remains of Christian Antiquity* as a riposte to the 'elegant and free
paraphrase of Mr. Gibbon' by which the circumstances of Cyprian's
death had become 'generally known'.[60]

III

By inviting the reader of *The Decline and Fall* to entertain doubt over the
received Anglican understanding of the life and work of Cyprian, and
with no matter how subtle a technique, in the eyes of the orthodox
Gibbon had conformed to what was for them a distressingly familiar
pattern. As Daniel Waterland had lamented, 'great Pains have been
taken by many to depreciate the Value of *Antiquity*, and to throw
contempt upon the primitive *Fathers*: Which is a very unjustifiable
Practice, and is wounding *Christianity* it self through their Sides.'[61] Even
some thirty years later, the memory was still green of how, in his
An Introductory Discourse . . . Concerning the Miraculous Powers (1747),
Middleton had acknowledged Cyprian to be the 'chief ornament' of
the Church in the third century, but then had slyly quoted him against

---

[59] In a footnote Gibbon directs us to 'the two lives of Cyprian, composed with equal accuracy,
though with very different views; the one by Le Clerc . . . the other by Tillemont' (*DF* i. 541 n.
76). Collation of these two accounts with the text of *The Decline and Fall* indicates that, although
Gibbon may have found Le Clerc's account in the *Bibliotheque Universelle*, xii. 208–378, more
congenial, he nevertheless relied to a greater extent on the more circumstantial account of
Tillemont, to be found in his *Memoires pour servir à l'histoire ecclesiastique*, IV. i. 76–326. However,
collation also reveals that while Gibbon retained anything in Tillemont which pointed to the
moderation of the Romans, he also suppressed some circumstances in which Tillemont insinuated that Cyprian's conduct was modelled on that of Christ before Pilate: this presumably on the
principle that one credits the praise of enemies and the blame of friends. Jortin had earlier
remarked of Cyprian that 'it hath been said of him that he was fond of spiritual power, and it
cannot be denied' (*Remarks on Ecclesiastical History*, ii. 296).

[60] Milner, *Gibbon's Account*, 61. [Eyre], *Remarks*, 72 and 72–88. Dalrymple, *Christian Antiquity*,
ii., p. ix and ii. 26–34; cf. also Dalrymple, *Secondary Causes*, 132–3.

[61] Waterland, *Importance of the Doctrine of the Trinity Asserted*, 395.

the cause of religious orthodoxy.[62] As a result of writings such as these, the withholding of reverence from the Fathers had come to be, in the eyes of orthodox Anglicans, one of the leading characteristics of both deists and those within the Church of England who, while being committed to revealed theology, were nevertheless uncomfortable with the orthodox doctrine of the Trinity.

The official teaching of the Church of England asserted that the Trinity, this 'Great and Sublime *Mystery*', was the 'Great and Fundamental' doctrine of Christianity.[63] Its primacy was reflected in the fact that it was the subject of the first of the thirty-nine articles.[64] According to Daniel Waterland, it was of the 'highest Concernment to all Christians'.[65] In the first place, it had been given prominence by Christ himself:

You will observe, that as soon as ever our Lord had given his Disciples Commission to form a Church, he instructs them to baptize in the Name of the *Father*, the *Son*, and the *Holy Ghost*.

This was the one short and important Lesson to be first instilled, and inculcated into the new Converts through every Nation. From whence we may justly infer, that the Faith in these Three Persons as *Divine*, in Opposition to all the *Gods* of the *Gentiles*, was to be the *Fundamental* Article of Christianity, the distinguishing *Character* of the true Religion. Such Care has been taken, to impress the Belief of the ever blessed Trinity upon the Minds of all Christ's Disciples.[66]

Secondly, it possessed great utility, as a defining and distinguishing doctrine: 'Upon the whole, I look upon it as exceedingly *useful*, and *necessary*, for every Church to have some such *Form* as this, or something equivalent, open and common to all its Members; that none may be led astray for want of proper Caution, and previous Instruction in what so nearly concerns the whole Structure and Fabrick of the Christian Faith.'[67] The historical fact of the centrality of the Trinity to Christianity was a point on which both the upholders and the

---

[62] Middleton, *Introductory Discourse*, 38–9. This work was later republished as part of Middleton's full-blown account of the topic, the notorious *A Free Enquiry into the Miraculous Powers* (1749). The detailed familiarity with Middleton's work evinced by Gibbon's detractors shows that the orthodox still read and pondered his work in the mid-1770s.

[63] Leslie, *Brief Account*, 10. Sherlock, *Vindication of the Doctrine of the . . . Trinity*, sig. A2ʳ.

[64] 'Of Faith in the Holy Trinity'. The text reads: 'There is but one living and true God, everlasting, without body, parts, or passions; of infinite power, wisdom, and goodness; the Maker, and Preserver of all things both visible and invisible. And in unity of this Godhead there be three Persons, of one substance, power, and eternity; the Father, the Son, and the Holy Ghost.'

[65] Waterland, *Familiar Discourse*, 4.

[66] Ibid. 19. The allusion is to Matthew 28: 19.

[67] Waterland, *Critical History of the Athanasian Creed*, 161–2.

impugners of the doctrine were agreed. William Whiston, for instance, bemoaned the fact that 'all the Christian Religion [has] been for many Ages esteem'd little more than the *Doctrine of the Trinity*: No *Mystery* at all so considerable in Religion as the *Mystery of the Trinity*; . . .'.[68]

For those who could accept the orthodox, or Athanasian, doctrine of the Trinity, it functioned in the way Waterland described: it was a doctrinal cornerstone and the basis of confessional self-definition.[69] But the challenge the doctrine posed to ordinary notions of philosophical clarity, in its insistence upon three consubstantial, co-present and co-eternal persons, meant that, in an age increasingly receptive to forms of explanation derived from mathematics and secular philosophy, the doctrine which the orthodox saw as the essence of their faith was also singled out by the heterodox as a weak point in the doctrinal edifice. It seemed to invite attack by those who wished to challenge doctrinal orthodoxy, either because they were unsympathetic to Christianity *tout court*, or because they wished to simplify its dogmatic content. So the doctrine of the Trinity came under critical pressure from both within and without the Church. As Thomas Randolph was to sigh in the middle of the century, the doctrine of the Trinity was '*a most important and fundamental Article of our Faith*', but unfortunately one which had been subject to '*fierce and repeated Attacks*'.[70] It is to the character of those attacks on the Fathers and the doctrine of the Trinity which they had framed which we must now turn.

In the eighteenth century Hobbes was widely regarded as one of the fountainheads of modern atheism (whether rightly or wrongly is, for our present purposes, of no importance). In *Leviathan* (1651) he had argued for a thorough-going Erastianism (that is, a subordination of Church to State) which was naturally hostile to the pretensions of the Fathers. He had explicitly denounced them at the end of that work as a conduit whereby error had contaminated the Christian religion:

Lastly, for the Errors brought in from false, or uncertain History, what is all the Legend of fictitious Miracles, in the lives of the Saints; and all the Histories of Apparitions, and Ghosts, alledged by the Doctors of the Romaine Church, to make good their Doctrines of Hell, and Purgatory, the power of Exorcisme, and other Doctrines which have no warrant, neither in Reason, nor Scripture; as also all those Traditions which they call the unwritten Word of God; but old Wives Fables? Whereof, though they find dispersed somewhat in the Writings of the ancient Fathers; yet those Fathers were men, that might too easily

[68] Whiston, *Primitive Christianity*, iv. 389.
[69] Clark, *English Society 1688–1832*, 277. Wiles, *Archetypal Heresy*, 142.
[70] Randolph, *Vindication*, pt. 1, p. 7.

beleeve false reports; and the producing of their opinions for testimony of the truth of what they beleeved, hath no other force with them that . . . examine Spirits, than in all things that concern the power of the Romane Church, (the abuse whereof either they suspected not, or had benefit by it,) to discredit their testimony, in respect of too rash beleef of reports; which the most sincere men, without great knowledge of naturall causes, (such as the Fathers were) are commonly the most subject to: For naturally, the best men are the least suspicious of fraudulent purposes.[71]

The blandly complimentary final sentence (which, after all, claims for the Fathers only natural goodness, rather than any special spiritual authority) does nothing to diminish the menace this passage poses to orthodoxy. Had not Hobbes earlier referred to no less important a Father than Cyprian himself, and explicitly elevated above his writings 'the Law of Nature (which is a better Principle of Right and Wrong, than the word of any Doctor that is but a man)'?[72] And had he not also propounded an heretical interpretation of the doctrine of the Trinity?

in the Trinity of Heaven, the Persons are the persons of one and the same God, though Represented in three different times and occasions. To conclude, the doctrine of the Trinity, as far as can be gathered directly from the Scripture, is in substance this; that God who is alwaies One and the same, was the Person Represented by Moses; the Person Represented by his Son Incarnate; and the Person Represented by the Apostles.[73]

Needless to say, this is very far from the orthodox, Athanasian doctrine, in which the Father, Son, and Holy Spirit are co-eternal, co-present, and consubstantial. Indeed, in its insistence that God is 'alwaies One and the same', Hobbes's understanding of the Trinity looks Arian, perhaps even Sabellian. As a result of passages such as these, the link between anti-Trinitarianism and contempt for the early Fathers was fixed in the minds of the orthodox as a mark of the beast.[74]

However, the most energetic assault on the credit and standing of the Fathers had been launched in the late 1740s by Conyers Middleton. At first in *An Introductory Discourse . . . Concerning the Miraculous Powers* (1747), then once again two years later in *A Free Inquiry into the Miraculous Powers, which are supposed to have subsisted in the Christian Church* (1749), Middleton had vigorously accused the Fathers of

---

[71] Hobbes, *Leviathan*, ch. 46, p. 473.

[72] Ibid. ch. 42, p. 393.

[73] Ibid. 340; cf. also Richard Tuck's comments, on p. xli of his introduction to this edition.

[74] From this standpoint one can appreciate the ingenuity of Middleton's malice when he accused Waterland of writing under the influence of Hobbes (Middleton, *Letter to Dr. Waterland*, 43).

credulity and imposture. Naturally, he had sported the customary
fig-leaf of well-intentioned piety. He claimed that his work was 'of the
greatest importance to the Protestant religion, and the sole expedient,
which can effectually secure it, from being gradually undermined, and
finally subverted by the efforts of *Rome*'.[75] For only if the Church of
England could be brought to repudiate the later, corrupt miraculous
traditions vouched for by the Fathers would it be safe from the 'railleries
of the Sceptics'.[76] Protestantism would be secure only when it rested
exclusively upon the foundation of the Bible, and eschewed 'the
authority of weak and fallible men [i.e. the Fathers], the detection of
whose errors, and the suspicion of whose frauds would necessarily give
a wound to Christianity itself'.[77]

Unsurprisingly, the orthodox viewed the author's own account of
the purpose of these works with suspicion, preferring instead to see
Middleton as a deist who sought disingenuously to undermine
Christianity in favour of natural religion. But no matter what
Middleton's true intentions actually were, it was nevertheless the
case, as he himself openly admitted, that his project in the *Free Inquiry*
'must necessarily *detract somewhat, from the characters of the Fathers, and the
implicit faith, which has been given to them in their reports of the primitive
miracles*', and that it was therefore only to be expected that he would
find himself accused of 'calumniating the Holy Fathers; misrepresenting their testimonies; and straining them to senses quite different from
their own'.[78] For in order to demolish the miraculous traditions of the
early Church, Middleton must also destroy 'the supposed integrity and
piety of the Fathers' who had attested to the truth of those traditions.[79]

The weapon around which Middleton's hand closed most readily
and comfortably was the cudgel of obloquy. The Golden Legend was
for him nothing more than the 'forgeries of a corrupt Clergy'.[80]
Athanasius, Basil, Jerome, and Chrysostom had spread 'lies and forged

---

[75] Middleton, *Free Inquiry*, p. iii.

[76] Ibid. p. cxli. Earlier Middleton has made clear his conviction that miraculous powers were
withdrawn from the Church quite early, 'while some of the Apostles were still living' (ibid.
p. xxix). It was a position he reaffirmed in his *A Preface to an Intended Answer to all the Objections
made against the Free Inquiry*, where he stated that '*we have no sufficient reason to believe, upon the
authority of the Primitive Fathers, that any miraculous powers were continued to the Church, after the days
of the Apostles*' (*Miscellaneous Works*, i. 376).

[77] Middleton, *Free Inquiry*, p. cxi.

[78] Middleton, *Preface to an Intended Answer* (*Miscellaneous Works*, i. 375 and 373). Cf. *Free
Inquiry*, 2, where Middleton states that he will impugn 'the particular characters and opinions of
the Fathers'.

[79] Middleton, *Free Inquiry*, p. xxxiv.

[80] Ibid., p. xlv.

miracles . . . in honor of the Monks'.[81] Athanasius in particular was berated for testifying to the truth of miracles which 'in the judgement of all the learned and candid Protestants, are manifestly fictitious, and utterly incredible', and for supporting his doctrine of the Trinity with palpable frauds.[82] But Middleton could also if necessary use the rapier of logical ambush. He disarmingly conceded that the Fathers may have had confused motives: 'the pretended miracles of the primitive Church were all mere fictions; which the pious and zealous Fathers, partly from a weak credulity, and partly, from reasons of policy; believing some perhaps to be true, and knowing all of them to be useful, were induced to espouse and propagate, for the support of a righteous cause.'[83] Middleton thus presented his reader with a choice. The Fathers were either credulous or deceitful, for 'it is common with men, out of crafty and selfish views, to dissemble and deceive; or, out of weakness and credulity, to embrace and defend with zeal, what the craft of others had imposed upon them'.[84] Given that, in the first place, miraculous powers were withdrawn at some point from the Church, and that, secondly, the Roman Catholic Church asserted a continual succession of these powers down to the Reformation, the only latitude Middleton extended to his Protestant reader was the freedom to decide at which particular point in history the character of the Fathers had either softened from mendacity to credulity, or sharpened from credulity to mendacity. It was an uncomfortable dilemma, but one upon which Middleton insisted:

I have shewn, by many indisputable facts, that the ancient Fathers, by whose authority that delusion was originally imposed, and has ever since been supported, were extremely credulous and superstitious; possessed with strong prejudices and an enthusiastic zeal, in favor, not onely of Christianity in general, but of every particular doctrine, which a wild imagination could ingraft upon it; and scrupling no art or means, by which they might propagate the same principles. In short; that they were of a character, from which nothing could be expected, that was candid and impartial; nothing, but what a weak or crafty understanding could supply, towards confirming those prejudices, with which they happened to be possessed; especially where religion was the subject, which above all other motives, strengthens every bias, and inflames every passion of the human mind.[85]

Although the *Free Inquiry* has been usually construed as a challenge to the reliance on miracles as supernatural endorsements of revelation, in

[81] Ibid., pp. lii–liv.
[83] Ibid., p. xci.
[85] Ibid., pp. xxxi–xxxii.

[82] Ibid., pp. lxxvi and 148–9.
[84] Ibid., pp. xiv–xv.

its own time the damaging implications of its argument for the patristic character of the Church of England was perhaps its most embarrassing feature. Middleton's attack on the credit of the Fathers lay on the surface of his work: frank, blunt, and unequivocal. His epistemological scepticism, on the other hand, was by contrast latent and implicit.

In the wake of Middleton's writings, the standing of the Fathers was further undermined, to the point where they might be openly scoffed at. In the 1760s a militia acquaintance of Gibbon's, John Wilkes, had defended himself against the charge that the *Essay on Woman* and the *Veni Creator* were 'a most scandalous, obscene, and impious libel; a gross profanation of many parts of the Holy Scriptures; and a most wicked and blasphemous attempt to ridicule and vilify the person of our blessed Saviour' by arguing that:

In my own closet I had a right to examine and even try by the keen edge of ridicule any opinions I pleased. If I have laughed pretty freely at the glaring absurdities of the most monstrous creed which was ever attempted to be imposed on the credulity of Christians, a creed which our great Tillotson wished the Church of England was fairly rid of, it was in private I laughed. I am not the first good Protestant who has amused himself with the egregious nonsense . . . of that strange, perplexed and perplexing mortal . . . Athanasius.[86]

Atheists and libertines had mocked the Fathers, and in particular Athanasius. So too, albeit from a different direction, had the 'modern Arians', heterodox theologians who had caused Waterland to sigh over 'the low Esteem which Those Gentlemen have of the *Fathers*.'[87] These were men such as William Whiston, whose *An Historical Preface to Primitive Christianity Revived* (1711) had claimed that the faith of the pre-Nicene Fathers had been anti-Trinitarian, and thus closer to the teaching of Arius than of Athanasius, and Latitudinarians such as Samuel Clarke.[88] Clarke himself (of whom it was noted by Waterland that he 'sets light by the Fathers, and lays no stress upon Them') had found

[86] Quoted in Clark, *English Society 1688–1832*, 310–11. Whiston believed that even those who outwardly supported Athanasius were privately scornful: 'I full well know, that those who pretend the greatest Zeal for the most Orthodox System of all, I mean, the *Athanasian* Creed, in publick, do privately banter and ridicule the same; a famous Instance whereof we have in a Letter of his late Excellency Mr. *Prior*, where the making an *Athanasian Business* or *Explanation*, is introduced as one of the greatest Examples of Absurdities, Contradiction, and Madness possible' (quoted in Clarke, *The Layman's Humble Address*, 32).

[87] Waterland, *Importance*, 460. See Wiles, *Archetypal Heresy*, *passim*. Amongst older studies in the general field of Arianism, Newman's *Arians of the Fourth Century* (London, 1833) is of enduring interest.

[88] In the words of J. H. Overton, anti-Trinitarians such as Whiston and Clarke 'constantly depreciate the value of patristic evidence' (Abbey and Overton, *English Church in the Eighteenth Century*, i. 503).

patristic evidence useless: 'Quotations from the Fathers being infinite, and generally ending in nothing but Personal Contests, whether this or the Other Writer understands the Languages best; which to the generality of Readers can be of no great importance; . . .'[89] And on the subject of the doctrine of the Trinity, Clarke had been evasive: 'Of this [the doctrine of the Trinity], I say; as there is nothing in bare Reason, by which it can be demonstrated that there is actually any such thing; so neither is there any Argument, by which it can be proved impossible or unreasonable to be supposed; and therefore when declared and made know to us by clear Revelation, it ought to be believed.'[90] This was surely less than a ringing endorsement, and the doubts it created were only strengthened seven years later when, in his *The Scripture-Doctrine of the Trinity*, Clarke had proceeded to call into question the extent to which the Trinity was indeed a scriptural, and hence a revealed as opposed to a man-made, doctrine. The champion of orthodoxy in this Trinitarian conflict[91] of the early decades of the eighteenth century had been Daniel Waterland, who had framed powerful arguments defending and defining the proper use of the Fathers. In the opinion of most, the forces of orthodoxy, led by Waterland, had prevailed.[92] However, during the Subscription Controversy of the 1770s certain aspects of the earlier arguments had been revived. Moreover, the ranks of those who had then busied themselves in the cause of orthodoxy included a number of clerics, such as Thomas Randolph, who were also engaged in organizing and stimulating the attacks on *The Decline and Fall*.[93]

As we have seen, anti-Trinitarian polemic frequently found *ad hominem* expression, since those who wished to question the orthodox conception of the Trinity found it convenient to employ 'Calumny and Detraction' against, in particular, Athanasius, the Father chiefly credited with dictating the Catholic form of the doctrine.[94] In part this

---

[89] Waterland, *Vindication of Christ's Divinity*, 442. Clarke, *Observations on Dr. Waterland's Second Defense*, 119.

[90] Clarke, *Being and Attributes of God*, 95–6.

[91] Of which the fullest account is still to be found in Abbey and Overton, *The English Church in the Eighteenth Century*, ch. 8, i. 480–529. For the general ecclesiological context, consult the essays collected in Walsh, Haydon, and Taylor (eds.), *The Church of England c.1689–c.1833*.

[92] 'Waterland was regarded with peculiar respect by the clergy as having encountered, and, as was generally supposed, crushed, the incipient Arianism of Clarke' (Stephen, *English Thought*, i. 257).

[93] On which see, most recently, Young, *Religion and Enlightenment*, ch. 2, '"Subscribe or Starve": The Subscription Controversy and its Consequences', 45–80.

[94] Thirlby, *An Answer*, p. i. But not all the participants lowered themselves to name-calling: Edward Stillingfleet and Samuel Clarke are both noteworthy for the comparatively austere and philosophical focus of their contributions.

was a consequence of the manner in which George Bull had pursued the argument of his great work defending the Catholic doctrine of the Trinity, *Defensio Fidei Nicænæ* (1685; second edition, 1688). Bull had sought to prove that the Catholic doctrine of the Trinity was not an innovation of the fourth century by demonstrating that the ante-Nicene Fathers had held substantially the same belief: 'He [Bull] showed that the crucial test of orthodoxy, the one single term at which Arians and semi-Arians scrupled—that is, the Homoousion or Consubstantiality of the Son with the Father—was actually in use before the Nicene Council, and that it was thoroughly in accordance with the teaching of the ante-Nicene Fathers.'[95] While this had the desired effect of making it difficult for the anti-Trinitarians to persist in the view that the doctrine of the Trinity had been first formulated in the fourth century, it also meant that the debate acquired a double focus. On the one hand, the substance of the doctrine might be questioned in a spirit of philosophy. On the other, the discussion might be directed towards the parallel historical and biographical questions of precisely when the doctrine had first assumed its Catholic form, and of the characters of the men who had upheld it.

Over time, the latter became the more frequented line of approach. Indeed, at times it seemed as if the whole controversy had resolved itself into 'the Question between the Vindicators of *Athanasius* and the *Unitarians*, Whether or no *Athanasius* was as vicious in his Life, and his Doctrine as erroneous, as it is said to be'.[96] Thus anti-Trinitarians might proceed by casting 'Indignities and Aspersions' on Athanasius, to the point where it might seem to the orthodox that 'the chief Object of [their] Spite is S. ATHANASIUS; as if it were the hard (shall I call it? or rather Kind and Glorious) Fate of that Great Person to have in all Ages the same Enemies with our most Holy *Faith*, and its ever Blessed *Author*'.[97] For example, an eye-catching element in Whiston's anti-Trinitarian theology was the section of his *Primitive Christianity Reviv'd* entitled 'Suspicions Concerning Athanasius'.[98] Whiston was adamant that Athanasius's character could inspire no confidence:

A Person of his General Character, which I take to be that of one Resolute, Ambitious, and Tyrannical; of admirable Parts, but little Learning, and small Appearance of Sincerity; who would never submit to either Emperor or Council; and who would rather set the Christian World in a Combustion on

[95] Abbey and Overton, *English Church*, i. 484–5.
[96] [Anon.], *The True History of the Great St. Athanasius*, 31.
[97] Savage, *An Answer*, 4. Thirlby, *An Answer*, p. v.
[98] Whiston, *Primitive Christianity*, i., pp. cxvi–cxxviii.

all Occasions than recede in the least from his Pretensions; who reasons generally very weakly; yet treats his Adversaries with the most unchristian Names of
Reproach and Scorn possible; and who still alter'd his Notions, or at least
his Language as he saw Occasion, and as Matters would bear, and yet us'd
plausible Words and Insinuations all along; a Person, I say, of this general
Character cannot but afford great Room for Suspicion to considering Men.[99]

In a more openly satirical work, such as *The Acts of Great Athanasius*, the
accusations might be more coarsely delivered: 'Here . . . *Athanasius* is
got into his *Altitudes*, or *Profundities*, which you will. Here 'tis that the
Ignorant think, they are taught *the Inmost Secrets* of Theological
Knowledg [*sic*] . . .'[100] But, in either mode, the gravamen of the charge
is the same. Athanasius is depicted as the source of all the 'Spurious and
Heretical' doctrines, and all the instances of 'Fraud, Interpolation and
Dishonesty' which are, in the eyes of the anti-Trinitarians, so prevalent
in the church history of the fourth century.[101] Any 'fair Method of
Enquiry', so it was argued, would uncover plentiful evidence of
Athanasius's 'Ignorance, Knavery, and Forgeries', and would leave no
alternative to the conclusion that '*Athanasius* was guilty of a known and
wilful Falsity and Interpolation . . . and of voluntarily propagating a
notorious Forgery over the Christian World'.[102] An awareness of how
and why the Trinitarian controversy of the late seventeenth and early
eighteenth centuries had taken a biographical turn, and of the language
and vocabularies in which that biographical turn had been pursued, is
necessary before one can understand what Gibbon was doing when in
chapter twenty-one of *The Decline and Fall* he wrote his account of the
life and character of Athanasius.

It is clear, then, that from the standpoint of doctrinally orthodox
members of the Church of England there was much to be concerned
about in the prospect that Gibbon was shortly to write on Athanasius,
and thus on the doctrine of the Trinity with which Athanasius was so
closely associated. This doctrine had been a recent and recurrent source
of conflict within the Church of England itself, while at the same time

---

[99] Ibid. i., p. cxviii. Whiston states that his suspicions were aroused by reading Montfaucon's
life of Athanasius (*Primitive Christianity*, i, pp. cxv–cxvi). However, his language here bears a
striking similarity to that of Isaac Newton, with whom we know Whiston discussed theology,
and who, in his manuscript 'Paradoxical Questions Concerning the Morals and Actions of
Athanasius and his Followers', wrote as follows of 'the seditious spirit of Athanasius': 'And this is
enough to let you see the spirit of the man. For this shews plainly how, for the sake of a bishopric,
he laboured to set the whole Roman world in a flame, and to make a civil war against his own
Emperor' (Newton, *Theological Manuscripts*, 109 and 106).
[100] [Anon.], *The Acts of Great Athanasius*, 13–14.
[101] Whiston, *Athanasius Convicted of Forgery*, 29.
[102] Ibid. 4 and 18–19.

being a favourite target for the sapping mockery of those outside the Church. Orthodox sensitivities, therefore, might well quiver in antici-pation. The Church of England had been plagued twice, once in the early years of the century and again in the Subscription Controversy of the 1770s, by a revival of the disputes of late antiquity concerning the doctrine of the Trinity—the doctrine upon which above all others rested the Church of England's claims for *sacerdotium*, and their sense of their separateness from Dissenters such as Unitarians and Socinians. No wonder that they contemplated with apprehension what an historian with an established reputation for irreligion would say about the contests over doctrine waged by the Fathers of the fourth century. For those contests were both the template for, and might be made the reflection of, the disputes which had disturbed their own peace over the past eighty years, and which indeed had revived with surprising vigour in the very recent past. The triumph of the orthodox over Clarke and Whiston and other anti-Trinitarians in the early decades of the century was therefore shortly to become a pyrrhic victory. For the effect of Waterland's 'brutal theology' had been to drive the debate on the doctrine of the Trinity into an historical form: 'It was thus his [Waterland's] natural tendency to ground the evidence of religion exclusively upon the testimony of facts, and to repudiate any theory which implied the possibility of constructing an independent test of his truth. The historical basis was the sole and sufficient basis . . .'.[103] Later in the century, discomfort was to swell from the historical spring whence comfort once had seemed to come.

IV

I have described why the critics of the first volume of *The Decline and Fall* had looked forward with keen and apprehensive interest to those parts of the second instalment of the history in which Gibbon would be obliged to consider the church history of the fourth century. The keen-ness of their interest explains why Gibbon took unusual pains in researching and composing this section of his narrative. His decision to immerse himself in the mud of the Trinitarian controversy is at one level understandable as a response to the menacing posture adopted by his critics. It remains for us now to turn to *The Decline and Fall* itself, and to consider the detail of how Gibbon met, eluded, or frustrated the expectations of his opponents. In the *Vindication*, which as we have

---

[103] Stephen, *English Thought*, i. 257–8.

noted Gibbon was probably composing at the same time as his chapters on Julian the Apostate and Athanasius, Walter Moyle was singled out for praise as 'a bold and ingenious critic, who read the Fathers as their judge, and not as their slave, and who has refuted, with the most patient candour, all that learned prejudice could suggest in favour of the silly story of the Thundering Legion'.[104] Boldness, ingenuity, independence, and candour were qualities which Gibbon always prized. But his own account of Athanasius relies rather upon guile, subtlety, and strategic brilliance. In his 'Memoirs' Gibbon would praise Bossuet as 'a master of all the weapons of controversy', and would specify as one of his skills the ability to fashion 'an happy mixture of narrative and argument'.[105] Gibbon was an apt pupil to the master. In chapter twenty-one, his own controversial ends were secured through the surreptitious embodiment of argument in narrative.

No historian walks untrodden paths. His imagination exists under constraints, whether of accepted fact or of prevailing interpretation. Naturally, either or both of these can be challenged (and indeed constraints of previous interpretation almost always are). But even if successfully overcome, the interpretation which has been driven out has, albeit in defeat, influenced and oriented the historian's flow of imaginative thought. And in historical writing, as so often elsewhere, a sign of mastery is the ability to turn constraint into advantage. In assessing the extent to which Gibbon was able to demonstrate mastery by converting constraint into advantage when writing on Athanasius, we need to identify those features of the subject as he found it which seem to have shaped his own account: features which a lesser mind might have seen as obstacles, but which under Gibbon's pen became opportunities. There are, I believe, three such features: one of fact, and two of interpretation.

The constraint of fact is the historical circumstance that Athanasius was a contemporary, and great foe, of Julian the Apostate. Anti-Trinitarian writers had naturally tended to ignore this coincidence, because it did not suit them to show Athanasius as one who had suffered persecution for the sake of the Church. But Trinitarian works such as *The History of the Life & Actions of Sᵗ. Athanasius* (1664) had for the opposite reason dwelt upon how, at the hands of Julian, Athanasius had 'suffered in his good name, his body, and mind'.[106] In the case of *The*

---

[104] *DF* iii. 1167. The comment seems designed to contrast in advance with Chelsum's dismay at Gibbon's 'general distrust of those respectable witnesses', the Fathers (*DF* iii. 1170–1).

[105] *A* 86.

[106] [Anon.], *History of the Life & Actions of Sᵗ. Athanasius*, 134: for Julian, see esp. pp. 170–83.

Decline and Fall, the fact that Julian was commonly seen as a hero of the freethinkers (he had been so marked out by Bentley) interacts tellingly with the expectation that Gibbon would adopt an anti-Trinitarian stance towards Athanasius.[107] As we shall see, Gibbon disappoints both the expectation that he would extol Julian and the expectation that he would denounce Athanasius. In the case of Julian, he substantially adopted Bentley's acute perception that Julian's religion was shot through with absurdities—absurdities which made him 'the most bigoted Creature in the World', and which meant that, according to Bentley, 'our modern Atheists can never reckon him on Their side, among the list of *Free-thinkers*'.[108] Moreover, the unexpected emphases in Gibbon's portrait of Julian fit snugly with the equally unexpected emphases in his portrait of Athanasius. As a result, the two portraits demand to be considered together as a diptych, in which certain details in one need to be read in the light of correspondent details in the other.[109]

As well as this leading factual circumstance, there were also two features of interpretation which Gibbon exploited in this section of *The Decline and Fall*. The first relates to the doctrine of the Trinity. Amongst anti-Trinitarian writers it was, if not an article of faith, then at least a common allegation, that the doctrine of the Trinity formed no part of primitive Christianity, but rather arose when the pure faith of the early Church had become corrupted by Platonic philosophy. Whiston was one who had insisted upon this interpretation. He had launched *Primitive Christianity Reviv'd* by proclaiming his adherence to 'that old plain Christianity or *Arianism* contain'd in [the Apostolical Constitutions], without the least Colour for any of those Novel Notions or Expressions which Philosophy began to introduce in the very Second Century; and which advanc'd to a mighty System in the Fourth, under the Conduct of *Athanasius*'.[110] Later in the work, when he considered the doctrine of the Trinity, he set out this position in more detail:

For I shall desire any one to shew me the least syllable in the first Ages, concerning this *Mystery of the Trinity*, till Philosophy crept into the Church, and men became so foolish as to leave the *wholesome Words of sound Doctrine*, deriv'd from Revelation, for the *vain Jangling*, and *metaphysical Jargon* of weak and bewildred Philosophers. And indeed 'tis a most sensible and affecting Change,

---

[107] Bentley, *Remarks*, 23.

[108] Ibid. 24.

[109] Unawareness of its interrelation with the portrait of Athanasius impairs existing accounts of Gibbon's treatment of Julian: a criticism from which I do not exempt my own earlier work.

[110] *Primitive Christianity*, i, p. xiv.

for an honest and pious Man to read a few Pages of an Original Christian Writer, before Philosophy came into the Church . . . and then to read as many in *Athanasius, Aquinas,* or the like Scholastick and metaphysick Reasoners . . . and to see what a vast difference there is in the present Case: The former containing plain, practical, serious, useful Truths; sufficient to affect and influence all Mankind: The latter involving deep, perplexing, puzling [*sic*] Subtilties, fit only for Metaphysical Genius's, and sufficient to make men doubt of everything, and to dispose them to reject the *plainness* of the *Duties*, on account of the *absurdity* of the *Doctrines* of *Christianity*.[111]

By the time Gibbon wrote *The Decline and Fall* it had become a recognized characteristic of anti-Trinitarian writers to attribute the origin of the doctrine of the Trinity to the infection of Christianity by Neoplatonism. Replying to Robert Clayton's *An Essay on Spirit* (1751), the High Church apologist and critic of Gibbon, Thomas Randolph, had recalled it as '*Not many Years ago it was pretended that this very* Justin [Justin Martyr] *was the first Person who introduc'd* the Doctrine of the Trinity *into the Christian Church, and that he learnt it in the Schools of the* Platonists'.[112]

On the basis of the first volume of *The Decline and Fall*, Gibbon's critics might with reason have judged that this was an interpretation of the development of theology in the early Church to which Gibbon himself subscribed. For at the end of chapter thirteen, as part of a review of intellectual culture in the Roman Empire at the beginning of the fourth century, he had considered the 'new Platonists':

Several of these masters . . . were men of profound thought, and intense application; but by mistaking the true object of philosophy, their labours contributed much less to improve than to corrupt the human understanding. The knowledge that is suited to our situation and powers, the whole compass of moral, natural, and mathematical science, was neglected by the new Platonists; whilst they exhausted their strength in the verbal disputes of metaphysics, attempted to explore the secrets of the invisible world, and studied to reconcile Aristotle with Plato, on subjects of which both these philosophers were as ignorant as the rest of mankind. Consuming their reason in these deep but unsubstantial meditations, their minds were exposed to illusions of fancy. They flattered themselves that they possessed the secret of disengaging the soul from

---

[111] *Primitive Christianity Reviv'd*, iv. 391. For another, later, example, see Jackson, *Christian Liberty Asserted*, 3.

[112] Randolph, *Vindication*, pt. 1, p. 7. Fontenelle, in his *Histoire des Oracles* (Amsterdam, 1687)—a book which we know Gibbon had read in 1762 (*J*1 121–2)—had advanced the same idea: 'Jamais Philosophie n'a esté plus à la mode qu'y fut celle de Platon pendant les premiers Siecles de l'Eglise', he wrote, identifying 'la sainte Trinité' as a significant point of contamination (p. 15).

its corporeal prison; claimed a familiar intercourse with dæmons and spirits; and, by a very singular revolution, converted the study of philosophy into that of magic. The ancient sages had derided the popular superstition; after disguising its extravagance by the thin pretence of allegory, the disciples of Plotinus and Porphyry became its most zealous defenders. As they agreed with the Christians in a few mysterious points of faith, they attacked the remainder of their theological system with all the fury of civil war. The new Platonists would scarcely deserve a place in the history of science, but in that of the church the mention of them will very frequently occur.[113]

That last sentence seems to proclaim the imminence of an account of church conflicts later in the fourth century which will have at its interpretative core the fact of intellectual miscegenation between Platonism and Christianity. But when Gibbon came eventually to write that account, the influence he attributed to Platonism, while fulfilling the letter of this promise (for it is indeed frequently mentioned), nevertheless eluded the further expectation that what he would write would be an account in the recognizably anti-Trinitarian mode of, for instance, Whiston.

The second circumstance of interpretation is an aspect of the language within which Athanasius had been discussed by his detractors. Anti-Trinitarian writers, so as to make more plausible their contention that the Catholic doctrine of the Trinity had been foisted on the Church by Athanasius in order to further his own personal ambition, had frequently committed themselves to the view that Athanasius's motivation was purely of this world, and that he was therefore to be viewed more as a politician than as a spiritual leader. For example, Whiston's 'Suspicions Concerning Athanasius' had maintained that Athanasius was an 'Ambitious, and Tyrannical' man who would stoop to any chicanery to promote his party and interest.[114] John Jackson, reviewing (as many anti-Trinitarians did) the variations in Athanasius's doctrines, noted that he had been to all appearances an Arian until he had acquired political authority: '*Athanasius*, in his first and best Writings, before he became the Head of a Party, strongly asserted the antient Doctrine of the Church, that the Father is *the only true God*, in Distinction to the Son.'[115] The anonymous anti-Trinitarian author of *The True History of the Great S^t. Athanasius . . . and of his Famous Creed* (1719) had painted the young Athanasius as 'too crafty for the honest

[113] *DF* i. 398–9.

[114] Whiston, *Primitive Christianity*, i, p. cxvi. Styan Thirlby noted that it was Whiston's intention to present Athanasius as 'an *Ambitious Ignorant Knave*' (*An Answer*, p. vii).

[115] Jackson, *Christian Liberty Asserted*, 118.

and legal Party'. As a result of these unworthy talents, he had contrived
to be elected bishop of Alexandria, and had then proceeded to lay down
a pattern of doctrinal and political corruption which would be followed
by the bishops of Rome: 'Thus, as was said of one of the Popes, *Intravit
ut Vulpes*: but how did he govern? Why, he out-did the rest of that
Pope's Character, *Regnavit ut Leo*.'[116] For Whiston, too, the career of
Athanasius demonstrated how doctrinal contamination had led to
political oppression. Athanasius's dishonesty had been at the root of 'all
the Corruptions which Pagan Philosophy and antichristian Tyranny
have brought in and impos'd upon the Church since the first Ages'.[117]
And the term Whiston had used to evoke Athanasius's improper
possession of these political talents was 'bold': 'This was a bold Stroke
with a witness; not only himself to Impose on the Church, by his
own Interpolated Copy, but to make the world believe, that the Great
Eusebius did attest to the same Interpolation, contrary to plain fact . . .'[118]
From the opposing camp, Styan Thirlby perceived that part of the
anti-Trinitarian case turned on presenting Athanasius as '*a Bold and
Daring Person*'.[119] For this reason (so Thirlby argued) they drew
attention to his ability to improvise in a crisis, implying that his self-
possession and resource indicated an expertise in the ways of this world
which was inappropriate in a spiritual leader: 'What should a lost
Man do? His desperate Case admits of nothing but a desperate Remedy;
and however that happens to succeed, he cannot be worse of it than
he is: Therefore *Athanasius* takes Post for *Constantinople* . . .'[120] The
Trinitarian riposte to this was to point out how throughout his life
Athanasius had repeatedly put himself at a political disadvantage—
strange behaviour, it was alleged, if Athanasius had really been the
consummate politician detested by the anti-Trinitarians. For William
Sherlock this shunning of political advantage therefore redounded to
Athanasius's credit: 'And if in that Age *Athanasius* were the only Man
who durst openly and boldly defend the Catholick Faith, against a prevailing Faction, supported by a Court Interest, and grown formidable
by Lies and Calumnies, and the most barbarous Cruelties, it is for his
immortal Honour, and will always be thought so by the Churches of

---

[116] [Anon.], *The True History of the Great S'. Athanasius*, 13 and 14. For further examples of
anti-Trinitarian assertions of the improperly political character of Athanasius, see e.g. *Brief Notes
on the Creed of St. Athanasius*, 2.
[117] Whiston, *Primitive Christianity*, i, p. xxiv. Again Thirlby was alert to this, blaming Whiston
for stigmatizing Athanasius as '*Resolute, Ambitious, and Tyrannical*' (*An Answer*, p. xxviii).
[118] Whiston, *Athanasius Convicted of Forgery*, 28.
[119] Thirlby, *An Answer*, p. xxii.
[120] *The True History of the Great S'. Athanasius . . . and of his Famous Creed*, 17.

Christ.'[121] Styan Thirlby agreed: 'Can it be suppos'd, that a *Tyrannical Man*, and one that sought nothing but his own private Ends, cou'd prefer Oppression to Power, Persecution to Honourable Repose, Want to Riches, and the Frowns of an Emperor to his Favour?'[122] Here again, Gibbon manoeuvred imaginatively within the languages he inherited and the positions to which they were attached. Whereas anti-Trinitarians had reviled the 'bold' Athanasius for his political acumen, and Trinitarians had commended him for his indifference to consider-ations of a political nature, Gibbon substantially endorsed the image of Athanasius as a man of exceptional political talent, and did not refrain from calling this talent boldness. But he found in this worldly accomplishment the basis for wholehearted admiration.[123]

We know that, in certain ways, Gibbon enjoyed being Delphic. The letter to Deyverdun in which he reported that both supporters of the royal prerogative and radical Whigs had found reflections of their widely divergent political sympathies in the first volume of *The Decline and Fall* is clearly an expression of satisfaction, rather than dismay.[124] But whereas in volume one that political ambiguity seems to have been created by the dispersal of seemingly contradictory opinions through-out the volume,[125] in the second instalment we are confronted by a more deeply pondered elusiveness: 'The schism of the Donatists was confined to Africa: the more diffusive mischief of the Trinitarian con-troversy successively penetrated into every part of the Christian world. The former was an accidental quarrel, occasioned by the abuse of freedom; the latter was a high and mysterious argument, derived from

---

[121] Sherlock, *Vindication*, 44.

[122] Thirlby, *An Answer*, p. xiv.

[123] See Barnes, 'Derivative Scholarship and Historical Imagination', esp. pp. 17–25, for a fascinating and learned account of the imperfection and incompleteness of Gibbon's acquain-tance with the life and writings of Athanasius. Barnes establishes that Gibbon imputed to Athanasius the political abilities which he then went on so lavishly to admire.

[124] 'Un historien est toujours jusqu'à un certain point, un politique; et chaque lecteur suivant ses opinions particulieres cherche dans les siecles les plus reculès les sentimens de l'ecrivain sur les hommes les Rois et les Gouvernemens differens. Un Sous-Ministre très attachè aux prerogatives de la Couronne m'a fait son compliment de ce que j'avois partout inculquè les plus saines maximes. M. Walpole d'un autre cotè et Mylord Cambden tous les deux partisans declarès de la libertè et meme de la Republique sont persuadès que je ne suis pas eloignès de leurs idèes: c'est une preuve de moins que j'ai observè une honnete neutralitè' (*L* ii. 107). For a similar sentiment, consider Pope's satisfaction in offending 'the *violent* of all parties' with the piece he co-wrote with Gay, *The Narrative of Dr. Robert Norris Concerning the Strange and Deplorable Frenzy of Mr John Dennis* (Pope, *Correspondence*, i. 179).

[125] For an example of Gibbon's measured support of monarchy, see his comments on the apparent disadvantages and real benefits of this form of government at the beginning of chapter seven (*DF* i. 187). For an apparently republican sentiment, consider his strictures on imperial despotism at the end of chapter three (*DF* i. 107).

the abuse of philosophy.'[126] When Gibbon says that the Trinitarian controversy was 'derived from the abuse of philosophy', is he saying that the controversy itself exemplified the abuse of philosophy and showed it in action, or rather that the controversy was occasioned by such abuse? The equivocation is not pointless, since what is at stake here is whether or not Gibbon is subscribing to the anti-Trinitarian view that the doctrine of the Trinity was nothing more than curdled Platonism. The effect achieved by the prose here is that of a slow movement, as what had seemed familiar—in this case, the well-known anti-Trinitarian interpretation which traced the doctrine of the Trinity to the consequences of Platonism—yields on closer inspection to something both less familiar and more ambiguous. Gibbon's style is deferring to the polemical imperative that critical aggression should, where possible, be anticipated and disarmed. The strategy is not one of simply belying the expected account by providing something completely opposed or different. Rather, the hostile expectation seems at first glance to be justified, only for the prose on closer scrutiny to qualify or move away from that position. And this strategy, of building something subtle and new from familiar elements, is visible not only at the level of the prose surface of these chapters in *The Decline and Fall*, but also at the level of historical interpretation. It is to this that we shall now turn.

Gibbon repeatedly uses the language of worldly prowess employed by anti-Trinitarian writers in their attempts to stigmatize Athanasius. For instance, Gibbon calls Athanasius's plan to appeal in person to Constantine in 336 AD 'a bold and dangerous experiment', and describes Athanasius 'boldly' encountering his emperor in the principal street of Constantinople.[127] His attendance at the councils of Rimini and Seleucia Gibbon views as a 'bold and dangerous . . . enterprise'.[128] Similarly, his behaviour during the sack of the church of St Theonas by the troops of Syrianus evinced, according to Gibbon, 'undaunted courage'.[129] He is, in short, 'the intrepid primate'.[130] But in Gibbon's eyes the fact that Athanasius was 'a prudent statesman' was grounds for praise, not blame.[131] As the empire mutated from a principate to a

---

[126] *DF* i. 770.

[127] *DF* i. 800: another instance of the point in question would be Gibbon's treatment of Athanasius's acumen in exploiting the political uses of stagecraft when he produced Arsenius at the synod of Tyre (*DF* i. 799).

[128] *DF* i. 814.

[129] *DF* i. 811.

[130] *DF* i. 814.

[131] *DF* i. 814. Note, too, Gibbon's willingness to exonerate Athanasius of responsibility for the notorious and inhumane creed which bears his name, on the grounds that 'it does not appear to have existed, within a century after his death' (*DF* ii. 442 n. 114).

monarchy, so political despotism became more prevalent and extended its pretensions, for Constantine and his sons 'presumed to extend their despotism over the faith, as well as over the lives and fortunes, of their subjects'.[132] However, from that very ambition arose relief, for one of the very few social forces which was capable of withstanding, to at least some degree, that rise in political despotism had come about as a result of theological dispute. *Odium theologicum* was not unambiguously friendly towards the cause of human liberty: 'The abuse of Christianity introduced into the Roman government new causes of tyranny and sedition; the bands of civil society were torn asunder by the fury of religious factions; and the obscure citizen, who might calmly have surveyed the elevation and fall of successive emperors, imagined and experienced, that his own life and fortune were connected with the interests of a popular ecclesiastic.'[133] But against that consideration needed to be set the fact that, as Gibbon acutely saw, the circum- spection with which a whole series of emperors had been obliged to proceed against Athanasius 'discovered to the world that the privileges of the church had already revived a sense of order and freedom in the Roman government'.[134] Thus when the bishop of Rome had defended Athanasius against Constantius, he had in the same breath asserted 'his own freedom'.[135] And when Athanasius, in exile, waged a pamphlet war against Constantius, the result was that 'the son of Constantine was the first of the Christian princes who experienced the strength of those principles, which, in the cause of religion, could resist the most violent exertions of the civil power'.[136] Athanasius thus emerges as a figure of effective resistance to overweening monarchy. In *The Decline and Fall* even monasticism (a religious practice which Athanasius did much to establish, and which Gibbon habitually deplores) is credited with indirectly serving the cause of liberty, since the monks gave Athanasius security in exile.

This startling insight is driven home by a series of telling recollections of republican Rome. Whereas, amongst the populace, 'ancient free- dom' endures only in the dwindled and trivial form of 'the right of treating their sovereign with familiar insolence',[137] amongst the more devout Christians the dignified aspects of the Roman republic enjoy an afterlife. Theological conflict renewed the disturbances of the republic, and thus 'the face of Rome, upon the return of a Christian bishop, renewed the horrid image of the massacres of Marius, and the pro-

[132] *DF* i. 789.   [133] *DF* i. 816.   [134] *DF* i. 805.
[135] *DF* i. 807.   [136] *DF* i. 814.   [137] *DF* i. 816.

scriptions of Sylla';[138] nevertheless, the strength of moral character in the face of violence which had characterized the patricians of the republic unexpectedly revives, in the fourth century, in monks (who die 'without a murmur', and who when captured 'silently stretched out their necks to the executioner') and in Athanasius himself, who awaits the troops of Syrianus 'seated on his throne . . . with calm and intrepid dignity'—an echo of the posture and the moral firmness of the patricians during the first sack of Rome.[139]

Gibbon, then, found a redemptive virtue in Athanasius's political prowess. In so doing, he endorsed the substance of the anti-Trinitarian analysis of Athanasius's character, but found that this analysis justified a degree (though not a quality) of praise which would not have been out of place in the writings of even so committed a Trinitarian as Waterland: 'Amidst the storms of persecution, the archbishop of Alexandria was patient of labour, jealous of fame, careless of safety; and although his mind was tainted by the contagion of fanaticism, Athanasius displayed a superiority of character and abilities, which would have qualified him, far better than the degenerate sons of Constantine, for the government of a great monarchy.'[140] The unexpected support for liberty which Gibbon saw arising from theological dogma made Athanasius a figure in whom, for Gibbon, secular strengths arose from religious partisanship. It is at this point that the juxtaposition with Julian the Apostate further advances Gibbon's eluding of his critics, so that, like the ministers of Pilate (at least according to the heresy of the Docetes), they wasted 'their impotent rage on an airy phantom'.[141]

The juxtaposition of Julian and Athanasius acquires salience, because Gibbon built on the historical accident that Athanasius and Julian were contemporaries by giving them certain characteristics in common. We have seen that Gibbon characterized Athanasius in part in terms of boldness. He did the same with Julian, who in his rebellion against Constantius conceived a 'bold enterprise', and who knew that as a rebel 'boldness only could command success'.[142] An aspect of Athanasius's boldness was his speed of executing what he had resolved upon.[143] Julian, too, was a man of 'vigorous and immediate resolution' who

[138] *DF* i. 817.
[139] *DF* i. 822, 812, and 811. For the behaviour of the patricians during the first sack of Rome, see Livy, *Ab Urbe Condita*, V. xli.
[140] *DF* i. 796.
[141] *DF* i. 774–5.
[142] *DF* i. 842 and 845.
[143] e.g. *DF* i. 800.

shared with Athanasius (at least in *The Decline and Fall*) a habit of 'unexpected arrival'.[144] The 'celerity of his motions' astonished his enemies, and elicited the admiration of his subjects:

Before the Barbarians were recovered from their amazement, the emperor appeared in arms on the banks of the Rhine . . .

The banks of the Danube were crowded on either side with spectators, who gazed on the military pomp, anticipated the importance of the event, and diffused through the adjacent country the fame of a young hero, who advanced with more than mortal speed at the head of the innumerable forces of the West.[145]

Even his administration displayed the same characteristic of unrelenting speed: 'He . . . signified his intentions more rapidly than they could be taken in short-hand by the diligence of his secretaries . . .'[146] However, although Gibbon attributed certain qualities to both Julian and Athanasius, the purpose of this limited point of contact was to make possible a more emphatic separation of the two men. Gibbon recorded Julian's particular aversion for Athanasius: 'Julian, who despised the Christians, honoured Athanasius with his sincere and peculiar hatred.'[147] That personal antipathy forms part of a broader array of respects in which *The Decline and Fall* sharply opposes the two men. It is an opposition which Gibbon developed in symbolic terms, as well as at the level of conscious action.[148] For instance, Athanasius is presented to the reader of *The Decline and Fall* in terms of self-possession and singleness of character. Gibbon has insinuated that it is a characteristic of the doctrine of the Trinity that, with its baffling contentions about the divine identity, it seems to unhinge the identity of those who contemplate it, so that even Constantine himself, 'in the midst of faction and fanaticism', was barely able to preserve 'the calm possession of his own mind'.[149] Only Athanasius, it seems, was proof against the disequilibration, the lapse from singleness into fragmentation and plurality, stimulated by contact with this doctrine:

We have seldom an opportunity of observing, either in active or speculative life, what effect may be produced, or what obstacles may be surmounted, by the force of a single mind, when it is inflexibly applied to the pursuit of a single

144 *DF* i. 842, 844.
145 *DF* i. 843; 840; 845.
146 *DF* i. 851.
147 *DF* i. 905.
148 For the actual conflict between the two men, see *DF* i. 904–6.
149 *DF* i. 790.

object. The immortal name of Athanasius will never be separated from the Catholic doctrine of the Trinity, to whose defence he consecrated every moment and every faculty of his being.[150]

As a result of this singleness of focus, Athanasius was able to preserve 'a distinct and unbroken view of a scene which was incessantly shifting'.[151] By contrast, Julian's character was deeply marked by that peculiar form of plurality which derives from vanity and affectation:

But with the fopperies, Julian affected to renounce the decencies, of dress; and seemed to value himself for his neglect of the laws of cleanliness. In a satirical performance, which was designed for the public eye, the emperor descants with pleasure, and even with pride, on the length of his nails, and the inky blackness of his hands; protests, that although the greatest part of his body was covered with hair, the use of the razor was confined to his head alone; and celebrates, with visible complacency, the shaggy and *populous* beard, which he fondly cherished, after the example of the philosophers of Greece. Had Julian consulted the simple dictates of reason, the first magistrate of the Romans would have scorned the affectation of Diogenes, as well as that of Darius.[152]

Julian possessed 'real or *affected* humanity'; his throne was 'the seat of reason, of virtue, and perhaps of *vanity*'; he viewed the luxury of the imperial court 'with *affected* surprise'; he 'placed his *vanity*, not in emulating, but in despising, the pomp of royalty'; his contempt of treason was 'the result of judgment, of *vanity*, and of courage'; his deference to the consuls was an '*affected* humility'; he regretted the execution of Theodoret, Count of the East, 'with real or *affected* concern'; his manners displayed a 'severe simplicity' which was 'always maintained, and sometimes *affected*'.[153] Even in death, Gibbon detected a disabling trace of self-consciousness: 'In his last moments he displayed, perhaps with some ostentation, the love of virtue and of fame, which had been the ruling passions of his life.'[154]

The source of this corruption of character in Julian was, according to Gibbon, the peculiar nature of his religious beliefs. Chapter twenty-three was devoted to a description of the emperor's idiosyncratic creed, and Gibbon insisted at the outset on the harmful consequences of the peculiar form of pagan belief which Julian had fashioned for himself: 'A devout and sincere attachment for the gods of Athens and Rome, constituted the ruling passion of Julian; the powers of an enlightened

[150] *DF* i. 796.
[151] *DF* i. 797.
[152] *DF* i. 855.
[153] *DF* i. 849; 851; 853; 854; 857–8; 859; 900; emphases added.
[154] *DF* i. 945.

understanding were betrayed and corrupted by the influence of superstitious prejudice; and the phantoms which existed only in the mind of
the emperor, had a real and pernicious effect on the government of the
empire.'[155] Julian did not renounce Christianity for simple paganism,
but rather for paganism overlaid by and interpreted through Neoplatonic philosophy. Acknowledging Plato for his 'master',[156] Julian
adopted a creed 'of the largest dimensions'.[157] In the first place, he
accepted without hesitation the most extravagant elements in the
'thousand loose and flexible parts' which comprised 'the mythology of
the Greeks':

> by a strange contradiction, he disdained the salutary yoke of the Gospel, whilst
> he made a voluntary offering of his reason on the altars of Jupiter and Apollo.
> One of the orations of Julian is consecrated to the honour of Cybele, the
> mother of the gods, who required from her effeminate priests the bloody
> sacrifice, so rashly performed by the madness of the Phrygian boy. The pious
> emperor condescends to relate without a blush, and without a smile, the
> voyage of the goddess from the shores of Pergamus to the mouth of the Tyber;
> and the stupendous miracle, which convinced the senate and people of Rome
> that the lump of clay, which their ambassadors had transported over the seas,
> was endowed with life, and sentiment, and divine power.[158]

But in addition to embracing and encouraging 'the superstition of the
people', Julian also indulged in esoteric interpretation of the pagan
mythology. Here he had fallen under the guidance of the 'philosophers
of the Platonic school', especially Ædesius, in whose company he
'silently withdrew from the foot of the altars into the sanctuary of
the temple'.[159] He had thus become enslaved to a cult in which both
philosophy and religion were perverted:

> This freedom of interpretation, which might gratify the pride of the Platonists,
> exposed the vanity of their art. Without a tedious detail, the modern reader
> could not form a just idea of the strange allusions, the forced etymologies, the
> solemn trifling, and the impenetrable obscurity of these sages, who professed to
> reveal the system of the universe. As the traditions of pagan mythology were

[155] *DF* i. 864.

[156] *DF* i. 850.

[157] *DF* i. 868.

[158] *DF* i. 868. In the course of this chapter Gibbon offers a wholesale condemnation of paganism: 'But the genius and power of Julian were unequal to the enterprise of restoring a religion,
which was destitute of theological principles, of moral precepts, and of ecclesiastical discipline;
which rapidly hastened to decay and dissolution, and was not susceptible of any solid or consistent reformation' (*DF* i. 879); a passage which it is instructive to compare with his sentiment of
1791, that 'The primitive Church, which I have treated with some freedom, was itself at that
time, an innovation, and *I* was attached to the old Pagan establishment' (*L* iii. 216).

[159] *DF* i. 868–9.

variously related, the sacred interpreters were at liberty to select the most convenient circumstances; and as they translated an arbitrary cypher, they could extract from *any* fable *any* sense which was adapted to their favourite system of religion and philosophy.[160]

It was this malign form of religion, an 'unnatural alliance of philosophy and superstition', which inserted into Julian's character the 'enthusiasm which clouded his virtues', and which ensured that 'the deadly spirit of fanaticism'—one of Gibbon's strongest terms of disapproval—'perverted the heart and understanding of a virtuous prince': 'In the caverns of Ephesus and Eleusis, the mind of Julian was penetrated with sincere, deep, and unalterable enthusiasm; though he might sometimes exhibit the vicissitudes of pious fraud and hypocrisy, which may be observed, or at least suspected, in the characters of the most conscientious fanatics.'[161] We need to pause at this point to gauge just how this strand of religious fanaticism in Julian's character interacts with the surrounding narrative. In the first place, it is clear that Gibbon has accepted Bentley's analysis of the imbecility of Julian's religion, and that he is therefore not pursuing the line of interpretation which would have been expected of a philosophical freethinker. Secondly, Gibbon's diagnosis of Platonic infection in Julian unfolds interesting implications in relation to Athanasius. As we have noted, it was a frequent assertion of the anti-Trinitarians that the Catholic doctrine of the Trinity, as forged by Athanasius, was traceable to the influence of Neoplatonic philosophy. Gibbon had begun chapter twenty-one with a review of the dissemination of Platonic doctrine through the near east in the centuries following the death of Plato himself, and had therefore encouraged his reader to view the Trinitarian controversy in the context of 'the progress of reason and faith, of error and passion, from the school of Plato to the decline and fall of the empire'.[162] But at no point does he suggest any Platonic affinities in the mind of Athanasius; and the result of this, when taken with the emphatic attribution of Neoplatonic enthusiasm to Julian, is that an expected element in Gibbon's account of the fourth century has been moved from its anticipated location. If you are looking for evidence of the corrupting influence of Platonism in this period, Gibbon implies, then it is in Julian, rather than in Athanasius, that you will find it. The migration of qualities from one figure to another is underlined and taken further when Gibbon finds in

---

[160] *DF* i. 869.

[161] *DF* i. 872; 864; 906; 872. Contrast the more limited extent to which Athanasius is said to have been affected by fanaticism: *DF* i. 796.

[162] *DF* i. 771 ff.

Julian the 'true spirit of a bigot' and even 'the skill of a Jesuit'.[163] It was
Athanasius whom the hard-line anti-Trinitarians had impugned as the
fount of all Roman Catholic corruptions, in an attempt to render
members of the Church of England uncomfortable with their defence
of him.[164] Gibbon, however, saw foreshadowings of the most egregious
forms of popery in Julian, rather than in Athanasius.

In this way the figures of Julian and Athanasius become linked
through opposition. And just as we find a transferral of expected philosophical allegiance between the two men, so we also find a similar
transferral of political qualities. Gibbon depicted Athanasius, who had
defied the despotism of successive emperors, as an unexpected but
nevertheless welcome champion of liberty: a surprising insight, because
of the importance of Athanasius in the pre-history of the Roman
Catholic Church, which in the minds of Englishmen at least earlier in
the eighteenth century had been closely linked with arbitrary government. In contrast, Julian, admired by the *philosophes* and freethinkers as
a hero who had tried to undo the incipient spiritual oppression of
Christianity,[165] is in Gibbon's account impelled towards political
tyranny by his religious fanaticism.[166] The 'partial spirit of his administration' results in a 'secret and vexatious tyranny'.[167] It is a characterization sealed by an allusion. Julian ordered Ecdicius, the præfect of Egypt,
to move against Athanasius:

> The death of Athanasius was not *expressly* commanded; but the præfect of
> Egypt understood, that it was safer for him to exceed, than to neglect, the
> orders of an irritated master. The archbishop prudently retired to the monas-
> teries of the Desert: eluded, with his usual dexterity, the snares of the enemy;
> and lived to triumph over the ashes of a prince, who, in words of formidable

---

[163] *DF* i. 892 n. 87; 879–80 n. 37.

[164] e.g.: 'So that at the same Time these Fathers restor'd *Athanasius*, they set up Anti-Christ. I
challenge all his Vindicators to deny, (if they can) that the Pope's Supremacy was first decree'd
and ordain'd by this *Sardican Conventicle* of *Western* Bishops, that restor'd *Athanasius*; and consequently, that *Popery* and *Athanasianism* were introduc'd at the same Time, and by the same
Persons' ([Anon.], *The True History of the Great S'. Athanasius . . . and of his Famous Creed*, 24); cf.
[Anon.], *The Acts of Great Athanasius*, 16.

[165] e.g. Montesquieu, *Considérations sur la grandeur des romains et de leur décadence*, ch. 17; cf. also
Womersley, *Transformation*, 158 n. 10. William Robertson, writing to Gibbon on 12 May 1781,
voiced his apprehension that '*you* might lean with some partiality towards him [Julian]; but even
bigots, I should think, must allow, that you have delineated his most singular character with a
more masterly hand than ever touched it before' (*MW 1796* i. 551).

[166] Note that Gibbon says that 'his superstition disturbed the peace, and endangered the
safety, of a mighty empire' (*DF* i. 958); and this is because 'before the emperor could have extinguished the religion of Christ, he must have involved his country in the horrors of a civil war'
(*DF* i. 908).

[167] *DF* i. 903; 894.

import, had declared his wish that the whole venom of the Galilæan school were contained in the single person of Athanasius.[168]

The recollection is of Caligula's famous wish, that the Roman people had only one neck.[169] Whereas the life of Athanasius puts Gibbon in mind of the turbulent liberty and moral firmness of the republic, Julian's petulant vindictiveness recalls some of the darkest days of the early principate. Although the emperor may use the forms of 'the expiring republic' in his letters to the senate, Gibbon's judgement was unequivocal: the essence of Julian's government was despotic.[170]

A repeated feature of Gibbon's portrait of Julian is the recurrent disquiet that, in some elusive way, he is flawed or disappointing:

An innumerable multitude pressed around him with eager respect; and were perhaps disappointed when they beheld the small stature, and simple garb, of a hero, whose unexperienced youth had vanquished the Barbarians of Germany, and who had now traversed, in a successful career, the whole continent of Europe, from the shores of the Atlantic to those of the Bosphorus.

When we inspect, with minute, or perhaps malevolent attention, the portrait of Julian, something seems wanting to the grace and perfection of the whole figure.

Our partial ignorance may represent him [Julian] as a philosophic monarch, who studied to protect, with an equal hand, the religious factions of the empire; and to allay the theological fever which had inflamed the minds of the people, from the edicts of Diocletian to the exile of Athanasius. A more accurate view of the character and conduct of Julian, will remove this favourable prepossession for a prince who did not escape the general contagion of the times.[171]

Whereas in the first of these examples, the disappointment experienced by the 'innumerable multitude' who pressed around Julian could be attributed to their unreasonable expectations, it is surely harder to dispense with the second and third. We should not read these naively as actual expressions of disappointment on Gibbon's part, but rather as moves towards a measured separation of *The Decline and Fall* from the tradition of philosophic eulogy of Julian.[172] And just as in *The Decline and Fall* Julian emerges as a somehow shrunken figure, so Athanasius takes on stature.

---

[168] *DF* i. 906.

[169] 'Utinam p. R. unam cervicem haberet!' (Suetonius, *Gaius Caligula*, XXX. 2).

[170] *DF* i. 847.

[171] *DF* i. 849; 863; 864.

[172] For other disengagements from the philosophic in these chapters, see e.g. *DF* i. 824 (Raynal and Montesquieu).

V

As we pause now to review how Gibbon met the pressures of controversy by which he had been surrounded as he composed his account of
relations between empire and Church in the fourth century, it may be
helpful to begin by focusing on a striking passage describing the education of the young Julian:

> But the independent spirit of Julian refused to yield the passive and unresisting
> obedience which was required, in the name of religion, by the haughty
> ministers of the church. Their speculative opinions were imposed as positive
> laws, and guarded by the terrors of eternal punishments; but while they
> prescribed the rigid formulary of the thoughts, the words, and the actions of the
> young prince; whilst they silenced his objections, and severely checked the
> freedom of his enquiries, they secretly provoked his impatient genius to dis-
> claim the authority of his ecclesiastical guides. He was educated in the Lesser
> Asia, amidst the scandals of the Arian controversy.[10] The fierce contests of the
> Eastern bishops, the incessant alterations of their creeds, and the profane
> motives which appeared to actuate their conduct, insensibly strengthened the
> prejudice of Julian, that they neither understood nor believed the religion for
> which they so fiercely contended. Instead of listening to the proofs of
> Christianity with that favourable attention which adds weight to the most
> respectable evidence, he heard with suspicion, and disputed with obstinacy
> and acuteness, the doctrines for which he already entertained an invincible
> aversion.[173]

And the text of note 10 reads as follows:

> See Julian apud Cyril. l.vi. p.206. l.viii. p.253. 262. 'You persecute,' says he,
> 'those heretics who do not mourn the dead man precisely in the way which
> you approve.' He shews himself a tolerable theologian; but he maintains that
> the Christian Trinity is not derived from the doctrine of Paul, of Jesus, or of
> Moses.

Here Gibbon sets out the connection between Julian the Apostate
and the doctrine of the Trinity. The corruption of the young prince's
religious sensibility is traced to the fact that he had been educated
'amidst the scandals of the Arian controversy'. His response, as presented by Gibbon in the text and note quoted above, recalls that of the
various kinds of anti-Trinitarians who had in more recent times subjected the doctrine of the Trinity and its adherents to hostile scrutiny.
Like Arians such as Whiston, Julian suspects that the doctrine of the
Trinity was a recent interloper into the fold of Christian theology, and

[173] *DF* i. 866–7.

was 'not derived from the doctrine of Paul, of Jesus, or of Moses'. Like the freethinkers and deists of the late seventeenth and early eighteenth centuries, he deplores the spirit of persecution which motivates the champions of doctrinal purity, and views the debates themselves as a mere logomachy, in which the disputants 'neither understood nor believed the religion for which they so fiercely contended'.

These implied comparisons between late antiquity and the religious history of the more recent past in England are laid as a delicate film over the historical narrative, but they are nevertheless there to be read, and their implications shed light on Gibbon's strategy as a controversialist in these chapters. Gibbon discovered in Julian the perceptions and the values which Gibbon's critics, scandalized by the irreligion of the first volume, had imputed to Gibbon himself. That Gibbon should then have gone on to dissect with such acuity how these perceptions and values generated, not enlightenment, but fanaticism in Julian, reflects back on the historian's own position in these chapters. As we have seen, Gibbon eluded his critics by manoeuvring brilliantly in the historical terrain where they encountered one another: like Athanasius himself, he frustrates and evades the clumsy attempts of those who would confine and imprison him. The positions where his clerical adversaries noisily expected him, he shunned. The ground they had assumed to be their own, he occupied. To that extent, these chapters of *The Decline and Fall* are a triumph, and it is therefore understandable that Gibbon should have voiced his sense of justifiable satisfaction with the intertwined portraits which lie at their centre. Of Julian, he recorded in draft 'E' of his 'Memoirs' that 'my impartial balance of the virtues and vices of Julian was generally praised'.[174] Of Athanasius, a footnote in chapter fifty-six concerning Gregory VII, 'a second Athanasius', expressed Gibbon's contentment with his portrait of the Apostate's antagonist: 'May I presume to add, that the portrait of Athanasius is one of the passages of my history . . . with which I am the least dissatisfied?'[175]

Yet contentment is not the whole story. There is a quality of incompleteness in Gibbon's claims. Just before his, perhaps complacent, recollection of the reception of his account of Julian, Gibbon touched more generally on the circumstances of publication of his second and third volumes: 'In this interval of my Senatorial life, I published the second and third Volumes of the decline and fall. My Ecclesiastical history still breathed the same spirit of freedom; but Protestant zeal is more indifferent to the characters and controversies of the fourth and fifth Centuries . . .'.[176] The analysis pursued in this chapter, which has traced both the keen interest in the characters and controversies of the fourth century evinced by controversialists in the Church of England from the late seventeenth century, and Gibbon's artful response to that keen interest, has given us good grounds for doubting both that Gibbon did in fact persist with 'the same spirit of freedom' in this second instalment, and that its subject matter was of less concern to the orthodox.

Conveniently enough, corroboration of both aspects of our doubt is available from contemporaries. On the publication of the second instalment of *The Decline and Fall* William Robertson wrote a note of congratulation to Gibbon, which culminated in the sentiment that 'I cannot conclude without approving of the caution with which the new volumes are written; I hope it will exempt you from the illiberal abuse the first volume drew upon you.'[177] So much for 'the same spirit of freedom'. And James Chelsum, writing in 1785, found that the second instalment of *The Decline and Fall* gave him no reason to moderate his opinion of Gibbon's irreligion: 'There may be found in them [volumes two and three], on due examination, much of the same species of poison as infected the former volume; much apparent spirit of prejudice, and much seeming eagerness to relate whatever may reflect either ridicule or disgrace upon the primitive Church.'[178] So much for greater indifference. Gibbon may have wished (for reasons which we shall consider below) to imply in draft 'E' of his 'Memoirs' that his difficulties with his critics were all now concluded business, and that the outstanding matters between them had now been adjusted to, if not the complete satisfaction of both parties, then at least their practical acquiescence—'my obstinate silence had damped the ardour of the polemics; Dr. Watson, the most candid of my adversaries, assured me that he had no thoughts of renewing the attack . . .'.[179] But the reality was different. Despite his adroit footwork, Gibbon knew that the discussions provoked by his work would continue, and would therefore continue to create difficulties for him which he would need to negotiate with great care. One such was the attempt by Priestley in *The Corruptions of Christianity* (1782) to conscript Gibbon to his own Unitarian and radical causes: an attempt which an alarmed Gibbon repulsed with vigour.[180] As we shall see when we examine the third instalment of

---

[176] *A* 322.
[177] *MW 1796* i. 552.
[178] Chelsum, *Reply*, 128.
[179] *A* 322.
[180] On which, see Turnbull, 'Gibbon's Exchange with Joseph Priestley'.

1788, the move to Lausanne in 1783 did little in practice to remove Gibbon from the attention of those who continued to be curious about both what he had written and what he would go on to write. We can now understand the trace of disquiet embodied in the allusion to *The Dunciad* with which we began. Gibbon had dived too deep into the mud of the Arian controversy, because traces of polemical mud had stuck to the historian's coat. We can now appreciate the justness of the allusion's implication. In allowing his critics to dictate his stance and mode of treatment of this period of the Roman past, Gibbon had in some measure allowed the historian to become submerged in the polemicist. The censure he had expressed concerning Epiphanius—a censure which reveals Gibbon's awareness of the separateness of the historian from the polemicist—might thus in some measure be applied to himself: 'we cannot but regret that he [Epiphanius] should soon forget the historian, to assume the task of controversy.'[181]

But if, while writing his 'Memoirs' and when reviewing the composition of this section of *The Decline and Fall*, Gibbon concealed some stubborn causes of dissatisfaction, he seems also to have overlooked elements of his achievement which, from our standpoint, are of particular interest and value. The doctrine of the Trinity is a rich source of paradoxes on not only the subject of identity, but also on those of affinity, interconnection, and aversion. In the words of a passage of Hilary quoted by Gibbon: 'Every year, nay every moon, we make new creeds to describe invisible mysteries. We repent of what we have done, we defend those who repent, we anathematise those whom we defended. We condemn either the doctrine of others in ourselves, or our own in that of others; and reciprocally tearing one another to pieces, we have been the cause of each other's ruin.'[182] In the midst of these vicissitudes of attraction and repulsion, those things which are separated can also be united, those things which are opposed can also be aligned. The antagonism between Gibbon and his critics lies on the surface of this episode in the composition of *The Decline and Fall*. But beneath that surface of aggression, those critics were also secret sharers in the business of historical composition. Unwelcome as their attentions may have initially seemed, the 'Watchmen of the Holy City' nevertheless stimulated Gibbon to become the historian he wished to be.[183] It was their monitory marking out of the obvious lines of interpretation—lines of

---

[181] *DF* i. 779 n. 43.

[182] *DF* i. 785. Cf. also Gibbon's comments on the '$\pi\epsilon\rho\iota\chi\omega\rho\upsilon\sigma\iota\varsigma$, or *circumincessio*' which is 'perhaps the deepest and darkest corner of the whole theological abyss' (*DF* i. 783 n. 59).

[183] I am grateful to John Pocock for this insight (private communication).

interpretation which the first volume of *The Decline and Fall*, and in particular chapter fifteen, suggests Gibbon might have been happy to pursue—which obliged Gibbon to discern and develop a more subtle vision of the relation between Church and emperor during the fourth century. And this more subtle vision shaped the chapters from the second instalment of *The Decline and Fall* which we have just examined. The resulting narrative thus invites consideration as (to use some of the technical language generated by the doctrine of the Trinity itself) a procession or emanation from the strong repulsion which existed between Gibbon and his clerical critics.

This strange conversion of adversaries into collaborators is also an aspect of the drama of Gibbon's reputation which we shall find repeated in the crucial chapters on Mahomet and Islam in the third instalment of *The Decline and Fall*.

4

'Enthusiasm and Imposture':
Gibbon and Mahomet

As a child and as a youth, Gibbon's imagination had been captured by Arabia and Islam.[1] It had been a boyish enthusiasm for the 'Arabian Nights'[2] which had enticed him towards more scholarly reading:

Mahomet and his Saracens soon fixed my attention, and some instinct of criticism directed me to the genuine sources. Simon Ockley, an original in every sense, first opened my eyes, and I was led from one book to another till I had ranged round the circle of Oriental history. Before I was sixteen I had exhausted all that could be learned in English of the Arabs and Persians, the Tartars and Turks; and the same ardour urged me to guess at the French of d'Herbelot, and to construe the barbarous Latin of Pocock's Abulpharagius.[3]

And during the brief period when he was resident at Magdalen College, Oxford, Gibbon had hoped to turn that childish enthusiasm into a regular course of study: 'Since the days of Pocock and Hyde, Oriental learning has always been the pride of Oxford, and I once expressed an inclination to study Arabic. His [Gibbon's first tutor, Dr. Waldegrave's] prudence discouraged this childish fancy; but he neglected the fair occasion of directing the ardour of a curious mind.'[4] Denied the chance to apply himself to Oriental learning, Gibbon bewildered himself in the mazes of Catholic theology, became a Roman Catholic, and was obliged to leave Oxford. But later, in March 1776, and when Gibbon was newly notorious as the author of *The Decline and Fall*, the vicissi-

---

[1] Two recent accounts of Gibbon's handling of Mahomet are noteworthy, although neither of them is sensitive to the polemical context within which this section of *The Decline and Fall* requires to be understood: Lewis, 'Gibbon on Muhammad', and Jallais, 'Gibbon et la pierre noire de l'Islam'. I owe my awareness of the latter article to the kindness of John Walsh.

[2] *A* 49, 118, 223, 296, and 393–4.

[3] *A* 58 (draft 'F'). Compare *A* 24 (draft 'C'): 'My curiosity was stimulated by the remoteness of time and place; and while I had a superficial knowledge of the modern transactions of Europe, I was familiarly conversant with the Arabian Caliphs, the Khans of Tartary, the outlying Empires (as Sir William Temple styles them) of China and Peru, and the dark and doubtful Dynasties of Assyria and Egypt.' [4] *A* 78–9.

tudes of his religious enthusiasms in the 1750s had somehow become public knowledge. I refer to the well-known conversation between Boswell and Johnson, recorded in the *Life*:

We talked of a work much in vogue at that time, written in a very mellifluous style, but which, under pretext of another subject, contained much artful infidelity. I said it was not fair to attack us thus unexpectedly; he should have warned us of our danger, before we entered his garden of flowery eloquence, by advertising, 'Spring-guns and men-traps set here.' The authour had been an Oxonian, and was remembered there for having 'turned Papist'. I observed, that as he had changed several times—from the Church of England to the Church of Rome,—from the Church of Rome to infidelity,—I did not despair yet of seeing him a methodist preacher. JOHNSON. (laughing,) 'It is said, that his range has been more extensive, and that he has once been Mahometan. However, now that he has published his infidelity, he will probably persist in it.' BOSWELL. 'I am not quite sure of that, Sir.'[5]

Gibbon's apostasy seems to have caused some comment at the time,[6] and so it is conceivable—though still perhaps surprising, given Gibbon's anonymity in the interim—that it might form part of Boswell and Johnson's conversation over twenty years later. But it is surely stretching the bounds of credibility to imagine that Johnson might have heard of Gibbon's fleeting undergraduate intention to study Arabic, and that he might be alluding to that when he spoke of Gibbon having once been 'Mahometan'. Yet, if not to that, then to what was Johnson referring when he used the word 'Mahometan'? At this point it is helpful to recall that, in eighteenth-century England, 'Mahometan' was a mildly abusive term for anti-Trinitarian Christians, such as the Socinians or Unitarians.[7] As Thomas Mangey wrote in reply to a work

---

[5] Boswell, *Life of Johnson*, 695. Gibbon alluded to this passage from the *Life* in his own 'Memoirs': *A* 88.

[6] 'By the keen protestants who would gladly retaliate the example of persecution, a clamour is raised of the encrease of popery, and they are always loud to declaim against the toleration of priests and Jesuits who pervert so many of his Majesty's subjects from their Religion and Allegiance. On the present occasion [that of Gibbon's own change of confession], the fall of one or more of her sons directed this clamour against the University; and it was confidently affirmed that Popish missionaries were suffered, under various disguises, to introduce themselves into the Colleges of Oxford' (*A* 87).

[7] Although the set of terms for non-Trinitarians (Socinians, Arians, Unitarians, Mahometans, etc.) was often used in the eighteenth century without any very great respect for the shades of theological difference between them, it is nevertheless useful at the outset to state those differences clearly. Orthodox Trinitarian Christians believe that Father, Son, and Holy Ghost are consubstantial and coeternal. Arians, named after the early Church Father Arius (*c.* 250–336), hold that, while the Son partakes of the Father's divine nature, He was ineffably generated from the Father at some time before the creation of the world, and is therefore not coeternal. Socinians, named after the Italian-born lay theologian Paolo Sozini, or Socinus (1539–1604),

of John Toland's which we shall consider later, 'Protestants have been formerly very watchful against the Growth of the *Unitarian* Notions, and have in their Discourses call'd them *Mahometans*.'[8] So Johnson was probably not revealing any inside knowledge about Gibbon's frustrated undergraduate ambitions when he speculated that he might have been a 'Mahometan' while at Oxford. Instead, he was glancing once more at Gibbon's general reputation for religious heterodoxy by endorsing the supposition—which, as we have seen in Chapter 3, Gibbon himself had tried energetically to muddy—that the historian of *The Decline and Fall* harboured unorthodox views on the doctrine of the Trinity. So Johnson and Boswell's conversation sends us back to the polemical use of writing on Islam from the late seventeenth century onwards: a field which we shall have to master if we wish to understand an important area of engagement between Gibbon and his critics in the 1780s.

II

Although interest in Islam had existed in medieval Christendom, it was only in the seventeenth century that scholarly study of the new religion, and the culture from which it had emerged, gathered momentum.[9] It was chiefly in the Protestant states of northern Europe—in England, Germany and Holland—that a confluence of motives impelled scholars to the acquisition of the Arabic language, and to the editing and translation of the most important Islamic texts, including of course the

maintain that the Son did not exist until He was born of the Virgin, and that therefore He is neither consubstantial nor coeternal. Unitarians might associate themselves to any hue of the spectrum of opinion extending from the Arians to the Socinians. On the significance of the doctrine of the Trinity in eighteenth-century England, see Young, *Religion and Enlightenment*.

[8] Mangey, *Remarks upon Nazarenus*, 49–50. It was in this sense that Henry Sacheverell had used the word 'Mahometan', in what was undoubtedly the most notorious English sermon of the eighteenth century (Holmes, *Trial of Doctor Sacheverell*, 67).

[9] General studies include: Ernest Renan, *Études d'histoire religieuse* (Paris, 1857); Pierre Martino, *L'Orient dans la littérature française au XVIIᵉ et au XVIIIIᵉ siècle* (Paris, 1906) and 'Mahomet en France au XVIIᵉ et au XVIIIᵉ siècle', in *Actes du XIVᵉ Congrès international des Orientalistes: Alger 1905*, part III (Paris, 1907), 206–41; Johann Fück, *Die arabischen Studien in Europa bis den Anfang des 20. Jahrhunderts* (Leipzig, 1955); N. A. Smirnov, *Islam and Russia* (London, 1956); Aldobrandino Malvezzi, *L'Islamismo e la cultura europea* (Florence, 1956); Dorothy Vaughan, *Europe and the Turk: A Pattern of Alliances* (Liverpool, 1954); G. E. von Grunebaum, 'Islam: The Problem of Changing Perspective', in Lynn White Jr. (ed.), *The Transformation of the Roman World: Gibbon's Problem After Two Centuries* (Berkeley and Los Angeles: University of California Press, 1966), 147–78; G. H. Bousquet, 'Voltaire et l'Islam', in *Studia Islamica*, fasc. 28 (1968), 109–26; P. M. Holt, *Studies in the History of the Near East* (London, 1973); Djavad Hadidi, *Voltaire et l'Islam* (Paris, 1974); N. Matar, *Islam in Britain 1558–1685* (Cambridge: Cambridge University Press, 1998); N. Matar, *Turks, Moors & Englishmen in the Age of Discovery* (New York: Columbia University Press, 1999).

Qur'ān.[10] Increased European trade in the Levant supplemented the
usual Spanish channels whereby Arabian culture had been disseminated
in Western Europe. This gave scholars the chance to visit these lands
and peoples, which were of interest to them partly because of the sidelights they might throw on the Hebrew text of the Old Testament, and
more opportunistically because here might be found allies against
the Church of Rome. In England, the major figures in this scholarly
tradition were Edward Pococke (1604–91), who in 1630 had been
appointed Chaplain in Aleppo by the Levant Company, who took up
the Laudian Chair of Arabic in Oxford in 1636, and whose *Specimen
Historiæ Arabum* (Oxford, 1648–50)—a translation of a fragment of the
Arabian chronicler Bar Hebraeus (or 'Abulpharagius' to Gibbon)—
Gibbon had read in the early 1750s; Simon Ockley (1678–1720),
Professor of Arabic in Cambridge, whose *History of the Saracens* in two
volumes (1708 and 1718) was, as we have seen, one of the books which
sharpened the young Gibbon's appetite for Oriental learning; and
George Sale (1697?–1736), an autodidact whose translation of the
Qur'ān was for long the most authoritative in any modern European
language. In Germany there was Johann Jakob Reiske (1716–74), who
had published at his own expense a Latin translation of the chronicle of
Abu'l-Fida (or 'Abulfeda' to Gibbon) under the title of *Annales*. In
Holland Adrian Reland (1676–1718) had written a treatise on Islamic
religion, the *De Religione Mohammedica* (Utrecht, 1717), praised by
Gibbon as 'an excellent treatise'.[11] Amongst French scholars, Jean
Gagnier (1670–1740) had published an edition of Abu'l-Fida, and also
La Vie de Mahomet, a biography of the prophet in two volumes
(Amsterdam, 1732), while the traveller and amateur orientalist Claude
Savary (1758–88) had published in 1783 a derivative translation of the
Qur'ān. The work on which Savary had mainly relied was that of the
Italian priest and scholar, Lodovico Marracci (1612–1700). His trans-
lation of the Qur'ān, accompanied by a refutation of Islam, had been
published in 1698, and was admired by Gibbon as 'virulent, but
learned'.[12]

As the example of Marracci shows, much of this scholarly activity
was far from dispassionate.[13] In particular, the patronage which the

[10] The footnotes to chapter fifty in *The Decline and Fall* record Gibbon's reading in this tradition of scholarship: cf. particularly *DF* iii. 190, n. 111.

[11] *DF* iii. 184, n. 101.

[12] *DF* iii. 189, n. 110.

[13] In this résumé of the polemical use of writing on Islam, I am greatly indebted to the work
of Justin Champion, especially chapter four of his *The Pillars of Priestcraft Shaken*, 99–132.

Church of England had extended to Arabic studies through the universities of Oxford and Cambridge suggests that Islam had been identified as a potential battleground between the forces of religious orthodoxy and their enemies. The fact that the creed of Mahomet insisted on the essential unity of God meant that it leant itself to being used as a stalking horse in disputes between various shades of Christian opinion. In the late seventeenth and early eighteenth centuries, as we have seen in Chapter 3, there were many in the Church of England who found the doctrine of the Trinity difficult to digest. They varied from the famous and preferred, such as John Locke, Thomas Firmin, Arthur Bury (the Rector of Exeter College, Oxford), and John Tillotson (who would in due course become archbishop of Canterbury), to lesser figures such as Stephen Nye, William Freke, and Henry Hedworth. For these men the doctrine of the Trinity was, as William Freke put it, the 'stumbling block in Christianity'.[14] Invented by Athanasius to meet a political emergency, it had been foisted upon primitive, pure, Christianity, and had obliterated the monotheistic nature of that religion with what they abusively dismissed with the term 'tritheism'. As Stephen Nye had pointed out, the doctrine of the Trinity (which he stigmatized in the customary way as putrescent Platonism) had not existed before the Council of Nicea in May 325; and he went on to argue that all the Roman Catholic doctrines most repugnant to Protestants had been derived from this original infection.[15] For these men, the religion promulgated by Mahomet, while of course corrupt and worldly in many respects, nevertheless was valuable to Christians in that, properly approached and handled, it might give them access to Christianity in its uncorrupted, monotheistic, form.

The riposte from the orthodox was prompt, and followed predictable lines. Works such as John Edwards's *Socinianism Unmasked* (1696), Francis Fullwood's *A Parallel: Wherein it Appears that the Socinian Agrees with the Papist* (1693), and Charles Leslie's *Socinian Controversy Discussed* (1708) and *Short and Easy Method with the Deists* (1704) turned the flank of the Unitarian alliance with the Mahometans. They reviled monotheism as heresy, pointing out its affiliations with dubious figures such as Simon Magus. At the same time, they laid heavy emphasis

---

[14] Freke, *Vindication of the Unitarians*, 6; quoted in Champion, *Pillars of Priestcraft*, 109.

[15] Nye, *Brief History of the Unitarians*; quoted in Champion, *Pillars of Priestcraft*, 109–10. Thomas Mangey would later retort, apropos of Toland's *Nazarenus*, that it was in fact Arianism which showed the clearest derivation from Platonism: 'The Christian Doctrine of the Trinity is so far from being owing to that Philosophy [Platonism], as some of late have unskilfully thought, that it is very contrary to it; the *Arian* Doctrine is the very Sentiment of *Plato*, who asserts that great Subordination that the *Arians* are so fond of' (Mangey, *Remarks upon Nazarenus*, 125–6).

upon the corruptions, absurdities, and impostures in the scriptures and traditions of the Mahometans. The apogee of this line of argument was reached with Humphrey Prideaux's *The True Nature of Imposture Fully Displayed in the Life of Mahomet* (1697), a popular work which ran through numerous editions. Arguing that the worldliness of Mahomet's methods and objectives marked out his religion as a human imposture designed simply to satisfy the ambitions and lusts of its founder, Prideaux construed the success of Islam as God's punishment for the theological divisions which had weakened the Eastern Church and which had provided Mahomet with his opening. Properly considered, then, the spectacle of Islam warned thoughtful Christians about the harmfulness of doctrinal disputes, while at the same time confirming them in their faith that Christianity—so different from Islam (according to Prideaux at least) in its repression of physical appetite and its employment of only peaceful persuasion—was a divine revelation, rather than a human fiction.

The battle-lines over Mahometanism were drawn up in this way within the Church of England, where, as has been suggested, the subject focused concerns about the truth or heresy of the doctrine of the Trinity. Beyond that, however, there were at least two other, more radical, strands of discussion. The first of these is to be found in works such as Henry Stubbe's *An Account of the Rise and Progress of Mahometanism* (1671), John Toland's *Nazarenus or, Jewish, Gentile, and Mahometan Christianity* (1718) and Henri de Boulainvilliers' *La Vie de Mahomed* (1730). These men admired Mahomet as a 'civil theologian'.[16] They repudiated the grosser aspects of the accounts of Mahomet and his religion as Christian calumny. This obfuscation, so they argued, was calculated to conceal the true origins of Christianity which, according to these writers, would when correctly understood have opened the way towards syncretism between Mahometanism and Christianity, such as the Mahometans themselves perhaps desired when they acknowledged Jesus to be a prophet. For instance, Toland's *Nazarenus* partly concerns the contents of the lost Gospel of St Barnabas, a manuscript of which Toland had discovered when studying in the Low Countries.[17] He summarized its contents in a way which emphasized its explosive potential: "'Tis in short, the ancient Ebionite or Nazaren System, as to the making of JESUS a mere man (tho not with them the Son of JOSEPH, but divinely conceiv'd by the Virgin MARY) and

[16] I borrow this phrase from Justin Champion, *Pillars of Priestcraft*, 120.
[17] This manuscript is now dismissed as a medieval forgery. For the most recent treatment, see Sox, *The Gospel of Barnabas*.

agrees in every thing almost with the scheme of our modern Unitarians . . .'.[18] Primitive Christianity, then, was a stranger to the doctrine of the Trinity. Moreover, it was a stranger, too, to the Pauline doctrine of justification by faith, a soteriology Toland rejected on the grounds that in its counter-intuitiveness it facilitated the impostures of priestcraft:

I leave all impartial persons to examine . . . whether all the barbarous stuff that's deliver'd in the Scholastic Systems concerning *faith* and *Justification*, be not an after-device of Priests to puzzle the cause; and so to raise scruples in mens consciences (to the bringing of them often into despair) that they may have recourse to them for the solution of their doubts, to the no small increase of their pay and their power?[19]

Toland encourages his reader to reject these later sophistries, and instead to embrace (as he puts it with audacious frankness at the end of the book) 'what the Mahometans believe concerning CHRIST and his doctrine': beliefs which were 'neither the inventions of MAHOMET, nor yet of those Monks who are said to have assisted him in the framing of his *Alcoran*', but which rather 'are as old as the time of the Apostles, having been the sentiments of whole Sects or Churches'.[20]

Henri de Boulainvilliers took a slightly different tack. Whereas Toland's *Nazarenus* had played the card of (as it happens, bogus) scholarship, Boulainvilliers chose instead to lead with the ironic tones of a deist. The balancing act he set himself in composing *La Vie de Mahomed* was to vindicate Mahomet from the charges of imposture, ambition, and lust which the orthodox had levelled at him, while at the same time making deferential gestures towards the greater completeness of the Christian revelation: 'En effet, tout ce qu'il [Mahomet] a dit est *Vrai*, par raport aux dogmes essentiels à la Religion; mais il n'a pas dit *tout* ce qui est *Vrai*: & c'est en cela seul que nôtre Religion diffère de la sienne.'[21] The Mahomet of Boulainvilliers is therefore an eighteenth-century *philosophe* some thousand years *avant la lettre*.[22] His opinions of

---

[18] Toland, *Nazarenus*, 16–17.

[19] Ibid. 68–9. The historical irony here, of course, is that the doctrine of justification by faith alone, when restated by Luther at the beginning of the sixteenth century, had been launched against a prevailing doctrine of justification by works which had fallen into discredit in part because of the ruthlessness with which its lucrative potential had been exploited by the Roman Catholic clergy, for instance through the medium of indulgences.

[20] Ibid. 84–5.

[21] Boulainvilliers, *Mahomed*, 246–7.

[22] Jean Gagnier, whose own biography of the prophet was offered to the reading public as a thorough rebuttal of that of Boulainvilliers, was very alive to the way in which Boulainvilliers had fashioned Mahomet in the image of his own fantasies: 'ne chargez pas le pauvre Mahomet de vos propres imaginations: il est déja assez coupable ailleurs' (*Vie de Mahomet*, i., p. xxxiv).

monks ('malheureuses victimes de leur propre crédulité') and priests ('un assemblage politique d'hommes réunis à ce point cy; de faire servir la Religion à leurs passions, convoitise, avarice, faste, domination; . . .') mark him out as the forebear of religious freethinkers such as Boulainvilliers himself.[23] The author's affinity with his subject is touched upon in a long, but central, passage:

Il est tems après cela d'en venir à moi-même, & de me justifier devant le Lecteur de l'impression que peut faire le stile Oriental & Arabe que j'employe dans ce récit. Je suis Chrétien comme lui, & j'en fais une profession aussi sincère; mais je suis opposé à deux principes sur lesquels a roulé jusqu'à présent nôtre controverse avec les Musulmans. Le premier est, *qu'il ne se trouve aucun motif raisonnable dans tout ce qu'ils croyent ou pratiquent; ensorte qu'il faille renoncer au sens commun pour s'y soumettre*. Le second, *que Mahomed aît été un imposteur si grossier, & si barbare, qu'il n'est point d'homme qui n'aît dû, & qui n'aît pû, s'appercevoir de sa tromperie, & de sa séduction*. Contre ces principes je soutiens 1°. Que sans la grace de la Révélation Chrétienne, qui nous éclaire bien au-delà de ce que Mahomed a voulu connoître & savoir, il n'y auroit sistème de Doctrine si plausible que le sien, si conforme aux lumieres de la Raison, si consolant pour les Justes, & si terrible aux pécheurs volontaires ou inapliquez; & que dans les pratiques de Culte qu'il a établi, on découvre manifestement la cause, & la démonstration de cet attachement invincible qu'ont les Musulmans pour leur Religion: attachement très connu par nos Missionaires, qui sont obligez d'avouer le peu de progrès qu'ils font parmi eux. 2°. Je soutiens que Mahomed, Imposteur, n'a été ni grossier ni barbare; qu'il a conduit son entreprise avec tout l'art, toute la délicatesse, toute la constance, l'intrépidité, les grandes vûes dont Alexandre & César eussent été capables dans sa place. Il est vrai que ses moeurs ont été plus simples que celles de ces deux Conquérans; qu'il a moins connu l'interêt, l'avarice, le luxe, & la prodigalité: au lieu desquels il a employé la Religion pour motif de ses exploits. Il n'a point non plus assujetti sa Patrie; au contraire il ne l'a voulu gouverner que pour la rendre Maîtresse du monde, & de ses diverses richesses, desquelles & lui, & ses premiers Successeurs ont fait un usage si desinteressé qu'ils doivent être admirez à cet égard par leurs plus grands ennemis. Au-reste comme le but de cet Ouvrage n'est que mon amusement particulier, après lequel je substitue celui d'un Lecteur équitable, je ne croi pas avoir besoin de justifier mon stile, & les termes que j'emprunte des Livres Arabes. Un pareil Ouvrage, où nous ne pouvons prendre que peu d'intérêt du côté de l'instruction, & de la connoissance de véritez dogmatiques, doit au moins essaïer de plaire par la singularité des expressions.[24]

A number of touches in this passage recall the techniques of the deist. The claim that 'Je suis Chrétien comme lui, & j'en fais une profession aussi sincère' is two-edged in its possibly tart reflection on the sincerity

[23] Boulainvilliers, *Mahomed*, 207.   [24] Ibid. 247–9.

of most men's professions of Christianity. The apparently pious remark about 'la Révélation Chrétienne, qui nous éclaire bien au-delà de ce que Mahomed a voulu connoître & savoir' holds the satirical charge that Mahomet might not have aspired to the degree of *éclaircissement* supplied by the Christian Revelation because he was well aware that, in those areas where it exceeded or conflicted with natural religion, Christian doctrine became mystification and falsehood. The final disavowal that the present work had any object beyond an innocent 'amusement particulier', and was free of any implication for 'la connoissance de véritez dogmatiques', would have been readily recognizable to the spokesmen for religious orthodoxy as exactly the kind of bland disclaimer which the deists had made their signature. This tradition, in which Mahomet is presented as the epitome of the philosophic legislator, was given vivid, concise, expression in the middle years of the century through Voltaire's *Essai sur l'Histoire Générale, et sur les Moeurs et l'Esprit des Nations* (1756); an account of Mahomet which was, a few years later, taken over almost verbatim in the article 'Mahométisme' in volume nine of the *Encyclopédie* (1765), and thereby given even wider currency.[25]

Beyond the tradition represented by Toland, Boulainvilliers, Voltaire, and the *Encyclopédie*, however, there lay a still more extreme twist on the significance of Mahomet and his religion. This was to be found in clandestine works such as the exuberantly irreligious and materialist *Traité des Trois Fameux Imposteurs* (a MS copy of which was to be found in Gibbon's library).[26] The three impostors of this cele-

---

[25] Voltaire, *Essai sur l'Histoire Générale, et sur les Moeurs et l'Esprit des Nations*, ch. 4, i. 32–51. *Encyclopédie*, ix. 864–8, 'Mahométisme': this article appeared over the name of the Chevalier de Jaucourt.

[26] For the discovery of the presence of the *Traité* in Gibbon's library, see Womersley, 'Gibbon's Religious Characters'. On the *Traité* more generally, see: M. Jacob, *The Radical Enlightenment* (1981); S. Berti *et al.* (eds.), *Contexts of Imposture* (Leiden, 1991); S. Berti, 'The first edition of the Traité des trois imposteurs and its debt to Spinoza's Ethics', in M. Hunter and D. Wootton (eds.), *Atheism from the Reformation to the Enlightenment* (Oxford: Oxford University Press, 1992), 183–220; S. Berti, F. Charles-Daubert, and R. H. Popkin (eds.), *Heterodoxy, Spinozism, and Freethought in Early Eighteenth-Century Europe: Studies on the Traité des Trois Imposteurs* (Klewer, 1996). Silvia Berti's Franco-Italian edition is the most useful: S. Berti (ed.), *Trattato dei Tre Impostori* (Torino: Einaudi, 1994). On the very complicated textual aspect of this work, and in particular on the tortuous relations between the printed and manuscript versions, see F. Charles-Daubert, 'Les Principales Sources de l'Esprit de Spinosa', in *Groupe de recherches spinozistes. Travaux et documents 1* (Paris, 1989), 61–107, 'Les Traités des trois imposteurs aux XVIIᵉ et XVIIIᵉ siècles', in G. Canziani (ed.), *Filosofia e religione nella letteratura clandestina secoli XVII e XVIII* (Milan, 1994), 291–336, and '*L'Esprit de Spinosa* et les *Traités des trois imposteurs*: rappel des différentes familles et de leurs principales caractéristiques', in S. Berti, F. Charles-Daubert, and R. H. Popkin (eds.), *Heterodoxy, Spinozism, and Freethought in Early Eighteenth-Century Europe: Studies on the Traité des Trois Imposteurs* (Klewer, 1996), 131–89.

brated and anonymous work were, of course, Moses, Christ himself, and Mahomet, all of whom were bitterly excoriated as charlatans and mountebanks. In the case of Mahomet, the imposture of the new religion was framed in order that he might 's'établir dans le poste de son Aieul'.[27] This ancestor was Obdol Motallab, Mahomet's grandfather, who was both the secular prince of his tribe and High Priest of the temple at Mecca. Mahomet had been robbed of the succession to these conjoined positions by the early death of his father, an event which had given his uncle an opportunity to interpose himself in Mahomet's place. With Mahomet's motivation satisfactorily explained as atavistic self-aggrandisement, it only remains for his methods to be described. They were, as it happens, exactly the same as those of his notable predecessors in imposture:

Les circonstances du tems ou il forma ce dessein lui etoient tres favorables; Car presque tous les Arabes degoutés du culte de leurs Idoles, etoient tombés dans une espece d'atheisme: C'est pour quoy Mahomet feignant au contraire d'etre pieux, commença par mener une vie retirée et exemplaire, cherchant la Solitude, et passant la plus grande partie du jour en prieres et en méditations. Lorsqu'il se fut fait des admirateurs avec cet extérieur composé, il commença a parler de visions celestes et de revelations divines. C'est par là qu'on gagne ordinairement la croiance de la populace. Ce fut par la que Moise et J.C. commencerent aussi. Mahomet se dit ensuite Prophete et envoyé de Dieu, et aiant autant d'adresse que ses predecesseurs pour faire des prodiges, il gagna d'abord l'attention, ensuite l'admiration, et bientôt après la confiance du peuple.[28]

Of the three impostors, Mahomet was the most successful. Because he had adapted his religion more closely to the appetites and inclinations of those to whom he preached it, he alone of the three great impostors saw his 'grand projet' reach fruition: 'Ainsi Mahomet fut plus heureux que J.C. car aprés avoir travaillé 23. ans a l'etablissem^t. de sa loy et de sa religion, il en vit les progrés avant sa mort, et put se flater de l'esperance que n'eut pas J.C., qu'elle subsisteroit longtems, puis qu'il l'avoit prudemment acommodèe au Genie et aux passions de ses Sectateurs.'[29] And finally Mahomet's greater accomplishment in imposture allowed him to make a better end than either Moses or Christ: 'Telle fut la fin de ces trois imposteurs: Moise se precipita dans un abime, par un excès d'ambition pour se faire croire immortel. J.C. fut honteusement

---

[27] *Traité*, 154. All quotations from and references to the *Traité* are keyed to Gibbon's MS copy, now in the library of the Athenaeum in London. In all cases the irregular orthography of the MS has been preserved.

[28] Ibid. 154–5.

[29] Ibid. 156 and 157.

crucifié avec deux Scelerats et ainsi couvert de honte pour recompense de ses impostures. Enfin Mahomet mourut a la veritè sur son lit, et au milieu de toute sa Grandeur . . .'.[30] Yet, despite his outward prosperity, Mahomet's death was agonizing. He expired 'les entrailles brulées du poison que lui avoit donné une jeune Juive pour eprouver s'il etoit veritablement Prophete'.[31] This was the natural retribution for the base trickery he shared with Moses and Christ:

> Voila tout ce que j'avois a dire de ces trois insignes fourbes, les trois plus fameux legislateurs de l'univers. Ils etoient tels que nous les avons représentés naturellement, et sans donner de fausses ombres a leurs portraits. Qu'on juge aprés cela s'ils meritent qu'on croie en eux, et si l'on est excusable de se laisser conduire par ces guides que l'ambition et la fourbe ont élevés, et que l'Ignorance a eternisès.[32]

Here, of course, the orthodox Christian and the radical materialist[33] could join hands (at least in respect of Mahomet). And it is indeed the case that certain books in this tradition might be translated into English, and offered to their readership as works of irreproachable orthodoxy: such, for instance, was the case with James Miller's translation of Voltaire's tragedy *Le Fanatisme, ou Mahomet le Prophète* (1741).[34]

III

Now that we have mapped out the terrain of polemical writing on Mahomet from the late seventeenth to the mid-eighteenth centuries, we are in a position to consider the particular circumstances surrounding the composition of Gibbon's account of Mahomet and Islam in the mid-1780s. In the first place, it is remarkable that during this decade in England the whole subject of Mahometanism had become freshly topical in the wake of the very public theological disputations between the Unitarian Joseph Priestley (1733–1804) and the High Church dogmatist Samuel Horsley (1733–1806). Gibbon would later recall these encounters in his 'Memoirs':

---

[30] Ibid. 157.

[31] Ibid. 157.

[32] Ibid. 157–8.

[33] The final section of the *Traité*, entitled 'Véritez Sensibles et Evidentes', states at the outset that 'Dieu est un etre Simple, d'une extension infinie, qui ressemble a ce qu'il contient: C'est a dire qu'il est materiel' (ibid. 159).

[34] James Miller, *Mahomet the Impostor. A Tragedy* (1744). Voltaire's play paints a significantly darker picture of Mahomet from the one he would depict some years later in the *Essai sur l'Histoire Générale*.

In his History of the Corruptions of Christianity (vol. ii.), Dr. Priestly throws down his two gauntlets to Bishop Hurd and Mr. Gibbon. I declined the challenge in a polite letter, exhorting my opponent to enlighten the World by his philosophical discoveries, and to remember that the merit of his predecessor Servetus is now reduced to a single passage, which indicates the smaller circulation of the blood through the lungs, from and to the heart . . . Instead of listening to this friendly advice, the dauntless philosopher of Birmingham continues to fire away his double battery against those who believe too little and those who believe too much. From *my* replies he has nothing to hope or fear; but his Socinian shield has repeatedly been pierced by the spear of the mighty Horsley, and his trumpet of sedition may at length awaken the magistrates of a free country.[35]

Between 1783 and 1790 virtually every year saw the publication of a defence of Unitarianism from Priestley and a riposte in the form of a witheringly sarcastic tract from Horsley. These latter were masterpieces of the polemicist's art, in which the deficiencies in Priestley's scholarship were mercilessly and precisely exposed. Taking advantage of the interest generated by this prominent theological dispute, anonymous pamphlets such as *The Life of Mahomet, the Imposter* (1784) were published, in which the main points of the orthodox tradition of commentary associated most closely with Humphrey Prideaux were tersely restated.[36] Mahomet was a wily charlatan, the governing principles of whose soul were 'ambition and lust'.[37] Driven by those appetites, he gauged the national character of the Arabs shrewdly and exploited it efficiently:

He [Mahomet] did indeed purge the religion of the Arabians . . . from some gross abuses . . . but in order to make his new system be the more easily received by his countrymen, he retained several of their old superstitious observances . . . The few things he proposed to their profession and belief certainly made it more easy for him to gain proselytes; the paradise he promised them was indeed very gross and sensual, as we shall see hereafter, but very well suited to the taste of the people he had to deal with: . . .[38]

---

[35] *A* 318, n. 38: compare *DF* iii. 437–9 and n. 42. On Gibbon and Priestley, see Turnbull, 'Gibbon's Exchange with Joseph Priestley'. The fact that Gibbon stands alongside Hurd as Priestley's target throws into vivid relief how the theological ground had moved since the 1760s and 1770s, when Gibbon himself tried to engage Hurd in controversy: see Womersley, 'Gibbon's Religious Characters'.

[36] This is possibly a reprinting of an earlier work which I have been unable to trace. The author says that Prideaux's work, first published in 1697, had appeared 'but a few years before' ([Anon.], *The Life of Mahomet, the Imposter*, 1). However, *The Life of Mahomet* could not have been written before 1730, since it shows knowledge of the work of Boulainvilliers.

[37] *Life of Mahomet*, 74.

[38] Ibid. 20.

The philosophical perspective on Mahomet, embodied for this author in the work of Boulainvilliers, is by contrast briskly dismissed as 'a kind of politico-theological romance'.[39]

This revival of public discussion of both the affinities between Unitarianism and Mahometanism, and the divergence between Mahometanism and Christianity, occurred between the publication of the second instalment of *The Decline and Fall* in 1781 and the third and final instalment in 1788. The second instalment, comprising volumes two and three in the quarto editions, had taken the history down to the fall of the Roman Empire in the West, an event which occurred towards the end of the fifth century AD.[40] It was therefore clear that Gibbon's third instalment—whenever it might appear—would contain an account of Mahomet and the rise of Islam. Indeed, as early as 1776 Gibbon had indicated as much in the 'Preface' to the first volume.[41] It was therefore natural for speculation to arise as to how Gibbon would treat this once more sensitive subject; natural, too, for those who wished to break a lance with Gibbon to mark out their ground in advance. Two publications of this kind are noteworthy: the first by William Godwin, who would later win fame as the author of the *Enquiry Concerning Political Justice* (1793) and *Caleb Williams* (1794), the second by Joseph White, the Laudian Professor of Arabic at Oxford.[42]

During the early 1780s Godwin worked as a minister in a variety of places, but his inclinations were turning from the Church towards literature, and he had begun to dabble in journalism. One of his earliest pieces is a clever *jeu d'esprit* called *The Herald of Literature*, which was advertised for sale in November 1783 (although the title page bears the date 1784).[43] This was a series of literary parodies masquerading as

[39] Ibid. 10.

[40] Gibbon is unsure whether Augustulus's renunciation of the Western Empire occurred in 476 or 479 AD (*DF* ii. 404).

[41] Gibbon there divided his subject into three periods, and gave the following advertisement for the second: 'The second period of the Decline and Fall of Rome, may be supposed to commence with the reign of Justinian, who by his laws, as well as by his victories, restored a transient splendour to the Eastern Empire. It will comprehend the invasion of Italy by the Lombards; the conquest of the Asiatic and African provinces by the Arabs, who embraced the religion of Mahomet; the revolt of the Roman people against the feeble princes of Constantinople; and the elevation of Charlemagne, who, in the year eight hundred, established the second, or German Empire of the west' (*DF* i. 1–2). Furthermore, and more recently, in the preface to the fifth, 1782, edition of volume one, Gibbon touched on the contents of the last volumes, and indicated that at the outset 'the conquests of the Mahometans, will deserve and detain our attention' (*DF* i. 3–4).

[42] On the amusing context of scandal surrounding the composition of White's Bampton lectures, see Womersley, 'Gibbon and Plagiarism'.

[43] Gibbon had left London to take up residence in Lausanne with his friend Georges Deyverdun on 1 September 1783. Nevertheless, books and newspapers were regularly sent over to him from London by the bookseller Elmsley (*L* iii. 210).

reviews of soon-to-be-published books, advance copies of which
the writer claimed surreptitiously to have acquired. In the manner of
eighteenth-century reviews, the individual articles contain large quotations, although of course in this case these 'quotations' are in fact
written by Godwin himself as parodies or imitations of the author in
question. At the level of style, then, they allow us to assess Godwin's
expertise as a parodist; while at the level of content they furnish useful
evidence of at least one man's judgement of the ideological allegiances
of the parodied author.

The first book Godwin 'reviewed' was the final instalment of *The
Decline and Fall*. He praised the history as 'one of the greatest ornaments
of the present age', and briefly described its contents, before selecting
for the subject of his first 'extract' the 'astonishing object' of 'the rise of
the Saracen khalifate, and the religion of Mahomet'.[44] The first 'quotation' is 'the character of the impostor, as sketched by the accurate and
judicious pencil of our historian', whose orientation towards his subject
Godwin described as follows: 'We will leave it to the judgment of our
readers, only observing, that Mr. Gibbon has very unnecessarily
brought Christianity into the comparison; and has perhaps touched the
errors of the false prophet with a lighter hand, that the disparity might
be the less apparent.'[45] There is already here a hint to the reader that
Godwin expects Gibbon's account to conform to the philosophic
tradition of Toland, Boulainvilliers, Voltaire, and the *Encyclopédie*. And
as we move on into the first of the 'extracts' from Gibbon's final
volumes, that is indeed what we find. Godwin makes Gibbon admire
the Arabs and their prophet in terms which, to a contemporary reader,
would have most immediately recalled the work of Voltaire:

Ingenious and eloquent, temperate and brave, as had been invariably their
national character, they had their exertions concentred, and their courage
animated by a legislator, whose institutions may vie, in the importance of their
consequences, with those of Solon, Lycurgus, or Numa. Though an impostor,
he propagated a religion, which, like the elevated and divine principles of
Christianity, was confined to no one nation or country; but even embraced a
larger portion of the human race than Christianity itself.[46]

Voltaire (contrasting himself with Bossuet, who had dismissed the
Arabs as nothing more significant than 'un déluge de Barbares') had
claimed that the advent of Islam was 'la plus grande & la plus prompte

---

[44] *Herald of Literature*, 17 and 20.
[45] Ibid. 20.
[46] Ibid. 21; cf. also 'His schemes were always laid with the truest wisdom' (ibid. 27).

révolution que nous connaissions sur la Terre'.[47] And in the *Encyclopédie*, Mahomet is repeatedly considered as a 'législateur':

Il n'altéra en rien la morale qui a toujours été la même dans le fond chez tous les hommes, & qu'aucun législateur n'a jamais corrumpue.

De tous les législateurs qui ont fondé des religions, il est le seul qui ait étendu la sienne par les conquêtes. D'autres peuples ont porté leur culte avec le fer & le feu chez des nations étrangeres; mais nul fondateur de secte n'avoit été conquérant. Ce privilege unique est aux yeux des Musulmans l'argument le plus fort, que la Divinité prit soin elle-même de seconder leur prophete.[48]

Moreover, in this tradition it is no qualification of Mahomet's secular merit that he was in religious terms an impostor. Although Voltaire and the authors of the *Encyclopédie* refrain from publishing materialist atheism, in the manner of the author or authors of the *Traité des Trois Imposteurs*, beneath their superficial deference to Christianity they seem to come close to that more radical strain, and appear content to hint that, since all founders of religions are necessarily impostors, it cannot be taken as a particular slur so to name any individual.[49]

Godwin goes on to make Gibbon praise the 'sublimity of his [Mahomet's] genius', and to present the theology of Islam as 'a sublime doctrine, of which the unity of God, the innocence of moderate enjoyment, the obligation of temperance and munificence, were the leading principles'.[50] Here again Godwin employs a key term from the vocabulary used by the *philosophes* when discussing Mahomet, whose doctrine is for instance praised in the *Encyclopédie* as 'd'un genre . . . véritablement sublime'.[51] When Godwin makes Gibbon praise the intensity of the verbal artistry deployed in the Qur'ān ('it is frequently figurative, frequently poetical, sometimes sublime') the cue is again to Voltaire and the *Encyclopédie*, where the poetic potency of the Arabic language is handsomely praised.[52] The military might of Islam is emphasized by Godwin's Gibbon: Mahomet led 'an intrepid and continually increasing army, inflamed with enthusiasm, and greedy of death'.[53] Similarly, the Islamic armies are presented as fearsome in the

---

[47] Voltaire, *Essai sur l'Histoire Générale*, i. 3 and 32.

[48] *Encyclopédie*, ix. 864 and 865.

[49] Consider how the *Encyclopédie* recounts Mahomet's death: 'Mahomet . . . expira peu de tems après, regardé comme un grand homme par ceux-même qui savoient qu'il étoit un imposteur, & révéré comme un prophete par tout le reste' (ix. 865).

[50] *Herald of Literature*, 22–3.

[51] *Encyclopédie*, ix. 864.

[52] *Herald of Literature*, 25; cf. Voltaire, *Essai sur l'Histoire Générale*, i. 51.

[53] *Herald of Literature*, 26.

Encyclopédie: 'Si jamais puissance a menacé toute la terre, c'est celle de ces califes; car ils avoient le droit du trône & de l'autel, du glaive & de l'enthousiasme. Leurs ordres étoient autant d'oracles, & leurs soldats autant de fanatiques.'[54] Finally, Godwin gives us a second 'extract' from *The Decline and Fall*. This is a character sketch of Saladin, and here again we find the language and the values of Boulainvilliers, Voltaire, and the *Encyclopédie*. Godwin makes Gibbon praise Saladin as the rival of the greatest hero of antiquity:

He has been compared with Alexander; and tho' he be usually stiled, and with some justice, a barbarian, it does not appear that his character would suffer in the comparison. . . . But the parallel is exceedingly far from entire. He possessed not the romantic gallantry of the conqueror of Darius; he had none of those ardent and ungovernable passions, through whose medium the victories of Arbela and Issus had transformed the generous hero into the lawless tyrant.[55]

Compare the *Encyclopédie*, where it is asserted that Mahomet possessed all 'l'intrépidité d'Alexandre', but conjoined with it 'la libéralité, & la sobriété dont Alexandre auroit eu besoin pour être grand homme en tout'.[56] It was a comparison which Boulainvilliers had earlier drawn, and to the advantage of Mahomet: 'Je soutiens que Mahomed, Imposteur, n'a été ni grossier ni barbare; qu'il a conduit son entreprise avec tout l'art, toute la délicatesse, toute la constance, l'intrépidité, les grandes vûes dont Alexandre & César eussent été capables dans sa place. Il est vrai que ses moeurs ont été plus simples que celles de ces deux Conquérans; qu'il a moins connu l'interêt, l'avarice, le luxe, & la prodigalité: au lieu desquels il a employé la Religion pour motif de ses exploits.'[57] It seems clear, then, that Godwin's implicit expectation in the *Herald of Literature* was that Gibbon would, in the final instalment of *The Decline and Fall*, continue to be what many had—perhaps mistakenly—imagined him to be since 1776: namely, the English Voltaire.[58]

The second of the anticipatory publications we shall consider, Joseph White's 1784 Bampton lectures, took a different line. If there is room

[54]   *Encyclopédie*, ix. 866.
[55]   *Herald of Literature*, 31 and 32.
[56]   *Encyclopédie*, ix. 864.
[57]   Boulainvilliers, *Mahomed*, 248.
[58]   For an account of how, where, and why this interpretation of Gibbon's work arose, see: Turnbull, ' "Une marionette infidèle" '. For arguments suggesting how, where, and why it is a mistaken (or at least an incomplete) representation of Gibbon's ideological outlook, see: Pocock, 'Superstition and Enthusiasm in Gibbon's History of Religion', and Robertson, 'Gibbon's Roman Empire as a Universal Monarchy', esp. p. 264. A measured justification for the allegations of affinity with Voltaire is to be found in Womersley, 'Gibbon's Religious Characters'.

to doubt whether Gibbon was aware of Godwin's parody of *The Decline and Fall*, it is by contrast quite certain that he knew about White's Bampton lectures. His library contained the second, 1785, edition of the lectures;[59] he refers to those lectures twice in the final instalment of *The Decline and Fall*;[60] and in draft 'E' of his 'Memoirs' he dwelt with amused urbanity on his assailant, touching obliquely in the reference to White's unacknowledged collaborator, Samuel Badcock, on the charges of plagiarism by which White's reputation had been so thoroughly damaged:

I have praised, and I still praise the eloquent sermons which were preached in St. Mary's pulpit at Oxford by Dr. White. If he assaults me with some degree of illiberal acrimony, in such a place and before such an audience, he was obliged to speak the language of the country. I smiled at a passage in one of his private letters to Mr. Badcock: 'The part where we encounter Gibbon must be brill[i]ant and striking.'[61]

White and his secret collaborator, Badcock, had chosen to encounter Gibbon in the following manner. The overall plan of White's lectures was very much in the idiom of the orthodox tradition of writing on Mahomet and his religion. As we have seen, this tradition had been, hitherto, best exemplifed in Prideaux's *The True Nature of Imposture Fully Displayed in the Life of Mahomet* (1697); but it was impressively brought up to date by White, who was an indolent writer with a weakness for quiet dissipation, but nevertheless also a genuine scholar well versed in the Oriental learning of the years since Prideaux had published his influential attack. White's strategy was to contrast the worldliness of Islam with the other-worldliness of Christianity, in order to underline the divine origin of the latter. However, the peroration of the third sermon was a substantial rebuttal of Gibbon's analysis of the five secondary causes which had contributed to the growth of Christianity—probably the most notorious aspect of his handling of religion in the first volume of *The Decline and Fall*.[62] The implication was that Gibbon had blundered. It was only Islam, not Christianity, which could be accounted for satisfactorily by reference to secondary causes:

---

[59] *K* 284.
[60] *DF* iii. 175 n. 70 and iii. 336 n. 30.
[61] *A* 318–19 n. 40. The earlier praise is to be found at *DF* iii. 336 n. 30.
[62] White, *Sermons*, 145–60; cf. *DF* i. 446–513. Gibbon's five secondary causes were: (1) the intolerant and unsocial zeal of the Jews; (2) the doctrine of a future life; (3) the miraculous powers ascribed to the primitive church; (4) the moral purity of the early Christians; and (5) the union and discipline of the early Christians.

Such then being the circumstances, and such the means by which the religion of Mahomet was so widely diffused, and so firmly established in the world; its success, however astonishing, is capable of being accounted for by merely human causes; and consequently to suppose any extraordinary and particular interposition of the Deity, is evidently unnecessary and absurd.[63]

The challenge to Gibbon was plain. If in his final volumes he were to extol Islam above Christianity, he would confirm his reputation as the English Voltaire—a reputation which the *Vindication* of 1779 had shown he was eager to reject. If, on the other hand, he were to extend to Islam the same kind of analysis he had used when approaching the early Christian Church, he would show himself to be blind to the broad array of significant differences between the two religions; differences which White had deployed in his sermons with a plausible show of scholarly power. To confront your opponent with such a dilemma was a classic strategy in the scholarly polemics of the eighteenth century.

IV

Considered in its broadest significance, the way Gibbon proceeded in his account of Mahomet illustrates conditions of authorship at the end of the eighteenth century; it shows how the reputation of an author might be produced, and the tendency of his writings influenced, as the result of a complex interplay of expectation and response with readers and critics. More narrowly, however, it also reveals Gibbon's growing mastery of the game of authorship. The techniques employed for the first time in the second instalment of 1781 when writing on Athanasius and Julian the Apostate are now refined and handled with new assurance. At the same time, we find a recurrence of the paradoxical outcome of the chapters on the Trinitarian controversy—namely, that Gibbon's mature character as an historian was forged in conflict. Gibbon's acuity in discerning the finer shade of historical fact was the foundation of both the enduring authority of his vision and the technical accomplishment of his writing. It was an acuity honed through controversy.

It was in the long fiftieth chapter of *The Decline and Fall* that Gibbon reviewed the '*Birth, Character, and Doctrine of Mahomet*'.[64] But this chapter ranges far more widely than the mere biography of the prophet. Prefacing his chapter with the recognizably *philosophe* emphasis that the origin and rapid growth of Islam formed 'one of the most memorable

---

[63] White, *Sermons*, 102–3.   [64] *DF* iii. 151–232.

revolutions, which have impressed a new and lasting character on the nations of the globe', he launched into a geographical description of Arabia and an anthropological description of the people who lived there.[65] It was only after about a quarter of the length of the eventual chapter that Gibbon turned to Mahomet himself. This method of proceeding could in itself be construed as a token of ideological affiliation, since the only work on Mahomet which had also begun with geography and anthropology before moving on to biography was Boulainvilliers' *Vie de Mahomed*:

> il est si nécessaire de donner quelque idée de l'Histoire du Païs, tant de l'ancienne qui renferme ce qui est arrivé en Arabie peu de temps après l'âge des Patriarches, que de celle qui a immédiatement précédé celui de Mahomed. Par-là le Lecteur sera mieux en état de juger des differentes circonstances du tems où il a paru; des préjugés qui lui ont été ou favorables ou contraires; des dispositions que la Providence, ou la Nature avoient préparées pour le prodigieux changement qu'un seul homme, foible & dépourvu de moyens, a porté dans l'Univers.[66]

We find such an insistence on the need for contextualizing knowledge to combat 'préjugés' nowhere else. Taken by itself, then, the fact that Gibbon chose so to initiate his account of Mahomet seems to confirm the expectation that he would align himself with those whom many in England insisted on seeing as his brother *philosophes*.

But Gibbon filled this *philosophe* template with unexpected, because un-*philosophe*, insight. A point of interpretation on which the orthodox and the philosophical agreed in relation to Mahomet was that, in framing his religion, he had been careful so to fashion its doctrine that it gratified the inclinations and offered no affront to the customs of the Arabs. For *philosophes* such as Boulainvilliers this had been the hallmark of Mahomet's accomplishment as a legislator:

> On pourra juger par là des fondements sur lesquels Mahomed a établi un sistème de Religion, non seulement propre aux lumieres de ses Compatriotes, convenable à leurs sentiments & aux moeurs dominantes du Païs; mais encore tellement proportionné aux idées communes du Genre humain, qu'il a entrainé plus de la moitié des Hommes dans ses opinions, en moins de XL.

---

[65] *DF* iii. 151. Compare Voltaire's insistence that the advent of Islam caused 'la plus grande & la plus prompte révolution que nous connaissions sur la Terre' (*Essai sur l'Histoire Générale*, i. 32); itself an echo of Boulainvilliers' claim concerning the magnitude of what he was about to narrate: 'aucune Histoire ne contient des événements plus sensibles à l'imagination, ni plus surprenants en eux-mêmes que ceux qui sont rapportez dans la vie des premiers Musulmans' (*Mahomed*, 5).
[66] Ibid. 96–7.

années: de sorte qu'il semble qu'il suffisoit d'en faire entendre la Doctrine pour soûmettre les esprits.[67]

Pierre Bayle, however, had noted how the same phenomenon—the nice adjustment of the doctrines of Islam to the Arabic character—had been interpreted to quite different effect: 'Il y a des gens qui . . . desaprouvent que l'on debite qu'il n'attira tant de sectateurs, qu'à cause que sa Morale s'accommodoit à la corruption du coeur, & parce qu'il promettoit aux hommes un Paradis sensuel.'[68] For the orthodox nothing better showed that Mahomet was an impostor than the worldliness of the appeal he made to his followers. Thomas Mangey, replying to Toland's *Nazarenus*, had made the point forcefully: 'we generally attribute greater Success to *Mahomet* than he really had; for he doth not seem so much to have establish'd a new Religion, as to have settled and put in Order an old one. He comply'd with the popular Notions of his Countreymen, and afterwards by the Assistance of their Arms propagated these Notions into the adjacent Parts.'[69] In this he was following the orthodox author of *Four Treatises Concerning the Doctrine, Discipline and Worship of the Mahometans* (1712), for whom Mahomet had merely adapted the precepts of his religion to suit 'the Notions the Country had of the greatest Happiness and the greatest Misery'.[70]

But from this point of interpretation, where the orthodox and the *philosophe* somewhat surprisingly joined hands, Gibbon quietly distanced himself. At the end of the *Natural History of Religion* (1757), Hume had offered guidance as to how the true philosopher should behave when trapped between squabbling factions: 'opposing one species of superstition to another, set them a quarreling; while we ourselves, during their fury and contention, happily make our escape, into the calm, tho' obscure, regions of philosophy.'[71] Such was Gibbon's strategy in chapter fifty of *The Decline and Fall*. For what he draws his reader's attention to is the way in which the demands of Islam cut across the established patterns of Arab behaviour as much as they gratified them. On the surface, of course, it was true that the Arabs to some extent persisted in the same grooves of conduct which had been worn in the centuries preceding the advent of Mahomet: 'The Arab continued to unite the professions of a merchant and a robber; and his petty excursions for the defence or the attack of a caravan insensibly prepared

[67] Boulainvilliers, *Mahomed*, 132–3.
[68] Bayle, *Dictionaire*, iii. 472–3.
[69] Mangey, *Remarks upon Nazarenus*, 47–8.
[70] *Four Treatises*, 33.
[71] Hume, *Natural History of Religion*, 95.

his troops for the conquest of Arabia.'[72] It was therefore true (although perhaps a banal truth) that Mahomet had 'invited the Arabs to freedom and victory, to arms and rapine, to the indulgence of their darling passions in this world and the other'; true, too, that the 'artful legislator indulged the stubborn prejudices of his countrymen'.[73] But these surface continuities masked deeper disjunctions, and more profound contradictions:

The intrepid souls of the Arabs were fired with enthusiasm: the picture of the invisible world was strongly painted on their imagination; and the death which they had always despised became an object of hope and desire. The Koran inculcates, in the most absolute sense, the tenets of fate and predestination, which would extinguish both industry and virtue, if the actions of man were governed by his speculative belief. Yet their influence in every age has exalted the courage of the Saracens and Turks. The first companions of Mahomet advanced to battle with a fearless confidence: there is no danger where there is no chance: they were ordained to perish in their beds; or they were safe and invulnerable amidst the darts of the enemy.[74]

The cross-grainedness of human nature easily twists 'speculative belief', wringing from it behaviour at variance with its obvious tendency. In the light of this human disposition to the perverse, what, then, could be easier to grant—what harder to deny?—than that the Arabs may have welcomed the subversion of their customs, even though that subversion was not offered to them in a spirit of calculation. So it might happen that 'the death which they had always despised became an object of hope and desire'. Gibbon, in common with other writers on the Arabs, points up their 'perpetual independence': only he, however, arranges his account so that the extinguishing of that independence in the discipline of Islam makes itself felt.[75] Gibbon dwells upon the natural unsociableness of the Arab:

The separation of the Arabs from the rest of mankind, has accustomed them to confound the ideas of stranger and enemy; . . . The temper of a people, thus armed against mankind, was doubly inflamed by the domestic licence of rapine, murder, and revenge. In the constitution of Europe, the right of peace and war is now confined to a small, and the actual exercise to a much smaller, list of respectable potentates; but each Arab, with impunity and renown, might point his javelin against the life of his countryman. The union of the nation consisted only in a vague resemblance of language and manners; and in each community, the jurisdiction of the magistrate was mute and impotent. Of the time of ignorance which preceded Mahomet, seventeen hundred battles are recorded by tradition: hostility was embittered with the rancour of civil

---

[72] *DF* iii. 198.　　[73] *DF* iii. 230 and 169.　　[74] *DF* iii. 198.　　[75] *DF* iii. 158.

faction; and the recital, in prose or verse, of an obsolete feud was sufficient to rekindle the same passions among the descendents of the hostile tribes. In private life, every man, at least every family, was the judge and avenger of its own cause.[76]

Yet it was they who were willing to renounce anarchy and submit to the authority of Mahomet. And what was true of the Arab's politics was even more true of his religion. Traditionally idolatrous, at the instigation of Mahomet the Arabs embraced a religion which forbade all representations of the divine. Moreover, the sequestered desert had, over centuries, offered refuge to the outcasts of all creeds. Vastness and desolation had been the parents of toleration: 'Arabia was free: the adjacent kingdoms were shaken by the storms of conquest and tyranny, and the persecuted sects fled to the happy land where they might profess what they thought, and practice what they professed. The religions of the Sabians and Magians, of the Jews and Christians, were disseminated from the Persian Gulf to the Red Sea.'[77] It was therefore natural that the freedom extended to refugees was claimed also by those who offered shelter: 'The liberty of choice was presented to the tribes: each Arab was free to elect or to compose his private religion: and the rude supersititon of his house was mingled with the sublime theology of saints and philosophers.'[78] Yet it was this people who welcomed the uncompromising pretensions of Islam, that curious hybrid of 'eternal truth, and . . . necessary fiction' summarized in the apothegmatic creed that 'THERE IS ONLY ONE GOD, AND THAT MAHOMET IS THE APOSTLE OF GOD'.[79] It was this paradoxical continuity and disjunction which also gave Gibbon the key to understanding the dynamic violence and simultaneous transience of their conquests. His commentary shows the historical imagination in action, and it makes the *philosophe* admiration for the force of Islam seem immediately shallow:

The idols of Arabia were broken before the throne of God; the blood of human victims was expiated by prayer, and fasting, and alms, the laudable or innocent arts of devotion; and the rewards and punishments of a future life were painted by the images most congenial to an ignorant and carnal generation. Mahomet was perhaps incapable of dictating a moral and political system for the use of his countrymen: but he breathed among the faithful a spirit of charity and friendship, recommended the practice of the social virtues, and checked, by his laws and precepts, the thirst of revenge and the oppression of widows and orphans. The hostile tribes were united in faith and obedience, and the valour which had been idly spent in domestic quarrels, was vigorously directed against a foreign

enemy. Had the impulse been less powerful, Arabia, free at home, and formidable abroad, might have flourished under a succession of her native monarchs.
Her sovereignty was lost by the extent and rapidity of conquest.[80]

The insight that the very success of Islam was instrumental in the
evanescence of its conquests is at one level an application of a familiar
civic humanist point about the natural history of republics—that they
eventually fall because of an excess of virtue. But it is here given a new
emotional colouring because of the way it chimes with Gibbon's (it
must be said, entirely book-derived) sense of the desert as a place in
which human energy is dissipated and absorbed. Attempting the conquest of Arabia, Augustus's legions 'melted away in disease and lassi-
tude'.[81] The traditional nomadic culture of the Bedoween had,
however, granted them a precarious tenure in this entropic zone. Islam
disrupted that customary existence, and for a while transformed the
Arab from a nomad to an imperialist. But such violent transformations
cannot endure, as the closing words of the chapter admonish us: 'After
the reign of three caliphs, the throne was transported from Medina to
the valley of Damascus and the banks of the Tigris; the holy cities were
violated by impious war; Arabia was ruled by the rod of a subject,
perhaps of a stranger; and the Bedoweens of the desert, awakening
from their dream of dominion, resumed their old and solitary independence.'[82] It is a wonderfully poetic coda, exemplifying beautifully
how in Gibbon historical judgement is wedded to imaginative apprehension. We are a world away, in terms both of quality of historical
insight and substantive assertion, from the brisk simplicities of
Boulainvilliers, Voltaire, and the *Encyclopédie*.

A sense of historical sequence as sophisticated and attuned to causal
nuance as was Gibbon's is naturally suspicious of both panegyric and
philippic. Set in the centre of this subtle account of the Arabs and their
religion, which shows up as caricature the vehement pieties of both the
orthodox and the *philosophe*—for the *philosophes*, too, as Gibbon well
understood, had their dogmas and their doctrines[83]—Gibbon's portrait
of Mahomet finds a truly historical way to surmount the crude dilemma
of impostor or philosophic hero in which his enemies had sought to

---

[80] *DF* iii. 231.
[81] *DF* iii. 159.
[82] *DF* iii. 232.
[83] Noting Voltaire's admiration for the Turkish sultan Amurath II, who abdicated the throne
and thereby earned from Voltaire the commendation of being 'le Philosophe Turc', Gibbon
comments: 'would he have bestowed the same praise on a Christian prince for retiring to a
monastery? In his way, Voltaire was a bigot, an intolerant bigot' (*DF* iii. 916, n. 13).

entrap him. In a long paragraph of balanced judgement, Gibbon vindi-
cates his own character as an historian at the same time as he evades the
clumsy ambushes of his enemies:

At the conclusion of the life of Mahomet, it may perhaps be expected, that I
should balance his faults and virtues, that I should decide whether the title of
enthusiast or impostor more properly belongs to that extraordinary man. Had
I been intimately conversant with the son of Abdallah, the task would still be
difficult, and the success uncertain: at the distance of twelve centuries, I darkly
contemplate his shade through a cloud of religious incense; and could I truly
delineate the portrait of an hour, the fleeting resemblance would not equally
apply to the solitary of mount Hera, to the preacher of Mecca, and to the
conqueror of Arabia. The author of a mighty revolution appears to have been
endowed with a pious and contemplative disposition: so soon as marriage had
raised him above the pressure of want, he avoided the paths of ambition and
avarice; and till the age of forty, he lived with innocence, and would have died
without a name. The unity of God is an idea most congenial to nature and
reason; and a slight conversation with the Jews and Christians would teach him
to despise and detest the idolatry of Mecca. It was the duty of a man and a
citizen to impart the doctrine of salvation, to rescue his country from the
dominion of sin and error. The energy of a mind incessantly bent on the same
object, would convert a general obligation into a particular call; the warm
suggestions of the understanding or the fancy, would be felt as the inspirations
of heaven; the labour of thought would expire in rapture and vision; and the
inward sensation, the invisible monitor, would be described with the form and
attributes of an angel of God. From enthusiasm to imposture, the step is
perilous and slippery: the dæmon of Socrates affords a memorable instance,
how a wise man may deceive himself, how a good man may deceive others,
how the conscience may slumber in a mixed and middle state between self-
illusion and voluntary fraud. Charity may believe that the original motives of
Mahomet were those of pure and genuine benevolence; but a human mission-
ary is incapable of cherishing the obstinate unbelievers who reject his claims,
despise his arguments, and persecute his life; he might forgive his personal
adversaries, he may lawfully hate the enemies of God; the stern passions of pride
and revenge were kindled in the bosom of Mahomet, and he sighed, like the
prophet of Niniveh, for the destruction of the rebels whom he had condemned. The injustice of Mecca, and the choice of Medina, transformed the
citizen into a prince, the humble preacher into the leader of armies; but his
sword was consecrated by the example of the saints; and the same God who
afflicts a sinful world with pestilence and earthquakes, might inspire for their
conversion or chastisement the valour of his servants. In the exercise of political government, he was compelled to abate of the stern rigour of fanaticism, to
comply in some measure with the prejudices and passions of his followers, and
to employ even the vices of mankind as the instruments of their salvation. The

use of fraud and perfidy, of cruelty and injustice, were often subservient to the propagation of the faith; and Mahomet commanded or approved the assassination of the Jews and idolaters who had escaped from the field of battle. By the repetition of such acts, the character of Mahomet must have been gradually stained; and the influence of such pernicious habits would be poorly compensated by the practice of the personal and social virtues which are necessary to maintain the reputation of a prophet among his sectaries and friends. Of his last years, ambition was the ruling passion; and a politician will suspect, that he secretly smiled (the victorious impostor!) at the enthusiasm of his youth and the credulity of his proselytes. A philosopher will observe, that *their* credulity and *his* success, would tend more strongly to fortify the assurance of his divine mission, that his interest and religion were inseparably connected, and that his conscience would be soothed by the persuasion, that he alone was absolved by the Deity from the obligation of positive and moral laws. If he retained any vestige of his native innocence, the sins of Mahomet may be allowed as an evidence of his sincerity. In the support of truth, the arts of fraud and fiction may be deemed less criminal; and he would have started at the foulness of the means, had he not been satisfied of the importance and justice of the end. Even in a conqueror or a priest, I can surprise a word or action of unaffected humanity; and the decree of Mahomet, that, in the sale of captives, the mothers should never be separated from their children, may suspend or moderate the censure of the historian.[84]

The central insight here is one which no one can make so properly as an historian. It is simply the commonplace observation (eagerly forgotten, however, by both the orthodox and the *philosophe* when they wrote on Mahomet) that all things, including the characters of men, change over time: 'could I truly delineate the portrait of an hour, the fleeting resemblance would not equally apply to the solitary of mount Hera, to the preacher of Mecca, and to the conqueror of Arabia.' It is the fact of change which makes the initial challenge to formulate a definitive judgement, to 'balance [Mahomet's] faults and virtues', a *question mal posée*. From this point of departure Gibbon unfolds a shrewd account of how, in a reciprocity of outward circumstances and inner disposition, Mahomet's motives and self-understanding changed during the course of his life:

The author of a mighty revolution appears to have been endowed with a pious and contemplative disposition: so soon as marriage had raised him above the pressure of want, he avoided the paths of ambition and avarice; and till the age of forty, he lived with innocence, and would have died without a name. The unity of God is an idea most congenial to nature and reason; and a slight conversation with the Jews and Christians would teach him to despise and detest the idolatry of Mecca. It was the duty of a man and a citizen to impart the doctrine of salvation, to rescue his country from the dominion of sin and error. The energy of a mind incessantly bent on the same object, would convert a general obligation into a particular call; the warm suggestions of the understanding or the fancy, would be felt as the inspirations of heaven; the labour of thought would expire in rapture and vision; and the inward sensation, the invisible monitor, would be described with the form and attributes of an angel of God. From enthusiasm to imposture, the step is perilous and slippery: the dæmon of Socrates affords a memorable instance, how a wise man may deceive himself, how a good man may deceive others, how the conscience may slumber in a mixed and middle state between self-illusion and voluntary fraud.

This passage shows clearly how in the later chapters of *The Decline and Fall* historical scholarship provides the materials and the framework for sympathetic and acute acts of imagination.

We find incorporated here the positions of both the *philosophe* (for instance, in the concession that 'the original motives of Mahomet were those of pure and genuine benevolence') and the orthodox (for instance, in the awareness that 'of his last years, ambition was the ruling passion; and a politician will suspect, that he secretly smiled (the victorious impostor!) at the enthusiasm of his youth and the credulity of his proselytes'). But both these simplifying extremes have been placed and transcended in Gibbon's more searching, wise, and imaginative synthesis. The passage concludes, appropriately, with the word 'historian'. In the final instalment of *The Decline and Fall*, Gibbon's entry into possession of his literary character is also a triumphal procession over the bodies of his critics.

PART II

AFTER *THE DECLINE AND FALL*

5

Gibbon's Unfinished History

Pope.   There is no one study that is not capable of delighting us
   after a little application to it.
Spence.   How true, even in so dry a thing as antiquities!

Gibbon embalmed the moment when the manuscript of *The Decline
and Fall* was completed in a famous passage of draft 'E' of the 'Memoirs':

> It was on the day, or rather the night, of the 27th of June, 1787, between the
> hours of eleven and twelve, that I wrote the last lines of the last page in a
> summer-house in my garden. After laying down my pen I took several turns
> in a *berceau*, or covered walk of Acacias, which commands a prospect of the
> country, the lake, and the mountains. The air was temperate, the sky was
> serene, the silver orb of the moon was reflected from the waters, and all Nature
> was silent. I will not dissemble the first emotions of joy on the recovery of my
> freedom, and perhaps the establishment of my fame. But my pride was soon
> humbled, and a sober melancholy was spread over my mind by the idea that I
> had taken my everlasting leave of an old and agreable companion, and that,
> whatsoever might be the future date of my history, the life of the historian must
> be short and precarious.[1]

It is possible to read this passage as musing on the interrelatedness of
composure and composition: the work, the author, and even Nature
herself have reached simultaneously a moment of repose. But the
moment of harmony is short-lived, yielding almost immediately to the
'sober melancholy' of divergence as Gibbon ponders the complicated
way in which he is now separated from his history. He has taken leave
of it, and is free now to apply himself to other projects; but in the longer
run, the history will take its leave of him, and will continue on its way
beyond the 'short and precarious' life of its author.

   It is no accident, I think, that the advent of these more sombre
reflections on the eventual disparity of art and life is heralded by the
word 'fame'. In one sense, Gibbon's fame was now assured. As his

[1] *A* 333–4.

handling of the subject of Islam and Mahomet demonstrated, in the final instalment of *The Decline and Fall* Gibbon's mastery of historical art had reached a new level of technical refinement and subtlety. He had become the writer of his wishes. The trials of controversy had played, as we have seen, a surprising and positive role in that process. But all previous discord was extinguished when Gibbon returned to England in the summer of 1787, bearing with him the manuscript of the last three volumes of the history, and ready to reap the harvest of fame:

All party resentment was now lost in oblivion; since I was no man's rival, no man was my enemy: I felt the dignity of independence, and as I asked no more, I was satisfied with the general civilities of the World. The house in London which I frequented with the most pleasure and assiduity was that of Lord North: after the loss of power and of sight, he was still happy in himself and his friends, and my public tribute of gratitude and esteem could no longer be suspected of any interested motive. Before my departure from England I assisted at the august spectacle of Mr. Hastings's tryal in Westminster hall: I shall not absolve or condemn the Governor of India, but Mr. Sheridan's eloquence demanded my applause; nor could I hear without emotion the personal compliment which he paid me in the presence of the British nation. . . . The day of publication was . . . delayed, that it might coincide with the fifty-first anniversary of my own birthday: the double festival was celebrated by a chearful litterary dinner at Cadell's house, and I seemed to blush while they read an elegant compliment from Mr. Hayley, whose poetical talent had more than once been employed in the praise of his friend.[2]

But all was not praise, festivity, and compliment. The final three volumes of the history were 'variously judged'; 'a religious clamour was revived; and the reproach of indecency has been loudly echoed by the rigid censors of morals.'[3] The contest over Gibbon's reputation was set to continue for several years yet, and to extend even beyond the 'short and precarious' life of the historian. And it was given, as we shall see, further impetus by the events of the following year. The French Revolution reinvigorated the debate over Gibbon's reputation, and in the ensuing controversy the topics of religious heterodoxy and indecency became entangled. So the works to which Gibbon turned after *The Decline and Fall* were not undertaken in the serene after-glow of the triumphs of 1787 and 1788. They, too, have their adversarial and combative aspects.

[2] *A* 335–7. The 'public tribute' Gibbon paid to Lord North was the dedication to him of the final three volumes of *The Decline and Fall* (*DF* ii. 520–1). Warren Hastings had been Gibbon's contemporary at Westminster School. The 'personal compliment' paid by Sheridan to Gibbon came when he condemned Hastings's crimes as surpassing anything to be found in 'the correct periods of Tacitus or the luminous page of Gibbon'. [3] *A* 337.

One such work is the 'unfinished history' of my title. For some three years towards the end of his life, between late 1789 and late 1792, Gibbon composed and revised a work he entitled *The Antiquities of the House of Brunswick*.[4] This (one of a projected series of 'historical excursions') was to be a genealogical essay setting out the European ancestry of the British royal family in three books: 'i THE ITALIAN DESCENT, ii THE GERMAN REIGN, and iii THE BRITISH SUCCESSION'.[5] We have only fragments of the first two books, and thus nothing concerning the Hanoverian succession in Great Britain, which Gibbon knew would be the most interesting part of his work.[6] Nevertheless, by reading those fragments in a context formed by contemporary European politics, Gibbon's correspondence, and earlier eighteenth-century studies of royal genealogy, we can reach probable conclusions concerning why Gibbon began this work, and why he abandoned it. In so doing we shall be led to examine how English men of property resisted the new 'French disease' of democratical principles; how the emotions and psychology of the English counter-revolution changed as perceptions of what was happening in France became more grave; and finally how the connotations of certain political vocabularies shifted under the pressure of events during the early 1790s.[7]

II

Had Gibbon completed and published the *Antiquities of the House of Brunswick* a contemporary reader would have placed it as another example of the plentiful literature celebrating the historical grandeur of the house of Hanover. What were the features of that literature, and why was it written?

Studies and celebrations of the genealogy of the royal family were not published uniformly throughout the period of the Hanoverian succession. They clustered around particular, crucial, dates: 1714 (the accession of George I), 1727 (the accession of George II), and the early 1740s (the beginning of the War of the Austrian Succession). At each of these crises, when either the legitimacy or the benefits of Hanoverian monarchy were called in question, 'some scribbler was employed . . . to

---

[4] For a recent theory of the status of the remaining manuscript fragments, see Patricia Craddock's comments in *EE* 594–7.

[5] For Gibbon's brief comments on this enterprise, see *L* iii. 203 and 211. *EE* 400.

[6] 'La succession de la maison de Brunswick au trone de la Grande Bretagne sera tres assurement la partie la plus interessante de mon travail' (*L* iii. 204).

[7] The reapplication of the phrase 'French disease' (for which Burke's *Reflections* is 'a most admirable medicine') is Gibbon's own (*L* iii. 216).

assert the hereditary right of the present family'.[8] This cannot but seem puzzling. In 1714 George I was, in terms of strict primogeniture, fifty-eighth in line to the throne; and yet in 1710 he had announced that he would ascend the throne by hereditary right.[9] There is, of course, no necessary contradiction here. An heir (particularly to the throne) need not be the closest in blood. Gilbert Nelson had set out the doctrine in 1717: 'The Law of *Hereditary Right* is not *unchangable*, but may be *explained*, *limited* or *qualified* by another succeeding Law'; and in England

the Succession has been limited to the *Protestant* Branches of the *Royal Family*. And this Succession has been confirm'd by several Laws, acknowledged by other Princes and signally vindicated by *Divine Providence*. So that His Majesty *King George* has the *best* Title to these Kingdoms by Law, and the *first Hereditary Right* above and before any Person, that is capable to Govern these Nations.[10]

Nevertheless, might it not have been wiser for the Hanoverians to have avoided the subject of hereditary right altogether? Would it not have been more prudent to have settled for the purely parliamentary title which some hardy spirits were eager to accord them?[11]

Clearly, the Hanoverians and their friends thought otherwise. The potency of ideas of hereditary right in the minds of Englishmen, the tenacity with which political thought was coloured by this sentiment (for such it essentially was, rather than a set of distinct propositions), obliged the Hanoverians 'to counter the Stuarts' dynastic claims with a dynastic title of their own, weak though it was'.[12] In mid-century Blackstone coolly presented this as the immemorial practice of English usurpers. Sensible of the credit enjoyed by such titles, they 'endeavoured to vamp up some feeble shew of a title by descent, in order to amuse the people, while they gained the possession of the kingdom'.[13]

Thus the Englishman's traditional respect for hereditary title, which

---

[8] The phrase is Bolingbroke's, and is taken from his *Idea of a Patriot King* (*Works*, iv. 264).

[9] This whole question has been illuminated by the research of Jonathan Clark; see his *English Society 1688–1832*, 119–98, 'The Survival of the Dynastic Idiom, 1688–1760: An Essay in the Social History of Ideas'.

[10] Gilbert Nelson, *King GEORGE's Right Asserted*, 25 and 28–9.

[11] Such as Daniel Defoe, in his ironical pamphlet *Reasons Against the Succession of the House of Hanover*; see especially sigs. G^v and G2^r.

[12] Clark, *English Society 1688–1832*, 132. On the propositional slipperiness—and consequent durability—of hereditary and divine right conviction ('a quasi-religious act of allegiance which could not easily by dispensed with, any more than could a religious faith or an obligation of personal honour'), see p. 143.

[13] Sir William Blackstone, *Commentaries on the Laws of England*, i. 197.

in 1823 Lord John Russell could dismiss as 'the bigotry of millions', was in the previous century a political actuality with which apologists for the royal family had to cope.[14] Toland might stigmatize a belief in divine right as evidence of 'want of thinking'; an anonymous pamphleteer of the 1740s might sigh that 'the Notion of Hereditary Right is sunk too deep in their weak Minds to be eradicated by Argument'.[15] The problem remained of how this stubborn delusion was to be managed. While some tried to weaken its hold on the popular mind through ridicule, and some sought through redefinition to reconcile divine right with an elective title, others chose the steeper, but more direct, path of harmonizing such belief with the fact of Hanoverian monarchy.[16]

At its simplest this might involve nothing more than an assertion that the Hanoverians enjoyed 'a double Claim' by virtue of their 'Descent from the Blood of *England*', and an assurance to George I that 'You are descended from the *First* of our KINGS of the PLANTAGENET Race, from the *First* of our KINGS of the TEUDOR Line, for the *First* of our KINGS of the STUARTINE Race'.[17] Others more subtly revived the scandal of the previous century, and found George I's title in terms of proximity of blood more probable than that of the Pretender because of the doubt as to whether the Pretender really was the son of James II.[18] The most ingenious, however, was the argument put forward in a pamphlet of 1729, *The True and Ancient Hereditary Right Consider'd and Explain'd*, where George II was accorded 'the best *Hereditary Right* to the Crown of *England* . . . of any Monarch that hath

[14] Lord John Russell, *History of the English Government and Constitution*, 212; quoted in Clark, *English Society 1688–1832*, 120 n. 7.
[15] John Toland, *Anglia Libera*, sig. G3ᵛ; [Anon.], *An Examine of the Expediency of Bringing over Immediately the Body of Hanoverian Troops taken into our Pay*, sig. Bᵛ.
[16] For the ridicule, see Defoe's *Reasons Against the Succession of the House of Hanover*, sigs. C2ᵛ–3ʳ; for the redefinition, Toland's *Anglia Libera*, where we learn that 'there is no Title equal to their [the people's] Approbation, which is the only divine Right of all Magistracy, for *the Voice of the People is the Voice of God*' (sig. C5ᵛ).
[17] [Anon.], *Memoirs of the House of Hanover*, sig. A2ᵛ; David Jones, *The History of the Most Serene House of Brunswick-Lunenburgh*, sig. A3ʳ. Compare also [Anon.], *A King and No King*, 8: 'have we not a Prince on the Throne immediately descended from the *Royal Blood of England*, (even the Line of the *STUARTS*) (if that be of such value to you) Great *Grandson* to King *James* the First, and great *Nephew* to King *Charles* I. just of the same Degree of Consanguinity with the late Queen of blessed memory; the next Protestant Prince of the whole World that is allied to us?' Other examples may be found in works selling at a variety of prices from 3d. to 2s.: *An Historical Account of our Present Sovereign George-Lewis* (1714), *The Glory of the Protestant Line, Exemplified . . . in His Most Excellent MAJESTY, GEORGE* (1714), and *The Whole Life, Burth and Character of his most Serene Highness Geoge* [sic] *Lewis Elector of Hanover* (n.d.).
[18] *King George's Title Asserted* (1716).

sat upon the Throne since *Richard* the First'.[19] The author was explicit that, in his opinion, the most secure foundation of the Hanoverian title was parliamentary.[20] Nevertheless, the Hanoverians *also* possessed the best hereditary right, because of a detail of medieval history: 'there was no Branch of the Royal Family of *Henry* the Second for the *Hereditary Right* to descend to, upon the death of the Princess *Eleanor*, and the Forfeiture of King *John*, but the Princess *Maud*, eldest daughter of King *Henry* the Second, and Mother of the first Royal Blood in the Ancestors of King *GEORGE*.'[21] In other words, the non-jurors needed to be shown that, even on their own contemptible terms, the Hanoverian succession had right on its side, and showed the 'astonishing Conduct of divine Providence, in restoring to the Throne of these Nations the Pure untainted Blood of the *Plantagenets*'.[22]

The genealogy of the Hanoverians was thus sometimes rehearsed in justification of a dynastic title. More often, however, it served panegyric purposes. The conviction that the Germans were 'the most despicable people in Europe', and the Hanoverians merely cocks of the midden, was countered with celebrations of the regality, distinction, and breeding of the Hanoverian line.[23] The British, so the argument ran, have not lost caste with their new royal family. If anything, the reverse is true:

I need say nothing on this Genealogy of the illustrious Family of *Brunswick* and *Hanover*, to prove it the most ancient and honourable in *Europe*: there is enough printed long before his late Majesty had any Views of coming to the throne of *Great-Britain*; which sufficiently demonstrates that this Family is the most ancient, honourable and glorious of any now subsisting in *Europe*, and therefore is so far from being the Object of Contempt, as many of my Countrymen have been deluded to think, that it is the greatest Ornament to the *British* Throne, of any Family that hath sat upon the throne of *England*, for these five hundred, (I may say) these thousand Years past.[24]

[19] It was this work of which George Ballantyne provided a partial, verbatim reprint in his *A Vindication of the Hereditary Right of his Present Majesty, King George II* (1743).

[20] 'But wou'd not have it understood, that by the following Argument I insinuate, That the Supreme Divine Right of his late, and present Majesty King *GEORGE* the Second, and his *Heirs* to the Crown of *Great-Britain*, is principally founded upon their strict *Hereditary Right* to the Crown of *England* and *Ireland*: No, that is founded upon the Acts of the States and the Supreme Legislative Power of the Nation, in their settling the *Crown* upon the Princess *Sophia*, and her Heirs, being *Protestants*' (sig. C2ʳ).

[21] Sig. B4ʳ.

[22] Sig. K2ʳ. In Ballantyne's reprint the pamphlet's ironic strategy is made plain on its title page: 'a full Answer to all the Arguments of the *NONJURORS* . . . in their OWN WAY, and upon their OWN PRINCIPLES.'

[23] [Anon.], *English Loyalty opposed to Hanoverian Ingratitude*, sig. A4ᵛ.

[24] [Anon.], *The True and Ancient Hereditary Right*, sig. Hʳ. Compare also 'Thus I have shewn

The poems of greeting for George I praise '*Brunswick's* Mighty Line' (aptly enough this phrase occurs in an alexandrine), admire the 'Celestial Progeny' of a 'Royal Line | In whom at once the Saint and Hero join', salute '*GEORGE* and his Illustrious Line', and enquire:

> What Place that ever was out-run by Fame,
> That has not heard of Mighty *BRUNSWICK's* Name?[25]

This emphasis is duplicated in the more academic and thorough works of Hanoverian genealogy which appeared after 1714. David Jones's *The History of the Most Serene House of Brunswick-Lunenburgh* (1715) aspired 'to Confirm our Veneration for Your PERSON, by a History of Your FAMILY'.[26] George I's ancestry was traced back to Odin, points of contact with the English throne indicated during the reigns of Alfred the Great and Henry II, and the House of Brunswick depicted as Imperial, rather than merely royal.[27] Henry Rimius's later and more sumptuous *Memoirs of the House of Brunswick* (1750)—an expensive book privately printed in small numbers, but exerting great influence by virtue of its being quoted extensively in the article on the Duke of Cornwall in Collins's often-reprinted *Complete Peerage of England*— contrived to make the whole course of European history seem merely an aspect of the family history of this 'Race of Heroes': 'There has scarcely been any Action of Consequence, during many Centuries, either relative to War or Peace, in which one or other of this Lineage has not acted a considerable Part, and its Antiquity is so great, that we find Traces of it long before the Birth of Christ, and can deduce it, without Interruption, for near Fourteen Hundred Years.'[28] In this respect accounts of the royal genealogy served to impart historical stiffening to a language of eulogy which might otherwise swell into laughable hyperbole:

To give you the Sum of what I think of our most gracious sovereign King GEORGE in general, he is every way so much more than Man, that he is no

---

the Descent and Pedigree of this most Noble and Illustrious House, by which it is evident that we have the Promise of a Race of Virtuous Princes to Rule over us in their Posterity' ([Anon.], *Memoirs of the House of Hanover*, sig. C3ᵛ). Other examples may be found in [Anon.], *An Examine of the Expediency*, sig. C4ʳ; Toland, *Anglia Libera*, sigs. F4ʳ⁻ᵛ; Harris, *Considerations on the Birth-day of his Most Sacred Majesty King GEORGE*, 29; Browne, *An Oration Upon the King's Happy Arrival*, 7.

[25] [Anon.], *An Ode Presented to the King*, 4; [Anon.], *A Poem Upon His Majesties Accession*, 3 and 4; Chapman, *Britannia Rediviva*, 10; [Anon.], *The Succession*, 4.

[26] Jones, *History of the Most Serene House of Brunswick-Lunenburgh*, sigs. A2ᵛ⁻3ʳ.

[27] Ibid., sig. A2ʳ⁻ᵛ.

[28] Rimius, *Memoirs of the House of Brunswick*, pp. iii and 2.

less in all things than himself. One whose rare Excellencies are such, as would make us believe his Breeding had been amongst the angels in another world, rather than among Royal Persons here in this, and that he was only lent us a while, as an universal Pattern for all Mankind to imitate, and to let us see how much of Heaven may dwell upon Earth.[29]

Flattery cannot often be made plausible. Yet with care it can be kept from becoming risible. This was one of the uses of royal genealogy in the first half of the eighteenth century.

After 1750, however, accounts of Hanoverian genealogy abruptly ceased.[30] In 1755 Shebbeare remarked that the Tories, despite their previous allegiance to the Stuarts, 'now defend the royal house on the throne, with as much zeal as the Whigs'.[31] The new security of the Hanoverian succession in the middle decades of the century permitted more frank avowals of both the parliamentary, legal, origins of the royal family's title, and of their personal failings. The independent Whig John Almon, writing in 1762 and convinced that the Hanoverians were 'firmly and immoveably seated on the throne', could calmly acknowledge of George II that 'the faculties of his understanding were not either lively or brilliant', and allow that his title was essentially not only parliamentary but popular.[32] That political candour and that indifferent tone (neither eulogistic nor satirical) were possible only when, after 1745, there was no longer any serious challenge to the Hanoverian monarchy.[33]

---

[29] [Anon.], *The History of the Lutheran Church, or, The Religion of our Present Sovereign King George Agreeable to the Tenets of the Church of England*, 4–5; cf. also [Anon.], *The Glory of the Royal Protestant Line, Exemplified* and *The Whole Life, Birth and Character of his most Serene Highness Geoge Lewis*, 7.

[30] After Rimius the bibliography of Hanoverian genealogy runs as follows: William Hamilton Reid, *A Concise History of the kingdom of Hanover, and of the house of Brunswick* (1816); Sir Andrew Halliday, *Annals of the House of Hanover* (1826); P. M. Thornton, *The Brunswick Accession* (1887).

[31] John Shebbeare, *Letters on the English Nation*, i. 22. The reasons for this shift have been explained by Jonathan Clark (*English Society, 1688–1832*, 50, 177, 184). It was noted by Gibbon who in his 'Memoirs' commented that the Tories had 'insensibly' transferred their loyalty to the house of Hanover (*A* 252). Over tea in 1773 Samuel Johnson made essentially the same point: 'the family at present on the throne has now established as good a right as the former family, by the long consent of the people; and that to disturb this right might be considered as culpable' (Boswell, *Life of Johnson*, 515).

[32] J. Almon, *A Review of the Reign of George II*, 258, 255. The popular foundations of the Hanoverian title are exposed in Almon's account of the central political transaction of the Glorious Revolution (p. 6): 'they [the people] dethroned him [James II], and by declaring the throne vacant, excluded from hereditary right his infant son. The people appointed for his successor his eldest daughter Mary, who was married to the Prince of Orange; but she declining to reign alone, and he to have any share in the government, unless invested with royalty for life, they were elected by the people king and queen.'

[33] 'After that defeat [of the Jacobites in 1745], the question of legitimacy was suddenly a non-

III

It would seem, then, that Gibbon's *Antiquities*, had they been published, would have revived a subject for which, since 1750, there had
been no call. However, they would have revived that subject in an
unfamiliar idiom. In his 'Memoirs' Gibbon defended the utility and
innocence of family genealogy from the scorn of philosophers.[34] Two
comparisons will show that he was not similarly indulgent towards
royal genealogy.

Henry Rimius had no doubt that the house of Brunswick could trace
its forebears back to the most glorious times and most dignified families
of the Roman republic:

> The *Actii, Atii,* or *Accii,* a noble Family of *Rome* in the Time of its Republican
> Government, retired to *Este,* or *Ateste,* an ancient city in that Part of *Italy,*
> which is now called the *Venetian Lombardy,* and from thence received the
> Name of *Atestina Domus,* or the House of *Este.* It appears, by authentic Authors,
> that this Family was long before in great Repute, and that *Romulus* had a Statue
> erected to them, an Honour the *Romans* never conferred, except on account of
> the highest Merit. One of that Family, named *Cajus Actius,* was known in the
> time of *Tarquinius Priscus,* about 600 Years before the Birth of *Christ;* and
> another, whose Name was *Marcus Actius Balbus,* according to *Suetonius,* had in
> Marriage *Julia,* Sister of *Cajus Julius Caesar,* and his Daughter *Actia* was the
> Mother of the Emperor *Octavius Augustus Caesar.*
>
> The Retirement of this Family is, without Doubt, the Reason, that we have
> no satisfactory Account of it to the Year 390 after the Birth of *Christ;* and the
> great Migrations of the many barbarous Nations, which soon after began to
> change the Face of *Italy,* appear to be the Occasion, that this warlike Family
> made itself known again, in the Defence of their Country. This much is
> certain, that the Genealogy of the House of *Este,* and consequently that of the
> House of *Brunswick,* can be deduced from that Time to this Day without
> Interruption.[35]

This seems urbane and learned. But, in fact, historical criticism has been
subordinated to flattery. The passage bears the true hallmark of panegyric genealogy: it depicts the past as a diminished image of the present.
Thus the connection with Augustus, besides making the ancestors of
George II the spine of the republic from Romulus until its mutation
into the principate, contrives to make his second name a patronym.

---

issue in British political thought; *de facto* and *de iure* merge after 1760' (Clark, *English Society 1688–1832,* 50).

[34] *A* 354–5.
[35] Rimius, *Memoirs,* 3. Compare also Jones, *History,* sigs. B^r–v.

Moreover, the interruption in the series of generations (which should really cast doubt on the whole story) is improved into an advantage. In that period of supposed retirement, ended by patriotic warlikeness, we can see the double image that the Hanoverians created for themselves in eighteenth-century England, of national bulwark and private, genteel family, superimposed on the enigmatic past.[36] Gibbon, asserting less and saying more, exposes the sandy foundations of this compliment:

In those happy times, when a Genealogical tree could strike its root into every soil, when the luxuriant plant could flourish and fructify without a seed of truth, the ambition of the house of Este-Brunswick was easily gratified with a Roman pedigree. The name of *Azo* or *Atto* so familiar to the Italian line was deduced as a manifest corruption from the Latin Original of *Attius* or *Accius* or *Actius*: and this fanciful identity an article of faith in the court of Ferrara, was not disputed in the sixteenth century by the rudeness of foreign criticism.[37]

This tendency to read earlier genealogy in terms of the political pressures exerted on it at the moment of its writing is, as we shall see, a central element of the *Antiquities*. But 'foreign criticism' need not always be rude. Gibbon, with amused learning, goes on to demonstrate how the connection with Augustus actually exposed to comment those it was designed to dignify:

But if the Praetor M. Attius Balbus, a real personnage of the seventh Century of Rome could have any possible affinity with our fabulous series, the genuine lustre of the Accii would be derived from their union with the human and Divine glories of the Julian race[.] Julia the sister of Julius Caesar was the wife of the Praetor Attius, and by their daughter Attia, their grandson Augustus himself might be claimed as a kinsman by the Duke of Modena, and the King of Great-Britain. A prudent Advocate may repeat with pleasure the verses of the Aeneid that celebrate the youthful command of the Trojan Atys, the founder, according to Virgil of the Atian family. . . . but he will dissemble the reproach of Antony, and the apology of Cicero, which may leave a stain on the maternal descent of Augustus.[38]

This sly hint at the futility of panegyric genealogy, its inevitable tendency to discover baseness the further it is prosecuted, is something to which we shall in a moment return. However, the glance at sexual impropriety, the 'stain' on Augustus' ancestry, is not prurient.[39] In the

[36] On images of royalty in the later eighteenth century, see Colley, 'Apotheosis of George III'.

[37] *EE* 405–6.

[38] *EE* 406–7.

[39] This charge is frequently levelled at *The Decline and Fall*, most wittily by Porson: 'nor does his humanity ever slumber, unless when women are ravished, or the Christians persecuted'

context of genealogy, sexual failure and transgression can sustain a more than impertinent interest, as the second comparison will show. We move forward with Henry Rimius to the eleventh century:

Guelph VI had the good Fortune to obtain in Marriage the richest Princess of her Time. It was *Mathildis*, above mentioned, only Daughter of *Boniface* Marggrave of *Este*, Heiress of *Ferrare*, *Mantua*, *Lucca*, *Parma*, *Modena*, *Placentia*, *Pisa*, *Spoleto*, *Ancona*, and *Tuscany*. This Princess, as a zealous Partizan of Pope Gregory VII. and of his Successors, in the Wars which these Popes had with the Emperors *Henry* IV. and *Henry* V, commanded whole Armies, conquered Cities, and did all that can be required of a consummate General. It is said, that one of the Reasons of her marrying *Guelph* VI. was to draw his Father *Guelph* V. from the Emperors Party. This Marriage subsisted but a few years, and was set aside so early as in the Life-time of *Guelph* V, whose Reconciliation with the Emperor probably was the Reason, that his Son lost *Mathildis*, whose Love to her Husbands was always proportioned to their Devotion to the Pope.[40]

Rimius accentuates Mathildis's opulence, as proper to add lustre to the house of Brunswick. But he then transforms her into a Catholic virago, as the failure of her marriage with Guelph is manipulated into an anticipation of the family's later status as Protestant heroes. It is left to Gibbon to uncover a more human explanation for that failure, an explanation probable to the same degree that it is unflattering:

By the Queen Dowager of England, the first Guelphic Duke of Bavaria had two sons, Guelph vii and Henry, surnamed the *black*. The eldest at the age of seventeen (1089) was sent into Italy and commanded by his parents to ascend the nuptial bed of Matilda the Great Countess of Tuscany who had attained the autumnal ripeness of forty three years. This Heroine the spiritual daughter of Gregory vii was twice married: but interest rather than love directed her choice, and her virginity was twice insulted by a crooked dwarf, and an impotent boy. The first and second night had been cold and inefficient: but as young Guelph still complained of some artifice or enchantment, the fairest tryal was offered him on the morning of the third day. The Countess (I soften the words of a Dean) spread herself on a table; and after striving to raise the husband by the display of her naked charms and lascivious motions, she dismissed him from her presence with a blow of contempt. Their conjugal union

---

(*Letters to Mr. Archdeacon Travis*, p. xxviii). There are a number of echoes of the earlier work in the *Antiquities*; Gibbon tells Langer that his interest in the House of Brunswick was kindled while working on *The Decline and Fall* (*L* iii. 204 and n. 7); and when Gibbon informs us that he possesses 'some experience of the way' we can see him reminding us of the authority which has accrued to him as a result of writing *The Decline and Fall* (*EE* 404). But the very different nature of the *Antiquities* means that features which the two works appear to share may not in fact be points of contact.

[40] Rimius, *Memoirs*, 25.

was hopeless; but six years (1089–95) elapsed between the marriage and the divorce; and the government of Tuscany was administered in their joint names, till the imperious temper of Matilda provoked the grandson of Azo to reveal a secret which her pride would have concealed from the World.[41]

This passage is, of course, informed by an alert comedy. But its edge derives from the fact that sexual performance is the perpetual, if unspoken, subject of genealogy. Consequently we are here not confronted with simple indecency on Gibbon's part. The passage's most unsettling feature is the final mention of concealment. It poses the question: how many more such failures shelter in the luxuriant family tree of the Brunswicks? The implicit answer (one of the ironic reversals of genealogy which Gibbon is pleased to discover and emphasize) is that the more successful the genealogist in extending the ramifications of a family, the greater the probability of a spurious inclusion.[42]

So, despite (for instance) Gibbon's scrupulously careful employment of the vocabulary of genealogy, the *Antiquities* seem to be placed at a measured angle to the whole subject and enterprise of genealogical study.[43] Comparison with Rimius indicates that Gibbon, had he published the *Antiquities*, would have prompted the sceptical thoughts which other genealogists tried to quell, and recounted the ungrateful truths they suppressed.

It is, however, most important that here we are as precise as possible concerning Gibbon's tone. For, although the *Antiquities* contain abundant materials for satire, they are not satirical. Rather, they are couched in a controlled, subtle idiom which demands to be understood as much in political, as historiographical, terms. In his 'Memoirs' Gibbon held that the 'study of hereditary honours is favourable to the Royal prerogative'.[44] The politics of his own genealogical study are not, however, so straightforward.

The *Antiquities* begin with the following, politically complex, sentence: 'An English subject may be prompted by a just and liberal curiosity to investigate the origin and story of the house of Brunswick; which, after an alliance with the daughters of our Kings, has been called by the voice of a free people to the legal inheritance of the

---

[41] *EE* 468–9.

[42] Cf. 'even the claim of our legal descent must rest on a basis not perhaps sufficiently firm, the unspotted chastity of *all* our female progenitors' (*A* 354).

[43] For instances of Gibbon's use of the characteristic vocabulary of genealogy, see *EE* 399, 407, 420, and 494.

[44] *A* 8. Gibbon was composing his 'Memoirs' at the same time as the *Antiquities*, and it seems that each work exerted an influence on the other.

Crown.'[45] Monarchical title may be settled by Parliament on behalf of the people (where authority fundamentally lies), and is then transmitted successively until another crisis demands parliamentary intervention.[46] Though apparently contradictory in its drawing together of both elective and hereditary principles, this is perfectly in accordance with the mid-century orthodoxy of Blackstone, expressed in a passage which the young Gibbon copied out *verbatim*:

The grand fundamental maxim upon which the *jus coronae*, or right of succession to the throne of these kingdoms, depends, I take to be this: 'that the crown is, by common law and constitutional custom, hereditary; and this in a manner peculiar to itself: but that the right of inheritance may from time to time be changed or limited by act of parliament; under which limitations the crown still continues hereditary.'[47]

Blackstone's account of the title and of its transmission was determined by his conviction that it was 'our duty at this distance of time to acquiesce' in the arrangements of 1688.[48] Consequently divine right was scorned as un-English folly.[49] The true English practice concerning monarchical title Blackstone established in a long historical digression, which was not primarily concerned to present that practice as intellectually coherent, but rather to establish that such indeed was English practice. The right of the legislature to 'exclude the immediate heir, and vest the inheritance in any one else' Blackstone found exemplified pre-eminently in the medieval monarchy; and so the Hanoverian succession emerged as representing both the recovery of 'our antient constitution and laws' after the absolutist interruption of the Tudors and Stuarts, and the coming to maturity of the institution of monarchy itself.[50]

---

[45] *EE* 493. Patricia Craddock considers this an early draft of the opening sentence, preferring the passage she prints on p. 398. Her arguments for doing so are to be found on pp. 595–7. The manuscripts furnish no conclusive evidence concerning priority, and so any argument will necessarily be internal and therefore probably inconclusive. That being so, I find that the balance of probability lies with this as Gibbon's final thought. In particular, the phrase 'by the voice of a free people' seems to me a careful, parliamentary revision of the earlier, simpler, less guarded and more popularly elective 'by a free people'. For comparison, see Rimius, *Memoirs*, 439 and [Anon.], *The British Hero*, 36–7.

[46] For Gibbon on the sanction of 'popular election', see *EE* 429.

[47] Blackstone, *Commentaries*, i. 190–1. Cf. *EE* 67.

[48] Blackstone, *Commentaries*, i. 212–13.

[49] Ibid. 191 and 209. In 1765 Gibbon pronounced divine right 'an incomprehensible absurdity' (*EE* 67).

[50] Blackstone, *Commentaries*, i. 195, 238, and 336–7. This synthesis of Blackstone's commanded such wide assent, and was allowed to mediate to Englishmen the political content of their 'Englishness', because it drew so heavily on notions already long current, but never before brought together and expressed so acceptably: cf. e.g. Toland, *Anglia Libera*, sigs.H7ʳff.; *Certain*

When, in 1765 or early 1766, Gibbon studied Blackstone, he imbibed the attitude towards the cardinal questions of English politics which stayed with him until the last eighteen months of his life: until, that is, he abandoned the *Antiquities*.[51] The three pillars of his political creed can be summarized as follows, and are all explicitly present in *The Decline and Fall*. First, hereditary monarchy, despite its apparent absurdity, is the most desirable form of government because of its avoidance of the tumults which necessarily arise in elective magistracies.[52] Second, the 'natural Aristocracy of a great Country' provides the 'only true foundation' of its government.[53] Finally, there is a necessary and salutary coincidence of political rights and possession of property.[54] A central paradox of *The Decline and Fall* is that it is a narration of the collapse of the greatest monarchy in world history by a firm supporter of both hereditary monarchy and the hegemony of an hereditary oligarchy.[55] It is a paradox to which even some of Gibbon's contemporaries were blind. Over dinner in Paris in 1777 the Abbé de Mably was astonished when Gibbon, instead of following the former's lead and championing republican government, 'generously' defended monarchy.[56]

However, it would be misleading to suggest that Gibbon's politics

---

Propositions humbly offered to the Consideration of a Person presumed to think too favourably of the present Rebellion against KING GEORGE, recto; *The Loyal Church-man* (1716); Nelson, *King GEORGE's Right Asserted*, 25, 28–9; John Somers, *A Brief History of the Succession of the Crown of England* (1688/9), 13.

[51] For the dating of the notes on Blackstone, see Gibbon, *EE* 558. Gibbon's library contained seventeenth- and earlier eighteenth-century works on the subject of monarchy, such as Philip Hunton's *A Treatise of Monarchy* (1680) and George Harbin, *The Hereditary Right of the Crown of England Asserted* (1713).

[52] *DF* i. 187–8. This is a very common position amongst eighteenth-century political men of letters: compare Hume, 'That Politics May be Reduced to a Science', *Essays Moral, Political and Literary*, p.18; Bolingbroke, *The Idea of a Patriot King, Works*, iv. 241; Blackstone, *Commentaries*, i. 192–3 and 218; Belsham, *Essays Philosophical, Historical and Literary*, 113–14.

[53] *L* iii. 184. Compare *DF* i. 85 and ii. 806–7; *EE* 520; Blackstone, *Commentaries*, i. 7; Toland, *Anglia Libera*, sig. E5ᵛ.

[54] *DF* i. 38–9; compare Blackstone, *Commentaries*, i. 33, Samuel Johnson in Boswell's *Life of Johnson*, 609–10 and 621, and Toland, *Anglia Libera*, sig.A4ᵛ. For the origins of this principle, see Pocock, *The Machiavellian Moment*, 331–552.

[55] The pro-monarchical orientation of *The Decline and Fall* is visible, too, in small details of its interpretation. In the *Esprit des Loix* Montesquieu had argued that in the Roman Empire those at the centre had enjoyed liberty, while those in the provinces suffered tyranny. This view, full of implications damaging to monarchy, was later adopted by the radical Richard Price (*Observations on the Nature of Civil Liberty*, 29). Gibbon, however, reverses this, and argues that although the principate was liable to create tyranny, this was endured only by those at the centre, while the provinces enjoyed the benefits of stable government (*DF* i. 157 and n. 33: compare Hume, *Essays*, 20 and Tacitus, *Annals*, I. 8).

[56] Gibbon, *A* 314–15. It is noticeable that Gibbon gives this anecdote great emphasis.

could accurately be represented by a series of articles of belief.[57] Such a
catalogue would entirely miss what was equally as important, namely
the peculiar manner in which these beliefs were held. The political
attitudes of the propertied in late eighteenth-century England may
accurately be called sophisticated, since they involved the unillusioned,
tactical support of political arrangements known to be at bottom
intellectually incoherent or without foundation, but valued for their
beneficial practical consequences.[58] Gibbon's way of putting this was
that 'positive institutions are often the result of custom and prejudice'.[59]
It was naturally put more explicitly by the radical Whig William
Belsham in 1789, while discussing the principle that the king can do
no wrong: 'How easy it would be pompously to declaim against the
political absurdity and dangerous tendency of this maxim! yet we see
that it is regarded as a mere political fiction, that no inconvenience in
fact results from it; but on the contrary, that it is productive of very
signal advantages.'[60] For John Campbell this sophisticated political
attitude was the product of English history. Through their collective
experience the English nation had been convinced 'of many Truths, to
a just Sense of which they could never have been persuaded by
Arguments'.[61] It is an attitude vividly exemplified in an episode of
Gibbon's political career. In April 1780 he had voted against Dunning's
famous motion calling for the power of the Crown to be diminished.
But some three weeks later he had supported an Address to the throne
humbly requesting that Parliament should not be dissolved until
measures had been taken to reduce the monarch's influence.[62] Abrupt
challenges (such as that of Dunning) to positive institutions must be
deplored and opposed, however much one may inwardly approve their
purpose, and even share the perception from which they arise.

Gibbon's great stroke of art in the *Antiquities* was to transpose that
distinctive mode of political belief into an historiographical idiom. The

---

[57] It is this shortcoming which above all mars what is to date the only study of Gibbon's
politics; Dickinson, 'The Politics of Edward Gibbon'.

[58] Consider Johnson's dinner-table sally of 1777, that a poll amongst the nation would produce a majority for the Stuarts ('the King who certainly has the hereditary right'), although no
one would run any risk to restore the exiled family, because the English 'have grown cold and
indifferent upon the subject of loyalty' (Boswell, *Life of Johnson*, 840–1).

[59] *DF* ii. 795. Compare also his famous comment on Roman religion; 'The various modes of
worship which prevailed in the Roman world were all considered by the people as equally true;
by the philosopher as equally false; and by the magistrate as equally useful' (*DF* i. 56). English
politics in the eighteenth century also required the endorsement of useful fictions.

[60] *Essays*, 129. Compare Shebbeare, *Letters*, ii. 12–13.

[61] *A Political Survey of Britain*, ii. 559.

[62] *L* ii. 398 n. 2.

opening sentence, as we have seen, established from the first that this work was written by, and from the perspective of, 'an English subject'. The 'Englishness' of the *Antiquities* was sustained, and further defined, in two main ways. First, Gibbon drew language from political vocabularies to describe his historiographic posture. Secondly, in a handful of introductory paragraphs he contrasted himself with his two great European predecessors in the field of Hanoverian genealogy: the German Leibnitz (librarian to the Dukes of Hanover from 1676 to 1716) and the Italian Muratori (librarian to the Dukes of Modena from 1700 to 1750).

When Sheffield published the remains of the *Antiquities* in 1796, his introduction singled out Gibbon's account of Leibnitz and Muratori as of special interest.[63] So indeed it is. But Sheffield's praise is unfortunate in its suggestion that these preliminary cameos are tangential to the main thrust of the *Antiquities*. In fact, despite their digressive appearance, they are an integral part of the text.

Henry Rimius exemplified the uncritical way with sources of the panegyrical genealogist. Every flattering conjecture was adopted, none was scrutinized, and the mere fact of there being previous commentators was cited as a tribute to the greatness of the house of Brunswick.[64] By contrast Gibbon opened the *Antiquities* with a review of the efforts of Leibnitz and Muratori which did not see all scholars aligned in a desire to immortalize the great house. Gibbon intended 'to erect a strong and substantial edifice of truth on the learned labours of Leibnitz and Muratori'.[65] But, in order that their 'learned labours' could support 'truth', Leibnitz and Muratori had first to be put in their place. Gibbon drew a diptych of two contrasting instances of intellectual imperfection: Leibnitz the impressive, but finally ridiculous, figure of intellectual hubris who 'ambitiously grasped the whole circle of human science', but whose 'powers were dissipated by the multiplicity of his pursuits'; Muratori the foot-soldier of scholarship whose *Antichita Estense* was 'a model of Genealogical criticism', but who nevertheless 'will not aspire to the fame of historical Genius'.[66] Gibbon used the work of both men, but not uncritically; and in the contextualizing of the work of Leibnitz

---

[63] Sheffield saw the *Antiquities* as one of the two major literary legacies of his friend (the other was the 'Memoirs'); *MW 1796* i. x ('Among the most splendid passages of that unfinished work may be enumerated the characters of Leibnitz and Muratori').

[64] 'There is no sovereign, no illustrious House on Earth, whose memorable Actions Authors in different Ages have more endeavoured to preserve from Oblivion, than those of the Most Serene House of BRUNSWICK' (Rimius, *Memoirs*, 1).

[65] *EE* 400.

[66] *EE* 400, 401, and 404; cf. also 506.

and Muratori which results we see, not only technical skills honed by twenty years of historical composition, but an enactment of the political liberty of an Englishman. For Leibnitz and Muratori were both, as Gibbon made plain, employees, and as such had no alternative to the panegyric genealogy in which (as Gibbon knew) 'the prospect is always closed by the fame [and] the virtues' of the living.[67] For Gibbon writing the *Antiquities*, on the other hand, 'the tone of panegyric' was always liable to 'prompt a suspicion'.[68] In consequence the *Antiquities* work against the grain of panegyric genealogy.[69]

The respect in which the *Antiquities* exceed the generic mould in which they seem to be cast is obliquely indicated in Gibbon's comment on Muratori, that he will not 'aspire to the fame of historical Genius'.[70] How would the productions of historical genius differ from those of the mere genealogist and compiler? The question is illuminated when Gibbon discusses the investiture of the first Duke of Brunswick by the Emperor Frederick II in the mid-thirteenth century: 'But our ideas are raised, and our prospect is opened by the discovery, that the first Duke of Brunswick was rather degraded than adorned by his new title, since it imposed the duties of feudal service on the free and patrimonial estate, which alone had been saved in the shipwreck of the more splendid fortunes of his House.'[71] The energy of historiography comes from that defeating of expectation which raises ideas and opens prospects. This comment on the psychology of historical composition reflects back brilliantly on the experience of writing *The Decline and Fall*. But it equally sheds light on the *Antiquities*. For this moment of degradation, in which Gibbon finds the impetus of study, is one in which the panegyric genealogist, for whom as we have seen the prospect must always be closed by praise of the living, cannot share, and from which he cannot benefit.

Genuinely and fully historical study on a subject as delicate as royal genealogy, then, was possible only for one who enjoyed the political liberty of an Englishman, as Gibbon suggested by bringing together the subject of historiography and the language of politics. Muratori's

---

[67] *EE* 411. Compare also 'an epitaph on the dead may prove somewhat more than a panegyric on the living' (*EE* 504).

[68] *EE* 482.

[69] We can therefore see the practised ironist of *The Decline and Fall* at work in the bland modesty of this disclaimer to Langer, '[suis] je en droit de supposer que mes ecrits puissent contribuer a son [that of the House of Brunswick] honneur?' (*L* iii. 205). It was never Gibbon's intention to write a work of royal compliment.

[70] *EE* 404.

[71] *EE* 403–4.

'victorious arguments in the dispute for Commachio, accustomed the slave to an erect posture and a bolder step'; nevertheless his intellect remained confined 'in the narrow circle of an Italian priest'.[72] Gibbon, however, as an English freeman, is motivated by 'a just and liberal curiosity'.[73] He need not confine himself to 'the rigid servitude of annals'.[74] He may 'assume the liberty of judgement' while not being 'unmindful of the duties of gratitude'.[75] He, and he alone, is free to 'disdain to be influenced by any partial regard for the interest or honour of the house of Brunswick' and to cultivate 'impartial criticism'.[76] Only he can expose the debasements of language which panegyric brings about.[77] Only he is free to pay due accord to 'the stubborn character of facts' and 'the order of time, that infallible touchstone of truth'.[78]

In a work composed at approximately the same time as the *Antiquities* Gibbon admired Britain as 'the only powerful and wealthy state, which has ever possessed the inestimable secret of uniting the benefits of order with the blessings of freedom'.[79] That ideal political poise is duplicated in the *Antiquities*. Gibbon offers beneficial and orderly support for established institutions by abstaining from satire, and by paying tribute (where it is due) to 'the majestic tree' formed by 'the male pedigree of the house of Brunswick'.[80] But he is also blessedly free to find in genealogy 'the annals of human vanity', and to allow his intelligence to play with amusement, but never indignation, over its ironic reversals and paradoxes.[81]

[72] *EE* 403.

[73] *EE* 493.

[74] *EE* 420.

[75] *EE* 404. 'Gratitude' is a term charged with political resonance in the context of Hanoverian literature. Opponents to the Hanoverian succession were regularly accused of ingratitude, particularly in the 1740s; see *The Advantages of the Hanover Succession, and English Ingratitude* (1744) and *English Loyalty Opposed to Hanoverian Ingratitude* (1744).

[76] *EE* 507 and 506.

[77] For examples, see *EE* 434 ('The French . . . Gallic chiefs.') and p. 492 ('The government . . . command of the silver mines').

[78] *EE* 506 and 507.

[79] *An Address &c* (*EE* 535). It was composed probably some time late in 1793 (*L* iii. 340–3).

[80] *EE* 399. For an example of such a compliment, see p. 400.

[81] *EE* 431. For examples of such reversals, see *EE* 412, 415, 430, 447, 448, 452, 458–9, 485, 489, 527 (the Persian tale). One suspects that this attitude towards royal genealogy was common amongst an elite, hegemonic oligarchy for whom questions of genealogy would often bear an immediate legal and financial importance (see Cannon, *Aristocratic Century* and L. Stone and J. C. Fawtier Stone, *An Open Elite? England 1540–1880*, 66–91). That very practical utility might throw a contrasting light over the essential vanity of royal genealogy in a period when monarchical title was known to be essentially parliamentary: James Anderson, author of *Royal Genealogies* (1732), had no takers for his project of a similarly ostentatious handling of aristocratic genealogies (sig. aᵛ); and Hervey despised George II for his interest in genealogy (Hervey, *Memoirs*, 71, 74–5, and 154).

That restraint, in which the literary playfulness of irony is separated from an overt hostility, may remind us of an earlier eighteenth-century historian and man of letters known personally to Gibbon: David Hume. In his *Essays* Hume had taken a form previously associated with the Whiggish views of Addison and Steele, and had availed himself of that association the better to insinuate his own, different, political attitudes. Gibbon was doing something similar in the *Antiquities*; and he indicated the lineage of his project, not with the pompousness of the genealogist, but through that touchstone of true propinquity, shared features. The language of his opening sentence, in which we learn that the Hanoverians have 'been called by the voice of a free people to the legal inheritance of the Crown', shows its descent when juxtaposed with the language of Hume's essay, 'Of the Protestant Succession': 'The princes of that family . . . have been called to mount our throne, by the united voice of the whole legislative body.'[82] In a phrase, the *Antiquities* give us the politics of Blackstone embodied in the literary sophistication of Hume.[83]

IV

It is only when we have recognized in the *Antiquities* a distinctively English treatment of Hanoverian genealogy, delivered from the standpoint of a mid-century politics based on Blackstone, that we can understand both why Gibbon began the work, and why he laid it to one side. Let us first set out the timetable, as we can reconstruct it from Gibbon's letters.

In September 1783 Gibbon had left England to set up home in Lausanne with the friend of his youth, Georges Deyverdun.[84] He played a full part in the society of Lausanne, and thereby met, as it happened, Charles George Augustus, hereditary prince of Brunswick: a virtual idiot he described as 'a soft and heavy piece of German dough'.[85]

---

[82] Hume, *Essays*, 511.

[83] There is evidence to suggest that Hume was in Gibbon's thoughts immediately before and at the time of writing the *Antiquities*, particularly in the various drafts of the 'Memoirs' (composed probably between 1789 and 1793). Beginning draft 'B' Gibbon refers to 'the philosophic Hume' as one of his 'masters' in autobiography (*A* 104). In draft 'E', having transcribed Hume's letter of congratulation on the publication of the first volume of *The Decline and Fall*, he notes that Hume died 'the death of a Philosopher' (*A* 313)—an example perhaps present to his mind when he wrote to Sheffield that Deyverdun 'beheld his approaching dissolution with the firmness of a philosopher' (*L* iii. 157).

[84] He arrived in Lausanne on 27 Sept. 1783 (*L* ii. 372).

[85] *L* iii. 11. For other references to the high society in which he moved, see *L* iii. 2, 9, 10, and 17.

Two years later, in 1785, the Furstenbund prompted Gibbon (as it did so many) to think afresh about Britain's connections with Germany.[86] His letters of the period show his awareness of the implications of that episode; and in 1788 and 1792 he socialized with the marquis of Carmarthen ('a fair and honourable man'). Carmarthen was the Secretary of State for Foreign Affairs in 1785 who had been calamitously 'compromised by the Elector of Hanover's German operations'.[87] These political and social circumstances were reinforced when the death of Deyverdun in July 1789, after a long period of illness, created in Gibbon the desire to occupy himself again in literary composition (the manuscript of *The Decline and Fall* having been completed almost exactly two years before).[88] Gibbon was profoundly shaken by the death of his friend ('the prospect before me is a melancholy solitude'); and the intellectual freedom in which he had at first revelled after completing *The Decline and Fall* now seemed less idyllic.[89]

All these circumstances served to nudge Gibbon towards the project to which he first alluded in December 1789, and which a year later, when he wrote to Ernst Langer (librarian to the Duke of Brunswick) asking for help with materials in the German language, was clearly well advanced.[90] In February 1791 Gibbon dangled before the nose of Cadell the possibility of his sending over 'for next Winter a thin quarto on an interesting subject'—presumably the *Antiquities*.[91] He seems still to have been working at it in April 1791, and referred to it as a possible source of money from Cadell in a letter of December 1791.[92] A reference in the text to 'Archduke Ferdinand the Emperor's brother' suggests that most of what we have was composed before the death of the emperor to whom this most probably applies (Leopold II) on 1 March 1792.[93] But by the end of September 1792 we can be sure that the *Antiquities* were dead. Gibbon abruptly snatched away the carrot with which he had tried to entice Cadell eighteen months before: 'You may

---

[86] On the Furstenbund see Blanning, '"That Horrid Electorate" or "Ma Patrie Germanique"? George III, Hanover and the *Furstenbund* of 1785'.

[87] *L* iii. 284; see also, for Gibbon's awareness of the Furstenbund, *L* iii. 35. Blanning, '"That Horrid Electorate" or "Ma Patrie Germanique"? George III, Hanover and the *Furstenbund* of 1785', 327.

[88] Deyverdun's death was announced in a letter to Salomon de Severy of 4 July 1789 (*L* iii. 156). Later in the same month, writing to Sheffield, he remarked on how he is eased by composition; 'yet I am less unhappy, since I have thrown my mind upon paper' (*L* iii. 165).

[89] *L* iii. 164. For Gibbon's intellectual freedom, see *L* iii. 130–1.

[90] *L* iii. 176 and 202–6.

[91] *L* iii. 211.

[92] *L* iii. 220 and 242.

[93] *EE* 453 and 598 n. 33. The Emperor could also conceivably be Joseph II.

perhaps be likewise disappointed at hearing that I shall probably come empty-handed. A variety of untoward circumstances have contributed to encrease my indolence.'[94] This is confirmed when we note that the *Antiquities* do not figure in the list of his current literary projects which Gibbon sent to Sheffield in January 1793.[95] How can we make sense of this timetable? What light does it throw on Gibbon's reasons for beginning the *Antiquities*? And what were the 'untoward circumstances' which finished the work off?

It may have been the death of Deyverdun which turned Gibbon once more towards his desk. It was perhaps the Vaudois society in which he moved and the politics of the mid-1780s which led him to his subject. But it was his response to the events of the first two years of the French Revolution which determined how that subject would be handled, and the political end it would be made to serve.

In December 1789 Gibbon's attitude towards events in France was divided. Conceding the need for change and therefore to some extent welcoming the direction of affairs, he yet foresaw that all might go— perhaps already had gone—horribly wrong:

What would you have me say of the affairs of France? We are too near and too remote to form an accurate judgment of that wonderful scene. The abuses of the court and government called aloud for reformation and it has happened as it will always happen, that an innocent and well-disposed prince pays the forfeit of the sins of his predecessors, of the ambition of Lewis XIV, of the profusion of Lewis XV. The French nation had a glorious opportunity, but they have abused and may lose their advantages. . . . How different is the prospect! Their King brought a captive to Paris after his palace had been stained with the blood of his guards: the Nobles in exile, the Clergy plundered in a Way which strikes at the root of all property, the capital an independent Republic, the union of the provinces dissolved, the flames of discord kindled by the worst of men . . .[96]

That apprehension was rapidly confirmed. In August 1790 he sighed to Sheffield 'Poor France, the state is dissolved, the nation is mad.'[97] And in May 1791 he was certain that the opportunity of 1789 had been forever missed: 'you cannot be indifferent to the strange Revolution which has humbled all that was high and exalted all that was low in France. The irregular and lively spirit of the Nation has disgraced their

[94] *L* iii. 273.

[95] *L* iii. 312.

[96] *L* iii. 183–4; cf. also 167, 171, and 176. By August 1792 Gibbon wrote of that missed opportunity as a fact (*L* iii. 265).

[97] *L* iii. 199.

liberty, and instead of building a free constitution they have only exchanged Despotism for Anarchy.'[98] However, although Gibbon now clearly had no hopes for the Revolution, its failure had not yet (as it soon would) thoroughly overturned his political views; at this time (1790–1) he still believed, for instance, that in certain circumstances the people might justly rise against their governors.[99] It was at this stage in his developing response to the French Revolution, when he could still view it with some equanimity as an adventure, largely confined to the realm of politics, which had sadly failed, that Gibbon became interested in literary remedies for what he called 'the French disease'.[100] Stimulated by his admiration for Burke's *Reflections*, Gibbon thought up his own project for a literary dyke against the flood of democratical principles:

The French spread so many lyes about the sentiments of the English nation, that I wish the most considerable men of all parties and descriptions would join in some public act declaring themselves satisfied with, and resolved to support, our present constitution. Such a declaration would have a wonderful effect in Europe, and were I thought worthy, I myself should be proud to subscribe it. I have a great mind to send you something of a sketch, such as all thinking men might adopt.[101]

Sadly, Gibbon on the British constitution is one of the great unwritten works. However, it is possible to see the *Antiquities* as an oblique fulfilment of just the need Gibbon indicated to Sheffield. As an inflection of a literary form away from the simple, emphatic loyalism by which it had been previously characterized, and towards the more sophisticated politics of the propertied in the 1780s, it would have been a work which embodied in itself the complex constitutional attitudes of the oligarchic elite during the first thirty years of the reign of George III. It would have been a work of celebration and exemplification which would have done for 'all thinking men' what the Associations did amongst the lower orders: it would have (in Sheffield's words) arranged their minds 'under a good Principle'.[102]

Having recognized in the *Antiquities* a work intended implicitly to

---

[98] *L* iii. 227.

[99] See the very interesting letter of 12 Oct. 1790 to Jean David Levade, professor of theology and morals at the Seminaire of Lausanne: 'Voici peut-etre l'example [*sic*] que vous cherchiez d'une revolte a la fois juste et malheureuse, celle des Bohemiens (en 1618) contre la tyrannie civile et Ecclesiastique de la maison d'Autriche' (*L* iii. 201).

[100] *L* iii. 216.

[101] For Gibbon's admiration for Burke, see *L* iii. 210, 216, 243, and 365 ('I passed a delightful day with Burke'). *L* iii. 216; cf. also 243.

[102] Prothero, ii. 352.

support the British constitution, we can understand why it was abandoned. For the European situation escalated with a swiftness which made the project seem not only an ineffectual half-measure, but one liable to being misread as lending comfort to the very principles it sought to oppose. In order to see why this was so, we need first to examine the new sombreness and extremity which stamped Gibbon's political thought in the closing months of 1792, at exactly the time he ceased to regard the *Antiquities* as worth continuing.

When Gibbon first moved to Lausanne in 1783 he presented its separation from English political life as a perfect match for (as he confessed to his erstwhile patron, Lord Eliot) his own ill-adaptedness to politics.[103] Once in Lausanne such interest as he took in English politics was motivated largely by private considerations: he was trying to raise funds by selling his estate at Buriton at a time when political circumstances had depressed the price of land.[104] This indifference to English politics per se was reinforced by his conviction that, after the early 1780s, the House of Commons had manifested a profound consensus on questions of policy overlaid with merely personal antagonisms. In a letter of August 1790 he reproached Sheffield for using 'those foolish obsolete, odious, words Whig and Tory. In the American War they might have some meaning, and then your Lordship was a Tory; since the coalition, all general principles have been confounded and if there ever was an opposition to men not measures it is the present.'[105] In all these comments Gibbon's perspective was, as he put it, that of a 'Citizen of the World'.[106] Free of the bias of nationhood, for most of the 1780s he posed as an indifferent spectator viewing European affairs from his Swiss vantage point.[107]

This poise was destroyed once Gibbon became aware of the extent of the rupture in the fabric of the European *ancien régime* made by events in France. The arrival of penniless French aristocrats in Lausanne made Gibbon forget his own, comparatively minor, problems over the sale of Buriton. He confessed that theirs 'are real misfortunes'.[108] Suddenly a

[103] 'I shall always remember with gratitude the friendly intentions of those who pushed me forwards into political life but I soon found by experience that it was a walk from whence I could derive neither benefit nor pleasure nor glory where it is not easy for a man of honour and delicacy to satisfy at the same time his public and his private connections . . .' (*L* iii. 19). For other, more openly disparaging remarks on English politics, see *L* iii. 12, 15, 21, and 29.

[104] *L* iii. 137–9.

[105] *L* iii. 195. The coalition in question is that of 1783 between Fox and North.

[106] *L* iii. 25.

[107] 'We are again spectators . . .' (*L* iii. 306).

[108] 'Yet I am almost ashamed to complain of some stagnation of interest when I am witness to the natural and acquired philosophy of so many French who are reduced from riches not to

new violence coloured his language when talking of the revolutionaries: they are 'tyrants and cannibals', 'miscreants'.[109] For Gibbon, as for
Wordsworth, it was the September Massacres which instilled 'a substantial dread' and which seem to have marked a turning point in his
understanding of the Revolution.[110] The ferocity of the revolutionaries
seemed unexampled, severing the present from the certainties of the
past and rendering the future wildly unpredictable.[111]

Gibbon's unease deepened the more clearly he realized that the
Revolution marked a social as well as a political epoch: 'Never did a
revolution affect [*sic*] to such a degree the private existence of such
numbers of the first people of a great Country.'[112] It was the fact that the
Revolution had initiated, as Gibbon came to realize, a new form of
private, as well as of public, life—that it had to a great extent *erased* the
separation between private and public—which most appalled him.[113] It
was an erasure Gibbon experienced with, for an Englishman, unusual
sharpness because of the proximity of Lausanne to France. On 14 May
1792 Sheffield warned Gibbon that Switzerland might be disturbed:
'the insane discontents of the Pais de Vaud may render Lausanne not
altogether an eligible and comfortable residence to you.'[114] This was
public life reaching into private life with a vengeance. Thereafter
Gibbon's letters mention two strong horses and 'a hundred Louis in
gold', telescopes to descry 'the Democratical aspect of twelve leagues of
the opposite coast which every morning obtrude themselves on my
view', and the daily task of running to the window to see if the French
were coming.[115] To be a Citizen of the World suddenly involved more
liabilities than benefits. Consequently Gibbon began to think of an
English refuge, 'a new system of life in my native Country' to which he
now professed himself 'truly attached' and which he saw (in early 1793)

---

indigence, but to absolute want and beggary. A Count d'Argout has just left us who possessed ten
thousand a year in the Island of St Domingo, he is utterly burnt and ruined, and a brother whom
he tenderly loved has been murdered by the Negroes' (*L* iii. 240).

[109] *L* iii. 265 and 319.

[110] *L* iii. 273 and 275. Sheffield had informed Gibbon that 'the late massacres are infinitely
more execrable than any French or English paper have stated' (Prothero, ii. 322).

[111] *L* iii. 277. Compare also *L* iii. 265, which suggests that Gibbon had felt this sense of
separation from the known ways of the past in a milder form before September 1792.

[112] *L* iii. 292.

[113] *L* iii. 311. For Gibbon's earlier sanguine assumption (which had indeed been exemplified
in the rest of his life) that the rhythm of private life was for the most part unaffected by public
events, see *DF* ii. 516. For a similar expression by Johnson, see his *False Alarm* (1770) in *Political
Writings*, 334.

[114] Prothero, ii. 295.

[115] *L* iii. 282, 276, 307, and 287.

as 'the sole great refuge of mankind against the opposite mischiefs of despotism and democracy'.[116]

Lausanne was in fact never invaded. The revolutionary army which had besieged Geneva in 1792 eventually withdrew, and its commander, the Marquis de Montesquiou, was driven to seek asylum in Rolle with (ironically enough) the Neckers.[117] Yet this was beside the point. Gibbon had already suffered a more intimate invasion: an invasion of the mind by public events. After January 1793 Gibbon's letters regularly complain that 'politics . . . till now never had such possession of my mind', a state of affairs he supposed general: 'politics . . . now engross the waking and sleeping thoughts of every feeling and thinking animal.'[118] It was certainly true of his main correspondent, Sheffield, who after the execution of Louis XVI was similarly possessed: 'I can hardly think on any other subject.'[119]

We can gauge the new dominion politics exerted over Gibbon by considering the increased urgency with which he set about gathering news. From his earliest days in Lausanne he had kept himself abreast of events in England, regularly having books and pamphlets sent out to him.[120] That continued through the early period of the Revolution, at which point Gibbon began also to read 'the French papers', particularly *Le Moniteur*.[121] In August 1792, however, his requests to Sheffield for news began to be couched in more pressing language: 'I must . . . again call upon you for a map of your political World'; 'I expect and require at this important crisis a full and confidential account'; 'I shall now expect . . . a regular political journal'; 'send me Woodfall's register . . . I now spare no expense for news.'[122]

Gibbon's main source of privileged information was, of course, Sheffield, who had sat in the House as a member for Bristol since 1790, and who had supported Pitt since 1792. His letters to Gibbon were one of the prime determinants of the historian's political awareness, and hence mood. A resolute anti-democrat and hearty denouncer of the French, after September 1792 even this competent, phlegmatic man of business was shaken to the uttermost.[123] In October 1792 he confided

---

[116] *L* iii. 299 and 307.

[117] *L* iii. 302–3.

[118] *L* iii. 308 and 325; cf. also 363 and 310.

[119] Prothero, ii. 365.

[120] *L* iii. 4 and 145–6. Consider also his satisfaction in being able to indicate to Sheffield that he had received confidential insights into French politics from Necker (*L* iii. 10).

[121] *L* iii. 199, 313, and 350.

[122] *L* iii. 264, 285, 307, and 313.

[123] For his opposition to democracy, see Prothero, ii. 253–4; for his denunciations of the French, Prothero, ii. 307 ('such execrable animals should be extirpated'), 321 ('I consider the

to Gibbon his own sense of separation from the familiar: 'all my specu-lations, moral, religious, political and military, are sent into a troubled sea without rudder or compass.'[124] By November that gloom had if anything deepened—'my political barometer never was so low'—as a result of the 'inexplicable phenomena of the later part of last September.'[125] From Sheffield's letters Gibbon would have heard dis-turbing home news; news of the spread of Jacobinism through 'many parts of the country', and of the consequent need to 'prevent the mass of the people from being inflamed'.[126] More significant than either, perhaps, was the change in the nature, almost in the texture of English political life, to which Sheffield testified. The political world reflected in his correspondence has moved far from the post-party consensus sketched by Gibbon in 1790. Sheffield's letters suggest that the effect of the Revolution on English party groupings was powerful but complex. It involved first, a degree of rallying round, which raised hopes even as late as July 1792 of the possibility of effective government by coalition, 'a junction of parties'; and second, a sharper recognition of fundamental dividedness resulting from the attempt at unity.[127] The tendency of the crisis to coerce men to simplify and reduce their politics Sheffield caught well when he wrote in January 1793 that 'the times will accelerate decision'.[128]

Gibbon responded alertly to this loss of what he called 'temper' in English political life.[129] Its sourness seems to have polluted even Lausanne.[130] Yet for Gibbon this was in part a welcome change, in that it signalled opposition to 'new democratical principles' and 'wild ideas of the rights and natural equality of man'.[131] Politeness, sophistication, indirection, irony, knowingness—these were all necessary casualties when politics had become a fight to the death, and when every battle was potentially the last battle: 'Will you not take some active measures

French affairs so far out of the line of common Politicks, that I wish the whole world to declare against them, and run them down as pestiferous wolves') and 364 ('that torrent of evil which was pouring in upon us from France').

[124] Prothero, ii. 320.

[125] Prothero, ii. 343. Sheffield's daughter had immediately before this written to Gibbon to say that 'Papa . . . is more alarmed than ever I saw him' (Prothero, ii. 342).

[126] Prothero, ii. 351 and 306.

[127] Prothero, ii. 305 and 330. This could not be more clearly illustrated than in the conduct of the erstwhile allies, Fox, Sheridan, and Burke in the House on 9 Feb. 1790 and 6 May 1791.

[128] Prothero, ii. 363. As examples of this one might cite the original support for, and subse-quent opposition to, the Revolution by, for instance, Richard Watson and Arthur Young.

[129] *L* iii. 229–30.

[130] *L* iii. 254 and 311.

[131] *L* iii. 257.

to declare your sound opinions and separate yourselves from your rotten members [reformers such as Charles Grey]? If you allow them to perplex government, if you trifle with this solemn business, if you do not resist the spirit of innovation in the first attempt, if you admit the smallest and most specious change in our parliamentary system, you are lost.'[132] Persuaded that the concession and compromise of reform would result in the country's being 'driven step by step from the disfranchisement of Old Sarum to the King in Newgate, the Lords voted useless, the Bishops abolished, and a house of Commons without articles', Gibbon embraced the politics of whole-hearted, overt commitment, and gloried 'in the character of an Englishman'.[133] His political language was at once enriched with terms of confrontation and extirpation.[134] The change was evident, too, in his habits of allusion. Resisting the democratic, republican appropriation of Milton, Gibbon repeatedly used *Paradise Lost* to express his trepidation ('I begin to fear that Satan will drive me out of my possession of Paradise'), his conviction that the Revolution was a type of original sin (a bite into 'the apple of false freedom'), and his hatred of the revolutionaries as devils.[135] Nowhere, however, was the change more evident than in the language and sentiment with which Gibbon discussed monarchy. Gibbon had long displayed that indifference, perhaps even secret contempt, towards monarchs typical of the eighteenth-century English oligarchic elite, and exemplified in an extreme form in Hervey's *Memoirs*.[136] In 1784 Gibbon had implied in a letter to Lord Eliot that it was un-English to possess 'an high reverence for the person and authority of Kings'.[137] During the illness of George III in 1788 he had written sympathetically, but also with the condescension proper to affection, of 'notre pauvre roi'.[138] Even when Louis XVI was recaptured at Varennes Gibbon's language had been unemotive, perhaps even callous: 'the Royal animal is again caught.'[139] But when Louis was

---

[132] *L* iii. 258; cf. also *L* iii. 308.

[133] *L* iii. 304 and 325.

[134] *L* iii. 261, 265, 337, and 321.

[135] *L* iii. 288 (cf. also 292 and 298), 292, and 311. The radical reading of Milton is most famously exemplified by Blake and Shelley. But it was shared by lesser figures: see e.g. Pigott's *A Political Dictionary*, in which Milton is one of the pantheon of '*true heroes*' who resisted '*tyrannic* power' (p. 25). Gibbon was aware of Milton's actual politics. His library contained Toland's biography.

[136] It is to be contrasted with what Lord Holland was to call 'the childish love of Princes so prevalent in England' amongst the lower orders (Colley, 'Apotheosis of George III', 94).

[137] *L* iii. 20.

[138] *L* iii. 136.

[139] *L* iii. 232.

executed, Gibbon bemoaned that the news was received in Lausanne 'with less horror and indignation than I could have wished'.[140] Certainly Gibbon's own emotions (as expressed to Lady Elizabeth Foster) did not lack warmth:

I have never approved the execution of Charles the First; yet Charles had invaded, in many respects, the ancient constitution of England, and the question had been judged in the field of Naseby before it was tried in Westminster-hall. But Louis had given and suffered every thing. The cruelty of the French was aggravated by ingratitude, and a life of innocence was crowned by the death of a saint, or, what is far better, of a virtuous prince, who deserves our pity and esteem.[141]

In 1818 Sir Samuel Romilly would argue that the French Revolution 'gave almost every description of persons who have any influence on public opinion an interest to adhere to, and maintain inviolably, an established Constitution and, above all, the Monarchy, as inseparably connected with, and maintaining everything valuable in the state'.[142] With Gibbon, however, this profound shift from *insouciance* to reverence was motivated at a level deeper than that of interested calculation. The image of suffering royalty undergoing extreme distress crystallized the developing change in Gibbon's vision of politics which had been under way since the early 1790s. After the events of late 1792 and early 1793 the field of political debate was for Gibbon less like a salon in which familiar and fundamentally like-minded players manoeuvred for slight advantages than a Manichaean struggle between right and wrong. We may suppose, then, that one of the 'untoward circumstances' which prompted Gibbon to discontinue work on the *Antiquities* was that the nuance and finesse with which they articulated their sophisticated politics no longer matched, in either mood or substance, the more simple, more fervent, attitudes into which he had been jolted by the September massacres, and which the execution of Louis XVI had later strengthened.

That change of heart would perhaps by itself have been sufficient to have made the *Antiquities* seem ill-conceived, and thus to have prompted Gibbon to abort them. It seems to have been reinforced, however, by two prudential considerations.

As we have seen, the *Antiquities* directed polite, but firm and shrewd scepticism at the genealogical pretensions, articulated by Leibnitz, of

---

[140] *L* iii. 318.

[141] *L* iii. 324–5.

[142] *Memoirs of the Life of Sir Samuel Romilly*, ii. 300–1; quoted in Colley, 'Apotheosis of George III', 106.

the German branch of the house of Brunswick. In June 1791 Gibbon had reported to Sheffield that 'the pulse of the Contre-Revolution beats high, but I cannot send you any certain facts'.[143] By mid-1792, however, one certain fact was that the hero of the Counter-Revolution was, as luck would have it, the Duke of Brunswick.[144] In August and September 1792 Gibbon fully expected Brunswick, at the head of the Prussian army, to become 'master of Paris'.[145] When the German forces were checked at Valmy Gibbon was amazed, and was able to explain 'this most unexpected failure' to himself only by supposing treason.[146] However, the *Antiquities* were abandoned before Gibbon could have known of the Duke's failure.[147] It seems likely, then, that one element in the decision to abandon the *Antiquities* was the consideration that it would have been inappropriate for 'a notorious aristocrate' such as Gibbon to publish in the early 1790s a work which, however politely, took at all in vain, or treated with anything less than unquestioning reverence, the family of the probable avenger of injured royalty.[148] Anti-Jacobin accounts of the Hanoverians read very differently from the *Antiquities*, and revive the eulogy of the early years of the century. Miss Askew, writing in 1792, argued that 'the natives of these isles never enjoyed lasting felicity, untill the house of Hanover succeeded to the government of this realm', an event which transformed Great Britain into 'the island of felicity' itself.[149] Moreover, after 1792 opponents of the Revolution emphasized that support for the constitution depended on reverence for the monarchy. Horsley and Watson explicitly united what the *Antiquities* would have deftly separated:

Such is the British Constitution, its Basis, Religion; its End, Liberty; its principal means and safe-guard of Liberty, the Majesty of the Sovereign.

---

[143] *L* iii. 231.

[144] The Brunswick Manifesto (threatening Paris with total destruction unless the royal family were respected and protected) was signed at Coblentz on 25 July 1792. On 19 August Brunswick crossed the frontier with Prussian forces, entering the Argonne Forest on 8 September. The battle of Valmy (20 September) put an end, for the time being, to hopes of a forcible re-establishment of the *ancien régime*.

[145] *L* iii. 269 and 268. This expectation was shared by those whose sympathies were on the other side: see *Letters of William Wordsworth*, 11. No one thought that the French forces would be able to check, let alone defeat, the Prussian army.

[146] *L* iii. 281, 283, 303. By April 1793 Brunswick was merely pitied as a failure (*L* iii. 325).

[147] The decisive letter to Cadell is dated 28 Sept. 1792, eight days after the battle of Valmy (*L* iii. 273). It seems, however, to have taken Gibbon about ten days at the earliest to learn of even the most sensational events in France. For instance, he appears first to be aware of the murder of Mme de Lamballe on 12 Sept. 1792, ten days after its occurrence (*L* iii. 270).

[148] The phrase is Sheffield's (Prothero, ii. 365).

[149] 'A Lady', *Review of the Reigns of George I. & II.*, pp. vi–vii and 130–1.

I cannot wish to see the splendour of the crown reduced to nothing, lest its proper weight in the scale of the constitution should be thereby destroyed.[150]

Had it been published in the early 1790s the *Antiquities* might thus have belied Gibbon's true political affiliations. Its reserve might have been confused with the sardonic amusement with which radicals such as Joseph Gerrald and Charles Pigott laced their resentment of aristocratic and hereditary privilege.[151]

This leads us to the second prudential consideration. Gibbon was obliged to take the possibility of the *Antiquities* being misread as a secretly hostile ironizing of royal pretension, and therefore of all hereditary systems, the more seriously, because of his own liability to be marked out as a friend to democratical principles, and that of his writings to be quoted by perceived radicals in support of their innovative views.

Sheffield, as one who fully knew the truth of the contrary, might jokingly reproach Gibbon as 'a renegado Englishman'.[152] Others might not be so sure. Even Burke, who knew Gibbon personally, suspected that there was something un-English about his language.[153] Others more straightforwardly found in his life and work support for democratical principles and political reform. In *The Jockey Club* Charles Pigott actually cited Gibbon as an example of how the stifling operation of nepotism and the hereditary principle in England obliged talent and genius to flee overseas: 'A man like Gibbon, whose writings have exalted the glory of his country, and whose great literary fame has reached the utmost extremities of the civilized world, is necessitated to live (an exile as it were) in a foreign clime, in obscurity and distress, while such a number of locusts, *nati consumere fruges*, are preying on its vitals, supported by this profligate dependence.'[154] *The Decline and Fall*, as well as its author, was susceptible to such perverse misrepresentation. In 1789 William Belsham had repeated virtually verbatim Gibbon's comments on the merely apparent disadvantages of hereditary mon-

---

[150] Samuel Horsley, *Sermon . . . Preached on 30 January 1793* (1793); Richard Watson, *Appendix to a Sermon* (1793), in Butler (ed.), *Burke, Paine, Godwin, and the Revolution Controversy*, 143 and 147.

[151] For their response to the defeat of the Duke of Brunswick, see Gerrald, *A Convention the Only Means of Saving us from Ruin*, 23 and Pigott, *Political Dictionary*, 7 and 74–5.

[152] In March 1793 (Prothero, ii. 374).

[153] Burke, *Correspondence*, vii. 502 and n. 2. Gibbon's brush with Catholicism and the French connections of his youth might also make him suspicious were they remembered in the 1790s, as also might his publishing the *Essai sur l'Étude de la Littérature* in French. It is interesting, in this context, that one of the aspects of his life that Gibbon is most at pains to stress in the 'Memoirs' (which were of course composed at this time) is his firm Englishness.

[154] Pigott, *The Jockey Club*, 182; cf. L iii. 257 for Gibbon's awareness of this work.

archy in an essay calculated to support political reform and a meddling attitude towards monarchy.[155] In the House on 1 February 1793 Belsham's friend, Samuel Whitbread, had quoted from *The Decline and Fall* while attacking the Duke of Brunswick's manifesto, and likening the Duke to Attila the Hun.[156] When a later generation of radicals such as Shelley quarried *The Decline and Fall* in search of useful materials they were following those in the 1790s who had distorted Gibbon into another Volney, and misread *The Decline and Fall* as an English *Ruines des Empires*.[157]

The publication of the *Antiquities* might have seemed to endorse that misreading with an authorial sanction. Gibbon's erudite and subtle embodiment of the complex views which had governed his own political career could have seemed more seditious than celebratory, more democratic than aristocratic, for so many features of its language and argument were, in the 1790s, to be found also in the utterances and writings of democrats and radicals. In 1794 Joseph Gerrald would articulate his defence against a charge of sedition through a Blackstonian constitutional rhetoric: Erskine based his defence of Paine on the same text.[158] In the 1790s it is primarily in the literature of political radicalism that we find antipathy to royal panoply, exposure of the fictions underlying the institution of monarchy, mockery of hereditary systems, suspicion of the German connections of the royal family, an assertion of the parliamentary nature of monarchical title.[159] To publish the *Antiquities* would have been to run the risk of being confused with Paine (who as early as 1776 had said that 'the plain truth is that the antiquity of English monarchy will not bear looking into') or with Fox, who (as an aghast Sheffield informed Gibbon) in February 1793, during the same debate in which Whitbread quoted *The Decline and Fall*, told the House 'distinctly that the Sovereignty was absolutely in the people, that the Monarchy was elective, otherwise the Dynasty of Brunswick had no right, and that the majority of the people, when-

---

[155] Belsham, *Essays*, 113–14; 'On Hereditary Succession'.

[156] Prothero, ii. 368 n. 2 and *L* iii. 319 n. 4.

[157] Another example of such appropriation is that of Adam Smith's *Wealth of Nations* by Paine.

[158] Thompson, *Making of the English Working Class*, 96 and 140.

[159] Antipathy to royal show; Pigott, *Jockey Club*, 2 and 13: knowingness concerning royal fictions; Gerrald, *Convention*, 35: hostility to hereditary systems; Pigott, *Jockey Club*, *passim*, *Political Dictionary*, 47, Wordsworth, 'A Letter to the Bishop of Llandaff': suspicion of German connections; Pigott, *Political Dictionary*, 57, [Anon.], *Sentiments on the Interests of Great Britain*, article xii of the *Address . . . to the Nation* by the L.C.S.: merely parliamentary nature of monarchical title; Gerrald, *Convention*, 39 and 88–9, Belsham, *Memoirs of the Kings of Great Britain*, i. 87–8, *Essays*, 114. They are of course all to be found in Part Two of Paine's *Rights of Man*.

ever they thought proper to change the form of Government, had a right to cashier the King.'[160] The risk was plainly too great to be run. Of course, Gibbon's work was not friendly to democratical principles. But developments in the language of politics since the work had been begun meant that it could easily be made to seem so. And were these anxious times propitious for the careful attention and nice discrimination of tone demanded by a true reading of the *Antiquities*? Is it not more likely that they would have been hastily misread, even by those whom Gibbon saw as his allies, and whose cause he wished to strengthen? How well would the subtleties of the *Antiquities* have suited the hectic temper of the counter-revolution, of which it was the purpose (in the words of Mackintosh) 'to inflame every passion and interest, real or supposed, that has received any shock in the establishment of freedom'?[161] How fastidiously would its personnel have weighed Gibbon's delicacies?

It is not surprising, then, that Gibbon locked away the manuscript of the *Antiquities* in his desk. He, as well as Pope's retired Hanoverian generals, was not 'fond of bleeding, ev'n in BRUNSWICK's cause'.[162] Moreover, he had another major project to occupy him, namely the composition of his 'Memoirs'. But if Gibbon turned to autobiography in the hope of some respite from the considerations which had hampered the *Antiquities*, he was to be disappointed.

---

[160] *Common Sense*, quoted in Thompson, *Making of the English Working Class*, 95: Prothero, ii. 368.

[161] The quotation is from *Vindiciae Gallicae*; Butler, *Revolution Controversy*, 92.

[162] *Imitations of Horace*, Ep. I. i, l. 10. By 1796, however, Sheffield felt able to print the *Antiquities* in Gibbon's posthumous *Miscellaneous Works*. And by 1814 he could even give presentation copies to George III and the Duke of York (Norton, 206).

6

The 'Memoirs': Autobiography in Time of Revolution

> Gibbon has finished his history; he has brought it down to the tak-
> ing of Constantinople, and now he says that he shall lay down his
> pen, having blotted paper enough.[1]

So wrote the exotic Anthony Storer to William Eden in September
1787.[2] But he was wrong. Gibbon could not forsake the pen, and the
major literary effort of his final years went into the drafts of his
'Memoirs of My Own Life'.

Gibbon did not complete the 'Memoirs' to his own satisfaction,
leaving at his death in 1794 six drafts, now identified by the letters 'A'
to 'F', which he had composed at various dates between 1788 and
1792.[3] His executor and friend, Lord Sheffield, produced in 1796 a
single account from these materials by a process of selection, emenda-
tion, and elision. Aside from Sheffield's own immediate circle, the
public did not have access to the manuscript drafts until 1894, when the
third Lord Sheffield sold them, together with the rest of the Gibbon
papers in his possession, to the British Museum. Although Sheffield had
been quite open that the version which he published in 1796 had been
elicited by him from the six drafts left by Gibbon, until 1894 only those
closest to him had the opportunity to judge the effect and tendency of
his editorial workmanship.

In 1896 John Murray published *The Autobiographies of Edward Gibbon*,
in which each of the six drafts was for the first time separately printed.
Serious study of Gibbon's 'Memoirs' begins at this point, and not

---

[1] Eden, *Journal and Correspondence*, i. 439.

[2] Storer, Anthony Morris (1746–99); dilettante, book collector, and diplomat. Eden,
William (1744–1814); first Lord Auckland; statesman and diplomat.

[3] The drafts were first dated in 1871 by W. A. Greenhill, to whom the second Lord Sheffield
had lent the box containing all the Gibbon papers. See Gibbon, *Memoirs of My Life*, ed. Bonnard,
pp. viii–x and xv–xix.

surprisingly scholars and critics have been fascinated by the archive of revision represented by the six drafts. How have they explained it? The discourses within which scholars have hitherto explored the drafts of the 'Memoirs' are of two kinds. The first is an idiom derived with more or less knowledge and fidelity from the language of psychoanalysis. Here Gibbon's repeated rewriting of the story of his life is taken to be the symptom of emotional uncertainties about identity. The second is the language of literary formalism. Here it is argued that the successive rewritings of the life were undertaken in order to overcome or resolve problems of a purely literary kind which arose in composition.[4]

Both approaches have their strengths, but on each I wish to enter a reservation. The bold anachronism of the turn to psychoanalysis, no matter how undoctrinaire the invocation, no matter how flexible the manner of its use, excludes its practitioners from approaching the 'Memoirs' as what we know from Gibbon's letters they certainly were, namely a literary work composed in full consciousness. For psycho-analysis can never equip us with the ideas in which to conceive, or the words in which to express, what Gibbon thought he was doing when he deliberately made six separate attempts to write his life.

In respect of formalism, my reservation concerns its will to igno-rance; namely, its determination to construe the changes of direction taken by the 'Memoirs' as draft succeeded draft purely in terms of the meditations on literary form of a mind abstracted from its social and political surroundings. Yet when Gibbon mentions his 'Memoirs' in his letters, he has usually either just broken off from, or is about to begin, discussing news from France. There surely were problems of literary form and method which Gibbon had to resolve or surmount in com-posing the 'Memoirs': shading of tone, placing of emphasis, choice of language, and sculpture of plot. But one can neither weigh the press-ingness, nor calculate the dimensions, of those problems, unless one is both sensitive to the context of European politics in the midst of which Gibbon picked up his pen and began to write the story of his life, and alert to the potency of that context to precipitate changes in Gibbon's understanding of the significance of his own life and of the tendency of his writings. As so many contemporaries noted, the French Revolution touched and transfigured everything.[5] From this revolutionary influ-

---

[4] For an example of the application of psychoanalysis, see W. B. Carnochan, *Gibbon's Solitude* (Stanford, Calif.: Stanford University Press, 1987). For an example of the application of literary formalism, see P. M. Spacks, *Imagining a Self: Autobiography and Novel in Eighteenth-Century England* (Cambridge, Mass.: Harvard, 1976).

[5] The all-embracing scope of the Revolution and its consequences was a matter on which

ence Gibbon's autobiographical project enjoyed no exemption. The result is that the formal problems which Gibbon encountered in composing his 'Memoirs' arose with the urgency and in the manner and shape they did only because of events which occurred outside—often, very far outside—his study.

So in considering Gibbon's 'Memoirs' we must keep at the centre of our attention those considerations incommensurable to psychoanalysis and formalism: that is to say, on the one hand the sequence of conscious decisions Gibbon made about the 'Memoirs', and on the other the influence exerted by contextual pressures in the taking of those decisions. When we do so, we shall find that through the six drafts of the 'Memoirs' we can see a silent struggle developing between Gibbon and Sheffield over the form in which the historian's life would be handed down to posterity, and that in this struggle a central point of contention was the worth or worthlessness of Burke's analysis of the French Revolution. On this matter the two friends disagreed, and their disagreement was full of implication. It dictated the twists and reversals in Gibbon's repeated recensions of the narrative of his life, and it eventually influenced the contents of the conflated text which Sheffield placed before the public in 1796.

II

The decision Gibbon had to take which was more important than any other in determining the content, tone, and tendency of each draft was the decision of whether to publish posthumously or non-posthumously. It was, however, a decision which he reversed on three occasions; and this indecision is itself perhaps a sign of his anxious awareness that major consequences would flow from the choice he made. Drafts 'A' to 'C', and possibly also 'D', were composed to be published posthumously. But by the time of draft 'E' Gibbon had clearly changed his mind, and wrote an account of his life which was manifestly intended to be published while its author was still alive. Draft 'F', however, represents a reversion to the earlier plan of posthumous publication. The third and final change of mind occurred, according to Sheffield, 'not long before [Gibbon's] death', when the historian

both the supporters and the detractors of the Revolution were of one mind. Compare Burke's opinion in *A Letter to a Noble Lord* that the French Revolution 'seems to have extended even to the constitution of the mind of man' (*Further Reflections on the Revolution in France*, 280) with Sir James Mackintosh's characterization of the Revolution controversy as 'so immense as to present the most various aspects to different understandings' (*Vindiciæ Gallicæ*, 'Advertisement').

apparently evinced an eager determination to publish his memoirs 'in his lifetime'; a most important circumstance whose significance, and the misleading use of it made by Sheffield, I discuss below.[6] As Sheffield put it in a letter to Gibbon of 6 January 1793 (to which I shall also return later): 'you should decide whether the book and the author are to see the light together, because it might be differently filled up according to that decision. A man may state many things in a posthumous work, that he might not in another; the latter often checks the introduction of many curious thoughts and facts.'[7]

In all the scholarly work on the 'Memoirs' known to me, this question of posthumous or non-posthumous publication is never mentioned. Yet, if one compares the shape and colouring which Gibbon gave to his life in the different drafts, the fundamental importance of the decision to publish, or not to publish, in one's own lifetime is plain. The form into which literary autobiography most naturally falls is that of relating a literary achievement which is public knowledge to a previously hidden private life.[8] It is a striking fact that, in the six drafts of the 'Memoirs', Gibbon constructed the links between the public literary achievement and the private man in two distinct forms. At times he wished to construct a recuperative account of his life, in which all reverses (such as the exile to Lausanne, the months wasted in the militia, and the years devoted to breathing 'the pestiferous air of St Stephen's Chappel') were depicted as having in the end contributed to his final success, and to the personal triumph which *The Decline and Fall* represented:

I shall always esteem that worthy man [Pavilliard] as the first father of my mind.

I read Homer in my tent, I compared the theory of ancient with the practise of modern tactics; and the Captain of Grenadiers . . . has not been useless to the historian of the Roman Empire.

[6] *MW 1796* i. 1 n. See below, pp. 239–40.

[7] Prothero, ii. 366. The Revolution controversy seems to have sensitized other writers in just the way Sheffield here imagines it will sensitize Gibbon. So critical were the issues raised by the controversy, that the balm offered by a form of publication for which one would not have to assume responsibility was attractive. For example, in the 'Advertisement' to his *Observations on the Appeal from the New to the Old Whigs and on Mr. Paine's Rights of Man* (1792), Sir Brooke Boothby explained that 'under the shade of an anonymous character, I have perhaps expressed myself with somewhat less reserve of men and things than I might have been inclined to use in my own person'.

[8] On this see John Sturrock's stimulating essays on instances of autobiography collected into *The Language of Autobiography* (Cambridge, 1993). His comments on Gibbon's *Memoirs*, at times acute, are in general hamstrung by the aversion of his attention from the textual complexities of the work, and his consequent endorsement of Bonnard's conflated text as 'the most rational to date' (p. 123 n. 10). The meaning of the word 'rational' here is unclear to me.

The eight sessions that I sat in Parliament were a school of civil prudence, the first and most essential virtue of an historian.

Shall I add that I never found my mind more vigorous or my composition more happy than in the winter hurry of society and Parliament?[9]

At other times, however, Gibbon suggested that the magnitude of *The Decline and Fall* exceeded all possible causes which might be adduced to explain it, save the genius of its author, who had triumphed over a series of impediments:

[At Westminster] I passed two years and a half . . . nor could I rise to the third form without improving my acquaintance with the Latin Classics. But my studies were interrupted by long and frequent illness; the labour of two masters . . . and of half a dozen Ushers was inadequate to the instruction of five hundred boys, and the slow march of public exercises must be proportioned to the lowest degree of ability and application.

I spent fourteen months at Magdalen College; they proved the fourteen months the most idle and unprofitable of my whole life.

By the habit of early rising I always secured a sacred portion of the day, and many scattered moments were stolen and employed by my studious industry. But the family hours of breakfast, of dinner, of tea, and of supper were regular and long: after breakfast Mrs. Gibbon expected my company in her dressing-room; after tea my father claimed my conversation and the perusal of the news-papers; and in the midst of an interesting work I was often called down to receive the visit of some idle neighbours.

As soon as the Militia business was agitated, many days were tediously consumed in meetings of Deputy-Lieutenants at Petersfield, Alton, and Winchester.

I had embraced the military profession . . . an active scene which bears no affinity to any other period of my studious and social life.[10]

There is vanity in both these contrasting ways of organizing an auto-biography, in that they both flatter the subject of it. But the flattery is in each case different. In the former, Gibbon was a blessed child whose life exhibited the benign coercion of misfortune into triumph. In the latter, the history which delivered that triumph was prodigious, the fruit of a hidden and ineffable disposition in the historian. The recuperative plot, in which *The Decline and Fall* has connections, albeit surprising ones,

---

[9] Breathing 'the pestiferous air of St Stephen's Chappel': that is to say, sitting in the House of Commons. L ii. 250. A 297, 299, 310, 316. Note that in the memorandum Gibbon drew up for himself in 1783 of the likely benefits and pains to be expected from a move to Lausanne, he referred to the House as 'a scene of business which I never liked' (BL Add. MSS 34882, fo. 256).

[10] A 116, 67, 163, 163, 177–8.

with the institutions of Hanoverian England, is to be found in draft 'E', which was intended for non-posthumous publication. It is also in this draft, as we shall see, that the influence of Burke is decisive. The plot in which *The Decline and Fall* has no filiations with the culture of Gibbon's native land, but is an achievement for which Hanoverian England can claim no credit, is to be found in those drafts which were intended for posthumous publication, and on which Burke left no trace.

The formal consequences of the decision about when to publish are therefore plain. But if one aspires to understand the reasons behind what might otherwise be misconstrued as the mere indecision of a plan overturned on three occasions, one must look beyond the horizon of literary form. One must attend to the sequence of Gibbon's responses to events in France, particularly as that sequence relates to the timetable of composition, and to the occurrence of the three changes of mind about posthumous as against non-posthumous publication.[11] Events in France were relevant to the composition of the 'Memoirs', not simply because of Gibbon's physical proximity to them (from his drawing room in Lausanne he could see the camp fires of the Revolutionary forces on the other side of the lake; from his terrace he could hear the artillery at the siege of Mayence some twenty miles away).[12] Their relevance flowed from the sudden delicacy the events of Gibbon's life took on in the aftermath of Burke's analysis of the Revolution. Gibbon's autobiography obliged its author to comment on many of the public institutions of the English *ancien régime*. Burke's *Reflections* encouraged its readers to view such institutions not as abuses but as elements in the palladium of the English nation; Burke's adversaries commented at length on his 'repeated encomiums on the British Constitution', in the folds of which he was said to have wrapped himself.[13] Yet in Gibbon's experience so many of these institutions had proved to be unprofitable; Oxford, the unreformed House of Commons, the militia. Indeed, for some Gibbon was a living embodiment of the harmful consequences of such institutions; he had been recruited into the regiments of radicalism (albeit by the radicals themselves) as one whose work and life formed a commentary on the corruption of Hanoverian England.[14] How was Gibbon to describe

---

[11] See below, Appendix 2 for a tabular arrangement of the most important circumstances and passages from Gibbon's correspondence.

[12] For the siege of Geneva by the Revolutionary army, see *L* iii. 275, 280–2, 282–4, 287–8, 290–1, 302–3; for the artillery at Mayence, see *L* iii. 332.

[13] Christie, *Letters on the Revolution of France*, 15; Macaulay, *Observations on the Reflections of the Right Hon. Edmund Burke*, 40.

[14] See the comments of Charles Pigott quoted above, p. 204.

his at best uneven experience of the pillars of Hanoverian England, without at the same time confirming the reading of his character offered by radicals such as Charles Pigott, and thereby seeming to line up with them against the author to whose prescient and hostile condemnation of the Revolution he had, as we shall see, fervently and promptly subscribed?

In writing the story of his life, Gibbon would also have to give an account of his difficult relationship with his father. How could he do so, without implicitly associating himself with all he most fervently wished to oppose, after Burke had linked together at the most fundamental level the possession of healthy political instincts and a lively sense of the sacredness of family ties?

We begin our public affections in our families. No cold relation is a zealous citizen

To be attached to the subdivision, to love the little platoon we belong to in society, is the first principle (the germ as it were) of public affections

we have given to our frame of polity the image of a relation in blood; binding up the constitution of our country with our dearest domestic ties; adopting our fundamental laws into the bosom of our family affections; keeping inseparable, and cherishing with the warmth of all their combined and mutually reflected charities, our state, our hearths, our sepulchres, and our altars.[15]

It would have been impossible for Gibbon, at work on the 'Memoirs' as he read these sentences from Burke's *Reflections*, not to have grasped their disruptive significance for the work under his hand.

Gibbon would need furthermore to explain his enthusiasm for the literary and intellectual culture of France in the heyday of that Enlightenment which had been attacked by Burke as a prime agent in the birth of the Revolution. Once again, there were sentences in the *Reflections* over which Gibbon must have paused in troubled thought:

We have not . . . lost the generosity and dignity of thinking of the fourteenth century; nor as yet have we subtilized ourselves into savages. We are not the converts of Rousseau; we are not the disciples of Voltaire; Helvétius has made no progress amongst us. Atheists are not our preachers; madmen are not our lawgivers.

---

[15] *Reflections on the Revolution in France*, 244, 97, and 84. Burke's defence of traditional family institutions was sufficiently plain to his first readers that it figured as a topic in the polemical answers provoked by *Reflections*. For example, Mary Wollstonecraft attacked Burke on this point (*Vindication of the Rights of Men*, 43).

[the nobility] countenanced too much that licentious philosophy which has helped to bring on their ruin.[16]

While Gibbon was by no means in the intellectual pocket of the French *philosophes* (he might remind his would-be critics that his first published work, the *Essai sur l'Étude de la Littérature* of 1761, had been a rebuke to the presumption of the *philosophes*) it would be idle for him to attempt to deny that he had read widely in their work, and had mingled with them socially.[17] Moreover, whatever the subtleties and reservations in his relationship with the *philosophes* from his own point of view, the more stubborn problem with which Gibbon had to wrestle was that, in the minds of the English reading public, *The Decline and Fall* had been a conduit whereby the ideas, values, and attitudes of the French Enlightenment had been ducted into English literary life.[18]

Lastly, there was perhaps the most difficult question of all, that of religion. In the *Reflections* Burke was adamant that one of the two spirits which had sustained European civilization was 'the spirit of religion'.[19] Religion was 'the basis of civil society, and the source of all good, and all comfort'. Christianity in particular Burke revered as 'our boast and comfort, and one great source of civilization amongst us'.[20] Modern religious scepticism he famously derided as in itself 'but the rotten stuff, worn out in the service of delusion and sedition in all ages, and which being newly furbished up, patched, and varnished, serves well enough for those who being unacquainted with the conflict which has always been maintained between the sense and nonsense of mankind, know nothing of the former existence and the antient refutation of the same follies'.[21] But the English public had too much good sense to be taken in by such a shabby passing off of the old for the new:

[16] *Reflections on the Revolution in France*, 137 and 187. For Burke's belief that *The Decline and Fall* was aligned with and reinforced the malign tendencies of that intellectual culture, see the record of his conversation with Arthur Young on 1 May 1796, where Burke accuses the religious scepticism of the history of 'contributing to free mankind from all restraint on their vices and profligacy, and thereby aiding so much the spirit which produced the horrors that blackened the most detestable of all revolutions' (Young, *Autobiography*, 258–9).

[17] Although it should be noted that Burke and Gibbon are often close in their response to the *philosophes*. Burke's comment that 'these Atheistical fathers have a bigotry of their own' may even be indebted to Gibbon's late, vehement, condemnation of Voltaire as 'a bigot, an intolerant bigot' (*Reflections on the Revolution in France*, 161; *DF* iii. 916 n. 13). For further discussion of Burke's reading of *The Decline and Fall*, see below, p. 232 n. 97.

[18] On this subject, see Turnbull, ' "Une marionette infidèle": the fashioning of Edward Gibbon's reputation as the English Voltaire'.

[19] *Reflections on the Revolution in France*, 130.

[20] Ibid. 142.

[21] *An Appeal from the New to the Old Whigs* (1791), in *Further Reflections on the Revolution in France*, 197.

'Who, born within the last forty years, has read one word of Collins, and Toland, and Tindal, and Chubb, and Morgan, and that whole race who called themselves Freethinkers? . . . Ask the booksellers of London what is become of all these lights of the world.'[22] Burke's detestation of irreligion (from which he was not always much concerned to distinguish religious dissent), and his location of religious establishments at the centre of the fabric of society, came together in his analysis of the causes of the Revolution.[23] In *A Letter to a Member of the National Assembly* (1791) he suggested how the erosion of faith in Christianity had permitted the Revolutionary government to act despotically: 'They know, that he who fears God fears nothing else; and therefore they eradicate from the mind, through their Voltaire, their Helvetius, and the rest of that infamous gang, that only sort of fear which generates true courage. Their object is, that their fellow citizens may be under the dominion of no awe, but that of their committee of research, and of their lanterne.'[24] In the *Letter to William Elliot*, he saw the undermining of religion as the key to the process whereby the Revolution, of itself unstable, established itself in France: 'Religion, that held the materials of the fabrick together, was first systematically loosened. All other opinions, under the name of prejudices, must fall along with it; and Property, left undefended by principles, became a repository of spoils to tempt cupidity, and not a magazine to furnish arms for defence.'[25] Gibbon was not as remote from Burke on the question of the social function of religion as was commonly believed. For instance, had he not insisted on the vital role played by Christianity in lenifying the manners of the barbarians who settled in the territories of the Western Empire?[26] But in assessing the likely impact of Burke's defence of religion on Gibbon as he meditated how best to tell the story of his life, one must bear in mind that, despite the *Vindication* and what Gibbon says in his 'Memoirs' about the effectiveness of this work of 1779 in silencing his clerical adversaries, the attacks on Gibbon's religious scepticism had peaked, not in the late 1770s, but in the late 1780s.[27] In other words, Gibbon's reputation for irreligion had been most frequently urged in the years immediately preceding the Revolution. It was therefore not a controversy of some fifteen years earlier. It was still a current controversy in the literary world, and the image of Gibbon

22 *Reflections on the Revolution in France*, 140.
23 For Burke's hatred of dissent, see ibid. 76.
24 *Further Reflections on the Revolution in France*, 55.
25 Ibid. 270.
26 See e.g. *DF* ii. 432–3 and 511.
27 See Norton, 88.

disseminated within it was one with which he would need to engage. Therefore Gibbon's autobiography, as well as that of Giannone (one of the three authors he would identify in the 'Memoirs' as his most important literary influences), was of necessity a work of justification and exculpation.[28] In it he had to oppose the political and religious misreadings of his life and work. But this was not a struggle in which Gibbon acted alone. The 'Memoirs', at least as the nineteenth century knew them, were the product of the efforts and prejudices, sometimes aligned, sometimes at variance, of two men. The second person who exercised a great influence over the content and polemical orientation of the 'Memoirs' (although it was not an influence always unopposed by the author) was also the person into whose hands Gibbon's untimely death deposited the whole matter of their editing and publication; namely, Lord Sheffield.[29]

III

John Baker Holroyd, as he then was, had met Gibbon at Lausanne in 1763, when they were both on the Grand Tour. The first mention of Holroyd in Gibbon's journal is not without its coolness: 'Nous [Gibbon, William Guise and Godfrey Clarke] avons tous soupé chez Holroyd, un des nouveaux debarqués. Il ne manque pas d'esprit, ni de connoissances mais il me paroit très suffisant. Manners son Compagnon est fils naturel du Duc de Rutland . . . Ils sont tous les deux militaires, et ils ont adopté tous les prejugés de leur etat contre la milice.'[30] But by the following spring, Gibbon could write: 'J'ai conçu une veritable amitié pour. [*sic*] Holroyd. Il a beaucoup de raison et de sentimens d'honneur avec un cœur des mieux placés.'[31] The friendship took and thrived.[32] By July 1772 Gibbon would frankly confess to Mrs Holroyd that her

---

[28] *A* 143.
[29] Holroyd, John Baker (1735–1821); 1st Earl of Sheffield; soldier, MP and statesman; writer on questions of commerce and agriculture. For a bibliography, see Appendix 3. A selection of his Grand Tour correspondence is published, with a linking commentary by Georges Bonnard, as 'John Holroyd in Italy' in *Études de Lettres: Bulletin de la Faculté des Lettres de l'Université de Lausanne*, ptie II, tom. 2 (1959), no. 3, 122–35. Collections of MS material are to be found in the British Library; the University of London Library; the Beinecke Library, Yale University; and the East Sussex Record Office. Insights into the political man can be gleaned from the correspondence of William Eden, 1st Baron Auckland (see above, n. 1). Domestic life at Sheffield Place is illuminated by J. H. Adeane (ed.), *The Girlhood of Maria Josepha Holroyd* (1896). Sheffield's was a life of great intrinsic interest, and deserves study in its own right.
[30] *J2* 21; entry for 1 Sept. 1763.
[31] *J2* 259; entry for 6 April 1764.
[32] Patricia Craddock evokes the 'particular ease of [Gibbon's] intimacy with Holroyd' well (Craddock, *Young Edward Gibbon*, 204).

son was 'the man in the world whom I love and esteem the most'.[33] And on the death of Lady Sheffield in 1793, Gibbon's letter of condolence began by reassuring Sheffield of his pre-eminent place in the historian's heart: 'My Dearest Friend, for such you most truly are, nor does there exist the person, who obtains or shall ever obtain a superior place in my esteem and affection!'[34] It was a declaration to which Sheffield responded warmly, although in a characteristically plainer style: 'We shall ever acknowledge that you are a right good friend.'[35]

What kind of man was Sheffield? How did his interests compare with Gibbon's? And how did such a strength of feeling develop between the two men? Lavater's reading of Sheffield's character from the evidence of his physiognomy is an irresistible point of departure:

La Physionomie d'un Inconnu, qui m'a été présenté par Mr le Chevalier Macpherson, m'a frappé d'abord comme une des plus décisives que j'aye jamais vû. C'est une Tête foncièrement bien organisée, pleine d'une mémoire immense, le Coup d'œil grand et juste, un jugement ferme et profond. Les yeux ne sont pas aussi bien exprimés comme le front le demandoit, mais assez décisifs pour une pénétration tout à fait singulière. Le Nez seul vaut une centaine de Nés ordinaires. J'en suis sûr, comme de mon existence, quand il est vrai, comme je le crois, c'est le Nez d'un homme 'prudentissime'. La bouche est plus juste que bon. Je ne voudrois comparoître devant lui, après avoir fait du mal.[36]

Lavater scores a number of hits. Certainly Sheffield's public character seems to have been deliberately positioned on the threshold between firmness and severity. Yet his private character was allowed to be blameless, even by his enemies, while the letter he wrote to William Eden before his marriage to Lucy Pelham in December 1794 reveals a capacity for self-mockery at which his public character had not hinted.[37] Emotionally reserved (Gibbon was astonished at his un-demonstrativeness on the death of his first wife), Sheffield was never-

---

[33] *L* i. 323. Gibbon's father had died two years before.

[34] *L* iii. 327.

[35] Prothero, ii. 382.

[36] Adeane, *Girlhood*, 111–12.

[37] 'I beg it to be observed, that I do not mean to throw any imputation on LORD SHEFFIELD's private character. He may have always been an excellent husband, and a tender father. There is every reason to believe that he has acted the part of a faithful friend; and I am glad to find that his services to Mr. Gibbon, the celebrated historian (though I dare say, not rendered with any such view) have been rewarded by a legacy, worth three thousand pounds' ([Anon.], *Propriety of Sending Lord Sheffield to Coventry*, 6–7; for another occurrence of the rumour that Sheffield benefited by £3,000 from Gibbon's will, see Walpole, *Correspondence*, xv. 331. For Sheffield's letter to Eden concerning his imminent marriage, see Eden, *Journal and Correspondence*, iii. 264.

theless full of unsentimental compassion.[38] In 1795 he worked tireless-
ly to raise money by subscription to provide bread for the 'Labourers'
families and the poor industrious'.[39] Although Sheffield was, as we shall
see, no admirer of Burke's, he did not allow this aversion to prevent
him collaborating with Burke on schemes to provide immediate and
practical assistance to *émigré* French clergy.[40]

In the words of the preamble to his report to the Lewes Wool Fair,
Sheffield had 'devoted a long and laborious life to the promotion of the
public welfare, by investigating the causes, and pointing out the best
means of forwarding, improving, and extending the Agriculture,
Manufactures, and Commerce of the Country'.[41] His publications
were chiefly on the Navigation Act, in which he unswervingly
defended England's monopoly of shipping to and from the colonies of
the empire, and on agriculture, particularly corn and wool. Sheffield's
constant character in his pamphlets was that of a 'well wisher to
the empire', a political body whose land settlements he saw as being
funded and secured by the military and financial consequences of the
Navigation Act. Although there is a degree of monomaniacal constancy
about Sheffield's arguments, these were nevertheless powerful inter-
ventions in important debates.[42] Even his adversaries in the pamphlet

[38] 'I found Lord S much better and even more chearful than I could have expected . . .' L iii.
337. A striking example of Sheffield's self-command at moments of danger is given by his
daughter, who was with him in a near-fatal boating accident in a lock: 'Papa very quietly
informed us we were going to sink' (Adeane, *Girlhood*, 294). During the Gordon riots of 1780
Sheffield had shown conspicuous gallantry and coolness (L ii. 243 and n. 2). The imputation of
an easy because unendangered bellicosity is quite wrong: 'His Lordship, knowing he should
never get a scar himself, has been always for the Sword . . . as well during the American war as the
present' ([Anon.], *The Propriety of Sending Lord Sheffield to Coventry*, 8).
[39] Adeane, *Girlhood*, 323 and 361.
[40] See Burke's letter to Sheffield of 17 Oct. 1792 (*Correspondence*, vii. 274). Sheffield's
letter to William Eden on the same subject earlier that month is no bad epitome of his
character. It shows his practicality, his independence of mind, his disdain for sentiment, and his
attentiveness to questions of economics: 'I have been particularly occupied (I did not want extra
work) in favour of the French clergy. About 1,200 have landed in this country. I have been useful. There is little prejudice with respect to Popish priests, but abundance of nonsense, even
among the better sort of people, in regard to the effect so many additional mouths will have on
the price of provisions' (Eden, *Journal and Correspondence*, ii. 448).
[41] Holroyd, *Report of the Earl of Sheffield to the Meeting at Lewes Wool Fair* (Dublin, 1816), 3.
[42] Sheffield wore his intellectual immobility as a badge of honour: 'The arguments I have
offered are, for the most part, the same as I used and expressed twenty-five years ago' (*A Letter on
the Corn Laws*, 58); 'These are the opinions I offered to the attention of the public, twenty-five
years ago, and every thing that has since happened proves that they were well founded' (*The
Orders in Council and the American Embargo*, 45). The experience of reading his pamphlets *seriatim*
confirms that these are not idle boasts. G.W. Jordan, the colonial agent for Barbados, was an
accurate reader of this side of Sheffield's character: 'You bring, my Lord, too many prejudices
into this question [of trade between Britain and the colonies of the empire], prejudices of ancient
growth, and of inveterate establishment, to be allowed to give any opinion upon it . . . You have,

wars in which he engaged allowed that Sheffield's writings 'had a very serious effect on the minds of the people in England'; they were 'quoted with symptoms of conviction and belief', and were deemed to 'predominate, in the British Cabinet'.[43] This influence was not unearned, for Sheffield's was by no means a shallow intellect. His *Observations on the Commerce of the American States* (1783) in some respects goes right to the heart of what is at stake in the matter of trade with the former colonies.[44] But his was a mind utterly uninterested in abstraction, and therefore liable to take a very narrow view of what was relevant to any particular issue. As he proudly proclaimed in relation to the Navigation Act: 'I rest my opinion on no abstract and theoretic grounds, but on the strong and stubborn evidence of experience and of fact.'[45]

Sheffield's mistrust of the abstract and faith in the concrete is vividly illustrated by his position on slavery. In 1790 he published his *Observations on the Project for Abolishing the Slave Trade*, a pamphlet striking for its refusal to acknowledge that this momentous question possessed any moral aspect. For Sheffield, the project of abolition was unworkable, and therefore not to be attempted: 'It is impossible to refrain from remonstrance against the inconsiderate and impracticable manner in

my Lord, to maintain a question, which it has been the great business of your life to establish. It has been the anxious business of a great part of your life to accumulate and to bend all facts and all arguments for and towards a particular purpose. The cause which you have thus advocated, you must not decide' (*Claims of the British West India Colonists*, 106–7).

[43] Bingham, *Letter from an American*, 4; [Coxe], *A Brief Examination*, 'Advertisement'; *Letter from an American*, 9. These adversaries were not push-overs. The anonymous author of *The Propriety of Sending Lord Sheffield to Coventry* held that Sheffield was 'totally wrong . . . in almost every one of his calculations on trade', and that his publications on America showed 'the forward pertness of ignorance' (5–6, 6).

[44] For an instance of Sheffield's fine eye for consequences, consider: 'The purpose [of the pamphlet], however, will be answered, if they should lead men, to see the necessity of maintaining the spirit of our navigation laws, which we seemed almost to have forgot, although to them we owe our consequence, our power, and almost every great national advantage. The Navigation act, the basis of our great power at sea, gave us the trade of the world: if we alter that act, by permitting any state to trade with our islands, or by suffering any state to bring into this country any produce but its own, we desert the Navigation act, and sacrifice the marine of England' (*Observations on the Commerce of the American States*, 120). Cf. *Observations on the Manufactures, Trade and Present State of Ireland*, p. viii. In a later pamphlet Sheffield would underline the importance of the marine in allowing England to resist the dreams of 'universal dominion' entertained by France (*Necessity of Inviolably Maintaining the Navigation and Colonial System of Great Britain*, 39–40).

[45] Ibid. 42. Cf. his even more explicit comments of 1815: 'It is mortifying to observe the attention of those, to whom the country looks up for relief, occupied by metaphysical inquiries, by dissertations on the division and price of labour, and by ringing the changes on the interests of the grower of corn and the consumer—modes of considering it by no means becoming the statesman' (*Letter on the Corn Laws*, 4).

which a great proportion of the community profess a disposition to relieve Negroes from slavery.'[46] For Sheffield the negroes are 'degraded' and 'depraved'; words which hover uneasily between the states of manifestly racist adjective (the negroes are by their very nature degenerate) and less injurious past participle (they have been made so by the life they have been forced to lead). Moreover, history furnished a warrant for the practice: the institution of slavery 'has existed at all times, and in the most enlightened times, even in a severe degree, and among the most civilized nations'.[47] Even the most volatile and irrational modern European nation, Sheffield goes on, would not dream of abolishing slavery: 'Little argument can be drawn from what may be said or done, *at this time*, by a neighbouring nation [France], which seems totally to have changed its character—a nation which has already abused, and may finally lose a glorious opportunity of founding an excellent constitution. . . . even in their wild career of extravagance they will not prohibit the trade in slaves; . . .'[48] The true interest of this passage emerges only when it is realized that Sheffield is borrowing almost verbatim the language of a letter of 15 December 1789 from Gibbon in which the historian had analysed the French Revolution in terms of a bungled chance: 'the French nation had a glorious opportunity, but they have abused and may lose their advantages.'[49] This was not to be the only time that Sheffield copied the language of this letter.[50] What is so striking in this instance, however, is Sheffield's annexation of Gibbon's words to a position from which his friend had explicitly distanced himself. Gibbon's views on the modern slave trade (as distinct from the institution of antiquity) had been made clear in 1781: 'Sixty thousand blacks are annually embarked from the coast of Guinea, never to return to their native country; but they are embarked in chains: and this constant emigration, which, in the space of two centuries, might have furnished armies to over-run the globe, accuses the guilt of Europe, and the weakness of Africa.'[51] Nothing could better illustrate the greater breadth of Gibbon's vision than the juxtaposition of this

---

[46] *Observations on the Project for Abolishing the Slave Trade*, 43, 1. Compare Sheffield's letter to William Eden of 20 Nov. 1786: 'I forgot to acknowledge in my late letter that no envoy or politician ever expressed himself so amiably and sentimentally as you—viz., that you would not promote the hellish trade in negroes. However, your amiability will not prevent the trade; you do not know what an immense business it is. Please to recollect that our islands could not be cultivated without them' (Eden, *Journal and Correspondence*, i. 395).

[47] *Observations on the Project for Abolishing the Slave Trade*, 56.

[48] Ibid. 53.

[49] *L* iii. 184.

[50] See below, pp. 225–6.

[51] *DF* i. 1008.

passage with the strictures of his friend. Moreover, Sheffield's attaching of Gibbon's language to a position to which the historian was a stranger is, as we shall see, proleptic of some of his practices when editing the 'Memoirs'.[52]

Sheffield was a free-trader in respect of manufactures, where he had, as far as I know, no financial interests. In 1785 he wrote: 'It is now well known among commercial nations, that manufactures, forced and supported by bounties and prohibitions, cannot long thrive, and are not only a loss to the community, in proportion to their expence, but are farther pernicious, by tempting away hands from the thriving manufactures.'[53] In 1799 he praised competition in manufactures because it encourages 'skill and industry, and promotes and enforces good regulations, and consequent cheapness of manufacture'.[54] But on the subject of agriculture he was a staunch protectionist, believing always that governments should introduce legal measures 'to secure the home market to the home grower', and consistently reminding his readers of the government's duty (as he saw it) 'to protect the British farmer'.[55] In the manner of both past and present advocates of price-support for agricultural products and producers, Sheffield sought to distinguish agriculture from manufactures on the grounds that in the former the interests of the consumer and the producer were finally identical: 'The interest of the grower is the interest of the consumer, as in the end it produces a steady subsistence by promoting tillage; therefore, for the sake of the consumer, the most liberal encouragement and protection should be given to the grower of corn.'[56] In other words, Sheffield accepted Scottish economic theory where it did not affect him, but consistently resisted the extension of its principles to areas where his

[52] Sheffield's views and language were not idiosyncratic. Responding to Burke's *Reflections*, the controversialist and then sub-Rector of Lincoln College, Edward Tatham, noted that the slave trade was 'a subject of present public discussion', and characterized his own position by remarking that the negroes, naturally destined to 'the extreme of servitude, to the hardest, to the meanest, to the ignoblest offices of society' should remain 'the property of their owners, but . . . as subjects, not as slaves' (*Letters to the Right Honourable Edmund Burke on Politics*, 81, 85–6).

[53] *Observations on the Manufactures, Trade and Present State of Ireland*, 3. Cf. his opinion of 1799, that competition in manufactures encourages 'skill and industry, and promotes and enforces good regulations, and consequent cheapness of manufacture' (*Union with Ireland*, 56).

[54] Ibid. 56. The language of Gibbon's refusal to endorse Sheffield's plan for his library to be kept entire at Sheffield Place as the Gibbonian Library suggests that Gibbon was aware of the limits of his friend's commitment to free trade: 'I am a friend to the circulation of property of every kind'—as Sheffield perhaps was not (*L* iii. 263 and n. 15).

[55] *Letter on the Corn Laws*, 54 and 14.

[56] *Observations on the Corn Bill*, 77 [italics reversed]; see also pp. 3–4 and 25 for similar sentiments. See also *Necessity of Inviolably Maintaining the Navigation and Colonial System of Great Britain*, 5 and 9.

own assets were committed.[57] By contrast, Gibbon's interest in such modern economic theory was profound and sophisticated, and *The Decline and Fall* shows that interest shaping at certain points his understanding of how modern societies emerged from the exhausted polities of antiquity.[58] Sheffield's pamphlets on trade, cast for the most part in the sternly arithmetical idiom of parliamentary report (many of them of course began life as just that) proudly ignore the economic thought of Hume and Smith, to which his friend had paid such serious attention.[59]

A recurrent emphasis in Sheffield's analysis of the burdens placed on the British farmer is his deploring of the effects of tithes. The domestic producer of fine wool is at a disadvantage because 'so heavily taxed and tithed', while virtually the only benign consequence of the French Revolution for Sheffield was its encouragement of the French farmer by its removal of the French clergy from his back.[60] It was at this point that Sheffield's economic thought touched his religious disposition (or, perhaps, his lack of religious disposition). A strain of anti-clericalism had been evident as early as the 1760s. On the Grand Tour Sheffield had mocked Catholic relics and superstitions with an energy fuelled more by irreverence than by Protestant piety.[61] By the 1790s, it was a matter of common agreement that Sheffield had no Christian faith. Arthur Young, who served as Secretary to the Board of Agriculture when Sheffield was President, confided in his *Autobiography* that 'Lord

[57] On this point of the relevance of freedom of trade to even the most central areas of a nation's agriculture, see Hume on England's staple of the wool trade in 'On the Jealousy of Trade' (*Essays*, 329–30).

[58] Cf. *DF* i, pp. lxxv–lxxvi.

[59] William Eden wrote to Sheffield in February 1787 and referred, presumably facetiously, to 'all the sound principles of national policy that I can trace in the writings of David Hume, Adam Smith, Lord Sheffield, M. Necker, etc. . . .' (Eden, *Journal and Correspondence*, i. 403). In October 1801 Sheffield would claim to have quoted Hume on the scarcity of grain (Eden, *Journal and Correspondence*, iv. 144). The 'Mr. Smith' whom Sheffield occasionally cites approvingly in the context of the Corn Laws is not Adam Smith, but rather Charles Smith, the author of *Three Tracts on the Corn Trade and Corn Laws* (2nd. edn., 1766); for Sheffield's references to Smith, see e.g. *Observations on the Corn Bill*, pp.52–3 and *A Letter on the Corn Laws*, 31. Adam Smith, however, praised him as 'very well informed' (*Wealth of Nations*, 508). Charles Smith was not the 'Mr. Smith' who managed Sheffield's Irish property (Adeane, *Girlhood*, 271).

[60] *Report of the Earl of Sheffield*, 7; *Letter on the Corn Laws*, 22. Cf. *Observations on the Corn Bill*, 14. Sheffield's admiration for the French abolition of tithes is arguably an anti-Burkean stance. In his attack on Burke, Stanhope had glanced approvingly at this act of the Revolution: 'In France, they have abolished Tythes: and so the Parliament ought to do in England, by substituting another mode of providing for the Clergy, less vexatious, less detrimental to Agriculture, more convenient for the Clergy, and less injurious to the Cause of *Religion*' (*Letter . . . to the Right Honourable Edmund Burke*, 31). There is a similar emphasis in J. Courtenay's attack on Burke, addressed to Priestley, the *Philosophical Reflections on the Late Revolution in France*, 7 ff.

[61] See Bonnard, 'John Holroyd in Italy', 125.

Sheffield never had a grain of religion'.[62] Sheffield seems not to have been above extracting amusement from this clash of belief between himself and his assistant. Perhaps out of mischief, perhaps out of indifference to beliefs he did not share, he manœuvred the devout Young into non-observance by obliging him to travel to Woburn on a Sunday to discuss the Board's business with the Duke of Bedford: 'Came [to Woburn] with Lord Sheffield yesterday. I detest this pro-fanation of the Sabbath, but he urged me so to accompany him that I yielded like a fool.'[63]

If Sheffield was not above bullying Arthur Young, he was also not above bullying Gibbon. At times this took the form of supplying Gibbon with the firmness of judgement he ought to have possessed himself. As we have seen, when the clerical attack on the first volume of *The Decline and Fall* was imminent, but not yet discharged, Gibbon had told Sheffield that he intended to delete chapters fifteen and sixteen from the second edition. Sheffield replied that to do so would be a blunder.[64] But occasionally such necessary bolstering could become something more brutal, and then Gibbon's letters have a miserable and cur-like tone: 'I feel and confess the true friendship which breathes through the apparent harshness of your style but is that harshness absolutely necessary? it can give you no pleasure and it sometimes gives me pain. If Hugonin's debt be desperate I must submit, but there is no *imbecillity* in saying that the loss will derange my plans . . .'[65]

It is beyond question that Sheffield did Gibbon enormous services

---

[62] *Autobiography of Arthur Young*, 469.

[63] Ibid. 469 and 395. Young also says that he has in general been comfortable working as Secretary to the Board with Sheffield as its President (ibid. 393). On the practice amongst the elite of travelling on the sabbath, note the censure of Vicesimus Knox: 'What think you then, my Lord, of the fashionable practice among Nobles, of selecting Sunday, in preference to all other days, for travelling?' (*Personal Nobility*, 275).

[64] For the two versions of this unused note by Sheffield see Appendix 1. It may be, then, that Sheffield's unbelief was of a more stubborn and open stripe than Gibbon's. Arthur Young had assumed that the peer had contracted his indifference to religion from the historian: 'his intimate connections with Gibbon would alone account for it', he wrote (*Autobiography of Arthur Young*, 469). It seems equally possible, however (particularly in the light of the cardinal importance of the early 1760s in Gibbon's intellectual development) that Gibbon might have been confirmed on the road of religious scepticism by the friendship he had struck up with Holroyd in Lausanne in 1763.

[65] *L* iii. 140; cf. also 185–6. The fact that Gibbon told Sheffield of his plan to retire to Lausanne by letter rather than to his face may suggest a desire on the part of the historian to avoid a direct experience of the peer's response to a scheme he had always opposed (*L* ii. 341–3). For Sheffield's view of Gibbon's departure, see his letter to William Eden of 7 Aug. 1783, in which good humour struggles with irritation; 'Gibbon has baffled all arrangements: possibly you may have heard at Bushy or Bedford Square, of a continental scheme. It has annoyed me much, and of all circumstances the most provoking is, that he is right; a most pleasant opportunity offered' (Eden, *Journal and Correspondence*, i. 56).

throughout his life. The two men were nevertheless of very different temperaments. That, of course, was one reason why their friendship was so strong. Had Sheffield been as incompetent a man of business as was Gibbon, one important source of that reciprocity of kindnesses by which their unlikely attachment was reinforced would have been removed.[66] Gibbon certainly knew this: 'You are in truth a wise active, indefatigable and inestimable friend and as our virtues are often connected with our faults, if you were more tame and placid you would be perhaps of less use and value.'[67] However, during the period when Gibbon was writing the 'Memoirs', the tensions between the two men had become more visible. Maria Holroyd, Sheffield's daughter, wrote to a friend in July 1793 during Gibbon's last visit to Sheffield Place expressing pleasure at the arrival of a new guest because 'I think both the Peer and the Historian began to grow tired of a Tête à Tête after Dinner'.[68]

This trace of late estrangement is understandable, and is to be explained by reference to the two men's diverging responses to the French Revolution. Although Gibbon and Sheffield both deplored the Revolution, their opposition to the 'French disease' of democratical principles took distinct forms. The attitudes of the two friends towards France before the Revolution were, of course, utterly different. Gibbon had as a young man spent so long in a French-speaking country that he had lost his fluency in English; while exiled on the borders of France, he had formed a great admiration for that nation's culture and had made the personal acquaintance of figures as celebrated as Voltaire; the occupations of his adulthood had entailed the most prolonged and deep engagement with French scholarship; and the three months he spent in Paris in 1777 he frankly confessed to be 'among the most agreeable of my life'.[69] In February 1787, however, William Eden, then negotiating

---

[66] Sheffield's services to Gibbon have left more documentary traces, but their friendship led to an exchange of benefits between the two men, as Maria Holroyd's lament for the dead historian reveals: 'the loss of that invaluable, sincere and well-judging friend Mr. Gibbon, is most sincerely felt by us for Papa, and I doubt not by Papa himself. Of what unspeakable consequence would his cool and unprejudiced advice have been to him at this critical time . . . even he could not entirely prevent Papa from taking some steps that he thought imprudent; but he had power to restrain him in some of his impetuosities; but this friend gone, who is there who has the least influence over him?' (Adeane, *Girlhood*, 269). (The phrase 'and I doubt not by Papa himself' nicely suggests Sheffield's outward unbendingness of manner: even his closest relations were reduced to conjecture about his emotions.) For a specific example of Gibbon's wise curbing of his more impetuous friend, see Craddock, *Luminous Historian*, 180–1.

[67] *L* iii. 153.

[68] Adeane, *Girlhood*, 225.

[69] Letter to David Garrick of 14 Aug. 1777; *L* ii. 159.

a commercial treaty with the French, mocked Sheffield for giving 'countenance to all the anti-Gallican nonsense which is encouraged in England'.[70] Eden had sent Sheffield privileged information on Louis XVI's banishment of the Parlement de Paris to Troyes. Sheffield replied by sketching how the news had been received:

Just as I was finishing [i.e. this letter], your interesting fragment on the banishment of the Parliament arrived. The Gibbon and I received it very greedily, graciously and gratefully; at least I did; and it immediately furnished us with a good subject. Considering the disposition towards liberality and bustle on the Continent, it is not clear that the constitution of France will remain exactly what it has been.[71]

'At least I did': the difference of outlook and opinion between the two friends is acknowledged in those words, and confirmed later in the letter when Sheffield confessed that he despaired of 'infusing a proper political zeal into [Gibbon]' on the question of relations with France.[72]

Nevertheless, and despite their quite different experiences of and attitudes towards the French, there is good reason to think that in the early months of the Revolution Sheffield and Gibbon were of almost one mind on French affairs. On 8 January 1790 Sheffield had shared his gloomy analysis of the turn taken by the Revolution with Eden:

At present there seems no symptom of attaining anything worthy the description of a government in France. I cannot conceive it possible that a Revolution, so managed as it is, can proceed smoothly. Progressive distress must produce a crisis, and probably a grand burst. As yet there is no appearance of a great man arising either to restore the monarchy or lead the commonwealth. If the silly nation, instead of abusing, had made use of their advantages; if they had been content with a liberal translation of our system; if they had respected the prerogatives of the Crown, and the privileges of the nobles, they might have raised a solid fabric on the only true foundation—the national aristocracy of a great country. How miserable is their prospect! and after a short time our trade

---

[70] Eden, *Journal and Correspondence*, i. 402. The anonymous author of *The Propriety of Sending Lord Sheffield to Coventry* explained Sheffield's change of mind in respect of Charles Fox by reference to his hatred of the French: '[Sheffield] had the sense or the luck to follow Mr. Fox in lesser questions', but when Fox argued against war with France and for the audience and redress of the grievances of the people, 'this infatuated busy-body of a politician slunk away from him, and joined his adversaries and yours' (p. 5). Sheffield's alarming allusion to the Channel Islands as 'the remains of our Norman dominions' suggests that even the Plantagenet claim to French territory was at least emotionally alive for him (*Observations on the Manufactures, Trade, and Present State of Ireland*, 53). Gibbon's *Mémoire Justificatif* (1779), although a work of remonstrance against the actions of the French, contains not a shred of vulgar anti-French prejudice.
[71] Eden, *Journal and Correspondence*, i. 436.
[72] Ibid.

and commerce, and a great part of Europe, will feel a check in consequence of the great distress of France.[73]

The latter part of this analysis is based very closely on the account of French affairs which Gibbon had sent Sheffield on 15 December 1789: 'The French nation had a glorious opportunity, but they have abused and may lose their advantages. If they had been content with a liberal translation of our system, if they had respected the prerogatives of the crown and the privileges of the Nobles, they might have raised a solid fabric on the only true foundation the natural Aristocracy of a great Country. How different is the prospect!'[74] Although Sheffield's substitutions of 'national' for 'natural', 'miserable' for 'different' and 'their' for 'the' are all worthy of comment, the clear significance of this borrowing is that, in the early months of 1790, Gibbon and Sheffield spoke with one voice on the French Revolution.[75] What divided them was an event which took place at the end of 1790; the publication in November of Burke's *Reflections on the Revolution in France.*

IV

Gibbon enlisted under Burke's colours with exceptional promptness. In February 1791, a very early date on which to express admiration for the *Reflections*, Gibbon wrote to Sheffield that 'Burke's book is an admirable medicine against the French disease, which has made too much progress even in this happy country. I admire his eloquence, I approve his politics, I adore his chivalry, and I can even forgive his superstition.'[76] He then went on to offer an explanation of that aspect

---

[73] Eden, *Journal and Correspondence*, ii.366.

[74] L iii. 184. It was also from this letter that Sheffield had borrowed for his pamphlet of 1790, *Observations on the Project for Abolishing the Slave Trade*; see above, n. 49. Such sentiments about the Revolution are, however, common at this time; cf. e.g. Goold, *Vindication of the Right Honourable Edmund Burke's Reflections on the Revolution in France*, 46: 'That the French government wanted correction and reformation, no one in any degree acquainted with it, will disallow.'

[75] The concept of a 'natural aristocracy' was important in Burke's revolutionary writings. In the *Reflections*, he criticized the composition of the *Tiers État* in the National Assembly for its exclusion of 'the natural landed interest of the country' (*Reflections on the Revolution in France*, 95). In *An Appeal from the New to the Old Whigs*, he gave his most extended description of how this class came into its existence, and explained its centrality to the existence of the nation (*Further Reflections on the Revolution in France*, 168). Chronology prevents both these works from providing a source for Gibbon's and Sheffield's use of the term 'natural aristocracy'.

[76] L iii. 216. The liking for chivalry, although perhaps surprising given Gibbon's physical ungainliness, is not out of keeping with the self-analysis he composed on his twenty-fifth birthday (8 May 1762): 'It appeared to me, upon this enquiry, that my Character was virtuous, incapable of a base action, and formed for generous ones; but that it was proud, violent, and disagreeable in society' (*J2* 69). We should also recall the anecdote about his quixotic

of his work which was perhaps most awkward in the light of his desire to present himself as an ally of Burke's, namely his insufficiently reverent handling of the early Christians: 'The primitive Church, which I have treated with some freedom, was itself at that time, an innovation, and *I* was attached to the old Pagan establishment.'[77] Whether or not one finds convincing Gibbon's attempt to discover or invent some common ground between his writings of the 1770s and Burke's views of the 1790s, it corresponds with other contemporary conjectures about how Burke would have behaved had he been a senator of Antonine Rome. Priestley had made just this point, in language very close to that used by Gibbon in his letter to Sheffield:

Had you lived at that time [i.e. during the period of the early Church], you would, according to your general maxim, have 'cherished your old' heathen 'prejudices, because they were old,' and have lived and died a humble worshipper of the Gods, and especially the *Goddesses*, of ancient Greece and Rome.

On this principle, Sir [attachment to old establishments] had you been a Pagan at the time of the promulgation of christianity, you would have continued one.[78]

Others besides Gibbon, then, had extrapolated from Burke's comments on eighteenth-century France to arrive at this image of him as a pagan senator. As we shall see, it is not untypical of Gibbon's experience of the Revolution controversy that, in trying to align himself with Burke, he should in doing so have selected language close to that of the very radicals from whom he was trying to dissociate himself.[79]

What Gibbon wished to present as a *rapprochement*, Burke reported to Arthur Young as a capitulation: 'Mr. Burke had not read Lord Sheffield's Memoirs of Gibbon. On my observing that Mr. Gibbon declares himself of the same opinion with him on the French Revolution, he said that Gibbon was an old friend of his, and he knew well that before he (Mr. G.) died, that he heartily repented of the anti-religious part of his work for contributing to free mankind from all restraint on their vices and profligacy, and thereby aiding so much the spirit which produced the horrors that blackened the most detestable of

challenges to travellers on the roads around Lausanne to deny the beauty of Suzanne Curchod. Gibbon's liking for chivalry colours his treatment of figures such as Richard I in *The Decline and Fall*; see e.g. *DF* iii. 640–3.

[77] *L* iii. 216.

[78] Priestley, *Letters to the Right Honourable Edmund Burke*, 61–2 and 113.

[79] On Gibbon's declining of a public controversy with Priestley in 1783, see Turnbull, 'Gibbon's exchange with Joseph Priestley'. For the letters to Priestley themselves, see *L* ii. 320–3.

all revolutions.'[80] The substance of this late meeting with Burke is
not independently corroborated by any third party. However, if one
imagines Gibbon's experience of reading Burke's *Reflections*, and the
other books in the Revolution controversy which he had had sent to
Lausanne, such a moment of conversion becomes readily compre-
hensible. The language and values of this writing must have challenged
Gibbon to reconsider in a very far-reaching manner the political
tendency of *The Decline and Fall*.

On publication of the first volume in 1776, Gibbon had congratulated himself on his adroit political footwork. Both supporters of the
royal prerogative and virtual republicans had seen in his history
confirmation of their very different political prejudices.[81] Sixteen years
later, the political character of ancient history as a field of study had
changed. The ambivalence behind which Gibbon had sheltered in 1776
had disappeared. For some, historical study of whatever period might
be expected to carry forward the work of political enlightenment. The
ironic radical John Courtenay began his *Philosophical Reflections on
the Late Revolution in France* by asserting that 'the visions of chimerical
speculation must disappear before the light of history, and truth and
reason again resume their empire over the human mind'.[82] But some
regions of the past might lend themselves more naturally to this work
than others, and during the 1790s the classical past was increasingly seen
as the most promising historical quarry for arguments to support the
tenets of radicalism and democracy.[83] The prohibition of lectures on
the laws and constitution of Britain meant that the classical past was
attractive as the ostensible subject of political discussions which all those
who heard or read them would nevertheless know well how to apply to

---

[80] *Autobiography*, 258–9. This interview might conceivably have occurred on the occasion
referred to by Gibbon in his letter of 25 Nov. 1793 to Sheffield: 'I passed a delightful day with
Burke; . . .' (*L* iii. 365). It is less likely to have occurred during his chance meetings with Burke
at the Lucans' (31 Nov. 1793: *L* iii. 367 n. 3) and Lord Loughborough's (7 Dec. 1793: *L* iii. 367
n. 2).

[81] See the letter to Georges Deyverdun of 7 May 1776: 'Un historien est toujours jusqu'à un
certain point, un politique; et chaque lecteur suivant ses opinions particulieres cherche dans les
siecles les plus reculès les sentimens de l'ecrivain sur les hommes les Rois et les Gouvernemens
differens. Un Sous-Ministre très attaché aux prerogatives de la Couronne m'a fait son compliment de ce que j'avois partout inculqué les plus saines maximes. M. Walpole d'un autre cotè et
Mylord Cambden tous les deux partisans declarès de la libertè et meme de la Republique sont
persuadès que je ne suis pas eloignès de leur idèes: c'est une preuve du moins que j'ai observè une
honnete neutralitè' (*L* ii. 107).

[82] John Courtenay (1741–1816), politician. *Philosophical Reflections on the Late Revolution in
France*, 3.

[83] Consider, for instance, Vicesimus Knox's opinion, expressed in a work dedicated to
C. J. Fox, that 'in public affairs you will, I conclude, from the principles you have imbibed in the
schools of antiquity, ever lean to the side of liberty and the people' (*Personal Nobility*, 359).

the contemporary world. Therefore, in proposing to give '*a Course of Lectures on Classical History*', John Thelwall knew that 'in treating the grand subjects which such a course would embrace' he might also 'investigate all the principles of Government, all the vices of oppression, and all the mischiefs of tyranny and corruption' in the confident expectation that the fruits of these investigations would be applied to Hanoverian Britain. The latest, as well as the earliest, periods of Roman history might be pressed into the service of radicalism: 'Nor is it one period alone of Roman history that furnishes us with interesting parallels. Every page is eloquent in condemnation of the present system. Let it be remembered, that the Empire, as well as the Regal Government, had its age of corruption and tyranny.'[84] The anonymous author of *Short Observations on the Right Hon. Edmund Burke's Reflections* drew his textbook examples of monarchical tyranny from the early Roman Empire.[85] Catherine Macaulay sought to justify the actions of the National Assembly by exploring their classical—specifically, Roman— pedigree.[86] Sir James Mackintosh, noting Burke's avowed enthusiasm for Lucan, claimed that:

the sublime genius whom Mr. Burke admires, and who sung the obsequies of Roman freedom, has one sentiment, which the friends of liberty in England, if they are like him condemned to look abroad for a free government, must adopt—

> Rediturque nunquam
> Libertas ultra Tigrim Rhenumque recessit
> Et toties nobis jugulo quaesita negatur
> Germanum, Scythicumque bonum.[87]

To sing the obsequies of Roman freedom, as Gibbon had so recently and famously done, was plainly to invite identification as a sympathizer with the cause of modern, French, freedom. It was a view of the natural affinity between a certain subject of study and certain political principles which was also held by some on the other side of the question, such as the vehement anti-Arian and anti-republican John Whitaker, who in his *The Real Origin of Government* of 1795 followed Hobbes in attributing England's mid-seventeenth-century commonwealth to a 'new fever of republicanism' induced by the intensive study

---

[84] Thelwall, *The Tribune*, iii. 261 and 331.

[85] [Anon.], *Short Observations on the Right Hon. Edmund Burke's Reflections*, 34–5.

[86] Macaulay, *Observations on the Reflections of the Right Hon. Edmund Burke*, 81.

[87] Mackintosh, *Vindiciæ Gallicæ*, 350. 'Freedom has retreated beyond the Tigris and the Rhine, never to return: often as we have wooed her with our life-blood, she wanders afar, a blessing enjoyed by Germans & Scythians.'

of the literature and history of classical Greece and Rome.[88] Burke, on the other hand, was habitually characterized by his adversaries in language which announced his opposition to the classical. His values and vision were 'Gothic', even 'monkish': terms which Burke himself used in a positive sense, but at least the second of which had been part of *The Decline and Fall*'s vocabulary of condemnation.[89] Thomas Christie spoke for many when he professed to marvel at Burke's resistance to the political messages of antiquity, despite having been thoroughly exposed to them:

Ancient learning never appeared to me valuable, because it taught the *art of words*, and the little *finesses of style*; but I was wont to honour it, because I believed it infused *manly sentiment* and *heroic principle*; because I had not met with a man who truly understood it, whom 'ancient learning had not warmed into the enlightened love of ancient freedom.' But Mr. Burke is an exception. He is proof, that a man may have studied the sentiments and history of the patriots of Greece and Rome, and yet be capable of cherishing in his mind the principles of gothic feudality, and of consecrating in his writings the unclassic jargon of lawyers, monks and sophists of the middle ages.[90]

In the 1790s, then, the choice of subject Gibbon had made some two decades before created expectations about his political sympathies which were widely different from his true allegiances. No matter that *The Decline and Fall* in fact hardly addressed itself to the classical period at all. In the public mind, Gibbon was the historian of Rome.

Gibbon was therefore in danger of acquiring a spurious, although convincing, radical character as a result of the way the political connotations of the classical past as a subject of study had developed after 1789; and his reading of the literature of the Revolution controversy must

---

[88] Whitaker, *Real Origin of Government*, 34; cf. Hobbes, *Behemoth*, 23, where the Great Rebellion is presented as (at least in part) a consequence of 'having read the glorious histories and the sententious politics of the ancient popular governments of the Greeks and Romans'. But not everybody accepted this linkage between the classical and the radical. For instance, George Rous held that the ancient republics afforded no precedents in contemplating modern politics, because conditions of life at the end of the eighteenth century were so different (*Thoughts on Government*, 6–7). However, such dissident voices, in their comparative loneliness, give oblique confirmation to the prevalence of the opposite opinion.

[89] For Burke as the champion of the 'gothic', see: Macaulay, *Observations on the Reflections of the Right Hon. Edmund Burke*, 34; [Anon.], *Heroic Epistle to the Right Honourable Edmund Burke*, 7, 77–8, 180, 305, 312; Wollstonecraft, *Vindication of the Rights of Men*, 9, 94; and Towers, *Thoughts on the Commencement of a New Parliament*, 100. For Burke's reverence for the constitution ascribed to 'monkish superstition', see Scott-Waring, *A Letter to the Right Hon. Edmund Burke*, 31. For Burke's positive use of this vocabulary, see *Reflections on the Revolution in France*, 150 (gothic), 206 (monastic), and 150 (monkish). For Gibbon's negative use of the word 'monkish'—a usage which is shared by the deists of the earlier eighteenth century—see *DF* ii. 411–29.

[90] Christie, *Letters on the Revolution of France*, 5.

have shown him that this was the case. However, that reading would also have confronted Gibbon with sharper, more intimate, admonitions of how the debates arising from the Revolution were drawing his writings within their scope, and thereby threatening further to determine his public reputation. The various writings which made up these debates frequently reveal the influence of *The Decline and Fall*, although the literary dynamics are complex and tantalizing. Sometimes it is simply a question of an author alluding to periods or episodes of the past which had been most recently and authoritatively addressed by Gibbon—for instance, when Priestley, in the course of attacking Burke, referred to Julian the Apostate, the conversion of the Roman Empire to Christianity, and the election of bishops in the early Church.[91] Sometimes, however, the linkage might be the stronger one of positive allusion. When Priestley touched on 'the common reproach of all histories, that they exhibit little more than a view of the vices and miseries of mankind', he was echoing Gibbon's famous sentence that history 'is, indeed, little more than the register of the crimes, follies, and misfortunes of mankind'.[92] When Priestley went on to explain this common aspect of all history by adducing the fact that, hitherto, all governments had been conspiracies of the few against the many, a recognizably Gibbonian sentiment had been harnessed to a radical argument (as it would be again when Sir James Mackintosh contrasted the moral nobility of the revolutionaries with 'the long catalogue of calamities and crimes which blacken human annals').[93] When Priestley, imagining a utopian future, reflected on the natural history of the military encounters between barbarism and civilization in these words —

Standing armies, those instruments of tyranny, will be unknown, though the people may be trained to the use of arms, for the purpose of repelling the invasion of Barbarians. For no other description of men will have recourse to war, or think of disturbing the repose of others; and till they become civilized, as in the natural progress of things they necessarily must, they will be sufficiently overawed by the superior power of nations that are so.

— he was recalling a position Gibbon had expounded more epigrammatically in the 'General Observations on the Fall of the Roman

---

[91] Priestley, *Letters to the Right Honourable Edmund Burke*, 68, 80–1. and 100.

[92] Ibid. 144: *DF* i. 102.

[93] Mackintosh, *Vindiciæ Gallicæ*, 125. Burke's similar comment, that 'History consists, for the greater part, of the miseries brought upon the world by pride, ambition, avarice, revenge, lust, sedition, hypocrisy, ungoverned zeal, and all the train of disorderly appetites' (*Reflections on the Revolution in France*, 189) is also a reworking of Gibbon.

Empire in the West': 'Cannon and fortifications now form an impregnable barrier against the Tartar horse; and Europe is secure from any
future irruption of Barbarians; since, before they can conquer, they
must cease to be barbarous.'[94] From Gibbon's standpoint, however, it
cannot have been comfortable to have his ideas incorporated into
Priestley's view of futurity. Uncomfortable, too, must have been his
reading of the allusion which served as the keynote to Sir Brooke
Boothby's attack on Burke — 'Belonging to no party, addicted to no
sect, and too old not rather to fear than to invite notoriety of any sort
. . .' — a profession which recalls Gibbon's declaration of independence
at the beginning of chapter forty-four of *The Decline and Fall*: 'Attached
to no party, interested only for the truth and candour of history, and
directed by the most temperate and skilful guides . . .'.[95] And when John
Courtenay discussed the literary character of Mosheim in the course of
his ironic sapping of Burke, he not only made him into a simulacrum of
Gibbon, but did so in a style and idiom redolent of *The Decline and Fall*:

> That bold and insidious writer, under the specious pretext of candour and
> moderation, inspires his readers with an aversion to all ecclesiastical power, and
> with indignation against the clergy, for having invariably fomented religious
> controversy on mysterious unintelligible tenets; for encouraging persecution,
> and promoting the misery of mankind in this world, by infusing into their
> minds a spirit of hatred, malice, and uncharitableness; which at last became the
> theological characteristick of every various discordant sect of Christianity.[96]

The attack on Burke by the English friends of Revolution was thus to
some extent carried forward in Gibbonian language, and through allusion to subjects with which Gibbon was publicly associated.[97] It is easy
to appreciate how this would have alarmed Gibbon, and how it might
naturally prompt him, when face to face with the author of *Reflections on
the Revolution in France*, into the contrition which Burke described to
Arthur Young.

Although as staunch an enemy of Revolution as was Burke, Sheffield
took his stand on very different ground: on the ground of the rights
of property, and, in the end, of force. He had no time for the (as he
probably thought) mystical ideas of the British constitution and of

---

[94] Priestley, *Letters to the Right Honourable Edmund Burke*, 151: *DF* ii. 514. For John Whitaker's
different response to this same passage in *The Decline and Fall*, see below, Ch. 9.

[95] Boothby, *A Letter to the Right Honourable Edmund Burke*, 1: *DF* ii. 779.

[96] Courtenay, *Philosophical Reflections on the Late Revolution in France*, 11–12.

[97] It may also be that Burke went back to *The Decline and Fall* when framing his replies to
his opponents. The comparison of the 'Republick of Algiers' with the 'Republick of the
Mammalukes in Egypt' in *Thoughts on French Affairs* repeats a comparison made by Gibbon
(*Further Reflections on the Revolution in France*, 236; *DF* i. 210 nn. 53 and 54).

prescription which Burke had disseminated, and was quite out of sympathy with Burke's relinquishing of rationality, and religious scepticism, to the supporters of democracy. Sheffield's suspicion of Burke was plain in his attitude towards the rumours which circulated after his death: 'As to Burke's disposition to excite the Roman Catholics against the Government in Ireland, I am perfectly satisfied it is true; nothing too extravagant or mischievous for that wild creature.'[98] For Sheffield, then, Burke had conceded far too much when he had surrendered the intellectual achievements of much of the earlier eighteenth century to the cause of revolution.

The emotional and psychological consequences of Gibbon's and Sheffield's different responses to the Revolution are themselves fascinating in human terms, independent of their textual and editorial afterlife. By subscribing to Burke's views on France, Gibbon swiftly furnished himself with an explanatory framework within which to understand, and therefore to some degree contain, even the most atrocious events of the Revolution.[99] This Burkean framework was of Manichaean simplicity, and the price of adopting it was the disowning of aspects of his earlier life and work. Nevertheless, it gave Gibbon points of reference in a world which otherwise threatened to overwhelm him. Sheffield, on the other hand, was equipped with no language or set of ideas which he might use to distinguish himself with the clarity he desired from the enemies of all he most valued. Therefore, although the Revolution disturbed him in some senses less profoundly than it did Gibbon (in that it touched him less intimately), in other respects its impact on his life was more prolonged and more disruptive. In October 1792 he wrote to Gibbon that European politics 'have totally deranged all my notions of dignity, generalship, preponderance of military discipline, &c., &c., and all my speculations, moral, religious, political, and military, are sent into a troubled sea without rudder or compass'.[100] Thus, although Sheffield's opposition to the French

---

[98] Letter to William Eden, 27 Oct. 1797 (Eden, *Journal and Correspondence*, iii. 383). There is probably also contempt for both the 'silly public' and the politician prepared to pander to them in Sheffield's noting to Eden that 'Burke's charges [against Warren Hastings] made a very considerable impression and alteration in the silly public' (Eden, *Journal and Correspondence*, i. 371). In the mid-1770s, Gibbon had viewed Burke with similar asperity. In 1774, writing to Sheffield about a debate on the government's American policy, he reported that 'Burke was a water mill of words and images' (*L* ii. 45).

[99] On this see above, Ch. 5. Gibbon's rereading of *Paradise Lost* at this juncture is a particularly suggestive circumstance.

[100] Prothero, ii. 319–20. The nautical language echoes Burke's metaphor for the consequences of an estrangement from inherited practice: 'When antient opinions and rules of life are taken away, the loss cannot possibly be estimated. From that moment we have no

Revolution was more grounded in practical realities than was that
of Burke and Gibbon, this paradoxically made it more fragile. His
dejection might easily curdle into resignation, as a bitter letter to
William Eden of April 1794 makes clear:

I certainly am no longer afraid of French politics; perhaps I am grown callous.
Events have happened to me within a year which have reduced me to an
eminent degree of philosophy, indifference, or whatever you please to call it. I
fear I care little about anything. I perceive that I hate politicians most heartily.
I am piqued, perhaps, into vigorous notions. I rather feel I am in train to
become what despots call a democrat, and in time by the engaging ways of Lady
Auckland and of *another*, I may slide further, and gradually become a friend of
the people and of reform.[101]

Beneath the playfulness, which asserts itself at the end, one can sense the
strain produced by opposition, when that stance of opposition has
required a continual assertion of the will, unbuttressed by any supporting ideology or myth. Gibbon (a shrewd reader of Sheffield's character,
as Maria Holroyd noted) may have known that he was not preaching
to the converted when he repeatedly warned his friend against 'the
specious name of Reform':

Will you not take some active measures to declare your sound opinions and
separate yourselves from your rotten members? If you allow them to perplex
government, if you trifle with this solemn business, if you do not resist the
spirit of innovation in the first attempt, if you admit the smallest and most
specious change in our parliamentary system, you are lost. You will be driven
from one step to another, from principles just in theory to consequences most
pernicious in practice, and your first concessions will be productive of every
subsequent mischief for which you will be answerable to your country and to
posterity. Do not suffer yourselves to be lulled into a false security.

Next winter may be the crisis of our fate and [if] you begin to improve the
constitution, you may be driven step by step from the disfranchisement of Old
Sarum to the King in Newgate, the Lords voted useless, the Bishops abolished,
and a house of Commons without articles (sans culottes).

compass to govern us, nor can we know distinctly to what port we steer' (*Reflections on the
Revolution in France*, 129). Burke is perhaps overhearing in his own mind Rosse's words to Lady
Macduff; 'when we hold rumour | From what we fear, yet know not what we fear, |
But float upon a wild and violent sea | Each way and move' (*Macbeth*, IV. ii. 19–22). (For
another allusion to this play, see *A Letter to a Noble Lord*, in *Further Reflections on the Revolution in
France*, 305; 'curses, not loud but deep': cf. *Macbeth*, V. iii. 29.) It was a metaphor which stuck in
the mind of other contemporaries; see Edward Tatham, *Letters to the Right Honourable Edmund
Burke on Politics*, 104. A letter from Sheffield to William Eden of the same month has the same air
of dejection of bewilderment (Eden, *Journal and Correspondence*, ii. 457–61). Cf. also Prothero, ii.
343; 'my political barometer never was so low.'

  [101] Eden, *Journal and Correspondence*, iii. 206–7.

You have now crushed the daring subverters of the Constitution, but I now fear the moderate well-meaning reformers. Do not, I beseech you tamper with Parliamentary representation. The present house of Commons forms in practise a body of Gentlemen who must always sympathize with the interest and opinions of the people, and the slightest innovation launches you without rudder or compass on a dark and dangerous ocean of Theoretical experiment. On this subject I am indeed serious.[102]

Not the least surprising aspect of this phase in Gibbon's and Sheffield's friendship is the sight of the historian for once supplying backbone to the peer.

Sheffield represents, then, a different strain of counter-revolutionary reaction from that of Burke and, in the event, from that of Gibbon. From Sheffield's standpoint the *Reflections* marked, not so much defiance, as a calamitous surrendering of territory. And here we return to the 'Memoirs', for occupying a prominent position in Sheffield's intentions when editing the drafts was the desire to conceal, wherever possible, Gibbon's crossing of the floor at the end of his life to stand

---

[102] *L* iii. 258 (30 May 1792), 304 (25 Nov. 1792) and 308 (1 Jan. 1793). In the last quoted passage Gibbon's nautical metaphor may be an allusion to either the language of Sheffield's letter to him of 17 Oct. 1792 (Prothero, ii. 319–22), or the language of Burke's *Reflections on the Revolution in France*, 129. The radical supporters of Revolution saw such hysteria as typical of counter-revolutionary sentiment: 'The French revolution, I perceive, has at the present moment an unhappy effect on the minds of men in this country. When any mention is made of *reform*, *improvement*, or *change* of any kind whatever, their feeble or frighted imaginations immediately conjure up the horrors of anarchy, riot, mobs, murders, burnings, &c.' (Christie, *Letters on the Revolution of France*, 30). There had been discussion of the need for parliamentary reform in the decades preceding the Revolution; Wilkes had proposed reform on 21 March 1776, Burke on 11 February 1780, Pitt on 7 May 1783 and again on 18 April 1785. There is a large scholarly litera-ture on movements for parliamentary reform before 1832: see especially I. R. Christie, *Wilkes, Wyvill and Reform* (1962), J. Dinwiddy, *Christopher Wyvill and Reform, 1790–1820* (York, 1971), J. A. Cannon, *Parliamentary Reform, 1640–1832* (Cambridge, 1972) and Clark, *English Society 1688–1832*, 336–46. The authoritative modern study of the unreformed electoral system is Frank O'Gorman, *Voters, Patrons and Parties: The Unreformed Electorate of Hanoverian England, 1734–1832* (Oxford: Clarendon Press, 1989). Professor O'Gorman's conclusions (pp. 384–93) corroborate Gibbon's and Burke's conviction that the unreformed House, despite its much-discussed short-comings, provided effectually for the representation of the people. As Burke put it, 'I shall only say here, in justice to that old-fashioned constitution, under which we have long prospered, that our representation has been found perfectly adequate to all the purposes for which a representa-tion of the people can be desired or devised' (*Reflections on the Revolution in France*, 107): see also Burke's contrasting of his own conduct towards the House of Commons with that of the ancestor of the Duke of Bedford in *A Letter to a Noble Lord* (*Further Reflections on the Revolution in France*, 305–6). John Scott-Waring found that Burke's enthusiasm for Parliaments in the 1790s smacked of hypocrisy: 'There is no part of your book which surprizes me more than the new-born zeal and affection displayed in it, for Parliaments; possibly you may have admired at all times the institution of the House of Commons; but of this I am sure, that there is no man in this king-dom who has treated the material part of that House, the Majority, with such sovereign contempt as you have done, for a long series of years' (*Letter to the right Hon. Edmund Burke*, 17).

shoulder to shoulder with Burke. When he set about editing the
'Memoirs', Sheffield wanted to present Gibbon as what, in his experience, Gibbon had been: namely, an opponent of democracy who yet
had had little in common with Burke.

V

We are now in a position to consider in an informed way the sequence
of decisions Gibbon took concerning the 'Memoirs', such as we can
ascertain them from the Gibbon–Sheffield correspondence and the
'Memoirs' themselves, touching at the same time where appropriate on
Gibbon's developing response to events in France. Then we shall put
this explanatory framework to the test with two examples from the
drafts of the 'Memoirs'. In the first place we shall compare the three
accounts Gibbon wrote of the death of Edward Gibbon senior; one
from draft 'C', which was to be published posthumously; one from
draft 'D', whose status in this respect is ambiguous; and the third from
draft 'E', which was manifestly intended for publication in Gibbon's
own lifetime. Secondly, we shall consider the five accounts he composed of his unhappy months at Oxford. The purpose of these instances
of practical criticism is to demonstrate the power of the preceding
examination of context to explain literary detail. To modify the maxim
of deconstruction: 'il n'y a pas de hors-contexte'.[103]

   As we have seen, Gibbon initially intended the 'Memoirs' to be
posthumous. Draft 'A', written in late 1788 or early 1789, begins by
informing the reader that 'if these sheets are communicated to some
discreet and indulgent friends, they will be secreted from the public eye
till the author shall be removed from the reach of criticism or
ridicule'.[104] Drafts 'B' and 'C' (and perhaps 'D'), which have evident
continuities with 'A', we can assume were also composed on this basis.
This repeated rewriting suggests dissatisfaction on Gibbon's part
without any clear sense of how to reconceptualize and recompose his
autobiography to circumvent or neutralize the sources of that dissatisfaction. It was the publication of Burke's *Reflections*, to the arguments
and sentiments of which, at once unsettling and alluring, Gibbon
responded so warmly, which broke the impasse and permitted the
innovative recension represented by 'E'.

   At some uncertain later stage—possibly just before the composition
of 'D', possibly just after—Gibbon decided that the 'Memoirs' should

---

[103] Derrida, *De la Grammatologie*, 158.   [104] *A* 353.

after all be published in his lifetime. 'E', at any rate, appears to have been composed with a view to non-posthumous publication; a decision presumably made easier when the publication of Burke's *Reflections* in November 1790 furnished Gibbon with an ideological framework within which to construct a version of the story of his life acceptable to English counter-revolutionary sentiment. Virtually at the end of this draft he used a tense which implied publication in his own lifetime: 'My friends, more especially Lord Sheffield, kindly relieve me from the cares to which my taste and temper are most adverse.'[105]

Gibbon then received a visit from Sheffield and his family at Lausanne during the summer and autumn of 1791. It is reasonable to assume that Gibbon and Sheffield discussed the project of the 'Memoirs' during this visit; the phrase 'I once mentioned' in the letter of 28 December 1791 seems naturally to refer to such conversations.[106] Gibbon had earlier that year completed 'E', and may even have described it to Sheffield, although he seems not to have allowed him to read it. It would be entirely in keeping with the nature of the friendship between the two men, and Gibbon's secretive behaviour over his writings, for him to have spoken of the version of his life embodied in 'E' as of a hypothetical project he might undertake, and to have sought Sheffield's valued opinion without fully confiding in him.[107] Sheffield at that point, I surmise, persuaded Gibbon to commit himself to posthumous publication, because he realized that, were publication non-posthumous, the narrative would coincide less with his own, non-Burkean values. He had two reasons for thinking this. First, Gibbon was in any event moving towards Burke's position, and was doing so with a remarkable promptness and completeness.[108] Second, Gibbon was now mentioning with greater frequency a plan to move back to England from Switzerland. He would have wished to do nothing to confirm the radicals' reading of his life and work, as an exposé of the corruption of England's *ancien régime*. Gibbon then began afresh, and set about composing 'F', although he seems not to have told Sheffield definitely that

---

[105] *A* 345. On this point of the decorum of tenses in autobiography, recall how Hume began his own autobiographical essay: 'I am, or rather, I was . . .'. In the manuscript this passage has been amended to read 'My friend Lord Sheffield has kindly relieved me' (BL Add. MS 34874 fo. 95ᵛ).

[106] *L* iii. 240.

[107] Sheffield wrote as if he were seeing Gibbon's papers for the first time when he informed Eden of their contents (Eden, *Journal and Correspondence*, iii. 237). For Gibbon's (very human) desire to be reassured about the likely reception of his work before irrevocably committing himself to publication under his own name, consider his anonymous soliciting of opinions concerning his aborted 'History of the Swiss': *A* 276–7 (draft 'C') and 408 (draft 'D').

[108] See column six, row five of the table in Appendix 2.

it was to be written for posthumous publication. Sheffield's letter of 23 January 1792 reveals the peer still trying to urge the historian towards posthumous publication: a plan we know Gibbon had already adopted. It was to the composition of 'F' that Gibbon alluded in his letter to Sheffield of 28 December 1791, when he confided in his friend that he was going to 'make the attempt' on the project of the 'Memoirs', and swore him to secrecy on the subject.[109]

Gibbon found the work difficult and put this draft to one side, but seems nevertheless to have been still committed to posthumous publication ('I much doubt whether the book and the author can ever see the light at the same time').[110] It is therefore beyond question that in this letter he is referring to 'F', which was in any case the draft on which he was then working. Gibbon was 'not satisfied' with 'F', I would suggest, because it was only in writing it out at length on the basis of posthumous publication that he realized quite how massive a challenge his life story, told in these terms, would mount to the Burkean values he had so recently adopted.

Sheffield replied on 23 January 1793, urging him not to abandon the project of the 'Memoirs', and restating the freedoms that would be possible only in a posthumous publication.[111] It is therefore clear that Gibbon did not take Sheffield fully into his confidence about either the progress of the 'Memoirs', or the fundamental decisions he had taken in regard to them. Sheffield wanted Gibbon to publish posthumously, as I have said, because he grasped the point that Gibbon's 'nerves' (as he was later to express it) would not allow him, in the raised political temperatures of the 1790s, to tell his life as the un-Burkean story Sheffield believed it to have been, were he still alive to witness and endure its reception.

Gibbon's correspondence with Nichols and Brydges of later in 1793 indicates that he did not throw up the 'Memoirs' altogether, but he seems not to have done any more writing in this period (unless perhaps a stray sheet justifying the pride of genealogy can be dated to these months).

The next significant event was Gibbon's death on 16 January 1794. Sheffield was his literary executor, and had his papers shipped over from Lausanne. His letter to Eden of 5 September 1794 reveals the frame of mind in which he approached his editorial task:

---

[109] *L* iii. 240.
[110] See the letters of 30 May 1792 and 6 Jan. 1793 (*L* iii. 264 and 312).
[111] Prothero, ii. 366.

I have been fully employed, the last ten days, with Mr. Hayley, in the examination of Gibbon's papers. I am much satisfied with the occupation, and it gave
me much pleasure to observe that he treated the business [of the 'Memoirs'?]
exactly as had appeared to me most advisable, and I think I may venture to
say that nothing is likely to appear that can disgrace Gibbon's literary fame,
prejudice society, or disgust the public, but, on the contrary, that the public
will be highly gratified.[112]

It is noteworthy that the well-being of society and the public are as
prominent in Sheffield's thoughts as Gibbon's literary fame: the
publication of the historian's *Miscellaneous Works* was to be as much a
political and social as a literary event.[113] Sheffield then compiled a
composite single narrative of the 'Memoirs' from the six drafts, in
which 'F' (that written on the basis of posthumous publication) was
given priority wherever possible, and 'E' (that written on the basis on
non-posthumous publication, and far more in line with Burkean sentiments and positions) was used only where there was no alternative;
namely, for the events in Gibbon's life after 1772. This selection of
material reveals very clearly where, in Sheffield's opinion, Gibbon had
treated the writing of his 'Memoirs' 'exactly as had appeared to
[Sheffield] most advisable'. Yet Sheffield placed this note at the head of
his conflated text:

Mr. Gibbon, in his communications with me on the subject of his Memoirs, a
subject which he had not mentioned to any other person, expressed a determination of publishing them in his lifetime; and never appears to have departed
from that resolution, excepting in one of his letters, in which he intimates a
doubt, though rather carelessly, whether in his time, or at any time, they would
meet the eye of the public.—In a conversation, however, not long before his
death, I suggested to him that, if he should make them a full image of his mind,
he would not have nerves to publish them, and that they should be posthumous;—He answered, rather eagerly, that he was determined to publish them
in his lifetime.[114]

The record of this conversation is a most important piece of evidence.
But it needs to be handled with the utmost care because of its potency
to mislead. First, we may note the simple inaccuracy. It was untrue
to say that Gibbon had never departed from the intention of non-

---

[112] Eden, *Journal and Correspondence*, iii. 237.
[113] Sheffield spoke of the publication of the third quarto volume of the *Miscellaneous Works*
almost in the same breath as he commented on the likelihood of the restoration of the Bourbons;
a circumstance strikingly expressive of the proximity of the literary and political realms for him
(Eden, *Journal and Correspondence*, iv. 408–9).
[114] *MW 1796* i. 1 n.

posthumous publication. The first three drafts, the sixth, and possibly the fourth were (as we have seen) written for posthumous publication. Moreover, some of the evidence for this, as we saw from the opening of draft 'A', is internal and thus would have been evident to Sheffield when he read the drafts, probably for the first time, on their arrival in Sussex. But the really misleading aspect of this note is its publication as footnote to the opening of Sheffield's conflated text, which wherever it can (and that includes the beginning) uses 'F'. For Gibbon's 'rather eager' wish at the end of his life that his 'Memoirs' should be published in his own lifetime can be read only as an implicit rejection of draft 'F', which the letter to Sheffield of 6 January 1793 shows he intended for posthumous publication, if publication were to occur at all, and with which he had explicitly declared himself to be dissatisfied. By placing this note where he did, Sheffield—it may have been done in innocence, but it certainly suited his book—contrived to suggest the very reverse of this. As Sheffield managed to make it seem, not only was Gibbon not rejecting the un-Burkean language and sentiments of 'F'; he was, on the contrary, determined to publish them, and resolved to face their reception.[115]

So it was that Gibbon's unexpected death allowed Sheffield to present the historian in his 'Memoirs' as the kindred, un-Burkean, spirit which for much of his life he had been. And so it was received, by Arthur Young at least, who wrote gloomily: 'alas! the whole volume has not one word of Christianity in it, though many which mark the infidelity of the whole gang.'[116]

---

[115] Further support for the view that the printed version of this note is deliberately misleading is provided by the MS draft, contained in the Sheffield papers at the Beinecke Library, Yale University. Sheffield expended much care on the wording of this note. The most interesting revision comes at the end. Sheffield originally wrote 'he was determined to publish them in his lifetime, and to enjoy the fruits of them—'. He then crossed out 'and to enjoy the fruits of them', thereby suppressing the fact that Gibbon's motive for non-posthumous publication was financial gain, not ideological defiance (MS Vault, Section 10, Drawer 3, Section B, B5).

[116] *Autobiography*, 469.

7

'As common as any the most vulgar thing to sense': Three Versions of the Death of a Father

The three versions of the death of his father which Gibbon composed for the 'Memoirs' offer us a particularly clear instance of the way in which successive drafts of the autobiography grew stylistically out of their predecessors. Gibbon retained phrases and sentences from the earlier, discarded drafts as he sat down and began once more to throw into written form his family life during the ten years between 1762 and 1772. It is therefore tempting (but I think mistaken) to consider this sequence of drafts in a formalist or aesthetic light, and to read the sequence of versions as a textual episode with no ramifications beyond or beneath the level of style. However, the movement from draft to draft, once set and explained in the context of the swift development in Gibbon's political sentiments which was happening at exactly the time he was composing these three accounts of the death of his father, suggests that stylistic choice was coordinated with the broader considerations which arose from his contemplation of the scene of European politics.

Before considering the detail of draft 'C', it is worth turning for a moment to the letter Gibbon wrote to Sheffield on 15 December 1789.[1] Two emphases should be carried over into a reading of the concurrently composed draft of the 'Memoirs'. The first is Gibbon's evocation of the predicament of Louis XVI: 'The abuses of the court and government called aloud for reformation and it has happened as it will always happen, that an innocent well-disposed prince pays the forfeit of the sins of his predecessors.'[2] That Gibbon should be alive to the damage that may follow from the 'sins of . . . predecessors', and

---

[1] See column six of the analytical table in Appendix 2.
[2] *L* iii. 183.

that he should locate the origin of 'abuses . . . [which call] aloud for reformation' in the period when those sinful predecessors held sway, is a perception of obvious pertinence to the account he gives in draft 'C' of his father's behaviour between the dissolution of the militia and his own dissolution. Like the earlier Bourbon monarchs, Edward Gibbon senior had behaved with a culpable heedlessness to the future.

The second pertinent emphasis is Gibbon's alertness to the slighting of vested interests by the revolutionaries, their disregard for 'the prerogatives of the crown and privileges of the Nobles'.[3] The mismanagement of the family finances by his father meant that Gibbon's own vested interests had suffered detriment, for the estate had been protected by an entail until Gibbon's father had persuaded him to consent to its removal in return for an allowance. As a result, Gibbon's own prospects were greatly different from what they would have been had his father not placed the immediate expenditure demanded by self-indulgence before both the future financial security of his son and the wishes of his own father, the architect of the family fortune and the settlement intended to protect and preserve it.[4]

Approaching the 'Memoirs' by way of this letter, then, we discover in Gibbon's attitude towards events in France a matrix of concerns which can focus our reading of the language of draft 'C'.[5] It would be as misguided to assume that the 'Memoirs' offered us a narrative *à clef* of the French Revolution as to assume that the account of Gibbon's family drama was conceived without any relation to the theatre of international politics. The connection between the two is definite, but flexible. The 'wonderful scene' of French politics displayed to Gibbon the endgame of a political system of which he had himself deduced the origins in *The Decline and Fall*. The 'Christian republic of nations' from within which, and on behalf of which, Gibbon had composed his great history was now being destroyed before his eyes by the eruption of internal agents whom wise government might have pacified with policy or suppressed with force.[6] The reflections prompted by this

---

[3] *L* iii. 184.

[4] The standard scholarly account of these issues is to be found in Sir John Habakkuk's Ford Lectures for 1985, now published as *Marriage, Debt and the Estates System: English Landownership, 1650–1950* (Oxford: Clarendon Press, 1994). Chapters 1 and 2 devote particular attention to the 'strict settlement', pithily defined as 'a form of legal arrangement which made it possible to tie up the succession of a specific landed estate for a generation ahead by ensuring that the apparent owner at any given time was only a tenant for life with very limited powers' (p. 1). I am very grateful to Sir John for his willingness to discuss the legal and financial aspects of the Gibbon family with me informally on many occasions.

[5] See Appendix 4 for transcripts of these passages from the drafts of the 'Memoirs'.

[6] *DF* ii. 511; cf. ii. 433. See also the Introduction to this edition, *DF* i, pp. lxv–lxvi.

unnecessary tragedy served to focus Gibbon's thoughts on his own life, in which substantial benefits had also been squandered through carelessness. His own earlier life displayed in miniature the potency for harm in those same toxins which now threatened to undermine the European body politic as a whole. There, the damaging agent had been his father, who had managed to combine the worst qualities of both sides in the revolutionary struggle, uniting the complacency of Louis XV to the disregard for the rights of property and the wishes of ancestors (in this case, the settlement constructed by his own father) typical of the revolutionaries.

The tone of draft 'C' is established by Gibbon's handling of his father's return to the family estate at Buriton after serving in the militia. Amusement plays about the reference to his father by his military rank ('the Major'), particularly since earlier in this draft Gibbon has written with ironic detachment of the 'bloodless and inglorious campaigns' of the Hampshire regiment as it marched to and fro over the tranquil fields of southern England.[7] It is confirmed and strengthened by what in this draft must be read as the plainly mock-heroic comparison with the martial hero of the Roman republic, Cincinnatus. Taken together with the allusion to Horace (whose ideal of happiness the Major only 'seemed to enjoy'), this invocation of the classical past creates a context of judgement around the figure of Gibbon's father more favourable to the dispassionate perception of discrepancy than to emotional sympathy. The two allusions to Roman literature and history work together in such a way that a perspective of deepening censure is created. Initially the reader assumes that the point of the glance at the conqueror of the Aequi at Mount Algidus is to mock the contrasting banality of the militia, whose nearest approaches to action came when it exercised within sight of the French coast, and took its turn in guarding French prisoners in Sissinghurst.[8] But Cincinnatus was as celebrated for his frugality as for his valour, and as the passage continues it becomes clear that Gibbon's father departed from the classical model in fiscal as well as military matters.[9]

The depiction of his father's financial embarrassments shows Gibbon's skill, polished over the years spent composing *The Decline and Fall*, in relating circumstances in such a way that judgement is implied

[7] *A* 252–4.

[8] *A* 253–4.

[9] Elsewhere in the literature of the 1790s the origin of Cincinnatus' poverty was accounted for by his having paid a fine incurred by his son; cf. William Godwin, *St. Leon*, 36. Such a circumstance would only intensify the latent satire of the comparison with Gibbon's father.

without needing to be stated. These embarrassments, Gibbon is clear, were the result of transgressions: 'the vanities of his youth were severely punished by the solicitude and sorrow of his declining age.' No matter that the adult is a reformed character ('his labours were useful, his pleasures innocent, his wishes moderate'). No matter that the penalty is severe. The reader of draft 'C' is nevertheless required to see the family misfortunes in the light of crime and punishment. As Gibbon specifies the separate components in the wreck of the family fortune, his father's responsibility for the debacle is confirmed:

The first mortgage, on my return from Lausanne (1758), had afforded him a partial and transient relief: the annual demand of interest and | allowance was an heavy deduction from ~~the~~ his income: the militia was a source of expence: the farm in his hands was not a profitable adventure: he was loaded with the costs and damages of an obsolete law suit; and each year multiplied the number, and exhausted the patience of his creditors.

This passage insists that Mr Gibbon was encumbered by the perfectly foreseeable consequences of his own actions. It is in the nature of things that mortgages must be serviced by payments of interest, and that allowances which permitted the raising of the mortgage in the first place have to be met. The passage further insists that Mr Gibbon exacerbated the harmfulness of those consequences by his own incompetence ('the farm *in his hands* was not a profitable adventure'). Moreover, the metaphorical charge of the language begins to look forward to the later section of the passage, in which Gibbon will recount his father's somatic collapse. The 'relief' afforded by the first mortgage and the load placed on him by the lawsuit introduce into the passage a sense of the physical body, and thus serve to link Mr Gibbon's moral weakness to the breaking of his constitution. His death thus already begins to take on that outline of a *felo de se* which, as we shall see, it in due course fully assumes. However, here again Mr Gibbon is no antique Roman. He undoes himself unintentionally, through incompetence and ineptitude. This is not the heroic and conscious resolution of a classical suicide.

In contrast, Gibbon's own behaviour conforms to the highest standards of positive rectitude: 'my own behaviour was not only guilt-less but meritorious.' He, at least, can banish from his mind all thought of 'personal advantages' and consent to the measures which might relieve the distress of a man whose 'vanities' have threatened the security of his son, even if those measures represent a calamitous dwindling of his patrimony ('an additional mortgage [and] the sale of Putney'). The genuinely classical stoicism and self-sacrifice of the younger generation finds no echo in the fast-declining behaviour of Mr Gibbon, who instead conforms to a pattern of degeneracy drawn from the troughs of imperial corruption:

he was no longer capable of a rational effort, and his reluctant delays postponed, not the evils themselves, but the remedies of those evils, (*remedia malorum potius quam mala differebat*). ~~But~~ The pangs of shame tenderness and self-reproach incessantly preyed on his vitals: his constitution was broken; he lost his strength and his sight; the rapid progress of a dropsy admonished him of his end, and he sunk into the grave on the tenth of November 1770, in the sixty fourth year of his age.

The Latin tag which Gibbon uses to illustrate his father's final state of imbecility is Tacitus's pithy analysis of the weakness of the Emperor Vitellius.[10] The defeat of Vitellius' forces at the battle of Cremona had effectively placed him in the power of Vespasian, and had initiated the protracted process of deposition which was to culminate in his capture, humiliation, and murder in the deserted imperial palace.[11] This is a passage of Tacitus which we know Gibbon particularly admired. In *The Decline and Fall* he had applied these very words to Maxentius, the worthless opponent of Constantine:

While Constantine signalized his conduct and valour in the field, the sovereign of Italy appeared insensible of the calamities and danger of a civil war which raged in the heart of his dominions. Pleasure was still the only business of Maxentius. Concealing, or at least attempting to conceal, from the public knowledge the misfortunes of his arms, he indulged himself in a vain confidence, which deferred the remedies of the approaching evil, without deferring the evil itself.

To which the footnote runs: 'Remedia malorum potius quam mala differebat, is the fine censure which Tacitus passes on the supine indolence of Vitellius.'[12] Gibbon does not, of course, expect the reader of his 'Memoirs' to recall this past use of the phrase, in a work published some thirteen years beforehand. But that earlier use is nevertheless of great value, because it reveals to us the significance of this Tacitean sentence to Gibbon. The source of the quotation is suppressed in draft 'C', but Gibbon must nevertheless have used it in the conviction that it was a 'fine censure . . . on supine indolence'. Moreover, when Gibbon had used the quotation before it had been part of a diptych formed by the weakness of Maxentius and the heroism of Constantine. When he turns once more to the phrase while composing his 'Memoirs', it again

---

[10] Tacitus, *Histories*, III. 54.   [11] Ibid. III. 84.   [12] *DF* i. 424–5.

points up the disparity between the firmness of a younger generation and the self-involved pusillanimity of its predecessors (Maxentius was of the same generation as Constantine's father).

The quotation is followed by a long sentence of multiple parts explaining the emotional and physical sequences of his father's final collapse: 'The pangs of shame tenderness and self-reproach incessantly preyed on his vitals: his constitution was broken; he lost his strength and his sight; the rapid progress of a dropsy admonished him of his end, and he sunk into the grave on the tenth of November 1770, in the sixty fourth year of his age.' This sentence echoes the earlier sentence of similar structure in which the various financial difficulties of Mr Gibbon were set out. The causal linkage between financial irresponsibility and physical decay is intimated through a stroke of style. At the same time, the suggestion hinted at earlier in the passage, that Mr Gibbon was the architect of his own undoing, is given quiet substantiation.

In *The Decline and Fall* Gibbon had introduced his final judgement on Julian the Apostate by explaining the practice of the ancient world on such occasions: 'It was an ancient custom in the funerals, as well as in the triumphs, of the Romans, that the voice of praise should be corrected by that of satire and ridicule; and, that in the midst of the splendid pageants, which displayed the glory of the living or of the dead, their imperfections should not be concealed from the eyes of the world.'[13] This principle shapes the next phase of this passage, when the satirical portrait of Mr Gibbon drawn by William Law (recalled in only this draft of the 'Memoirs') is 'corrected' by Gibbon's tribute to his father's personal qualities:

A family tradition insinuates that Mr. William Law has drawn his pupil in the light and inconstant character of <u>Flatus</u>, who is ever confident and ever disappointed in the chace of happiness. But these constitutional failings are were amply compensated by the virtues of the head and heart, by the warmest sentiments of honour and humanity. His graceful person, polite address, gentle manners, and unaffected chearfulness, recommended him to the favour of every company: and in the change of times and opinions, his liberal spirit had long since delivered him from the zeal and prejudice of a Tory education[14]

Criticism of the youth delivered by an outsider seems to be moderated by the son's much more positive testimony to the virtues of the adult.

---

[13] *DF* i. 957.

[14] The non-juror William Law (1686–1761) had been employed by Gibbon's grandfather as a tutor to his children. The character of Flatus occurs in his *A Serious Call to a Devout and Holy Life* (1728).

But Gibbon's praise of his father supplements Law's critique without ever supplanting it, and the apparently innocent comment that the identification of Mr Gibbon with Flatus is a 'family tradition' gives Law's censure more force. Such a tradition can hardly come into being without a number of well-positioned people being persuaded of its accuracy.

The way is thus prepared for the final phase of the passage. This is a speech put into the mouth of a Hamlet whom Claudius has managed to persuade that the loss of a father was indeed 'as common | As any the most vulgar thing to sense':

The tears of a son are seldom lasting: I submitted to the order of Nature; and my grief was soothed by the conscious satisfaction, that I had discharged all the duties of filial piety: Few, perhaps, are the children, who, after the expiration of some months or years, would sincerely rejoyce in the resurrection of their parents; and it is a melancholy truth, that my father's death, not unhappy for himself, was the only event that could save me from an hopeless life of obscurity and indigence.[15]

The central concern of these closing sentences is summed up in the question (as urgent to Gibbon as to Hamlet) 'what is a son to do?' The repeated movement between the general example and the particular behaviour of Gibbon himself suggests a measuring of his performance against a model of appropriateness. It is a test which Gibbon fully satisfies. The transience of filial grief is made decorous as a submission to 'the order of Nature', while the acknowledgement of the final, 'melancholy truth' is also, in its firm turning away from the dead to the needs of the living, a natural transition, the 'natural' here perhaps to be understood in opposition to the religious, implied by the connotations of the undesiderated 'resurrection' of the parent. In this draft, filial piety and grief have no permanent claim on Gibbon's attention and emotions. They are a stage it is proper to enter, but also to leave behind as one moves on to a sober attention to one's self-interest. The naturalness of such attention is quietly insisted on by the unobtrusive broadening of the general examples Gibbon juxtaposes to his own behaviour: first a son, second children as a whole. The transition from a half to the entirety of the human race mounts a latent, but formidable, challenge to the reader to censure Gibbon's attitude as callously self-interested, or his implicit resentment of his father's conduct as ungrateful. But that Gibbon's attitude to his father in 'C' is un-Burkean is beyond dispute. For was it not Burke who had urged men to 'approach the faults of

[15] *Hamlet*, I. ii. 98–9.

the state as to the wounds of a father, with pious awe and trembling solicitude'?[16]

A letter Gibbon wrote to his aunt Hester at the time of his father's death is relevant here:

Economy was not amongst my father's Virtues. The expences of the more early part of his life, the miscarriage of several promising schemes, and a general want of order and exactness involved him in such difficulties as constrained him to dispose of Putney and to contract a Mortgage so very considerable that it cannot be paid unless by the sale of our Buckinghamshire Estate. The only share I have ever taken in these transactions has been by my sensibility to my father's wants and my compliance with his inclinations, a conduct which has cost me very dear, but which I cannot repent. It is a satisfaction to reflect that I have fulfilled, perhaps exceeded my filial duties, and it is still in my power with the remains of our fortunes to lead an agreable and rational life. I am sensible that as no Estate will answer the demands of Vice and folly, so a very moderate Income will supply the real wants of Nature and Reason.[17]

Gibbon retained a copy of this letter, which is to be found amongst his papers in the British Library.[18] The comment that he has 'fulfilled, perhaps exceeded [his] filial duties' may thus be the origin of the comment in 'C' that he had 'discharged all the duties of filial piety'. It is therefore interesting that these words immediately precede the implicit stigmatizing of his father's conduct as 'Vice and folly', in contrast to the 'Nature and Reason' of his own temperament.

When Gibbon came about a year later to rewrite the account of his father's death in draft 'D', he retained much of the language and phrasing of 'C'.[19] However, in the later version, the emotional colouring of the death of Mr Gibbon is very different. Once again, Gibbon's correspondence of the time concerning the French Revolution offers us guidance in our reading. In the first place, it is important to recognize that at this time Gibbon was eager to read Burke on events in France, but had not yet seen a copy of the *Reflections*, as the letter to Cadell of 7 November 1790 makes clear: 'I thirst for Mr Burke's Reflections on the Revolutions of France. Intreat Elmsley, in my name, to dispatch it to Lausanne with care and speed, by *any* mode of conveyance less expensive than the post.'[20] The suggestion behind this letter of the desire to make a transition in political sentiment, without there being as yet any

---

[16] *Reflections on the Revolution in France*, 146.
[17] L i. 273–4.
[18] BL Add. MSS 34883, fos. 170–1.
[19] A 412–13.
[20] L iii. 210.

clear idea of to exactly what one might be moving, is a helpful notion to bear in mind as we read draft 'D', because there we will find a muting of some of the emphases of draft 'C' without their place being taken by other, equally clear, emphases. Gibbon's eagerness to read Burke was preceded, and perhaps therefore caused, by his darkening view of the course of the Revolution. The letter of 7 August 1790 to Sheffield shows that his tentative hopes for a positive outcome ('the French nation had a glorious opportunity, but they have abused and may lose their advantages') have disappeared to be replaced by a vision of inexplicable disorder: 'Poor France, the state is dissolved, the nation is mad.'[21] His 'Memoirs' are in their turn touched by this new sensitivity to disorder. The naturalness of his father's death in 'C' is replaced in the subsequent draft by an insinuation that it arose from the workings of a capricious and blind fortune. In 'D' the Gibbons, father and son, are the victims of chance, and what in 'C' had been Gibbon's firmness against sentiment, in 'D' is changed into a solidarity with his father. In 'D' the generations stand together to defy, even if they cannot deflect, the fickleness of this world.

The first sentence of the new version possesses obvious continuities with its predecessor, but it also contains revisions of equal importance:

The dissolution of the militia at the close of the War (1762) had restored my father, a new Cincinnatus, to his Hampshire farm. His labours were useful, his pleasures innocent, his wishes moderate: the neighbourhood enjoyed the presence of an active magistrate and charitable landlord: his polite address and chearful conversation recommended him to his equals: he was not dissatisfied with his son, and he had been fortunate or rather judicious in the choice of his two wives. In this retirement he <u>seemed</u> to enjoy the state of life which is praised by philosophers and poets . . .

The potentially mock-heroic comparison of his father with Cincinnatus is retained. But the changes Gibbon makes around it soften its impact until it seems less satirical, and more a raillery compatible with affection, even perhaps esteem. The substitution of 'my father' for 'C's 'the Major' places the family bond before the professional role, and suggests that this account is written from a less distanced, less dispassionate, standpoint. That movement towards a greater mildness is reinforced by the long insertion which follows the bare statement of Mr Gibbon's rural usefulness, innocence, and moderation which is common to both drafts. In 'D' Mr Gibbon's country life is carefully evoked in a series of clauses which map out his life in a series

---

[21] *L* iii. 184 and 199.

of oppositions. These give substance to the praise which in 'C' had been too cursory to offer any effective correction to the implicit criticism by which it was surrounded: 'the neighbourhood enjoyed the presence of an active magistrate and charitable landlord: his polite address and chearful conversation recommended him to his equals: he was not dis-satisfied with his son, and he had been fortunate or rather judicious in the choice of his two wives.' The claims of society are balanced by the pleasures of domesticity, and each of those realms of existence is further divided. The 'neighbourhood' of dependants and inferiors benefits from Mr Gibbon's activity on the bench and charity as a landlord (it is possible that 'charitable' may be a litotes for 'indulgent'). His 'equals' (those who made up the county, rather than the neighbourhood) enjoy his social graces. In his domestic life, he could take satisfaction in both his son and his well-chosen wives. The chiastic organization of these clauses by itself evokes a complete and harmonious life. But the inser-tion, already positive in its own right, serves also to fend off a critical implication which the different arrangement of 'C' had allowed to come forward. By separating the allusion to Cincinnatus from the quotation of Horace which follows, and which again in 'D' serves to introduce the question of Mr Gibbon's difficult financial situation, the secondary satiric charge in the comparison of Mr Gibbon with Cincinnatus, which contrasts the frugality of the Roman with the spendthrift Hampshire squire and which the organization of 'C' had encouraged the reader to form, is neutralized. Indeed, the more thorough account of Mr Gibbon's Hampshire life supplied in 'D' sends the reader back to the comparison with Cincinnatus to quite different effect. The Hampshire squire and the Roman farmer may now be genuinely compared as each being an exemplar—*mutatis mutandis*, given their very different historical situations—of rural obligations properly discharged. In 'D', then, the revisions Gibbon makes to the opening of this paragraph create a perspective in which amusement at his father's military life is overshadowed by the much more detailed evocation of the utility and decorum of his social duties and domestic occupations. The result is that the comparison with Cincinnatus, which one reads initially as ironic, gradually loses that character of irony. In one respect Mr Gibbon actually does revive the essential virtues of the ancient Roman, although in a form appropriate to a sophisticated modern society more commercial than agrarian, rather than to a classical republic sustaining itself by subsistence farming.[22]

---

[22] Gibbon's awareness of the differing customs proper to the various stages of society has been explored by Pocock in his 'Gibbon and the Shepherds'.

To approach the rehearsal of Mr Gibbon's financial embarrassments via the opening sentences of 'D' is to see them in a very different context from that established in 'C'. In the earlier draft the various elements which combined to form Mr Gibbon's difficulties were separately stated, and his mismanagement of the Buriton estate was identified as one of them ('the farm in his hands was not a profitable adventure'). In 'C', then, it is made clear that the incompetence of the adult Mr Gibbon contributed to his poverty. In 'D', however, Mr Gibbon is not a bungling countryman. He is something of a pattern for how the gentry should involve themselves in rural communities. His lack of money in the later draft is therefore solely (rather than partially, as in 'C') a hangover from an earlier period of folly: 'the vanities of his youth were severely expiated by the accumulation of solicitude and sorrow.' This is the wording of 'C', with one important exception: 'punished' has been replaced by 'expiated'. The revision is transforming because it completely alters the ethical aspect of Mr Gibbon's financial difficulties. In 'C' we were invited to contemplate transgressions which received condign, if severe, punishment. In 'D' Mr Gibbon's youthful vanities are more errors than crimes, for which he does not so much suffer punishment as offer expiation. With the substitution of 'expiated' for 'punished' we have moved from a juridical to a religious model, and the implications are profound. In 'C' Mr Gibbon's troubles are the natural consequence of his culpable failings. Like his early death, they are part of 'the order of Nature'. In 'D', however, they overwhelm him despite his competence as magistrate, landlord, father, and husband. Like the hero of a Greek tragedy, he is pursued by furies who eventually destroy him. The tonal quality of the later version is therefore inflected. What in 'C' had appeared the melancholy but just consequences of a carelessness which amounted to criminality, in 'D' we are invited to see as unmerited suffering. Mr Gibbon had contributed to the causes of his misfortunes, but had done so innocently.

The transformation of Mr Gibbon from the pitiable architect of his own undoing to the well-nigh guiltless victim of undeserved calamities is matched by revisions in the depiction of the response of Gibbon himself to his father's nemesis. In 'C', as we have seen, there is a contrast established between the rectitude of the son and the fecklessness of the father. In 'D' we read not of contrast but of compassion: 'There can be no merit in the discharge of a duty: but, alone, in my library, at such a distance of time and place, without a witness or a judge, I should be pursued by the bitterness of remembrance; had I not obeyed the dictates of filial piety, had I not consented to every sacrifice that might promise some relief to the distress of a parent.' 'There can be no merit in the discharge of a duty': how trenchantly that criticizes the language and sentiments of 'C', where Gibbon's 'grief was soothed by the conscious satisfaction that I had discharged all the duties of filial piety'. The greater sentimental warmth of 'D' makes the rectitude Gibbon had assumed in 'C' look cold-hearted. In 'D' Gibbon requires a more ample consolation than could be provided by the mere consciousness of having fulfilled a contract, which is what we seem to have in 'C'. The imagined scene of the solitary Gibbon in his library is an emblem of moral judgement compatible with the ethical thought of his friend Adam Smith, where the moral sense is entrusted to 'the impartial spectator, and [to] the representative of the impartial spectator, the man within the breast'.[23] In this reflective solitude Gibbon is not haunted by 'the bitterness of remembrance'; but he is equally free of the calm sense of separation from the predicament of his father which is communicated by the placid judiciousness of 'C'.

The account of his father's physical collapse is, as was the earlier part of this passage in 'D', built upon the foundations of 'C', but once again it is decisively influenced by thoughtful suppressions and substitutions:

His mind, alas was no longer capable of a rational effort, and his reluctant delays postponed, not the evils themselves, but the remedies of those evils (remedia malorum potius quam mala differebat). The pangs of tenderness and self-reproach incessantly preyed on his vitals: he lost his strength and his sight: a rapid dropsy admonished him of his end, and he sunk into the grave in the sixty-fourth year of his age.

'D's portrait of Mr Gibbon as victim is intensified by the replacement of 'C's 'He was no longer capable . . .' with 'His mind, alas was no longer capable . . .'. To locate the failure in the mind, rather than making it a failure of the whole individual, makes Gibbon's father the helpless and unwilling prey of one part of his identity, while the exclamation solicits the reader's pity. The injurious implications of the quotation from Tacitus are thereby diluted, and the progressive stages of the decline into death are to be read as a series of betrayals of the man by his physical body, not as the natural consequence of his own guilt, as they were in 'C'. An important deletion at this stage reinforces Gibbon's steady exoneration of his father. In 'C' Mr Gibbon's guiltiness was implied by the inclusion of the pangs of 'shame' amongst the variety of ills which 'preyed upon his vitals', but in 'D' that word has been

---

[23] Adam Smith, *The Theory of Moral Sentiments*, 215. Gibbon owned copies of the third (1767) and sixth (1790) editions of this work. It had been first published in 1759.

removed to leave only 'tenderness and self-reproach'. It now seems
almost as if Mr Gibbon's constitution was undermined by an excess of
moral sensitivity.

The conclusion of the passage is considerably shortened from the
equivalent in 'C', and bears quite a different emphasis: 'His death was
the only event that could have saved me from a life of obscurity and
indigence; yet I can declare to my own heart, that on such terms, I
never wished for a deliverance.' Gibbon is here the involuntary
beneficiary of an unwanted release. The unwarranted sufferings of the
father are followed, in an inversion of capricious fortune, by the un-
desired relief of the son. The emotional alignment with his father's
death (a difficult subject handled with more subtlety than sentiment in
'C') is suppressed, and the impression created that he is even now ('I can
declare to my own heart') unreconciled to it. Here the suppression in
'D' of the word 'hopeless' plays a part. Gibbon's equanimity in the face
of his father's death in 'C' is justified both through the unrelieved
bleakness of the alternative ('an *hopeless* life of obscurity and indigence'),
and by the observation that Mr Gibbon's death was 'not unhappy for
himself'. When that bleakness has been moderated by the suppression
of 'hopeless', there is correspondingly less at stake for Gibbon himself in
his father's fate, and so his distaste for the deliverance it represented
becomes more believable; note that Gibbon rearranges the elements of
the final sentence to allow the paragraph to end with this detail.
Moreover, the suppression of 'hopeless' implies different values on
Gibbon's part. In 'C' there is the frank acknowledgement, compatible
with that draft's freedom from sentiment, that obscurity and indigence
make life hopeless. In 'D', with its more emotional colouring, the mind
is not so determined by the body's material circumstances.

The revisions of 'D' therefore show Gibbon dissatisfied with 'C', but
without as yet any clear alternative conception of how the death of his
father was more satisfactorily to be put into words. The rearrangements,
substitutions, and suppressions of 'D', though cumulatively powerful in
shifting the tone of the account towards leniency, and successful in
placing Mr Gibbon in the light of victim rather than fool, all fall into the
category of surface changes. It was only with draft 'E' that Gibbon
entirely abandoned the structural blueprint for this paragraph which he
had laid down in 'C' and followed in 'D'.[24] As was the case with 'C' and
'D', Gibbon's letters once again throw light on the contemporary
developments in these manuscripts. 'E' was composed just at the
moment of Gibbon's instantaneous conversion to Burke's view of the

[24] *A* 306.

French Revolution, and that clarification of his allegiances and convictions was immediately expressed in his letters.[25] The attachment to old establishments professed in the letter to Sheffield of 5 February 1791 and the deploring of inversion in the letter to his stepmother of 18 May 1791 were both explicitly related to his reading of Burke, and both are compatible with the replotted version of his father's death which we find in 'E'. The 'naturalness' of 'C', which was a naturalness of cause and effect, an unsentimental necessitarianism, was replaced in 'E' by a sociable naturalness, articulated through a decent, manly, and reticent, yet profound, sentiment. In 'E' the passage is compressed and unforthcoming as to detail, in a way which is quite in keeping with its greater charge of emotion. All the particularity concerning his father's immiseration is removed, as is the approach to his death via the mock heroic perspective created by the disembodying of the militia; and the passage of property from one generation to another is, not the hair's-breadth 'scape of 'C', or the capricious reversal of fortune of 'D', but a decorous transferral of 'patrimony' (the connotations of the word are not unwanted) which ensures, on this small scale at least, social immobility. If 'C' verges on satire and 'D' is tinctured with tragedy, 'E' is an exercise in counter-revolutionary euphemism.

The paragraph in 'E' falls into two almost exactly equal parts, the first discussing the death of Mr Gibbon and the second the new arrangements made by his son and widow after his death. The organization of the paragraph therefore invites us to conceptualize Mr Gibbon's decease, not as the termination of an individual life, but as a transaction between generations and within a family. Mr Gibbon's death and its aftermath could have been told as a story of the catastrophic break-up of a family and the ruinous dispersal of much of its property. Indeed, that was how it had presented itself to Gibbon at the time.[26] In 'E', however, it occurs at the proper season, when Gibbon was 'upwards of thirty-three years of age, the ordinary term of an human generation'. (Note that this last phrase was an afterthought, added in the margin by Gibbon after the body of the passage had been drafted: it thus bears a particular weight of intention.) Decorum is strong in the three following sentences, in which the death is obliquely alluded to, rather than directly narrated, in prose as remarkable for its tonal control as its lack of detail:

[25] Compare columns two and six in the table reprinted in Appendix 2.

[26] 'Vous comprenez, mais vous ne pouvez pas comprendre assez, le cahos d'affaires dans lequel je me vois plongè'; letter to Georges Deyverdun of 2 Dec. 1770 (*L* i. 267). Cf. also *L* i. 263, 270, and 273–4.

My grief was sincere for the loss of an affectionate parent, an agreeable companion, and a worthy man. But the ample fortune which my grandfather had left was deeply impaired, and would have been gradually consumed by the easy and generous nature of his son. I revere the memory of my father, his errors I forgive, nor can I repent | of the important sacrifices which were chearfully offered by filial piety.

Here we find no criticism of Mr Gibbon. The fact that his father's 'easy and generous nature' (how cosmetic a phrase!) was responsible for the deep impairment of the family fortune is admitted only as the dark side of a syntactical ambiguity which the punctuation of the passage invites us to dismiss for its brighter alternative, namely that his father was the innocent heir of a situation with which his good nature did not equip him to cope, and merely threatened to exacerbate. Similarly Mr Gibbon's son is the embodiment of filial reverence, now no longer merely consenting to sacrifices (as in 'C' and 'D'), but cheerfully offering them. The transition to a new plan of life is, in writing as we know it was not in life, smooth, despite the small delay occasioned by 'the web of rural œconomy' (another masterly concealment of his father's agency in the wreck of the family estates):

Domestic command, the free distribution of time and place, and a more liberal measure of expence were the immediate consequences of my new situation: but two years rolled away before I could disentangle myself from the web of rural œconomy, and adopt a mode of life agreeable to my wishes. From Buriton Mrs Gibbon withdrew to Bath; while I removed myself and my books into my new house in Bentinck Street Cavendish Square, in which I continued to reside ab near eleven years.

That this was a process of dispersal and impoverishment is not allowed to make itself felt. This is an account of the death of Mr Gibbon composed by a man who has been awakened by Burke to the importance of 'a permanent landed Gentry, continued in greatness and opulence by the laws of primogeniture, and by a protection given to family settlements', and who wishes as far as possible so to arrange the story of his life that it supports, rather than undermines, this pillar of English society.[27]

The strength of that wish can be measured by the magnitude of the rearrangements necessary to gratify it. Gibbon did not scruple to seal this audaciously positive account of his father's death with a bold lie: 'The clear untainted remains of my patrimony have been always sufficient to support the rank of a Gentleman, and to satisfy the desires

[27] *Thoughts on French Affairs*, in *Further Reflections on the Revolution in France*, 214.

of a philosopher.' The fictiveness of this assertion will need no under-
lining to those who have read the corpus of the historian's letters, and
who therefore know how frequently, and with what bewilderment and
exasperation, Gibbon was obliged after 1770 to address the complexities and inadequacies of his assets. But in the early months of 1791
telling the truth about one's life may have seemed less important than
making one's life serve the truth.

8

'Fourteen months, the most barren and unprofitable of my whole life': Five Versions of Residence in Oxford

Although Gibbon's period of residence at Oxford and his conversion to Catholicism occurred before the death of his father, it is better to examine out of their chronological sequence the five versions of his abortive university career and his apostasy which he composed in drafts 'B' to 'F' of his 'Memoirs'. In part this is because the upshot of the analysis of the different versions of Gibbon's residence in Oxford leads conveniently into the subject of the next chapter, namely, Sheffield's editing of the *Miscellaneous Works*. However, the different versions of the death of Gibbon's father are also in every respect a simpler instance of what I contend Gibbon was doing when he composed the six narratives which make up the archive of the 'Memoirs'. Simpler, in the first place, because there we have only three manuscript versions of broadly similar extent, rather than the five versions recounting Gibbon's time at Oxford which vary in length from 95 words ('E') to over 7,000 words ('F'). Simpler, in the second place, because the contextual dimension of the passages dealing with the death of Gibbon's father is comparatively slender. Their emotional colouring and vocabulary repay reading in the light of Burke's *Reflections*; but there was no contemporary debate about the deaths of fathers within which we would be obliged to situate Gibbon's accounts of this particular dissolution. The variant versions of the death of Gibbon's father therefore provide, in terms of both text and context, a more controllable example of the complex nature of the 'Memoirs'. They can therefore properly serve as an introduction to those areas in which the complexity of the 'Memoirs' is more richly expressed.

It is to one of those more richly expressive areas that we turn when we consider the accounts of Gibbon's time at Magdalen. Its greater textual complexity is evident simply in the larger number of manuscript versions, and in the much greater discrepancies between them, while its greater contextual complexity emerges, as we shall see, as an aspect of its textual dynamics. When he narrated his career as an Oxford undergraduate, Gibbon drew upon and contributed to a debate over the origins, nature, and purpose of Oxford University which had been continuing since the mid-seventeenth century, and which itself was only a province of a broader field of imaginative engagement with this provoking and fascinating institution.[1] However, although it is clear within which general context we should situate our discussion of these manuscripts—the context of writing about Oxford from the Restoration to the end of the eighteenth century—it is not clear what the appropriate micro-context is. Gibbon was in residence from 3 April 1752 to 8 June 1753 (the date of his conversion to Rome), and he alludes to salient events in that period, such as the approaching general election and the 'great Oxfordshire contest' which was part of it.[2] However, the years in which he composed the different accounts of his residence— 1788 to 1793—were a period in which Oxford (in common with many of the institutions of Hanoverian England) came under intense criticism. When we examine the detail of Gibbon's rewritings of this period of his life, we shall see that, in respect of tone and content, they move around between the earlier and the later of these micro-contexts. Once we have plotted this movement, we will be in a position to understand more intimately the shifting motives governing the successive revisals of the narrative of this period in Gibbon's life. In particular, we will be able to glimpse the divided, and in the last analysis incoherent, motivation lying behind the last and (as it promised to

---

[1] The first port of call for those who wish to explore this field is E. H. Cordeaux and D. H. Merry, *Bibliography of Printed Works Relating to the University of Oxford* (Oxford: Clarendon Press, 1968). It may be accompanied by the appropriate volume or volumes of *The History of the University of Oxford* (Oxford: Clarendon Press, 1984–), and should be supplemented by searches in the on-line pre-1920 Bodleian catalogue and a survey of equivalent material relating to Cambridge, since the two universities were often discussed together, especially in the eighteenth century. John Gascoigne's 'Church and State allied: the failure of parliamentary reform of the universities, 1688–1800' in A. L. Beier, David Cannadine, and James M. Rosenheim (eds.), *The First Modern Society: Essays in English History in Honour of Lawrence Stone* (Cambridge: Cambridge University Press, 1989), 401–29 is a lively survey of an important aspect of the subject. Two recent publications are also of interest: Graham Midgley, *University Life in Eighteenth-Century Oxford* (New Haven and London: Yale University Press, 1996) and John Dougill, *Oxford in English Literature: The Making, and Undoing, of 'The English Athens'* (Ann Arbor: The University of Michigan Press, 1998). Why Oxford has been so much more written about than Cambridge is an interesting subject of speculation. On the specific subject of Gibbon and Oxford, J. A. W. Bennett's 'Gibbon and the Universities' in his *Essays on Gibbon* is a graceful study.

[2] *A* 76 (draft 'F').

be) the most elaborate of Gibbon's autobiographical narratives, draft 'F'. Consequently we will be able to understand why Gibbon abandoned that draft when and where he did, and why he wrote to Sheffield on 6 January 1793 professing himself dissatisfied with it.[3]

We shall begin by taking an overview of writings on Oxford from the Interregnum to the French Revolution, pointing out the recurrent topics of concern and the broad lines of development. We shall then turn to the manuscript drafts, and consider their textual detail in the light of the dynamics of the context, for much of that detail is either dumb or enigmatic until it is positioned within its context. Finally, we will assess how Sheffield presented this episode to the reading public in 1796, and how the public responded to it, thereby opening up a perspective on the subject of the final chapter of this book, the strategy behind Sheffield's editing of the *Miscellaneous Works*.

II

In 1750 the editors of *The Student, or the Oxford Monthly Miscellany* launched their fledgling magazine by remarking how widely discussed, and how widely censured, the university had recently become: 'OXFORD we know has for some time been used as a term of reproach, and become a bye-word amongst many. Pamphlets have been designedly written, and measures industriously pursued, to lessen her credit.'[4] Then, as now, the public had great curiosity about an institution in which private wealth was reputed to protect and underwrite a style of living either alluringly *louche* or scandalously corrupt, depending on your point of view. 'Abuse of this University is with some People become a fashionable Topick of Conversation' huffed the anonymous author of *A Letter from a member of the University of Oxford, to a Gentleman in the Country* (1755), but (again as now) the university's resentment of being 'the Subject of Conversation in the Great World; the Eyes of which are fixed upon us' rang false.[5] When John Ayliffe was engaged in his struggle with the Warden and Fellows of New College, he followed the strategy adopted by many before and since, and took great care to ensure that his case '*made so much Noise at Oxford, and other Places*'.[6]

[3] L iii. 312.
[4] *The Student, or the Oxford Monthly Miscellany*, i. 5.
[5] [Anon.], *A Letter from a member of the University of Oxford, to a Gentleman in the Country*, 4; [Anon.], *A Serious Inquiry into Some Late Proceedings in Vindication of the Honour, Credit, and Reputation of the University of Ox———D, Relative to an Offence of a Certain Member of the same* (1751).
[6] *The Case of Dr Ayliffe at Oxford*, pp. iv–v.

Oxford, then, had been much discussed, indeed from or for hack as John Hall's Baconian and Miltonic 'Areopagitick' pamphlet of 1649, *An Humble Motion to the Parliament of England concerning the Advancement of Learning: And Reformation of the Universities.* The public function of the universities was a recurrent topic in these early pamphlets, sometimes finding figurative expression through the trope of a potentially fertile field rendered sterile as a result of neglect:

Universities well govern'd, do certainly conduce very much to the publick Welfare of any Nation, wherein they are instituted: For it is there that the Seeds of a good Education are sown . . . But if a Government shou'd once suffer this Field of Knowledge to be over-grown with Thorns and Thistles . . . the Consequences of such a neglect must be very fatal to a Commonwealth, from the evil produce it affords. The Principles of the young Nobility and Gentry will thereby become debauch'd; Ignorance and Barbarism will soon invade that People, and overshadow all their Affairs . . .[7]

More often, however, those professing concern for the university chose the image of a fountain to express its potential for good, and also to enforce the urgency of its reformation, should it ever become a poisonous rather than salubrious influence:

The University is like a Fountain, which when once Corrupted its Branches can never remain Untainted; . . . The thought of this National Degeneracy which must necessarily Ensue from a University Corruption, I cou'd wish wou'd have so great an Influence over our Academicks, as to occasion a General Reformation and Amendment of their Manners.[8]

If these fountains grow corrupt, and instead of virtue, religion and learning, vice, impiety and ignorance gain the prevalency in them; then nothing but dirty and filthy streams will flow from thence, all over the island, and every part of it will be tainted and polluted with the corruptions thereof.[9]

It will take but little Labour to prove, why a Stream is muddy and foul that flows from a corrupt and degenerate Fountain. Can any one bring a clean Thing from an unclean? *No not one!* What wonder will it be, that the inferior Clergy are debauch'd in Morals, disloyal in Politicks, heretical in Principles, prophane in Conversation, when we shall trace them back to their Erudition, and find that they were bred up in all these at the Colleges, where they were placed to be finish'd with Learning and good Morals, and where they suck in Vice instead of Virtue, profligate Manners instead of Piety.[10]

---

[7] *The Case of Dr Ayliffe at Oxford*, pp. xxii–xxiii.

[8] [Anon.], *A Step to Oxford*, 9–10.

[9] Humphrey Prideaux, in a paper on the reform of the universities prepared in 1715 at the request of Lord Townshend; quoted in Ketton-Cremer, *Humphrey Prideaux*, 28–9.

[10] [Anon.], *Reasons for Visiting the Universities*, 15. The image is to be found less often in pamphlets from later in the century. The only example I have found occurs in [Anon.], *Remarks*

However, we should not confuse uniformity of metaphor with any deeper constancy of outlook. The century and a half between the Interregnum and the French Revolution saw development and change in the public understanding of Oxford's proper function, and hence of the criteria which should be applied when trying to decide whether or not the university was corrupt or in a state of health. The period as a whole resolves itself into two phases of comment, characterized by subtly different concerns. The first extends from the mid-seventeenth century to a little after the mid-eighteenth century, the second occupies the following forty or so years, until the project of practical reform of the university got seriously under way in the later 1790s.[11]

In the placing of both its emphases and its silences, Hall's *Humble Motion* is typical of the phase of comment it initiates. Beginning by echoing Milton and deploring that 'the body of learning lyes scattered in as many peeces as ever Medea cut her little Brother into', Hall charges the university with malversation of endowment.[12] Noting their 'outward Magnificence, and . . . large if not luxurious liberality', Hall recommends reformation of the universities as part of a wholesale remodelling of the kingdom made possible, necessary, and seemly by the execution of Charles I, in order that the colleges' benefactions should tend 'to a publicke advantage, then to the private fostering of . . . idle pedantick Brotherhoods'.[13] As part of this reform the number of fellowships was to be reduced, and the number of university professorships increased. Aside from this, however, Hall says nothing about how the university was to discharge its duty of educating the young.[14] There is a similar silence on questions of education in *Sundry Things from Several Hands Concerning the University of* Oxford (1659). Urging Parliament to 'take into your Care the two Universities' and suppress 'whatever is Monarchical, Superstitious, or Oppressive', and also recommending in general terms 'a more strict Way of Exercise, suited to the Preserving and Upholding us as a Republick' so that the university's graduates 'may be serviceable to the Nation, and not grow old in their Colleges, which thereby become as it were Hospitals and Monasteries', the anonymous author nevertheless has nothing to say

on the Enormous Expence in the Education of Young men in the University of Cambridge, 19: 'The Purity of the Church, and the Purity of its doctrines are to flow from this Fountain, the Universities.'

[11] Sutherland and Mitchell, *The History of the University of Oxford*, vol. v: *The Eighteenth Century*, 622–8.

[12] Hall, *Humble Motion*, 5–6.

[13] Ibid. 16–17. Apparently a Committee for the Reformation of the Universities was formed in 1651.

[14] Ibid. 29.

about either the content or the delivery of an Oxford education.[15] In the early years of the next century the Earl of Macclesfield was equally unconcerned about Oxford's curriculum, and the procedures for imparting it to the young.[16] Exercised instead by 'the disloyal behaviour of the Universities, since his Majesty's happy accession to the Crown', he sought to bring the colleges into line by having every head of house elected, not by the fellowship of the college they were to govern, but by 'the great Officers of State, and such of the Archbishops and Bishops as shall be thought proper'.[17] His concern was simply for the political docility of the regent bodies—hence his proposal of 'a well chosen set of Commissioners, constantly residing in each University' to super-intend the good behaviour of the resident members.[18] Provided there was conformity and no sedition, all was well.

It is characteristic of the earlier discussion of Oxford that the univer-sity should be considered as more a political entity than an educational machine. Disturbances in the town in 1715 and 1745 had confirmed the university's already established reputation as a nest of 'Jacobites *and* Non-Jurors'.[19] A character in Thomas Baker's *An Act at Oxford* of 1704 would announce that 'I have no Opinion of *Oxford* Education, it breeds nothing but Rakes, and rank Tories'.[20] And as early as 1681 'Oxford' principles had been resolved into a catechism: 'You know my meaning well enough; Are you for the Prerogative and Government in Church and State? As for the People, it's their business to obey their Superiors, to pay their Tythes, and their Taxes; and, if occasion be, to fight for the Glory and honour of their Prince, and the Church of *England*.'[21]

---

[15] [Anon.], *Sundry Things*, 79–80.

[16] Thomas Parker (1666?–1732), first Earl of Macclesfield: Lord Chancellor, 1718; staunch Whig and Hanoverian; adversary of Francis Atterbury; created Earl of Macclesfield, 1721; impeached, and found guilty, 1725; personal favourite of George I. The most likely author of 'A Memorial Relating to the Universities', reprinted in J. Gutch, *Collectanea Curiosa*, 2 vols. (Oxford: Clarendon Press, 1781), ii. 53–75.

[17] Ibid. 53, and 55.

[18] Ibid. 66.

[19] *Case of Dr. Ayliffe*, p. viii.

[20] Thomas Baker, *An Act at Oxford*, 4; cf. also [Anon.], *The University Answer to the Pretended University Ballad* and [Anon.], *The Oxford Dialogue Between a Master of Arts and a Stranger*, 3 and 7–8. Initially Cambridge was considered just as pro-Stuart as Oxford (*Case of Dr. Ayliffe*, p. xiii; *Reasons for Visiting the Universities*, 33; Shaftesbury, *Several Letters Written by a Noble Lord to a Young man at the University*, 31); and even in mid-century George Coade would complain that 'the Seeds of Disloyalty and disaffection had for a long Time been sowing, in our Universities', drawing no distinction in this regard between Oxford and Cambridge (*A Blow at the Root*, p. v). However, gradually the more Whiggish and Latitudinarian character of Cambridge was recognized: cf. [Anon.], *The University of Cambridge Vindicated*, 1, and Thomas Tyrwhitt, *An Epistle to Florio at Oxford*, 17. Gibbon would himself point this out at the very end of draft 'F': *A* 95.

[21] [Anon.], *A Dialogue at Oxford between a Tutor and a Gentleman, formerly his Pupil, concerning*

The Tory, High Church, character of Oxford was intensified in the 'Church and State' disputes of the early eighteenth century.[22] It was embodied in such official pronouncements as the university's retort to Hoadly, which required of all

> Readers, Tutors, Catechists, and others to whom the care and Trust of *Institution* of *Youth* is committed, that they diligently instruct and ground their *Scholars* in that most necessary *Doctrine*, which in a manner is the *Badge* and *Character* of the Church of *England*, Of submitting to every Ordinance of man for the Lords sake, whether it be to the King as supreme, or unto Governours as unto them that are sent by him, for the Punishment of *Evil Doers* and for the praise of them that *Do well*. Teaching that this Submission and Obedience is to be clear, absolute, and without any exception of any State or Order of Men.[23]

So ruthless an imposition of a political creed might amongst some, and in due course, breed a reaction. Writing in 1749, Thomas Tyrwhitt composed a palinode to his Oxford education, and to the political indoctrination he had undergone there:

> 'Tis true, my Friend, what busy Fame has told,
> My *Oxford* Tenets I no longer hold:
> Broke from the slavish Bond of lineal Right,
> I bow to Liberty's cœlestial Light.

And he recollected the arts of political seduction to which he and 'Florio' (to whom the poem is addressed) had succumbed:

> The sad, the truly shameful Change you know,
> When first we bow'd to Freedom's exil'd Foe;
> Led by false Teachers, by ourselves betray'd,
> By fancy'd Right, and weak Compassion sway'd,
> For oft' exploded Lies we quitted Truth,
> For Factions guilty Cares the Joys of Youth.[24]

Tyrwhitt's second thoughts occur at at time when, as we shall see, the extinguishing of the Jacobite option in English political life had destroyed the attraction of such a creed in the minds of all but fanatics. Nevertheless, his act of contrition testifies to the political temper of the university in the earlier part of the century.

Government, 2. The pupil, who has spent some time in London, replies with some moderate Whig principles, such as 'Government as by Law Establisht' (p. 2), and the upshot of the dialogue is that the now Whiggish pupil educates his erstwhile tutor out of his extreme Tory prejudices.

[22] On which see Bennett, *Tory Crisis*.

[23] [Anon.], *The Oxford Decree: Being an Entire Confutation of Mr. Hoadley's Book, of the Original of Government*, 7. Cf. also Tyrwhitt, *An Epistle to Florio*, 5 and 7, and William Mason, *Isis. An Elegy*, 13–14.   [24] Tyrwhitt, *An Epistle to Florio*, 5 and 7.

As the university spoke and taught, so did it also act. The allegations of Tory and even Jacobite sympathy were corroborated by egregious acts of persecution directed at those whom Edmond Miller would characterize in 1717 as 'in favour of the present Government'.[25] The case which made the most noise was that of John Ayliffe, a Fellow of New College. Ayliffe claimed to have suffered '*Trouble and Vexation . . . from Law-Suits and other Persecutions, for the sake of my adhering to the Principles of the Revolution; which shall be the Test of my Loyalty so long as I live*', and complained bitterly of the '*various Afflictions of Pain and other Oppressions under which I have labour'd for almost 10 Years together, from the Malice of such as are ever promoting arbitrary Power in the Prince*'.[26] This seems principally to have been the Warden of New College, whose 'supine Negligence' and alleged malversation of endowment Ayliffe resolved to expose.[27] In 1716 he published *The Antient and Present State of the University of Oxford*, a two-volume history and survey of the university, intended to correct the '*evident Partiality*' of Anthony Wood ('*a known Friend to the Church of Rome*').[28] Dedicated to the Whig grandee John Somers, whom Ayliffe praised for ridding the nation of the 'pestilential Air of Arbitrary Power', this alternative account of the university displayed the '*foul and scandalous Corruptions*' which arose from the '*insufferable Tyranny*' of the heads of house.[29] As might have been expected, this publication attracted the attention of the university authorities, and Ayliffe was deprived of his fellowship by the 'arbitrary Sentence' of a 'tyrannous and unpresidented [*sic*] Method of proceeding'.[30] Nor was Ayliffe the only Whig to be so persecuted. Other notorious cases were those of Mr Lavington, again at New College, of Mr Ayscough at Corpus Christi, and of Mr Parkinson at Lincoln. In these instances, as well as in the case of Ayliffe, the language in which they were reported insisted on arbitrariness and tyranny on the one side, and allegiance to Revolution

---

[25] Miller, *An Account of the University of Cambridge*, 183–4.

[26] Ayliffe, *The Antient and Present State of the University of Oxford*, i. sig. A6ʳ. For Ayliffe's pronounced Whig and Hanoverian loyalties, see *Case of Dr. Ayliffe*, p. xxv, 54 and 90 (where Ayliffe, writing to the bishop of Winchester, styles himself a martyr to the 'late happy Revolution').

[27] Ayliffe, *Antient and Present State*, i. 323.

[28] Ibid. i. sig. A4ᵛ.

[29] Ibid. i. sig. A6ʳ. Nicholas Amhurst would later pillory the overbearing habits of the heads of house in the character of Dr Drybones, who 'exercised an absolute authority in his college, in contempt of all *statutes*, which were no more than *dead letters* in his eyes; trampling under his feet the will of his *Founder* and *Benefactors*; laughing at the opposition of his *Fellows*, and indulged himself in the most arbitrary proceedings' (*Terræ-Filius*, 173–4). The most likely real-life model for such figures was, of course, Richard Bentley, whose disputes with the fellows of Trinity College, Cambridge were so protracted and bitter.

[30] [Anon.], *Case of Dr. Ayliffe*.

principles on the other. The division of a particular college on party
lines was particularly vivid in the case of Mr Parkinson: 'They [the other
Fellows of Lincoln] thought *the King was Absolute*; he was of another
opinion. They said, *The Legislative Power was lodg'd solely in the King*; he
believ'd it was not: *They were against the Bill of Exclusion*, he was for it.
They were for Dr. Hick's *Passive Obedience*, he was for Mr. *Johnson's.*'[31]
According to Nicholas Amhurst, the experience of Parkinson and
Ayliffe was repeated in a multitude of less lurid cases, to the point where
'to call yourself a WHIG at OXFORD, to act like one, or to lie under the
suspicion of being one, is the same as to be attainted and outlaw'd;
you will be discourag'd and browbeaten in your own college, and dis-
qualify'd for preferment in any other'.[32] In the pages of *Terræ-Filius*
Amhurst refracted Oxford's reputation into its constituent elements,
breaking down the general charges of corruption and sedition into
different kinds of actual behaviour. The indignation which fuelled the
composition of *Terræ-Filius* arose from the experience of perpetual
moral affront:

to see ignorance, superstition, tyranny and priestcraft riding rampant in the
seminaries of religion; to see barefaced, fraudulent actions daily committed by
the hands that ought to administer justice; to see perjury and rebellion
publickly preached and inculcated into the minds of youth; to see the virtuous
munificence of founders and benefactors squandered away at *gaming-tables*, and
amongst *stockjobbers*, or guzzled down in hogsheads of wine, or tost up in
fricasees and venison pasties: I say to see all this, and to see no publick remedy
apply'd or propos'd to be apply'd to this complication of evils, would extort
satire and indignation from the most lukewarm breast.[33]

The 'complication of evils' Amhurst depicted in Oxford emanated
from its central core of political disaffection. From this sprang the moral
casuistry which permitted the malversation of endowments and the
ignoring of solemn oaths, while it also encouraged the initiation and
corruption of youth in similar practices, and smiled benignly on the
riotous self-indulgence financed by benefactions perverted from the

---

[31] [Anon.], *An Account of Mr. Parkinson's Expulsion from the University of Oxford*, 4–5. The
charges against Parkinson were that he had upheld the following propositions: (1) That exclusion
was lawful. (2) That if a Prince did not discharge his duty, then his subjects were absolved of
theirs. (3) That monarchy might be abolished in England by parliament (pp. 7–9).

[32] *Terræ-Filius*, 175; cf. pp. 235–6 for Amhurst's account of the stigmatizing of suspected
Whigs in the 'Black Book'. Paper no. XLV (19 June 1721) is given over to a Whig's experiences
of persecution in Oxford (*Terræ-Filius*, 247–53). One college which appears to have been receptive to Whigs was Merton, at this time allegedly a focus of Hanoverian loyalism (*Terræ-Filius*, 27,
32, and 123).

[33] *Terræ-Filius*, 4.

benefactors' intentions. It was on these three areas—the corruption of students (which might even extend as far as Catholic entrapment), malversation, and the pursuit of sensual pleasure—that Oxford's earlier critics chose to concentrate.[34]

It is at this point, however, that this first phase of commentary begins to reveal some of its ambivalence, for its major theme of censure is varied by undertones of Rabelaisian celebration. The occasional exuberance of the writing alone indicates that the purposes of Oxford's critics were not confined to satire: 'And 'tis to be hop'd, that in a little time, for his impudent and unmannerly declaring against the Celebration of the King's Birthday, &c. he will become the Pissing-post of Chair and Hackney Coachmen in *London*, as he is already the Jest and Scorn of all Persons of better Rank and Quality in other Parts of the Kingdom.'[35] Wendeborn would remark at the end of the century that *alumni* were plentiful among the universities' detractors, and that 'many who have resided in them [Oxford and Cambridge], and have afterwards acquired celebrity, frequently join in the censure and the satire that is thrown out against these seats of learning'.[36] Their complicated position of affiliation and detachment might easily create an outlook in which those features of university life which their more serious thoughts insisted were important failings could at the same time be relished as the most characteristic and pleasurable aspects of a period of freedom before the responsibilities of adult life had to be shouldered. Like Justice Shallow, eighteenth-century critics of Oxford seem also to have hugged their memories of the chimes at midnight. Squire Calf of Essex, in Thomas Baker's *An Act at Oxford*, returns to Oxford for the Encænia and 'to be drunk with my old Fellow-Collegiates, and to hear the *Turræ filius*, they say he designs to be violently witty, and I love an *Oxford Turræ filius* better than *Merry Andrew* in *Leicester Fields*'. On arrival he goes 'first to visit my Mistress, and then to meet some honest

---

[34] For the corruption of students, see: *Case of Dr. Ayliffe*, p. xxiv; *Reasons for Visiting the Universities*, 45. For malversation, see: Ayliffe, *Antient and Present State*, i. sig. A5ʳ; *Case of Dr. Ayliffe*, pp. v–vi; *Terræ-Filius*, 17 ff.; most amusingly, James Miller, whose *The Humours of Oxford* includes the following tirade from one fellow, Haughty, to a colleague, Conundrum: 'Besides, don't I know how much thou hast embezled [*sic*] of the College-Money, whilst thou wert Steward?—how many Legacies, which were bequeathed to the College, thou hast put into thy own Pocket' (p. 49). For self-indulgence, see: *Sundry Things*, 83; *Case of Dr. Ayliffe*, p. xi; *Humours of Oxford*, 23; *Terræ-Filius*, 218; *A Step to Oxford* (1704), 6; *Idler*, 33 (2 Dec. 1758). The occasional attempts by senior members to sodomize the junior members—a complicated evil indeed—combined aspects of the first and third categories: cf. [Anon.], *A Serious Inquiry into Some Late Proceedings in Vindication of the Honour, Credit, and Reputation of the University of Ox———D*.

[35] *Case of Dr. Ayliffe*, 64.

[36] Wendeborn, *A View of England*, ii. 141.

Fellows of *All-Soul's College*, who resolve to be staggeringly drunk in opposition to *Lilly's* Grammar, that says *Homo*'s a Noun Substantive'.[37] Such characters embodied, in the form of caricature, the recognition that the university was in origin pre-modern and a stranger to considerations of educational utility. In common with other medieval institutions (at least as they were understood in a period of 'enlightenment'), it embraced episodes of inversion and excess. The very existence of the Terræ Filius, whose speeches at the Encænia were unsparing of personalities and contained rich detail of the customary academic foibles of lechery and drunkenness (but who never attacked the university itself, and who went out of his way to extol Oxford over Cambridge) suggests as much. Even when the persona of the Terræ Filius was taken over by Nicholas Amhurst and used as the vehicle of a more severe satire, the celebratory content of the form could not be quite suppressed. (Even supposing that Amhurst wished to suppress it: ambivalence is always a possibility in the writings of this self-proclaimed Whig who was also so instrumental in the composition of most of Bolingbroke's *Craftsman*.)[38]

Accusations are hurled for only so long as they are damaging. They are tolerated for only so long as there remains the possibility that changing circumstances may transform the imputation from a liability to an asset. In the fifteen or so years between Culloden and the accession of George III, when the restoration of the Stuarts was gradually eliminated from the realm of the possible in English politics, three developments broadly coincided in the literature about Oxford.[39] Firstly, accusations

---

[37] Baker, *An Act at Oxford* (1704), 7 and 20.

[38] Nicholas Amhurst (1697–1742); poet, journalist, and political writer; expelled from St John's College, 29 June 1719; satirized the university in *Terræ-Filius* (Jan.–July 1721); editor-in-chief of *The Craftsman*; died in penury. For an example of Amhurst's complexity of standpoint and the resulting discursive ambivalence, consider his *Oculus Britanniae: an Heroi-Panegyrical Poem on the University of Oxford* (1724), which is both critical and affectionate.

[39] Burke described that process of elimination in two passages of his *Thoughts on the Present Discontents* (1770): '[George III] came to the throne of these kingdoms with more advantages than any of his predecessors since the Revolution. Fourth in descent, and third in succession of his Royal family, even the zealots of hereditary right, in him, saw something to flatter their favourite prejudices; and to justify a transfer of their attachments, without a change in their principles. The person and cause of the Pretender were become contemptible; his title disowned throughout Europe, his party disbanded in England'; and '[George II] overcame a dangerous rebellion, abetted by foreign force, and raging in the heart of his kingdoms; and thereby destroyed the seeds of all future rebellion that could arise upon the same principle. . . . he left his succession resting on the true and only true foundations of all national and all regal greatness; affection at home, reputation abroad, trust in allies, terror in rival nations' (pp. 262 and 266–7). It was a judgement endorsed by Gibbon (interestingly enough, by reference to Burke) in draft 'B' of the 'Memoirs': 'The most beneficial effect of this institution [the militia] was to eradicate among the Country gentlemen the relicks of Tory, or rather of Jacobite prejudice. The accession of a British king

of Tory and Jacobite allegiance become markedly less common. Secondly, we begin to come across vehement denials of 'the stale Cry of *Popery* and *Jacobitism*', and protestations that Oxford was 'most firmly and unalterably attach'd to the Church of *England*, and to its great Support, the Protestant Succession'.[40] At mid-century Edward Bentham wrote two Whiggish tracts upholding 'Revolution Principles' and pointing out how little a restoration of the Stuarts and the forcible re-establishment of Roman Catholicism would be in the interests of the universities.[41] Thirdly, the focus of critical discussion moved away from the realm of the political, and from the colourful and even festive instances of personal and institutional corruption by which it had been for so long preoccupied. Oxford's critics began instead to concentrate on the detail of what Oxford taught, and how it set about its teaching.

An early straw blowing in this wind was the anonymous *Letter to the Heads of the University of Oxford* (1747). The keynote of this pamphlet— a keynote seldom encountered at this time—was the fear that, if the colleges were not to take seriously their duty of providing education, then 'an University Education [will be] looked upon, by all the sober honest part of the World, as the Bane of Virtue, Morality, and even of those very Sciences they were established to promote'.[42] The author's concern that Oxford might be overrun by 'a most wretched Depravity of Taste, Morals, and Behaviour' is of course a line of filiation to the *topoi* of excess and sensual indulgence characteristic of the earlier phase of comment on Oxford.[43] What is unusual is his greater alertness to the

reconciled them to the government, and even to the court; but they have been since accused of transferring their passive loyalty from the Stuarts to the family of Brunswick; and I have heard Mr. Burke exclaim in the house of Commons, "They have changed the Idol, but they have preserved the Idolatry"' (*A* 182). It also shapes the concluding sentiment of draft 'F': 'The last generation of Jacobites is extinct; "the right Divine of Kings to govern wrong" is now exploded, even at Oxford; and the remains of Tory principles are rather salutary than hurtful, at a time when the Constitution has nothing to fear from the prerogative of the Crown, and can only be injured by popular innovation' (*A* 94–5). For a scholarly exploration and explanation of this transformation in mid-eighteenth-century English politics, see Clark, *English Society, 1688–1832*.

[40] [Anon.], *Letter from a Member of the University of Oxford*, 12; cf. [Anon.], *The Principles of the University of Oxford, As far as relates to Affection to the Government, Stated* (1755). A little over a decade later, Oxford could even be the (mildly startling) setting for an anonymous poem, *The Complaint of Liberty* (1768).

[41] Edward Bentham, *A Letter to a Young Gentleman of Oxford* (1748); *A Letter to a Fellow of a College, the sequel of A Letter to a Young Gentleman of Oxford* (1749). In the latter Bentham explained that his purpose in writing the earlier work had been to disabuse its readership of un-Whiggish principles, such as 'that Subjects are the absolute Property of their Sovereign; and further, that a Right of Dominion here in *England* is indefeasibly inherent in Princes by lineal Descent' (*Letter to a Fellow*, 8).

[42] [Anon.], *Letter to the Heads of the University of Oxford*, 12.

[43] Ibid. 7.

educative, rather than political, consequences of such depravity: an alertness exemplified in his admiration of the 'exact Regulation, Discipline, and Oeconomy observed in the Universities of *Scotland*', and his praise for Dr Cockman, the Master of University College, who kept an unusually close eye on both the progress of the college's undergraduates and the quality of the guidance they received from the college's tutors.[44]

The shift in emphasis away from questions of political allegiance and towards the detail of the university's practical arrangements for the education of the young is altogther more pronounced in Richard Davies's 1759 tract on *The General State of Education in the Universities*. Davies called for 'a more liberal provision for general Knowledge' in the universities, which he thought could be achieved by 'some enlargement in their plan of Education; some emancipation from established forms'.[45] His specific proposals included an increase in the number of professorships, the abolition of the requirement for heads of house and fellows to take holy orders, a reduction in the tenure of fellowships from their current status as perpetual freeholds, and measures to invigorate the desire for learning amongst the young by means of emulation.[46]

That the site of struggle had moved decisively to the question of the university's effectiveness and utility as a provider of education was, by the 1770s, unmistakable. At exactly the same time that Jebb was demanding that Cambridge examine, and if necessary reform, the spirit and content of its education,[47] in Oxford John Napleton argued that, surrounded as she was by criticism, the university could do no better than to make clear by her actions that she took her duty of education very seriously:

As Public Establishments of every kind will always be objects of envy and reproach, if there be any persons so little acquainted with the true interests of their Country, as to entertain unfavourable sentiments of a University, which has ever done honour to the English Nation, and contributed largely to the

---

[44] Ibid. 20.

[45] Davies, *General State of Education in the Universities*, 5–6 and 18.

[46] Ibid. 12, 30, 31, and 38. These were not all novel demands; for instance, John Hall had called for an increase in the number of university professorships, and a corresponding reduction in the number of college fellowships, as early as 1649 (*Humble Motion*, 29).

[47] Jebb, *Remarks Upon the Present Mode of Education in the University of Cambridge* (Cambridge, 1773); *A Proposal for the Establishment of Public Examinations in the University of Cambridge* (Cambridge, 1774). Jebb's writings are premised upon the assumption that the universities 'ought to be considered as seminaries for the information of youth in those studies, which have a tendency to fit them for the various scenes of social life' (*Proposal*, 1); a utilitarian premiss which was not to the fore in the later seventeenth and earlier eighteenth centuries.

Public Good, she cannot, I conceive, better refute the unkind suggestions of her enemies, or more surely engage the countenance and protection of her friends, than by reviving and improving the true salutary spirit of her ancient discipline and institutions, and rendering them every day more eminently conducive to the advancement of Religion and Learning.[48]

Although this presents itself as a project of restoration, of the revival of the university's 'ancient discipline and institutions', there is no doubt that what it looks for is the reform the need for which in 1791 Wendeborn could still say was 'very visible'.[49]

This general movement involved in the passage from the first to the second phase of criticism of Oxford in the long eighteenth century—a movement away from the politics of the university and towards the detail of its arrangements for education—is reflected in the topics on which censure chose to dwell. In the first phase, the question of subscription was exceptionally prominent. All junior members were required to subscribe the Thirty-Nine Articles, as well as the oath of allegiance. Edmond Miller's pungently Whiggish *An Account of the University of Cambridge* focused on what he called the 'difficult and obscure Oaths' demanded of those entering the university, and he gave an account of the likely consequences of such a requirement which implied unmistakably how such a regime both suited the Jacobites who administered it and was likely to breed further Jacobites: 'Such an Initiation into the University, is too apt to teach its Young Members either a mean Quibling to avoid the plain Words of an Oath; or else a disregard of the Sacredness of it, thro' Despair of not being able to act according to the Purport of it.'[50] Miller was followed by the author of *Reasons for Visiting the Universities*. The anonymous author traced the 'Immorality, and scandalous Lives of those Wretches who call themselves at this Time of the Clergy' to 'the present degenerate State of the Universities where they are bred, and where they imbibe Principles of Levity and Prophaneness, instead of Piety and Learning'.[51] A decade later, Nicholas Amhurst was also troubled by the fact that at matriculation the freshman perjured himself in one of two ways; he swore either impossible oaths, or oaths of the meaning of which he was ignorant, as a mere matter of form. The political damage done by such a climate

[48] Napleton, *Considerations on the Public Exercises for the First and Second Degrees in the University of Oxford*, 61.

[49] Wendeborn, *View of England*, ii. 142.

[50] Miller, *Account*, 4 and 6.

[51] For the author's acknowledgement of Miller's arguments, see *Reasons for Visiting the Universities*, 16. Ibid. 7.

of casual oath-taking was that it calloused the young to any sense of obligation by making 'insincerity and immorality . . . the first rudiments of their education'.[52] It was an analysis confirmed at mid-century by Thomas Tyrwhitt, who in his penitent *An Epistle to Florio, at Oxford* confessed that the 'blackest Deed' of his Oxford career had been to subscribe, for 'thus to Treason Perjury we join'd, | And prostituted God to cheat Mankind'.[53] In the same year Edward Bentham indicated how the imputation of Jacobitism was linked to the question of subscription when he expressed the pious hope that 'the Opinion of the Disloyalty of our University hath few Instances of such sober Villany [i.e. casuistical subscription] to support it'.[54] Nevertheless, some tender souls seem in fact to have been troubled by their non-performance of the obsolete but nevertheless compulsory oaths which they had been obliged to swear on matriculation.[55]

However, by the 1770s more sophisticated notions of what was involved in subscription had begun to prevail. The author of *A Collection of Papers, Designed to Explicate and Vindicate the Present Mode of Subscription Required by the University of Oxford* (1772) noted that the 'Affair of the Subscription has been much agitated', and wrote 'to skreen the University from the Reproach of an absurd and arbitrary Conduct, in requiring from young People a formal Assent to the Truth of Propositions which they knew it was impossible for them to understand'.[56] But the outcry misconceived what subscription entailed (perhaps, he darkly insinuated, more out of secret irreligion than because of any 'tender Concern for the Consciences of our Youth'). An '*Acquiescence* . . . is all that is, or ever was intended': 'All that he [the matriculand] is supposed to know of the Doctrines is, that they are the Doctrines of the Church of which he has been educated a Member; and that for the Present, he acquiesces in them as such, suspending any farther Judgment of them, till he shall be better able to examine them.'[57] It was therefore simply an error to imagine that 'a formal and explicit Assent to the Sense of the Doctrines' was ever implied by the act of subscription.[58] It was in this spirit that in the 1780s a father might

[52] *Terræ-Filius*, 12, 15, and 16; cf. also pp. 94 and 100, in which a fictional correspondent confirms Amhurst's gloomy diagnosis of the consequences of subscription.

[53] Tyrwhitt, *Epistle to Florio*, 8.

[54] Bentham, *Letter to a Fellow of a College*, 58.

[55] See e.g. Bonwicke, *A Pattern for Young Students in the University*, 28–9.

[56] [Anon.], *A Collection of Papers, Designed to Explicate and Vindicate the Present Mode of Subscription Required by the University of Oxford*, 21 and 10.

[57] Ibid. 22, 17, and 7.

[58] Ibid. 6.

write to his son at the university and congratulate him on his filial (if not necessarily religious) piety: 'my dear Charles, you have acted in Obedience to your Father in subscribing the Articles.'[59] And by the 1790s foreign observers of the English universities would be in agreement that subscription, although from one point of view indefensible, was by now a trite and, in comparison with the urgent practical consideration of how a university education was to be pursued and what it was to teach, even an unimportant question.[60] It was now only dissenters such as Priestley who hoped to make an issue out of university subscription.[61]

For the practical question which had focused the broader, ideological, concerns of the first phase of comment on Oxford had indeed been that of subscription. In the second phase, characterized less by politics than by education more narrowly conceived, comment clustered around how learning was to be imparted, and how its possession was to be assessed. That is to say, it clustered around the tutorial system and the method of examination. Of course, neither the effectiveness of the college tutors, nor the appropriateness of the forms of examination, had hitherto escaped without severe comment. Nicholas Amhurst had censured them both in *Terræ-Filius*, when they were both already topics which the university's critics had recognized as weak spots in its armour.[62] But as the century moved into its middle decades, there arose a strengthening consensus that it was on these practical aspects of university education that the sharpness of comment, and thereafter the energy of reform, should be trained. Criticism was levelled at these

---

[59] [Anon.], *A Letter from a Father to his Son at the University*, 22.

[60] Berkenhout, *A Volume of Letters from Dr. Berkenhout to his son at the University*, 30; Wendeborn, *View of England*, ii. 139.

[61] Priestley deplored the fact that students have gone on 'from generation to generation, subscribing what they have not considered, and then maintaining it because they have subscribed it', and he urged matriculands not to subscribe 'before you have carefully considered what each of those articles is, and have really satisfied yourselves that you see the evidence on which the truth of them is founded' (*Letters to the Young Men who are in a Course of Education for the Christian Ministry*, pp. ix and 47).

[62] Amhurst, *Terræ-Filius*, 113 and 227 (examinations), and 260 (tutors). Earlier indictments of the university examinations known as 'exercises' include [Anon.], *A Step to Oxford*, where a fellow of a college says he 'prefers an half a Goose with a Plum Pudding for his Dinner, to the unprofitable exercise of Bantering Quibles and Academical Distinctions' (p. 7). During the 1710s the tutorial system had been attacked in *The Case of Dr. Ayliffe*, where '*such Tutors, who seldom read to their Pupils more than once a Quarter, to put them in mind of their Quarters [sic] Payment*' (p. xx) are reproached, and also in *Reasons for Visiting the Universities*, where it is a source of political as well as personal corruption: 'Tutors, who, God knows, are in many Colleges perfectly negligent of the Morals of their Pupils; nay, rather Promoters, than Restrainers of their Vices, and only careful to instil disloyal Principles into them, and busie their Heads with Politicks instead of Philosophy, to the ruin of the Peace of the University, and indeed of the whole Nation' (p. 24).

aspects of Oxford's organization for the same reasons that it had been in earlier decades. As the century wears on, one encounters no new arguments about why the tutorial system was a disgrace and the examinations a farce. What changed in the final three decades of the century was the frequency, and hence the cumulative force, of the accusations.

In respect of the university's examinations, it is natural to begin with Napleton's *Considerations on the Public Exercises* of 1773. Deploring the 'low condition into which they [the public exercises] were fallen', he noted 'how little they answer the salutary purposes they were intended to promote' now that they were declined into 'lifeless unedifying formalities'.[63] He was followed in 1781 by Vicesimus Knox, who in *Liberal Education* (a most important publication which we will consider more fully when we turn to the detail of Gibbon's manuscripts) attacked the 'frivolous exercises required for the attainment of academical honours'.[64] Knox would return to the charge some years later in *Winter Evenings*, in which essay LVI, 'On Some Effects of a regular and University Education', recounts the fortunes of Jack Hearty, the clever son of a middlingly wealthy family who goes to Oxford.[65] Jack's tutor gives him 'some strings of arguments' on which to rely in his exercises, as well as other material which undermines what little value the exercises had for assessing educational attainment: 'Dr. Hunter, my tutor, has given me an old Latin sermon that I am sure will do for the exercise, because it has done already a dozen times at least, and is almost worn out in the service.'[66] These comments are typical of the strengthening view that the university had to demonstrate its commitment to its educative role by instituting a form of examination which could properly measure the accomplishment (or lack of it) in its students.

In the person of the worldly Dr Hunter, Knox connected the uselessness of the university's examinations to the corruption of its tutors. In so doing he drew together the two main themes in the later phase of the eighteenth century's criticism of Oxford, and it is to the second of these themes—the failures of the tutorial system—that we now turn. In James Miller's *Humours of Oxford* the feckless student, Ape-All, complains in the following terms of his tutor:

---

[63] Napleton, *Considerations*, pp. i, 1, and 2.
[64] Knox, *Liberal Education*, 320–1.
[65] Knox, *Winter Evenings*, i. 478–98.
[66] Ibid. i. 490 and 495.

my first two Years, indeed, I spent very vilely I confess—I had a good-for-nothing, musty Fellow for a Tutor, who made me read *Latin* and *Greek*, and would certainly have ruin'd me, if two or three honest Fellows had not got me out of his Clutches, carried me to Town, and show'd me the World—but I think I have pretty well recover'd my self. I hope, I neither talk nor look now, as if I had ever read *Greek*.[67]

Committed, if not necessarily effective, tutors, then, did exist,[68] and there were accordingly many attempts to clear the tutorial system of any blame for such shortcomings as there might be in an Oxford education. *Observations on the Present State of the English Universities* (1759) is typical. Notwithstanding what some allege, the author assures us, additional university professorships are not required because of 'that most excellent provision of college *tutors*; where, by a course of instruction in the catechetical way, with constant examinations, every part and degree of science is in the best manner adapted to the several capacities of students, and their respective progress in it most effectually discovered'.[69] Such reassurances seem not to have been effective in stemming the flow of charges of graspingness and neglect directed at the university's tutors. Another character in Miller's *Humours of Oxford*, Conundrum, is the epitome of the negligent and rapacious tutor, as his colleague Haughty reveals when he claims to know 'how many of thy Pupils thou hast abominably defrauded, by converting the Money which was sent to thee (by their Friends) for their Use—to thy own—and how horribly thou dost Impose on them, by never giving them any Lectures, nor letting them come nigh unto thee, but at the Quarter's End, when they are to pay thee for doing nothing'.[70] It was a character-

---

[67] Miller, *Humours of Oxford*, 25.

[68] Although even fair-minded commentators such as Wendeborn would 'not presume to assert' that such 'able, learned and deserving men' constituted the majority of tutors (*View of England*, ii. 146). Edward Bentham's self-characterization, as one who had 'now for the space of more than five and forty years carefully watched over the morals and education of youth, and never absented myself from the duties of my station, even one term, but constantly discharged them to the utmost of my abilities' (*The Honor of the University of Oxford Defended*, 36), is the complaint of a man who knows that the public mind does not customarily associate tutors with such selfless diligence.

[69] [Anon.], *Observations*, 10; cf. 'there never were more able tutors, nor more properly and worthily employed, than at present. Never, I believe, were more pains taken in the diligent instruction of the youth committed to them; never was a larger portion of true useful science taught, nor in so good a method; many not contenting themselves with reading and explaining some of the best authors on each subject, but likewise drawing up particular plans of their own, of which they have found the benefit by long experience' (p. 17). For other exculpations of the tutors, see: [Anon.], *Free Thoughts Upon University Education*, 9; [Edward Bentham], *Advices to a Young Man of Fortune and Rank*, 19 and 28 ff.

[70] Miller, *Humours of Oxford*, 49.

ization of the college tutor which would be echoed and endorsed in 1788 by the author of *Remarks on the Enormous Expence in the Education of Young Men*, as well as by Knox in *Winter Evenings*.[71] And at the same time as this portrait of the college tutor was being purged of the festive connotations it had initially enjoyed, and was coming to be seen as an abuse requiring reform, so we also encounter more frequent comparisons between the dissipation of student life at Oxford and the allegedly more regular discipline to be found in foreign universities, including those of Scotland.[72] The growing prevalence of international comparison is a sign that Oxford's corruptions and excesses are now no longer being viewed, even in part, within an indulgent and even festive conception of Englishness, but are being more dispassionately measured against utilitarian *criteria* of educational effectiveness.

III

Without an awareness of how the tone and focus of writing on Oxford had altered over the century preceding Gibbon's composition of his 'Memoirs', and without some sensitivity to the changes in the vocabulary in which those shifting preoccupations had found expression, much of the rewriting and rethinking which we find in the five manuscript versions of his residence at Oxford would necessarily seem insignificant, or be positively misleading, to even the most discerning critical eye. We may now turn to the verbal detail of that series of parallel texts from a standpoint of informed awareness, and parse their language in relation to the context whose evolutions we have just plotted. Before we do so, however, it should be noted that the period of Gibbon's residence—3 April 1752 to 8 June 1753—occurred on the very cusp of the change from the first to the second phase of eighteenth-century criticism of Oxford. That Gibbon was in Oxford as an older outlook waned and a newer outlook waxed is a circumstance which the textual dynamics created by the various drafts of his 'Memoirs' endows with powerful suggestive force.

Appendix 5 displays the relevant sections of drafts 'B', 'C', 'D', and 'E', while Appendix 6 does the same for draft 'F' and the text as published in the 1796 *Miscellaneous Works*. In both appendices the

---

[71] [Anon.], *Remarks*, 9; Knox, *Winter Evenings*, i. 489–90.

[72] *Letter to the Heads of the University of Oxford*, 20; *Collection of Papers*, 28; *Free Thoughts Upon University Education*, 21; 'Memorial Relating to the Universities', ii. 62 and 63. The university's defenders, as usual, provide indirect testimony to the prevailing sentiment: cf. Bentham, *Honor of the University of Oxford*, 4.

information has been organized in a tabular form, so that it can be read both vertically (the text of each separate draft) and horizontally (parallel passages from the various drafts and the *Miscellaneous Works*). Given that we will be for the most part concerned to examine the rewriting of sections as Gibbon moved from draft to draft, the text has been divided into sections, so that parallel passages in all five drafts and in the *Miscellaneous Works* can be conveniently located; this also has the advantage that deletions, new material, and the rearrangement of existing material are rendered easily visible. Since the analysis which follows will inevitably make repeated and detailed reference to the information displayed in these appendices, readers may find it convenient to have them bookmarked for ease of consultation.[73]

The general outline of what these appendices reveal is plain. In drafts 'B', 'C', and 'D' we have three texts which display a strong family resemblance. The plentiful continuities of wording indicate that 'B' has served as the base text for 'C' and 'D', and their mere visual appearance when displayed in parallel might suggest that these later drafts represent two stages of steadily greater compression. It would be an error, however, to conclude from this general outline of what we might call the architecture of these passages that as we move from 'B' to 'D' we get a progressively more pithy expression of essentially the same vision of Gibbon's time at Oxford and his conversion to Catholicism. Nevertheless, this would be an error hard to avoid were one not previously aware of the developments in the discursive context which had taken place during the eighteenth century. For the elisions which the uninformed eye could not escape construing as the elements of two acts of mere précis in fact serve to move drafts 'C' and 'D' to different positions within the discursive field; a mobility which was taken further, as we shall see, by the striking act of rearrangement in draft 'D', namely the movement of sections 8 and 9 so that they follow section 12.

In draft 'E'—written we must remember when Gibbon either was reading or had just read Burke's *Reflections*—we see a further and quite extraordinary condensation. Again, a reader innocent of context but aware of the increasing conciseness of the text in drafts 'B' to 'D' might assume that the drastic shrinkage evident in draft 'E' was just another stage in the same process of striving for greater terseness. In fact, draft 'E' represents a further move on Gibbon's part, as a result of which he occupies a fresh position within the discursive field. When we turn to

[73] References to passages in the appendices will take the form '('B': 3)', where the letter indicates the draft and the number the section. The published text in the *Miscellaneous Works* of 1796 will be referred to by the letters '*MW*'.

draft 'F', we see an equally extraordinary expansion of the passage. Here, once again, 'B' provides the template, but the addition of much new material, the substantial reshaping of what is preserved, an engagement with different near-contemporary writings, and a likely responsiveness on Gibbon's part to the reception at the time of composition of other writings attacking Oxford, reveal and explain a further movement of perspective and tone on Gibbon's part. Moreover this is where draft 'F' breaks off, and so it was presumably at or close to this point of composition that Gibbon wrote to Sheffield on 6 January 1793 and professed himself 'not satisfied' with the progress of the 'Memoirs'.[74] Our analysis of what will emerge, on the showing of this passage at least, as the conflicting ends which Gibbon had set himself in draft 'F' will allow us to understand why it was that, with the section on Oxford, he had reached an impasse, and could neither take this draft further nor embark upon another—a putative draft 'G'. That is, we shall arrive at an understanding of the probable causes of the dissatisfaction Gibbon felt in the early days of 1793 with both draft 'F', and also the entire project of autobiography.

Since, as this résumé makes clear, our close readings of Gibbon's prose will take place within an enabling and controlling awareness of context, it would be best to begin by setting out how insistently these passages from the drafts of the 'Memoirs' evoke the language and topics of the discursive context within which we will read them. Once we have registered how frequently Gibbon draws upon, and seems to play into, the context of writing on Oxford (and further examples will be produced in the course of our analysis of the various drafts), the value of using that context as an interpretative matrix for the 'Memoirs' will become clear.

Many of the topics on which Gibbon touches in this section of his 'Memoirs' had also figured in earlier writing on Oxford, to the point where his writing seems almost a collection of commonplaces. When, for instance, he recalls his 'elegant apartment of three rooms in the new buildings' ('B':2), 'a spacious apartment' ('C':2) and 'three elegant and well-furnished rooms in the new building, a stately pile, of Magdalen College' ('F':2), this would have been for the contemporary reader an unsurprising emphasis, since the New Buildings at Magdalen were a celebrated structure to which tourists to Oxford were particularly directed by guides published at exactly the time of Gibbon's residence.[75] When Gibbon explained that 'since the days of Pocock and Hyde, Oriental learning has always been the pride of Oxford, and I once expressed an inclination to study Arabic' ('F':8), he implied his own willingness as a student by reference to a well-known strength of the university; a magazine published just before Gibbon came up had remarked on the 'great and almost general pursuit of *Oriental* Learning in this University'.[76] Gibbon mocked the want of publications by Oxford's and Cambridge's academics: 'If I enquire into the manufactures of the monks of Magdalen, if I extend the enquiry to the other Colleges of Oxford and Cambridge, a silent blush, or a scornful frown, will be the only reply.' ('F':6a; cf. 'B':10 and 'C':10) But in this he had been anticipated by Nicholas Amhurst, who in the 1720s had jeered at the silence of the Clarendon Press.[77] In all five manuscript drafts Gibbon found room to include an allusion to Adam Smith's indictment of the Oxford professoriat as having 'given up altogether even the pretence of teaching' ('B'–'F':6). This, too, however, was a topic of complaint reaching back to the 1720s and Amhurst;[78] it had been more recently repeated by Wendeborn (who mildly remarked that the 'labour of the professors is very easy');[79] and in the previous year (and notwithstanding the acknowledgement that these 'articles of accusation . . . have been frequently brought forward') it had been discussed also by Berkenhout, in language close to that of Gibbon and Smith:

foreigners . . . are astonished to find that our professorships are commonly sinecures; that there is no continued series of public lectures in arts or sciences; and that college tutors are almost the only sources of information. [By contrast, professors in continental universities] are paid by their auditors, who are under no obligation to attend them; consequently their emoluments depend on their reputation.[80]

And when Gibbon adverted to the social and educational indulgences

---

[75] *Pocket Companion for Oxford*, 30; the New Buildings were one of the few subjects illustrated with a cut in this guide. Designed it is thought by Dr George Clarke, Fellow of All Souls, and probably constructed by William Townesend (assisted by Gibbs) in 1733, the New Buildings were more warmly appreciated by connoisseurs in the eighteenth century than they have always been by their successors in the twentieth: for an especially grudging evaluation, see Pevsner, *The Buildings of England: Oxfordshire*, 154. By contrast, in the 1770s Edward Tatham urged the fellows of Magdalen to remove 'those irregular Offices on the east of the Quadrangle' in order to 'open the new building to the bridge. This will be a magnificent object to those who hourly pass and repass; . . .' (*Oxonia Explicata & Ornata*, 17).

[76] *The Student*, i. 41.

[77] Amhurst, *Terræ-Filius*, 58.

[78] Ibid. 51–2.

[79] Wendeborn, *View of England*, ii. 154.

[80] Berkenhout, *Volume of Letters*, 34; cf. 'F':6.

extended to the Gentlemen Commoners, he again touched on a subject which Oxford's detractors had long recognized as a propitious spot upon which to train their artillery. Amhurst once more provides a good comparison: 'the education of a person of distinction at Oxford, instead of being, as it ought, the most strictly taken care of, is of all the most neglected; . . . A gentleman-commoner, if he be a man of fortune, is soon told, that it is not expected from one of his form to mind exercises: . . .'[81]

If the subjects on which Gibbon took Oxford to task would have seemed familiar to contemporary readers, those readers would also have found little to surprise them in the vocabulary in which Gibbon attacked his old university. The university's detractors over the previous century had created not only a list of recurrent topics, but also an idiom which acted almost as a shorthand for their sense of how and why the university had become corrupted. It was an idiom in which the fellows were monks, the colleges monasteries or convents, and in which the traditional customs and practices of the university—educational, political and social—were stigmatized as monkish. At one level, this language insinuated that the shortcomings of the English universities (for it was a language used also of Cambridge) were the result of vestiges of Roman Catholicism which had escaped reformation.[82] This was the opinion of Dr. Berkenhout:

the entire system is too obviously Gothic to escape the ridicule of strangers, who visit Oxford and Cambridge with the idea that the *Ecclesia Anglicana* is a *reformed* Church, and that these formal seminaries are appropriated to the education of nobility, of gentlemen, statesmen, lawyers, physicians, and divines. . . . It is indeed very extraordinary that, in discarding the absurdities of the Romish creed and religious ceremonies, we should have retained so much of the ancient mode of education, both in our schools and universities. . . . It

[81] Amhurst, *Terræ-Filius*, 47; cf. also [Anon.], *Free Thoughts Upon University Education*, 9. For a Cambridge parallel, see the strictures on Fellow-Commoners (the Cambridge equivalent) in John Jebb, *Remarks Upon the Present Mode of Education in the University of Cambridge*, 7; [Anon.], *Remarks on the Enormous Expence in the Education of Young Men in the University of Cambridge*, 7, 8, and 25; and the author of *A Letter to the Author of the Proposal for the Establishment of Public Examinations* (Cambridge, 1774), who comments that the 'order of Fellow-Commoners has by immemorial usage a kind of prescriptive right to idleness; and fashion has inspired it with an habitual contempt of discipline' (p. 5).

[82] For example, by Richard Davies, who moved smartly from the historical fact that the 'two Universities were originally founded in the times of Monkish Superstition' to the more judgemental view that they 'have been too much permitted to creep on in the same lazy channel, which was marked out for them in the days of Gothic ignorance and superstition' (*General State of Education*, 5 and 9), and by the author of *Remarks on the Enormous Expence*, who saw the effects of 'Popery' in the malfunctioning areas of the university (p. 10).

cannot be denied, that the Colleges in our English Universities retain an obvious similitude to Roman Catholick Convents.[83]

But this language could also be used in a broader and more swash-buckling fashion.[84] It dropped naturally from the lips of freethinking Whigs, who found in it an idiom which allowed them in a single breath to pillory Oxford for both its clericalism (deemed favourable to priest-craft) and its alleged endemic Jacobitism (the Roman Catholicism of the Stuarts being of course notorious), while at the same time castigating fellows of colleges for their unwholesome renunciation of the world.[85] As Nicholas Amhurst had commented: 'In many colleges the *Fellow-ships* are so considerable, that no preferment can tempt some persons to leave them: they prefer this *monastick*, and (as they call it) *retired* life to any employment, in which they would be obliged to take some pains, and do *some good*.'[86] Therefore when Edward Bentham defended Oxford against Burke in 1781, he did so in full awareness of the impli-cations of the customary language in which Oxford had been, was, and would be, attacked: 'If we listen to the insinuations of our shameless Defamer, the nature of our Education is better adapted to fit us for the inglorious solitude of a Monastic cell, than for the busy scenes of public life.'[87] Gibbon's employment of this language issued an invitation to his

---

[83] Berkenhout, *Volume of Letters*, pp. ii, 14, and 31; cf. also his censure of the 'Gothic absurdity' of the system of education at Oxford and Cambridge (p. 141). Wendeborn repeated the allegation: 'The students . . . live in colleges, greatly resembling monasteries'; a resemblance hardly surprising, since the colleges were indeed derived from 'monastic institutions', and were 'modelled upon a monastic plan' (*View of England*, ii. 140, 160, and 161; cf. also his comparison of heads of house to 'abbots', ii. 143).

[84] For evidence that the idiom of monkishness had become detached from its precise origins, and had passed into the general language in which Oxford was discussed, consider the naming of the character 'Monkwell' in *The Humours of the Road: Or, a Ramble to Oxford* (1738), Tyrwhitt's castigation of the 'monkish pray'r' of Oxford (*Epistle to Florio*, 11) and the dismissing of college discipline as 'monkish nonsense' in *A Few General Directions*, 7. An additional, though minor, strand of meaning relates to the dominant architectural style of the older colleges, a style characterized by Edward Tatham in the phrase 'monastic recluseness' (*Oxonia Explicata & Ornata*, p. 2).

[85] This was the view of the author of the 1659 pamphlet, *Sundry Things*, who demanded that the university's graduates be employed outside the university, 'so as they may be serviceable to the Nation, and not grow old in their Colleges, which thereby become as it were Hospitals and Monasteries' (*Harleian Miscellany*, vi. 80). Shaftesbury (that epitome of freethinking Whiggery) also placed monkishness in opposition to a healthy worldliness: 'the highest Principle, which is *the love of* GOD, is best attained not by dark Speculations and *Monkish Philosophy*, but by moral Practice, and love of Mankind, and a Study of their Interests' (*Several Letters*, 7).

[86] Amhurst, *Terræ-Filius*, 219; cf. 258 (where the colleges are condemned as '*monkish* societies') and p. 222—of especial interest in relation to Gibbon—where Amhurst refers to the 'monks of MAGDALEN'.

[87] Bentham, *Honor of the University of Oxford defended*, 6.

readers to condition their understanding of the text of the 'Memoirs' by reference to this context: a conditioning given, of course, additional vividness by the circumstance of Gibbon's having actually become a Catholic as a result of his residence in this still monkish, and (as this language implicitly and constantly reminded his readers) originally popish, university.

Now that we have registered the extent to which Gibbon's prose in this section of the 'Memoirs' establishes relationships between context and text, we can move into the first part of our comparative analysis of the different accounts Gibbon composed of his residence in Oxford; namely, an analysis of the textual dynamics arising from a juxtaposition of drafts 'B', 'C', and 'D'. Before we immerse ourselves in the detail of the comparison, section by section, it might be helpful to indicate in general terms what we shall discover. What will emerge from our analysis is a movement the logic of which can be understood only in relation to the dynamics of the context we have sketched in the preceding pages. As we move from 'B' to 'D', we move from a base text in which a degree of equipoise is achieved between the educational earnestness of the second phase of the context and the festive overtones of the first phase, to a text in which that equipoise has been destroyed by the almost complete elimination of the detailed pedagogic concern which was characteristic of other writing about Oxford at the time Gibbon composed his 'Memoirs'. In other words, the two successive acts of revision which produced drafts 'C' and 'D' show Gibbon seeming to move backwards in time, and imaginatively recovering a way of writing about Oxford more typical of the period of his actual residence than it was of the moment at which he was writing.

In section 1 what is most striking is the virtually verbatim preservation across all three drafts of the marvellous phrase Gibbon coined to express the excellence and the inadequacy of the intellectual equipment he brought to the university: 'I arrived at Oxford with a stock of Erudition which might have puzzled a Doctor and a degree of ignorance of which a school-boy would have been ashamed' ('B'–'D':1).[88] However, the phrase exists in different verbal company in each draft, and its impact is accordingly various. In 'B', the balance of praise and

---

[88] It is interesting to note that, owing to the absence of this phrase from draft 'F' (which Sheffield used to the exclusion of all others in his conflated text of the 'Memoirs' for this period of Gibbon's life), the general public became aware of this memorable sentence only with the publication in 1894 of Murray's edition of the six drafts. It therefore formed no part of the Victorian response to Gibbon, although it has been for twentieth-century readers one of the most discussed and quoted sentences of the 'Memoirs'.

blame created by the acknowledgement of both Gibbon's erudition and his ignorance is sustained in the following sentence about his 'litterary projects'. They were at once 'far above my strength', and yet, although precocious, not therefore entirely misconceived; for Aurelian and Selim 'may indeed support some kind of resemblance' ('B':1). In 'D', however, these projects seem less substantial. We are told that 'Several projects of composition already floated in my mind', and 'floated', especially when taken with the vaguely plural 'several', insinuates dilettantism and infirmity of purpose. This change is almost a keynote for the tendency of the revision revealed by drafts 'B', 'C', and 'D'. In 'B', Gibbon is a boy of vast but rude promise who stands in need of responsible guidance from the university he has just entered. In 'D' his literary appetite is treated with a shade more detachment, and as a result in this draft 'the erudition that my̶ might have puzzled a Doctor' seems less deserving of our admiration ('D':1). In this light the chief significant detail of 'C'—the increase in the number of Gibbon's projects from the two of 'B' to the three listed in the next draft—marks a transitional stage towards the attenuation of the young Gibbon's literary accomplishment which we see in 'D'. It is a stroke in a maquette for 'D's more self-deprecating portrait of a youth of ill-founded confidence who has spread himself too thin.

In drafts 'B' and 'C' section 2 is an account of beguiling, but ultimately deceptive, first impressions. That emphasis is entirely suppressed in 'D', which offers a plain statement of fact as to the age at which Gibbon entered Oxford, followed by some polite but general words about the university. The elision in 'D' of the preparation for censure of Oxford which is apparent in 'B' and 'C' is clearly in keeping with the overall tendency of revision we have indicated above. However, it would be wrong to overlook the changes which Gibbon made for draft 'C', for they are full of significant rewriting and rethinking. In the first place, we should note the deletion of the final limb of this section in 'B', 'and the key of the College-library, which I might use or abuse without much interruption from the fellows of the Society' ('B':2), and its replacement by the less accusative and more circumspect phrase, 'the libraries are appropriated to the use of a studious and contemplative life' ('C':2). The allegation of intellectual indolence, made unmistakable in 'B' by the use of mordant sarcasm, is thus suppressed in 'C'. However, this is but one element in 'C's' more general reshaping of the affective aspect of Gibbon's arrival in Oxford. In 'B' Gibbon's entry to Magdalen is accompanied by 'surprize and satisfaction', and we are told that these 'sentiments were naturally produced' ('B':2). It is not clear quite what force we should attach to 'naturally' here. It might be taken to imply Gibbon's innocence (one of the imaginative templates for Gibbon's narration of this episode in his life is unmistakably *Paradise Lost*). The word might equally be being used in a less approbatory, more neutral, manner. That implication of innocence, however, is strengthened by the touch of menace with which draft 'B' imbues Oxford—a menace plainly there in the temptation afforded by 'a decent allowance in my own disposal with a ~~large~~ loose and *dangerous* credit' (my emphasis), but also latently present in the 'sudden promotion' to a standing for which he was ill-equipped and in which it was impossible that he could acquit himself creditably. In 'B', then, a steadily more definite portrait is emerging of Gibbon as a victim.

It is, however, a portrait over which in draft 'C' Gibbon draws a sponge. The most obvious revision scoring through an implication of threat comes when 'B's' 'decent allowance in my own disposal with a ~~large~~ loose and dangerous credit' becomes 'a competent allowance'. The striking addition in the later draft of the perspective of the 'stranger', whose 'admiration' is excited by the appearance of Oxford, and whose emotions are echoed at a distance by the elation of 'childish vanity' felt by Gibbon diminishes 'B's' air of entrapment. By aligning the affections of the young Oxonian with those of an anonymous everyman, 'C' reduces 'B's' menacing sense of Gibbon's having been in some way marked out. Furthermore, the suppression in 'C' of Gibbon's unusually early entry (no mention is made of his precise age in this draft; though naturally the reader could have worked it out from the dates supplied) also serves to dissipate the atmosphere around Gibbon's entry to Oxford which 'B' creates, an atmosphere of atypicality pregnant with mishap.

So much by way of strict practical criticism of section 2. As far as it goes, it is not misleading, but it is incomplete, because an additional richness of significance in these variants can be seen and understood only when they are positioned within their context. It is in this section that Gibbon begins to touch on issues handled by both Oxford's assailants and her defenders, and it is therefore at this point that his account of his residence at Magdalen begins to root itself in its discursive soil. It is worth juxtaposing with this section of Gibbon's 'Memoirs' a passage from Amhurst's *Terræ-Filius* on a similar subject: 'Raw, unthinking young men, having been kept short of money at school, and sent, perhaps, to the university with a small allowance, are notwithstanding strangely flushed with the change of their condition, and care not how extravagant they are, whilst they can support their extravagances upon *trust* . . .'.[89] The revolution in the newly matriculated student's outlook, and the aptness of that revolution to find expression in financial imprudence, was, then, a theme in writing about Oxford long before Gibbon composed his 'Memoirs', and this is a consideration which must complicate our thoughts about the extent to which Gibbon here is transcribing, at a distance of some forty years, the emotions of the moment, or whether he is rather concocting a career for himself from the available contextual materials, and then draping it around a spare (and therefore versatile) factual framework. However, if Amhurst shows that in this section Gibbon was addressing a *topos* of long standing in writing about Oxford, it was nevertheless a much more recent book, Knox's *Liberal Education*, that Gibbon's prose most closely shadowed. Knox was unsurprised that 'a number of young men, just emancipated from school, and from a parent's authority, should break out into irregularities, when encouraged by mutual example', and when 'many had money at command'.[90] In these circumstances, early entry to the university was rash: 'I consider the sending a son thither at present, without particular precautions, as a most dangerous measure; a measure which may probably make shipwreck of his learning, his morals, his health, his character, and his fortune, if he has one . . .'. Therefore: 'In the first place, boys should not be sent to the university so young as they often are. It is really cruel to let a boy of fifteen be precipitated into drunkenness and debauchery. By a too early entrance, his health will be injured, his peace of mind broken, his learning lost, and his morals depraved.' And the temptations were intensified by the inner changes effected in the new student by his transplantation to the university, for 'Every one, on putting on the academical dress, commences a man in his own opinion, and will often endeavour to support the character by the practice of manly vices'.[91] The closeness between what Knox had published in 1781 and what Gibbon was writing at the end of the decade is striking. We know from a footnote in draft 'F' that Gibbon was aware of Knox's writings on the English universities.[92] It would seem, therefore, that Gibbon was almost casting his career at Oxford in the mould of Knox's strictures on the university's shortcomings, as an exemplification of what Knox had

---

[89] Amhurst, *Terræ-Filius*, 180. At the end of the century undergraduates would be ironically warned against feebly complying with demands for payment from tradesmen: 'If the tradesmen are weak enough to let you run into their debt, you will not be weak enough to pay them' ([Anon.], *A Few General Directions*, 8).

[90] Knox, *Liberal Education*, 322.

[91] Ibid. 324–5.

[92] *A* 70, n. 9.

diagnosed as unhealthy. The almost complete erasure in 'C' of the details which invited comparison with Knox is of a piece with the muting in that draft of the specifically educational complaints of 'B'. The same is true of the complete deletion from 'C' and 'D' of section 3 (the consequent removal from 'C' and 'D' of Locke's name is especially telling, since according to George Coade 'the great, the wise, the learned Mr. *Locke*' had suggested the project of reforming the universities to William III, and was therefore strongly aligned with the outlook of 'B').[93]

In section 4 we have an excellent example of Gibbon as a reader of his own prose. Common to all three accounts is the sense of barrenness in Gibbon's period of residence in Oxford, although the nature of that barrenness shifts as we move from draft to draft. And in 'B' and 'C', this barrenness is evoked through the metaphor of a failed parent/child relationship between Gibbon and the university. Taking these two elements in turn, we notice firstly in the case of Gibbon's handling of the barrenness of his time at Oxford that this gradually becomes a less specifically educational barrenness, and indeed is mildly weakened in the successive revisions. Consider the sequence: 'totally lost for every purpose of study or improvement' ('B':4); 'most compleatly lost for every purpose of improvement' ('C':4); and 'the most barren and unprofitable of my whole life' ('D':4). With the discarding of 'B's' 'study', the only unambiguously educational word is removed from the passage, a process taken further when 'C's' residual 'lost for every purpose of improvement' is condensed into 'unprofitable': 'improvement' may be educational (though it need not be, as 'B's' 'study or improvement' implies), and improvement is itself not the only kind of profit (in that it is possible to conceive of benefits which are not improving). The waste Gibbon suffered therefore becomes steadily less specific and more general with each successive act of revision. At the same time, the degree of waste undergoes a mild diminution, from 'B's' unmitigated 'totally lost for every purpose of study or improvement'; to 'C's' more guarded and ambiguous 'most compleatly lost for every purpose of improvement' (where 'most' can be read as either intensifying or reducing—if it is given the readily available contemporary meaning of 'almost'[94]—the force of 'compleatly'); to 'D's' 'fourteen months, the most barren and unprofitable of my whole life', which at first glance seems more extreme, but which exchanges an absolute standard of waste for a comparative one—Gibbon's time at Magdalen might be the

[93] [George Coade], *Blow at the Root*, 25–6.
[94] *OED* B.3.

'most barren and unprofitable' period of his life, and nevertheless fall short of 'B's' utterly unqualified 'totally lost for every purpose of study or improvement'.

This process of removing the sharply educational complaint we find in 'B' is abetted by the apparently minor revision of the substitution in 'D' of 'consumed' for 'B' and 'C's' 'spent'. In those earlier drafts one reads 'spent' most readily as meaning simply 'passed'; and if any aspect of the word's metaphorical potential is activated in drafts 'B' and 'C', it is the word's fiscal rather than somatic side which is given salience by the discussion in section 3 of the extent of Gibbon's allowance and credit. However, if we imagine Gibbon reviewing 'B' and 'C', and perhaps even having them before him on his desk as he composed 'D', then it would seem that his mind fastened on the bodily implications of 'spent' when he replaced it with 'consumed'.[95] With this word we see introduced into 'D' the image of the festive, consuming body which later becomes more prominent, and which of course is characteristic of the first phase of the context, towards which, as I have suggested, Gibbon was to some extent harking back in the sequence of revisions which produced 'D'.

The gradual muting of 'B's' educational stridency is visible, too, in the changing way Gibbon handles the metaphor of parent and child to express the relationship between university and student. It is, of course, a metaphor drawn from the official idiom of the university itself, as the technical term for the admission of a student, 'matriculation', reminds us.[96] In both 'B' and 'C' Gibbon uses this metaphor to suggest the failure of this parental bond, but each draft implies a different attribution of responsibility for the failure, and configures the emotional estrangement between Gibbon and the university in a slightly distinctive manner. In 'B', we have a mutual, symmetrical, and apparently simultaneous aversion: 'the University will as gladly renounce me for her son as I shall disclaim her for my mother.' In 'C', however, we encounter revised wording which positions Gibbon's renunciation of the university before any reciprocal rejection: 'the University *will* not be ambitious of a son who disclaims all sense of filial piety and gratitude' (my emphasis). The revision in 'C' creates the possibility, guarded

---

[95] We possess very little direct information about exactly how Gibbon composed his 'Memoirs', but it is difficult to account for the often verbatim transmission of material from one draft to another except on the supposition that Gibbon had his earlier manuscripts by him when composing.

[96] The root word, 'matricula', meaning the register of a body such as a university, is a diminutive of 'matrix', meaning 'womb' or 'mother'.

against in 'B' by the symmetrical use of future tenses, that the university's renunciation of Gibbon is a response to his prior renunciation of the university. This in its turn may suggest that the cause of the offence lay with Gibbon, a possibility plainly there in 'C's' opening formula of 'I must blush for myself or for my teachers', which in retrospect thereby comes to seem more of a genuine choice of possible alternatives.

The apportionment of blame between the student and the university is the leading theme of section 5, and here again we see a movement from a precision of resentment to a version at once less detailed and more equivocal in tone. The most striking change, as one looks across at the parallel passages, is the deletion from 'C' and 'D' of the second half of 'B'. The deleted passage consists of three sentences: the third serves merely to introduce section 6, but the first presents an idealized image of what an Oxford education could be, and the second checks that ideal image against both the advantages Gibbon derived from his European exposure and the monkish actuality he experienced at Oxford. The language of the first sentence seems close to the terms in which Oxford's defenders had fought off the allegations of its critics. For instance, Gibbon's image of a carefully graduated *cursus* of study had been used in 1759 against the criticisms of Richard Davies, when the universities had been extolled as in truth places 'Where youth are gently led from sounds to sense; their notions formed, and their attentions fixed, and both gradually introduced into the more complex relations and abstruse connections of things: . . .'.[97] If Gibbon borrows the accents of Oxford's apologists here, he does so only for a moment. In 'B' these pleasing tones can exist only within a conditional mood: 'my youthful ardour *would* have been encouraged', 'I *should* gradually have risen'. As soon as the mood reverts to the indicative, however, we move from the soothing tones of those who wished to extenuate, or even deny the existence of, the university's failings, to a favourite topic and the customary language of its critics; namely, European comparison and the idiom of monkishness. These two sentences, then, give us *in petto* the conflict we have seen played out in the context, and Gibbon's loyalties in that conflict are clearly implied, not only by the fact that he gives the last word to Oxford's critics, but by the more subtle, grammatical, alignment of their perspective with actuality, and that of Oxford's defenders with only the hypothetical.

Common to all three versions of section 5 is a passage in which

---

[97] [Anon.], *Observations on the Present State of the English Universities*, 11.

Gibbon attempts to allocate appropriate proportions of responsibility for his disappointment at Oxford to the shortcomings of the university and his own unpreparedness. In 'B' the concession that his own lack of readiness to benefit from what Oxford could offer should 'operate with [its] proper weight' (however great or trifling) is immediately followed and checked by an uncompromising affirmation of his 'capacity and application' ('B':5). In 'C', that affirmation is complicated into the mock modesty of the 'presumptuous belief that neither my temper nor my talents were averse to the lessons of science'; a circumspection of tone which springs the trap of the litotes at the end of the section, when Gibbon suggests that 'some share of reproach will adhere to the Academical institution which could damp every spark of industry in a curious and active mind' ('C':5). If 'C' is therefore tonally more guarded than 'B', and if that tonal shrewdness is the signature of a more disingenuous strategy for insinuating authorial judgement, nevertheless drafts 'B' and 'C' are close in their shared, fundamental, conviction, that it is to Oxford, rather than to Gibbon, that the lion's share of responsibility must be attributed. In 'D', however, the introduction of a measure of tonal equivocation in 'C'—even if it seems not to betoken any hesitation of judgement—has hardened into a more substantial openness. The choice and placing of word in 'D' does little to guide the reader, aside from the point that, Gibbon having made at the outset an acknowledgement that a portion of the blame must rest with him, any reader not already a partisan of the university is liable to (and, it is implied, should) attribute the balance of blame to the university and 'the misconduct of my Academic guides'. But notice how that acknowledgement has evolved over the three drafts, from 'B's' consideration of a stranger ('If I am reminded . . .'), to 'C's' 'reasonable abatement', to 'D's' 'fair abatement'. That shedding of a degree of defensiveness, and the consequent allaying of the tone of accusation in 'D', is of a piece with the tendency of the revisions to earlier sections.

Sections 6 and 7 are best taken together. In all three drafts the subject here is Oxford's educational failure, and in all three the core of the charge is Adam Smith's attack on the Oxford professoriat in *The Wealth of Nations*.[98] In 'B' and 'C' this is accompanied by the exceptions which prove the rule, namely Lowth and Blackstone. It is a show of fair-mindedness and scruple which does nothing substantially to blunt the attack on Oxford's shortcomings, particulary as in both drafts it is

---

[98] Smith, *The Wealth of Nations*, ii. 761. This is virtually the only element common to all five drafts of this part of the 'Memoirs'.

immediately followed by Gibbon's quietly hostile account of Oxford's tutorial system. The unstated but nevertheless plain insinuation here is that such a system could never have arisen in any place which took seriously the business of education. Here again we see Gibbon coming close to the language and sentiments of Oxford's most recent critics:

foreigners . . . are astonished to find that our professorships are commonly sinecures; that there is no continued series of public lectures in arts or sciences; and that college tutors are almost the only sources of information.

in England, they [professors] live in luxury, in colleges resembling palaces, and their annual income is secured without the assistance of industry.

The college tutors are often, it is to be presumed, men of judgment as well as learning and morals, and are well qualified to direct the student in every part of his conduct. It is at the same time to be lamented, that from the number of pupils usually allotted to one, he is incapable of paying all that attention to each, which a tender parent must desire.[99]

In draft 'D', however, section 7 has been deleted, and so Smith's accusation stands alone. Once again the conciseness of 'D' has been purchased at the expense of energy and vigour of criticism. Moreover, quite how the reader takes Smith's resentment of Oxford's sinecures in 'D' is conditioned by the radical decision Gibbon took when he revised the next five sections for that draft.

In drafts 'B' and 'C' the inclusion of section 7, on the tutorial system, leads naturally in to Gibbon's account of his experiences with Dr Waldegrave, 'one of the best of the Tribe'. The Appendix shows this to have been far more elaborate in 'B', although what the Appendix cannot reveal is how securely the detail of this passage anchors it in the literature surrounding Oxford. The apparently inert circumstance of the 'our evening walks to the top of Heddington hill', for instance, reverberates through the discursive context back as far as 1681, where we hear of a tutor taking his pupils on a 'walk to *Heddington*, or *Shot-over hill*';[100] it figures in the idealized and unshadowed portrait of under-graduate life we find in the *Epistle to a College-Friend, Written in the Country Some Years After the AUTHOR had left the University* (1775); Knox included such activities in his regime for tutors and their charges; 'a private tutor of character must be engaged. A compensation must be

---

[99] Berkenhout, *Volume of Letters*, ii. 34; cf. Berkenhout's contrasting account of professors at foreign universities, where Smith's ideas were put into practice: 'They are paid by their auditors, who are under no obligation to attend them; consequently their emoluments depend on their reputation.' Wendeborn, *View of England*, ii. 141–2. Knox, *Liberal Education*, 328.

[100] [Anon.], *Dialogue at Oxford*, 13.

made him sufficient to induce him to inspect his pupil not only in the
hours of study, but also of amusement; and I would give particular
directions, that the pupil should never take a walk or a ride, but in the
company of the private tutor . . .'.[101] And in 1795 the ironic pamphlet
*A Few General Directions for the Conduct of Young Gentlemen in the
University of Oxford* included this amongst the rites of passage that the
freshman had to endure: 'After being indulg'd by your destin'd Tutor
with an entertaining walk to the top of Headington Hill, or through
St. John's Garden, you are now Sir, to all intents and purposes a
Gownsman.'[102] Similarly, although there is no reason to doubt that
Gibbon actually did read 'two or three comedies of Terence' ('C':8)
with Waldegrave, it is equally the case that the anonymous *Advice to a
Young Student* of 1755 had stipulated Terence as the book on which new
undergraduates should cut their teeth.[103] Once this passage is returned
to its context in this way, it reinforces what Gibbon hints at when he
calls Waldegrave 'one of the best of the Tribe' ('B':8); namely, that his
experience of Oxford conformed to the best that even the university's
defenders and apologists would claim. In 'B', the deficiencies
of Gibbon's education at Magdalen are then enforced through the
dramatized encounter with Waldegrave:

During the first weeks | I regularly attended these lessons in my tutor's room,
but as they were equally devoid of profit and pleasure I was once tempted to
make the experiment of a formal apology. The apology was accepted with a
smile: I repeated the offence with less ceremony; the excuse was accepted with
the same indulgence: the slightest motive of laziness or indisposition, the most
trifling avocation at home or abroad was a sufficient obstacle; my visits became
rare and occasional, nor did my tutor appear conscious of my absence or
neglect.[104]

This almost becomes an allegory: 'The corruption of innocent willingness'. In 'C' the detail is cut back hard, but the essence of the serious
charge of neglect is preserved. In 'D' Waldegrave is perhaps made to
seem a shade less blameworthy by the change in wording to 'at full
liberty to attend or forget' ('D':8).

But the most striking and consequential change in 'D' is the reorganization of the material in this part of the narrative, namely the
placing of sections 8 and 9 after sections 10 to 12. This is the sole

[101] Knox, *Liberal Education*, 327.

[102] [Anon.], *A Few General Directions*, 4–5.

[103] [Anon.], *Advice to a Young Student*, 22 (allegedly the work of Waterland). Terence is
recommended for January and February of the first year.

[104] 'B':8.

instance of reorganization to be found in this family of three manuscripts, and as such it has a particular claim on our attention, as likely to be the result of unusually careful thought on Gibbon's part, and therefore at least potentially of unusual utility in suggesting his intentions when he set about composing draft 'D'.

The suppression in 'D' of section 7, which as a general account of the tutorial system had served in 'B' and 'C' to introduce Gibbon's experiences with his particular tutor, means that this rearrangement of material in 'D' could be accomplished without the jerkiness which would have resulted from the topic of Oxford's tutors being first raised, then dropped, then raised again. However, the deeper significance of this reordering comes into focus only when we note that the subject of sections 10 to 12 is the sensuality in which Oxford's senior members were supposed to indulge themselves. The decision to place in draft 'D' his account of the pleasurable sloth of the fellows of Magdalen before the failures of its tutors means that, not only does the Rabelaisian aspect of the university take literal precedence over the pedagogic issues (which were, at the time of composition, being urged with new insistence, as we have seen) but that we tend to see those educational failures as a consequence of that self-indulgence, rather than the other way around. 'B' and 'C' imply an analysis of the university's failings in which the radical problem is pedagogic, and the self-indulgence a secondary sign of that. In 'D', it is the self-indulgence which is primary, and through which the reader then approaches the educational neglect from which Gibbon suffered. Furthermore, the rearrangement in 'D' also unfolds implications backwards to our reading of section 6, namely Adam Smith's exposure of the indolence of Oxford's professors. In 'D', it seems that the professors have given up lecturing out of sensuality rather than mere indifference to the welfare of their charges. Taken together, these changes underline the movement in 'D' away from pure educational critique, and towards the partial reinstatement of an earlier, more festively satirical image of the university. That image had, of course, always embraced an element of complaint about how Oxford set about discharging its educational function. But at the same time it held back from the full, utilitarian implications of that complaint in its willingness also to recognize that what the pure educationalist would condemn outright as the university's old abuses and corruptions might, in a broader and less monocular perspective, be seen to perform comic and positive roles. This more relaxed and tolerant standpoint was therefore open to the thought that those who had experienced Oxford's educational shortcomings could in some way have benefited from them, and were in consequence not mere victims of an unreformed and scandalous institution.

If we turn now to sections 10 and 11, and bearing in mind always the effect of the reordering of material in draft 'D', it is clear that as the process of revision and composition moves forwards the language of monkishness, which is common to all three drafts, becomes progressively less a language connoting educational neglect. Where 'B' is explicit in citing the intellectual nullity of the fellowship and its blighting effect on the young—

the example of the ^old Monks (I mean the fellows)^ ~~senior members of the society~~ was not likely to incite the emulation and diligence of ~~Youth their~~ the novices and undergraduates. The forty principal members of our opulent foundation who had been ~~were~~ amply endowed with the means of study and subsistence, were content to slumber in the supine enjoyment of these benefits; they had absolved themselves from the labour of reading, ~~of~~ or thinking, or writing, and the first shoots of learning or genius rotted on the ground without producing any fruits either for the owners or the public.

—'C' mollifies the tone of the passage by suppressing the notion of public inutility, and by presenting the influence of the idle fellows as a neutral absence of encouragement, rather than an established practice of neglect which leads to the wasteful rotting of what might have been of use and value: 'Instead of animating the under-graduates by the example of diligence, they enjoyed in tranquil indolence the benefactions of the founder, and their slumbers were seldom disturbed by the labour of writing, of reading or thinking.' But that slight movement of withdrawal from the vehemence of 'B' is greatly amplified in 'D', where the significance of the fellows being in some sense monks is left inexplicit. Whereas in 'B' and 'C' it is accompanied by Whiggish, secular, overtones, in 'D' the pruning of the detail which might justify the slur means that it could be a simple allusion to the pre-Reformation origins of Oxford. Without actually exonerating the fellows of Magdalen from the charges levelled at them in 'B' and 'C', this nevertheless suffers the door of interpretation to stand more open to the possibility of innocence—a possibility reinforced by 'D's' moderation of 'B's' and 'C's' allegations of Jacobitism into the more unexceptionable phrase, 'Tory politics'.

Section 12 brings together the two topics (which we have already considered in a cursory fashion) of the special status of the Gentlemen Commoners and the value of Oxford's system of examinations. In 'B', and perhaps also (although to a lesser extent) in 'C', Gibbon's dissatisfaction with the exercises and disputations of the Schools derives from the utilitarian consideration that they do not serve their proper function of stirring up by means of 'rewards and censures' the academic energies of the students. In a similar spirit of impatience Knox had earlier complained of 'the relaxation of discipline, and the useless and frivolous exercises required for the attainment of academical honours'.[105] In 'D', however, the expression has a curious effect of diminishing clarity: 'no model or motive or example of study was proposed to the under-graduates: and the silk gown, the velvet cap, was a badge of protection against the formal exercises of the common hall.' This might seem to be unequivocally censorious. But it will in fact be so only if we have assumed beforehand that the sole, or even the prime, business of a university is academic instruction. That this was a strengthening assumption in the later eighteenth century, but that it had not as yet driven out entirely the earlier, broader conception of the purpose of a university and the methods by which it pursued that purpose, is made clear by a passage of exceptional clarity and interest from James Williamson's 1774 defence of the current practice of sub-scription at matriculation:

Such as have leisure and opportunity to examine the statutes of the University, will be enabled to form a proper notion of its importance to the nation, and must at the same time be convinced that all the objections raised against it have no other foundation, than a total ignorance of its intention and use; for the pre-vailing opinion is, that an University should consist only of professed teachers; and as strangers observe that very few are employed in such a manner as to answer their idea of the end of the institution, the obvious clamour is, that the supernumeraries are entirely useless, and that the money arising from the fellowships &c. should be applied to some national purpose. This no doubt is the idea which a superficial observer would be apt to form, and his regulations are quite consistent with this idea. But a more particular attention to this subject will convince us, that we form a very inadequate notion of the University, if we consider it in the diminutive light of a School: it ought rather to be considered as a Republic constituted for the destruction of ignorance and error; whether they appear in the shape of folly and absurdity, or in the more dangerous form of new discoveries and self-conceit; a republic governed by its own laws, and under the protection of a great state, which in return for this protection receives supplies of learned and well-principled subjects; . . .[106]

While Williamson does not renounce the notion of the public utility of

[105] Knox, *Liberal Education*, 320–1.
[106] Williamson, *Opinions Concerning the University of Oxford and Subscription to the Thirty-Nine Articles*, 2–3.

the university (as his idea of 'a republic governed by its own laws, and under the protection of a great state, which in return for this protection receives supplies of learned and well-principled subjects' makes explicit), he embraces it in such a way that the possibility of any mechanism being devised to measure the performance of Oxford in achieving its objectives looks like a dangerous shallowness. In Williamson's view, Oxford will discharge its public duties best if it is left to its own devices and considered almost in the light of an autotelic body. That certainly is the light which 'D' seems increasingly to throw over Oxford, a light intensified by the act of rearrangement which places sections 8 and 9 after section 12.

   Gibbon's account of Oxford, prior to the narrative of his apostasy, is concluded in sections 13 and 14. Common to section 13 in all three of drafts 'B' to 'D' is the topic of Gibbon's 'excursions' to London and Bath. Such elopements formed a vivid part of the public image of particularly the Oxford undergraduate, as Wendeborn would comment in 1791: 'They [undergraduates] are particularly fond of taking trips to London, where they indulge themselves liberally in the pleasures of the metropolis. A short play, called the *Oxonian in Town*, which is not unfrequently acted on the London theatres, represents their manner of living in lively colours, but it is said, that they are not yet sufficiently strong.'[107] The allusion is to Colman's comedy, *The Oxonian in Town*, premiered at Covent Garden on 7 November 1767 and published in 1769. It was a play to which Gibbon would himself allude in draft 'F'.[108] In it one Oxford undergraduate saves another from falling into the snares which have been spread for him in the very locality where the play was staged. Considered in isolation, the circumstance of these excursions is ambivalent: it might figure on a charge-list detailing the university's culpable neglect of its students' academic welfare; on the other hand, as the happy outcome of Colman's play makes clear, it might reinforce that celebratory and festive image of the university, in which such excesses could ultimately be seen in a positive light. In 'D', where Gibbon's acknowledgement of his expeditions to London and Bath is presented in a bare and unsupported manner, that ambivalence is not closed down. In 'B' and 'C', however, it is accompanied by a very

---

[107] Wendeborn, *View of England*, ii. 160. The prevalence of the abuse is attested by the following stipulation in the regime of an ideal university: 'Any Undergraduate absenting himself from his College Duty on Pretence of Illness, who shall be seen out of the Walls of his College, or, at any Time, be absent when visited by those in Authority, shall be expelled, *ipso facto*' (*Remarks on the Enormous Expence*, 28–9).

[108] 'F':13 n. 21.

interesting passage, abbreviated in 'D', which reaches out into the context in a telling manner: 'Yet I eloped from Oxford, I returned; I again eloped in a few days; as if I had been an independent stranger in an hired lodging, without once hearing the voice of admonition or once feeling the hand of controul.'[109] This is a cardinal element in 'B' and 'C', because Oxford and Cambridge's defenders had cited the arrangements made for the lodging of students at these universities as one of the clearest signs of the seriousness with which they took their pastoral responsibilities. When students were 'restrained within their own college walls, and immediately under the eye of the governours and tutors', then the scope for misbehaviour and waste of time was substantially eliminated.[110] Gibbon's inclusion in 'B' and 'C' of his own rather different experience of college discipline is another occasion on which he depicts Oxford being untrue to the terms in which it had been defended. In 'D', however, the failing educational institution of 'B' and 'C' is replaced by one which is, in a curious way, simply *un*-educational; and this muting of reproach is accompanied (as it was also in section 5) by changes of phrasing which hint at a greater willingness on Gibbon's part to bear some responsibility himself. In particular, the change from 'B's' 'idle and dangerous follies', to 'C's' 'costly and dangerous follies', to 'D's' 'my foolish frequent excursions', in its movement from noun to adjective, presents them less as individual episodes and more as the expressions of a disposition to foolishness in Gibbon himself. It is a hint amplified by the deletion in 'D' of the phrase which Gibbon had used in both 'B' and 'C' to indicate that he was someone towards whom an unusual degree of attention could and should have been directed: 'my tender years [in 'C', 'childish years'] might have justified a more than ordinary restraint.'

With section 14 the question of reform arises directly. Most of Oxford's critics were persuaded that the university, through either infirmity of purpose or (more probably) guile, was incapable of reforming itself:

The University then must be reformed. But it cannot reform itself. The assistance then of the legislative is *necessary* to its reformation.

Much rust has been contracted in them by time, many evils deeply rooted, which cannot be eradicated but by the legislative arm; . . .

You remember Æsop's fable of the mice and the cat. Who will hang the bell?

---

[109] 'B':13. The passage is virtually identical in 'C', with the exception of the added final sentence, which I discuss above.

[110] [Anon.], *Observations on the Present State of the English Universities*, 31–2.

A first Reformer is sure to create many enemies. It is very difficult to stem and divert into another channel, a torrent of prejudice that has been so many years accumulating, without being carried down with the stream. But such a reformation requires a power which the Universities themselves do not possess. It must be the act of the Legislature; . . .[111]

As we shall see, in draft 'F' Gibbon explicitly commits himself to this position. In 'B' and 'C', however, it is nevertheless latently present. The greater detail in 'B' concerning the 'vices' which are 'inherent' to Oxford enforce the point that the university cannot change without ceasing to be itself, while in 'C' the important substitution of 'introduced' (for 'has taken place') suggests that the impulse to reform has arisen outside the university. In 'D', however, the reversion to 'has taken place', when not followed by 'B's' detail about the ingrained viciousness of Oxford, takes no stance on the question of whether or not Oxford can reform itself, and contributes to the more lenient picture of the university painted in that draft.[112]

We now move on to Gibbon's account of his conversion to Rome. Given that the general direction of revision in drafts 'B', 'C', and 'D' has been established in some detail in the earlier sections, and given also that it seems remarkably consistent and coherent, we may give a more succinct account of the final eleven sections (15 to 25). We shall therefore focus on two issues. In the first place, we shall consider Gibbon's handling of the question of his subscription to the Thirty-Nine Articles, and how that handling varies over the three drafts. Secondly, we shall consider the account he gives of what stimulated his conversion to Catholicism.

As we have seen from our review of the contextual writing on Oxford, subscription was a central issue in the first phase (fuelled presumably by the broader theological dispute on the question of clerical relief from subscription between Samuel Clarke and Daniel Waterland).[113] However, the issue revived strongly in the 1760s and

---

[111] *Series of Papers*, 16; Knox, *Liberal Education*, 323; Berkenhout, *Volume of Letters*, 32; cf. p. 35: 'the fortuitous events necessary to bring forward so consequential a revolution, depend on so singular a coalition of circumstances, that many ages may yet roll on, before our Universities are perfectly reformed.'

[112] It is worth noting that, in all the revisions he made on the four occasions on which he revised the text of the first volume of *The Decline and Fall*, Gibbon never reinstated an old reading (*DF* i. 1084–105). Consequently a revision such as this runs strongly counter to his established habits of recension. It therefore merits particular attention.

[113] Clarke, *The Scripture-Doctrine of the Trinity* (1712); Waterland, *The Case of Arian-Subscription Consider'd* (Cambridge, 1721) and *A Critical History of the Athanasian Creed, representing the opinions of antients and moderns concerning it* (Cambridge, 1724). See Young, *Religion and*

1770s.[114] On the side of the anti-subscriptionists we find John Jebb (who, as we have seen, was shortly to busy himself as a fellow of Peterhouse with educational reform at Cambridge), Francis Blackburne (whom Gibbon would cite in his support in draft 'F'),[115] and Edmund Law. Opposing them, there was a platoon of orthodox clergyman, such as Josiah Tucker and Gibbon's later adversary Thomas Randolph, whose voices were tuned by the archbishop of Canterbury, Thomas Secker.

In the context of Gibbon's 'Memoirs', three observations on this controversy are of particular importance. First, Gibbon was himself a member of the Commons when the 'Feathers Tavern' petition of the anti-subscriptionists that clergymen, lawyers, and physicians might be relieved from the obligation to subscribe was debated on 6 February 1772. Two days later, he wrote to Sheffield and reported on what had transpired:

> Though it is very late, and the bell tells me that I have not above ten minutes left, I employ them with pleasure in congratulating you on the late Victory of our Dear Mamma the Church of England. She had last Thursday 71 rebellious sons who pretended to set aside her will on account of insanity: but 217 Worthy Champions headed by Lord North, *Burke*, Hans Stanley, Charles Fox, Godfrey Clarke &c, though they allowed the thirty nine Clauses of her Testament were absurd and unreasonable supported the validity of it with infinite humour.[116]

Secondly, the anti-subscriptionist stance was surrounded with penumbral political connotations of a radical Whig stripe. Thirdly, the figure of Chillingworth (whom of course Gibbon introduces for purposes of comparison into this episode of the 'Memoirs') was summoned into the lists by anti-subscriptionists such as Blackburne.[117] Furthermore, it was the case that in the popular mind, and given the public character he had acquired as a result of the controversy surrounding the first volume

---

Enlightenment, esp. ch. 1, 'Enlightened Ecclesiastics: The Shaping of an Antidogmatic Tradition', 19–44.

[114] See ibid. ch. 2, 45–80.

[115] 'F':18 n. 22.

[116] L i. 305. The conceit of the will which Gibbon employs here perhaps derives from Swift's *Tale of a Tub*. Note his admiring comments on the writers of the reign of Anne, to whom on his return from Lausanne in 1758 he was directed by the freethinker David Mallet, and who 'breathe the spirit of reason and liberty': 'By the judicious advice of Mr. Mallet, I was directed to the writings of Swift and Addison: wit and simplicity are their common attributes; but the style of Swift is supported by manly original vigour; that of Addison is adorned by the female graces of elegance and mildness; and the contrast of too coarse or too thin a texture is visible even in the defects of these celebrated authors' (*A* 166).

[117] Young, *Religion and Enlightenment*, 49–51.

of *The Decline and Fall*, Gibbon was perceived as the natural ally and likely beneficiary of anti-subscriptionist success, as this pseudonymous verse attack on Edmund Law by 'Pasquin' reveals:

> But chief, O L–w, to thee be honours paid!
> Well sits the mitre on thy hoary head:
> Wonder of Bishops! still pursue thy plan,
> Man to brute . . . and God degrade to man.
> How can I count the labours of thy life?
> With Creeds and Articles at constant strife;
> With Blackburne leagued, in many a motley page,
> Immortal war with Mother Church to wage;
> Each fence that guards her altar to pull down,
> And take Geneva's cloak, to Prelate's gown.
> Nor ere thy zeal for comprehension ends,
> Jews, Deists, Musselmen, thy love befriends,
> Blends Christ and Belial at one sacred table—
> Delightful mass of an united Babel!
> O! envied change! when, freed from faith's strict rules,
> Law's latitude of doctrine guides my schools!
> When, benefic'd by Pitt's all-powerful hand,
> Socinian preachers swarm throughout the land!
> Paul's mysteries, when each wrangler disbelieves,
> And Hume's and Gibbonses may wear lawn sleeves![118]

On the basis of this material, two assumptions seem safe. Firstly, as a man involved in public life at the time of the Feathers Tavern petition, Gibbon had at the very least the opportunity to become well acquainted with the issues underlying and surrounding the subscription controversy, and the language and *topoi* in which the various protagonists expressed their attitudes towards those issues. Secondly, this was a controversy with which in the public mind he might be connected, not in his capacity as a legislator, but as one whose religious character (as inferred from *The Decline and Fall*) would incline him towards the anti-subscriptionists.

It is therefore striking that in 'D' the matter of Gibbon's subscription to the Thirty-Nine Articles is passed over in a generalization about Oxford's even-handed neglect of both her pupils' religion and literary studies.[119] It is a silence which unfolds its implications in two directions: it deletes from 'D' an item which figured frequently in indictments of

---

[118] 'Pasquin', 'Cambridge Triumphant', in J. Almon (ed.), *An Asylum for Fugitive Pieces*, iii. 136–8; quoted in Young, *Religion and Enlightenment*, 55.

[119] Gibbon did in fact subscribe the articles. But the silence about subscription in 'D' is no access of honesty, since the assertion that he did not subscribe will return in 'F'.

the university, and which painted Gibbon in Whiggish colours. In addition, in 'D' Gibbon's conversion to Catholicism emerges as more purely accidental than in 'B' and 'C', because the precise nature of Oxford's neglect of her pupils' religion is left vague. The consequence of this is clear if we examine the rewriting of section 17. Gibbon is obviously pleased with the image of himself 'groping' his way to religion by the 'light [in 'C' and 'D', the 'dim' light] of my Catechism', since he retains this image and these words in all three drafts. But in 'B' and 'C', because the neglect of the university and college authorities is initially emphasized, the insufficiency of light seems largely a consequence of their failure to discharge their responsibilities. In 'D', however, the dimness is more intrinsic to Gibbon, and there is accordingly a more even distribution of responsibility between the student and the university for the resulting unsatisfactory state of affairs.

We turn now to the stimulus which impelled Gibbon towards Catholicism. I will return to this in relation to draft 'F', with its startling substitution of Conyers Middleton for 'some Popish treatises of Controversy' in the role of midwife to Gibbon's conversion; a dramatic revision which is full of significance for what Gibbon is trying to do in draft 'F'. For the time being, however, I wish to pause on two aspects of this portion of Gibbon's narrative: the use made of Chillingworth, and the exculpation of the university from the 'false supposition' that Jesuits were actively proselytizing amongst the student body. Chillingworth had been brought forward by Shaftesbury as a prophylactic against Romish inclinations: 'CHILLINGWORTH *against Popery* is sufficient Reading for you, and will teach you the best Manner of that Polemick Divinity.'[120] It was a prescription endorsed by Dr Waldegrave, Gibbon's first tutor, who, when he heard of Gibbon's reconversion to the Church of England and return from Lausanne, had written to him explaining how he dealt with confessional restiveness:

I have read nothing for some time (and I keep on reading still) that has given me so much pleasure as your letter, which I received by the last post. I rejoice at your return to your country, to your father, and to the good principles of truth and reason. Had I in the least suspected your design of leaving us, I should immediately have put you upon reading Mr. Chillingworth's Religion of Protestants; any one page of which is worth a library of Swiss divinity.[121]

There is therefore some piquancy in Gibbon's citing as a precedent for

---

[120] Shaftesbury, *Several Letters*, 25.

[121] 7 Dec. 1758; *MW 1796* i. 417. The letter from Gibbon to which Waldegrave is replying has not survived. The warmth and good nature so evident in this letter should be kept in mind when we consider Gibbon's account of his first tutor.

his own religious misadventures this figure who, in the opinion of some, ought to have prevented them; once again, the insinuation is launched that Oxford's apologists know not of what they speak. The textual dynamics, however, present at first glance a confusing picture. In 'B', the probable heterodoxy in Chillingworth's private faith is brought out explicitly: 'It was with deep reluctance that Chillingworth subscribed the thirty nine articles several parts of which he disbelieved: his acute understanding was repeatedly vanquished by itself, and his last opinions were most probably those of an Arian or Socinian.'[122] There is no allusion to Chillingworth at all in 'C', and in 'D' this parsing of Chillingworth's religious inclinations is silently gathered up into his 'acute understanding'. This looks rather like a progressive, if uneven, attenuation of criticism, and slightly disturbs what we have hitherto suggested was the relationship between 'B' and 'C'. However, this set of variants needs to be viewed in the light of the charge levelled at Oxford at the very moment Gibbon was composing his 'Memoirs', that it was a place on which the energies of the Reformation had left only slight and superficial traces. The university was therefore still vestigially Catholic, and 'monkish' in a more precise sense than the wielders of that term of abuse frequently intended: 'It is indeed very extraordinary that, in discarding the absurdities of the Romish creed and religious ceremonies, we should have retained so much of the ancient mode of education, both in our schools and universities.'[123] Therefore, when Gibbon denied that Jesuits had actively solicited his conversion, what looks on the surface to be a word said in defence of Oxford implicitly suggests something rather more damaging, namely that Gibbon had instead simply succumbed to the Romish atmosphere of the place. The removal of that detail from 'D' is therefore of a piece with that manuscript's muting and complication of criticism directed at the university.

At this point we can review the apparent tendency of revision embodied in manuscripts 'B', 'C', and 'D'. In terms of tone, this can be described as a movement away from stridency, and towards a more ambiguous colouring, in which it is less clear that Gibbon was a pure victim of a corrupt institution. Considered in terms of movement within the discursive context, Gibbon's revisions move back in time, away from the sharply educational concerns prevalent at the time he was composing the 'Memoirs', and towards the more equivocal qualities visible in the writing about Oxford published earlier, at about the time of his actual residence at the university, and beforehand.

---

[122] 'B':22.

[123] Berkenhout, *Volume of Letters*, 14.

It was at exactly this point, with draft 'D' completed and draft 'E' in progress,[124] that Gibbon read, with much avidity, Burke's *Reflections*. There he would have found a passage of obvious relevance to the portion of his 'Memoirs' dealing with his period of residence at Oxford. As part of his defence of the institutions of England's *ancien régime*, and as an aspect of what he wished to persuade his reader was a characteristically English cherishing of both the religious and the traditional, Burke entered the lists as a champion of the customary forms of English education:

Our education is so formed as to confirm and fix this impression. Our education is in a manner wholly in the hands of ecclesiastics, and in all stages from infancy to manhood. Even when our youth, leaving schools and universities, enter that most important period of life which begins to link experience and study together, and when with that view they visit other countries, instead of old domestics whom we have seen as governors to principal men from other parts, three-fourths of those who go abroad with our young nobility and gentlemen are ecclesiastics; not as austere masters, nor as mere followers; but as friends and companions of a graver character, and not seldom persons as well born as themselves. With them, as relations, they most commonly keep up a close connexion through life. By this connexion we conceive that we attach our gentlemen to the church; and we liberalize the church by an intercourse with the leading characters of the country.

So tenacious are we of the old ecclesiastical modes and fashions of institution, that very little alteration has been made in them since the fourteenth or fifteenth century; adhering in this particular, as in all things else, to our old settled maxim, never entirely nor at once to depart from antiquity. We found these old institutions, on the whole, favourable to morality and discipline; and we thought they were susceptible of amendment, without altering the ground. We thought that they were capable of receiving and meliorating, and above all of preserving the accessions of science and literature, as the order of Providence should successively produce them. And after all, with this Gothic and monkish education (for such it is in the ground-work) we may put in our claim to as ample and early a share in all the improvements in science, in arts, and in literature, which have illuminated and adorned the modern world, as any other nation in Europe; we think one main cause of this improvement was our not despising the patrimony of knowledge with was left us by our forefathers.[125]

It will be immediately clear how vigorously this cuts across the accounts

---

[124] See Appendix 2, where the composition of the drafts is correlated with Gibbon's responses to both events in France and Burke's *Reflections*.

[125] Burke, *Reflections*, 149–50. There is an obvious congruence between this passage and Burke's parallel defence of French monastic instititutions against what he portrays as the rapacity of the revolutionaries (*Reflections*, 194–212).

of Oxford which Gibbon had framed in drafts 'B', 'C', and 'D'. Burke's cool acknowledgement and neutralizing of the monkishness of England's educational provision might be expected to have exerted a powerful effect on Gibbon because of the way it arose within a contexture of political argument with which Gibbon profoundly sympathized. If we turn now to draft 'E', we shall see that it diverges radically from the three preceding drafts, in a manner which it is hard not to construe as the consequence of the irruption of Burke's counter-revolutionary tract into Gibbon's still-fluid thoughts about the shape and significance of his life.

As we have noticed, the sequence of manuscripts from 'B' to 'D' reveals a process of, on one level, steady précis, and, on another, of increasing tonal complication as the bitterly precise criticism of Oxford which is so typical of 'B' is gradually muted into the more equivocal expressions which characterize 'D'. However, that double process of compression and lenification is so amplified in 'E' that it cannot sensibly be seen as an extension of the same tendency at work in 'B', 'C', and 'D'. The account in 'E' is so short that it can conveniently be quoted in full:

At an unripe age I was matriculated, as a Gentleman Commoner at Magdalen College in the University of Oxford, where I lost fourteen valuable months of my youth. The reader will ascribe this loss to my own incapacity, or to the vices of that ancient institution.[9]

And the footnote reads:

[9] The revenues, ~~and~~ monopoly, and idleness of these Ecclesiastical corporations are justly censured by Dr Adam Smith (Riches of Nations vol. ii p 340–374), who affirms that most of the professors of Oxford have given up even the pretence of public teaching.

The first, and most eye-catching, revision occurs in the opening words: 'At an unripe age . . .'. If we examine how this passage has been rewritten by Gibbon, we see that 'B's' 'my tender years, my short residence and my imperfect præparation' is rearranged into 'C's' 'my tender age, insufficient preparation, and short residence', before being more substantially rephrased in 'D's' 'my tender age, unripe studies, and hasty removal'. Although one can sense in this progression a gradually increasing willingness on Gibbon's part to shoulder some responsibility for what happened to him at Oxford, the constant element—the qualification of his age with the adjective 'tender'—insists on the countervailing consideration, that his youth demanded and deserved particular protection. It is therefore particularly important that, in 'E', Gibbon should have dropped 'tender', and preferred the word 'unripe', a word which enters this passage with draft 'D', where it is applied to Gibbon's studies. When transferred to Gibbon's age, however, it tacitly implies that the unsatisfactory outcome of Gibbon's period of residence at Magdalen was attributable, either wholly or in part, to his being placed there too early. In consequence, when the reader is asked to adjudicate on the portions of blame to be ascribed to the student and the university, this seems to be a much more genuine dilemma than is the case in any of the earlier drafts. Furthermore, when Oxford is described as 'that ancient institution' (a phrase which in the mid-1780s might confidently be understood as referring to an institution which was shot through with vices requiring urgent reform, but which in the early 1790s, and following on from Burke's redescription of the ancient and the monkish as virtuous rather than vicious, would carry different connotations) the reader acquainted with Burke's *Reflections* must be disposed to discount those 'vices' as at least potentially salutary. The footnote containing Smith's censure of Oxford is, of course, a powerful contrary element; but perhaps the most significant circumstance here is the decision to place this material in a footnote. Having completed *The Decline and Fall*, Gibbon was more aware than most authors of the potential for offence possessed by footnotes; nevertheless, such material is to some degree relegated. Gibbon cannot altogether renounce the idea that Oxford was culpable. At the same time, he now chooses not to draw attention to it in quite the way he was keen to do before.

Here we are at the very edges of what Gibbon felt was negotiable in the account of his time at Oxford. What was beyond extenuation has been passed over in silence; what could not be passed over in silence has been, as far as was possible, de-emphasized. The account which emerges from this strategy is, as a result, under an immense tension: a tension arising from the pressure behind the wall of containment, which Gibbon's prose has necessarily become in draft 'E', of all that has not been said. That pressure leaves its mark on his writing in this section through the bifurcation between narrative and note. In *The Decline and Fall* Gibbon had practised and refined the art of exploiting the different levels and registers of narrative and note in pursuance of a single strategy.[126] In this draft of his 'Memoirs', by contrast, the note is not the

---

[126] For examples of this, consider his handling of the footnotes in the various revisions to chapters fifteen and sixteen, discussed above in Chapter 1.

obedient auxiliary of the narrative, but instead provides an outlet for the emotions and judgements which now cannot be tolerated within the more strictly policed political economy of the main body of the draft. It should be clear, then, that draft 'E' is different from the earlier drafts in nature, as well as in political orientation. The latitude of viewpoint which (as we have seen in the case of the different accounts of Oxford in drafts 'B', 'C', and 'D') was earlier manifested in the variations and evolutions *between* the different drafts, has now become a tension *within* a single draft. As we turn now to draft 'F', we will see that it too is marked by self-division, and that it can be seen as what we might call the mirror-image of 'E'. What before was subordinated is now elevated; what before received priority is now appended or in other ways subdued. Drafts 'E' and 'F' are therefore at once parallel and opposed: parallel in form, opposed in tendency. Taken together, they suggest why Gibbon was in the end unable to write his autobiography in a form which satisfied him. Beyond that, they also throw light on the much broader issue of how the French Revolution disrupted the self-identification of those who lived through it.

V

From the mere extent of Appendix 6 it will be immediately clear that draft 'F' is by some way the longest account Gibbon composed of his period of residence at Oxford. Furthermore, the analysis of that draft into sections reveals that for this draft Gibbon rearranged the topics of the earlier drafts;[127] it also demonstrates that he now included some entirely fresh material.[128] Nevertheless, it is also substantially clear that for draft 'F' Gibbon returned to draft 'B', and used that as his template, not only for the structure of individual sections, but more importantly for one element which shapes the tone of draft 'F'. For after the almost complete Burkean suppression of 'E', and the gradually more pronounced subsuming of educational critique within the more equivocal phrasing of 'C' and 'D', we find in 'F' that Gibbon restates the educational indictment of Oxford with fresh detail and greater sharpness.

---

[127] The degree of rearrangement is indicated by the degree of disruption of sequential numbering in the sections of 'F' (in 'B', which for the purposes of this analysis was taken as the base text, the sections are naturally in numerical order).

[128] The sections marked with the suffix '*a*' contain new material (5*a*, 6*a*, 19*a*); of course, this does not reflect the full extent of the additions, since sections 26–30 are entirely new in this draft, and furthermore sections which are recognizably developments of sections in earlier drafts, and hence are given the same number in the Appendix, may nevertheless be substantially enlarged; compare, for instance, 'F':2 with 'B':2.

Two examples will suggest how this was done. In the first place, we might look at one of the rearrangements of material Gibbon made for this draft. By moving sections 10, 11, and 12 to a much earlier position in the overall narrative, in 'F' Gibbon makes section 13 follow directly on from section 9. In other words, the young Gibbon's neglect of his studies and his adventures to London and Bath are presented immediately after his discussion of the conduct of his second tutor, Dr Winchester. In consequence the sequence of topics carries the strong implication that the folly of the student was given opportunity only as a result of the indolence of the tutor. Secondly, we might consider how Gibbon handles the question of his subscription to the articles in draft 'F' (sections 16–18). In the first place, we note the introduction in section 18 of the sharp judgement that Oxford was guilty of 'incredible neglect' which gave rise to 'the worst mischiefs'. This, as has already been suggested, is the keynote of draft 'F', and it suggests Gibbon's open alignment of himself in this draft with those who wanted Oxford to be reformed so as better to discharge its educational mission. However, it needs to be read alongside Gibbon's clarifying of some of the wording of draft 'B', to which he returned. In 'B' Gibbon had said that Oxford required the articles to be subscribed by her students 'either with or without reading them'.[129] That phrase, and with it the damaging implication of the university's indifference to whether or not the substance of the articles was understood and believed by those who subscribed, disappeared from drafts 'C', 'D', and of course 'E' (where the whole topic of subscription is ignored). In 'F', however, the sentiment behind the phrase returns in a more openly heterodox form, and with a new crispness of expression: 'According to the statutes of the University, every student, before he is matriculated, must subscribe his assent to the thirty nine articles of the Church of England, which are signed by more than read, and read by more than believe them.'[130] What had been an insinuation of the university's merely formal attitude towards subscription is now deepened into a suggestion of the religious scepticism of the majority who silently conformed. This, when taken together with the parenthetic comment about Aunt Kitty's puzzlement at Gibbon's 'objections to the mysteries which she strove to believe', and the indication that Blackburne's *Confessional* would be placed under contribution in support of Gibbon's opinions in this section,[131] suggests that, whatever Gibbon's opinions about the Feathers Tavern petition may have been when the matter was debated in his presence in the

---

[129] 'B':16.   [130] 'F':16.   [131] 'F':18 and n. 22.

Commons, he now wished to present himself as someone whose
religious opinions would have led him to enlist on the more radical side
of that question.[132]

It would, however, be a mistake to see draft 'F' as nothing more than
an enlarged and sharpened version of the trenchantly critical draft 'B'.
For draft 'F', just as much as draft 'E', was clearly written in the knowledge of how and in what terms Burke had analysed the French
Revolution, although (as we shall see) that knowledge shaped 'F' very
differently from the way it had shaped 'E'. In 'E', Gibbon had capitu-
lated to Burke's analysis. The result was a version of his life which,
although completed (it is, paradoxically enough, the only completed
version amongst the six drafts of the 'Memoirs'), nevertheless is deeply
marked by deliberate acts of forgetting and a tendentious policy of
redescription, as comparison with the earlier drafts makes evident. In
order to reach towards an understanding of the emotional and psychological conditions which attended the composition of 'F', we must
postulate first of all an awareness on Gibbon's part that 'E' was unsatisfactory in the extent of the violence it did to Gibbon's understanding of
the significance of his life, as he had experienced it. Of course, the very
existence of draft 'F' indicates that Gibbon was not content to repose on
draft 'E', but believed that another attempt had to be made to bring his
life into alignment with post-revolutionary realities and to reconcile the
square of his new Burkean allegiances with the philosophic circle of his
adult life. Draft 'F' is that attempt. But how was it to be done? Defiance
of Burke was, in the present menacing circumstances of European
politics, unthinkable. Capitulation, on the model of draft 'E', had evidently done too much violence to memory and sentiment. Was there,
however, yet some third way, in which Gibbon might at once insist
on his present alignment with Burke while nevertheless not being so
egregiously false to the man he had been? It is important to recall, at this
juncture, that Gibbon had entertained Sheffield and his family at
Lausanne in between finishing 'E' and beginning 'F'.[133] Sheffield's own
response to the Revolution, as we have explored above, brought
together uncompromising resistance to the revolutionary imperative
that all social structures should be remodelled, and a refusal to accept
Burke's diagnosis that philosophical scepticism had created the conditions in which revolution had been able to prosper. Although it seems
from their letters that Gibbon did not show Sheffield draft 'E' while
they were together in Switzerland, there is no doubt that they discussed

---

[132] See above, pp. 297–8.   [133] See above, Ch. 6.

the Revolution, and good reason to believe that they also touched on the project of the 'Memoirs'.[134] If we approach draft 'F' on the premiss that it represents Gibbon's recension of the story of his life dictated from a standpoint adjacent to Sheffield's, much of the textual innovation which we discover in 'F' becomes legible.

We should begin by registering the much greater bibliographical specificity of draft 'F'. In this draft Gibbon used many more footnotes than he had in earlier drafts, and the references they contain provide us with valuable information about his reading in the eighteenth-century debate about the universities in general and Oxford in particular.[135] As we shall see presently, these references are not unambiguous, and, in at least one instance (that of the reference to Vicesimus Knox), they have in the past been almost certainly misinterpreted. Nevertheless, the notion that this draft is more overtly engaged with its discursive context seems secure. Now, when we pick out some of the more striking proximities between new material in 'F' and contextual writings, it is striking that they are to be found most often on the positive side of the account. For instance, when Gibbon begins the narrative of his residence in Oxford by putting before us the impression it makes on a traveller—

A traveller who visits Oxford or Cambridge is surprized and edified by the apparent order and tranquillity that prevail in the seats of the English muses. In the most celebrated Universities of Holland, Germany, and Italy, the students, who swarm from different countries, are loosely dispersed in private lodgings at the houses of the burghers: they dress according to their fancy and fortune . . . Instead of being scattered in a town, the students of Oxford and Cambridge are united in Colleges: their maintenance is provided at their own expence or that of the founders; and the stated hours of the hall and the chappel represent the discipline of a regular and, as it were, a Religious community. The eyes of the traveller are attracted by the size or beauty of the public edifices; and the principal colleges appear to be so many St palaces which a liberal nation has erected and endowed for the habitation of Science.[136]

—this recalls works such as *The Spy at Oxford and Cambridge* (1744), which had praised the visual impact made by the city ('whether we look on the Uniformity of private Houses, or Magnificence of the publick

---

[134] For an account of what we can infer about what they did (and did not) discuss together, see above, Ch. 6.

[135] These footnotes, which are still in the form of elliptical and frequently inexplicit jottings, provide valuable information about how Gibbon composed his footnotes which, given that the manuscript of *The Decline and Fall* has disappeared, we can come by in few other ways.

[136] 'F':2.

Structures, it must be allow'd to be one of the finest Cities in *England*'),
while also drawing just the comparison with the different arrangements
to be found in European universities which would later be made by
Gibbon: 'That *Oxford* was a Place of publick Studies before the *Saxon*
Conquest, is past all Doubt; but then the Students lived in the Citizens
Houses, and had only Meeting-places, to hear Lectures and Disputations, as is the Custom of several foreign Universities, and without any
Distinction of Habit or Dress; . . .'[137] Or again, when Gibbon refers to
the Vinerian bequest as one of the most important of recent developments at the university—

The Vinerian professorship is of far more serious importance; the laws of his
country are the first science of an Englishman of rank and fortune, who is called
to be a Magistrate, and may hope to be a Legislator. This judicious institution
was coldly entertained by the graver Doctors, who complained, I have heard
the complaint, that it would take the young people from their books: but
Mr. Viner's benefaction is not unprofitable, since it has at least produced the
excellent commentaries of Sir William Blackstone.[138]

—he was echoing those many earlier commentators who had recognized the importance of this 'ample endowment for the study of the
common law of our country', and the value to civil society of a course
of study which 'discovers the just grounds of our obedience to civil
government, and prescribes the bounds both of civil and religious
liberty'.[139]

How should we explain the presence in 'F' of these emphases
normally encountered in the writings of Oxford's apologists? Their
presence requires comment because, as we have seen, elsewhere draft
'F' recapitulates and even intensifies the astringent criticism of Oxford
which we find in draft 'B'. It is at this point that we can see how 'F', just
as much as 'E', is a piece of writing which tries to accommodate
Gibbon's life to Burke's doctrine on the French Revolution. In 'F' the
voices of Oxford's defenders, which after 1790 are unmistakably
Burkean, are not directly attacked or discredited, but rather are folded
into a narrative which nevertheless has room for other perspectives.

---

[137] *The Spy at Oxford and Cambridge*, 37 and 38. Amhurst also compares the continental practice of students lodging privately with the English institution of colleges (*Terræ-Filius*, 66–7); it
was not, therefore, an entirely fresh comparison when Gibbon revisited it in 1791.

[138] 'F':30. Gibbon had himself studied and written an abstract of the first volume of
Blackstone as a young man in 1765: *EE* 59–87.

[139] *Observations on the Present State of the English Universities*, 28–9 and 24. Positive comments
on the Vinerian bequest can be found also in Bentham, *The Honor of the University of Oxford
defended*, 5, and Napleton, *Considerations*, 5.

This juxtaposition of what elsewhere at this time might have been vigorously antagonistic elements is part of an attempt to soften dichotomies and to rediscover a wholeness which the ideological polarization consequent upon the Revolution had destroyed. In draft 'F' Gibbon acknowledges Burke's ideals of social deference and political tradition, but takes implicit issue with the central contention in Burke's analysis of how the Revolution had arisen in France, namely that religious scepticism and philosophic rationality necessarily pose mortal threats to those ideals.[140] He is trying to recover the identity he had possessed before 1790, in which the social and political conservative had coexisted peaceably with the philosopher.

We can see this policy of ideological rapprochement most openly at work in two places in this portion of draft 'F': in what Gibbon now says of the role played by Middleton in his conversion to Catholicism, and in the paired characters of Chillingworth and Bayle, whom he places in apposition to his own religious mobility.[141]

The identification of Middleton's *Free Inquiry*[142] as the pre-eminent catalyst in his conversion to Catholicism is the most arresting discrepancy between draft 'F' and the other manuscripts, at least in the portions of them all devoted to Gibbon's time at Oxford. It seems also to have startled Sheffield, who was moved to append a note which, if it does not exactly contradict what Gibbon says, nevertheless makes it clear that Sheffield cannot endorse it: 'Mr. Gibbon never talked with me on the subject of his conversion to popery but once; and then, he imputed his change to the works of Parsons the jesuit, who lived in the reign of Elizabeth, and who, he said, had urged all the best arguments in favour of the Roman catholic religion. S.'[143] There are thus some grounds for thinking that this unprecedented involvement of Middleton in Gibbon's apostasy is a detail included to meet the emergencies of the 1790s rather than to report the realities of the 1750s. That it might play a role in Gibbon's later management of his reputation is obliquely indicated by the moment when the subsequent association of Gibbon and Middleton is alluded to: 'Many years afterwards when the name of Gibbon was become as notorious as that of Middleton, it was industriously whispered at Oxford that the historian had formerly

---

[140] For Burke's indictment of the French *philosophes* as a 'literary cabal [which] had some years ago formed something like a regular plan for the destruction of the Christian religion', see *Reflections*, 160 ff.

[141] 'F':19*a* and 'F':27–8.

[142] Conyers Middleton, *A Free Inquiry into the Miraculous Powers, which are supposed to have subsisted in the Christian Church* (1749).

[143] *MW 1796*, sect. 21.

"turned Papist": my character stood exposed to the reproach of inconstancy; and this invidious topic would have been handled without mercy by my opponents, could they have separated my cause from that of the University.'[144] This passage shows, not only that Gibbon is fully aware of how the entanglement of his name with Middleton's after 1776 by opponents such as Davis and Chelsum[145] forms part of the context within which the revelation he now makes about the consequences of his youthful reading of the *Free Inquiry* will be interpreted, but also that (as the phrase 'could they have separated my cause from that of the University' hints) Gibbon is alert to how, in the wake of the French Revolution, the question of university reform had become an aspect of those more general and prevalent conflicts over religious conformity and political stability which were then being so vigorously debated. Furthermore, it also reveals that Gibbon realized that he himself was now a convenient focus for all three issues, and that therefore in the particular circumstances of the early 1790s the narrative of his life possessed an unusual public and political significance.

In this light, Gibbon's attribution of responsibility for his Catholicism to the influence of Middleton's most notorious essay in religious scepticism has a double implication. In the first place, Gibbon is hoping to discredit the insinuations of his adversaries, that in chapters fifteen and sixteen of *The Decline and Fall* he is 'but the Echo of D[r]. Middleton',[146] by challenging his reputation as an unrepentant avatar of religious scepticism. In fact, so draft 'F' maintains, Gibbon's reading in the literature of religious heterodoxy was a youthful indiscretion. Moreover, the opportunity for that indiscretion arose not from any inclination to deism on his part, but rather out of Oxford's neglect of its students; and the consequences of it gave him little reason to feel veneration for the writer by whose 'bold criticism' he had been bewildered into Catholicism.[147] This detail of Gibbon's intellectual

---

[144] 'F':26.
[145] For a discussion of this depiction of Gibbon as a latter-day Middleton, see above, Ch. 2.
[146] CUL Add. MS 8530 fo. 15[v].
[147] 'F':19a. The quotation from the *Aeneid* I shall discuss more fully in a moment, but in this connection it is worth remarking that, as it can be applied to Gibbon's situation, it presents Gibbon as Aeneas and Middleton as his enemy, the Greeks. Nor, in the light of the divided and nuanced motivation of draft 'F', can it plausibly be argued that the allusion is 'ironic', and therefore to be reversed. Tones of disingenuousness are certainly present, but at this stage of his life Gibbon has ceased to employ irony (for want of a better word) as a means of sarcastic dismissal, and instead uses it as a way of suspending his prose between a number of more simple positions, each of which is partially true (and therefore not to be renounced) but none of which is entirely the case.

biography thus undermines one of the recurrent and, on the basis of at least Davis's *Examination*, one of the textually best-supported allegations of his enemies—namely, that the historian was a disciple of Middleton—by acknowledging a period of such influence, but depicting its outcome as unhappy and locating it well before Gibbon had even conceived of the project of *The Decline and Fall*.[148] Secondly, Gibbon invites his reader to entertain notions, both of the likely outcome of philosophical freethinking on religious matters and of how human agents respond to cultural influences, which are more complicated than those which served as the premises for Burke's indictment of the French *philosophes* as the agents of revolution. In the highly coloured

---

[148] For the avoidance of confusion, it may be helpful if I state here my beliefs about the extent, timing, and nature of Gibbon's reading of Middleton (as distinct from the tracing of implication in his writings about that reading, which is what I am concerned with in my text). In the first place, it seems to me indisputable that Middleton was strong in Gibbon's mind as he composed the first volume of *The Decline and Fall*: the echoes, borrowings, and proximities set out by Davis in his *Examination* (a work more derided than read) put this, in my opinion, beyond doubt. The question therefore arises as to when Gibbon read Middleton. The claim that there was a period of exposure and influence in the early 1750s which led to his apostasy is to be mistrusted on three counts. First, it occurs in only one of the five relevant manuscript drafts of the 'Memoirs'. Second, it is implicitly discredited by Sheffield (*MW 1796* i. 45 n. *). Third, it suits Gibbon's book, in the aftermath of the Burkean response to the French Revolution and his desire to appear as the friend to all that the Revolution menaced, to depict himself as yet another who suffered at the hands of religious freethinking. At this point we turn to the evidence of Gibbon's letters and minor publications. There are no references to Middleton in the correspondence, in the English journal, and in the Grand Tour journal. There are, however, four references in the Lausanne journal, one of which is of great interest and perhaps decisive import (*J2* 114, 167, 214, and 224). The first is a polite reference to Middleton's work on the history of printing, the second an unpartisan allusion to Middleton's difference of opinion with Warburton on the significance of the similarities between the religious culture of Roman Catholicism and paganism, and the third a note recording that he had read Middleton's *A Treatise on the Roman Senate* (1747). The fourth, however, is to be quoted in full: 'Recherches Libres sur les Miracles par le Docteur Middleton. Cet homme avoit bien de la netteté et de la penetration. Il voyoit bien jusqu'ou l'on pouvoit pousser les consequences de ses principes mais il ne lui convenoit pas de les tirer' (*J2* 224: 25 Feb. 1764). These journal entries do, of course, tend to the laconic. Nevertheless, it is remarkable that, if this book had indeed played such a decisive role in Gibbon's intellectual life ten years previously, such previous exposure should not now either receive explicit comment or influence the tone of the journal entry, which seems strikingly dispassionate—a comment on a book like any other. Moreover, it is clear that the Gibbon of 1764 has no difficulty in construing correctly the significance of Middleton's abstention from following up 'les consequences de ses principes'. If we turn now to Gibbon's other writings (excluding the *Vindication*), we find that the warmest references to 'my ingenious friend Dr Middleton' occur in works composed in the 1760s: the 'Index Expurgatorius' and the 'Hints' (*EE* 91 and 115). The balance of the evidence therefore inclines me to the following position: (a) the allegation that the conversion to Catholicism was due to a reading of Middleton is a fiction of 1791, calculated to meet the needs of the moment of its composition; (b) the period when Gibbon was demonstrably reading Middleton—probably for the first time—was the mid- to late 1760s: a period when there are good grounds for believing that he was exploring religious heterodoxy more broadly (see Womersley, 'Gibbon's Religious Characters'), and when he was also approaching composition of *The Decline and Fall*, in which the traces of Middleton's influence are manifest.

mental landscape of the *Reflections*, philosophy (at least that degraded philosophy practised by the *philosophes*) leads directly to social dissolution, and those who are exposed to it are uniformly contaminated by its toxins. However, what Gibbon says of his reading of Middleton challenges Burke's analysis at a number of points:

The progress of my conversion may tend to illustrate, at least the history of my own mind. It was not long since th Dr Middleton's free Enquiry had sounded an alarm in the Theological World; much ink and gall had been spilt in the defence of the primitive miracles; and the two dullest and most angry of their champions were crowned with Academic honours by the University of Oxford. The name of Middleton was unpopular; and his proscription very naturally tempted me to peruse his writings and those of his antagonists. His bold criticism, which approacheds the precipice of infidelity produced on my mind a singular effect; and had I persevered in the communion of Rome I should now apply to my own fortune the prediction of the Sibyll.

————— Via prima salutis,
Quod minimum reris, Graeâ [Graiâ] pandetur ab Urbe.

The elegance of style and freedom of argument were repelled by a shield of prejudice. I still revered the characters, or rather the names, of the Saints and fathers whom Dr Middleton exposeds, nor could he destroy my implicit belief, that the gift of miraculous powers was continued in the Church during the first four or five [Centuries] of Christianity. But I was unable to resist the weight of historical evidence, that within the same period, most of the leading doctrines of Popery were already introduced in Theory and practise: nor was my conclusion absurd, that Miracles are the test of truth, and that the Church must be orthodox and pure, which was so often approved by the visible interposition of the Deity. The marvellous tales, which are so boldly attested by the Basils and Chrysostoms, the Austins and Jeroms, compelled me to embrace the superior merits of Celibacy, the institution of the monastic life, the use of the sign of the cross, of holy oil, and even of images, the invocation of Saints, the worship of relicks, the rudiments of purgatory in prayers for the dead, and the tremendous mystery of the sacrifice of the body and blood of Christ, which insensibly swelled into the prodigy of Transubstantiation.[149]

Gibbon's perverse misreading of Middleton—for such it surely was—resonates subtly and unexpectedly within the context of Burke's denunciation of freethinking as a menace to social cohesion. In the first place, Gibbon makes the Shaftesburyan point that the suppression of heterodox writings can operate as an enticement: 'the name of Middleton was unpopular; and his proscription very naturally tempted me to peruse his writings and those of his antagonists.'[150] Secondly, the 'singular effect' which the *Free Inquiry* had on Gibbon's mind (scepticism innoculating Gibbon against scepticism) is broadened by means of the quotation from the *Aeneid* into an example of a more general cross-grainedness in human affairs.[151] A principle of paradoxical consequences seems often to ensure, as it did for Aeneas as well as Gibbon, that comfort can swell from that spring whence discomfort seemed to come, and vice versa. If that is so, then it may be possible to endorse Burke's social and political conservatism, while at the same time disputing what now looks like his over-simple assertion that religious scepticism will uniformly operate as a solvent of existing social relations and political structures. The opposite was true in Gibbon's case and might—so the litotes of 'the progress of my conversion may tend to illustrate, *at least* the history of my own mind' hints to us—be more generally true. It might, for instance, have been true of *The Decline and Fall*, which lurks here as a ghostly presence summoned by the parallel circumstance Gibbon notes in the reception of Middleton's writings: 'the two dullest ~~and most angry~~ of [his adversaries] were crowned with Academic honours by the University of Oxford.' In draft 'E' Gibbon had noted how his own assailants had received, as a foretaste of future benefits, a measure of earthly meed: 'My antagonists, however, were rewarded in this World: poor Chelsum was indeed neglected, and I dare not boast the making Dr. Watson a Bishop; but I enjoyed the pleasure of giving a Royal pension to Mr. Davies, and of collating Dr. Apthorpe to an Archiepiscopal living.'[152] Middleton's *Free Enquiry* gave rise to perverse outcomes, and so did *The Decline and Fall*. After all, what is disruptive about the advancement of the orthodox to positions of influence and emolument, no matter how indirect or even unintended the agency?

The implication that religious heterodoxy is not necessarily socially explosive is supported by the characters Gibbon gives in 'F' of the two precedessors in scepticism, Chillingworth and Bayle. In 'B', 'D', and 'E' Gibbon had alluded to the struggles of their 'acute understandings' to break through the 'sophistry' by which they had been ensnared.[153] In 'F', those allusions are greatly expanded into thumbnail biographies

---

[150] Compare the comments on freethinking and authority in Shaftesbury's 'Sensus Communis: an Essay on the Freedom of Wit and Humour' (1709), reprinted in *Characteristicks* (1711).

[151] The quotation is *Aeneid*, vi. 96–7; the Sibyl informs Aeneas that 'the path of safety shall be opened from a Grecian city, however little you think so now'.

[152] *A* 317 (draft 'E').

[153] 'B', 'D', and 'E':22.

which focus on the progress of Bayle and Chillingworth's religious opinions. In the case of Chillingworth, Gibbon emphasizes how religious enquiry had as its outcome conformity and quietude:

From this middle region of the air, the descent of his reason would naturally rest on the firmer ground of the Socinians: and, if we may credit a doubtful story and the popular opinion, his anxious enquiries at last subsided in Philosophic indifference. So conspicuous however were the candour of his Nature, and the innocence of his heart, that this apparent levity did not affect the reputation of Chillingworth. His frequent changes proceeded from too nice an inquisition into truth. His doubts grew out of himself, he assisted them with all the strength of his reason: he was then too hard for himself: but finding as little quiet and repose in those victories, he quickly recovered by a new appeal to his own judgement; so that in all his sallies and retreats, he was, in fact, his own convert.[154]

In the case of Bayle, religious vicissitude generated a temper of mind in which impartiality and independence came together to proclaim the virtue of 'custom and education':

Had Bayle adhered to the Catholic Church, had he embraced the Ecclesiastic profession, the Genius and favour of such a proselyte might have aspired to wealth and honours in his native country; but [the Hypocrite] he would have found less happiness in the comforts of a benefice, or the dignity of a mitre than he enjoyed at Rotterdam, in a private state of exile, indigence, and freedom. Without a country, or a patron or a prejudice, he claimed the liberty, and subsisted by the labours of his pen: the inequality of his voluminous works is explained and excused by his alternately writing for himself, for the booksellers, and for posterity, and if a severe critic would reduce him to a single folio, that relick, like the books of the Sybill would become still more valuable. A calm and lofty spectator of the Religious tempest, the Philosopher of Rotterdam | condemned with equal firmness the persecution of Lewis XIV; and the Republican maxims of the Calvinists; their vain prophecies and the intolerant bigotry which sometimes vexed his solitary retreat. In reviewing the controversies of the times, he turned against each other, the [arguments] arms of the disputants: successively wielding the disputants arms of the Catholics and protestants, he proves that neither the way of authority, nor the way of examination can afford the multitude any test of Religious truth; and dexterously concludes, that custom and education must be the sole grounds of popular belief. The ancient paradox of Plutarch, that Atheism is less pernicious than superstition acquires a tenfold vigour when it is adorned with the colours of his wit, and pointed with the acuteness of his logic.[155]

Gibbon's portrait of Bayle, in which an un–Burkean freedom of attach-

---

[154] 'F':27.　　　[155] 'F':28.

ments to little platoons feeds a social conservatism which Burke would nevertheless not have wished to repudiate, points to the delicately balanced and self-exculpating end which Gibbon has in view in draft 'F': namely, that of showing Burkean outcomes arising from un-Burkean roots.

At this point in our argument, we can see why Gibbon's engagement with the writings of Vicesimus Knox is of particular importance.[156] Knox was one of the most prominent writers on education of the later eighteenth century, and although it would have been less than reckless to have assumed from drafts 'B' to 'E' that Gibbon was aware of his work, a footnote to draft 'F' puts the matter beyond doubt.[157] On methods of examination, Gibbon noted that recent intended reforms had missed their aim: 'The <u>Arts</u>' are supposed to include the liberal knowledge of Philosophy and litterature: but I am informed that some tattered shreds of the old Logic and Metaphysics compose the exercises for a Batchelor and Master's degree; and that modern improvements, instead of introducing a more rational tryal, has [have] only served to relax the forms which are now the object of general contempt.'[158] To this a note is appended: 'Here Vicesimus Knox must be used.' But which of Knox's many writings did Gibbon intend to press into service at this point? The most natural assumption is that made by John Murray in his edition of the various drafts of the 'Memoirs', where we find Gibbon's note itself annotated: 'This probably refers to *Liberal Education* . . .'[159] As the work whose title most obviously proclaims Knox's interest in education, and in which there is moreover a chapter on the universities, this is an easy assumption to make, although (as is the case with many easy assumptions) closer inspection suggests that it is wrong. Furthermore, it is not clear from Murray's note that he has read either *Liberal Education* or Knox's other writings ('probably' reads like an admission). A review of the progress of Knox's opinions on education and politics as revealed in his publications will indicate another candidate for the book Gibbon had in mind when writing that enigmatic note. In the process, light will be shed from another angle on the

---

[156] Vicesimus Knox (1752–1821), Whig, teacher, and popular writer; St John's College, Oxford; BA, 1775; MA, 1779; Fellow, 1775–8; headmaster, Tonbridge School, 1778–1812. The more important of his writings include: *Essays Moral and Literary* (1778), *Liberal Education* (1781), *Elegant Extracts* (1783), *Winter Evenings* (1788), *Family Lectures* (1791–5), *Personal Nobility* (1793), *Antipolemus* (1794), and *The Spirit of Despotism* (?1795).

[157] There are no references to Knox in Gibbon's letters or (this is unsurprising) *The Decline and Fall*, and Keynes's catalogue of Gibbon's library does not include any works by Knox.

[158] 'F':5a.

[159] *A* 70 n. *.

experience which was also Gibbon's, of the French Revolution's violent separation of the elements of a life which had before 1789 cohered well enough at the level of practice, whatever the latent tensions and conflicts at the level of theoretical implication.

Knox's first important publication on education, *Liberal Education*, has already been cited in this chapter as evidence of that more disciplined focus on pedagogy which we discover in the second half of the eighteenth century. What has not been brought out, however, is the marked prudence which overtakes the book in its closing pages. For *Liberal Education* concludes by praising the universities (which are, of course, the subject of only one chapter in a book which takes for its subject the whole realm of education in England at that time). Knox's admiration is qualified only by his sense of the need for 'a few public alterations'; but he separates himself vigorously from the cause of radicalism: 'And I cannot help thinking, that their [the universities'] declared enemies, those who wish to destroy or totally alter their constitution, are of that description of men who envy the advantages which they have never shared, or who, from an unfortunate mode of thinking, endeavour to overturn all the antient establishments, civil and ecclesiastical.'[160] Here Knox explicitly denies that the measures he was advocating in *Liberal Education* should be taken as evidence that he was a friend to reform in any broader political sense. However one construes that gesture—as the sincere wish of a troubled friend to Oxford, or as an attempt disingenuously to deflect censure from outraged conservatives—it is nevertheless valuable further evidence that, in the 1780s, calls for reform in the universities might be seen as stalking horses for larger causes.

Whatever Knox's motives, the gesture was unavailing. On its publication in 1781 *Liberal Education* provoked discussion and dissent, to which Knox offered ripostes in two of the essays he published in 1788 as *Winter Evenings, or Lucubrations on Life and Letters*. The first came in essay LVI, entitled 'On Some Effects of a regular and University Education'. This narrates the fortunes of Jack Hearty, the promising son of a moderately wealthy family who goes to Oxford, told in the form of a letter from his father, Francis Hearty. At first, all is promising: 'On our entrance into Oxford we were wonderfully struck with the sight of the handsome buildings, and the appearance of young men in square caps, with pig-tails, leather breeches, and shoe-strings, strutting about with gowns on their backs, like that of our good old vicar.'[161] The congruence with the opening of draft 'F' is already striking, although it is a

---

[160] Knox, *Liberal Education*, 329.   [161] Knox, *Winter Evenings*, i. 481.

closeness of subject rather than of phrasing.[162] However, Jack goes off the rails almost immediately. He spends the first week of his first Long Vacation 'at the Hummums in Covent Garden' (a hummum being a Turkish bath or brothel).[163] He begins to despise his parents for their lack of fashion, and falls into habits of inconsiderate expense. His tutor, the appropriately named Dr Hunter, is assiduous in giving Jack tips on how to care for sick horses and on where he can buy 'cheap stirrups'.[164] His educational efforts, however, are confined to supplying Jack with 'some strings of arguments' for the Schools exercises, and 'an old Latin sermon that I [Jack] am sure will do for the exercise, because it has done already a dozen times at least, and is almost worn out in the service'.[165] The result is a disaster on every level, as his father explains:

I have paid out two thousand pounds for five or six years of this university education, and I am confidentially told, my son has incurred a debt of more than half that sum, with wine-merchants, horse-dealers, taylors, and the honourable fraternity of gamblers. He has lost his health, and the little school learning he took with him to college; I have lost the comfort of a good son, and a quiet contented house.[166]

Although in *Liberal Education* Knox had complained that while a Fellow of St John's he had seen 'immorality, habitual drunkenness, idleness, ignorance, and vanity, openly and boastingly obtruding themselves on public view [and] triumphing without controul over the timidity of modest merit', such general reproaches were necessarily less vivid than this particular—albeit fictionalized—instance of the harm which a period of residence at Oxford might produce. Although the substance of what Knox has to say here by way of reproach to the university is very similar to what he had said in *Liberal Education*, the change of form implies a return to the assault with different, and perhaps sharper weapons. Certainly there is nothing in this essay remotely parallel to the careful, sweetening, paragraph of praise and reassurance of loyalty which Knox inserts at the end of *Liberal Education*.

Still less did Knox abate his acerbity in the second essay of *Winter Evenings* which revisited the territory of *Liberal Education*. The final

---

[162] Compare 'F':2; 'A traveller who visits Oxford or Cambridge is surprized and edified by the apparent order and tranquillity that prevail in the seats of the English muses. . . . the uniform habit of the Academics, the square cap and black gown: is adapted to the civil and even clerical profession: and from the Doctor in Divinity to the under-graduate, the degrees of learning and age are externally distinguished. . . . The eyes of the traveller are attracted by the size or beauty of the public edifices; and the principal colleges appear to be so many st palaces which a liberal nation has erected and endowed for the habitation of Science.'

[163] Knox, *Winter Evenings*, i. 483.   [164] Ibid. i. 489–90

[165] Ibid. i. 490 and 495.   [166] Ibid. i. 487.

essay in the collection, 'LXXII. On the Superiority of the English Universities, *as Places of Education*, over all other Seminaries in the World; and on the Animadversions on them contained in a Book entitled "LIBERAL EDUCATION"', sees Knox confessing, with heavy-handed irony, to 'my heinous crime . . . to have censured the present state of those hallowed universities'.[167] This is an important essay for our purposes, because it covers much of the same ground as Gibbon would later when composing draft 'F', and furthermore because it specifically mentions Gibbon as someone who had suffered from Oxford's educational carelessness, thereby corroborating what Gibbon himself had said towards the end of draft 'F', that the controversy over his writings had become entangled with that over Oxford.[168]

This essay of Knox's is also close to Gibbon, in the sense that it touches on many of the topics, and employs some of the vocabulary, which Gibbon would later incorporate into his 'Memoirs of my Life'. Knox anticipates Gibbon in directing his reader (albeit with the caveat that he 'cannot approve the whole' of Smith's writings) to Adam Smith's 'Remarks on the Universities of England', which 'suggest matter for serious consideration on the expediency of their present forms and establishments'.[169] Just as Gibbon grudgingly admits the possibility of reform—'It will perhaps be asserted that in the lapse of forty years many improvements have taken place in the College and the University'—so Knox reports (although without evident conviction) that he has 'been informed that since [the publication of *Liberal Education*], a few changes in collegiate discipline have been made, and a few improvements adopted'.[170] Like Gibbon, he notes that the establishment of the Vinerian Lecture, which had borne the fruit of Blackstone's *Commentaries*, would 'be immediately brought forward' as evidence of progress.[171] However, also like Gibbon, who will be unrepentantly convinced that 'the inveterate evils which are derived from their birth and character must still cleave to our Ecclesiastical corporations', Knox asserts that such piecemeal tinkering as has taken place amounts more to sophisticated deflection of the pressure to reform than a desire thoroughly to cleanse Oxford's Augean stables:

---

[167] Knox, *Winter Evenings*, ii. 551.

[168] 'As to history, Hume indeed is dead, and I am chiefly confined to living instances; but Gibbon, notwithstanding his principles are to be reprobated, has great fame, whether I think he deserves it or not, as an historian; and what did Hume, or what did Gibbon derive from a residence in Oxford or Cambridge?' (ibid. ii. 572–3); compare 'F':26.

[169] Knox, *Winter Evenings*, ii. 553, n. *; cf. sect. 6, in all drafts.

[170] 'F':14; Knox, *Winter Evenings*, ii. 554–5.

[171] Ibid. 569; 'F':30.

It is now many years since I resided at Oxford, and since I wrote my offensive animadversions. Alterations in little matters may have taken place since I was able to make ocular remarks, and wrote the result of them. A few things, therefore, that were strictly true when I wrote, may now be no longer true; I say a few things, for I know, and all the world knows, that a general reform has not taken place, and that the great and leading observations of my treatise, the only ones which are worth maintaining, are still applicable.[172]

Just as Gibbon was unimpressed by the literary productivity of eighteenth-century Oxford ('If I enquire into the manufactures of the monks of Magdalen, if I extend the enquiry to the other Colleges of Oxford and Cambridge, a silent blush, or a scornful frown, will be the only reply'), so Knox asks rhetorically whether 'any of the great literary works of this day, in any department, [are] produced by the university?'[173] And, finally, just as Gibbon would later declare his emotional independence of the university ('To the University of Oxford I acknowledge no obligation, and she will as chearfully renounce me for a son, as I am willing to disclaim her for a mother'), so Knox with an equal pride proclaims that 'I ask no favours of them, I want no indulgence'.[174]

Knox assures his reader that it is as 'places of EDUCATION only, I have considered the universities, unconnected with politics, unconnected with the temporal interest of civil or religious establishments'.[175] But such political abstraction, at this time and on this subject, would have been inconceivable, and is in any case belied by Knox's stated determination to write in a style 'not adapted to the timid caution of an academic conclave, but to the bold genius of Englishmen, enlightened by liberal inquiry, warmed with the spirit of liberty, and judging of institutions conducive to general benefit, without the bias of private, partial and unmanly policy'.[176] It is interesting to see where this commitment to rational Whiggery leads Knox. In the first place, it dictates a pungent scorn for 'the academic dread of innovation' which protects 'great corruptions, preserved by prejudice and authority, and almost SANCTIFIED BY ANTIQUITY'.[177] Secondly, in a significant shift of position from 1781 and *Liberal Education*, Knox insists not only on the 'necessity of an academical reform', but that that reform must be

---

[172] 'F':30; Knox, *Winter Evenings*, ii. 567.
[173] 'F':6a; Knox, *Winter Evenings*, ii. 574; see also the long section (pp. 568–76) in which Knox examines the full extent of Oxford and Cambridge's under-production.
[174] 'F':4; Knox, *Winter Evenings*, ii. 578.
[175] Ibid. 577.
[176] Ibid. 564.
[177] Ibid. 563 (cf. p.565) and 561.

thoroughgoing and complete.[178] The time when 'a few public alterations' would have sufficed has long since departed: 'I now repeat, with
additional and most perfect conviction of my mind, that the universities
are so much degenerated by the lapse of ages, and the want of occasional
amendments adapted to the exigencies of succeeding times; that they
stand in need of a reform so complete and general, as to resemble a total
renovation.'[179] Knox is manifestly aware of the potential vulnerability
of this stance. He understands that 'reformation is in its nature
invidious; and the very name of reformer has been artfully rendered
obnoxious to hatred'; he deplores and distances himself from 'the turbulence of the demagogue, and the mischievous activity of the wanton
innovator', with which he evidently fears he may become associated.[180]
Nevertheless, in the end he unambiguously takes his stand on the
rational ground of educational utility and dismisses the claims of political prescription:

I can neither adopt nor approve that academical POLICY, which seems at
first sight to evidence a greater regard for a state system, than for education; a
greater regard for a church, than for Christianity; a greater regard for its own
dull dignity, and the conservation of its own idle forms, than for the advantage
of a whole people, for whose benefit alone an university can be supposed, on
rational principles, to have been originally designed, and constantly supported.[181]

What must be registered here is the sense the conclusion of this essay
evokes, of a man being driven with equal measures of reluctance and
resolve towards a position both more simple and more extreme than
that he would prefer. That impression of Knox committing himself
through gritted teeth to a position of unwelcome exposure is accompanied by what seems like an apprehension of imminent struggle, and
by decreasing faith in the power of the arts of political accommodation
to find a way through. Whereas in *Liberal Education* it seemed there
might be some point in trying to build alliances, by the end of the 1780s
it is more a question of making choices. That is certainly the mood of
Knox's last publication of the decade on the subject of education, his *A
Letter to the Right Hon. Lord North* (1789). The extremity of tone which
had marked the end of *Winter Evenings* is once again evident, and
perhaps even sharpened, when Knox deplores the resistance to reform

---

[178] Knox, *Winter Evenings*, ii. 581 (cf. also p. 582).
[179] Knox, *Liberal Education*, 329; Knox, *Winter Evenings*, ii. 552.
[180] Ibid. 558 and 560.
[181] Ibid. 577.

within the university, now presented as a local manifestation of broader and more serious moral failings: 'authority, in the hands of those who enjoy emolument in the present disarranged state of the University, shuddering at innovation, will determine to withstand it with the whole weight of corrupt influence; pride will despise, and malice traduce, a reform, of which they have neither sentiment to feel, nor manliness to acknowledge, the necessity.'[182] Given the importance of the object—for 'the welfare of the nation greatly depends on [the university's] being rightly conducted'—nothing less than an exertion of executive authority is required (North had been Chancellor of the University since 1772): 'The faults and defects of the university are so gross, as not to require any great sagacity, either to discover, or amend and supply them. Nothing is wanting to reform it, but an earnest desire in those who possess the power.'[183] There are tempting grounds for believing, then, that when Gibbon wrote the cryptic note to remind himself that 'Here Vicesimus Knox must be used', it was the later, more acerbic *Winter Evenings* he had in mind, rather than its more clement predecessor, *Liberal Education*. Not only was the actual subject under discussion at that point in the text of the 'Memoirs'—the system of university examination—much more explicitly handled in *Winter Evenings* than in *Liberal Education*; as we have seen, the language and topics of the later work coincide much more closely with the 'Memoirs' than does *Liberal Education*, while Knox's evident inward strain in *Winter Evenings* suggests something like the internal division which we have discerned in draft 'F', even if Knox had responded to that self-division in a different way. In draft 'E' Gibbon had suppressed much of his identity in order to appear more Burkean than in fact he was or had been. In *Winter Evenings* Knox is Gibbon's *doppelgänger*: a man whom the polarizing of debate in the wake of the French Revolution induces to suppress his conservative leanings, and enlist ever more emphatically under the colours of radicalism. *Winter Evenings* therefore sees Knox taking a path which Gibbon might have chosen, but which in fact he declined—a circumstance which might explain the claim such a book could have exerted upon Gibbon's attention.

   The most sustained *riposte* to Knox's strictures on Oxford came from the pseudonymous 'Philalethes', in the form of *A Letter to the Rev. Vicecimus [sic] Knox on the Subject of his Animadversions on the University of Oxford* (1790). Although this pamphlet appears to have been published

---

[182] Knox, *A Letter to the Right Hon. Lord North*, p. iii.
[183] Ibid., p. xii.

before Burke's *Reflections*,[184] it nevertheless employs Burkean principles and Burkean vocabulary in its attempt to discredit Knox. Furthermore, a striking similarity of phrasing and subject matter suggests that Gibbon may have read the pamphlet before composing draft 'F'.[185] If so, then the treatment Knox received at the hands of 'Philalethes' would have given Gibbon some warning about how his own criticisms of Oxford might be received once they were published.

When 'Philalethes' opened his pamphlet by asserting that Knox's attacks on Oxford had duplicated 'the common errors of Voltaire and of Smith', he partly associated him with that French philosophy which Burke would shortly indict as a cause of the Revolution.[186] He also struck the keynote of his tract, which dismissed without discussion Knox's claim to have bracketed all political questions when considering the universities. For 'Philalethes', this was cant. The question of the universities was not to be separated from the profound issues of government which were at that very moment being fought over in France. 'Philalethes' thus merged the question of university government into that of national government. For him, reverence for the university's statutes and constitution was an aspect of the 'first principles of government'; such bracketing as Knox pretended to was simply impossible. The result was a profoundly prescriptive vision of English politics, as that was focused in the life of Oxford:

The Statutes of private Colleges, which we bind ourselves to observe at our Admission upon a Foundation, cannot with propriety be changed or diminished by any Power on Earth: They may be considered as a Sacred Deposit committed to our Trust by a confiding Founder and Ancestor: He has bestowed on us an ample Reward to compensate for the Observance of them:

---

[184] The letter is dated 6 Feb. 1790 (*A Letter to the Rev. Vicecimus [sic] Knox*, 36). Burke's *Reflections* was published on 1 Nov. 1790.

[185] Gibbon opens his account of Oxford in draft 'F' by drawing a contrast between its outward orderliness and the comparative turmoil of its counterparts in Europe: 'In the most celebrated Universities of Holland, Germany, and Italy, the students, who swarm from different countries, are loosely dispersed in private lodgings at the houses of the burghers: they dress according to their fancy and fortune: and in the intemperate quarrels of youth and wine, their swords, though less frequently than of old, are sometimes stained with each other's blood' ('F':2). 'Philalethes' draws a similar contrast, again to Oxford's advantage: 'It [Oxford] is not, like its own commended Ancestry, distracted by internal and party commotions, defending the Errors of Science with unmanly, and even personal acrimony, bathed in the frequent blood of its own slaughtered Members, and recurring perpetually to the Interposition of Royal Authority' (*Letter to Knox*, 28). Although Gibbon was in Switzerland in 1790, he had regular parcels of English books on subjects of interest to him ('works of merit, history, travels, litterature, philosophy and even extraordinary novels') sent out by Peter Elmsley: *L* iii. 273–4.   [186] *Letter to Knox*, 5.

And we have no more right to amend or abridge them, than to alienate the Benefices, to which they are affixed.[187]

Here we find, in an almost fully developed form, the Burkean doctrine of the contract between generations. Burkean, too, is 'Philalethes's apprehension of the way the precedent of reform might over generations develop an unstoppable momentum:

The Statutes of the University, as they are of a more public Nature, may be excepted from this sacred severity of Observance. But every Establishment, in this and every other Kingdom, possesses its own peculiar Rights and Privileges: and the Exaction of an Oath, for the preservation of those Rights and Privileges, from every new admitted Member, is consistent with the dictates of Reason, and the first principles of Government. The Statutes, which this Amendment [the detailed proposals for reform in Knox's *Letter to the Right Hon. Lord North*, p. xii] advises us to alter, were formed by the greatest Modellers of the present European Institutions; and have produced their proposed Utility through many an illustrious Generation. They were carefully observed by those Characters of earlier Ages, whom our Reformer [Knox] proposes as the Subjects of our Eulogies, and the Objects of our Imitation: And surely it is presumption in us, an unworthy and degenerate Race, to condemn, from tenderness of Conscience, those very Ceremonies, to which the most moral of our Ancestors submitted with chearfulness. But an Alteration in the fundamental Principles of an antient Establishment endangers the Peace and Security of that Establishment for ever. When an inroad has been once made into its original Forms and Institutions, a precedent is established for the propositions of every dangerous Innovator. We cannot presume to hope, that Posterity will abide by our Amendments. They will doubtless vindicate a Right of superseding them, and of erecting on their Ruins their own fancied Model of Perfection. And then the Peace and Security, which are so peculiarly required for the Pursuits of an Academic Retirement, will be perpetually violated by useless attempts at Innovation and ideal Improvement.[188]

It was by reference to these more general notions of convenience, rather than to the criterion of 'utility', that 'Philalethes' defended the utility of Oxford's system of examination, the 'exercises': 'I mean not to defend the utility of those Exercises in the present state of Learning: But I am unwilling to infringe upon antient Establishments, when a compliance with their original Forms and Customs does not materially affect the Welfare of the Institution. Upon these grounds, and on these grounds only, I beg leave to recommend an adherence to the antient Exercises of the Schools.'[189] With mordant sarcasm, the language of monkishness was dismissed as yet more cant, and Knox's busyness in the

---

[187] Ibid. 16.   [188] Ibid. 17–18.   [189] Ibid. 22.

matter of reform mocked as self-importance trying to pass itself off as something nobler:

I applaud the judicious Amendment; and every Englishman of the eighteenth Century will surely aid the patriotic Design of exterminating from our Territories the Papists, Slaves, Monks, and Goths, who have dared to plant themselves in the very Centre of the Kingdom, and with a matchless effrontery have stood forth as the Guardians of the British Youth. The celebrated Atchievements of the Great Reformer of the North will be lost in the Fame of his illustrious Descendant. Even the glorious Feats of early Knighthood will be revived and eclipsed by our daring and intrepid Adventurer. Let him but sound his Trumpet before our Battlements, and the prophane and disgraceful abodes of Ancient Superstition will tremble to their Foundations, and, like the visionary Castle of Enchantment, vanish at the Blast.[190]

Writing with the 'mild and amiable Earnestness of an affectionate Son', 'Philalethes' made a robust claim for Oxford's healthiness:

The University of Oxford stands eminently distinguished by the advantages it holds forth. The Retirement of Situation, the Assistance of Tutors, both public and private, the Classical Exercises and Examinations, the Regularity of Religious Duties, the Attention to Morality, the Regulation and Moderation of Expences, and the variety of Scholarships, Exhibitions and Fellowships, reserved for the rewards of Merit, all tend to invigorate the literary exertions of Youth, and to form the susceptible mind by the sacred principles of Knowledge and Morality.[191]

As 'Philalethes' exclaims, 'what a gloomy Reverse to this amiable Picture has our Reformer drawn!'[192] That Oxford might even at the end of the eighteenth century have possessed such determined and politically sophisticated advocates, who were alive to the tactical advantages created for their cause by the French Revolution, is a circumstance worth recollecting and exploring in some detail if we wish to understand the ideological conditions prevailing when Gibbon was composing his 'Memoirs'.

Knox's next publication, *Personal Nobility: or, Letters to a Young Nobleman, on the Conduct of his Studies, and the Dignity of the Peerage* (1793), shows him once more trying to maintain a balance between support for causes of reform and social conservatism which 'Philalethes' had denied was possible. Dedicated—with an engaging maladroitness, given its vision that aristocracy may be preserved only by personal integrity—to Charles Fox, and critical of those 'who shrunk from [his]

---

[190] *Letter to Knox*, 25.   [191] Ibid. 33–4 and 27.   [192] Ibid. 29.

side in the hour of danger' (a clear allusion to Burke),[193] this work demands parliamentary reform, intemperately denouncing those who oppose it as 'that description of men, who, like some noisome insects, can only subsist in corruption. They feed and fatten in filth, and cleanliness is their bane.'[194] However, it also explicitly separates itself from the cause of violent revolution. Its central contention is that aristocratic title is by itself an insufficient claim for deference, and that it needs to be reinforced by personal merit: 'Would you preserve the magnificent Gothic pile of our ancestors uninjured? Then add personal merit to the aristocracy. Let genius, learning, and virtue, outshine the pearls and jewels of the peer's coronet; and this country will still, such are its prepossessions in favour of nobility, honour and support it.'[195] That Knox should now use 'Gothic' as a term of praise, and that he should acknowledge the centrality of deference to the English character, reveals a significant change of political stance following the September massacres of 1792 and the execution of Louis XVI in January 1793. It was difficult, in the light of those events, to dismiss Burke's *Reflections* as hysterical and alarmist. What Knox therefore attempted in *Personal Nobility* was to cloak with Burkean trappings what was in reality an increasingly radical core of doctrine. After all, the demand for personal merit in aristocracy struck hard at the principle which served as the taproot of Whiggism: namely, that political authority flowed from the possession of property, independent of the personal characteristics of the possessor. Knox opened up a line of communication with Burke's thought when he acknowledged the salutary consequences of the 'awe' which surrounds noble birth, and when he presented the English character as one particularly apt to look up to aristocracy: 'The English are still attached to illustrious birth, and if it is accompanied with any virtue, pay it great respect.'[196] He also echoed Burke when he contended that the English were a particularly religious people. However, at this point the divergence between Burke and Knox becomes apparent. Whereas Burke had suggested in *Reflections* that habits of religious reverence amongst the English reinforced habits of political

---

[193] Knox, *Personal Nobility*, p. vi. The conflicts of the early 1790s amongst the Whigs are described from different standpoints, and with different heroes, by Conor Cruise O'Brien in *The Great Melody* (London: Sinclair Stevenson, 1992) and by L. G. Mitchell in *Charles James Fox* (Oxford: Oxford University Press, 1992).

[194] Knox, *Personal Nobility*, p. xiv.

[195] Ibid. 219–20; cf. also p. 288, where Knox asserts that aristocracy cannot last long in England if 'unsupported by personal merit'.

[196] Ibid. 200 and 284.

deference,[197] Knox depicts the religious sensibility of the English as a much more Protestant, and even idealistic, matter. It may as easily fuel radicalism as social conformity: 'Should an aristocracy thus insult a generous and *religious* people, let it not imagine itself founded on a rock.'[198] Here Knox struck a clear note of menace, while at the same time turning the flank of the use Burke had made of the religious disposition of the English in *Reflections*.

Personal Nobility thus reveals Knox to have been a shrewd literary tactician, possessing a keen sense of the lie of the polemical land in the early 1790s. Beneath that superficial adroitness, however, we sense an identity under increasing inward strain. In Knox's next publication of the 1790s, *The Spirit of Despotism* (1795), strain has become shrillness.[199] Knox's affinities with radicalism now emerge more plainly, with details which recall Rousseau, Paine, and Godwin.[200] Nevertheless, he accepts Burke's diagnosis that 'philosophy' was the parent of revolution, although not without giving the indictment an ingenious twist: 'Liberty is the daughter of Philosophy; and they who detest the offspring, do all they can to vilify and discountenance the mother. . . . But it is modern philosophy, and *French* philosophy, which gives such umbrage to the lovers of old errors, and the favourers of absolute power; . . .'[201] According to Knox, the pillorying of sceptical philosophy for its supposedly corrosive effects on society was inherently improbable, given the abstruseness of much of the writing, and its limited readership. The allegation could be explained only as a diversionary tactic on the part of the truly guilty. For the 'TORY and JACOBITE SPIRIT, under other more plausible names, is still

[197] In the 1770s when writing on the war with the colonies Burke had shown an awareness that religious spirit might be politically disruptive: note his comments on the religion of the colonists as 'the dissidence of dissent; and the protestantism of the protestant religion' (*Speech on Conciliation with the Colonies*, 353).
[198] Knox, *Personal Nobility*, 277: Knox's emphasis. Knox identified Chesterfield's *Letters* as a book which had seriously damaged the standing of the aristocracy in the eyes of the common people (Knox, *Personal Nobility*, 316).
[199] The bibliography of this work is mysterious, complex, and suspect. The earliest extant copies were published by William Hone in 1821, where it is asserted that the work was first privately printed in London in 1795, and thereafter suppressed with only three copies surviving. It was never published with Knox's name on the title page in his lifetime, but was included in the 1837 edition of Knox's works. I shall discuss it as a work of 1795, but in doing so I am acutely aware of all that might be urged on the other side of the question.
[200] For an echo of Rousseau on natural simplicity, see *The Spirit of Despotism*, 'second edition' (1821), 5; for echoes of Paine's perception of the necessary linkage between despotism and war, see *Spirit of Despotism*, 24, 41, and 68 ('despots make war their first study and delight'); for a judgement similar to Godwin's footnote on Burke in the third edition of *Political Justice*, see *Spirit of Despotism*, 63.
[201] Knox, *Spirit of Despotism*, 10.

alive, and has increased of late'.[202] The result was the polluting of the
state by its very guardians:

The Tindals, the Collins's, the Bolingbrokes, the Humes, the Gibbons, the
Voltaires, the Volneys, the *miscreant* philosophers of France, never did so much
injury to the cause of Christianity, as those English ministers of state, who,
while they shed the blood of thousands for the sake of law, order, and *religion*,
prostitute the church and the CURE OF SOULS to the corruption of the
senate.

The corruption of the church for the purpose of corrupting the legislature, is
an offence far more injurious to the general happiness of mankind and the
interests of a Christian community, than any of those which have banished the
offenders to Botany Bay, or confined them for years within the walls of the
prison-house. Both the corrupters and the corrupted, in this case, are more
injurious to Christianity than all the tribes of sceptics and infidels; than Tindal,
Toland, Bolingbroke, Hume, Rousseau, Voltaire, and Gibbon. The *common
people* do not *read* them, and perhaps could scarcely *understand* them.[203]

However, this corruption amongst the great courted its own correction, as Knox explained by touching on the themes of his earlier publications, notably those on education:

The constitution of England is founded on liberty, and the people are warmly
attached to liberty; then why is it even in danger, and why is a constant
struggle necessary to preserve it uninfringed? Many causes combine, and
perhaps none is more operative, than a corrupt education, in which pride is
nourished at the tenderest period, and the possession or expectation of wealth
and civil honours is tacitly represented, even in the schools of virtue, as superseding the necessity of personal excellence.[204]

When Knox touches again on the theme with which he had launched
himself as a popular writer—namely, corrupt education—it is difficult
for the reader not to reflect on how much has changed since the publication of *Liberal Education* in 1781. Then, it seemed possible to be both
a reforming Whig and, in the main, a supporter of established forms. As
the 1790s wore on, such a position became less and less tenable. Forced
to choose, Knox cleaved to his reforming, Whiggish self, and made
steadily fewer attempts to conciliate or avoid affronting the defenders of
(in Godwin's phrase) 'things as they are'.

Quite what Gibbon had read of Knox's we cannot be sure, but given
the eagerness with which he kept up with his reading on the revolution
controversy, it would hardly be surprising had he read everything up to
and including *Personal Nobility*. If so, he might have sensed that he and

---

[202] Ibid. 10.   [203] Ibid. 74 and 82.   [204] Ibid. 11–12.

Knox were increasingly opposed on all the most important issues of the day, and yet also bound together by a shared experience of violated identity. With his intention, in draft 'F', that 'Vicesimus Knox must be used' Gibbon revealed a desire to incorporate Knox's increasingly radical voice within his own.[205] But it would never have been allowed to dominate, as the extraordinary modulations of draft 'F's' final words indicate:

The manners and opinions of our Universities must follow at a distance the progressive motion of the age; and some prejudices, which reason could not subdue, have been slowly obliterated by time. The last generation of Jacobites is extinct: "the right Divine of Kings to govern wrong" is now exploded even at Oxford: and [the] some remains of Tory principles are rather salutary than hurtful, at a time when the Constitution has nothing to fear from the prerogative of the Crown, and can only be injured by popular innovation. But the inveterate evils which are derived from their birth and character must still cleave to our Ecclesiastical corporations: the fashion of the present day is not propitious, in England, to discipline and œconomy; and even the [exceptionable] praeposterous mode of foreign education has been lately preferred by the highest and most respectable authority in the Kingdom. I shall only add that Cambridge appears to have been less deeply infected than her sister with the vices of the Cloyster: her loyalty to the house of Hanover is of a more early date; and the name and authorit philosophy of her immortal Newton were first honoured in his [native] own Academy.[206]

The years spent composing *The Decline and Fall* had constituted a thorough training in the essential historiographical technique of combining and softening originally disparate materials, and the skills acquired in that long apprenticeship are on display in this passage. It begins with a sentiment that Burke might have endorsed; qualifies that emphasis by acknowledging the 'inveterate evils' which might cling to the customary; and concludes, in an inspired and brilliant move, by fusing admiration for loyalty to the Hanoverians with renewed implicit criticism of Oxford. In this way Gibbon found, momentarily, a voice at once critical and conservative, and so brought off what had been beyond Knox. But for how long could such an equivocating style be maintained? And how would it cope with the subject to which it would next have to impart legible form, namely the years of Gibbon's exile in Lausanne, which included theatrical evenings at the home of the age's most notorious infidel? The evidence of the earlier drafts suggests that here even Gibbon's art might not have sufficed:

The wit and philosophy of Voltaire, his table and theatre, refined in a visible degree the manners of Lausanne; and, however addicted to study, I enjoyed my share of the amusements of Society. After the representations of Montrepos I sometimes supped with the Actors: . . .

my love of the French Drama was gratified by a very singular event: a succession of Tragedies and comedies . . . was acted on a private theatre by a company of Gentlemen and Ladies, and the great leader, Voltaire himself, declaimed his own verses with the enthusiasm of an author. . . . I was introduced, without being known, to that extraordinary man, 'Virgilium vidi tantum:' he reigned two winters at Lausanne by the double influence of his wit and fortune (in 1757 and 1758), and the Clergy was scandalized by the visible progress of luxury and Deism.[207]

That draft 'F' breaks off where it does, then, is hardly accidental. On the basis of draft 'F', there was no way forward with the project of the 'Memoirs'. In 1823 Carlyle would praise *The Decline and Fall* as 'a kind of bridge which connects the antique with the modern ages. And how gorgeously does it swing across the gloomy and tumultuous chasm of those barbarous centuries.'[208] But the abandoned stem of draft 'F' of the 'Memoirs' marks the moment in 1793 when Gibbon had withdrawn, daunted and defeated in the project of finding an amenable form for the story of his life by the no less tumultuous chasms of the modern world.

A pamphlet published after Gibbon's death in 1794 but before the publication of Sheffield's edition of the 'Memoirs' in the *Miscellaneous Works* of 1796 confirms that, if Gibbon did indeed abandon the project of autobiography for the reasons I have inferred above, he acted prudently. *A Few General Directions for the Conduct of Young Gentlemen in the University of Oxford* (1795) is a work of irony which, in the guise of advice, exposes the dissipation and disregard for education prevalent at Oxford. For instance, the Oxonian's creed is reduced to the following propositions: 'learning . . . is a farce . . . Religion is a *Bore*, your Tutor a *Quiz*, and College discipline, monkish nonsense; all which you will find by experience to be fact.'[209] As to the tradesmen of the town, they are the well-bred undergraduate's legitimate prey: 'If the tradesmen are weak enough to let you run into their debt, you will not be weak enough to pay them.'[210] To frown at drunkenness is a sign of insufficient enlightenment: 'I confess myself surprized that any one in attempting to dissuade men from it [drunkenness] should be silly enough to attack that practice as a breach of the moral or Christian law, stuff that no body minds at this enlightened period of the world.'[211] As

---

[207] *A* 149 (draft 'B') and p. 238 (draft 'C').
[209] [Anon.], *General Directions*, 7.
[211] Ibid. 10.

[208] Carlyle, *Early Letters*, ii. 180.
[210] Ibid. 8.

such, drunkenness is but one aspect of the approved Oxonian practice of 'turning Religion into ridicule', which is itself but one element in a dissolute way of life best acquired from the company of 'those virtuous and well-inclined companions who have sense enough to absent themselves from Chapel or lecture'.[212] Tutors easily grant exeats, and as a result the undergraduate is freed from the dullness of being tethered to one spot: 'nothing gives a higher flavor to the enjoyments of an Oxford life, than retiring from it now and then for a short time. To do this in the most sensible and salutary manner, you must not run off to Woodstock or Abingdon, but go directly to London.'[213] Moreover the library of the Oxonian contains only works compatible with this way of life, namely the eighteenth century's primers of irreligion, amorality, and radicalism: 'L. Bolingbroke will teach you to be an Atheist, Ld. Chesterfield will disencumber you of principle, and Tom Paine afford you a clear and expeditious method of becoming a good Politician.'[214] The value of this pamphlet, from the standpoint of the student of Gibbon's 'Memoirs', is not simply that it confirms that the topics and even the language of Gibbon's account of his time at Oxford were common property, but more specifically that it suggests so vividly how the account of Gibbon's university career given in draft 'F' would have recalled the radical, libertine atheist undergraduate depicted in *A Few General Directions*, and thus defeated his intentions of forging in his own remembered past an alliance between resistance to revolution and enlightenment.

It was precisely to fend off such interpretations of Gibbon as a reforming radical that Sheffield, in his edited text of the 'Memoirs', was so careful to make clear that these strictures on Oxford did not represent Gibbon's final view of the university, concerning which there had at the very end been significant development:

This was written on the information Mr. Gibbon had received, and the observation he had made, previous to his late residence at Lausanne. During his last visit to England, he had an opportunity of seeing at Sheffield-place some young men of the college above alluded to [i.e. Christ Church]; he had great satisfaction in conversing with them, made many inquiries respecting their course of study, applauded the discipline of Christ Church, and the liberal attention shewn by the Dean, to those whose only recommendation was their merit. Had Mr. Gibbon lived to revise this work, I am sure he would have mentioned the name of Dr. Jackson with the highest commendation. There are

[212] [Anon.], *General Directions*, 10 and 12.
[213] Ibid. 15–16 and 15.
[214] Ibid. 14–15.

other colleges at Oxford, with whose discipline my friend was unacquainted, to which, without doubt, he would willingly have allowed their due praise, particularly Brazen Nose and Oriel Colleges; the former under the care of Dr. Cleaver, bishop of Chester, the latter under that of Dr. Eveleigh.[215]

When James Hurdis took up the cudgels on behalf of Magdalen and Oxford against the account of both the college and the university which Gibbon had offered in his 'Memoirs', he was aware of this late—but in his view insufficient—modification of opinion on Gibbon's part.[216] Hurdis's line of attack on Gibbon has its weak sides. Few readers, now or then, one imagines, would feel the need seriously to revise Gibbon's censure of the diligence and productivity of Oxford's professors in the light of this catalogue of mishap:

The late Professor of Botany—*did* read, but Botany not being much in fashion among the younger members of either University, he, for want of pupils, employed the latter part of his life in collecting materials for a Flora Græca, the probable utility of which cannot be disputed. Dying in consequence of a disorder contracted in Greece, he bequeathed this work for completion to his able friend Dr. Wenman, then Professor of Civil Law, but who was soon afterwards drowned by accident in the river Cherwell.[217]

Nevertheless, Hurdis's pamphlet is valuable in two respects. Firstly, a low kind of polemical shrewdness is evident in the way Hurdis manoeuvres across the polemical terrain formed by the context of eighteenth-century attacks on Oxford. For, although he associated Gibbon with that general critical tendency, he also employed against Gibbon one of the points upon which one of Gibbon's best-known colleagues in the attack on Oxford had most insisted. Knox had, as we have already seen, counselled strongly against boys being sent to the university too early.[218] Hurdis blandly adopted the principle of his enemy: 'Nothing however can excuse the imprudence of sending boys so hastily into the society of men, but unusual sobriety and discernment on their part, united to a more than common proportion of attainments, and a well-settled habit of application.'[219] It was, of course, the perfect standpoint from which to retort the responsibility for Gibbon's disappointing academic career on those who were levelling the charge: for 'every consequent imprudence ought to be imputed to his friends and to himself, and not to the waves which overwhelmed and wrecked

[215] *MW 1796* i. 52.
[216] Hurdis, *A Word or Two in Vindication of the University of Oxford*, 8.
[217] Ibid. 37.
[218] See above, pp. 284–5.
[219] Hurdis, *Vindication*, 1.

him'. Indeed, 'what could his ill-judging parent expect from committing so shallow a novice to the boisterous element of a public
University?'[220] By turning Knox against Gibbon, Hurdis sought to
drive a wedge amongst Oxford's critics. It was not a particularly inven-
tive or brilliant polemical move, and of course Gibbon was not alive to
reply. But in its very obviousness Hurdis's lumbering advance has the
merit of pointing clearly to the discursive context within which
Gibbon's account of Oxford was received, construed, and eventually
attacked.

Secondly, Hurdis was alive to the broader political implications
which often lay buried within complaints about the university. His
repudiation of utility as a criterion against which Oxford's professors
should be judged may have been unfortunately worded, and his vision
of the consequences was surely implausibly extreme: 'If the mere plea
of inutility were admitted as sufficient cause of deprivation, estates and
offices would soon be in a state of continual transfer at the will of the
factious and dissatisfied, and society would be a mere whirlpool of
revolution.'[221] Nevertheless, there is a kind of acuity here. As we have
seen in the case of Knox, there might be a path from educational
modernization to political radicalism. And Hurdis was cleverer than he
could possibly know when he pointed out that in respect of Oxford
Gibbon 'adopts those Gallic principles, which he has always sense
enough to abhor, but when speaking of the University or Church'.[222]
Cleverer than he could know, because although he was aware of the
fact that Gibbon had composed six accounts of his life,[223] Hurdis was
necessarily unaware of the discrepant contents and divergent tendencies
of each of the manuscripts, and thus could not be aware of the fact that
this apparent playing fast and loose with 'Gallic principles' was a consequence of Sheffield's editing as much as Gibbon's ambivalence. As
well, therefore, as confirming that Gibbon's 'Memoirs' were received
as well as composed within a milieu conditioned by the French
Revolution, Hurdis's shrewd nose for the contradictions within the
product of Sheffield's editorial handiwork encourages us to assess the
tendency of Sheffield's editing of these manuscripts, and to view his
manipulations of Gibbon's autobiographical writings in the broader
setting formed by the *Miscellaneous Works* as a whole.

[220] Hurdis, *Vindication*, 2: for further censure on this theme, see pp. 3 and 4.
[221] Ibid. 40.
[222] Ibid. 40.
[223] Ibid. 44, where he mockingly refers to the 'six treatises of his own military and historical
exploits'. Sheffield had disclosed the existence of the six drafts in his prefatory remarks to the first
edition of the *Miscellaneous Works* (MW 1796 i, p. iv).

PART III

MISCELLANEOUS WORKS

9

The Making of Gibbon's Miscellaneous Works

In 1795, in the wake of rioting at home and deepening crisis abroad, John Whitaker published *The Real Origin of Government*, a denunciation of the French Revolution so sulphurous that it was deplored by Sheridan in the House of Commons.[1] It was material which Whitaker had used during the previous year for a sermon, as he had explained to his friend Richard Polwhele in a letter of 14 November 1794:

> I preached at the Visitation a sermon, upon the origin of government. The idea is not novel, but founded upon the everlasting pillars of the Scriptures, and sub-versive of all the common theories at once. I concluded this with as pointed a description of the present state of France as my pen and my zeal could compose; and I am now going to publish all, as a pamphlet; in opposition to French anarchy and French Atheism. I fear no censures, no contradiction, no malice. Even the guillotine is nothing to him who would be proud to die a martyr for the religion of the Gospel.[2]

In the course of this vehement restatement of traditional political pieties,[3] Whitaker depicted the revolutionaries of France as barbarians who were all the more dangerous because they were equipped with the refinements of civilization:

> They [the revolutionaries] are thus become a horde of Tartars breaking out from the wilds of Scythia; Tartars in a barbarian's ferociousness of spirit, in a barbarian's disdain of treaties, in a barbarian's defiance of dangers, and in a barbarian's ostentation of bravery; but ten times more formidable than any

---

[1] John Whitaker (1735–1808); historian, antiquarian, clergyman, and controversialist. On his relationship with Gibbon, see in particular two brief articles in *Notes and Queries*, 5th ser., 7 (1877), 444–5 and 489–90.

[2] Polwhele, *Biographical Sketches*, iii. 95.

[3] Whitaker's arguments, he realized, 'were more familiar to the nation eighty or ninety years ago, than they are at present'. Therefore he undertook 'to arrange them in a new form, and to exhibit them in a new dress, calculated immediately for the present times' (*Real Origin of Government*, 'Advertisement').

Tartars ever were, by their knowledge of all the arts of life, by their acquaintance with all the laws of tacticks, and by their familiarity with all the practices of engineering. A refined nation reduced into barbarism by some prevailing venom, unites at once all the martial violence of nature, and all the military discipline of art, together. The Anti-christian, the Atheistical republicans of France, are thus acting at present; equalling the nations that they have obliged to engage them, in all the science of war; excelling them in the national masses of men, which, like true Tartars, they bring into the field; and, if we of this nation had not been forced by them to come into the contest, *sure*, we may say, to have thrown the whole circuit of the nations around them, perhaps the whole continent of Europe, into the most frightful convulsions of Liberty, Republicanism, Infidelity, and Atheism.[4]

The overt aggression of this passage conceals also a hidden sting, although the man for whom it was intended had died the previous year. In the 'General Observations on the Fall of the Roman Empire in the West', which he had appended to chapter thirty-eight of *The Decline and Fall*, Gibbon had reflected, with perhaps ill-judged complacency, on the security of the civilization of Western Europe.[5] In particular, he had suggested an ingenious argument against the possibility of any future incursion of barbarians, such as those which had overrun the western provinces of the Roman Empire. Advances amongst the civilized nations in the technologies of war had contributed to the present security of the West. But they were not in truth its surest safeguard:

Cannon and fortifications now form an impregnable barrier against the Tartar horse; and Europe is secure from any future irruption of Barbarians; since, before they can conquer, they must cease to be barbarous. Their gradual advances in the science of war would always be accompanied, as we may learn from the example of Russia, with a proportionable improvement in the arts of peace and civil policy; and they themselves must deserve a place among the polished nations whom they subdue.[6]

It was against this (perhaps over-sanguine) assumption on Gibbon's part that material refinement could never exist alongside moral barbarism that Whitaker had silently directed his analysis of the peculiar evil embodied in the French revolutionaries.[7] And when Whitaker had

[4] Whitaker, *Real Origin of Government*, 53–4.

[5] *DF* ii. 508–16.

[6] *DF* ii. 514–15.

[7] Gibbon's assumption about the incompatibility of material refinement and moral coarseness might be thought to reveal the influence of Hume, in particular the argument of the essay 'Of Refinement in the Arts'. In general the Humean character of Gibbon's thought weakens over the period in which *The Decline and Fall* was composed: see, in this connection, what Gibbon says in his 'Memoirs' about the early date of composition of the 'General Observations' (*A* 324 n. 48; cf. also *DF* i, pp. lxv–lxvi and ii. 1009).

gone on to follow Burke's lead and to depict the revolutionaries as the spawn of philosophic enlightenment, the anti-Gibbonian subtext of his sermon had been reinforced.

Whitaker had nursed a grievance against Gibbon for many years, although the origin of their estrangement is disputed. The two men were acquainted at least by correspondence in 1773 when they had exchanged letters on the subject of Ossian,[8] a subject on which they both had sceptical reservations, although the manner of their expression was widely divergent.[9] Thereafter the two men exchanged further letters, and acquaintance seems slowly to have ripened into friendship. At least, Gibbon was prepared to exploit his position as a member of the House of Commons and to supply Whitaker with franks.[10] They seem also to have met,[11] although to judge from the careful formality of the style they seem always to have used to each other, they never became truly intimate.[12] However, there was sufficient confidence between them for Whitaker to be one of the few whom Gibbon was prepared to entrust with foreknowledge of the existence of *The Decline and Fall*. Whitaker's appetite was whetted: 'In the mean while, I hope you are engaged in the usefuller business of preparing your history for the public: no time, I think, should be lost, in justice to yourself as well as the public; and I should have been glad, if I could have been of half the service to you in it, that you have been of to me.'[13] According to

---

[8] *MW 1815* 587–93. Whitaker's reference to 'our old subjects' (*MW 1815* 592) suggests earlier exchanges of letters. Gibbon's letter, to which this is a reply, has not survived. In later life Whitaker was ostentatiously indifferent about the fate of the letters he had received from Gibbon: see the anecdote recounted in *L* ii. 90 n. 1.

[9] Compare the suave and learned precision of *DF* i. 152 n. 14 with the intemperance of Whitaker's *Genuine History of the Britons*.

[10] Cf. *MW 1815* 595 and 598.

[11] 'I should be very sorry to have our acquaintance, and (I hope I may add) our friendship, even suspended for the long interval of my absence from London,' Whitaker assured Gibbon in 1773 (*MW 1815* 592); and in 1775 Gibbon enquired as to Whitaker's 'intentions, with regard to London, for the ensuing Winter' (*L* ii. 90). But the language and tone of Whitaker's letter to Gibbon of 26 March 1776 suggests that their meetings never became either regular or relaxed: 'Cannot Mr. Gibbon and I, therefore, contrive to spend an hour together upon the subject [Gibbon's references to Whitaker's *History of Manchester* in *The Decline and Fall*]? I shall be very happy in waiting upon Mr. Gibbon at his own appointment, and either in Bentinck-street, Fetter-lane, or a coffee-house. And I shall be glad to cultivate the acquaintance of a gentleman . . .' (*MW 1815* 596).

[12] For the only surviving letter from Gibbon to Whitaker, see *L* ii. 90–1. Whitaker's surviving letters to Gibbon were printed by Sheffield in the second edition of the *Miscellaneous Works* (*MW 1815* 587–93, 595–600).

[13] *MW 1815* 592. This letter from Whitaker is dated 20 July 1773. The first allusion to *The Decline and Fall* in Gibbon's correspondence occurs in a letter to Sheffield dated 10 Sept. 1773 (*L* ii. 377: 'my great Work'). So Whitaker seems to have been taken into Gibbon's confidence at an early stage.

Whitaker, Gibbon availed himself of this offer of service, and sent him an advance copy of *The Decline and Fall* for comment, but held back the controversial final two chapters on Christianity, thereby eliciting approval on false pretences.[14] So, in any event, did Whitaker represent what had happened, in an *obiter dictum* written a decade after the death of 'my late unhappy friend, Mr. Gibbon':

with whom I afterwards spent many an hour, and exchanged many a letter of literary friendliness, during an intercourse of four or five years; by whom . . . the poor scepticism of his spirit was carefully kept a secret to me all the time, though I began to suspect it at last; from whom I even received the favour of perusing, at my own leisure, his History in manuscript, then prosecuted into a part of the second volume, but industriously gutted of every thing *very* offensive; and to whom I remonstrated upon his sending me the first *volume* printed in 1776, so boldly and so keenly in a couple of letters, on his impious effrontery against Christianity, as broke off our friendly intercourse for ever; . . .[15]

We know that Gibbon did selectively canvas opinion about *The Decline and Fall* before publication.[16] However, when Whitaker thanks Gibbon for his presentation copy of volume one of the history, he writes of it as a work encountered for the first time, and makes no allusion to any prior reading of a bowdlerized version (although he indeed vigorously deplores what he takes to be Gibbon's attacks on 'the religious system of your country').[17] Moreover, Whitaker was concealing other reasons for breaking off his friendship with Gibbon: the less reputable and less high-minded reasons of authorial vanity and frustrated acquisitiveness. In the first place, in 1787 Whitaker had been

[14] This may be the 'fairy favour' alluded to in the letter from Whitaker to Gibbon of 26 March, which Sheffield placed in 1776, but which seems on internal evidence to be earlier than that, therefore probably 1775 (*MW 1815* 596). Whitaker's comment that the 'obliging communication' contained 'two remarks' on the *History of Manchester* is corroborative. There are four references to the *History of Manchester* in vol. i of *The Decline and Fall*, but only two of them incorporate comments on the history (*DF* iii. 1274, *sub* 'Whitaker, John'). If in this letter Whitaker is indeed thanking Gibbon for a manuscript copy of the history, it would explain why the text of the two final chapters was not included. They had not yet received their final revision (*L* ii. 81). On 29 June 1775 (according to Sheffield's dating: the letter was not dated by Gibbon himself) Gibbon wrote to Sheffield to say that 'the Press is just set to work' on *The Decline and Fall* (*L* ii. 76).

[15] Whitaker, *Ancient Cathedral of Cornwall*, ii. 315–16.

[16] See e.g. the letter to Gibbon from George Lewis Scott of 29 Dec. 1775, thanking Gibbon for 'the liberty of perusing part of your work' (*MW 1796* i. 496). Gibbon also showed the manuscript of vol. i to Georges Deyverdun and his friend the barrister John Batt (*L* ii. 81; and see below, n. 27).

[17] *MW 1815* 597–600; quotation on p. 597. Whitaker's comments on the 'new shape' which Gibbon has imparted to deism are of particular interest (*MW 1815* 600).

piqued on hearing that Gibbon had mocked his work on Mary Queen of Scots.[18] Then injury was added to insult. Whitaker had wanted Gibbon to solicit Lord North for preferment on his behalf, but the expected patronage was never received.[19]

Whitaker first vented his accumulated spleen against Gibbon in his reviews of the final instalment of *The Decline and Fall*. These he had first published in the *English Review*, and then later collected as *Gibbon's History of the Decline and Fall of the Roman Empire . . . reviewed* (1791). It was a performance singled out by Sheffield as the most 'malignant and illiberal' of all those provoked by Gibbon's history.[20] But even this still left Whitaker with some debt of malice unpaid, some residue of un-expressed resentment. So in 1795 he took aim at Gibbon once again. It was an act of petty spite which there would be little point in excavating, were it not for the broader significance it can be made to yield. Coming a year after Gibbon's death and a year before the first publication of the *Miscellaneous Works*, Whitaker's covert sniping at a vulnerable passage of *The Decline and Fall* demonstrates that when composing his 'Memoirs' Gibbon had been right to suspect that attempts would be made to conscript him into the ranks of those held responsible for creating the possibility of the French Revolution. Whitaker's sermon is just such an attempt. It marks the shoals of public opinion around which Sheffield had carefully to navigate when preparing his friend's *Miscellaneous Works* for publication.

The story of how Gibbon's *Miscellaneous Works* were arranged for publication is by itself a subject on which a book could be written. In 1940 Jane Norton noted that the 'bibliographical history of Gibbon's *Miscellaneous Works* must be almost unique in the extent of its documentation', and listed the following materials:

1. In the British Museum, most of the author's own manuscripts, including the six separate drafts from which the single printed version of the memoirs was compiled.

[18] 'When Mr. Gibbon came to England, in 1787, he read Whitaker's Mary Queen of Scots, and I have heard him VERY *incautiously* express his opinion of it. Some *good natured friend* mentioned it to Mr. Whitaker. It must be an extraordinary degree of resentment that could induce any person, of a liberal mind, to scrape together defamatory stories, true or false, and blend them with the defence of the most benign religion, whose precepts inculcate the very opposite practice. Religion receives her greatest injuries from those champions of the church who, under the pretence of vindicating the Gospel, outrageously violate both the spirit and the letter of it' (*MW 1814* i. 243 n).
[19] Whitaker sought the wardenship of Manchester Collegiate Church; see Aston, 'A "Disorderly Squadron"?', 257 n. 20.
[20] *MW 1814* i. 243 n.

2. In the British Museum and in the collection of Sheffield Papers at Yale, a
   mass of letters and notes written to the editor advising about the publication
   of both the first and second editions.
3. Among the Sheffield Papers at Yale, a number of drafts made from the
   original manuscripts in preparation for printing, with alterations and
   emendations by the editor, and of drafts of the editor's own introduction
   and notes.
4. The printed letters of the editor's daughter, written at the time that the first
   edition was preparing.
5. In the British Museum, the editor's correspondence with the publishers of
   the first edition.
6. At Chicago University, the proof sheets of the first edition.
7. At Yale, the editor's copy of the first edition with additions and emendations for the second edition interleaved.
8. Among the Sheffield Papers at Yale, letters to the editor from the printers of
   the second edition.

And she reasonably concluded, 'in few cases can so much of the
original material used in editing and publishing an important book have
survived.'[21] That being the case, what I intend to do in this chapter is
simply to slice into the archive at a number of selected points. What will
result is no complete account of how Gibbon's *Miscellaneous Works*
were put together, but rather a maquette of such an account, albeit one
which will not I hope be positively misleading.[22]

II

At some point in 1789, while composing draft 'C' of his 'Memoirs',
Gibbon recalled an important episode in the studies which had prepared the way for *The Decline and Fall*:

As I believed, and as I still believe, that the propagation of the gospel and
triumph of the Church are inseperably [sic] connected with the decline of the
Roman Monarchy, I weighed the causes and effects of the Revolution, and
contrasted the narratives and apologies of the Christians themselves, with the
glances of candour or enmity which the Pagans have cast on the rising sect. The

---

[21] Norton, 198. Some small additions and corrections might be made to Norton's list of
materials. It is noteworthy, for instance, that Gibbon's manuscripts at the British Museum bear
in places pencil markings made by Sheffield as part of the process of preparing the *Miscellaneous
Works*. And the papers at Chicago are not simply the proof sheets of the first edition.

[22] Other accounts of the making of the *Miscellaneous Works* and of Sheffield's editorial handiwork can be found in Norton, 177–214 and Harrison, *Proceedings*, 18–35. Incidental comments
on the handling of particular texts are scattered through the standard accounts of Gibbon's life
and work, e.g. the 'Recueil géographique', in Craddock, *Young Edward Gibbon*, 182 ff., or the
'Journal' in *J1*, pp. xxii and xxv–xxix.

Jewish and Heathen testimonies, as they are collected and illustrated by Dr. Lardner, directed, without superseding my search of the originals; and in an ample dissertation on the miraculous darkness of the passion, I privately drew my conclusions from the silence of an unbelieving age.[23]

After Gibbon's death in January 1794 Sheffield put together a conflated text of his friend's 'Memoirs' from the six manuscript drafts, and published it in 1796 as the most substantial element in the two quarto volumes of *Miscellaneous Works*. The passage from draft 'C' was one of those that Sheffield selected for publication, but what he printed was this:

As I believed, and as I still believe, that the propagation of the Gospel, and the triumph of the church, are inseparably connected with the decline of the Roman monarchy, I weighed the causes and effects of the revolution, and contrasted the narratives and apologies of the Christians themselves, with the glances of candour or enmity which the Pagans have cast on the rising sects. The Jewish and Heathen testimonies, as they are collected and illustrated by Dr. Lardner, directed, without superseding, my search of the originals; and in an ample dissertation on the miraculous darkness of the passion, I privately withdrew my conclusions from the silence of an unbelieving age.[24]

It is a thoroughly inaccurate transcription, although its inaccuracies are not all of equal gravity. The changes in punctuation and capitalization would, at the time of publication, have been thought to fall within the legitimate discretion of an editor (or even of a printer).[25] More substantial is the substitution of the plural 'sects' for Gibbon's singular 'sect'—a substitution which seems intended to absolve Gibbon from the implication that Christianity was itself a sect. But most striking of all is the transformation of Gibbon's phrase 'drew my conclusions' for the very different 'withdrew my conclusions'.

Is this a simple case of editorial carelessness? It certainly falls short of what we would now regard as best editorial practice. But if we dismiss

---

[23] *A* 285. This dissertation on the passion is mentioned only once elsewhere in the 'Memoirs', in draft 'D', where however Gibbon gave no indication of the sceptical tendency of his work: 'These various studies were productive of many remarks and memorials, and in this supplement I may perhaps introduce a Critical dissertation on the miraculous darkness of the Passion' (*A* 412). In *The Decline and Fall* itself Gibbon handled the darkness of the passion with notorious freedom at the end of the fifteenth chapter (*DF* i. 512–13); it is reasonable to suppose that this passage in the history may be a heavily reduced version of the 'ample dissertation' recollected in the 'Memoirs'. In draft 'E' of the 'Memoirs' Gibbon recorded that the fifteenth and sixteenth chapters 'have been reduced, by three successive revisals, from a large Volume to their present size, and they might still be compressed without any loss of facts or sentiments' (*A* 308).

[24] *MW 1796* i. 140.

[25] As an example of the freedoms which printers might take, consider the changes made for the 5th edn. of vol. i of *The Decline and Fall*, in which Gibbon had no hand (*DF* i. 1084–105).

it as a *mere* error, and do not pause to wonder how it came about, we suffer in two respects. We run the risk of cleaving to our contemporary editorial protocols in an illiberal and dogmatic spirit, and we overlook the absorbing human stories which can, on occasion, be elicited from what seem like nothing more than blunders, such as the printing of 'withdrew' for 'drew'. Once we understand the story of which that slip was a part, we will be able also to understand why it was not, in fact, a pure and meaningless error.

In London on 16 January 1794 Edward Gibbon died, suddenly and unexpectedly, of post-operative peritonitis. Under the terms of Gibbon's will his executors were entrusted with all his manuscripts, and were empowered to publish any that appeared 'sufficiently finished for the public eye'.[26] The two executors were friends of long standing, John Batt and Lord Sheffield, and they seem to have agreed between themselves that it would be Lord Sheffield who took possession of the manuscripts, arranged for their publication, and received the resulting financial benefits.[27] It was towards the end of that month that Sheffield first had leisure to examine the papers in his friend's possession at the time of his death.[28] Gibbon had of course expected to return to Lausanne, where he had made his home since 1783, and so had travelled only with those manuscripts on which he was presently working.[29] Sheffield brought these manuscripts down to Sheffield Place, his family home in Sussex, and by early March was reading passages from them out loud to entertain his family.[30] At the same time Sir John Legard had been commissioned to bring over from Switzerland the remainder of Gibbon's papers, and the picture of Lord Sheffield by Reynolds which had hung in Gibbon's drawing room. These duly arrived in Sussex before the end of July 1794 (a month later than expected).[31]

[26] *A* 423.

[27] John Batt (1746–1831); barrister and commissioner in bankruptcy; friend of Dr Johnson as well as Gibbon; one of the few who read the manuscript of vol. i of *The Decline and Fall* (*L* ii. 81). For the financial benefits generated by the first edition of the *Miscellaneous Works*, see Norton, 190.

[28] Letter from Maria Josepha Holroyd to Ann Firth, 26 Jan. 1794, in Adeane, *Girlhood*, 267.

[29] These included four of the six drafts of the *Memoirs*, including drafts 'E' (that ending at 1791) and 'F' (that which ends with his leaving Oxford), as we learn from a letter dated 9 March 1794 from Maria Josepha Holroyd to Ann Firth: 'he has left Four [drafts of his *Memoirs*]; the last coming down no later than his leaving Oxford, and that which finishes at 1791 is only Heads and Notes, but infinitely curious' (Adeane, *Girlhood*, 274).

[30] Maria Josepha Holroyd to Ann Firth, 2 March 1794: 'Papa has read us several parts of Mr. Gibbon's Memoirs, written so exactly in the Style of his Conversation that, while we felt delighted at the Beauty of the Thoughts and Elegance of the Language, we could not help feeling a severe Pang at the Idea we should never hear his instructive and amusing Conversation any more' (Adeane, *Girlhood*, 273).

[31] Ibid. 280, 286, and 293. The far from perfect conditions of manuscript conservation at

In March 1794 Sheffield was still in doubt as to whether or not he should publish anything from these manuscripts, as his daughter confided to her friend, Ann Firth:

I believe I told you in my last scrap that we had read all the Memoirs, and that they were, as you may imagine, in the highest Degree interesting. There are many Passages that would be very unfit to Publish. . . . and if published would produce many Scribblers and much abuse, now that his ready Pen is no more there to answer them. Papa and Mr. Darrell agree the Memoirs are in much too unfinished a State for Publication; but they both think, with the help of his Letters to Papa, a very curious Book might be made out of them.[32]

But by early June he had firmly resolved 'to undertake the Arrangement of Mr. Gibbon's Memoirs and letters for the Public Eye', and went so far as to employ a secretary to deal with the clerical drudgery.[33] By September 1794 a small committee (including Sheffield himself and the poet William Hayley) were sitting in regular session on the 'Memoirs', deciding what could be printed and what should be suppressed or modified.[34] This process of editing by committee went on until the summer of the following year.[35] By September 1795 the edited text seems to have been in the hands of the printers.[36] The early months of 1796 were occupied in the correction of the proofs,[37] and on 31 March 1796, after some last-minute difficulties between Sheffield and the

Sheffield Place are unintentionally revealed by a letter of 29 July 1816 from Sheffield to Edward Maunde-Thompson, who had enquired concerning the whereabouts of a volume of Gibbon's 'Journal'. Sheffield replied that he was 'aware of the existence' of the volume, but went on to confess that he had 'not seen it,—I think for 30 or 40 years . . . I have seen it,—and it is, I hope, still in existence somewhere in this house: I will have another search made for it—and I will not leave anything undone, towards discovering it,—and I hope I may be successful —' (BM Add. MS 34876).

[32] Maria Josepha Holroyd to Ann Firth, 9 March 1794 (Adeane, *Girlhood*, 274). The Darells were Gibbon's bankers, as well as being related to the Gibbon family through marriage.

[33] Maria Josepha Holroyd to Ann Firth, 7 June 1794: 'His name is Socket; he is about 16; has had a good education; can read Latin and French; and is to have £20 a year and to live with the Servants' (Adeane, *Girlhood*, 286).

[34] Ibid. 303–4; Norton, 183–4.

[35] 'the Memoirs . . . are hastily drawing to a conclusion. I suppose there cannot be more than twenty pages wanting to finish the second volume'; 'The Gibbonian Memoirs go on swimmingly' (Adeane, *Girlhood*, 320 (12 May 1795) and 327 (19 July 1795)).

[36] Maria Josepha Holroyd to Ann Firth, 30 Sept. 1795: 'The Memoirs are in a progressive state, and I should hope Papa's being in Town may help to forward the Publication, as Printers are people who want much spurring' (Adeane, *Girlhood*, 336–7).

[37] Maria Josepha Holroyd to Serena Holroyd, 25 Jan. 1796: 'I broke off to correct the Press . . .'; Maria Josepha Holroyd to Ann Firth, 30 Sept. 1795: 'The 1st vol. of the Gibbonian Memoirs is quite printed off and the 2nd so far advanced that I now begin to hope, with some confidence,the work may come out soon after Easter. Milady and I are excellent Devils, and corrected yesterday 3 sheets of 16 pages each' (Adeane, *Girlhood*, 363 and 365).

publishers, and some three weeks later than expected, the two quarto volumes of the first edition of the *Miscellaneous Works* were finally published.[38] The first volume contained Sheffield's edition of the 'Memoirs', supported by a number of letters from and to Gibbon. The second comprised the texts of the works Gibbon had published before *The Decline and Fall*, together with a very careful selection of his hitherto unpublished writings.

It is essential to have this timetable clear in our mind, even though by itself it takes us only a little way towards understanding the forces which motivated and informed this act of publication. The key to moving beyond this—to grasping why Sheffield published what he did in 1796, why he felt able to publish more in the enlarged second edition, and why he edited the 'Memoirs' with the freedom which scandalized so many, once the scale and nature of his textual surgery became generally known at the end of the nineteenth century—is to understand that the publication of the *Miscellaneous Works* was yet another engagement in the struggle over Gibbon's reputation which had already been under way for nearly twenty years, which would last well into the nineteenth century, and which has been the subject of this book. It was a struggle in the first place between Gibbon himself and his detractors. But after Gibbon's death his place was taken by those, such as Sheffield, who saw themselves as the custodians of his fame.

The publication of the *Miscellaneous Works* was therefore an attempt to seize the prize which untimely death had denied to Gibbon himself: namely, the purification of his public reputation from the besmirching allegations which had tainted it since 1776, and which had been refreshed by the controversy arising from the French Revolution. From the very outset it was recognized by the committee who sat in editorial judgement on Gibbon's papers that nothing less than 'the fame and character of a common friend' was at stake.[39] The same note was struck by Sheffield in the short preface he placed at the head of the volumes:

I am persuaded, that the Author of them [the Memoirs] cannot be made to appear in a truer light than he does in the following pages. In them, and in his different Letters, which I have added, will be found a complete picture of his talents, his disposition, his studies, and his attainments. . . . I must, indeed, be blinded, either by vanity or affection, if they [the letters] do not display the

---

[38] Norton, 188–90. Advance copies seem to have been distributed to Sheffield's family a few days beforehand. His sister Serena at Bath had the books in her possession on 29 March 1796 (Adeane, *Girlhood*, 372).

[39] Maria Josepha Holroyd to Ann Firth, 10 Sept. 1794 (Adeane, *Girlhood*, 304); cf. also her awareness from the outset of the likelihood of controversy (Adeane, *Girlhood*, 274).

heart and mind of their Author, in such a manner as justly to increase the number of his admirers.[40]

Are the *Miscellaneous Works* then a straightforward act of extenuation? In part, yes; but towards the end of Gibbon's life Sheffield's ideas about how Gibbon's reputation might best be cleared were, as we have seen, slightly at variance with Gibbon's own. This divergence between the two men might naturally lead to Sheffield's attempting to vindicate Gibbon's character, after Gibbon's death, in ways that Gibbon himself might not have chosen. In fact, however, the space between Sheffield's and Gibbon's position on the revolution seems to have narrowed between Gibbon's death in January 1794 and publication of the first edition of the *Miscellaneous Works* in March 1796. These were years of virtually unrelieved setback for the cause of the counter-revolution, and Sheffield's morale suffered some heavy blows.[41] He had ended 1793 in low spirits, as his letter to Lord Auckland of 25 October reveals: 'I was scarce ever more anxious. . . . It seems to me to be too late to expect anything from counter-revolution at Brest. The death of the Queen [16 Oct. 1793] elevates me to such a pitch that I am equal to conflagration, murder, &c. I wish it were in my power to burn everything com-bustible and overturn every stone at Paris.' The new year brought no improvement. On 5 January Sheffield confided to Auckland that 'in truth I never was more disturbed by the state of things', and by April the sardonic tone of his letters shows that the iron had entered his soul:

I certainly am no longer afraid of French politics; perhaps I am grown callous. Events have happened to me within a year which have reduced me to an eminent degree of philosophy, indifference, or whatever you please to call it. I fear I care little about anything. I perceive that I hate politicians most heartily. I am piqued, perhaps, into vigorous notions. I rather feel I am in train to become what despots call a democrat, and in time, by the engaging ways of Lady Auckland and of *another*, I may slide further, and gradually become a friend of the people and of reform.

It was a mood which persisted until at least September: 'As to public affairs, I trouble myself not about them, nor do those employed in them trouble themselves in any degree or shape about me. . . . I have hardly even looked in a newspaper for some time. There is nothing pleasant to hear.'[42] Moreover, just before the *Miscellaneous Works* came out private

---

[40] *MW 1796* i, pp. v and vi–vii.

[41] See Appendix 7 below, for a tabular arrangement correlating the stages in the production of the *Miscellaneous Works* with the political and military context.

[42] The dates of the letters from which these extracts are taken are given in Appendix 7; the

anxiety was added to public despondency, as Lady Sheffield began to succumb to the consumption which would eventually kill her on 18 January 1797 (little over two years after their marriage).

In his preface Sheffield was frank about the adversity with which he had contended while working on Gibbon's papers: 'The melancholy duty of examining the Papers of my deceased Friend devolved upon me at a time when I was depressed by severe afflictions.'[43] An unpublished first draft of the beginning of the preface, in the Beinecke Library at Yale, is however significantly more forthcoming:

> The melancholy duty of examining my friends papers fell to my Lot at a Time, when my Mind labouring under severe Depression, was but little inclined to such a Task; From this Cause & a belief that the publick (entirely engrossed by the great Events which with such rapidity press upon their Minds & wholly occupy their thoughts) woud be little disposed to attend to the Memoirs of an Individual; I had nearly abandoned the idea of preparing his Manuscripts for the press: But when I reflected on the uncommon Anxiety & Solicitude he had ever shown about preparing "Memoires of his own Life & Writings" the loss it woud be to the lettred World to be deprived of what so admired an Author had taken pains to compose & the Apprehension that others woud publish a Life which might have been disgraced by an Attempt for which they coud have no in no Degree been prepared I determined to undertake the Work.[44]

What is of interest here is not only the stronger language which Sheffield uses of his own mental state ('my Mind labouring under severe Depression'), but also the explicit linkage with developments in the theatre of European conflict ('the great Events which with such rapidity press upon their Minds & wholly occupy their thoughts'). That Sheffield toyed with a more open confession of his own 'severe afflictions', and a more explicit relation of the *Miscellaneous Works* to the war with revolutionary France suggests that he found himself in a dilemma between more and less impetuous editorial paths.

A number of documents in the archive created by the publication of the *Miscellaneous Works* allow us to see Sheffield in the very act of hesitating in this dilemma. In the first place, we might consider the broader significance of the note on Gibbon's irreligion, which Sheffield drafted, then redrafted, but finally did not print.[45] I have already

full texts from which they are taken can be found in the appropriate place in Eden, *Journal and Correspondence*. Appendix 7 also reproduces passages from the letters of Maria Holroyd which indicate that Sheffield's low spirits were general at Sheffield Place.

[43] *MW 1796* i, p. iii.

[44] Beinecke Library, MS Vault, Sect. 10, Drawer 3, Sect. B 2 vii, f.

[45] Beinecke Library, MS Vault, Sect. 10, Drawer 3, Sect. B 11 i and ii; transcribed in Appendix 1, below.

discussed this important manuscript in terms of what we might call its primary significance: that is to say, what it suggests to us about Gibbon's state of mind concerning the imminent attacks on *The Decline and Fall* early in 1776.[46] However, it also tells us something about Sheffield's state of mind in the mid-1790s when he was preparing his friend's papers for publication. The encounter between the peer and the historian, at least as Sheffield dramatizes it in this note, is a clash between indecision and intransigence. Gibbon is prepared to bend before the imminent blast of public censure, but Sheffield stands firm. However, no matter how resolute Sheffield had been in 1776, the existence of two drafts of this note, and still more the eventual decision not to publish it, show that in the 1790s the peer had been infected with some of the historian's doubt. The very strategy of exculpation which Sheffield is toying with in the note also suggests divided purposes. On the one hand, Gibbon did not mean to offend: 'Mr Gibbon was not, in the first instance, aware how offensive his Irony, and manner of mentioning the Christian Religion, must be.' On the other, the reason for his having done so was that with him irreligion was somehow natural and automatic: 'He was so habituated to the infinitely more extravagant writings of Voltaire and others, and to the extreme levity of conversation, among the generality of those with whom he had lived, that he thought himself comparatively decent.' The argument Sheffield uses to exonerate Gibbon from the charge of deliberate offensiveness has the unfortunate effect of relying on his earlier intimacy with French *philosophes* such as Voltaire: an episode in Gibbon's life concerning which those protective of his reputation might not, in the 1790s and in the wake of Burke's indictment of French philosophy as the midwife of the Revolution, have wished to remind the public. Moreover, if as seems likely sheet ii is a first draft of the longer and more polished text on sheet i, then Sheffield had some significant second thoughts about the precise wording of this note. For instance, in the first draft he wrote that Gibbon 'had often' spoken to him about the 'Difficulty & Delicacy' of the religious aspect of *The Decline and Fall*. In the second draft, the indication of frequency is suppressed: 'while it was in hand, he said to me that there would be much difficulty and Delicacy in respect

---

[46] See above, Ch. 1. Sheffield's memory of the event is not wholly reliable. If the conversation with Gibbon indeed took place when the second edition was 'at the Press', then it cannot also have occurred 'some time after the Attack on the 15th and 16 Chapters had commenced', since nothing was published against *The Decline and Fall* until after the second edition of volume one had already appeared. For the actual timetable, see above, Ch. 1. Nevertheless, there is no reason to mistrust the substance of what Sheffield tells us in this note.

to that part which gives the History of the Christian Religion.' In such revisions we can see Sheffield becoming aware, as if for the first time, of the difficulty and delicacy of the task of vindicating the 'fame and character' of his friend. It was an awareness which conferred literary benefits as well as bringing the disquiet of anxiety. One of the passages in draft 'E' of the 'Memoirs' over which Sheffield may have raised an eyebrow was Gibbon's verdict on his literary talents: 'my friend has never cultivated the arts of composition.'[47] But the manuscripts which lie behind the *Miscellaneous Works* show Sheffield struggling to acquire those arts. As he wrestled with his editorial labours, he became sensitive to the importance of choice of word and arrangement of material in a way which he had previously not needed to be.

Sheffield's editorial decisions were not uniformly on the side of caution, as a small drama of revisal concerning a letter from Gibbon to Deyverdun will show. In this letter, written on 1 July 1783, Gibbon wrote with relaxed freedom of the woman who, when the *Miscellaneous Works* were published, was the close friend of the then Duchess of Devonshire, and who in 1809 would become Duchess of Devonshire herself: 'Quand retournez vous à Lausanne vous même? Je pense que vois y trouverez une petite bête bien aimable, mais tant soit peu méchante, qui se nomme Milady Elizabeth Foster; parlez lui de moi, mais parlez en avec discrétion; elle a des correspondances partout. Vale.'[48] That is the text as eventually published in the *Miscellaneous Works*. The proof-sheet, however, shows that Sheffield had qualms about this passage which he expressed with some vigorous strokes of the pen: 'Quand retournez vous à Lausanne vous même? Je pense que vois y trouverez une petite ~~bête~~ bien aimable, mais tant soit peu méchante, qui se nomme Milady Elizabeth Foster; parlez lui de moi, ~~mais parlez en avec discrétion; elle a des correspondances partout.~~ Vale.'[49] Both deletions are of interest, but it is the first, the suppression of the word 'bête', which is the more rich in implication. It looks like nothing more than the elision of a mildly insulting term. However, the word 'animal' had recently been associated with a woman of noble birth in a way which suggests a much sharper and more precise motive for the deletion than that offered by just general considerations of courtesy. In one of the most notorious passages of the *Reflections* Burke had memorably characterized the degrading outlook of the revolutionaries: 'On this scheme of things [that of the revolutionaries], a King is but a man; a queen is but a woman; a woman is but an animal; and an animal not of

[47] *A* 335 n. 56.   [48] *MW 1796* i. 592.   [49] Regenstein.

the highest order.'[50] We cannot know for a fact whether or not these words of Burke's were running through Sheffield's mind as he drew his pen through the word 'bête'. What we can say is that it would be unsurprising if they had been, because elsewhere his editorial policy involved the careful minimizing of those elements in Gibbon's life which might have suggested an affinity with the forces of revolution. It was an editorial policy which operated on a number of fronts, all of which were dictated by Burke's febrile but increasingly persuasive understanding of the revolutionary temperament. It consequently (and unsurprisingly) focused on irreligion. But it also deliberated anxiously over any suggestions of sexual irregularity, and of less than warm attitudes towards the family.

The unpublished note which we have already discussed indicates that Sheffield was well aware that Gibbon's reputation for irreligion was, in many respects, a battle which had been already lost and which was therefore to some extent not worth fighting. The connection between Gibbon and religious heterodoxy was so much a fixture in the literary public's mind that it must have seemed unshakeable. Nevertheless, something might still be done on the margin, and there was no need unnecessarily to confirm the reputation. So Sheffield did what he could to suppress Gibbon's links with those perceived to be the advocates of atheism, both at home and abroad.

An example occurs in the section of Sheffield's edition of the 'Memoirs' in which Gibbon is discussing his first published work, the *Essai sur l'Étude de la Littérature* of 1761, and in particular the section of the essay in which he offered some 'general remarks on the study of history and of man'. This is what Sheffield printed: 'I am not displeased with the inquiry into the origin and nature of the gods of polytheism, which might deserve the illustration of a riper judgment.'[51] But what Gibbon had written in draft 'B' of the 'Memoirs' was much longer:

I am not displeased with the enquiry into the origin and nature of the Gods of Polytheism. In a riper season of judgement and knowledge, I am tempted to review the curious question whether these fabulous Deities were mortal men or allegorical beings: perhaps the two systems might be blended in one; perhaps the distance between them is in a great measure verbal and apparent. In the rapid course of this narrative I have only time to scatter two or three hasty observations. *That* in the perusal of Homer a naturalist would pronounce his Gods and men to be of the same species, since they were capable of engender-

---

[50] Burke, *Reflections*, 128. Compare Gibbon's application of the word 'animal' to Louis XVI (above, p. 201).

[51] *MW 1796* i. 92.

ing together a fruitful progeny. *That* before the Reformation St. Francis and the Virgin Mary had almost attained a similar Apotheosis; and that the Saints and Angels, so different in their origin, were worshipped with the same rites, by the same nations. *That* the current of superstition and science flowed from India to Egypt, from Egypt to Greece and Italy; and that the incarnations of the Cœlestial Deities, so darkly shadowed in our fragments of Egyptian theology, are copiously explained in the sacred books of the Hindoos. Fifteen centuries before Christ, the great Osiris, the invisible agent of the Universe, was born or manifested at Thebes, in Bœotia, under the name of Bacchus; the idea of Bishen is a metaphysical abstraction; the adventures of Kishen, his perfect image, are those of a man who lived and died about five thousand years ago in the neighbourhood of Delhi.[52]

This passage could have alarmed Sheffield because of its proximity, in approach, language, and some points of interpretation, to Hume's writings on religion, in particular his *Natural History of Religion* (1757). Gibbon's chosen persona in this passage, that of the 'naturalist', might easily remind the reader of this work of Hume's, in which it had been postulated that Hercules, Theseus, and Bacchus were 'originally founded in true history, corrupted by tradition', and in which Hume had also expounded the anthropomorphism of the typical polytheist: 'They suppose their deities, however potent and invisible, to be nothing but a species of human creatures, perhaps raised from among mankind, and retaining all human passions and appetites, along with corporeal limbs and organs.'[53] That Gibbon and Hume had been friends was not something which could now be concealed. But nevertheless as editor of Gibbon's autobiographical papers Sheffield still enjoyed considerable power to disguise the extent of the intellectual affinity between the two men by means of deletions such as this.

A similar, and if anything more defensive, suppression occurs in the section of the 'Memoirs' devoted to Gibbon's first visit to Paris in 1763. The nature of Gibbon's involvement in the French social and intellectual circles of the mid-century was always going to be difficult biographical terrain after 1789, and so it proved for both the historian and his editor. Having recorded the fact that Gibbon had a 'place, without invitation, at the hospitable tables of Mesdames Geoffrin and du Bocage, of the celebrated Helvetius, and of the Baron d'Olbach', Sheffield's text goes on to evoke in purely general terms the society and conversation of these *salons*: 'In these symposia the pleasures of the table were improved by lively and liberal conversation; the company was

---

[52] *A* 173–4.
[53] Hume, *Natural History of Religion*, 29 and 35.

select, though various and voluntary.'[54] In draft 'B' of the 'Memoirs', however, Gibbon himself had been much more specific:

. . . the company was select, though various and voluntary, and each unbidden guest might mutter a proud, an ungrateful sentence.

Αυτοματοι δ'αγαθοι δειλων επι δαιτας ιασιν

Yet I was often disgusted with the capricious tyranny of Madame Geoffrin, nor could I approve the intolerant zeal of the philosophers and Encyclopædists the friends of d'Olbach and Helvetius; they laughed at the scepticism of Hume, preached the tenets of Atheism with the bigotry of dogmatists, and damned all believers with ridicule and contempt.[55]

It is not remarkable that after 1789 Gibbon should so explicitly have sought to separate himself from the compromising thinkers with whom he was so regularly associated (though the strength of the disavowal is noteworthy). Yet it surely is remarkable that Sheffield should have decided to suppress this passage. Even a vehement rejection of dogmatic atheism might, it seems, do damage; it would confirm the fact of social contact.

A disposition to scoff at established religion was but one expression of that more generalized antipathy towards traditional pieties which counter-revolutionary writers such as Burke had imputed to the revolutionaries. Others included libertinism, and here again Sheffield was vigilant. Gibbon's life gave few grounds for suspicion on this score, but on the first visit to Paris there was a liaison of sorts with a good-time girl of literary tastes called—in an uncanny prolepsis of twentieth-century idiom—Madame Bontemps.[56] In the *Miscellaneous Works*, Sheffield suppressed all mention of Madame Bontemps, moving immediately from Gibbon's evaluation of the histrionic skills of the great Parisian actresses of the day to the recollection of a neglected impulse towards permanent residence in Paris—an impulse which, in that juxtaposition, looks like the result of a purely cultural appetite: 'For my own part, I preferred the consummate art of the Clairon, to the intemperate sallies of the Dumesnil, which were extolled by her admirers, as the genuine voice of nature and passion. Fourteen weeks insensibly stole away; but had I been rich and independent, I should have prolonged, and perhaps have fixed, my residence at Paris.'[57] In

---

[54] *MW 1796* i. 115–16.

[55] *MW 1796* i. 203–4. Eupolis, χρυσουν γενος.

[56] Marie Jeanne de Chatillon (1718–68); wife of Pierre Henri Bontemps, paymaster of the forces.

[57] *MW 1796* i. 117.

draft 'B' of the 'Memoirs', however, Gibbon had interposed the sketch of a romance between his appreciation of Parisian theatre and his regretful departure:

. . . genuine voice of nature and passion. I have reserved for the last the most pleasing connection which I formed at Paris—the acquisition of a female friend, by whom I was sure of being received every evening with the smile of confidence and joy. I delivered a letter from Mrs. Mallet to Madame Bontems, who had distinguished herself by a translation of Thomson's Seasons into French prose: at our first interview we felt a sympathy which banished all reserve, and opened our bosoms to each other. In every light, in every attitude, Madame B. was a sensible and amiable Companion, an author careless of litterary honours, a devotee untainted with Religious gall. She managed a small income with elegant economy: her apartment on the Quai des Theatins commanded the river, the bridges, and the Louvre; her familiar suppers were adorned with freedom and taste; and I attended her in my carriage to the houses of her acquaintance, to the sermons of the most popular preachers, and in pleasant excursions to St. Denys, St. Germain, and Versailles. In the middle season of life, her beauty was still an object of desire: the Marquis de Mirabeau, a celebrated name, was neither her first nor her last lover; but if her heart was tender, if her passions were warm, a veil of decency was cast over her frailties. Fourteen weeks insensibly stole away: but had I been rich and independent, I should have prolonged, and perhaps have fixed, my residence at Paris.[58]

Although the vocabulary here hovers delicately between the sentimental and the physical, it is nevertheless hard not to read the concluding sentence quite differently in Gibbon's manuscript from the reading it demands in Sheffield's edited text: as the record of an erotic, rather than a cultural, sacrifice. In the manuscript, the need for wealth on Gibbon's part seems necessary in order to compensate for Madame Bontems' 'small income', while the fourteen weeks of insensibility seems to be the result of an emotional, not a theatrical rapture. And when the passage draws to a close on the note of what cannot be expressed through the 'veil of decency', it is natural to construe the information that the Marquis de Mirabeau was 'neither her first nor her last lover' as an oblique encouragement to see Gibbon himself as the Marquis's successor. This is far from any frank avowal of libertinism. But even so subtly expressed a recollection of the sexual freedom of Paris in the 1760s was material too dangerous to receive Sheffield's *imprimatur* in the 1790s.

---

[58] *A* 204–5. Gibbon himself slightly compressed this passage for draft 'C', but retained the language which hints, albeit coyly, at a physical relationship (*A* 263). There is no mention of Madame Bontemps in drafts 'D' and 'E'.

The need to trim away such passages was strengthened by the otherwise unsatisfactory nature of Gibbon's family life. Burke had insisted that the family was the matrix of our political attitudes, which would be healthy or corrupt in so far as the family in which we were bred was so too. We have already seen Gibbon wrestling in the three versions of the death of his father with the consequences of the sudden politicizing of the family which Burke's *Reflections* had brought about.[59] It also evidently gave Sheffield pause for thought. In the *Miscellaneous Works* the death of Gibbon's natural mother is related in these words:

My studies were too frequently interrupted by sickness; and after a real or nominal residence at Kingston-school of near two years, I was finally recalled (December 1747) by my mother's death, which was occasioned, in her thirty-eighth year, by the consequences of her last labour. I was too young to feel the importance of my loss; and the image of her person and conversation is faintly imprinted in my memory.[60]

Gibbon himself, however, had in draft 'F' of the 'Memoirs' been more forthcoming about the nature of his feelings at this loss:

My studies were too frequently interrupted by sickness; and after a real or nominal residence at Kingston school of near two years, I was finally recalled (December, 1747) by my mother's death, which was occasioned, in her thirty-eighth year, by the consequences of her last labour. As I had seldom enjoyed the smiles of maternal tenderness she was rather the object of my respect than of my love: some natural tears were soon wiped. I was too young to feel the importance of my loss, and the image of her person and conversation is faintly imprinted in my memory.[61]

The main motive for Sheffield's deletion of the central sentence must have been an anxiety over how so frigid a declaration of emotional self-possession at the death of a parent would be received. A secondary consideration might also have been the Miltonic allusion in 'some natural tears were soon wiped', since the public had recently been reminded of Milton's republicanism by Johnson in his *Lives of the Poets* (1779–81).[62]

Johnson, and his reputation in the 1790s, is also a factor in the final

---

[59] Above, Ch. 6.
[60] *MW 1796* i. 23.
[61] *A* 45.
[62] 'Some natural tears they dropped, but wiped them soon; . . .' (*Paradise Lost*, xii. 645). Gibbon seems to have reread *Paradise Lost* during the Revolution crisis; cf. above, Ch. 5. However, to allude in this way to these words of Milton might by this time have become commonplace; in *Rambler*, 170 (2 Nov. 1751) they had already been quoted in the context of a parting between parents and child.

example I wish to discuss to illustrate Sheffield's editing of the 1796 volumes. Towards the end of the text of the 'Memoirs' as printed in the *Miscellaneous Works*, Gibbon muses in these words on the possible causes of his literary success: 'I cannot boast of the friendship or favour of princes; the patronage of English literature has long since been devolved on our booksellers, and the measure of their liberality is the least ambiguous test of our common success. Perhaps the golden mediocrity of my fortune has contributed to fortify my application.'[63] But in draft 'E', Gibbon's thoughts had run on: '. . . fortify my application: few books of merit and importance have been composed either in a garret or a palace. A Gentleman, possessed of leisure and competency, may be encouraged by the assurance of an honourable reward; but wretched is the writer, and wretched will be the work, where daily diligence is stimulated by daily hunger.'[64] The motives for this deletion are harder to discern, at least on the surface. But we might begin by recalling that Boswell's *Life of Johnson* had recently informed the reading public about Johnson's very high esteem for booksellers. It had been the subject of a memorable conversation between the two men: 'I once said to him, "I am sorry, Sir, you did not get more for your *Dictionary*." His answer was, "I am sorry, too. But it was very well. The booksellers are generous, liberal-minded men." He, upon all occasions, did ample justice to their character in this respect. He considered them as the patrons of literature; . . .'.[65] It is a judgement echoed by Gibbon's opinion that 'the patronage of English literature has long since been devolved on our booksellers'. But thereafter Gibbon's views diverge sharply from an equally well-known precept of Johnson's concerning composition. Boswell had cited Johnson's almost unintermitted composition of *The Rambler* as a 'strong confirmation of the truth of a remark of his, which I have had occasion to quote elsewhere, that a "man may write at any time, if he will set himself doggedly to it."'[66] This is at variance with Gibbon's judgement, that the literary imagination works better when free rather than when flogged: 'A Gentleman, possessed of leisure and competency, may be encouraged by the assurance of an honourable reward; but wretched is the writer, and wretched will be the work, where daily diligence is stimulated by daily hunger.' Gibbon's view on this point is hardly in conflict with the

---

[63] *MW 1796* i. 184.

[64] *A* 347.

[65] Boswell, *Life of Johnson*, 217; cf. p. 310.

[66] Ibid. 144. The earlier citation was in the *Journal of a Tour to the Hebrides*, under 16 Aug. 1763.

greater emphasis upon the value of gentility which arose, at least amongst counter-revolutionary circles, in the 1790s. But Johnson's reputation also developed in interesting ways after the outbreak of revolution in France. At his death, it had proved impossible to raise sufficient funds for a monument in Westminster Abbey.[67] But in the 1790s he was being praised by Arthur Murphy as 'the great moral teacher of his countrymen', and by Anna Seward as a 'sublime teacher of perfect morality'.[68] Moreover, Boswell had offered the second, 1793, edition of the *Life* to the public specifically as a remedy for the French disease of political radicalism:

His [Johnson's] strong, clear, and animated enforcement of religion, morality, loyalty, and subordination, while it delights and improves the wise and the good, will, I trust, prove an effectual antidote to that detestable sophistry which has been lately imported from France, under the false name of Philosophy, *and with a malignant industry has been employed against the peace, good order, and happiness of society, in our free and prosperous country; but thanks be to* GOD, *without producing the pernicious effects which were hoped for by its propagators.*[69]

Clearly, the cause of Sheffield and his collaborators to vindicate Gibbon's reputation from the taint of, if not exactly revolutionary sympathies, then at least of having trodden the path which had paved the way to revolution, would not be helped were he to be discovered in the 'Memoirs' dissenting from the man who was now being made to embody in his own person the English resistance to the regicide regime in France. It is a deletion which illustrates the vigilant policing of potentially damaging details which is the hallmark of Sheffield's editing of the 1796 edition of the *Miscellaneous Works*.

III

Sheffield seems from the outset to have considered the possibility of a second edition of the *Miscellaneous Works* in which Gibbon's unpublished writings would be more completely represented.[70] However,

---

[67] Boswell, *Life of Johnson*, 1396.

[68] Boulton, *Johnson: The Critical Heritage*, 69 and 413.

[69] Boswell, *Life of Johnson*, 7.

[70] One of the points of contention with the publishers of the 1796 volume, Strahan and Cadell, which had delayed the appearance of the books was Sheffield's wish to include a list of writings which might be published at some future date (Norton, 189–90). In their letter to Sheffield of 12 March 1796, Strahan and Cadell feared, not unreasonably, that the proposed list of unpublished manuscripts would 'have the Effect of making the Public not so ready to purchase as if they were completing Mr. Gibbon's Works by their Publication; and, by throwing out the Idea of a Continuation, make them shy of the First Expence for these two Volumes' (B.M. Add.

serious planning of the second edition seems to have begun only in 1807.[71] Therefore the years in which the second edition of the *Miscellaneous Works* were planned and put together were years in which the tide of success gradually turned against Napoleonic France. It is not surprising, then, that these years also witnessed a dramatic recovery in Sheffield's spirits. The decade between 1796 and 1806 had given him little satisfaction. In September 1796 he had gloomily sensed that the future would be even worse than the past: 'I probably shall soon be obliged to acknowledge that the evils I feared are nothing when compared to those which are coming on.' Even Trafalgar applied no balm to his shattered nerves: 'What say you to the present state of things? Can anything be more frightful?' Napoleon's victory at Austerlitz a few months later merely confirmed to him that he had been right to accept no comfort: 'Our situation is desperate. There is nothing to look to.' But the disintegration of the Grande Armée in the course of its retreat from Russia, and then the victories of the Grand Alliance over Napoleon during the following year, completely changed his mood: 'I am so exceedingly exalted that I begin to flatter myself with the expectation of the restoration of the Bourbons,' he wrote in January 1814.[72]

The effect of this improvement of the international situation upon the contents of the volumes published in 1815 was, at one level, simple and obvious. It removed many of the concerns which had restricted the range of what Sheffield had been prepared to publish in 1796. The imminent defeat of Napoleon and restoration of the *ancien régime* in the person of the Bourbons, to which Sheffield looked forward with such enthusiasm, meant that the French Revolution must have seemed almost like concluded business. As a result, opinions, associations, and interests on Gibbon's part which, in the more ominous circumstances of the mid-1790s, had seemed to Sheffield too compromising to acknowledge, might now find a place in the published record without exposing his dead friend to unwelcome comment. So new manuscript material was introduced, as well as new letters from 'very considerable personages', some of which had been elicited by personal appeals for fresh material from Sheffield.[73]

MS 34887, fo. 332ʳ). Nevertheless, Sheffield's will prevailed. A list of unpublished manuscripts was included at the beginning of the second volume of the first edition (*MW 1796* ii, pp. iv–v), introduced by the proclamation that 'there still remain in my possession many Papers which I think equally worth attention'.

[71] Norton, 192.

[72] The dates of the letters from which these extracts are taken are given in Appendix 7: cf. n. 42 above.

[73] Eden, *Journal and Correspondence*, iv. 409; Norton, 193–4.

For the most part, the additional material suggests greater confidence and extinguished inhibitions. For example, Sheffield now included for the first time Gibbon's early unpublished writings in French, such as the essay 'Sur la Monarchie des Mèdes', in which his familiarity with, and deep reflection on, the concerns of the French *philosophes* were obvious.[74] It would be wrong, however, to imagine that what we have in 1815 is a simple case of restraint removed. Some of the reviewers of the 1796 volumes had complained of the extent to which the financial minutiae of Gibbon's life were recorded in the letters published as part of the first edition; Sheffield accordingly deleted a number of letters from Gibbon to his publisher in which occurred allusions to the monetary aspects of publication of *The Decline and Fall*.[75] That suggestion of continued sensitivity to public opinion is further attested by some of the most interesting documents in the Sheffield papers at the Beinecke Library. A number of them record an initial impulse towards disclosure, which is then either completely or substantially stifled. For instance, the Beinecke papers indicate that Sheffield intended originally to include some additional letters written by him to Gibbon in 1792, in which he commented on European politics, either despairingly or with what turned out to be ungrounded optimism.[76] But in the event he decided against them, and they were not included.

A similar, small drama of indecision can be inferred from a detail in the interleaved set of the first edition of the *Miscellaneous Works* which Sheffield used in the preparation of the second edition, and which is now kept in the Beinecke Library at Yale.[77] In the first edition, Sheffield had included the text of a long letter written to Gibbon by his daughter Maria Josepha in November 1791. In the letter she describes the massacre of the priests and of the archbishop of Arles, which they had heard about from a group of *émigré* French clergymen who had landed on the Sussex coast in an open boat, and who had been brought to Sheffield Place. In the first edition, the letter ends as follows:

[74] Peel's inability to speak fluent conversational French when visiting Paris shows how little French culture might be possessed by even a well-educated Englishman in the early nineteenth century (Thomas, *Macaulay and Croker*, 96). In the context of that cultural sundering of England from France, only imminent victory could neutralize the damaging implications of Gibbon's immersion in French *mœurs*, literature, and language.
[75] Norton, 191. Given that Sheffield had by this time fallen out with Strahan and Cadell (the second edition being published by John Murray), it may be that personal pique contributed to his determination to suppress these letters; Norton, 189–90.
[76] Beinecke Library, Im G352 and C796, I. i. 246–7 (ungrounded optimism)—cf. Prothero, ii. 304–8, letter from Sheffield to Gibbon of 30 July 1792. I. i. 252–3 (despair)—cf. Prothero, ii. 319–22, letter from Sheffield to Gibbon of 17 Oct. 1792.
[77] Beinecke Library, Im G352 and C796.

'There can be no doubt that the whole business of the massacres was concerted at a meeting at the Duke of Orleans's house. I shall make you as dismal as myself by this narration. I must change the style.' ★ ★ ★ ★ ★ ★ ★ ★ ★ ★[78]

The row of asterisks indicates an elision of text. On the blank, facing interleaved page in the Beinecke volumes, Sheffield copied out the suppressed text, presumably with the intention of printing it in the second edition:

Mon ame est sans culotes; you must not be shocked; it is perfectly classic since the new order of things. Such was the opening of an exquisite piece of Eloquence lately in the assembly, and a speech is nothing unless sans culoterie is interlarded.

Citoyen Gibbon, je suis ton Egale

M.J. Holroyd

It is clear why Sheffield had decided against printing this in 1796. Even so mordantly sarcastic an adoption of revolutionary language might have been open to misinterpretation in the feverish political climate of the mid-1790s. By 1814, however, it seemed safe to let the original language of the letter stand. Except that the intention to restore the full text of the letter, preserved in the annotation in the Beinecke volumes, did not take effect. The second edition of the *Miscellaneous Works* prints more than was tolerated for the first edition, but it still stops short of a full restoration:

'There can be no doubt that the whole business of the massacres was concerted at a meeting at the Duke of Orleans' house. I shall make you as dismal as myself by this narration. I must change the style.' ★ ★ ★ ★ ★ ★ ★ ★ ★ ★ Citoyen Gibbon, je suis ton égal. MARIA J. HOLROYD.[79]

Even now, with the restoration of the Bourbons just over the political horizon, the revelation of his daughter's playful *sans culoterie* is, on reflection, better suppressed.

Two further annotations in the Beinecke volumes also illustrate the smothered candour which stamped Sheffield's editing of the second edition of the *Miscellaneous Works*. Both of them reveal Sheffield's returning to a letter of Gibbon's on which he had performed some editorial surgery for the first edition of the *Miscellaneous Works*, and being tempted towards a fuller disclosure. The first annotation occurs in the text of Gibbon's letter to Sheffield of 25 November 1792. Gibbon touches on the prospect, revealed to him by Sheffield, of a 'firm and

---

[78] *MW 1796* i. 260–2; quotation on p. 262.
[79] *MW 1814* i. 376.

honourable union of parties', and then adds ruefully (at least as it was printed in 1796): 'Yet what can such a coalition avail? Where is the champion of the constitution?'[80] The actual text of the letter, however, made reference to living personages. Gibbon in fact wrote: 'Yet what can such a coalition avail? if Fox be detestable and Pitt democratical, where is the champion of the Constitution.'[81] In the Beinecke volumes, Sheffield made the following annotation on the interleaved page facing the text of the letter. Firstly he restored the deleted text, by transcribing what had been suppressed: '^ If Fox be detestable and Pitt democratical, yet where'. And then below this he added his own comment on what he took to be the implication of Gibbon's phrasing: 'these expressions were not used by me in any letter to Gibbon'. But once more Sheffield thought better of his candour. The second edition of the *Miscellaneous Works* prints exactly the same text of this letter as had the first edition.[82]

There is a similar annotation in the text of Gibbon's letter to Sheffield of 6 January 1793. Once again, the delicacy arises from some comments on English politics. In 1796 Sheffield had printed this text: 'Before I conclude, we must say a word or two of parliamentary and pecuniary concerns. 1. We all admire the generous spirit with which you damned the assassins ★ ★. I hope that ★ ★ ★ ★ ★'[83] The asterisks once again indicate where some text has been excised. What Gibbon actually wrote was this: 'Before I conclude, we must say a word or two of Parliamentary and pecuniary concerns. 1. We all admire the generous spirit with which you damned the Assassins; but I hope that your abjuration of all future connection with Fox was not quite so peremptory as it is stated in the French papers. Let him do what he will I must love the dog.'[84] In the Beinecke volumes Sheffield once again restored the text he had cut out in 1796 by transcribing it on the facing, interleaved page: '^ your abjuration of all future connection with Fox was not quite so peremptory as it is stated in the French papers. Let him do what he will I must love the dog.' And once again he appended his own comment on this text, by writing below it: 'I never abjure all future all future connection with him altho' I vigorously reprobated his conduct—S.' Sheffield's choler is perhaps discernible in the emphatic repetition of the phrase 'all future'. If so, it was an intemperance from which he recovered. In the second edition of the *Miscellaneous Works*,

[80] *MW 1796* i. 268.
[81] BM Add. MS 34885, fos. 184–5; *L* iii. 303–4.
[82] *MW 1814* i. 383.
[83] *MW 1796* i. 275.
[84] BM Add. MS 34885, fos. 190–2; *L* iii. 313.

Gibbon's comments on Fox are restored, but the putative annotation clarifying Sheffield's attitude towards Fox was never printed.[85]

What these annotations capture so vividly, when juxtaposed with the texts of the first and second editions of the *Miscellaneous Works*, is the volatility of mood in which Sheffield set about his editorial tasks when preparing the enlarged second edition. It is a volatility which asks at one level to be related to the precariousness of the international situation, with victory over Napoleonic France in sight but yet not quite within reach. In so suspended a situation, Sheffield's editorial guard could not drop completely. He still had measures to keep, and so submitted himself to the prudential discipline which stood sentinel over his candour.

He continued to do so on behalf of his dead friend, as well as on his own account, as the last set of examples we shall consider illustrates. One of the works which Sheffield published for the first time in the second edition of the *Miscellaneous Works* was Gibbon's 'Remarks' on Blackstone's *Commentaries*.[86] The manuscript of this work bears pencilled annotations which show Sheffield's censoring of comments he considered to be of too free a nature for publication. On the first page of the manuscript Gibbon had composed three notes to his own annotations, in which with a mocking courtliness he had smiled over both the worldly wiles of clergymen and the irrational, customary character of the English common law:

This excellent work, of which, we have only the first volume is extracted which Mr. B. read as Vinerian Professor, and may be considered as a rational System of the English Jurisprudence digested into a natural method, & cleared of the pedantry the obscurity and the superfluities which rendered it the unknown horror of all men of taste.

Perhaps Mr. B might have shewn the reasons of the preference with the Clergy gave to the Civil and Canon, and have given us some instances how well they suited the Views and Interest of the Ecclesiastical Order.

Mr. B touches upon this neglect [the defects of English legal education], with the becoming tenderness of a pious son who would wish to conceal the infirmities of his parent.[87]

---

[85] *MW 1814* i. 392. Fox had died in 1806. See Low, *Edward Gibbon*, 116 for discussion of another example of Sheffield's printing material only after the death of the subject of an anecdote (in this case, Wilkes, who died in 1797). Compare *MW 1796* i. 100 n. with *MW 1814* i. 142 n to see the later addition.

[86] *MW 1814* v. 545–7. The full text has been reprinted in *EE* 59–87. BM Add. MS 34881, fos. 216ᵛ–41.

[87] BM Add. MS 34881, fo. 216ᵛ; cf. *EE* 63. The anticipation in this last note, written in 1765 (*EE* 55), of the subject matter of Chapter 7 above is striking. The corrupt grammar of the first note is as Gibbon wrote it.

Sheffield eventually published the first of these notes, but suppressed the others.[88] The same motive, of concealing from sight the frank anti-clericalism of the young Edward Gibbon, urged him to delete the following passage, which speculates that the clergy prefer traditional to written law, because its confusions create more opportunities for the operation of priestcraft: 'I think the Clergy of all religions have as constantly preferred the traditional to the written law; and perhaps too from the same motives.'[89] In 1814 anti-clericalism was still too damaging an attribute to be openly confessed. But Sheffield's second thoughts had evidently reassured him that the rationalist, anti-prescriptive aspect of Gibbon's thinking in the mid-1760s could after all be placed before the public in 1814, notwithstanding the fact that it flew in the face of the premisses of Burke's *Reflections*. It is an editorial judgement which calibrates with some precision the degree of additional relaxation which Sheffield permitted himself in preparing the second edition of the *Miscellaneous Works*.

IV

Let us return to the example of Sheffield's editorial workmanship with which we began; namely, the printing of 'withdrew my conclusions' for 'drew my conclusions.' By allowing 'withdrew' to stand in place of 'drew', Sheffield inverted the sense of the passage. In Gibbon's manuscript, the 'unbelieving age' is Mediterranean society at the time of the Crucifixion. When he says that he 'drew [his] conclusions from the silence of an unbelieving age', what he means is that, when he noted that no contemporary non-Christian witnesses had recorded the darkness of the Passion, he inferred that it had never in fact taken place, but instead was yet another of those fictitious prodigies with which credulous men embroider the deaths of political or religious leaders. As he had put it at end of the fifteenth chapter of *The Decline and Fall* some thirteen years earlier:

But how shall we excuse the supine inattention of the Pagan and philosophic world, to those evidences which were presented by the hand of Omnipotence, not to their reason, but to their senses? . . . Under the reign of Tiberius, the whole earth, or at least a celebrated province of the Roman empire, was involved in a præternatural darkness of three hours. Even this miraculous

---

[88] The first note corresponds to the first paragraph of the text as published in the second edition of the *Miscellaneous Works* (*MW 1814* v. 545).

[89] BM Add. MS 34881, fo. 217ᵛ; *EE* 63; cf. *MW 1814* v. 547. For another such suppression, see Craddock, *Young Edward Gibbon*, 92.

event, which ought to have excited the wonder, the curiosity, and the devotion of mankind, passed without notice in an age of science and history. It happened during the lifetime of Seneca and the elder Pliny, who must have experienced the immediate effects, or received the earliest intelligence, of the prodigy. . . . A distinct chapter of Pliny is designed for eclipses of an extraordinary nature and unusual duration; but he contents himself with describing the singular defect of light which followed the murder of Cæsar, when, during the greatest part of a year, the orb of the sun appeared pale and without splendour. This season of obscurity, which cannot surely be compared with the præternatural darkness of the Passion, had been already celebrated by most of the poets and historians of that memorable age.[90]

But when 'withdrew' takes the place of 'drew', the meaning of the passage is reversed from impiety to piety. The 'unbelieving age' now becomes Gibbon's own time, and the implication is that Gibbon concealed and withdrew his entirely orthodox conclusions about the darkness of the Passion to prevent their being scoffed at by his irreligious contemporaries.

If the printing of 'withdrew' was an error, it is difficult to see it as an entirely random one. For, as we have seen when analysing the considerations which prevailed over the composition of the first edition of the *Miscellaneous Works*, there must have been a part of Sheffield which indeed wished that Gibbon had either been orthodox in the matter of religion, or, if that was beyond him, had indeed withdrawn his conclusions (no matter how much he himself may have shared them). If he had done so, then the editorial dilemma with which Sheffield had been forced to grapple on two occasions—namely, how much of Gibbon's ancillary writing was to be published, and when—would have been much abated.

From our standpoint, and no matter what his conscious or unconscious motives, Sheffield's handling of Gibbon's manuscript was scandalous.[91] And, confining ourselves still for the moment to this present example, one might say that the fact that Sheffield corrected the slip for the second edition[92] and printed the correct 'drew my conclusions', supports an uncompromising view of his editing as simply defective. Against which, we may say that Sheffield's editing was neither narrowly self-interested nor ignoble in its motives. The presiding concern of any editor must be fidelity, but fidelity to what? For

[90] *DF* i. 512–13.
[91] 'By all the standards of scholarship, Lord Sheffield's conduct was deplorable' (Norton, 186).
[92] *MW 1814* i. 214.

the modern editor of a work of literature, the distraction of wider allegiances seldom arises. We can afford the luxury of narrow views, because we live in a time in which literature—certainly past literature, and for the most part contemporary literature, too—has become decoupled from public life. But the case of the *Miscellaneous Works* was very different. Its fashioning was conditioned by the most markedly ideological conflict in Europe and the Mediterranean basin since the Crusades. Unsurprisingly, Sheffield took wide views and pondered consequences. But he did not merely surrender to the pressures which in 1795 and 1796 came close to crushing him. On both occasions when he edited the writings of his dead friend, he took his bearings shrewdly from the prevailing circumstances, and tried to balance his duty to the truth against his desire to offer as little purchase as possible to mischievous calumny. If we find more to blame than to admire in Sheffield's editorial workmanship, we can do so only from a position of great ethical strangeness.

Conclusion

The implications of this study extend in two directions. In respect of Gibbon himself, tracing the influence of reputation on creativity has led to fresh insights concerning Gibbon's experience of authorship. By reviewing Gibbon's various engagements with his critics in the period extending from the anxious weeks spent preparing the revisions to volume one of *The Decline and Fall* during the spring of 1776 until the fatal illness of January 1794 which cut short both the historian's life and the project of autobiography which had preoccupied and perplexed him till the very end, we have been obliged often to supplement, and at moments to challenge and correct, the accounts of his experience as an author supplied by Gibbon himself, whether in his 'Memoirs', or in his letters, or in works such as *A Vindication*. Paying attention to the dramas of the shaping, contesting, and redemption of reputation which run so strongly through Gibbon's career has allowed us also to advance more circumstantial and persuasive explanations than were previously available for the complicated and shifting motives which produced the extraordinary process of repeated composition and revision embodied in the six drafts of the 'Memoirs'. As a corollary of this, Gibbon's friendship with Lord Sheffield has been analysed with new fullness, and the tensions as well as the affinities between the two men, together with their literary consequences in the editing of the 'Memoirs' and more broadly in the construction of the *Miscellaneous Works*, have been brought to light. Turning to *The Decline and Fall*, by following the clew of reputation a previously hidden aspect of the serial publication of the history has been made visible; namely, the way in which the reception of earlier instalments shaped the conception, framing, and narration of later episodes.

Gibbon's, then, was not simply a great historical intelligence voyaging through seas of silent thought alone. After all, what could be more natural than that the controversy of 1776 should have operated to attune Gibbon with some precision to the reception of his work? As he

himself said of the attacks on his history, 'as soon as I saw the advertisement, I generally sent for them.'[1] But we have also observed a strange
alchemy of literary composition, whereby aggression has been trans-
muted into collaboration. In the case of both Gibbon's portrait of
Athanasius and his account of the rise of Islam, angry reproof was the
spur to a greater subtlety, and even audacity, of historical imagination
and literary construction. The works of Chelsum, Davis, *et al.* have
never, I think, enjoyed justice from scholars, who have been too ready
to allow the superbly imperious Gibbon of *A Vindication* to dictate to
them. My own view, argued for at some length above, is that the attacks
on *The Decline and Fall* are often more considerable, both as examples of
polemical art and as critical responses to Gibbon's history, than has been
recognized. But if, as I believe, these hostile pamphlets were furthermore the grit around which some of the most lustrous historiographical
pearls of *The Decline and Fall* slowly accumulated, then even those who
cannot join with me in thinking, for instance, that there are moments
of acuity in Davis's *Examination*, or that the revisions for the second edition of Chelsum's *Remarks* reveal a writer learning with impressive
speed about the art of literary polemic, might nevertheless permit
themselves to think more kindly about the 'Watchmen of the Holy
City' than they have done up to now.[2]

But there is also a broader implication in the story of Gibbon's
reputation, which the unexpected and unintended fruitfulness of the
criticisms levelled at *The Decline and Fall* brings into focus. It is that
authorship may not be the pure creation of an author, but can be produced dialectically out of engagements, whether hostile or amicable,
with a readership. The relationship between a writer and a readership
can thus take on a strongly tactical quality, to the point where it might
even be analysed under the rubric of game theory. Writers and readers
may try to second-guess the next moves of their adversaries who are—
such is the ambivalent nature of a game—also their collaborators. It is
an approach to authorship which can surely be applied to many writers
beyond Gibbon, although we cannot often expect the evidence of
response to be quite so plentiful, and the engagement of the author with
his readership to be so prolonged, and to take such various forms.

In pursuing this approach in the case of Gibbon, it has been necessary
to range over almost the whole extent of the 'long eighteenth century',
from the reign of William III to the early years of the Regency, and to

[1] In *A Vindication* (*DF* iii. 1109).
[2] Although see, as honourable exceptions, Bowersock, *Gibbon's Historical Imagination*, 8–9, and Barnes, 'Derivative Scholarship and Historical Imagination'.

review material as diverse as, for instance, the Church and State disputes
of the late seventeenth century, the standing and importance of the
Fathers in the Church of England, traditions of literary polemic from
the dispute between the Ancients and Moderns until the late 1770s,
accounts of Islam from the later seventeenth century until the debates
between Priestley and Horsley, attacks on and defences of the universities of Oxford and Cambridge from the Great Rebellion to the French
Revolution, and the reverses of morale amongst England's governing
elite during the war with Napoleonic France. There is exhilaration in
such transitions. Moreover, they suggest how it became possible to
write this book, because they explain how the question of Gibbon's
reputation became divorced from his achievement as an historian. In
the world of the early Regency, a world of 'non-party loyalism' in
which ideological affiliations tended to be less important than a reliance
upon one another born of the knowledge of character engendered by
the eventually successful conduct of a continental war,[3] the conflicts
which were the crucible for much of *The Decline and Fall* dropped
below the horizon of men's attention. So Gibbon's writing became
separated from some of its most immediate stimulants and provoca-
tions, and his achievement was admired as something simpler, more
disinterested, and perhaps purer, but also certainly less human, and also
I think less absorbing, than the achievement which I have just described
and analysed.

[3] Thomas, *The Quarrel of Macaulay and Croker*, 33.

APPENDICES

APPENDICES

I. THE TWO DRAFTS OF SHEFFIELD'S
UNPUBLISHED NOTE ON CHAPTERS
FIFTEEN AND SIXTEEN

Source: Beinecke Library, Yale University, MS vault, section 10, drawer 3, section B, B 11 i and ii

A: MS vault, section 10, drawer 3, section B, B 11 i

On two pieces of paper; all text diagonally scored through in pen in both directions. Text within carets is inserted above the line.

[Sheet 1]

P 213

Note

Where he says Had he believed the Majority of English Readers were attached to the shadow of Christianity he might have softened the invidious Chapters

I mention the following Anecdote to shew that Mr Gibbon was not, in the first instance, aware how offensive his Irony, and manner of mentioning the Christian Religion, must be; and that he did not mean to outrage Society in the Degree that has been supposed – Some time after the Attack on the 15th and 16 Chapters had commenced, he said to me that he had flattered himself his History (the first Vol) would be rated somewhat above mediocrity, that he was not less surprized to find it valued so highly as it was, by one set of Men, than that it should be so much ~~abused~~ ^ reprobated ^ by another and then asked whether I thought it advisable to withdraw the offensive passages from the second Edition then at the Press –

[Sheet 2 recto]

He was answered that the mischief was done, and he was asked how he could suppose it possible to withdraw them: did he not know that such an Attempt would only raise the demand for the first Edition. Possibly he only wished to know my Opinion, but before the publication of the Work, and while it was in hand, he said to me that there would be much difficulty and

Delicacy in respect to that part which gives the History of the Christian Religion. When the mischief and wantonness of disregard to established Opinions was mentioned, he exceeded in expression all that was said. He was so habituated to the infintely more extravagant writings of Voltaire and others, and to the extreme levity of conversation, among the generality of those with whom he had lived, that he thought himself comparatively decent; and has often expressed great surprize that ~~it~~

[Sheet 2 verso]

~~should be so reprobated~~ ^ He had given so much Offence ^. He had always shewn more civility than is common to Age and situation, and, particularly in mixed Company, avoided saying any thing that could shock or offend; but many were now disposed to pronounce him not only a Deist, but an Atheist, (which he was not) and he has since often jocosely remarked, the bad effect of <u>taking away a persons Character</u>, as to Religion, as well as in other respects, and that it could answer no worldly purpose to him, longer to put himself under restraint of any kind.

[Vertically in the left hand margin of the verso of Sheet 2, in the hand of William Hayley]

suppress the whole Note – the Ground does not admit of any very solid & satisfactory defence – a slight palliation will only provoke more Severity against the delinquent –

B: MS vault, section 10, drawer 3, section B, B 11 ii

One sheet; apparently a first draft of MS vault, section 10, drawer 3, section B, B 11 i. Text within carets is inserted above the line.

[recto]

(213) ~~I mention~~ ^ The ^ the following ^is mentioned to ^ Anecdote to shew that Mr Gibbon was not in the first instance aware how Offensive his Irony & ~~manner of mentioning~~ ^ would & must be to the religious [illegible] ^ the Christian Religion must be, & that he did not mean to outrage Society in the degree that has been supposed – Some time after the attack on the 15 & 16th Chapters had commenced he said to me that he had flattered himself, his History (The first Vol:) would be rated somewhat above mediocrity, that he was not less surprized to find it valued so highly as it was by one set of men; than that it should be so much abused by another – and then asked whether I thought it adviseable to withdraw the Offensive Passages from the second Edition then ~~at~~ ^ going to ^ the Press – He was answered That the Mischief was done & he was asked; how he could suppose it possible to withdraw them – Did he not know that such an Attempt would only raise the demand for the first Edition – possibly he only wished to know my Opinion

[verso]

but before the publication of the Work & while it was in hand He ^ had
often ^ said ~~to me~~ there would be much Difficulty & Delicacy in respect to
that part which gives the History of The Christian Religion – When the
Mischief & Wantonness of Disregard to established Opinions was
mentioned, he exceeded in Expression all that was said – He was so
habituated to the infinitely more extravagant Writings of Voltaire & others,
& to the extreme levity of Conversation amongst the generality of those
with whom he had lived, that he thought himself comparatively decent ^ &
has often expressed great surprize that he shd be so reprobated ^ – He had
always shewn more respect & civility, than is common to Age & Situation,
and particularly in mixed company avoided saying any thing that could
shock or offend – but ~~when he found~~ many were ^ now ^ disposed to
pronounce him, not only a Deist but an Atheist (which he was not –) And
he has ^ since ^ often jocosely ~~said that as the Public~~ remarked the bad
effect of taking away a person's character as to Religion, as well as in other
respects; and that it could answer no ^ worldly ^ purpose to him, longer to
put himself under restraint of any kind –

2. GIBBON'S 'MEMOIRS OF MY LIFE': DRAFTS, CORRESPONDENCE, AND CONTEXT

Draft	Date of Composition*	Scope	Length†	References to 'Memoirs' in Letters etc.	Responses to Events in France
A	Late 1788 and early 1789: posthumous publication.	Early records of the family to 1761	38	21 Nov. 1787, to Lord Sheffield [L iii. 82]: allusion to John Gibbon the herald. 17 June 1788, to J. C. Brooke [L iii. 110]: enquiry concerning John Gibbon. 27 June 1788, to J. C. Brooke [L iii. 114]: another request to investigate his family history. 'My own amusement is my motive, and will be my reward; and if these sheets are communicated to some discreet and indulgent friends, they will be secreted from the public eye till the author shall be removed from the reach of criticism or ridicule' (A 353; draft 'A').	
B	1788–1789: posthumous publication.	Birth of E. G. (1737) to 1764	107		
C	1789: posthumous publication.	Birth to 1772	82		15 Dec. 1789, to Lord Sheffield [L iii. 183–4]: 'What would you have me say of the affairs of France? We are too near and too remote to form an accurate judgment of that wonderful scene. The abuses of the court and government called aloud for reformation and it has happened as it will always happen, that an innocent well-disposed prince pays

	Publication	Content	Age	Events / Letters
D	1790: possibly non-posthumous publication.	Birth to 1770 (death of E. G. senior)	25	the forfeit of the sins of his predecessors . . . The French nation had a glorious opportunity, but they have abused and may lose their advantages. If they had been content with a liberal translation of our system, if they had respected the prerogatives of the crown and the privileges of the Nobles, they might have raised a solid fabric on the only true foundation the natural Aristocracy of a great Country. How different is the prospect!' 7 Aug. 1790, to Lord Sheffield [*L* iii. 199]: 'Poor France, the state is dissolved, the nation is mad. Adieu.' 7 Nov. 1790, to Thomas Cadell [*L* iii. 210]: 'I thirst for Mr Burke's Reflections on the Revolutions of France. Intreat Elmsley, in my name, to dispatch it to Lausanne with care and speed, by *any* mode of conveyance less expensive than the post.'
E	January and February 1791: completed, 2 March 1791: non-posthumous publication.	Early history of the family to 1789	60	5 Feb. 1791, to Lord Sheffield [*L* iii. 216]: 'Burke's book is a most admirable medicine against the French disease, which has made too much progress even in this happy country [the Pays de Vaud]. I admire his eloquence, I approve his politics, I adore his chivalry, and I can even forgive his superstition. The primitive Church, which I have treated with some freedom, was itself at

Draft	Date of Composition*	Scope	Length†	References to 'Memoirs' in Letters etc.	Responses to Events in France
					that time, an innovation, and *I was* attached to the old Pagan establishment.' 18 May 1791, to his stepmother [*L* iii. 227]: 'In the moving picture of this World, you cannot be indifferent to the strange Revolution which has humbled all that was high and exalted all that was low in France. The irregular and lively spirit of the Nation has disgraced their liberty, and instead of building a free constitution they have only exchanged Despotism for Anarchy. . . Burke, if I remember right is no favourite of yours, but there is surely much eloquence and much sense in his book. The prosperity of England forms a proud contrast with the disorders of France . . .'.
F	1792–3: posthumous publication.	Early records to 1753	103	28 Dec. 1791, to Lord Sheffield [*L* iii. 240]: 'I have much revolved the plan of the Memoirs I once mentioned, and as you do not think it ridiculous I believe I shall make the attempt: if I can please myself I am confident of not displeasing: but let this be a profound secret between us: people must not be prepared to laugh: they must be taken by surprise.' 24 Feb. 1792, to John Nichols (of *Gentleman's Magazine*) [*L* iii. 246]: enquiry about family history.	

10 Nov. 1792, to Lady Sheffield [*L* iii. 299]: speculates as to 'a new system of life in my native Country, for which my income though improved and improving would be probably insufficient.'

1 Jan. 1793, to Lord Sheffield [*L* iii. 307]: 'My own choice has indeed transported me into a foreign land, but I am truly attached from interest and inclination to my native country: and even as a Citizen of the World, I wish the stability of England, the sole great refuge of mankind against the opposite mischiefs of despotism and democracy.'

30 May 1792, to Lord Sheffield [*L* iii. 264]: 'the work appears far more difficult in the execution than in the idea, and as I am now taking my leave for some time of the library, I shall not make much progress in the Memoirs of P P. till I am on English ground.'

6 Jan. 1793, to Lord Sheffield [*L* iii. 312]: 'And now approach, and let me drop into your most private ear a literary secret. Of *the Memoirs* little has been done, and with that little I am not satisfied: they must be postponed till a mature season, and I much doubt whether the book and the author can ever see the light at the same time.'

23 Jan. 1793, Lord Sheffield in reply to Gibbon's of 6 Jan. 1793 [Prothero, ii. 366]: 'I shall never consent to your dropping the Memoirs. Keep that work always going: but you should decide whether the book and the author are to see the light together, because it might be differently filled up according to that decision. A man may state many things in a posthumous work, that he might not in another; the latter often checks the introduction of many curious thoughts and facts.'

16 Jan. 1793, 4 Apr. 1793 and ? July 1793, to John Nichols [*L* iii. 314–15, 323–4 and 344–5]: matters relating to family history.

Draft	Date of Composition*	Scope	Length†	References to 'Memoirs' in Letters etc.	Responses to Events in France
				7 Aug. 1793, to Samuel Egerton Brydges [L iii. 344–5]: enquiries about the early history of the Gibbon family in Kent. 'This passage [the passage concerning posthumous publication from draft 'A' above] is found in one only of the six sketches, and in that which seems to have been the first written, and which was laid aside among loose papers. Mr. Gibbon, in his communications with me on the subject of his Memoirs, a subject which he had never mentioned to any other person, expressed a determination of publishing them in his lifetime; and never appears to have departed from that resolution, excepting in one of his letters annexed [that of 6 Jan. 1793 (L iii. 312)], in which he intimates a doubt, though rather carelessly, whether in his time, or at any time, they would meet the eye of the public. – In a conversation, however, not long before his death, it was suggested to him, that, if he should make them a full image of his mind, he would not have nerves to publish them in his lifetime, and therefore that they should be posthumous; – He answered, rather eagerly, that he was determined	

* The drafts were first dated by William Alexander Greenhill in 1871–2. The dating adopted here follows G. A. Bonnard's revision of Greenhill's findings (G. A. Bonnard (ed.), *Edward Gibbon: Memoirs of My Life* (1966), pp. viii–xix). to publish them *in his lifetime*' (note by Sheffield to *Memoirs*; Edward Gibbon, *Miscellaneous Works* [1796], i, 1).

† These are the number of pages occupied in John Murray (ed.), *The Autobiographies of Edward Gibbon* (1896).

3. JOHN BAKER HOLROYD, 1ST EARL OF
SHEFFIELD (1735–1821): A BIBLIOGRAPHY

A. WORKS BY LORD SHEFFIELD
(OTHER THAN EDITIONS OF GIBBON)

Observations on the Commerce of the American States (1783). [Many editions; the sixth, enlarged, edition was published in 1784.]

Observations on the Manufactures, Trade and Present State of Ireland (Dublin, 1785).

Observations on the Project for Abolishing the Slave Trade (1790).

Observations on the Corn bill, now Depending in Parliament (1791).

Substance of the Speech [. . .] *of Lord Sheffield* [. . .] *upon the Subject of Union with Ireland* (Dublin, 1799). [Three editions in 1799.]

Remarks on the Deficiency of Grain Occasioned by the Bad Harvest of 1799 (1800).

Observations on the Objections made to the Export of Wool from Great Britain to Ireland (1800).

Strictures on the Necessity of Inviolably Maintaining the Navigation and Colonial System of Great Britain (1804). ['New' edition, with appendix, 1806.]

The Orders in Council and the American Embargo Beneficial to the Political and Commercial Interests of Great Britain (1809).

Lord Sheffield's Present State of the Wool Trade (Dublin, 1811).

On the Trade in Wool and Woollens (1813).

Report [. . .] *to the Meeting at Lewes Wool Fair* (1813).

Observations on the Impolicy, Abuses, and False Interpretation of the Poor Laws (1813: second edition, 1818).

On the Trade in Wool and Woollens, including an Exposition of the Commercial Situation of the British Empire (1813).

A Letter on the Corn Laws (1815). [Two editions in 1815.]

Report [. . .] *to the Meeting at Lewes Wool Fair* (Dublin, 1816).

Remarks on the Bill of the Last Parliament for the Amendment of the Poor Laws (1819).

B. REPLIES TO WORKS BY LORD SHEFFIELD

Anon., *Cursory Remarks on Lord Sheffield's Pamphlet Relative to the Trade and Manufactures of Ireland* (Cork, 1785).

Anon., *Considerations on the Corn Laws, with Remarks on the Observations of Lord Sheffield on the Corn Bill* (1791).

Anon., *The Propriety of Sending Lord Sheffield to Coventry* (1796). [A pamphlet from the general election of May, 1796, in which Sheffield was opposed at Bristol by 'Mr. Hobhouse [. . .] a man of most violent Democratic and Republican Principles, supported by all the Mob very vehemently; but not by one respectable person [. . .]' (J. H. Adeane (ed.), *The Girlhood of Maria Josepha Holroyd* [1896], 372).]

J. Allen, *Considerations on the present state of the intercourse between his majesty's sugar colonies and the dominions of the United States of America* (1784). [Allen was Secretary of the West India planters. This work was an answer to Sheffield's *Observations* of 1783.]

W. Bingham, *A letter from an American* [. . .] *to a member of parliament, on* [. . .] *the restraining proclamation, and containing strictures on lord Sheffield's pamphlet on the Commerce of the American states* (Philadelphia, 1784).

T. Broughton, *A Letter to Lord Sheffield* (1815).

S. Cock, *An answer to lord Sheffield's pamphlet, on the subject of the navigation system* (1804).

T. Coxe, *A brief examination of lord Sheffield's Observations on the commerce of the United States* (Philadelphia, 1791).

G. W. Jordan, *The Claims of the British West India Colonists* (1804). [Jordan was the colonial agent for Barbados. His work was a reply to Sheffield's *Strictures* of 1804.]

Sir. L. O'Brien, *Letters concerning the Trade and Manufactures of Ireland* [. . .] *in which Certain Facts and Arguments Set Out by Lord Sheffield* [. . .] *are Examined* (1785).

4. THE THREE VERSIONS OF THE DEATH
OF EDWARD GIBBON SENIOR

| indicates a page break. ^ on either side of a word or passage indicates an
insertion. [ ] indicates material added in the margin.

1. Draft 'C' (BL Add. MS 34874, fos. 77ʳ⁻ᵛ)

The disembodying of the Militia at the close of the War (1762) had restored the
Major, a new Cincinnatus, to a life of Agriculture. His labours were useful, his
pleasures innocent, his wishes moderate: and my father <u>seemed</u> to enjoy the
state of happiness which is celebrated by poets and philosophers as the most
agreable to Nature, and the least accessible to Fortune.

> Beatus ille, qui, procul negotiis
> (Ut prisca gens mortalium)
> Paterna rura bubus exercet suis,
> Solutus omni fœnore.

But the last indispensable condition, the freedom from debt, was wanting to eo
my father's felicity: and the vanities of his youth were severely punished by the
solicitude and sorrow of his declining age. The first mortgage, on my return
from Lausanne (1758) had afforded him a partial and transient relief: the annual
demand of interest and | allowance was an heavy deduction from the his
income: the militia was a source of expence: the farm in his hands was not a
profitable adventure: he was loaded with the costs and damages of an obsolete
law suit; and each year multiplied the number, and exhausted the patience of
his creditors. Under these painful circumstances, my own behaviour was not
only guiltless but meritorious. Without stipulating any personal advantages, I
consented at a mature and well-informed age to an additional mortgage, to the
sale of Putney, and to every sacrifice that could alleviate his distress: but he was
no longer capable of a rational effort, and his reluctant delays postponed, not
the evils themselves, but the remedies of those evils, (remedia malorum potius
quam mala differebat). But The pangs of shame tenderness and self-reproach
incessantly preyed on his vitals: his constitution was broken; he lost his strength
and his sight; the rapid progress of a dropsy admonished him of his end, and he
sunk into the grave on the tenth of November 1770, in the sixty fourth year of
his age. A family tradition insinuates that Mr William Law has drawn his pupil
in the light and inconstant character of <u>Flatus</u>, who is ever confident and ever
disappointed in the chace of happiness. But these constitutional failings are
were amply compensated by the virtues of the head and heart, by the warmest
sentiments of honour and humanity. His graceful person, polite address, gentle
manners, and unaffected chearfulness, recommended him to the favour of

every company: and in the change of times and opinions, his liberal spirit had long since delivered him from the zeal and prejudice of a Tory education The tears of a son are seldom lasting: I submitted to the order of Nature; and my grief was soothed by the conscious satisfaction, that I had discharged all the duties of filial piety: Few, perhaps, are the children, who, after the expiration of some months or years, would sincerely rejoyce in the resurrection of their parents; and it is a melancholy truth, that my father's death, not unhappy for himself, was the only event that could save me from an hopeless life of obscurity and indigence.

2. *Draft 'D' (BL Add. MS 34874, fo. 85ᵛ)*

The dissolution of the militia at the close of the War (1762) had restored my father, a new Cincinnatus, to his Hampshire farm. His labours were useful, his pleasures innocent, his wishes moderate: the neighbourhood enjoyed the presence of an active magistrate and charitable landlord: his polite address and chearful conversation recommended him to his equals: he was not dissatisfied with his son, and he had been fortunate or rather judicious in the choice of his two wives. In this retirement he <u>seemed</u> to enjoy the state of life which is praised by philosophers and poets, as the most agreable to Nature, and the least accessible to Fortune

> Beatus ille qui procul negotiis
> (Ut prisca gens mortalium)
> Paterna rura bubus exercet suis
> <u>Solutus omni fænore</u>."

But the last indispensable condition, the freedom from debt was wanting to my father's happiness: and the vanities of his youth were severely expiated by the accumulation of solicitude and sorrow on his declining. There can be no merit in the discharge of a duty: but, alone, in my library, at such a distance of time and place, without a witness or a judge, I should be pursued by the bitterness of remembrance; had I not obeyed the dictates of filial piety, had I not consented to every sacrifice that might promise some relief to the distress of a parent. His mind, alas was no longer capable of a rational effort, and his reluctant delays postponed, not the evils themselves, but the remedies of those evils (remedia malorum potius quam mala differebat). The pangs of tenderness and self-reproach incessantly preyed on his vitals: he lost his strength and his sight: a rapid dropsy admonished him of his end, and he sunk into the grave in the sixty-fourth year of his age. His death was the only event that could have saved me from a life of obscurity and indigence; yet I can declare to my own heart, that on such terms, I never wished for a deliverance.

3. *Draft 'E' (BL Add. MS 34874, fos. 88ᵛ–89ʳ; note on fo. 98ʳ)*

At the time of my father's decease I was upwards of thirty-three years of age [the ordinary term of an human generation]. My grief was sincere for the loss of an affectionate parent, an agreeable companion, and a worthy man. But the ample fortune which my grandfather had left was deeply impaired, and would have been gradually consumed by the easy and generous nature of his son.[26] I revere the memory of my father, his errors I forgive, nor can I repent of | the important sacrifices which were chearfully offered by filial piety. Domestic command, the free distribution of time and place, and a more liberal measure of expence were the immediate consequences of my new situation: but two years rolled away before I could disentangle myself from the web of rural œconomy, and adopt a mode of life agreable to my wishes. From Buriton Mrs Gibbon withdrew to Bath; while I removed myself and my books into my new house in Bentinck Street Cavendish Square, in which I continued to reside ~~ab~~ near eleven years. The clear untainted remains of my patrimony have been always sufficient to support the rank of a Gentleman, and to satisfy the desires of a philosopher.

[26] In his ~~rural~~ [Hampshire] retirement, my father might seem to enjoy the state of primitive happiness; "Beatus ille qui procul negotiis, etc. But alas he was not "solutus omni fœnore" and without such freedom there can be no content

5. RESIDENCE IN OXFORD AND CONVERSION TO CATHOLICISM: MSS 'B', 'C', 'D', AND 'E'

| indicates a page break. ^ on either side of a word or passage indicates an insertion. [ ] indicates material added in the margin.

	'B' BL Add MS 34874, fos. 28ᵛ–31ʳ	'C' BL Add MS 34874, fos. 61ᵛ–62ᵛ	'D' BL Add MS 34874, fos. 80ᵛ–81ʳ	'E' BL Add MS 34874, fo. 87ʳ, note fo. 97ᵛ.
1	I arrived at Oxford with a stock of Erudition which might have puzzled a Doctor and a degree of ignorance of which a school-boy would have been ashamed. To complete this account of my puerile studies, I shall here observe that I soon attempted and soon abandoned two litterary projects far above my strength; a critical enquiry into the age of Sesostris, and the paralel lives of the Emperor Aurelian and Selim the Turkish Sultan, who in their cruelty, valour, and Syrian victories, may indeed support some kind of resemblance.	I arrived at Oxford with a stock of Erudition that might have puzzled a Doctor, and a degree of ignorance of which a school-boy	would have been ashamed. My first litterary attempts were a new plan of Chronological tables, the paralel lives of Aurelian and Selim, and a critical enquiry into the age of Sesostris.	Several projects of composition already floated in my mind; and I arrived at Oxford, with a stock of	erudition that my might have puzzled a Doctor and a degree of ignorance of which a school-boy would have been ashamed.	At an unripe age I was matriculated, as a Gentleman Commoner at Magdalen College
2	I entered on my ^life^ at Magdalen College in the University of Oxford, with surprize and satisfaction. These sat sentiments were naturally	The stately buildings of Oxford and especially of Magdalen College excite the admiration of a stranger: the ex apparent decencies of habit and order solicit his reverence; and the cloysters,	Before I had accomplished my fifteenth year I was matriculated as a Gentleman-Commoner of Magdalen College in the ancient and famous university of Oxford	

'B'	'C'	'D'	'E'
			in the University of Oxford,
produced by my sudden promotion before the age of fifteen to the rank of a man; the general civility ∧with∧ which I was treated; the silk gown and velvet cap of a Gentleman-Commoner; a decent allowance in my own disposal with a large loose and dangerous credit; an elegant apartment of three rooms in the new buildings; the beauty of the walks and public edifices; and the key of the College-library, which I might use or abuse without much interruption from the fellows of the Society.	the walks, and the libraries are appropriated to the use of a studious and contemplative life. I was delighted with the novelty of the scene: my dress and rank of a gentleman-commoner, a competent allowance and a spacious apartment elated my childish vanity with the idea of manly independence.		

3 I may wish that the fruits of my noviciate had corresponded with this flattering appearance, and ∧that∧ I could now proclaim my gratitude in the well-chosen words of Dr. Lowth the late Bishop of London |
   "I was educated in the University of Oxford. I enjoyed all the advantages, both public and private, which that famous seat of learning so largely affords. I spent many happy years in that illustrious society, in a well-regulated course of useful discipline and studies, and in the agreeable and improving commerce of Gentlemen and scholars; in a society where

where I lost fourteen valuable months of my youth.

in which I consumed fourteen t months, the most barren and unprofitable of my whole life.

The reader will ascribe this loss to my own incapacity, or to the vices of that ancient institution.[9]

After every fair abatement for my tender age, unripe studies, and hasty removal the reader will impute this loss of time either to my own incapacity or to the misconduct of my Academical guides.

But I must blush for myself or for my teachers, when I declare that of all the years of my life the fourteen months which I spent at Oxford were most compleatly lost for every purpose of improvement: and the University will not be ambitious of a son who disclaims all sense of filial piety and gratitude.

I am willing to make every reasonable abatement for my tender age, insufficient preparation, and short residence. Yet I must confess the presumptuous belief that neither my temper nor my talents were averse to

emulation without envy, ambition without jealousy, contention without animosity, incited industry and awakened Genius; where a liberal pursuit of knowledge and a generous freedom of thought was raised encouraged and pushed forward by example, by commendation, and by authority: I breathed the same atmosphere that the Hookers, the Chillingworths, and the Lockes had breathed before, etc —" It may indeed be observed that the Atmosphere of Oxford did not agree with Mr. Locke's constitution, and that the Philosopher might justly despised the Academical bigots who expelled his person and condemned his principles.

4   For me the University will as gladly renounce me for her son as I shall disclaim her for my mother; since I am compelled to acknowledge that the fourteen months which I spent in Magdalen College were totally lost for every purpose of study or improvement.

5   If I am reminded, that my tender years, my short residence and my imperfect preparation could not derive much benefit from the institution of that learned body, I am willing that such reasons should

'B'	'C'	'D'	'E'
operate with their proper weight. Yet I may affirm that at the age of fifteen I was not destitute of capacity and application and, that even my childish reading had proved an eager early though blind propensity to books and learning, and that the shallow flood might have easily been taught to flow in a deep and regular channel. In the discipline of a well-constituted society, and under the discipline guidance of a skillful teacher, my youthful ardour would have been encouraged and directed; I should gradually have risen from translations to originals, from the Latin to the Greek Classics, from dead language to living science; and the six years which my father had alotted for my ⟨&⟩ Academical education might have been successfully employed in the labour of learning. Yet when I reflect ^When I reflect indeed^ on the advantages which I gained in a liberal acquaintance with the nations the manners and the idiom of ^Europe,^ the modern World I must rather rejoyce than repine at my early deliverance	from the habits and prejudices of an English Cloyster. But instead of speculating on what might	the lessons of science; that the discipline of well-regulated studies might have inflamed the ardour and restrained the wanderings of youth: and that some share of reproach will adhere to the Academical institution which could damp every spark of industry in a curious and active mind. —		

have been the colour of my life and opinions, I shall now state with simple sincerity the result of my personal experience of Magdalen College in the university of Oxford.

6 The elegant Dissertations of Lowth on the Hebrew poetry, and the useful commentaries of Blackstone on the laws of England were first delivered in the form of Academical lectures. But the assertion of Mr. Adam Smith is generally true, that in the University "of Oxford the greater part of the public professors have given up all for these many years past have given up altogether even the pretence of teaching."

A great master of moral and political wisdom has observed that "in the University of Oxford the greater part of the public professors, for these many years past, have given up altogether even the pretence of teaching" (Riches of nations Vol ii p 343); nor is and this melancholy truth, which sounds almost incredible in foreign Academies, is not disproved by the rare and honourable exceptions of Blackstone and Lowth.

Yet I will take leave to repeat, after a philosopher and a friend, that "in the University of Oxford the greater part of the public professors, for these many years past, for have given up, altogether, even the pretence of teaching," (Riches of Nations Vol II. p 343).

7 Instead of a course of lectures by the masters of each particular science to a greater number of disciples, the task of instruction is abandoned to the College-Tutors, who teach or undertake to teach the whole circle, at least, of elementary knowledge in separate lessons to their private pupils.

The silence of the professors is imperfectly supplied by the College tutors who instruct, or pr wh promise to instruct, their pupils in language and science.

The diligence of my College Tutors was confined to a morning lecture of an hour which I was at full liberty to attend or forget: with the first, one of the best of the tribe, I read in two or three months two or three plays of Terence;

8 The first Tutor to whose care I was resigned appears to have been one of the best of the Tribe: Dr. Waldegrave was a learned and pious man, of strict morals, and a mild though reserved disposition, who seldom mingled either in the business or the jollity of

My first tutor, Dr. Waldegrave, was one of the best of the tribe; we read in two or three months two or three comedies of Terence; he gave me every morning an hour at his chambers; but my absence was excused on the slightest pretence, and

9 The revenues, and monopoly, and idleness of these Ecclesiastical corporations are justly censured by Dr Adam Smith (Riches of Nations Vol. ii p 340–374), who affirms that most of the professors of Oxford have given up even the pretence of public teaching.

'B'

the College. He soon gained my regard and confidence; I preferred his company to that of the younger students, and in our evening walks to the top of Heddington hill, we freely conversed on a variety of topics. But this respectable tutor was a stranger to the polite or philosophic world: his temper was indolent; his faculties, which were not of the first-rate, had been relaxed by the climate; and he was content, like the rest of his fellows, with a slight and superficial performance of an important trust. No plan of study was formed: no litterary exercises were prescribed; he suffered me to waste my leisure without account or advice; his morning lessons were confined to the space of a single hour, and that hour was filled by an easy task for the master and the pupil. We read together the Comedies of Terence: the whole sum of my improvement at Oxford may be reduced to the perusal of two or three Latin plays; and even this employment, which might of have been productive of so much Philosophical reflection and critical remark consisted only of a cold dry interpretation of the text and

'C'

I soon discovered that my ^attendance^ absence and my apologies were equally superfluous.

'D'

'E'

metre. During the first weeks | I regularly attended these lessons in my tutor's room, but as they were equally devoid of profit and pleasure I was once tempted to make the experiment of a formal apology. The apology was accepted with a smile: I repeated the offence with less ceremony; the excuse was accepted with the same indulgence: the slightest motive of lazyness or indisposition, the most trifling avocation at home or abroad was a sufficient obstacle; my visits became rare and occasional, nor did my tutor appear conscious of my absence or neglect.

9 ^Before^ On my return to Oxford, after spending the vacation in Hampshire, Dr. Waldegrave was removed to a College-living; but I was transferred, with the rest of his pupils, to his Academical heir a Dr. Winchester whose only science was supposed to be that of a broker and salesman. From my own person experience I am not, indeed, qualified to represent his character; his person I scarcely knew, and in the eight months for which he ^demanded^ received a salary I never received a word of lesson or advice from the Director of my studies.

His successor Dr. Winchester never deserved the annual stipend of twenty Guineas by a single word of instruction of enquiry or of advice.

but I was never called in a much longer space to visit the chambers of the second.
[In Gibbon's MS 'D', sections 8 and 9 follow rather than precede sections 10, 11, and 12.]

	'B'	'C'	'D'	'E'
10	The defects of private tuition might have been supplied by public discipline and example; but the example of the ^old Monks (I mean the fellows)^ senior members of the society was not likely to incite the emulation and diligence of Youth their the novices and undergraduates. The forty principal members of our opulent foundation who had been were amply endowed with the means of study and subsistence, were content to slumber in the supine enjoyment of these benefits; they had absolved themselves from the labour of reading, or thinking, ef or writing, and the first shoots of learning or genius rotted on the ground without producing any fruits either for the owners or the public.	I compliment our English Fellows when I compare them to the Monks of a Benedictine Abbey. Instead of animating the under-graduates by the example of diligence, they enjoyed in tranquil indolence the benefactions of the founder, and their slumbers were seldom disturbed by the labour of writing, of reading or thinking.	The monks or fellows of our wealthy foundation	
11	Their conversations to which I have sometimes listened in the common room stagnated within the narrow circle of Uni College-business, and Tory politics; their deep and dull compotations left them no right to blame the warmer intemperance of youth, and their constitutional toasts were not expressive of the most sincere loyalty to the house of Hanover.	Their ^discourse^ conversation in the common room, to which I was sometimes admitted stagnated in the narrow circle of College business and Tory politicks: their deep and dull compotations left them no right to censure the warmer intemperance of youth; and their constitutional toasts were not expressive of the most sincere loyalty to the house of Hanover.	were immersed in Port wine, and Tory politics;	

12 The discipline of the society I neither felt nor observed: a tradition still remained that Latin declamations had been spoken by the Gentlemen-Commoners in the Hall; but in my time the custom was abolished: the obvious methods of rewards and censures, of exercises and examinations, were unknown; nor could I learn that the conduct of Tutors and pupils had ever awakened the attention of the President.

I have heard that Latin declamations were formerly pronounced by the Gentlemen commoners in the hall: but in my time the silk gown, velvet cap | were sacred from all duty of exercise or examination.

no model or motive or example of study was proposed to the under-graduates: and the silk gown, the velvet cap, was a badge of protection against the formal exercises of the common hall.

13 For my own part, the want of occupation and experience soon led me into some irregularities of bad company, late hours, and improper expence. My debts might be secret, my absence was visible: four a tour into Buckinghamshire, an excursion to Bath, four excursions to London were idle and dangerous follies; | and my tender years might have justified a more than ordinary restraint. Yet I eloped from Oxford, I returned, I again eloped in a few days, as if I had been an independent stranger in a hired lodging without once hearing the voice of admonition, or once feeling the hand of controul. —

Idleness and inexperience soon led me into some disorders of late hours, bad company, and improper expence: my debts might be secret, my absence was notorious: a tour into Buckinghamshire, an excursion to Bath, four excursions to London were costly and dangerous follies; and my childish years might have justified a more than ordinary restraint. Yet I eloped from Oxford, I returned; I again eloped in a few days; as if I had been an independent stranger in an hired lodging, without once hearing the voice of admonition or once feeling the hand of controul. Such was my Academical life.

The idleness of a boy was easily betrayed into some irregularities of company and expence; but after my foolish frequent excursions to London, Bath, &c. I never felt the hand of authority or ever heard the voice of admonition

14 I am told, and I am willing to believe that since the year fifty three some reformation has taken place. The

I shall rejoyce to hear that any reformation has been since introduced into the University or the College.

— I shall rejoyce to learn, that, since my time any reformation has taken place either in the university, or in the college.

'B'

'C'

'D'

'E'

essential vices of the University are however inherent to its dark Antiquity, to the spirit of an Ecclesiastical corporation, to the fixed salaries of the professors, and to the lazy opulence of the Colleges, which I flatter by comparing them to so many Abbeys of Benedictine monks.

15 It might at least be expected that an Ecclesiastical school should have diligently inculcated on the minds of youth the study of Religion, and the arguments that established the truth of the Christian and protestant Systems.

16 But the University of Oxford had contrived to unite the opposite extremes of bigotry and indifference. According to her statutes, every student, on his matriculations, subscribes either with, or without reading them, the thirty-nine articles of the Church of the En England; but this ceremony was post-poned on account of my age, and the Vice-Chancellor directed me to return so soon as I had accomplished my fifteenth year, referring me in the mean while to the Religious instructions of my College.

In religious matters the University of Oxford united the extremes of bigotry and indifference. As I had not compleated, at the time of my matriculation, the my fifteenth year of my age, I was excused from the legal obligation of subscribing the thirty nine articles of the Church of England;

As the university of Oxford had contrived to unite the opposite extremes of bigotry in her doctrines, and of indifference in her practise, the religion of her pupils was not less neglected than their litterature;

17.

My College forgot to instruct; I forgot to return, and was ~~in my return~~ myself forgotten by the Vice-Chancellor; and thus without signing any symbol of faith, without being sanctifyed by any rites of confirmation, I groped my way by the light of my Catechism to the Chappel and the Communion table.

but my Academical teachers were as careless of spiritual, as of litterary, instruction, and I groped my way to the chappel and the communion-table by the dim light of my catechism.

and I was left by the dim light of my Catechism to grope my way to the Chappel and the Communion-table.

18.

Like most children who are born with any natural sense, I had formerly puzzled my aunt by my questions and objections on the mysteries of Religion, and the heavy atmosphere of Oxford ~~was now~~ had not totally broken the elasticity of my mind.

~~Religion~~ I Religion had often been the theme of my infant curiosity: the shrewdness of my questions and objections had sometimes puzzled my pious aunt; nor had the dull atmosphere of Oxford compleatly broken the elasticity of my mind.

But the dull weight of the Atmosphere had not totally broken the elasticity of my mind.

19.

Without guide or preparation, my idle curiosity was unluckily directed to the study of the disputes between the Protestants and the Papists: and I soon persuaded myself that victory and salvation were on the side of the Church of Rome.

Some Popish books unluckily fell into my hands: I was bewildered in the maze of controversy, and my understanding was oppressed by their specious arguments, till I believed that I believed in the stupendous mysteries and infallible authority of the ^Catholic^ ~~Church of Rome.~~

~~Gts~~ Accident threw into my hands and curiosity tempted me to peruse some Popish treatises of Controversy. I read till I was deluded by the specious sophistry, till I believed that I believed all the tremendous mysteries of the Catholic creed;

Without a master or a guide I unfortunately stumbled on some books of Popish controversy: nor is it a matter of reproach, that I a boy should have believed that he believed, &c.

20.

The University of Oxford which ^has^ suffered some reproach from my short apostacy was insulted by the false supposition that some Jesuits, some Romish Wolves must have been permitted to steal into the fold and to

As the University has suffered some reproach on my account, truth and justice oblige me to declare that such books were the sole instruments of my conversion, and that I never saw any emissary of Rome within the precincts of Oxford.

394

	'B'	'C'	'D'	'E'
	was asleep. | In truth and justice, I must affirm that I never conversed at Oxford with a priest or even with a Catholic till my resolution was irrevocably fixed;			I was seduced like Chillingworth and Bayle; and, like them, my growing reason soon broke through the toils of sophistry and superstition.
21	and it was fixed by some books of controversy the first of which I borrowed from a young Gentleman of the College who secretly inclined to the same opinions. I read till my ignorance was confounded in a labyrinth ^entangled in the net^ of texts of scripture and passages of the Fathers. The hard doctrine of transubstantion was smoothed by the protestant belief in the mystery of the trinity: the vices of the Reformation were triumphantly urged, and I yielded to the specious argument that a wise legislator would provide a supreme and visible Judge for the interpretation of his laws.			
22	If I now smile or blush at the recollection of my folly, I may derive some countenance from the example of Chillingworth and Bayle, who at a riper age were seduced by similar argumen sophistry to embrace the same system of superstition. I may claim the merit of treading in their		and my folly may be excused by the examples of Chillingworth and Bayle, whose acute understandings were seduced at ¤ a riper age by the same arguments.	

footsteps, when after a transient delusion they broke their fetters and resumed the command of their captive reason. But, in their return to the Religion of their fathers, my two predecessors were carried beyond the term from whence they had departed. It was with deep reluctance that Chillingworth subscribed the thirty nine articles several parts of which he disbelieved: his acute understanding was repeatedly vanquished by itself, and his last opinions were most probably those of an Arian or Socinian. The free and comprehensive Genius of Bayle balanced the Religions of the Earth in the scales of his sceptical philosophy, till the adverse quantities, if I may use the language of Algebra, had annihilated each other.

23 No sooner was my reason subdued than I resolved to approve my faith by my works and to enter without delay into the pale of the Church of Rome. In my last excursion to London, I addressed myself to a Catholic bookseller in Russell street Covent Garden: he recommended me to a priest of whose name and order I am at present ignorant, and by his p exhortations I was confirmed in my pious design.

But no sooner had I resolved to save my soul at the expence of my fortune, than I eloped to London and addressed myself to Mr Lewis a Popish bookseller in Russel street, who introduced me to a priest, perhaps a Jesuit, of his acquaintance.

With the ardour of a youth and the zeal of a proselyte I was impatient to enter into the pale of the Church: some acquaintance in London introduced me to a priest,

	'B'	'C'	'D'	'E'
24	The conversion of a young Englishman of family and fortune could not fail of making much noise and might be attended with some danger, but his zeal overlooked these worldly considerations,	That zealous missionary exposed his life to the rigour of our intolerant laws;		
25	and at his feet, on the eighth of June 1753 I solemnly, though privately abjured the errors of heresy.	and on the eighth of June 1753 I solemnly though privately abjured at his feet the errors of heresy.	and at his feet I solemnly abjured the heresy of my ancestors.	

6. RESIDENCE IN OXFORD AND CONVERSION TO CATHOLICISM: MS F AND *MW 1796*

| indicates a page break. ^ on either side of a word or passage indicates an insertion. [ ] indicates material added in the margin.

'F'	*MW 1796* i. 32–53
BL Add MS 34874, fos. 116ᵛ–123ᶠ (notes, fos. 126ᵛ–127ᵛ)	

2

A traveller who visits Oxford or Cambridge is surprized and edified by the apparent order and tranquillity that prevail in the seats of the English muses.[1] In the most celebrated Universities of Holland, Germany, and Italy, the students, who swarm from different countries are loosely dispersed in private lodgings at the houses of the burghers: they dress according to their fancy and fortune: and in the intemperate quarrels of youth and wine, their <u>swords</u>, though less frequently than of old, are sometimes stained with each other's brothers blood.[2] The use of arms is banished from our English Universities; the uniform habit of the Academics, the square cap and black gown is adapted to the civil and even clerical profession: and from the Doctor in Divinity to the under-graduate, the degrees of learning and age are externally distinguished. Instead of being scattered in a town, the students of Oxford and Cambridge are united in Colleges: their maintenance is provided at their own expence or that of the founders; and the stated hours of the hall and the chappel represent the discipline of a regular, and, as it were, a Religious community. The eyes of the traveller are attracted by the size or beauty of the public edifices; and the principal colleges appear to be so many st palaces which a liberal nation has erected and endowed for the habitation of Science. My own introduction to the University of Oxford forms a new æra in my life, and at the distance of ^four^ forty years I still remember my first emotions of surprize and satisfaction.

A traveller, who visits Oxford or Cambridge, is surprised and edified by the apparent order and tranquillity that prevail in the seats of the English muses. In the most celebrated universities of Holland, Germany, and Italy, the students, who swarm from different countries, are loosely dispersed in private lodgings at the houses of the burghers: they dress according to their fancy and fortune: and in the intemperate quarrels of youth and wine, their *swords*, though less frequently than of old, are sometimes stained with each other's blood. The use of arms is banished from our English universities; the uniform habit of the academics, the square cap, and black gown, is adapted to the civil and even clerical profession; and from the doctor in divinity to the under-graduate, the degrees of learning and age are externally distinguished. Instead of being scattered in a town, the students of Oxford and Cambridge are united in colleges; their maintenance is provided at their own expence, or that of the founders; and the stated hours of the hall and chappel represent the discipline of a regular, and, as it were, a religious community. The eyes of the traveller are attracted by the size or beauty of the public edifices; and the principal colleges appear to be so many palaces, which a liberal nation has erected and endowed for the habitation of science. My own introduction to the university of Oxford forms a new æra in my life; and at the distance of forty years I still remember my first emotions of surprise and satisfaction. In my fifteenth year I felt myself suddenly raised from a boy to a man: the

'F'

At the In my fifteenth year, I felt myself suddenly raised from a boy to a man: the persons whom I respected as my superiors in age and Academical rank entertained me with every mark of attention | and civility; ^and^ my vanity was flattered by the velvet Cap and silk gown which discriminate a Gentleman-Commoner from a plebeian student. A decent allowance, more money than a school-boy had ever seen, was at my own disposal, and I might command among the tradesmen of Oxford, an indefinite and dangerous latitude of credit. A key was delivered into my hands which gave me the free use of a numerous and learned library: my apartment consisted of three elegant and well-furnished rooms in the new building, a stately pile, of Magdalen College: and the adjacent walks, had they been frequented by Plato's disciples, might have been compared to the Attic shade on the banks of the Ilissus.[3] Such was the fair prospect of my entrance (April. 3: 1752) into the University of Oxford.

[1] Le nombre des Etudians d'Oxford va à 2000. Ils ne portent ni bâton ni épée. Tous portent la robe et le bonnet quarré, l'habillement differe suivant le degré et la qualité … Tout est bien reglé dans cette Université: les desordres n'y regnent pas comme dans celles d'Allemagne (Voyage Litteraire en 1733. par M. Jordan (the correspondent of Frederic), pp.174.175

[2] Quarrels of the students — Padua deserted by stranger — unsafe after sunset (Burnet's travels p. 102 — At Oxford North and South, Greeks and Trojans — Duels at Ox Gottingen.

[3] Praised by Hurd. (Dialogues iii. p165–169) — Spartan halls, Attic symposia are or may be united

3   A venerable prelate, whose taste and erudition must reflect honour on the society in which they were formed has drawn an a very interesting picture of his Academical life. "I was educated (says Bishop Lowth in the University of Oxford. I enjoyed all the advantages both public and private, which that famous seat of learning so largely

persons, whom I respected as my superiors in age and academical rank, entertained me with every mark of attention and civility: and my vanity was flattered by the velvet cap and silk gown, which discriminate a gentleman commoner from a plebeian student. A decent allowance, more money than a schoolboy had ever seen, was at my own disposal; and I might command, among the tradesmen of Oxford, an indefinite and dangerous latitude of credit. A key was delivered into my hands, which gave me the free use of a numerous and learned library: my apartment consisted of three elegant and well-furnished rooms in the new building, a stately pile, of Magdalen College; and the adjacent walks, had they been frequented by Plato's disciples, might have been compared to the Attic shade on the banks of the Ilissus. Such was the fair prospect of my entrance (April 3, 1752) into the university of Oxford.

A venerable prelate, whose taste and erudition must reflect honour on the society in which they were formed, has drawn a very interesting picture of his academical life. — "I was educated (says Bishop Lowth) in the UNIVERSITY OF OXFORD. I enjoyed all the advantages, both public and private, which that famous seat of learning so largely affords. I spent many years in that illustrious society, in a well-regulated course of useful discipline and studies, and in the agreeable and improving commerce of gentlemen and of scholars; in a society where emulation without envy, ambition without jealousy, contention without animosity, incited industry, and awakened genius: where a liberal pursuit of knowledge, and a genuine freedom of thought, was raised, encouraged, and pushed forward by example, by commendation, and by authority. I breathed the same atmosphere that the HOOKERS, the CHILLINGWORTHS, and the LOCKES had breathed before; whose benevolence and humanity were as extensive as their vast genius and comprehensive knowledge; who always treated their adversaries with civility and respect; who made candour, moderation, and liberal judgment as much the rule and law as the subject of their discourse. And do you reproach me with my education in this place, and with my relation to this most respectable body, which I shall always esteem my greatest advantage and my highest honour?" I transcribe with pleasure this eloquent passage, without examining what benefits or what rewards were derived by Hooker, or Chillingworth, or Locke, from their academical institution; without inquiring, whether in this angry controversy the spirit of Lowth himself is purified from the intolerant zeal, which Warburton had ascribed to the Genius of the place.

The expression of gratitude is a virtue and a pleasure: a liberal mind will delight to cherish and celebrate the memory of its parents; and the teachers of science are the parents of the mind. I applaud the filial piety, which it is impossible for me to imitate; since I must not confess an imaginary debt, to assume the merit of a just or generous retribution. To the university of Oxford I acknowledge no obligation;

---

affords. I spent many years in that illustrious Society, in a well-regulated course of useful discipline and studies; and in the agreeable and improving commerce of Gentlemen and of Scholars; in a society where emulation without jealousy envy, ambition without jealousy, contention without animosity, incited industry, and awakened genius: where a liberal pursuit of knowledge, and a generous freedom of thought was raised encouraged and pushed forward, by example, by commendation, and by authority. I breathed the same atmosphere. that the Hookers, the Chillingworths, and the Lockes H had breathed before: whose benevolence and humanity were as extensive as their vast Genius and comprehensive Knowledge. who always treated their adversaries with civility and respect, who made candour, moderation, and liberal judgement as much the rule and law as the subject of their discourse. — And do you reproach me with my education in This place, and with my relation to This most respectable Body; which I shall always esteem my greatest advantage, and my highest honour?"⁴ I transcribe with pleasure this eloquent passage, without examining what benefits or what rewards were derived by Hooker, or Chillingworth or Locke from their Academical institution, without enquired ^ing^ whether in this angry controversy the spirit of Lowth himself is purified from the intolerant Zeal which Warburton had ascribed to the Genius of the place.⁵

⁴ Letter of a late professor at Oxford (p 62–65) – by an happy quot. from Clarendon charges W. with having been an attorney's clerk Clerk.
⁵ Idolatry excluded from toleration p34–51 — and Bengal — the Lingam, Suicide? Inquisition at Calcutta? Ha!

4

The expression of gratitude is a virtue and a pleasure: a liberal mind will delight to cherish and celebrate the memory of its parents, and the the teachers of science are the parents of the mind.⁶ I applaud the filial piety which it is impossible for me to imitate: since I must not confess an imaginary debt, to assume the merit of a just or generous retribution. To the University of Oxford I acknowledge no obligation, and she will as chearfully renounce me for a son, as I am willing to disclaim her for a mother. I spent fourteen months at Magdalen College: they proved the fourteen months the most idle and unprofitable of my whole life:

6 Locke owed no thanks — Student of Christ-Church, expelled never restored after Revol (Biograph. Brit. Vol. v.) — Heads of houses. no public censure — He laughed ^Locke^ a good jest, a recommendation, yet was anxious to know (His Works. 4° Edit Vol. iv. p. 618. 19. in his letters.

5 the reader will pronounce between the school and I the scholar: but I cannot affect to believe that Nature had disqualified me for all litterary pursuits. The specious and ready excuse of my tender age, imperfect preparation, and hasty departure may doubtless be alleged, nor do I wish to defraud such excuses of their proper weight. Yet in my sixteenth year I was not devoid of capacity or application; ray even my childish reading had displayed an early though blind propensity for books; and the shallow flood might have been taught to flow in a deep channel and a clear stream. In the discipline of a well-constituted Academy, under the guidance of skillful and vigilant professors, I should gradually have risen from translations to originals, from the Latin to the Greek Classics, from dead languages to living science: my hours would have been occupied by useful and agreable studies: the wanderings of fancy would have been restrained, and I should have precipitated my departure from Oxford.

5a Perhaps, in a separate annotation I may coolly examine the fabulous and real antiquities of our sister Universities, a question which has kindled such fierce and foolish disputes among their fanatic sons. In the mean while, it will be acknowledged that these venerable bodies are sufficiently old to partake of all the prejudices and infirmities of

and she will as cheerfully renounce me for a son, as I am willing to disclaim her for a mother. I spent fourteen months at Magdalen College; they proved the fourteen months the most idle and unprofitable of my whole life:

the reader will pronounce between the school and the scholar; but I cannot affect to believe that Nature had disqualified me for all literary pursuits. The specious and ready excuse of my tender age, imperfect preparation, and hasty departure, may doubtless be alleged; nor do I wish to defraud such excuses of their proper weight. Yet in my sixteenth year I was not devoid of capacity or application; even my childish reading had displayed an early though blind propensity for books, and the shallow flood might have been taught to flow in a deep channel and a clear stream. In the discipline of a well-constituted academy, under the guidance of skilful and vigilant professors, I should gradually have risen from translations to originals, from the Latin to the Greek classics, from dead languages to living science: my hours would have been occupied by useful and agreable studies, the wanderings of fancy would have been restrained, and I should have escaped the temptations of idleness, which finally precipitated my departure from Oxford.

Perhaps, in a separate annotation I may coolly examine the fabulous and real antiquities of our sister universities, a question which has kindled such fierce and foolish disputes among their fanatic sons. In the mean while it will be acknowledged, that these venerable bodies are sufficiently old to partake of all the prejudices and infirmities of age. The schools of Oxford and Cambridge were founded in a dark age of false and barbarous science; and they are still tainted with the vices of their origin. Their primitive discipline was adapted to the education of priests and monks; and the goverment still remains in the hands of the Clergy, an order of men, whose manners are remote from the present World, and whose eyes are dazzled by the light of Philosophy. The legal incorporation of these societies by the charters of Popes and Kings, had given them a monopolisty of the public instruction; and the spirit of monopolists is narrow, lazy and oppressive; their work is more costly and less productive, than that of independent artists; and the new improvements so eagerly grasped by the competition of freedom, are admitted with slow and sullen reluctance in those proud corporations, above the fear of a rival, and below the confession of an error. We may scarcely hope that any reformation will be a voluntary act,[7] and so deeply are they rooted in law and prejudice that even the omnipotence of Parliament would shrink from an enquiry into the state and abuses of the two Universities.

The use of Academical degrees, as old as the thirteenth century, is visibly borrowed from the mechanic corporations; in which an apprentice, after serving his time, obtains a testimonial of his skill, and a license to practise his trade and mystery. It is not my design to depreciate those honours which could never gratify or disappoint my ambition: and I should applaud the institution, if the degrees of Batchelor or licentiate were bestowed as the reward of [manly and] successful study: if the name and rank of Doctor or Master were strictly reserved for the professors of science who have approved their title to the public esteem. The mysterious faculty] of Theology must not be scanned by a profane eye, a shadow [the cloak] of reason sits awkwardly on our fashionable Divines and in the Ecclesiastical studies of the fathers and councils, their modesty will yield to the Catholic universities. Our English civilians and canonists have never been famous: their real business is confined to a small circle; and the double

age. The schools of Oxford and Cambridge were founded in a dark age of false and barbarous science; and they are still tainted with the vices of their origin. Their primitive discipline was adapted to the education of priests and monks; and the government still remains in the hands of the clergy, an order of men whose manners are remote from the present world, and whose eyes are dazzled by the light of philosophy. The legal incorporation of these societies by the charters of popes and kings had given them a monopoly of the public instruction; and the spirit of monopolists is narrow, lazy, and oppressive; their work is more costly and less productive than that of independent artists; and the new improvements so eagerly grasped by the competition of freedom, are admitted with slow and sullen reluctance in those proud corporations, above the fear of a rival, and below the confession of an error. We may scarcely hope that any reformation will be a voluntary act; and so deeply are they rooted in law and prejudice, that even the omnipotence of parliament would shrink from an enquiry into the state and abuses of the two universities.

The use of academical degrees, as old as the thirteenth century, is visibly borrowed from the mechanic corporations; in which an apprentice, after serving his time, obtains a testimonial of his skill, and a licence to practise his trade and mystery. It is not my design to depreciate those honours, which could never gratify or disappoint my ambition; and I should applaud the institution, if the degrees of bachelor or licentiate were bestowed as the reward of manly and successful study: if the name and rank of doctor or master were strictly reserved for the professors of science, who have approved their title to the public esteem.

jurisprudence of Rome is overwhelmed by the enormous profession of common lawyers, who, in the pursuit of honours and riches, disdain the mock majesty of our budge Doctors.[8] We are justly proud of the skill and learning of our physicians: their skill is acquired in the practise of the hospitals: they seek their learning in London, in Scotland, or on the continent; and few patients would trust their pulse to a medical student, if he had passed the fourteen years of his noviciate at Oxford or Cambridge, whose degrees however, are exclusively admitted in the Royal College. The Arts are supposed to include the liberal knowledge of Philosophy and litterature: but I am informed that some tattered shreds of the old Logic and Metaphysics compose the exercises for a Batchelor and Master's degree; and that modern improvements, instead of introducing a more rational tryal, has [have] only served to relax the forms which are now the object of general contempt.[9]

[7] Lord Townshend. wished to reform — severe scheme (B.B. tom. v. Prideaux (A.A.) — never heard of more. ^Whiston (p 42–45) Emendenda, always tutors and old fellows^

[8] The budge Doctors of the Stoic fur – (Comus, 795 707. and Warton's notes p 220). I do not apply lean and sallow abstinence

[9] Here Vicesimus Knox must be used.

6   In all the Universities of Europe except our own, the languages and sciences are distributed among a numerous list of effective professors: the students, according to their taste, their calling, and their diligence apply themselves to the proper masters, and in the annual repetition of public and private lectures, these masters are assiduously employed.[10] Our curiosity may inquire what number of professors has been instituted at Oxford, (for I shall now confine myself to my own University), by whom are they appointed, and what may be the probable chances of merit or incapacity? how many are stationed to

In all the universities of Europe, excepting our own, the languages and sciences are distributed among a numerous list of effective professors: the students, according to their taste, their calling, and their diligence, apply themselves to the proper masters; and in the annual repetition of public and private lectures, these masters are assiduously employed. Our curiosity may inquire what number of professors has been instituted at Oxford? (for I shall now confine myself to my own university:) by whom are they appointed, and what may be the probable chances of merit or incapacity? how many are stationed to the three faculties, and how many are left for the liberal Arts? what is the form and what the substance, of their lessons? But all these questions are silenced by one short and singular answer. "That in the University of Oxford, the greater part of the public professors have, for these many years, given up altogether even the pretence of teaching."[11] Incredible as the fact may appear I must rest my belief on the positive and impartial evidence of a Philosopher who had himself resided at Oxford. Dr Adam Smith assigns as the cause of their indolence, that, instead of being paid by voluntary contributions, which would urge them to encrease the number, and to deserve the gratitude, of their pupills, the Oxford professors are secure in the enjoyment of a fixed stipend, without the necessity of labour, or the apprehension of controul.[12] It has indeed been observed, nor is the observation absurd, that except in experimental sciences, which demand a costly apparatus and a dextrous hand, the many valuable treatises wh that have been published on every subject of learning may now supersede the ancient mode of oral instruction. Were this principle true in its utmost latitude, I should only infer that the offices and salaries which are become useless ought, without delay, to be abolished.[13] But there still remains a material difference between a book and a professor: the hour of the lecture enforces attendance: attention is fixed by the presence, the voice, and the occasional questions of the teacher: the most idle will carry something away; and the more diligent will compare the instructions which they have heard in the school, with the volumes which they peruse in their chamber. The advice of a skillful professor will adapt a course of reading to every mind and every situation; his learning will remove difficulties, and solve objections: his authority will discover, admonish, and at last chastise the negligence of his disciples; and his vigilant enquiries will ascertain the steps of their litterary progress. Whatever science he professes, he may illustrate in a series of discourses, composed in the leisure of his closet, pronounced on public occasions and finally delivered to the press. I observe with

the three faculties, and how many are left for the liberal arts? what is the form, and what the substance, of their lessons? But all these questions are silenced by one short and singular answer, "That in the university of Oxford, the greater part of the public professors have for these many years given up altogether even the pretence of teaching." Incredible as the fact may appear, I must rest my belief on the positive and impartial evidence of a master of moral and political wisdom, who had himself resided at Oxford. Dr. Adam Smith assigns as the cause of their indolence, that, instead of being paid by voluntary contributions, which would urge them to increase the number, and to deserve the gratitude of their pupils, the Oxford professors are secure in the enjoyment of a fixed stipend, without the necessity of labour, or the apprehension of controul. It has indeed been observed, nor is the observation absurd, that excepting in experimental sciences, which demand a costly apparatus and a dexterous hand, the many valuable treatises, that have been published on every subject of learning, may now supersede the ancient mode of oral instruction. Were this principle true in its utmost latitude, I should only infer that the offices and salaries, which are become useless, ought without delay to be abolished. But there still remains a material difference between a book and a professor; the hour of the lecture enforces attendance; attention is fixed by the presence, the voice, and the occasional questions of the teacher; the most idle will carry something away; and the more diligent will compare the instructions, which they have heard in the school, with the volumes, which they peruse in their chamber. The advice of a skilful professor will adapt a course of reading to every mind and every situation; his authority will discover, admonish, and at last chastise the negligence of his disciples; and his vigilant inquiries will ascertain the steps of their literary progress. Whatever science he professes he may illustrate in a series of discourses, composed in the leisure of his closet, pronounced on public occasions, and finally delivered to the press. I observe with pleasure, that in the university of Oxford Dr. Lowth, with equal eloquence and erudition, has executed this task in his incomparable *Prelections* on the Poetry of the Hebrews.

The college of St. Mary Magdalen was founded in the fifteenth century by Wainfleet bishop of Winchester; and now consists of a president, forty fellows, and a number of inferior students. It is esteemed one of the largest and most wealthy of our academical corporations, which may be compared to the Benedictine abbeys of catholic countries; and I have loosely heard that the estates belonging to Magdalen College, which are leased by those indulgent landlords at small quit-rents and occasional fines, might be raised, in the hands of private avarice, to an annual revenue of nearly thirty thousand pounds. Our colleges are supposed to be schools of science, as well as of education; nor is it unreasonable to expect that a body of litterary men, devoted to a life of celibacy, exempt from the care of their own subsistence, and amply provided with books, should devote their leisure to the prosecution of study, and that some effects of their studies should be manifested to the world. The shelves of their library

---

pleasure, that in the University of Oxford, Dr Lowth, with equal eloquence and erudition, has executed this task, in his incomparable *Prelections* on the poetry of the Hebrews.[14]

[10] Sm Information from Gottingen. — Professors — Lectures &c.

[11] Smith W. of N. Vol. ii. L v. C i. P iii. Article iii. p 343 — himself a P. at Glasgow. — His Theory a small part of his lectures.

[12] Gray Prof. of modern hist at Cambridge. £400 a year (Mem. p 333.) in three years never once read — his remorse, Mason's excuses. p 395–399. never admonished by any superiors.

[13] Dodwell. Præl. Camden — read on the August. hist. 25 lectures only for the authors and private life of Hadrian (Life. Vol 190–217 by Brokesby), must be now worth (since 1722) at least £400 per annum (B. B. p 168, new edit. Camden. Ayliffe. Vol. ii. p 186).

[14] Lowth de sacrâ Hebræorum poesi. Prælect. Academ. 1775. 8°. 3ᵈ Edit. — the first in 4° in 1753 — When delivered? Interesting without Hebrew or faith — good abstract in Blair (Lectures on Rh. Vol. ii p 385–406).

6a (inc. old 10, 11 and 12) The College of Sᵗ Mary Magdalen (it is vulgarly pronounced Maudlin) was founded in the fifteenth Century by a Bishop of Winchester,[15] and now consists of a President, fellows, and a number of inferior students. It is esteemed one of the largest and most wealthy of our Academical corporations, which may be compared to the Benedictine Abbeys of Catholic countries: and I have loosely heard that the estates belonging to Magdalen College, which are leased by those indulgent landlords at small quit-rents and occasional fines, might be raised in the hands of private avarice, to an annual revenue of near thirty thousand pounds. Our Colleges are supposed to be schools of science as well as of education: nor is it unreasonable to expect that a body of litterary men, addicted to a life of celibacy, exempt from the care of their own subsistence, and amply provided with books, should devote their leisure to the prosecution of study, and that some [effects] fruits of their studies should be given to the

groan under the weight of the Benedictine folios, of the editions of the fathers, and the collections of the middle ages, which have issued from the single abbey of St. Germain des Préz at Paris. A composition of genius must be the offspring of one mind; but such works of industry, as may be divided among many hands, and must be continued during many years, are the peculiar province of a laborious community. If I enquire into the manufactures of the monks of Magdalen, if I extend the enquiry to the other colleges of Oxford and Cambridge, a silent blush, or a scornful frown, will be the only reply. The fellows or monks of my time were decent easy men, who supinely enjoyed the gifts of the founder: their days were filled by a series of uniform employments; the chappel and the hall, the coffee-house and the common room, till they retired, weary and well satisfied, to a long slumber. From the toil of reading, or thinking, or writing, they had absolved their conscience; and the first shoots of learning and ingenuity withered on the ground, without yielding any fruit to the owners or the public. As a gentleman commoner, I was admitted to the society of the fellows, and fondly expected that some questions of literature would be the amusing and instructive topics of their discourse. Their conversation stagnated in a round of college business, Tory politics, personal anecdotes, and private scandal: their dull and deep potations excused the brisk intemperance of youth; and their constitutional toasts were not expressive of the most lively loyalty for the house of Hanover. A general election was now approaching: the great Oxfordshire contest already blazed with all the malevolence of party-zeal. Magdalen College was devoutly attached to the old interest! and the names of Wenman and Dashwood were more frequently pronounced, than those of Cicero and Chrysostom. The example of the senior fellows could not inspire the under-graduates with a liberal spirit or studious emulation; and I cannot describe, as I never saw, the discipline of college. Some duties may possibly have been imposed on the poor scholars, whose ambition aspired to the peaceful honours of a fellowship (*ascribi quietis ordinibus - - - Deorum*);

public [manifested to the World.] The shelves of their library groan under the weight of the Benedictine folios, of the editions of the fathers, and the Collections of the middle ages, which have issued from the single Abbey of St Germain des Préz at Paris.[16] A composition of Genius must be the offspring of [one] ~~a single~~ mind: but such works of industry as may be divided among many hands, and must be continued during many years are the peculiar province of a laborious community. If I enquire into the manufactures of the monks of Magdalen, if I extend the enquiry to the other Colleges of Oxford and Cambridge, a silent blush, or a scornful frown, will be the only reply. The fellows or monks of my time were decent easy men who supinely enjoyed the gifts of the founder: their days were filled by a ~~series of uniform employments; a long breakfast at no early hour, the chappel, the dinner in the Hall, their walk regular walk, afternoon prayers, the Coffee-house, the evening assembly in the common-room~~ [the Chappel and the Hall, the Coffee-house, and the common room,] till they retired, weary and well satisfied, to a long slumber. From the toil of reading or thinking, or writing they had absolved their conscience, and the first shoots of learning and ingenuity withered on the ground without yielding any fruit to the owners or the public. The only student was a young fellow, (a future Bishop) who was deeply immersed in the follies of the Hutchinsonian system: the only author was an half-starved Chaplain, Ballard was his name | who begged subscriptions for some Memoirs concerning the learned ladies of Great Britain. As a Gentleman-Commoner, I was sometimes admitted to the society of the fellows, and fondly expected that some q questions of litterature would be the amusing and instructive topics of their discourse. Their conversation stagnated in a round of College business, Tory politics, personal stories and private scandal: their dull and deep potations excused the brisk intemperance of Youth; and their constitutional toasts were not expressive of the most lively loyalty for the house of Hanover.[17] A general election was now approaching: the great Oxfordshire contest already blazed with all the

'F'

malevolence of party-zeal: Magdalen College was devoutly attached to the Old interest; and the names of Wenman and Dashwood were more frequently pronounced than those of Cicero and Chrysostom. The example of the senior fellows could not inspire the under-graduates with a liberal spirit a studious emulation; and I cannot describe, as I never knew, the discipline of Magdalen [the] College, Some duties may possibly have been imposed on the poor scholars, whose ambition aspired to the peaceful honours of a fellowship (ascribi quietis ordinibus ... Deorum): but no independent members were admitted, below the rank of a Gentleman-Commoner; and our velvet cap was the cap of liberty. A tradition prevailed that some of our predecessors had spoken Latin declamations in the Hall, but of this ancient [custom] no vestige remained: the obvious methods of public exercises and examinations were totally unknown; and I have never heard that either the President or the Society interfered in the private œconomy of the Tutors and their pupils.

15 William Patten of Wainfleet. Lord Chancell. B. of Winchester – founded Magdalen 1458 — merit under James ii, zeal, privileges. Ayliffe Hist. of Oxford. Vol p i. p. 342 &c.

16 Lively picture in Hist de l'Acad. tom. 27. p. 219 (from Quirini's own Comment. Tom. 1. p. 853) Artificumq. manus inter se operumq. laborem | miratur. burnt till extinction more or less.

17 Fellow's Journal. Idler, N°. 33. not by Dr Johnson. his awe, nonsense, air.!

8 The silence of the Oxford professors, which deprives the Youth of public instruction is imperfectly supplied by the Tutors as they are styled of the several colleges. Instead of confining themselves to a single science which had satisfied the ambition of Burman or Bernouilli, they teach or promise to teach either History or Mathematics, or ancient literature or moral philosophy; and as it is

MW 1796 i. 32–53

but no independent members were admitted below the rank of a gentleman commoner, and our velvet cap was the cap of liberty. A tradition prevailed that some of our predecessors had spoken Latin declamations in the hall; but of this ancient custom no vestige remained: the obvious methods of public exercises and examinations were totally unknown; and I have never heard that either the president or the society interfered in the private œconomy of the tutors and their pupils.

The silence of the Oxford professors, which deprives the youth of public instruction, is imperfectly supplied by the tutors, as they are styled, of the several colleges. Instead of confining themselves to a single science, which had satisfied the ambition of Burman or Bernouilli, they teach, or promise to teach, either history or mathematics, or ancient literature, or moral philosophy; and as it is possible that they may be defective in all, it is highly probable that of some they will be ignorant. They are paid, indeed, by private contributions; but their appointment depends on the head of the house: their diligence is voluntary, and will consequently be languid, while the pupils themselves, or their parents, are not indulged in the liberty of choice or change. The first tutor into whose hands I was resigned appears to have been one of the best of the tribe: Dr. Waldegrave was a learned and pious man, of a mild disposition, strict morals, and abstemious life, who seldom mingled in the politics or the jollity of the college. But his knowledge of the world was confined to the university; his learning was of the last, rather than the present age; his temper was indolent; his faculties, which were not of the first rate, had been relaxed by the climate, and he was satisfied, like his fellows, with the slight and superficial discharge of an important trust. As soon as my tutor had sounded the insufficiency of his disciple in school-learning, he proposed that we should read every morning from ten to eleven the comedies of Terence. The sum of my improvement in the university of Oxford is confined to three or four Latin plays; and even the study of an elegant classic, which might have been illustrated by a comparison of ancient and modern theatres, was reduced to a dry and literal interpretation of the author's text. During the first weeks I constantly attended these lessons in my tutor's room; but as they appeared equally devoid of profit and pleasure, I was once tempted to try the experiment of a formal apology. The apology was accepted with a smile. I repeated the offence with less ceremony; the excuse was admitted with the same indulgence: the slightest motive of laziness or indisposition, the most trifling avocation at home or abroad, was allowed as a worthy impediment; nor did my tutor appear conscious of my absence or neglect. Had the hour of lecture been constantly filled, a single hour was a small portion of my academic leisure. No plan of study was recommended for his inspection; and, at the most precious season of youth, whole days and weeks were suffered to elapse without labour

possible that they may be defective in all, it is highly probable that of some they will be ignorant. They are paid indeed by private contributions; but their appointment depends on the head of the house: their diligence is voluntary, and will consequently be languid, while the pupills themselves and their parents are not indulged in the liberty of choice or change. The first Tutor into whose hands I was resigned, appears to have been one of the best of the tribe: Dr Waldegrave was a learned and pious man, of a mild disposition, strict morals and abstemious life, who seldom mingled in the politics or the jollity of the College. But his knowledge of the World was confined to the University; his learning was of the last, rather than the present age, his temper was indolent; his faculties, which were not of the first-rate, had been relaxed by the climate; and he was satisfied, like his fellows with the slight and superficial discharge of an important trust. As soon as my tutor had sounded the insufficiency of his disciple he in school-learning he proposed that we should read every morning from ten to eleven the comedies of Terence: the sum of my pr improvement in the University of Oxford is confined to three or four Latin plays; and even the study of an elegant Classic which might have been illustrated by a comparison of ancient and modern theatres was reduced to a dry and literal interpretation of the Author's text During the first weeks I r constantly attended these l lessons in my tutor's room; but as they appeared equally devoid of profit and pleasure, I was once tempted to try the experiment of a formal apology. The apology was accepted with and a a smile: I repeated the offence with less ceremony, the excuse was admitted with the same indulgence: the slightest motive of laziness or indisposition, the most trifling avocation at home or abroad was allowed as a worthy impediment and nor did my tutor appear conscious of my absence or neglect. Had the hour of lecture been constantly filled, a single hour was a small portion of my Academic leisure. No plan of study was recommended for my use; no exercises were prescribed for his inspection; and at the most precious season of Youth whole days and weeks were suffered to elapse without labour or amusement, without advice or account. I should have listened to the voice of reason and of my tutor: his mild behaviour had gained my confidence: I preferred his society to that of the younger students, and in our ~~fr~~ evening walks to the top of Heddington hill we freely conversed on a variety of subjects. ~~Or~~ Since the days of Pocock and Hyde, Oriental learning has always been the pride of Oxford, and I once expressed an inclination to study Arabic. His prudence discouraged this childish fancy; but he neglected the fair occasion of directing the ardour of a curious mind. During my absence in the summer vacation, Dr. Waldegrave accepted a College living at Washington in Sussex, and on my return I no longer found him at Oxford. From that time I have lost sight of my first tutor: but at the end of thirty years (1781) he was still alive, and the ~~continual~~ practise of exercise and temperance had entitled him to an healthy old-age.

1   The long recess between the Trinity and Michaelmas terms empties the Colleges of Oxford as well as the courts of Westminster. I spent at my father's house at Buriton in Hampshire the two months of August and September, which, in the year 1752, were curtailed, to my great surprize, of eleven days, by the alteration of the style. It is whimsical enough that as soon as I left Magdalen college my taste for books began to revive, but it was the same blind and boyish taste for the pursuit of exotic history. Unprovided with original learning, unformed in the habits of thinking, unskilled in the arts of composition, I resolved — to write a book. The title of this first Essay, the Age of Sesostris was perhaps suggested by Voltaire's Age of Lewis XIV which was new and popular, but my sole object was to investigate the probable date of the life and reign of the Conqueror of Asia. I was then enamoured of Sir John Marsham's Canon Chronicus,[18] an elaborate work of whose merits and defects I was not

or amusement, without advice or account. I should have listened to the voice of reason and of my tutor; his mild behaviour had gained my confidence. I preferred his society to that of the younger students; and in our evening walks to the top of Heddington-hill, we freely conversed on a variety of subjects. Since the days of Pocock and Hyde, Oriental learning has always been the pride of Oxford, and I once expressed an inclination to study Arabic. His prudence discouraged this childish fancy; but he neglected the fair occasion of directing the ardour of a curious mind. During my absence in the Summer vacation, Dr. Waldegrave accepted a college living at Washington in Sussex, and on my return I no longer found him at Oxford. From that time I have lost sight of my first tutor; but at the end of thirty years (1781) he was still alive; and the practice of exercise and temperance had entitled him to a healthy old age.

The long recess between the Trinity and Michaelmas terms empties the colleges of Oxford, as well as the courts of Westminster. I spent, at my father's house at Buriton in Hampshire, the two months of August and September. It is whimsical enough, that as soon as I left Magdalen College, my taste for books began to revive; but it was the same blind and boyish taste for the pursuit of exotic history. Unprovided with original learning, unformed in the habits of thinking, unskilled in the arts of composition, I resolved — to write a book. The title of this first Essay, the Age of Sesostris, was perhaps suggested by Voltaire's Age of Lewis XIV., which was new and popular; but my sole object was to investigate the probable date of the life and reign of the conqueror of Asia. I was then enamoured of Sir John Marsham's Canon Chronicus; an elaborate work, of whose merits and defects I was not yet qualified to judge. According to his specious, though narrow plan, I settled my hero about the time of Solomon, in the tenth Century before the

According to his specious, though narrow plan, I settled my Hero about the time of Solomon, in the tenth Century before the Christian Æra. It was therefore incumbent on me, unless I would adopt Sir Isaac Newton's shorter Chronology, to remove a formidable objection; and my solution, for a youth of fifteen, is not devoid of ingenuity. In th his version of the sacred books, Manetho the High priest has identified Sethosis or Sesostris with the elder brother of Danaus who landed in Greece, according to the Parian marble fifteen hundred and ten years before Christ.[19] But in my supposition the High-priest is guilty of a voluntary error: flattery is the prolific parent of falsehood, and falsehood, I will now add, is not incompatible with the sacerdotal | Character. Manetho's history of Egypt is dedicated to Ptolemy Philadelphus who derived a fabulous or illegitimate pedigree from the Macedonian Kings of the race of Hercules.[20] Danaus is the ancestor of Hercules; and after the failure of the elder branch his descendants the Ptolemies are the sole representatives of the Royal family and may claim by inheritance the Kingdom which they hold by conquest. Such were my juvenile discoveries; at a riper age I no longer presume to connect the Greek, the Jewish, and the Egyptian antiquities which are lost in a distant cloud: nor is this the only instance in which the belief and knowledge of the child are superseded by the more rational ignorance of the man. During my stay at Buriton, my infant labour was diligently prosecuted without much interruption from company or country diversions; and I already heard the music of public applause. [The discovery of my own weakness was the first symptoms of taste: but on my return to Oxford, the Age of Sesostris was wisely relinquished; but the imperfect sheets remained twenty years at the bottom of a drawer, till in a general clearance of papers (November 1772) they were committed to the flames. After the departure &c] ~~But on my return to Oxford, in the beginning of October (1752), I nodded to the Genius of the place, and gently rep relapsed into my former lethargy.~~

[18] Best Edit. London 1672 in folio — Hebrew Chronology.

Christian æra. It was therefore incumbent on me, unless I would adopt Sir Isaac Newton's shorter chronology, to remove a formidable objection; and my solution, for a youth of fifteen, is not devoid of ingenuity. In his version of the Sacred Books, Manetho the high priest has identified Sethosis, or Sesostris, with the elder brother of Danaus, who landed in Greece, according to the Parian Marble, fifteen hundred and ten years before Christ. But in my supposition the high priest is guilty of a voluntary error; flattery is the prolific parent of falsehood. Manetho's History of Egypt is dedicated to Ptolemy Philadelphus, who derived a fabulous or illegitimate pedigree from the Macedonian kings of the race of Hercules. Danaus is the ancestor of Hercules; and after the failure of the elder branch, his descendants, the Ptolemies are the sole representatives of the royal family, and may claim by inheritance the kingdom which they hold by conquest. Such were my juvenile discoveries; at a riper age I no longer presume to connect the Greek, the Jewish, and the Egyptian antiquities, which are lost in a distant cloud. Nor is this the only instance, in which the belief and knowledge of the child are superseded by the more rational ignorance of the man. During my stay at Buriton, my infant labour was diligently prosecuted, without much interruption from company or country diversions; and I already heard the music of public applause. The discovery of my own weakness was the first symptom of taste: on my return to Oxford, the Age of Sesostris was wisely relinquished; but the imperfect sheets remained twenty years at the bottom of a drawer, till, in a general clearance of papers (November 1772,) they were committed to the flames.

'F'

[19] Fragments in Joseph. contra Apion. Li. C15. Tom ii. p 447. Edit. Havercamp. real loss. see Fabricius. Bibl and Gerard Vossius.

[20] Quidam Phillippo genitum esse credebant, certum pellice ejus ortum constabat Q. C. Lix. C8, cum not. Fre^i^nshein.

9   After the departure of Dr Waldgrave, I was transferred with the rest of his live stock to a senior fellow, whose literary and moral character did not command the respect of the College. Dr Winchester well remembered that he had a salary to receive, and only forgot that he had a duty to perform. Instead of guiding the studies and watching over the behaviour of his [disciple] pupill, I was never summoned to attend even the ceremony of a lecture; and was never summoned to attend even the ceremony of a lecture; and, except one voluntary visit to his rooms, during the eight months of his titular office, the tutor and pupil lived in the same College as strangers to each other.

13   The want of experience, of advice, and of occupation soon betrayed me into some improprieties of conduct, ill-chosen company, late hours, and inconsiderate expence. My growing debts might be secret: but my frequent absence was visible and scandalous: and a tour to Bath, a visit into Buckinghamshire, and four excursions to London in the same winter, were costly and dangerous frolicks. They were indeed without a meaning, as without an excuse: the irksomeness of a cloystered life repeatedly tempted me to wander: but my chief pleasure was that of travelling; and I was too young and bashful to enjoy, like a manly Oxonian in town, the taverns and bagnios of Covent Garden.[21] In all these excursions, I eloped from Oxford; I returned to College; in a few days I eloped again, as if I had been an independent stranger [in a hired lodging,] without once hearing the voice of admonition, without once feeling the hand of controul. Yet my time was lost, my expences were multiplied, my behaviour abroad was unknown; folly as well as vice should have awakened the

---

After the departure of Dr. Waldgrave, I was transferred, with his other pupils, to his academical heir, whose literary character did not command the respect of the college. Dr. ★ ★ ★ ★ well remembered that he had a salary to receive, and only forgot that he had a duty to perform. Instead of guiding the studies, and watching over the behaviour of his disciple, I was never summoned to attend even the ceremony of a lecture; and, excepting one voluntary visit to his rooms, during the eight months of his titular office, the tutor and pupil lived in the same college as strangers to each other.

The want of experience, of advice, and of occupation, soon betrayed me into some improprieties of conduct, ill-chosen company, late hours, and inconsiderate expence. My growing debts might be secret; but my frequent absence was visible and scandalous: and a tour to Bath, a visit into Buckinghamshire, and four excursions to London in the same winter, were costly and dangerous frolics. They were, indeed, without a meaning, as without an excuse. The irksomeness of a cloistered life repeatedly tempted me to wander; but my chief pleasure was that of travelling; and I was too young and bashful to enjoy, like a Manly Oxonian in Town, the pleasures of London. In all these excursions I eloped from Oxford; I returned to college; in a few days I eloped again, as if I had been an independent stranger in a hired lodging, without once hearing the voice of admonition, without once feeling the hand of control. Yet my time was lost, my expences were multiplied, my behaviour abroad was unknown; folly as well as vice should have awakened the attention of my superiors, and my tender

411

attention of my superiors, and my tender years would have justified a more than ordinary degree of restraint and discipline.

[21] See Conoisseur No XI. worked up in Colman's farce Pallas quas condidit arces | ipsa colat, –good.

15 It might at least be expected that an Ecclesiastical school should inculcate the orthodox [principles] system of Religion.

16 But our venerable Mother had contrived to unite the opposite extremes of bigotry and indifference: an heretic or unbeliever was a monster in her eyes; but she was always, or often, or sometimes, remiss in the spiritual education of her own children. According to the statutes of the University, every student, before he is matriculated, must subscribe his assent to the thirty nine articles of the Church of England, which are signed by more than read, and read by more than believe them; My insufficient age excused me however from the immediate performance of this legal ceremony: and the Vice-Chancellor directed me | to return, so soon as I should have accomplished my fifteenth year; recommending me in the mean while to the instruction of my College.

17 My College forgot to instruct: I forgot to return, and was myself forgotten by the first Magistrate of the University. Without a single lecture, either public or private, either Christian or protestant, without any Academical subscription, without any episcopal confirmation, I was left, by the dim light of my Catechism, to grope my way to the Chapel and communion-table; where I was admitted without a question how far, or by what means I might be qualified to receive the sacrament.

18 Such almost incredible neglect was productive of the worst mischiefs.[22] From my childhood I had been fond of Religious disputation: my poor aunt has been often puzzled by [my] objections to the mysteries which she strove to believe; nor had the elastic spring been totally broken by the weight of the Atmosphere of Oxford.

years would have justified a more than ordinary degree of restraint and discipline.

It might at least be expected, that an ecclesiastical school should inculcate the orthodox principles of religion.

But our venerable mother had contrived to unite the opposite extremes of bigotry and indifference: an heretic, or unbeliever, was a monster in her eyes; but she was always, or often, or sometimes, remiss in the spiritual education of her own children. According to the statutes of the university, every student, before he is matriculated, must subscribe his assent to the thirty-nine articles of the church of England, which are signed by more than read, and read by more than believe them. My insufficient age excused me, however, from the immediate performance of this legal ceremony; and the vice-chancellor directed me to return, as soon as I should have accomplished my fifteenth year; recommending me, in the mean while, to the instruction of my college.

My college forgot to instruct: I forgot to return, and was myself forgotten by the first magistrate of the university. Without a single lecture, either public or private, either christian or protestant, without any academical subscription, without any episcopal confirmation, I was left by the dim light of my catechism to grope my way to the chapel and communion-table, where I was admitted, without a question, how far, or by what means, I might be qualified to receive the sacrament.

Such almost incredible neglect was productive of the worst mischiefs. From my childhood I had been fond of religious disputation; my poor aunt has been often puzzled by the mysteries which she strove to believe; nor had the elastic spring been totally broken by the weight of the atmosphere of Oxford.

The blind activity of idleness urged me to advance without armour into the dangerous mazes of controversy; and at the age of sixteen, I bewildered myself in the errors of the church of Rome.

The progress of my conversion may tend to illustrate, at least, the history of my own mind. It was not long since Dr. Middleton's free inquiry had sounded an alarm in the theological world: much ink and much gall had been spilt in the defence of the primitive miracles; and the two dullest of their champions were crowned with academic honours by the university of Oxford. The name of Middleton was unpopular; and his proscription very naturally led me to peruse his writings, and those of his antagonists. His bold criticism, which approaches the precipice of infidelity, produced on my mind a singular effect; and had I persevered in the communion of Rome, I should now apply to my own fortune the prediction of the Sibyl,

— Via prima salutis,

Quod minimè reris, Graiâ, pandetur ab urbe.

The elegance of style and freedom of argument were repelled by a shield of prejudice. I still revered the character, or rather the names, of the saints and fathers whom Dr. Middleton exposes; nor could he destroy my implicit belief, that the gift of miraculous powers was continued in the church, during the first four or five centuries of christianity. But I was unable to resist the weight of historical evidence, that within the same period most of the leading doctrines of popery were already introduced in theory and practice: nor was my conclusion absurd, that miracles are the test of truth, and that the

---

22 Ignorance religious of under graduates, who are soon ordained — complaint of Dr Prideaux — Dr Busby offered to endow two Catechists — rejected by both Univers. — Confessional. p 435–440.

19 The blind activity of ~~indolence~~ idleness urged me to advance without armour into the dangerous mazes of controversy, and at the age of sixteen I bewildered myself in the errors of the Church of Rome.

19a The progress of my conversion may tend to illustrate, at least the history of my own mind. It was not long since ~~th~~ Dr Middleton's free Enquiry had sounded an alarm in the Theological World; much ink and gall had been spilt in the defence of the primitive miracles; and the two dullest ~~and most angry~~ of their champions were crowned with Academic honours by the University of Oxford. The name of Middleton was unpopular; and his proscription very naturally tempted me to peruse his writings and those of his antagonists. His bold criticism, which approaches the precipice of infidelity produced on my mind a singular effect; and had I persevered in the communion of Rome I should now apply to my own fortune the prediction of the Sibyll.

———— Via prima salutis,

Quod minimum reris, Graeâ [Graiâ] pandetur ab Urbe

The elegance of style and freedom of argument were repelled by a shield of prejudice. I still revered the characters, or rather the names, of the Saints and fathers whom Dr Middleton exposeds, nor could he destroy my implicit belief, that the gift of miraculous powers was continued in the Church during the first four or five [Centuries] of Christianity. But I was unable to resist the weight of historical evidence, that within the same period, most of the leading doctrines of Popery were already introduced in Theory and practise: nor was my conclusion absurd, that Miracles are the test of truth, and that the Church must be orthodox and pure, which was so often approved by the visible interposition of the Deity. The marvellous tales, which are so boldly attested by the Basils and Chrysostoms, the Austins and Jeroms, compelled me to embrace the superior merits of Celibacy, the institution of the monastic life, the use of the sign of the cross, of holy oil, and even of images, the invocation of Saints, the worship of relicks, the rudiments of purgatory in prayers for the dead, and the tremendous mystery of the sacrifice of the body and blood of Christ, which insensibly swelled into the prodigy of Transubstantiation.

21 In these dispositions, and already more than half a convert, I formed an unlucky intimacy with a young Gentleman of | our College whose name I shall spare. With a character less resolute Mr —— had imbibed the same Religious opinions, and some Popish books, I know not through what channel, were conveyed into his possession. I read, I applauded, I believed: the English translations of two famous works of Bossuet, Bishop of Meaux, the Exposition of the Catholic doctrine, and the history of the Protestant variations, achieved my conversion; and I surely fell by a noble hand. I have since examined the originals with a more discerning eye, and shall not hesitate to pronounce that Bossuet is indeed a master of all the weapons of controversy. In the Exposition, a specious Apology, the Orator assumes, with consummate art, the tone of candour and simplicity; and the ten-horned Monster is transformed at his magic touch into the milk-white hind, who must be loved as soon as she is seen. In the history, a bold and well-aimed attack, he displays with an happy mixture of narrative and argument, the vices faults and follies, the changes and contradictions of our first Reformers; whose Variations, (as he dextrously contends), are the mark of heretical error, while the perpetual Unity of the Catholic Church is the sign and test of infallible truth. To my actual feelings it seems incredible that I could ever believe that I believed in Transubstantion! But my

church must be orthodox and pure, which was so often approved by the visible interposition of the Deity. The marvellous tales which are so boldly attested by the Basils and Chrysostoms, the Austins and Jeroms, compelled me to embrace the superior merits of celibacy, the institution of the monastic life, the use of the sign of the cross, of holy oil, and even of images, the invocation of saints, the worship of relics, the rudiments of purgatory in prayers for the dead, and the tremendous mystery of the sacrifice of the body and blood of Christ, which insensibly swelled into the prodigy of transubstantiation.

In these dispositions, and already more than half a convert, I formed an unlucky intimacy with a young gentleman of our college, whose name I shall spare. With a character less resolute, Mr. ★★★★ had imbibed the same religious opinions; and some Popish books, I know not through what channel, were conveyed into his possession. I read, I applauded, I believed: the English translations of two famous works of Bossuet Bishop of Meaux, the Exposition of the Catholic Doctrine, and the History of the Protestant Variations, achieved my conversion, and I surely fell by a noble hand.★ I have since examined the originals with a more discerning eye, and shall not hesitate to pronounce, that Bossuet is indeed a master of all the weapons of controversy. In the Exposition, a specious apology, the orator assumes, with consummate art, the tone of candour and simplicity; and the ten-horned monster is transformed, at his magic touch, into the milk-white hind, who must be loved as soon as she is seen. In the History, a bold and well-aimed attack, he displays, with a happy mixture of narrative and argument, the faults and follies, the changes and contradictions of our first reformers; whose variations (as he dexterously contends) are the mark of historical error, while the perpetual unity of the catholic church is the sign and test of infallible truth. To my present feelings it seems incredible that I should ever believe in transubstantiation. But my conqueror oppressed me with the sacramental words, "Hoc est corpus

conqueror oppressed me with the sacramental words "Hoc est corpus meum", and dashed against each other the figurative half-meanings of the Protestant sects: every objection was resolved into Omnipotence; and after repeating at S.ᵗ Mary's the Athanasian creed, I humbly acquiesced in the Mystery of the real presence.

To take up half on trust, and half to try,
Name it not faith, but bungling bigotry.
Both knave and fool the merchant we may call
To pay great sums and to compound the small
For who would break with Heaven, and would not break for all?

No sooner had I settled my new Religion, than I resolved to profess myself a Catholic: Youth is sincere and impetuous; and a momentary glow of Enthusiasm had raised me above all temporal considerations.

20 By the keen toleration protestants who would gladly retaliate the example of persecution, a clamour of the encrease of popery: and they are always loud to declaim against the toleration of priests and Jesuits who pervert so many of his Majesty's subjects from their Religion and Allegiance. On the present occasion the fall of one, or more, of her sons, directed this clamour against the University: and it was confidently affirmed that Popish missionaries were suffered, under various disguises to introduce themselves into the Colleges of Oxford. But the love of truth and justice enjoyns me to declare, that, as far as relates to myself, this assertion is false, and that I never conversed with a priest or even with a papist, till my resolution from books was absolutely fixed.

meum,'' and dashed against each other the figurative half-meanings of the protestant sects; every objection was resolved into omnipotence, and after repeating at St. Mary's the Athanasian creed, I humbly acquiesced in the mystery of the real presence.

"To take up half on trust, and half to try,
"Name it not faith, but bungling bigotry.
"Both knave and fool, the merchant we may call,
"To pay great sums and to compound the small;
"For who would break with Heaven, and would not break for all?"

No sooner had I settled my new religion than I resolved to profess myself a catholic. Youth is sincere and impetuous; and a momentary glow of enthusiasm had raised me above all temporal considerations★.
★ Mr. Gibbon never talked with me on the subject of his conversion to popery but once; and then, he imputed his change to the works of Parsons the jesuit, who lived in the reign of Elizabeth, and who, he said, had urged all the best arguments in favour of the Roman catholic religion. S.
★ He described the letter to his father, announcing his conversion, as written with all the pomp, the dignity, and self-satisfaction of a martyr. S.

By the keen protestants, who would gladly retaliate the example of persecution, a clamour is raised of the increase of popery: and they are always loud to declaim against the toleration of priests and jesuits, who pervert so many of his majesty's subjects from their religion and allegiance. On the present occasion, the fall of one or more of her sons directed this clamour against the university; and it was confidently affirmed that popish missionaries were suffered, under various disguises, to introduce themselves into the colleges of Oxford. But justice obliges me to declare, that, as far as relates to myself, this assertion is false; and that I never conversed with a priest, or even with a papist, till my resolution from books was absolutely fixed.

23   In my last excursion to London, I addressed myself to a Roman Catholic bookseller in Russel-street Covent Garden, who recommended me to a priest of whose name and order I am at present ignorant. In our first interview, he soon discovered that persuasion was needless; and, after sounding the motives and merits of my conversion, he consented to admit me into the pale of the Church:

25   and at his feet on the eighth of June, 1753, I solemnly, though privately abjured the errors of heresy.

24   The seduction of an English | Youth of family and fortune was an act of as much danger as glory; but he bravely overlooked the danger of which I was not then sufficiently informed. "Where a person is reconciled to the see of Rome, or procures others to be reconciled, the offence, (says Blacks Blackstone amounts to High-treason." And if the humanity of the age would prevent the execution of this sanguinary statute there were other laws, of a less odious cast, which condemned the priest to perpetual imprisonment, and transferred the proselyte's estate to his nearest relation.

26   An elaborate controversial Epistle approved by my director, and addressed to my father, announced and justified the step which I had taken. My father was neither a bigot nor a philosopher; but his affection deplored the loss of an only son; and his good sense was astonished at my strange departure from the Religion of my Country. In the first sally of passion, he divulged a secret, which prudence might have suppressed: and the gates of Magdalen College were for ever shut against my return. Many years afterwards when the name of Gibbon was become as notorious as that of Middleton, it was industriously whispered at Oxford that the historian had formerly "turned Papist": my character stood exposed to the reproach of inconstancy; and this invidious topic would have been handled without mercy by my opponents, could they have separated my cause from that of the University.

In my last excursion to London, I addressed myself to a Roman Catholic bookseller in Russell-street, Covent Garden, who recommended me to a priest, of whose name and order I am at present ignorant. In our first interview he soon discovered that persuasion was needless. After sounding the motives and merits of my conversion, he consented to admit me into the pale of the church;

and at his feet, on the eighth of June 1753, I solemnly, though privately, abjured the errors of heresy.

The seduction of an English youth of family and fortune was an act of as much danger as glory; but he bravely overlooked the danger, of which I was not then sufficiently informed. "Where a person is reconciled to the see of Rome, or procures others to be reconciled, the offence (says Blackstone) "amounts to high-treason." And if the humanity of the age would prevent the execution of this sanguinary statute, there were other laws of a less odious cast, which condemned the priest to perpetual imprisonment, and transferred the proselyte's estate to his nearest relation.

An elaborate controversial epistle, approved by my director, and addressed to my father, announced and justified the step which I had taken. My father was neither a bigot nor a philosopher; but his affection deplored the loss of an only son; and his good sense was astonished at my strange departure from the religion of my country. In the first sally of passion he divulged a secret which prudence might have suppressed, and the gates of Magdalen College were for ever shut against my return. Many years afterwards, when the name of Gibbon was become as notorious as that of Middleton, it was industriously whispered at Oxford, that the historian had formerly "turned papist:" my character stood exposed to the reproach of inconstancy; and this invidious topic would have been handled without mercy by my opponents, could they have separated my cause from that of the university.

'F'

22 For my own part, I am proud of an honest sacrifice of interest to conscience; I can never blush that [if] my tender mind was entangled in the sophistry [that] which seduced the acute and manly understandings of Chillingworth and Bayle, who [afterwards emerged from superstition to scepticism]

27 While Charles the first governed England, and was himself governed by a Catholic Queen, it cannot be denied that the Missionaries of Rome laboured with impunity and success in the Court, the country, and even the Universities. One of the sheep –

――― Whom the grim Wolf, with privy paw,
Daily devours apace, and nothing said, –

is Mr. William Chillingworth, master of arts, and fellow of Trinity College, who, at the ripe age of twenty-eight years was persuaded to elope from Oxford to the English seminary of Douay in Flanders. Some eonv disputes with Fisher, a subtle Jesuit might first awaken him from the prejudices of education, but he yielded to his own victorious argument "That there must be somewhere an infallible judge and that the Church of Rome is the only Christian society, which either does or can pretend to that character." After a short tryal of a few months, Mr Chillingworth was again tormented by his own spirit [religious scruples]: he returned home, resumed his studies, unravelled his mistakes, and delivered his mind from the yoke of authority and superstition. His new creed was build on the principle that the Bible is our only [sole] judge, and private reason our sole interpreter: and he ably defends this maintains this principle in the Religion of a protestant, a book (1638) [(1634)] which, after startling the Doctors of Oxford, is still esteemed the most solid defence of the Reformation. The learningnng the virtue, the recent merits of the author entitled him to fair preferment, but the slave had now broke

---

For my own part, I am proud of an honest sacrifice of interest to conscience. I can never blush, if my tender mind was entangled in the sophistry that seduced the acute and manly understandings of Chillingworth and Bayle, who afterwards emerged from superstition to scepticism.

While Charles the First governed England, and was himself governed by a catholic queen, it cannot be denied that the missionaries of Rome laboured with impunity and success in the court, the country, and even the universities. One of the sheep,

— Whom the grim wolf with privy paw
Daily devours apace, and nothing said,

is Mr. William Chillingworth, Master of Arts, and Fellow of Trinity College, Oxford; who, at the ripe age of twenty-eight years, was persuaded to elope from Oxford, to the English seminary at Douay in Flanders. Some disputes with Fisher, a subtle Jesuit, might first awaken him from the prejudices of education; but he yielded to his own victorious argument, "that there must be somewhere an infallible judge; and that the church of Rome is the only christian society which either does or can pretend to that character." After a short trial of a few months, Mr. Chillingworth was again tormented by religious scruples: he returned home, resumed his studies, unravelled his mistakes, and delivered his mind from the yoke of authority and superstition. His new creed was build on the principle, that the Bible is our sole judge, and private reason our sole interpreter: and he ably maintains this principle in the Religion of a Protestant, a book which, after startling the doctors of Oxford, is still esteemed the most solid defence of the Reformation. The learning, the virtue, the recent merits of the author, entitled him to fair preferment: but the slave had now broken his fetters; and the more he weighed, the less was he

his fetters, and the more he weighed, the less was he disposed to subscribe the thirty-nine articles of the church of England. In a private letter he declares, with all the energy of language, that he could not subscribe them without subscribing to his own damnation; and that if ever he should depart from this immoveable resolution, he would allow his friends to think him a madman or an atheist. As the letter is without a date, we cannot ascertain the number of weeks or months that elapsed between this passionate abhorrence and the Salisbury Register, which is still extant. "Ego Gulielmus Chillingworth, … omnibus hisce articulis, … et singulis in iisdem contentis volens, et ex animo subscribo, et consensum meum iisdem præbeo. 20 die Julii 1638." But, alas! the chancellor and prebendary of Sarum soon deviated from his own subscription: as he more deeply scrutinized the article of the Trinity, neither scripture nor the primitive fathers could long uphold his orthodox belief; and he could not but confess, "that the doctrine of Arius is either a truth, or at least no damnable heresy." From this middle region of the air, the descent of his reason would naturally rest on the firmer ground of the Socinians: and if we may credit a doubtful story and the popular opinion, his anxious inquiries at last subsided in philosophic indifference. So conspicuous, however, were the candour of his nature and the innocence of his heart, that this apparent levity did not affect the reputation of Chillingworth. His frequent changes proceeded from too nice an inquisition into truth. His doubts grew out of himself; he assisted them with all the strength of his reason: he was then too hard for himself; but finding as little quiet and repose in those victories, he quickly recovered, by a new appeal to his own judgment: so that in all his sallies and retreats, he was in fact his own convert.

Bayle was the son of a Calvinist minister in a remote province of France, at the foot of the Pyrenees. For the benefit of education, the protestants were tempted to risk their children in the catholic universities; and in the twenty-second year of his age, young Bayle

28   his fetters, and the more he weighed, the less was he disposed to subscribe the thirty-nine articles of the Church of England. In a private letter he declares, with all the energy of language, that he could not subscribe them, without subscribing his own damnation, and that if ever, he should depart from this | immoveable resolution, he would allow his friends to think him a madman or an atheist. As the letter is without a date, we cannot ascertain the number of weeks or months that elapsed between this passionate abhorrence, and the Salisbury register, which is still extant "Ego Gulielmus Chillingworth, … omnibus hisce articulis et singulis in iisdem contentis, volens et ex animo subscribo, et consensum meum iisdem præbeo. 20 die Julii 1638." But, alas! the Chancellor and prebendary of Sarum soon deviated from his own subscription; and as he more deeply scrutinized the doctr article of the Trinity, neither Scripture nor the primitive fathers, could long uphold his orthodox belief; "and he could not but confess that the doctrine of Arius is either a truth, or at least no damnable heresy." From this middle region of the air, the descent of his reason would naturally rest on the firmer ground of the Socinians: and, if we may credit a doubtful story and the popular opinion, his anxious enquiries at last subsided in Philosophic indifference. So conspicuous however were the candour of his Nature, and the innocence of his heart, that this apparent levity did not affect the reputation of Chillingworth. His frequent changes proceeded from too nice an inquisition into truth. His doubts grew out of himself; he assisted them with all the strength of his reason: he was then too hard for himself; but finding as little quiet and repose in those victories, he quickly recovered by a new appeal to his own judgement; so that in all his sallies and retreats, he was, in fact, his own convert.

Bayle was the son of a Calvinist minister in a remote province of France at the foot of the Pyrenees. For the benefit of education, the Protestants were tempted to risk their children in the Catholic Universities; and in the twenty second year of his age (1669) young

Bayle was seduced by the arts and arguments of the Jesuits of Tholouse. He remained about seventeen months (19th March 1669 – 19th August 1670) in their hands, a voluntary captive; and a letter to his parents, which the new convert composed or subscribed (15th April 1670) is darkly tinged with the spirit of Popery. But Nature had designed him to think as he pleased and to speak as he thought: his piety was offended by the excessive worship of creatures; and the study of physics convinced him of the impossibility of Transubstantiation, which is abundantly refuted by the testimony of our senses. His return to the communion of a falling sect was a bold and disinterested step, that exposed him to the rigour of the laws, and a speedy flight to Geneva protected him from the resentment of his spiritual tyrants, unconscious as they were of the full value of the prize which they had lost. Had Bayle adhered to the Catholic Church, had he embraced the Ecclesiastic profession, the Genius and favour of such a proselyte might have aspired to wealth and honours in his native country; but [the Hypocrite] he would have found less happiness in the comforts of a benefice, or the dignity of a mitre than he enjoyed at Rotterdam, in a private state of exile, indigence, and freedom. Without a country, or a patron or a prejudice, he claimed the liberty, and subsisted by the labours of his voluminous works is explained and excused by his alternately writing for himself, for the booksellers, and for posterity, and if a severe critic would reduce him to a single folio, that relick, like the books of the Sybill would become still more valuable. A calm and lofty spectator of the Religious tempest, the Philosopher of Rotterdam | condemned with equal firmness the persecution of Lewis XIV; and the Republican maxims of the Calvinists; their vain prophecies and the intolerant bigotry which sometimes vexed his solitary retreat. In reviewing the controversies of the times, he turned against each other,

was seduced by the arts and arguments of the jesuits of Thoulouse. He remained about seventeen months (19th March 1669 – 19th August 1670) in their hands, a voluntary captive; and a letter to his parents, which the new convert composed or subscribed (15th April 1670), is darkly tinged with the spirit of popery. But Nature had designed him to think as he pleased, and to speak as he thought: his piety was offended by the excessive worship of creatures; and the study of physics convinced him of the impossibility of transubstantiation, which is abundantly refuted by the testimony of our senses. His return to the communion of a falling sect was a bold and disinterested step, that exposed him to the rigour of the laws; and a speedy flight to Geneva protected him from the resentment of his spiritual tyrants, unconscious as they were of the full value of the prize, which they had lost. Had Bayle adhered to the catholic church, had he embraced the ecclesiastical profession, the genius and favour of such a proselyte might have aspired to wealth and honours in his native country: but the hypocrite would have found less happiness in the comforts of a benefice, or the dignity of a mitre, than he enjoyed at Rotterdam in a private state of exile, indigence, and freedom. Without a country, or a patron, or a prejudice, he claimed the liberty and subsisted by the labours of his pen: the inequality of his voluminous works is explained and excused by his alternately writing for himself, for the booksellers, and for posterity; and if a severe critic would reduce him to a single folio, that relic, like the books of the Sybil, would become still more valuable. A calm and lofty spectator of the religious tempest, the philosopher of Rotterdam condemned with equal firmness the persecution of Lewis the Fourteenth, and the republican maxims of the Calvinists; their vain prophecies, and the intolerant bigotry which sometimes vexed his solitary retreat. In reviewing the controversies of the times, he turned against each other the arguments of the disputants; successively wielding the arms of the catholics and protestants, he proves that neither the way of authority, nor the way of examination can afford the multitude any test of religious truth; and dexterously concludes that custom and education must be the sole grounds of popular belief. The ancient paradox of Plutarch, that atheism is less pernicious than superstition, acquires a tenfold vigor, when it is adorned with the colours of his wit, and pointed with the acuteness of his logic. His critical dictionary is a vast repository of facts and opinions; and he balances the *false* religions in his sceptical scales, till the opposite quantities (if I may use the language of algebra) annihilate each other. The wonderful power which he so boldly exercised, of assembling doubts and objections, had tempted him jocosely to assume the title of the νεφεληγερετα Ζευς, the cloud-compelling Jove; and in a conversation with the ingenious Abbé (afterwards Cardinal) de Polignac, he freely disclosed his universal Pyrrhonism. "I am most truly (said Bayle) a protestant; for I protest indifferently against all systems and all sects."

The academical resentment, which I may possibly have provoked, will prudently spare this plain narrative of my studies, or rather of my idleness; and of the unfortunate event which shortened the term of my residence at Oxford. But it may be suggested, that my father was unlucky in the choice of a society, and the chance of a tutor.

It will perhaps be asserted, that in the lapse of forty years many improvements have taken place in the college and the university.

I am not unwilling to believe, that some tutors might have been found more active than Dr. Waldgrave, and less contemptible than Dr. ****. About the same time, and in the same walk, a Bentham was still treading in the footsteps of a Burton, whose maxims he had adopted, and whose life he had published. The biographer indeed preferred the school logic to the new philosophy, Burgursdicius to Locke; and the

---

the ~~[arguments]~~ arms of the disputants: successively wielding the ~~disputants~~ arms of the Catholics and protestants, he proves that neither the way of authority, nor the way of examination can afford the multitude any test of Religious truth; and dexterously concludes, that custom and education must be the sole grounds of popular belief. The ancient paradox of Plutarch, that Atheism is less pernicious than superstition acquires a tenfold vigour when it is adorned with the colours of his wit, and pointed with the acuteness of his logic. His critical Dictionary is a vast repository of facts and opinions; and he balances the false Religions in his sceptical scales till the opposite quantities (if I may use the language of Algebra) annihilate each other. The wonderful power, which he so boldly exercised of assembling doubts and objections, had tempted him jocosely to assume the title of the νεφεληγερετα Ζευς, the cloud-compelling Jove; and in a conversation with the ingenious Abbé, (afterwards Cardinal) de Polignac, he freely disclosed his universal Pyrrhonism. "I am most truly (said Bayle) a protestant; for I protest indifferently against all Systems, and all Sects."

29 The Academical resentment, which I may possibly have provoked, will prudently spare this plain narrative of my studies, or rather of my idleness; and of the unfortunate event which shortened the term of my residence at Oxford. But it may be suggested that my father was unlucky in the choice of a society and the chance of a tutor.

14 It will perhaps be asserted that in the lapse of forty years many improvements have taken place in the College and the University.

30 I am not unwilling to believe that some Tutors might have been found more active than Dr Waldegrave, and less contemptible than Dr Winchester. About the same time, and in the same walk, a Bentham was still treading in the footsteps of a Burton, whose maxims he had adopted and whose life he has published. The Biographer indeed preferred the school-logic to the new Philosophy, Burgersdicius to

hero appears, in his own writings, a stiff and conceited pedant. Yet even these men, according to the measure of their capacity, might be diligent and useful; and it is recorded of Burton, that he taught his pupils what he knew; some Latin, some Greek, some ethics and metaphysics; referring them to proper masters for the languages and sciences of which he was ignorant. At a more recent period, many students have been attracted by the merit and reputation of Sir William Scott, then a tutor in University College, and now conspicuous in the profession of the civil law: my personal acquaintance with that gentleman has inspired me with a just esteem for his abilities and knowledge; and I am assured that his lectures on history would compose, were they given to the public, a most valuable treatise. Under the auspices of the present Archbishop of York, Dr. Markham, himself an eminent scholar, a more regular discipline has been introduced, as I am told, at Christ-Church★, a course of classical and philosophical studies is proposed and even pursued, in that numerous seminary: learning has been made a duty, a pleasure, and even a fashion; and several young gentlemen do honour to the college in which they have been educated. According to the will of the donor, the profits of the second part of Lord Clarendon's History has been applied to the establishment of a riding-school, that the polite exercises might be taught, I know not with what success, in the university. The Vinerian professorship is of far more serious importance; the laws of his country are the first science of an Englishman of rank and fortune, who is called to be a magistrate, and may hope to be a legislator. This judicious institution was coldly entertained by the graver doctors, who complained (I have heard the complaint) that it would take the young people from their books: but Mr. Viner's benefaction is not unprofitable, since it has at least produced the excellent commentaries of Sir William Blackstone.

Locke; and the Hero appears in his own writings a stiff and conceited Pedant. Yet even these men m according to the measure of their capacity, might be diligent, and useful; and it is recorded of Burton that he taught his pupills what he knew, some Latin, some Greek, some Ethics and Metaphysics, referring them to proper masters for the languages, and sciences of which he was ignorant. At a more recent period many students have been attracted by the merit and reputation of Sir William Scott, then a tutor in University College, and now conspicuous in the profession of the Civil law: my personal acquaintance with that Gentleman has inspired me with a just esteem for his abilities and knowledge; and I am assured that his Lectures on history would compose, were they given to the public, a most valuable treatise. Under the auspices of the present Archbishop of York, Dr Markham, himself an eminent scholar, a more regular discipline has been introduced, as I am told at Christ-Church: a course of Classical and philosophical studies is proposed and even pursued in that numerous seminary: Learning has been made a duty, a pleasure and even a fashion; and several young Gentlemen | who do honour to the College in which they have been educated. According to the will of the Donor the profits of the second part of Lord Clarendon's history has been applied to the establishment of a riding school, that the polite exercises might be taught, I know not with what success, in the University. The Vinerian professorship is of far more serious importance; the laws of his country are the first science of an Englishman of rank and fortune, who is called to be a Magistrate, and may hope to be a Legislator. This judicious institution was coldly entertained by the graver Doctors, who complained, I have heard the complaint, that it would take the young people from their books: but Mr. Viner's benefaction is not unprofitable since it has at least produced the excellent commentaries of Sir William

Blackstone. The manners and opinions of our Universities must follow at a distance the progressive motion of the age; and some prejudices, which reason could not subdue, have been slowly obliterated by time. The last generation of Jacobites is extinct: "the right Divine of Kings to govern wrong" is now exploded even at Oxford: and [the] some remains of Tory principles are rather salutary than hurtful, at a time when the Constitution has nothing to fear from the prerogative of the Crown, and can only be injured by popular innovation. But the inveterate evils which are derived from their birth and character must still cleave to our Ecclesiastical corporations: the fashion of the present day is not propitious, in England, to discipline and oeconomy; and even the [exceptionable] praeposterous mode of foreign education has been lately preferred by the highest and most respectable authority in the Kingdom. I shall only add that Cambridge appears to have been less deeply infected than her sister with the vices of the Cloyster: her loyalty to the house of Hanover is of a more early date; and the name and authorit authority of her immortal Newton were first honoured in his [native] own Academy.

* This was written on the information Mr. Gibbon had received, and the observation he had made, previous to his late residence at Lausanne. During his last visit to England, he had an opportunity of seeing at Sheffield-place some young men of the college above alluded to; he had great satisfaction in conversing with them, made many inquiries respecting their course of study, applauded the discipline of Christ Church, and the liberal attention shewn by the Dean, to those whose only recommendation was their merit. Had Mr. Gibbon lived to revise this work, I am sure he would have mentioned the name of Dr. Jackson with the highest commendation. There are other colleges at Oxford, with whose discipline my friend was unacquainted, to which, without doubt, he would willingly have allowed their due praise, particularly Brazen Nose and Oriel Colleges; the former under the care of Dr. Cleaver, bishop of Chester, the latter under that of Dr. Eveleigh. It is still greatly to be wished that the general expence, or rather extravagance, of young men at our English universities may be more effectually restrained. The expence, in which they are permitted to indulge, is inconsistent not only with a necessary degree of study, but with those habits of morality which should be promoted, by all means possible, at an early period of life. An academical education in England is at present an object of alarm and terror to every thinking parent of moderate fortune. It is the apprehension of the expence, of the dissipation, and other evil consequences, which arise from the want of proper restraint at our own universities, that forces a number of our English youths to those of Scotland, and utterly excludes many from any sort of academical instruction. If a charge be true, which I have heard insisted on, that the heads of our colleges in Oxford and Cambridge are vain of having under their care chiefly men of opulence, who may be supposed exempt from the necessity of oeconomical controul, they are indeed highly censurable; since the mischief of allowing early habits of expence and dissipation is great, in various respects, even to those possessed of large property; and the most serious evil from this indulgence must happen to youths of humbler fortune, who certainly form the majority of students both at Oxford and Cambridge. S.

7. EDITING GIBBON'S *MISCELLANEOUS WORKS*: TEXT AND CONTEXTS

Year	Editing and publishing events	Morale at Sheffield Place	Political, military, and diplomatic events
1793		(25 Sept.) 'I cannot be delighted with the state of things' (LS to LA). (25 Oct.) 'I was scarce ever more anxious. … It seems to me to be too late to expect anything from counter-revolution at Brest. The death of the Queen [16 Oct.] elevates me to such a pitch that I am equal to conflagration, murder, &c. I wish it were in my power to burn everything combustible and overturn every stone at Paris' (LS to LA).	
1794	(16 Jan.) Gibbon dies in London. (Mar.) Gibbon MSS brought down to Sheffield Place.	(5 Jan.) 'In truth I never was more disturbed by the state of things' (LS to LA). (11 Jan.) 'How very gloomy the Prospect is at present! I hate to think on the subject, for who can pretend to guess what the year '94 may produce' (MJH). (19 Jan.) 'I am glad Parliament will employ Papa, it will prevent his thinking' (MJH). (23 Mar.) Sheffield apprehensive of French invasion, according to MJH. (1 Apr.) Sheffield 'low', says MJH. (21 Apr.) 'I certainly am no longer afraid of French politics; perhaps I am grown callous. Events have happened to me within a year which have reduced me to an eminent degree of philosophy, indifference, or	(2 Apr.) Trial of Danton begins. (5 Apr.) Execution of the Dantonists.

(May) Suspension of Habeas Corpus.

(8 June) Festival of the Supreme Being. Law of 22 *Prairial* (broadening the definition of 'public enemy').

(27–28 June) Fall and execution of Robespierre.

Committee of Public Safety stripped of its powers.

(Aug.) Riots in London.

(27 June) 'How very bad affairs appear on the Continent!' (MJH).

(3 July) 'Lord Auckland writes very much out of spirits about foreign affairs, and says he quite gives up any hopes of our Allies performing their Engagements properly' (MJH).

(30 July) 'How very bad affairs are going on, on the Continent! What will become of poor England?' (MJH).

(24 Aug.) 'Elmsley is alarmed at the Riots in London, and does not like to quit the protection of his house and property. The Riots have been very alarming I believe ...', (MJH).

(5 Sept.) 'As to public affairs, I trouble myself not about them, nor do those employed in them trouble themselves in any degree or shape about me. .... I have hardly even looked in a newspaper for some time. There is nothing pleasant to hear' (LS to LA).

whatever you please to call it. I fear I care little about anything. I perceive that I hate politicians most heartily. I am piqued, perhaps, into vigorous notions. I rather feel I am in train to become what despots call a democrat, and in time, by the engaging ways of Lady Auckland and of *another*, I may slide further, and gradually become a friend of the people and of reform' (LS to LA).

(June) Sheffield resolved to publish *MW*. Secretarial assistance for editing of MSS arranged.

(July) Remainder of Gibbon MSS delivered to Sheffield Place from Lausanne by Sir John Legard.

(5 Sept.) 'I have been fully employed, the last ten days, with Mr. Hayley, in the examination of Gibbon's papers. I am much satisfied with the occupation, and it gave me much pleasure to observe that he treated the business [the *Memoirs*] exactly as had appeared to me most advisable, and I think

Year	Editing and publishing events	Morale at Sheffield Place	Political, military and diplomatic events
	I may venture to say that nothing is likely to appear that can disgrace Gibbon's literary fame, prejudice society, or disgust the public, but, on the contrary, that the public will be highly gratified. My ten days with Hayley have pleased me much. He appears to me an eminently amiable man' (LS to LA).	(26 Dec.) Sheffield marries his second wife.	
1795	(7 Jan.) Editorial work drawing to a close. (30 Sept.) Press set to work.	(1 Aug.) 'the State of the West Indies terrifies me . . .' (SH). (Sept.) Letter received at Sheffield Place from Hamilton, Governor of Bermuda, describing French atrocities in the West Indies.	(1 Nov.) Attempted assassination of George III.
1796	(Jan.–Feb.) Correction of proofs. (31 Mar.) First edition of *MW* published in two quarto volumes.	(Feb.) Lady Sheffield unwell: 'spasms in her throat.' (18 Mar.) 'Milady has got a fresh Cold and coughs dreadfully; she was so well before that it is very provoking, she has not eat a bit of meat or been out even in the carriage for four days' (MJH) (26 June) 'but I know not why I laugh, for I	(7 Feb.) Stone flung into the carriage of George III. (2 Mar.) Bonaparte becomes General of the Army of Italy. (10 May) Bonaparte defeats the Austrians at Lodi.

1801	was never less disposed to it – I never was thoroughly alarmed before. Surely we are utterly unfit to conduct the affairs of Europe, or the war, and surely those are now fortunate who are not mixed in public affairs' (LS to LA). (23 Sept.) 'I probably shall soon be obliged to acknowledge that the evils I feared are nothing when compared to those which are coming on . . .' (LS to LA).	(16 Nov.) Bonaparte's victory at Arcola. (6 June) Portugal cedes territory to Spain and France. (1 Oct.) Preliminary convention to establish peace between Britain and France.
1802	(18 Oct.) 'We sacrifice so many conquests for a peace [the Peace of Amiens] which gives no security in future. We have yielded every point and every principle' (LS to LA).	(27 Mar.) Treaty of Amiens. (Apr.) French fleet claims Australia as *Terre Napoléon*.
1804	(29 Nov.) 'we are in complete jeopardy . . . non-resistance to such a devil as Bonaparte is submission . . . I begin most cordially to wish for the apotheosis of Bonaparte. He is too much for modern mortals' (LS to LA).	(15 Mar.) Arrest and execution of the Duc d'Enghien. (18 May) Bonaparte created Emperor as Napoleon I.
1805		(Aug.) Formation of the Third Coalition against Napoleon.

Year	Editing and publishing events	Morale at Sheffield Place	Political, military and diplomatic events
1805		(29 Oct.) 'What say you to the present state of things? Can anything be more frightful?' (LS to LA).	(20 Oct.) Austrian army capitulates at Ulm. (21 Oct.) Battle of Trafalgar. (13 Nov.) French troops enter Vienna. (2 Dec.) Austro-Prussian army defeated at Austerlitz: Third Coalition wrecked.
1806		(1 Jan.) 'Our situation is desperate. There is nothing to look to' (LS to LA).	(23 Jan.) Death of Pitt (dying words: 'Oh my country! how I leave my country!'). (14 Oct.) French victories at Jena and Auerstadt. (28 Oct.) Napoleon enters Berlin.
1807			(June) Peace of Tilsit between Russia and France. (Nov.) Russia declares war on Britain.
1808			(May) Napoleon declares his brother Joseph king of Spain.
1811			Franco–Russian alliance breaks down.
1812			(4 June) Napoleon invades Russia; English/Russian alliance. (Sept.) Moscow captured and burnt. (Nov.–Dec.) Retreat from Moscow of the 'Grande Armée'.
1814		(13 Jan.) 'I am so exceedingly exalted that I begin to flatter myself with the expectation of the restoration of the Bourbons' (LS to LA). (4 Mar.) 'I have never ceased my execrations of those poor creatures who have not the	Victories of the Grand Alliance against Napoleon. Castlereagh's policies adopted by the Grand Alliance. (9 Mar.) Treaty of Chaumont: unification of the Grand Alliance.

(30 Mar.) Fall of Paris.

genius to rise with the great events of the times, and see that now or never permanent peace may be acquired by the restoration of the Bourbons. . . . You say the conduct of the campaign in France is certainly not edifying. I see nothing to blame in the military part, except the obvious folly of separating the several corps, and giving Bonaparte the only chance he had of beating them in detail' (LS to LA).

(13 Apr.) Treaty of Fontainebleau.
(20 Apr.) Napoleon leaves for Elba.
(30 May) First Peace of Paris (France returned to the frontiers of 1 January 1792).
(June) Leaders of the Grand Alliance celebrate in London.
(Sept.) Opening of the Congress of Vienna.
(Dec.) Tensions emerge within the Grand Alliance.

1815   (15 Feb.) Publication of second, '1814' edition of *MW*.

(4 Apr.) Publication of the supplementary, third quarto volume of *MW*.

(Mar.) Return of Napoleon: the 'Hundred Days'.

(9 June) 'Acte finale' of Congress of Vienna.
(18 June) Battle of Waterloo; final defeat of Napoleon.
(7 July) Allies re-enter Paris.

LS = John Baker Holroyd, Lord Sheffield.
LA = William Eden, Lord Auckland.

MJH = Maria Josepha Holroyd (Sheffield's daughter).
SH = Serena Holroyd (Sheffield's sister).

BIBLIOGRAPHY

A. MANUSCRIPTS

Beinecke Library, Yale University
MS vault, section 10, drawer 3, section B.
Im. G352, C796.

British Library
Add. MSS 34874–34887.

Cambridge University Library
CUL Add. MS 8530.

Regenstein Library, University of Chicago
D 7 fo. 6419.

B. WRITINGS BY GIBBON

Essai sur l'Étude de la Littérature (1761).
Critical Observations on the Sixth Book of the Aeneid (1769).
The History of the Decline and Fall of the Roman Empire, 6 vols. (1776–88).
The History of the Decline and Fall of the Roman Empire, vol. i, second quarto edn.
    (1776).
The History of the Decline and Fall of the Roman Empire, vol. i, third quarto edn.
    (1777).
Mémoire Justificatif (1779).
Miscellaneous Works, ed. Lord Sheffield, 2 vols. (1796).
Miscellaneous Works, ed. Lord Sheffield, 5 vols. (1814).
Miscellaneous Works . . . In Three Volumes, ed. Lord Sheffield, vol. iii (1815).
The Autobiographies of Edward Gibbon, ed. J. Murray (London: John Murray,
    1896).
The History of the Decline and Fall of the Roman Empire, ed. J. B. Bury, 7 vols.
    (London: Methuen, 1896–1900).
Gibbon's Journal to January 28th. 1763, ed. D. M. Low (London: Chatto and
    Windus, 1929).

Le Journal de Gibbon à Lausanne, ed. G. A. Bonnard (Lausanne: Librairie de l'Université, 1945).

Miscellanea Gibboniana, ed. G. R. de Beer, L. Junod, and G. A. Bonnard (Lausanne: Librairie de l'Université, 1952).

The Letters of Edward Gibbon, ed. J. E. Norton, 3 vols. (London: Cassell and Company, 1956).

Gibbon's Journey from Geneva to Rome, ed. G. A. Bonnard (London: Thomas Nelson and Sons, 1961).

A Vindication [. . .], ed. Hugh Trevor-Roper (Oxford, 1961).

Edward Gibbon: Memoirs of My Life, ed. G. A. Bonnard (London: Thomas Nelson and Sons, 1966).

The English Essays of Edward Gibbon, ed. P. B. Craddock (Oxford: Clarendon Press, 1972).

The History of the Decline and Fall of the Roman Empire, ed. D. J. Womersley, 3 vols. (London: Allen Lane, 1994).

C. WORKS ORIGINALLY PUBLISHED BEFORE 1900

Anonymous pre-1900 works are listed first, in alphabetical order of title.

An Account of Mr. Parkinson's Expulsion from the University of Oxford (1689).

The Acts of Great Athanasius, With Notes, by Way of Illustration on his Creed (1690).

The Advantages of the Hanover Succession, and English Ingratitude (1744).

Brief Notes on the Creed of St. Athanasius (1690).

A Brief State of Dr. Ayliffe's Case at Oxford (n.p., n.d.).

The British Hero (1715).

Certain Propositions humbly offered to the Consideration of a Person presumed to think too favourably of the present Rebellion against KING GEORGE (1715).

A Collection of Papers, Designed to Explicate and Vindicate the Present Mode of Subscription Required by the University of Oxford (1772).

The Complaint of Liberty (1768).

A Dialogue at Oxford between a Tutor and a Gentleman, formerly his Pupil, concerning Government (1681).

English Loyalty opposed to Hanoverian Ingratitude (1744).

An Examine of the Expediency of Bringing over Immediately the Body of Hanoverian Troops taken into our Pay (1746).

A Few General Directions for the Conduct of Young Gentlemen in the University of Oxford (1795).

Four Treatises Concerning the Doctrine, Discipline and Worship of the Mahometans (1712).

Free Thoughts Upon University Education (1751).

The Glory of the Protestant Line, Exemplified . . . in His Most Excellent MAJESTY, GEORGE (1714).

An Heroic Epistle to the Right Honourable Edmund Burke (1791).

An Historical Account of our Present Sovereign George-Lewis (1714).

The History of the Life & Actions of S^t. Athanasius (1664).

The History of the Lutheran Church, or, The Religion of our Present Sovereign King George Agreeable to the Tenets of the Church of England (1715).

The Humours of the Road: Or, a Ramble to Oxford (1738).

A King and No King (1716).

King George's Title Asserted (1716).

A Letter from a Member of the University of Oxford, to a Gentleman in the Country (1755).

A Letter from a Father to his Son at the University (Oxford, 1787).

Letter to the Heads of the University of Oxford (1747).

A Letter to the Author of the Proposal for the Establishment of Public Examinations (Cambridge, 1774).

The Life of Mahomet, the Imposter (1784).

The Loyal Church-man (1716).

Memoirs of the House of Hanover (1713).

Observations on the Present State of the English Universities (1759).

An Ode Presented to the King (1714).

The Oxford Decree: Being an Entire Confutation of Mr. Hoadley's Book, of the Original of Government (1710).

The Oxford Dialogue Between a Master of Arts and a Stranger (1705).

A Pocket Companion for Oxford (1753).

A Poem Upon His Majesties Accession (1714).

The Principles of the University of Oxford, As far as relates to Affection to the Government, Stated (1755).

The Propriety of Sending Lord Sheffield to Coventry (179?).

Reasons for Visiting the Universities (1717).

Remarks on the Enormous Expence in the Education of Young men in the University of Cambridge (1788).

Sentiments on the Interests of Great Britain, with Thoughts on the Politics of France (1787).

A Serious Inquiry into Some Late Proceedings in Vindication of the Honour, Credit, and Reputation of the University of OX—D, Relative to an Offence of a Certain Member of the same (1751).

Short Observations on the Right Hon. Edmund Burke's Reflections (1790).

The Spy at Oxford and Cambridge (1744).

A Step to Oxford: In Which is Comprehended an Impartial Account of the University (1704).

The Succession, a poem, humbly inscrib'd to his sacred Majesty, King George (1714).

Sundry Things from Several Hands Concerning the University of Oxford (1659), reprinted in *The Harleian Miscellany* (1745), vi. 79–84.

The True History of the Great St. Athanasius . . . and of his Famous Creed (1719).

The University Answer to the Pretended University Ballad (1705).

The University of Cambridge Vindicated (1710).

The Whole Life, Birth and Character of his most Serene Highness Geoge [sic] Lewis Elector of Hanover (n.d.).

ABBEY, C. J. and J. H. OVERTON. *The English Church in the Eighteenth Century*, 2 vols. (London: Longmans, Green and Co., 1878).

ADEANE, J. H. (ed.), *The Girlhood of Maria Josepha Holroyd* (1896).

ALMON, J. *A Review of the Reign of George II* (1762).

—— (ed.). *An Asylum for Fugitive Pieces in Prose and Verse, Not in any other collection*, 4 vols (1785–95).

AMHURST, NICHOLAS. *Oculus Britanniae: an Heroi-Panegyrical Poem on the University of Oxford* (1724).

——. *Terræ-Filius*, 2nd edn. (1726).

ANDERSON, JAMES. *Royal Genealogies* (1732).

APTHORP, EAST. *Letters on the Prevalence of Christianity* (1778).

AYLIFFE, JOHN. *The Case of Dr. Ayliffe at Oxford* (1716).

——. *The Antient and Present State of the University of Oxford*, 2 vols. (1716).

BAKER, THOMAS. *An Act at Oxford* (1704).

BALLANTYNE, GEORGE. *A Vindication of the Hereditary Right of his Present Majesty, King George II* (1743).

BARBEYRAC, JEAN. *Traité de la Morale des Pères de l'Eglise* (Amsterdam, 1728).

BAYLE, PIERRE. *Dictionaire Historique & Critique*, 2 vols. in 4 (Rotterdam, 1697).

BELSHAM, WILLIAM. *Essays Philosophical, Historical and Literary* (1789).

——. *Memoirs of the Kings of Great Britain*, 2 vols. (1793).

BENTHAM, EDWARD. *A Letter to a Young Gentleman of Oxford* (1748).

——. *A Letter to a Fellow of a College, the sequel of A Letter to a Young Gentleman of Oxford* (1749).

[——.] *Advices to a Young Man of Fortune and Rank, Upon his Coming to the University* (Oxford, 1762; first published, 1760).

——. *The Honor of the University of Oxford Defended* (1781).

BENTLEY, RICHARD. *A Dissertation Upon the Epistles of Phalaris* (1699).

——. *Remarks Upon a Late Discourse of Free-Thinking* (1713).

——. *Remarks Upon a Late Discourse of Free-Thinking . . . Supplemented with a Third Part* (1743).

——. *A Dissertation Upon the Epistles of Phalaris* (1777).

BERKENHOUT, JOHN. *A Volume of Letters from Dr. Berkenhout to his son at the University* (Cambridge, 1790).

BINGHAM, WILLIAM. *A Letter from an American . . .* (Philadelphia, 1784).

BLACKSTONE, SIR WILLIAM. *Commentaries on the Laws of England*, 4 vols. (Oxford, 1770).

BOLINGBROKE, FIRST VISCOUNT. *See* St John, Henry.

BONWICKE, AMBROSE. *A Pattern for Young Students in the University* (1729).

BOOTHBY, SIR BROOKE. *A Letter to the Right Honourable Edmund Burke* (1791).

——. *Observations on the Appeal from the New to the Old Whigs and on Mr. Paine's Rights of Man* (1792).

BOSSUET. *Histoire des Variations* (1688).

BOSWELL, JAMES. *The Correspondence of James Boswell and William Johnson Temple 1756–1795*, vol. i: 1756–1777, ed. Thomas Crawford (Edinburgh and New Haven: Edinburgh University Press and Yale University Press, 1997).

———. *Life of Johnson*, ed. R. W. Chapman, corr. J. D. Fleeman (Oxford: Oxford University Press, 1976).

BOULAINVILLIERS, HENRI DE. *La Vie de Mahomed* ('Londres', 1730).

BOYLE, CHARLES. *Dr. Bentley's Dissertations . . . Examin'd* (1743).

BROWN, JOHN. *Essays on the Characteristics of the Earl of Shaftesbury* (1751).

———. *An Estimate of the Manners and Principles of the Times* (1757).

BROWNE, J. *An Oration Upon the King's Happy Arrival* (1714).

BULL, GEORGE. *Defensio Fidei Nicænæ* (1685; 2nd edn., 1688).

BURGH, WILLIAM. *An Inquiry into the Belief of the Christians of the First Three Centuries* (York, 1778).

BURKE, EDMUND. *The Correspondence of Edmund Burke*, ed. T.W. Copeland *et al.*, 10 vols. (Cambridge: Cambridge University Press, 1958–78).

———. *Thoughts on the Cause of the Present Discontents* (1770), in *The Writings and Speeches of Edmund Burke*, vol. ii: *Party, Parliament and the American Crisis, 1766–1774*, ed. P. Langford (Oxford: Clarendon Press, 1981).

———. *Speech on Conciliation with the Colonies* (1775), in Edmund Burke, *A Philosophical Enquiry into the Sublime and Beautiful and Other Pre-Revolutionary Writings*, ed. David Womersley (Harmondsworth: Penguin Books, 1998).

———. *Reflections on the Revolution in France* (1790), in *The Writings and Speeches of Edmund Burke*, vol. iii: *The French Revolution 1790–1794*, ed. L. G. Mitchell (Oxford: Clarendon Press, 1989).

———. *Further Reflections on the Revolution in France*, ed. D. E. Ritchie (Indianapolis: Liberty Fund, 1992).

CAMPBELL, JOHN. *A Political Survey of Britain*, 2 vols. (1775).

CARLYLE, THOMAS. *Early Letters*, ed. C. E. Norton (London and New York: Macmillan, 1886).

CHAPMAN, R. *Britannia Rediviva* (1714).

CHELSUM, JAMES. *Remarks on the Two Last Chapters of Mr. Gibbon's History* (1776).

———. *Remarks on the Two Last Chapters of Mr. Gibbon's History*, 2nd edn. (1778).

———. *A Reply to Mr. Gibbon's Vindication* (Winchester, 1785).

CHRISTIE, THOMAS. *Letters on the Revolution of France* (1791).

CLARKE, SAMUEL. *A Demonstration of the Being and Attributes of God* (1705).

———. *Scripture-Doctrine of the Trinity* (1712).

———. *The Layman's Humble Address* (1717).

———. *Observations on Dr. Waterland's Second Defense* (1724).

[COADE, GEORGE]. *A Blow at the Root* (1749).

COOPER, ANTHONY ASHLEY, third earl of Shaftesbury. *Characteristicks*, 3 vols. (1711).

[———.] *Several Letters Written by a Noble Lord to a Young man at the University* (1732).

COURTENAY, JOHN. *Philosophical Reflections on the Late Revolution in France*, 2nd edn. (1790).

[COXE, TENCH]. *A Brief Examination of Lord Sheffield's Observations on the Commerce of the United States* (Philadelphia, 1791).

DAILLÉ, JEAN. *Traicté de l'Employ des Saincts Peres* (Geneva, 1632).

DALRYMPLE, SIR DAVID. *Remains of Christian Antiquity*, 3 vols. (Edinburgh, 1776–80).

——. *An Inquiry into the Secondary Causes which Mr. Gibbon has assigned for the Rapid Growth of Christianity* (Edinburgh, 1786).

DAVIES, RICHARD. *The General State of Education in the Universities* (Bath, 1759).

DAVIS, HENRY. *An Examination of the Fifteenth and Sixteenth Chapters of Mr. Gibbon's History* (1778).

——. *A Reply to Mr. Gibbon's Vindication* (1779).

DEFOE, DANIEL. *Reasons Against the Succession of the House of Hanover* (1713).

EDEN, WILLIAM, LORD AUCKLAND. *The Journal and Correspondence of William, Lord Auckland*, ed. J. Eden, 4 vols. (1861–2).

EDWARDS, JOHN. *Socinianism Unmasked* (1696).

Encyclopédie, ou dictionaire raisonné des arts, des sciences et des lettres, 31 vols. (Paris, 1751–80).

[EYRE, FRANCIS]. *A Few Remarks on the History of the Decline and Fall* (1778).

——. *A Short Appeal to the Public. By the Gentleman who is particularly addressed in the Postscript of the Vindication* (1779).

FELL, JOHN. *Of the Unity of the Church* (Oxford, 1681).

—— (ed.). *Sancti Cæcilii Cypriani Opera, recogn. & illustr. per Ioannem Oxoniensem episcopum* (Oxford, 1682).

FONTENELLE, BERNARD LE BOVIER DE. *Histoire des Oracles* (Amsterdam, 1687).

FREKE, WILLIAM. *Vindication of the Unitarians* (1690).

FULLWOOD, FRANCIS. *A Parallel: Wherein it Appears that the Socinian agrees with the Papist* (1693).

GAGNIER, JEAN. *La Vie de Mahomet*, 2 vols. (Amsterdam, 1732).

GERRALD, JOSEPH. *A Convention the Only Means of Saving us from Ruin* (1794).

GODWIN, WILLIAM. *The Herald of Literature; or, a review of the most considerable publications that will be made in the course of the ensuing winter: with extracts* (1784).

——. *Enquiry Concerning Political Justice*, 2nd edn. (1793).

——. *St. Leon*, ed. P. Clemit (Oxford: Oxford University Press, 1994).

GOOLD, THOMAS. *A Vindication of the Right Honourable Edmund Burke's Reflections on the Revolution in France* (1791).

GRAY, THOMAS. *Poems and Memoirs*, ed. William Mason (York, 1775).

HALL, JOHN. *An Humble Motion to the Parliament of England Concerning the Advancement of Learning, and Reformation of the Universities* (1649).

HALLIDAY, SIR ANDREW. *Annals of the House of Hanover* (1826).

HARBIN, GEORGE. *The Hereditary Right of the Crown of England Asserted* (1713).

HARRIS, J. *Considerations on the Birth-day of his Most Sacred Majesty King GEORGE* (1715).

HARRISON, FREDERICK. *Proceedings of the Gibbon Commemoration 1794–1894* (1895).

HERVEY, JOHN. *Lord Hervey's Memoirs*, ed. R. Sedgwick (London: William Kimber, 1952).

HOBBES, THOMAS. *Leviathan*, ed. R. Tuck (Cambridge: Cambridge University Press, 1996).

——. *Behemoth, or the Long Parliament*, ed. Ferdinand Tönnies, intro. Stephen Holmes (Chicago and London: University of Chicago Press, 1990).

HOLROYD, JOHN BAKER, LORD SHEFFIELD. *Observations on the Commerce of the American States* (1783).

——. *Observations on the Manufactures, Trade and Present State of Ireland* (Dublin, 1785).

——. *Observations on the Project for Abolishing the Slave Trade* (1790).

——. *Observations on the Corn bill, now Depending in Parliament* (1791).

——. *Substance of the Speech* [. . .] *of Lord Sheffield* [. . .] *upon the Subject of Union with Ireland* (Dublin, 1799).

——. *Remarks on the Deficiency of Grain Occasioned by the Bad Harvest of 1799* (1800).

——. *Observations on the Objections made to the Export of Wool from Great Britain to Ireland* (1800).

——. *Strictures on the Necessity of Inviolably Maintaining the Navigation and Colonial System of Great Britain* (1804).

——. *The Orders in Council and the American Embargo Beneficial to the Political and Commercial Interests of Great Britain* (1809).

——. *Lord Sheffield's Present State of the Wool Trade* (Dublin, 1811).

——. *On the Trade in Wool and Woollens* (1813).

——. *Report* [. . .] *to the Meeting at Lewes Wool Fair* (1813).

——. *Observations on the Impolicy, Abuses, and False Interpretation of the Poor Laws* (1813).

——. *On the Trade in Wool and Woollens, including an Exposition of the Commercial Situation of the British Empire* (1813).

——. *A Letter on the Corn Laws* (1815).

——. *Report* [. . .] *to the Meeting at Lewes Wool Fair* (Dublin, 1816).

——. *Remarks on the Bill of the Last Parliament for the Amendment of the Poor Laws* (1819).

HORSLEY, SAMUEL. *Tracts in Controversy with Dr. Priestley* (1789).

——. *Sermon . . . Preached on 30 January 1793* (1793).

HOWES, THOMAS. *A Discourse on the Abuse of the Talent of Disputation in Religion, Particularly as practiced by Dr. Priestly, Mr. Gibbon, And others of the modern Sect of Philosophic Christians* (1784).

HUME, DAVID. *Essays Moral, Political and Literary*, ed. E. F. Miller (Indianapolis, 1985).

——. *The Natural History of Religion* (1757), in A. W. Colver and J. V. Price (eds.), *David Hume on Religion* (Oxford: Clarendon Press, 1976).

HUNTER, CHRISTOPHER. SCEPTICISM *not separable from* IMMORALITY*, illustrated in the instances of* HUME *and* GIBBON*, a sermon* (1799).

HUNTON, PHILIP. *A Treatise of Monarchy* (1680).

HURD, RICHARD. Q. *Horatii Flacci Epistolæ, ad Pisones et Augustum*, 2nd edn. (Cambridge, 1757).

——. *A Discourse, by way of General Preface to . . . Warburton's Works, containing some Account of the Life, Writings, and Character of the Author* (1794).

——. *Works of Richard Hurd, DD, Lord Bishop of Worcester*, 8 vols. (1811).

HURDIS, JAMES. *A Word or Two in Vindication of the University of Oxford and of Magdalen College in Particular from the Posthumous Aspersions of Mr. Gibbon* (n.p., n.d.: Bishopstone?, *c.*1800).

JACKSON, JOHN. *Christian Liberty Asserted* (1734).

JEBB, JOHN. *Remarks Upon the Present Mode of Education in the University of Cambridge* (Cambridge, 1773).

——. *A Proposal for the Establishment of Public Examinations in the University of Cambridge* (Cambridge, 1774).

JOHNSON, SAMUEL. *Political Writings*, ed. D. J. Greene (New Haven: Yale University Press, 1977).

——. 'Preface' to Shakespeare, in B. H. Bronson (ed.), *Selections from Johnson on Shakespeare* (New Haven and London: Yale University Press, 1986).

JONES, DAVID. *The History of the Most Serene House of Brunswick-Lunenburgh* (1715).

JORDAN, G. W. *The Claims of the British West India Colonists* (1804).

JORTIN, JOHN. *Remarks on Ecclesiastical History*, 5 vols. (1751–73).

KILVERT, FRANCIS. *Memoirs of the Life and Writings of the Right Rev. Richard Hurd, D.D.* (1860).

KNOX, VICESIMUS. *Essays Moral and Literary* (1778).

——. *Liberal Education: or, a Practical Treatise on the Methods of Acquiring Useful and Polite Learning* (1781).

——. *Elegant Extracts* (1783).

——. *A Letter to the Right Hon. Lord North* (1789).

——. *Winter Evenings: Or, Lucubrations on Life and Letters*, 2 vols., 2nd edn. (1790).

——. *Personal Nobility: or, Letters to a Young Nobleman, on the Conduct of his Studies, and the Dignity of the Peerage*, 2nd edn. (1793).

——. *Family Lectures* (1791–5).

——. *Antipolemus* (1794).

——. *The Spirit of Despotism*, 2nd edn. (1821).

'A LADY'. *A Review of the Reigns of George I. & II.* (Berwick, 1792).

LAW, WILLIAM. *A Serious Call to a Devout and Holy Life* (1728).

LE CLERC, JEAN. *Bibliotheque universelle et historique* (Amsterdam, 1686–93).

LELAND, JOHN. *Reflections on the late Lord Bolingbroke's Letters on the Study and Use of History* (1753).

LELAND, JOHN. *A View of the Principal Deistical Writers*, 3 vols. (1754, 1755, 1756).

——. *A Supplement to the First and Second Volumes of the View of the Deistical Writers* (1756).

LESLIE, CHARLES. *A Brief Account of the Socinian Trinity* (1695).

——. *Short and Easy Method with the Deists* (1704).

——. *Socinian Controversy Discussed* (1708).

LOFTUS, SMYTH. *A Reply to the Reasonings of Mr. Gibbon* (Dublin, 1777).

'London Corresponding Society'. *Address . . . to the Nation* (1798).

MACAULAY, CATHERINE. *Observations on the Reflections of the Right Hon. Edmund Burke* (1790).

MACKINTOSH, JAMES. *Vindiciæ Gallicæ: Defence of the French Revolution and its English Admirers Against the Accusations of the Right Hon. Edmund Burke* (1791).

MACLAINE, ARCHIBALD. *A Series of Letters Addressed to Soame Jenyns* (1777).

MANGEY, THOMAS. *Remarks upon Nazarenus* (1718).

MARVELL, ANDREW. *A Short Historical Essay Touching General Councils, Creeds, and Impositions in Religion* (1676).

——. *The Rehearsal Transpros'd*, ed. D. I. B. Smith (Oxford: Clarendon Press, 1971).

MASON, WILLIAM. *Isis. An Elegy* (1749).

MIDDLETON, CONYERS. *A Letter to Dr. Waterland* (1731).

——. *A Defence of the Letter to Dr. Waterland* (1732).

——. *An Introductory Discourse . . . Concerning the Miraculous Powers* (1747).

——. *A Free Inquiry into the Miraculous Powers, which are supposed to have subsisted in the Christian Church* (1749).

——. *Miscellaneous Works*, 4 vols. (1752).

MILLER, EDMOND. *An Account of the University of Cambridge* (1717).

MILLER, JAMES. *The Humours of Oxford* (1730).

——. *Mahomet the Impostor. A Tragedy* (1744).

MILNER, JOHN. *Letters to a Prebendary . . . With Remarks on the Opposition of Hoadlyism to the Doctrines of the Church of England* (1802).

MILNER, JOSEPH. *Gibbon's Account of Christianity Considered* (York, 1781).

MONK, JAMES HENRY. *The Life of Richard Bentley*, second, revised edition, 2 vols. (1833).

MONTESQUIEU, CHARLES DE SÉCONDAT, BARON DE. *Considérations sur la grandeur des romains et de leur décadence*, ed. J. Ehrard (Paris: Garnier-Flammarion, 1968).

NAPLETON, JOHN. *Considerations on the Public Exercises for the First and Second Degrees in the University of Oxford* (1773).

NELSON, GILBERT. *King GEORGE's Right Asserted* (1717).

NEWMAN, JOHN HENRY. *Arians of the Fourth Century* (1833).

NEWTON, SIR ISAAC. *The Chronology of Ancient Kingdoms Amended* (1728).

——. *Observations Upon the Prophecies of Daniel, and the Apocalypse of St. John* (1733).

———. *Theological Manuscripts*, ed. H. McLachlan (Liverpool, 1950).

NYE, STEPHEN. *Brief History of the Unitarians, called also Socinians* (1687).

OGILVIE, JOHN. *An Inquiry into the Causes of the Infidelity and Scepticism of the Times* (1783).

PAINE, TOM. *Common Sense* (1776).

———. *Rights of Man* (1791).

PARKER, THOMAS. 'A Memorial Relating to the Universities', reprinted in J. Gutch (ed.), *Collectanea Curiosa*, 2 vols. (Oxford: Clarendon Press, 1781), ii. 53–75.

PARSONS, PHILIP. *Dialogues of the Dead with the Living* (1779).

PATTISON, MARK. *Essays*, 2 vols. (Oxford, 1889).

'PHILALETHES'. *A Letter to the Rev. Vicecimus [sic] Knox on the Subject of his Animadversions on the University of Oxford* (1790).

PIGOTT, CHARLES. *The Jockey Club* (1792).

———. *A Political Dictionary* (1795).

POLWHELE, RICHARD. *Biographical Sketches in Cornwall*, vol. iii (Truro, 1831).

POPE, ALEXANDER. *The Works of Alexander Pope Esq. . . . together with the Commentarites and Notes of Mr. Warburton*, 9 vols. (1751).

———. *The Correspondence of Alexander Pope*, ed. G. Sherburn, 5 vols. (Oxford, 1956).

PORSON, RICHARD. *Letters to Mr. Archdeacon Travis* (1790).

PRICE, RICHARD. *Observations on the Nature of Civil Liberty* (1776).

PRIDEAUX, HUMPHREY. *The True Nature of Imposture Fully Displayed in the Life of Mahomet* (1697).

PRIESTLEY, JOSEPH. *Letters to the Young Men who are in a Course of Education for the Christian Ministry, at the Universities of Oxford and Cambridge* (Birmingham, 1787).

———. *Letters to the Right Honourable Edmund Burke* (1791).

RANDOLPH, THOMAS. *A Vindication of the Doctrine of the Trinity* (1754).

———. *The Proof of the Truth of the Christian Religion* (Oxford, 1777).

REID, WILLIAM HAMILTON. *A Concise History of the kingdom of Hanover, and of the house of Brunswick* (1816).

RENAN, ERNEST. *Études d'histoire religieuse* (Paris, 1857).

RICHARDSON, S. *Clarissa, or the History of a Young Lady*, ed. A. Ross (Harmondsworth: Penguin Books, 1985).

RIMIUS, HENRY. *Memoirs of the House of Brunswick* (1750).

ROBERTSON, WILLIAM. *The Situation of the World at the Time of Christ's Appearance* (Edinburgh, 1755).

ROMILLY, SIR SAMUEL. *Memoirs of the Life of Sir Samuel Romilly*, 3 vols. (1840).

ROUS, GEORGE. *Thoughts on Government*, 4th edn. (1791).

RUSSELL, LORD JOHN. *An Essay on the History of the English Government and Constitution* (1823).

SAINTE-BEUVE, C. A. DE. *Causeries du Lundi* (Paris, 1854).

ST JOHN, HENRY, FIRST VISCOUNT BOLINGBROKE. *Works*, 8 vols. (1809).

SALISBURY, WILLIAM. *A History of the Establishment of Christianity* (1776).

SAVAGE, J. *An Answer to an Anonymous Pamphleteer* (1690).

SCOTT-WARING, JOHN. *A Letter to the Right Hon. Edmund Burke, in Reply to his "Reflections on the Revolution in France, &c."* (1790).

SHAFTESBURY, THIRD EARL OF. See Cooper, Anthony Ashley.

SHEBBEARE, JOHN. *Letters on the English Nation*, 2 vols. (1755).

SHEFFIELD, LORD. See Holroyd, John Baker.

SHERLOCK, WILLIAM. *A Vindication of the Doctrine of the . . . Trinity* (1690).

SMITH, ADAM. *The Theory of Moral Sentiments*, ed. D. D. Raphael and A. L. Macfie (Oxford: Oxford University Press, 1976).

———. *An Inquiry into the Nature and Causes of the Wealth of Nations*, 2 vols., ed. R. H. Campbell, A. S. Skinner, and W. B. Todd (Oxford: Oxford University Press, 1976).

SOMERS, JOHN. *A Brief History of the Succession of the Crown of England* (1688/9).

STANHOPE, CHARLES, THIRD EARL STANHOPE. *A Letter from Earl Stanhope to the Right Honourable Edmund Burke* (1790).

STEPHEN, LESLIE. *English Thought in the Eighteenth Century*, 2 vols. (1876).

STEPHENS, WILLIAM. *An Account of the Growth of Deism in England* (1696).

STUBBE, HENRY. *An Account of the Rise and Progress of Mahometanism* (1671).

The Student, or the Oxford Monthly Miscellany, 2 vols. (Oxford, 1750–1).

TATHAM, EDWARD. *Oxonia Explicata & Ornata* (Oxford, 1773).

———. *Letters to the Right Honourable Edmund Burke on Politics* (Oxford, 1791).

TAYLOR, HENRY. *Thoughts on the Nature of the Grand Apostacy* (London, 1781).

THELWALL, JOHN. *The Tribune*, 3 vols. (1795, 1796, 1796).

THIRLBY, STYAN. *An Answer to Mr. Whiston's Seventeen Suspicions Concerning Athanasius* (Cambridge, 1712).

THORNTON, P. M. *The Brunswick Accession* (1887).

TILLEMONT, SÉBASTIEN LE NAIN DE. *Memoires pour servir à l'histoire ecclesiastique des six premiers siécles*, 5 vols. (Brussels, 1695–1707).

TOLAND, JOHN. *Anglia Libera* (1701).

———. *Nazarenus or, Jewish, Gentile, and Mahometan Christianity* (1718).

TOWERS, JOSEPH. *Thoughts on the Commencement of a New Parliament* (Dublin, 1791).

TRAVIS, GEORGE. *Letters to Edward Gibbon Esq.* (Chester, 1784).

TREVELYAN, SIR GEORGE OTTO. *The Life and Letters of Lord Macaulay*, 2 vols. (1876).

TYRWHITT, THOMAS. *An Epistle to Florio at Oxford* (1749).

VOLTAIRE, F. M. A. DE. *Letters on England*, tr. L. Tancock (Harmondsworth: Penguin Books, 1980).

———. *Le Fanatisme, ou Mahomet le Prophète* (1741).

———. *Essai sur l'Histoire Générale, et sur les Moeurs et l'Esprit des Nations*, 7 vols. (n.p., 1756).

WALPOLE, HORACE. *Correspondence*, ed. W.S. Lewis *et al.*, 48 vols. (New Haven and Oxford: Yale University Press and Oxford University Press, 1937–83).

WARBURTON, WILLIAM. *Letters from a Late Eminent Prelate to one of his Friends*, ed. Richard Hurd (Kidderminster, 1808).

WATERLAND, DANIEL. *A Vindication of Christ's Divinity* (1719).

——. *The Case of Arian Subscription Considered* (1721).

——. *A Familiar Discourse Upon the Doctrine of the Holy Trinity* (1723).

——. *A Critical History of the Athanasian Creed* (Cambridge, 1724).

——. *Importance of the Doctrine of the Holy Trinity Asserted* (1734).

[——.] *Advice to a Young Student* (1755).

WATSON, RICHARD. *An Apology for Christianity, in A Series of Letters Addressed to Edward Gibbon, Esq.* (Cambridge, 1776).

——. *Appendix to a Sermon* (1793).

WENDEBORN, F. A. *A View of England*, 2 vols. (1791).

WHISTON, WILLIAM. *Primitive Christianity Reviv'd*, 5 vols. (1711).

——. *Athanasius Convicted of Forgery* (1712).

WHITAKER, JOHN. *The History of Manchester* (1771).

——. *The Genuine History of the Britons Asserted*, 2nd, corr., edn. (1773).

——. *Gibbon's History of the Decline and Fall of the Roman Empire . . . reviewed* (1791).

——. *The Origin of Arianism Disclosed* (1791).

——. *The Real Origin of Government* (1795).

——. *The Ancient Cathedral of Cornwall Historically Surveyed*, 2 vols. (1804).

WHITE, JOSEPH. *Sermons Preached before the University of Oxford* (Oxford, 1784).

WILLIAMSON, JAMES. *Opinions Concerning the University of Oxford and Subscription to the Thirty-Nine Articles* (1774).

WOLLSTONECRAFT, MARY. *A Vindication of the Rights of Men* (1790).

WORDSWORTH, WILLIAM. *Letters of William Wordsworth*, ed. and sel. A. G. Hill (Oxford, 1984).

WOTTON, WILLIAM. *Reflections Upon Ancient and Modern Learning* (1697).

YOUNG, ARTHUR. *The Autobiography of Arthur Young*, ed. M. Betham-Edwards (1898).

D. WORKS PUBLISHED AFTER 1900

ASTON, NIGEL. 'Horne and Heterodoxy: The Defence of Anglican Beliefs in the Late Enlightenment', *English Historical Review*, 108 (1993), 895–919.

——. 'A "Disorderly Squadron"? A Fresh Look at Clerical Responses to *The Decline and Fall*', in D. Womersley (ed.), *Gibbon: Bicentenary Essays* (Oxford: The Voltaire Foundation, 1997), 253–77.

BARNES, T. D. 'Derivative Scholarship and Historical Imagination: Edward Gibbon on Athanasius', in Emmet Robbins and Stella Sandahl (eds.), *Corolla Torontonensis: Studies in Honour of Ronald Morton Smith* (Toronto: University of Toronto Press, 1994), 13–28.

BENNETT, G. V. *The Tory Crisis in Church and State 1688–1730: The Career of Francis Atterbury Bishop of Rochester* (Oxford: Clarendon Press, 1975).

BENNETT, J. A. W. *Essays on Gibbon* (Cambridge: privately printed, 1980).

BERTI, S. *et al.* (eds.). *Contexts of Imposture* (Leiden, 1991).

——. 'The First Edition of the Traité des trois imposteurs and its Debt to Spinoza's Ethics' in M. Hunter and D. Wootton (eds.), *Atheism from the Reformation to the Enlightenment* (Oxford: Oxford University Press, 1992), 183–220.

——. *Trattato dei Tre Impostori* (Torino: Einaudi, 1994).

——, F. CHARLES-DAUBERT, and R. H. POPKIN (eds.). *Heterodoxy, Spinozism, and Freethought in Early Eighteenth-Century Europe: Studies on the Traité des Trois Imposteurs* (Dordrecht and London: Klewer, 1996).

BETTENSON, H. (ed.). *The Early Christian Fathers* (Oxford: Oxford University Press, 1956).

BLANNING, T. C. W. ' "That Horrid Electorate" or "Ma Patrie Germanique"? George III, Hanover and the *Furstenbund* of 1785', *Historical Journal*, 20 (1977), 311–44.

BONNARD, GEORGES. 'John Holroyd in Italy', *Études de Lettres: Bulletin de la Faculté des Lettres de l'Université de Lausanne*, ptie II, tom. 2 (1959), no. 3, 122–35.

BOULTON, J. T. (ed.). *Johnson: The Critical Heritage* (London: Routledge and Kegan Paul, 1971).

BOUSQUET, G. H. 'Voltaire et l'Islam', *Studia Islamica*, fasc. 28 (1968), 109–26.

BOWERSOCK, GLEN. *Gibbon's Historical Imagination* (Stanford, Calif.: Stanford University Press, 1988).

BROWNING, REED. *Political and Constitutional Ideas of the Court Whigs* (Baton Rouge, La.: Louisiana State University Press, 1982).

BRUYN, FRANS DE. *The Literary Genres of Edmund Burke: The Political Uses of Literary Form* (Oxford: Clarendon Press, 1996).

BUTLER, MARILYN (ed.). *Burke, Paine, Godwin, and the Revolution Controversy* (Cambridge: Cambridge University Press, 1984).

CANNON, JOHN. *Parliamentary Reform, 1640–1832* (Cambridge: Cambridge University Press, 1972)

——. *Aristocratic Century* (Cambridge: Cambridge University Press, 1984).

CARNOCHAN, BLISS. *Gibbon's Solitude* (Stanford, Calif.: Stanford University Press, 1987).

CHAMPION, JUSTIN. *The Pillars of Priestcraft Shaken: The Church of England and its Enemies 1660–1730* (Cambridge: Cambridge University Press, 1992).

CHARLES-DAUBERT, F. 'Les Principales Sources de l'Esprit de Spinosa', in *Groupe de recherches spinozistes. Travaux et documents 1* (Paris, 1989), 61–107.

——. 'Les Traités des trois imposteurs aux XVIIᵉ et XVIIIᵉ siècles', in G. Canziani (ed.), *Filosofia e religione nella letteratura clandestina secoli XVII e XVIII* (Milan: Franco Angeli, 1994), 291–336.

——. 'L'Esprit de Spinosa et les Traités des trois imposteurs: rappel des différentes familles et de leurs principales caractéristiques' in S. Berti, F. Charles-Daubert, and R. H. Popkin (eds.), *Heterodoxy, Spinozism, and Freethought in*

Early Eighteenth-Century Europe: Studies on the Traité des Trois Imposteurs (Dordrecht and London: Klewer, 1996), 131–89.

CHRISTIE, I. R. *Wilkes, Wyvill and Reform* (London: Macmillan, 1962).

CLARK, J. C. D. *English Society 1688–1832: Ideology, Social Structure and Political Practice during the ancien regime* (Cambridge: Cambridge University Press, 1985).

——. *English Society 1660–1832: Religion, Ideology and Politics during the ancien regime*, 2nd edn. (Cambridge: Cambridge University Press, 2000).

COLLEY, LINDA. *In Defiance of Oligarchy: The Tory Party 1714–60* (Cambridge: Cambridge University Press, 1982).

——. 'The Apotheosis of George III: Loyalty, Royalty and the British Nation 1760–1820', *Past and Present*, 102 (1984), 94–129.

CORDEAUX, E. H., and D. H. MERRY. *Bibliography of Printed Works Relating to the University of Oxford* (Oxford: Clarendon Press, 1968).

COSGROVE, P. W. 'Undermining the Footnote: Edward Gibbon, Alexander Pope, and the Anti-Authenticating Footnote', in S. Barney (ed.), *Annotation and Its Texts* (Oxford: Oxford University Press, 1991), 130–51.

CRADDOCK, PATRICIA. *Young Edward Gibbon, Gentleman of Letters* (Baltimore and London: The Johns Hopkins University Press, 1982).

——. *Edward Gibbon: A Reference Guide* (Boston: G. K. Hall and Co., 1987).

——. *Edward Gibbon, Luminous Historian 1772–1794* (Baltimore and London: The Johns Hopkins University Press, 1989).

DERRIDA, J. *De la grammatologie* (Paris, 1967), tr. Gayatri Chakravorty Spivak, *Of Grammatology* (Baltimore: The Johns Hopkins University Press, 1976).

DICKINSON, H. T. 'The Politics of Edward Gibbon', *Literature and History*, 8/4 (1978), 175–96.

DINWIDDY, J. *Christopher Wyvill and Reform, 1790–1820* (York: St Anthony's Press, 1971).

DOUGILL, JOHN. *Oxford in English Literature: The Making, and Undoing, of 'The English Athens'* (Ann Arbor: The University of Michigan Press, 1998).

EVANS, A. W. *Warburton and the Warburtonians: A Study in Some Eighteenth-Century Controversies* (Oxford: Clarendon Press, 1932).

FÜCK, JOHANN. *Die arabischen Studien in Europa bis den Anfang des 20. Jahrhunderts* (Leipzig: O. Harrassowitz, 1955).

FURET, FRANÇOIS. 'Civilization and Barbarism in Gibbon's History', *Dædalus*, 105/3 (1976), 209–16.

GASCOIGNE, J. *Cambridge in the Age of the Enlightenment* (Cambridge: Cambridge University Press, 1988).

——. 'Church and State Allied: The Failure of Parliamentary Reform of the Universities, 1688–1800', in A. L. Beier, David Cannadine, and James M. Rosenheim (eds.), *The First Modern Society: Essays in English History in Honour of Lawrence Stone* (Cambridge: Cambridge University Press, 1989), 401–29.

GHOSH, P. R. 'Gibbon's Dark Ages: Some Remarks on the Genesis of *The Decline and Fall*', *Journal of Roman Studies*, 73 (1983), 1–23.

GHOSH, P. R. 'Gibbon's First Thoughts: Rome, Christianity and the *Essai sur l'Étude de la Littérature* 1758–61', *Journal of Roman Studies*, 85 (1995), 148–64.

——. 'Gibbon's Timeless Verity', in D. Womersley (ed.), *Gibbon: Bicentenary Essays* (Oxford: The Voltaire Foundation, 1997), 121–63.

GOLDGAR, ANNE. *Impolite Learning: Conduct and Community in the Republic of Letters, 1680–1750* (New Haven and London: Yale University Press, 1995).

GRAFTON, ANTHONY, *The Footnote: A Curious History* (London: Faber and Faber, 1997).

GRUNEBAUM, G. E. VON. 'Islam: The Problem of Changing Perspective', in Lynn White Jr. (ed.), *The Transformation of the Roman World: Gibbon's Problem After Two Centuries* (Berkeley and Los Angeles: University of California Press, 1966), 147–78.

HABAKKUK, SIR JOHN. *Marriage, Debt and the Estates System: English Landownership, 1650–1950* (Oxford: Clarendon Press, 1994).

HADIDI, DJAVAD. *Voltaire et l'Islam* (Paris: Association Langues et Civilisations, 1974).

HOLMES, GEOFFREY. *The Trial of Doctor Sacheverell* (London: Eyre Methuen, 1973).

HOLT, P. M. *Studies in the History of the Near East* (London: Cass, 1973).

HUNTER, M., and WOOTTON, D. (eds.). *Atheism from the Reformation to the Enlightenment* (Oxford: Oxford University Press, 1992).

HURD, RICHARD. *The Correspondence of Richard Hurd and William Mason* (Cambridge: Cambridge University Press, 1932).

JACOB, M. *The Radical Enlightenment: Pantheists, Freemasons, and Republicans* (London: Allen and Unwin, 1981).

JALLAIS, THÉRÈSE-MARIE. 'Gibbon et la pierre noire de l'Islam: Quelques remarques sur le chapitre L de *The Decline and Fall of the Roman Empire*', in *Quand religions et confessions se regardent* (Paris: Didier-Erudition, 1998), 167–77.

JARVIS, SIMON. *Scholars and Gentlemen: Shakespearian Textual Criticism and Representations of Scholarly Labour, 1725–1765* (Oxford: Clarendon Press, 1995).

JEBB, SIR RICHARD CLAVERHOUSE. *Bentley* (London: Macmillan, 1902).

JORDAN, DAVID. *Gibbon and His Roman Empire* (Urbana, Ill.: University of Illinois Press, 1971).

KETTON-CREMER, R. W. *Humphrey Prideaux* (privately printed, 1955).

LEVINE, J. M. *Humanism and History: Origins of Modern English Historiography* (Ithaca, NY: Cornell University Press, 1987).

——. *The Battle of the Books: History and Literature in the Augustan Age* (Ithaca, NY: Cornell University Press, 1991).

LEWIS, BERNARD. 'Gibbon on Muhammad', *Daedalus*, 105/3 (Summer, 1976), 89–101.

LOW, D. M. *Edward Gibbon 1737–1794* (London: Chatto and Windus, 1937).

McCLOY, S. T. *Gibbon's Antagonism to Christianity* (London: Williams and Norgate, 1993).

McKENZIE, D. F. '*Mea Culpa*: Voltaire's Retraction of his Comments Critical of Congreve', *RES* 49 (1998), 461–5.

——. 'Richard van Bleeck's Painting of William Congreve as Contemplative (1715)' *RES*, 51 (2000), 41–61.

MALVEZZI, ALDOBRANDINO. *L'Islamismo e la culture europea* (Florence: Sansoni, 1956).

MARTINO, PIERRE. *L'Orient dans la littérature française au XVIIe et au XVIIIe siècle* (Paris: Hachette, 1906).

——. 'Mahomet en France au XVIIe et au XVIIIe siècle', in *Actes du XIVe Congrès international des Orientalistes: Alger 1905*, part III (Paris, 1907), 206–41.

MATAR, N. *Islam in Britain 1558–1685* (Cambridge: Cambridge University Press, 1998)

——. *Turks, Moors & Englishmen in the Age of Discovery* (New York: Columbia University Press, 1999).

MIDGLEY, GRAHAM. *University Life in Eighteenth-Century Oxford* (New Haven and London: Yale University Press, 1996).

MITCHELL, L. G. *Charles James Fox* (Oxford: Oxford University Press, 1992).

MOMIGLIANO, ARNALDO. 'Gibbon's Contribution to Historical Method', in *Studies in Historiography* (London: Weidenfeld and Nicolson, 1966), 40–55.

NOCKLES, PETER B. *The Oxford Movement in Context* (Cambridge: Cambridge University Press, 1994).

O'BRIEN, CONOR CRUISE. *The Great Melody* (London: Sinclair Stevenson, 1992).

O'GORMAN, FRANK. *Voters, Patrons and Parties: The Unreformed Electorate of Hanoverian England, 1734–1832* (Oxford: Clarendon Press, 1989).

PALMERI, F. 'The Satiric Footnotes of Swift and Gibbon', *The Eighteenth Century*, 31 (1990), 245–62.

PAULSON, RONALD (ed.). *Henry Fielding: The Critical Heritage* (London: Routledge and Kegan Paul, 1969).

PEVSNER, N. *The Buildings of England: Oxfordshire* (Harmondsworth: Penguin, 1974).

POCOCK, J. G. A. *The Machiavellian Moment: Florentine Political Thought and the Atlantic Republican Tradition* (Princeton: Princeton University Press, 1975).

——. 'Gibbon and the Shepherds: The Stages of Society in the *Decline and Fall*', *History of European Ideas*, 2 (1981), 193–202.

——. 'Superstition and Enthusiasm in Gibbon's History of Religion', *Eighteenth-Century Life*, 8 (1982), 83–94.

——. 'The Varieties of Whiggism from Exclusion to Reform', in *Virtue, Commerce, and History* (Cambridge: Cambridge University Press, 1985), 215–310.

——. 'Edward Gibbon in History: Aspects of the Text in *The History of the Decline and Fall of the Roman Empire*', *The Tanner Lectures on Human Values* (Salt Lake City: University of Utah Press, 1990).

PORTER, ROY. *Edward Gibbon: Making History* (London: Weidenfeld and Nicolson, 1988).

QUANTIN, JEAN LOUIS. 'The Fathers in Seventeenth Century Anglican Theology', in Irena Backus (ed.), *The Reception of the Church Fathers in the West: From the Carolingians to the Maurists* (Leiden, New York, Köln: E. J. Brill, 1997), 987–1008.

REDFORD, BRUCE. *Venice and the Grand Tour* (New Haven and London: Yale University Press, 1996).

RIVERS, ISABEL. *Reason, Grace and Sentiment: A Study of the Language of Religion and Ethics in England, 1660–1780*, vol. i: *Whichcote to Wesley* (Cambridge: Cambridge University Press, 1991).

———. *Reason, Grace and Sentiment: A Study of the Language of Religion and Ethics in England, 1660–1780*, vol. ii: *Shaftesbury to Hume* (Cambridge: Cambridge University Press, 2000).

ROBERTSON, JOHN. 'Gibbon's Roman Empire as a Universal Monarchy: the *Decline and Fall* and the Imperial Idea in Early Modern Europe', in Rosamond McKitterick and Roland Quinault (eds.), *Edward Gibbon and Empire* (Cambridge: Cambridge University Press, 1997), 247–70.

RUPP, E. G. *Religion in England, 1688–1791* (Oxford: Clarendon Press, 1986).

SMIRNOV, N. A. *Islam and Russia* (London: Central Asian Research Centre, 1956).

SOX, D. *The Gospel of Barnabas* (London: Allen and Unwin, 1984).

SPACKS, P. M. *Imagining a Self: Autobiography and Novel in Eighteenth-Century England* (Cambridge, Mass.: Harvard University Press, 1976).

SPURR, JOHN. *The Restoration Church of England 1646–1689* (New Haven and London: Yale University Press, 1991).

STONE, L. and J. C. FAWTIER STONE. *An Open Elite? England 1540–1880*, abridged edn. (Oxford: Oxford University Press, 1986).

STURROCK, JOHN. *The Language of Autobiography* (Cambridge: Cambridge University Press, 1993).

SUTHERLAND, L. S. and L. G. MITCHELL (eds.). *The History of the University of Oxford*. vol. v: *The Eighteenth Century* (Oxford: Clarendon Press, 1986).

THOMAS, WILLIAM. *The Quarrel of Macaulay and Croker: Politics and History in the Age of Reform* (Oxford: Oxford University Press, 2000).

THOMPSON, E. P. *The Making of the English Working Class* (Harmondsworth: Penguin Books, 1980).

TURNBULL, PAUL. 'The Supposed Infidelity of Edward Gibbon', *The Historical Journal*, 5 (1982), 23–41.

———. 'Gibbon's Exchange with Joseph Priestley', *BJECS*, 14 (1991), 139–58.

———. ' "Une marionette infidèle": The Fashioning of Edward Gibbon's Reputation as the English Voltaire', in David Womersley (ed.), *Edward Gibbon: Bicentenary Essays* (Oxford: The Voltaire Foundation, 1997), 279–307.

VAUGHAN, DOROTHY. *Europe and the Turk: A Pattern of Alliances* (Liverpool: Liverpool University Press, 1954).

WALSH, J., C. HAYDON and S. TAYLOR (eds.). *The Church of England c.1689–c.1833* (Cambridge: Cambridge University Press, 1993).

WILES, MAURICE. 'The Theological Legacy of St Cyprian', *JEH*, 25 (1963).

——. *Archetypal Heresy: Arianism through the Centuries* (Oxford: Clarendon Press, 1996).

WOMERSLEY, DAVID. 'A Complex Allusion in Gibbon's Letters', *British Journal for Eighteenth-Century Studies*, 10 (1987), 55–7.

——. *The Transformation of the Decline and Fall of the Roman Empire* (Cambridge: Cambridge University Press, 1988).

——. 'Gibbon's Apostasy', *British Journal for Eighteenth-Century Studies*, 11 (1988), 51–70.

——. 'A Complex Allusion in Gibbon's *Memoirs*', *Notes and Queries*, 36 (1989), 68–70.

——. 'From Polybianism to Perfectibilism: Gibbon and the Chevalier de Chastellux', *British Journal for Eighteenth-Century Studies*, 13 (1990), 47–58.

——. 'Gibbon and Classical Example: The Age of Justinian in *The Decline and Fall*', *British Journal for Eighteenth-Century Studies*, 19 (1996), 17–31.

——. 'Gibbon and Plagiarism', *Times Literary Supplement*, no. 4872, 16 Aug. 1996, 14–15.

——. *Gibbon: Bicentenary Essays* (Oxford: The Voltaire Foundation, 1997).

—— (ed.). *Augustan Critical Writing* (Harmondsworth: Penguin Books, 1997).

——. 'Gibbon's Religious Characters', in *History, Religion, and Culture: British Intellectual History 1750–1950*, ed. S. Collini, R. Whatmore, and B. Young (Cambridge: Cambridge University Press, 2000), 69–88.

——. 'An Annotated Copy of Gibbon's *Miscellaneous Works* (1796)', *Notes and Queries*, 47 (2000), 216–18.

YOUNG, B. W. ' "The Religious Accuracy of the Historian": Gibbon and Newman', in D. Womersley (ed.), *Gibbon: Bicentenary Essays* (Oxford: The Voltaire Foundation, 1997), 309–30.

——. *Religion and Enlightenment in Eighteenth-Century England: Theological Debate from Locke to Burke* (Oxford: Clarendon Press, 1998).

INDEX